The Korean Presidents

Leadership for Nation Building

For Karen Knudsen
with the author's compliments

THE KOREAN PRESIDENTS

LEADERSHIP FOR NATION BUILDING

Choong Nam Kim

EastBridge
Norwalk

EastBridge

Signature Books

Copyright © 2007 by EastBridge

All rights reserved.
No part of this book may be reproduced in any form
without written permission from the publisher
EastBridge
64 Wall Street
Norwalk, CT 06850 USA

EastBridge is a nonprofit publishing corporation,
chartered in the State of Connecticut and tax-exempt under
Section 501(c)(3) of the United States tax code.

This book was supported in part by a
generous grant from the Korea Foundation

This book was supported in part by a
grant from the East-West Center

Library of Congress Cataloging-in-Publication Data

Kim, Choong Nam, 1940-
The Korean Presidents : Leadership for nation building / Choong
Nam Kim. -- 1st ed.
    p. cm.
  Includes bibliographical references.
  ISBN 1-59988-003-2 (pbk. : alk. paper)
1. Political leadership--Korea (South)--History. 2. Presidents--Korea
(South)--History.
3. Korea (South)--Politics and government. 4. Korea (South)--
Economic policy. I. Title. II.
Title: The Korean presidents
  JQ1725.K5564 2007
  951.9504092'2--dc22
                                                        2007019200

Printed in the United States of America

Contents

FOREWORD ....*ix*
PREFACE AND ACKNOWLEDGEMENTS ....*xi*

CHAPTER ONE
    INTRODUCTION
        THE BLUE HOUSE BLUES *3*
        LEADERSHIP FOR NATION BUILDING *7*

CHAPTER TWO
    SOUTH KOREA AFTER LIBERATION
        THE LEGACY OF JAPANESE RULE *21*
        AMERICAN MILITARY RULE *25*

CHAPTER THREE
    SYNGMAN RHEE FOUNDER OF THE REPUBLIC
        LIFE AND CHARACTER OF A GREAT PATRIOT *34*
        ESTABLISHMENT OF THE REPUBLIC *36*
        TASKS AND CHALLENGES OF STATE BUILDING *40*
        STRUGGLE FOR POLITICAL SURVIVAL *46*
        THE STRUGGLE FOR EXTERNAL ASSISTANCE *48*
        THE ANTI-COMMUNIST STRUGGLE *50*
        WARTIME LEADERSHIP *54*
        DIPLOMACY FOR NATIONAL SURVIVAL *63*
        POST-WAR RECONSTRUCTION *69*
        DEMOCRACY ON TRIAL *75*
        LEADERSHIP FOR NATIONAL SURVIVAL *83*

CHAPTER FOUR
    PARK CHUNG HEE ARCHITECT OF MODERN KOREA
        FAILURES OF THE CHANG REGIME *94*
        THE ROOTS OF A GREAT REVOLUTIONARY *98*
        THE MILITARY GOVERNMENT (1961-63) *99*
        THE THIRD REPUBLIC (1963-1972) *106*
        MODERNIZATION OF THE FATHERLAND *112*
        DIPLOMACY FOR ECONOMIC GROWTH *119*
        THE FOURTH REPUBLIC (1972-79) *126*
        LEADERSHIP FOR MODERNIZATION *145*

CHAPTER FIVE
    CHUN DOO HWAN PUSHING KOREA TOWARD THE FIRST WORLD
        A TURBULENT TRANSITION *158*
        THE MAN AND HIS CHARACTER *167*
        THE FIFTH REPUBLIC (1981-1987) *169*
        THE SECOND ECONOMIC TAKEOFF *178*
        DIPLOMACY FOR SECURITY AND THE OLYMPICS *191*
        TOWARD DEMOCRATIC TRANSITION *198*
        LEADERSHIP FOR NATIONAL REVITALIZATION *204*

Contents

CHAPTER SIX
ROH TAE WOO PRESIDENT OF DEMOCRATIC TRANSITION
LIFE AND CHARACTER OF THE "ORDINARY MAN" 216
TURBULENT VOYAGE TO FULL DEMOCRACY 218
THE ECONOMY DURING DEMOCRATIC TRANSITION 230
THE NORTHERN POLICY 235
POLITICS OF PRESIDENTIAL SUCCESSION 246
LEADERSHIP FOR DEMOCRATIC TRANSITION 251

CHAPTER SEVEN
KIM YOUNG SAM PRESIDENT OF DEMOCRATIC REFORM
THE MAN AND HIS CHARACTER 259
ASCENT TO THE PRESIDENCY 262
AN ALL-OUT REFORM DRIVE 265
REFORMS FOR A "NEW ECONOMY" 272
THE NORTH KOREAN CRISIS 279
THE KOREAN FINANCIAL CRISIS 287
LEADERSHIP FOR REFORM POLITICS 300

CHAPTER EIGHT
KIM DAE JUNG GROPING FOR REUNIFICATION
THE MAN AND HIS CHARACTER 312
POLITICS OF THE ECONOMIC CRISIS 314
ECONOMIC REFORM DRIVE 321
THE SUNSHINE POLICY 331
FROM ECONOMICS TO POLITICS 336
FROM A HERO TO A LAME DUCK 341
LEADERSHIP FOR FUNDAMENTAL CHANGE 352

CHAPTER NINE
ROH MOO HYUN A LEADER WHO ATTEMPTED A SOCIAL REVOLUTION
BEGINNING OF A "NEW ERA"? 363
EARLY TURBULENCE FOR THE PRESIDENCY 365
THE POLITICS OF A NEW GENERATION 368
ON THE BACK-BURNER: THE ECONOMY 371
PEACE AND PROSPERITY POLICY 376
LEADERSHIP FOR A RADICAL REFORM 380

CHAPTER TEN
LESSONS AND IMPLICATIONS
LESSON ONE: PRIORITY SETTING FOR NATIONAL GOALS
  IS MORE CRUCIAL IN DEVELOPING NATIONS. 391
LESSON TWO: MAINTENANCE OF NATIONAL SECURITY AND
  POLITICAL STABILITY IS A PREREQUISITE FOR POLITICAL LEADERSHIP
  IN NEWLY ESTABLISHED STATES. 393
LESSON THREE: EFFECTIVENESS IS AS IMPORTANT AS LEGITIMACY
  FOR NATION BUILDING. 395

LESSON FOUR: A STRONG AND DETERMINED LEADER IS MORE LIKELY
TO SUCCEED IN THE INITIAL PHASE OF NATION BUILDING. 397
LESSON FIVE: LONG-TERM GOAL-SETTING IS REQUIRED
FOR SUCCESSFUL LEADERSHIP FOR NATION BUILDING. 398
LESSON SIX: DOMESTIC POLICY SUCCESS OUTWEIGHS
DIPLOMATIC PERFORMANCE. 400
LESSON SEVEN: INTEGRITY IS AN IMPORTANT QUALITY
FOR SUCCESSFUL LEADERSHIP...400
LESSON EIGHT: INSTITUTIONALIZING THE ROLE OF CHIEF EXECUTIVE
IS A KEY TO SUCCESSFUL PRESIDENTIAL GOVERNMENT..............................402

ENGLISH BIBLIOGRAPHY 407
KOREAN BIBLIOGRAPHY 418
PERSONS CITED 421

Foreword

CHARLES E. MORRISON
PRESIDENT, THE EAST-WEST CENTER

In this book, Dr. Kim Choong-nam undertakes a valuable and neglected task – a comprehensive study of the leadership styles and achievements of the Republic of Korea's first presidents[1]. He begins with a central paradox: The Republic of Korea as a nation is typically given high marks for its performance, including the dramatic growth of its economy and its transition to democracy over the past half century. However, each of Korea's presidents has typically been judged severely deficient, both by scholars and by their constituents, despite their leadership roles in a successful developing nation. One might assume that the Korean economic and political transformations occurred despite the country's chief executives rather than because of them. Dr. Kim believes, however, that executive leadership has been an essential part of the Korean success story and that critics have consistently undervalued achievements of Korea's presidents by measuring them against unrealistic standards of another place or time.

Dr. Kim provides a comparative, analytical assessment of each president, both to provide a more detached perspective from which to judge their performance as well as to set out a model for broader studies of executive leadership in third world countries. Dr. Kim's criteria for evaluation are vision, agenda setting, quality of appointees, managerial skill, crisis management, commitment, integrity, and net achievements. In the case of each president, he sketches the challenges they faced in order to better understand restraints as well as potentials. Some of these are fairly unique to Korea, such as the division of the country, the ever-present security threat, and the particular legacy of Korea's colonial experience. Many of the other economic and political challenges are similar to those of other developing countries. And not surprisingly, Dr. Kim finds weaknesses and strengths among all the incumbents. Aside from the individual assessments, this study helps the reader understand the progression of Korea's political and economic development and how achievements at one period of time may have led to new challenges in another period.

This book also makes clear that there has been no Korean president who could be considered a puppet of outside powers. Most had humble origins, all took pride in Korea, and all took significant political and personal risks to move into the top position and push forward a vision of Korea's future. While they sought power, most sought power or used their power for some strong conviction about Korea and its needs. Syngman Rhee was a devoted nationalist committed to a unified Korea. Park Chung Hee was also deeply committed to transforming the Korean economy to provide a basis of security, unification, and even democracy. Chun Doo Hwan, although no democrat, and Roh Tae Woo played significant roles in the democratic transition and in developing

---

[1] Only the seven full-term presidents are considered in depth.

Foreword

new relations with the socialist world. Kim Young Sam and Kim Dae Jung were committed to democracy and the latter also transformed the relations with the North. Except for Roh, Dr. Kim believes that the Korean presidents sought to be active agents of change, although not necessarily effectively. Tragically, however, all in some way betrayed the hopes and trust initially placed in them. Whether or not one agrees with interpretation Dr. Kim gives of each president and his decisions, his accounts provide rich detail and fresh and comparative perspectives.

This book gives special emphasis to the security threat, which Dr. Kim believes has been often discounted by critics focused mainly on adherence to western democratic principles. Today, North Korea is usually regarded as a frail and weak country, desperately seeking a nuclear status but hardly in a position to launch an aggressive war against the much more populous and wealthy South Korea. Dr. Kim reminds us that the image of North Korea and the relative capabilities of North and South were quite different through much of the history of the divided peninsula. Pyongyang had inherited the larger share of the industrial wealth of the country, it had launched a war of unification, it maintained a hostile and aggressive posture toward the South for decades, and it sought to exploit weaknesses in the South's political system. As recently as 1983, the North Korean regime sought to assassinate one South Korean president, Chun Doo Hwan, in a terrorist attack in Burma, killing instead 17 very senior officials. For a succession of South Korean presidents, the North has been a significant military threat that Korean presidents could not take lightly.

As a scholar and a former Blue House official, Dr. Kim is almost uniquely qualified for this task. He served as an assistant to three of the presidents of whom he writes, and thus has a solid understanding of institution of the presidency in Korea as well as personal knowledge of the challenges faced by the presidents he served and their immediate advisers. Given this experience, it perhaps is not surprising that Dr. Kim emphasizes that in the end effective leadership depends not so much on good intentions as on matching vision with prioritizing, choosing a good team, and achieving outcomes. The two most successful Korean presidents, in his view, were Park and Chun because they "managed the government by institutions rather than personal whim." Since these skills came from their military backgrounds, it raises the intriguing question of whether the career politicians and lawyers from which more recent presidents have been drawn are much less likely to be effective managers of Korea's on-going political transformation.

During the past nine years, Dr. Kim has been at the East-West Center, where he has administered the Posco Fellowship program while conducting his research on Korean presidents. We continue to be honored by his presence and enlightened by his insights into Korean society. We believe that this volume will contribute to the understanding within and outside of Korea of the institution of the presidency in Korea, Korean political history, and the challenges of executive leadership in developing countries in times of rapid change.

Preface and Acknowledgements

Writing a book on South Korean presidents is a difficult and dangerous task. It is difficult because there are few existing studies and little material on the subject. It is dangerous because Korean views of their former leaders are sharply divided. Any author dealing with the Korean presidency will inevitably be criticized for either praising or degrading his subject, for being either a sycophant or a traitor. Nevertheless, I thought it a worthwhile attempt for the very simple reason that leadership matters. During times of crisis, the quality of a nation's leader can be decisive. Ever since the establishment of the Republic of Korea in 1948, Korea has been a nation full of crises.

In many ways, South Korea presents an important case study among developing countries. Yet analysis of Korea has been lacking and as a result the country remains greatly misunderstood. Most studies of Korean politics and leadership—in both Korea and the West—have come from what one might call a Western liberal democratic viewpoint. As a result, Korean presidents have been traditionally regarded as authoritarian and as poor leaders; and consequent Korean distrust in their government continues to be a serious problem. One leading South Korean journalist recently wrote: "Perhaps no other country has seen its elected president become the object of so much ridicule among citizens as ours.... The president's prestige is at a low ebb, and the shame is the country's."[1]

The Korean people have long debated the identity of South Korea. Some, like me, view it as a successful state, while many others, including a great number among the post-Korean War generations, tend to view their country as a failed state. Younger generations are by nature idealistic and tend to stress the darker side of their contemporary history. They do not deny the realities of remarkable economic and social development, but they stress the prices paid for them—an authoritarian political order, inter-Korean confrontation, labor sacrifices, income gaps, and moral decadence. I believe this persistent distrust in past and present political leaders threatens the very foundation of Korean democracy.

Past Korean leaders viewed and analyzed from a Western liberal perspective were frequently labeled undemocratic and authoritarian. But considering the dire and threatening conditions the country has faced since 1945, we cannot place sole blame for the turbulent history of Korean democracy on its leaders. Such a perspective pays little attention to the security dilemma and the economic poverty the Korean people experienced. Although security has been one of the most critical issues in Korea, most experts on Korea almost totally neglect the national security aspect of Korean politics and political leadership. As a frontline country in the Cold War, relative economic prosperity was also a crucial factor for the survival and legitimacy of the Republic of Korea.

Thanks in part to the decade-long North Korean nuclear crisis, the world now understands more clearly what sort of country North Korea is. During half a century of the Cold War, the world paid little attention to North Korea, which continued to

---

[1] Kim Dae-joong, "A President Reviled Means a Country Shamed", *Chosun Ilbo*, October 9, 2005.

threaten South Korea. Confrontation and competition with North Korea are a salient characteristic of the contemporary history of South Korea. Since 1948 the fragile democracy in the South faced a Stalinist regime in the North intent on the military subjugation of the South. Had past decisive leaders not rallied the Korean people, the Republic of Korea might very well have perished. It is important not to forget that post-1945 South Korea was lacking in almost everything that counted in the West. After a half-century struggle on the part of the Korean people, Korean economic and political development is regarded as one of the twentieth century's most remarkable achievements. Today's South Korea is a leading industrial and democratic state. If for no other reason than this, previous Korean governments and presidents could be judged less critically.

Under strong American influence, South Korea once regarded everything American or Western as good, even superior. Korean scholars tended to blindly accept foreign perspectives, which were often based on completely alien contexts. Many South Korean intellectuals became victims of Western "intellectual imperialism." I have long thought we needed a new perspective to understand the politics and leadership of developing nations and have given much thought to what sort of leadership is appropriate for developing countries. After all, the world has no shortage of failed or failing states.

Regardless of one's political stand, if one looks at the course of Korean history over the last half-century, it is clear that Korea's path to the present is strewn with both successes and failures. Before passing final judgment on the meaning of Korea's nation-building, however, one ought to try to understand what happened and why. Not to do so means falling into an ahistorical praise-and-blame approach to history, which judges people and nations of the past by standards they themselves did not accept or regard as appropriate. I have thus tried to develop an alternative perspective on the leadership of developing countries. It endeavors to analyze Korean leadership in terms of the interplay of three factors: security, economics, and politics. It is assumed that different historical, social, and political contexts make different demands on leaders. In the social sciences objectivity is important. Although I have attempted throughout this process to remain objective, it is important to recognize my biases. Such biases come from being Korean, from having experienced the turbulent process of post-1945 Korean history: the legacy of colonial rule, national division, a devastating war, the continued confrontation across the DMZ, abject poverty, and the struggle for democracy. I have also had the privilege, rare among Korean writers, to have served for over nine years as an assistant to three South Korean presidents.

During the Roh Tae Woo and Kim Young Sam administrations, I witnessed the difficult transition to full democracy. But South Korea's leaders, their advisors, and even the Korean people were ill-prepared to deal with the challenges of the democratic era. In late 1990 I resigned from my post in the office of President Roh Tae Woo and went to the United States to spend a year studying presidential leadership. Returning to Korea, I wrote and published in Korean *Successful Presidents, Unsuccessful Presidents* (1992), and went on to publish a revised edition in 1998. Following this, President Kim Young Sam asked me to join his Blue House staff, to which I reluctantly agreed. After serving him for more than two years, I resigned my post in 1996 under serious disenchantment. In early 1997 I came to the East-West Center with the renewed intention of dedicating myself to a thorough study of South Korean presidential leadership. Since then I have focused my time and energies on research and writing on Korean political leadership.

Although I may not be the most qualified person to write such a book, I have given my utmost effort. I felt my full commitment was especially required as this is probably the first book to evaluate all seven full-term South Korean presidents. Although I am a typical scholar, my extensive real world experience in three presidencies has changed my views on Korean leadership. This work was an ambitious and daunting task, because it covers the entire period from 1945 to early 2007. Although there are no doubt shortcomings and problems with my book, it is my hope that it provides a more thorough analysis of contemporary Korean politics and leadership than what is already available, and that it contributes to a more balanced understanding of South Korean presidents and the dynamic changes of post-1945 Korea.

* * *

In this book, meant not only for scholars and students of Korea but also for the general reader, I have tried to avoid academic jargon as much as possible. For much the same reason, to the extent possible I have steered clear of Korean words and terms. Naturally, the inclusion of a large number of Korean names was inevitable. With the exception of Syngman Rhee (the version of his name by which he is widely known outside of Korea), I have always put the family name first, as is Korean custom. For the names of South Korean presidents from Park Chung Hee to Kim Dae Jung, as well as with other well-known Koreans like Kim Il Sung and Kim Jong Il, I have romanized the name as those individuals do or did. Other Korean names are rendered in English using the official standards for romanization promulgated by the South Korean government in 2000 (for example, as Kim Jong-pil).

I began my research for this book with my arrival at the East-West Center in 1996. My stay as a visiting scholar accorded me a comfortable and prestigious scholarly perch. The Center is located on the campus of the University of Hawaii at Manoa, and the university's main library, the Hamilton Library, is well known for its wealth of material on Asia, including Korea. I am particularly grateful to the East-West Center, which put me in charge of the POSCO Visiting Fellowship, a position that allowed me to meet many distinguished scholars. I extend my heartfelt thanks to Dr. Charles E. Morrison, President of the East-West Center, Dr. Lee-Jay Cho, Dr. Muthiah Alagappa, and my many other colleagues at the Center for their support, encouragement, and friendship. Research grants from the Samsung Economic Research Institute and the Y. S. Mae Foundation of Los Angeles made it possible for me to concentrate more fully on this effort. I am indebted to those institutions. I wish to thank the librarians of Hamilton Library, University of Hawaii, the Korean National Assembly Library, the Blue House Library, and the U. S. National Archives for assisting my research.

I express my special thanks to my interviewees, senior advisers or former presidential ministers. In-Sang Song, Minister of Finance and Hyun-Hwack Shin, Minister of Reconstruction during the Syngman Rhee administration, Dr. Duck-Woo Nam, Minister of Finance and then of the Economic Planning Board, Chung-Yum Kim, Blue House Chief of Staff, and Suk-Jae Lee, Minister of Government Administration during the Park Chung Hee administration, Dr. Il Sakong, senior economic advisor to President Chun Doo Hwan, and Dr. Myung Oh, Minister of Telecommunications during the Chun administration, Dr. Chong-Whi Kim, National Security Advisor to President Roh Tae

Preface and Acknowledgements

Woo, and Dr. Hakjoon Kim, presidential spokesman of the Roh administration, Dr. Chong-Wook Chung, National Security Adviser to President Kim Young Sam, and Dr. Se-Il Park, Senior Adviser for Social Welfare to President Kim Young Sam, Bong-Kyun Kang, Senior Economic Adviser to President Kim Dae Jung, and Dong-Won Lim, National Security Adviser to President Kim Dae Jung, and Dr. Jong-Chan Lee, former National Assemblyman and adviser to several presidents.

Professors Yonhyok Choe, University College of South Stockholm, Russell J. Dalton, University of California at Irvine, Hong Nack Kim, West Virginia University, Hans-Dieter Klingemann, Director of Social Science Research Center in Berlin, Philippe E. Schmitter, European University Institute, Doh C. Shin, University of Missouri, and David I. Steinberg, Georgetown University read part or all of my manuscript and offered their valuable input. Dr. Roger W. Benjamin, my former academic adviser and currently president of the Council for Aid to Education in New York, Professor Emeritus Ilpyong J. Kim, University of Connecticut, Professor Jungmin Seo, University of Hawaii at Manoa, and Dr. Sheila Smith and Dr. Terrance Bigalke of the East-West Center, were also generous enough to read the manuscript and provide their valued input. Professor Victor D. Cha, Georgetown University, Larry Diamond, Senior Research Fellow at the Hoover Institution, Professor David Kang, Dartmouth College, Professor Hong Yung Lee, University of California at Berkeley, Professor Emerson M.S. Niou, Duke University, Professor Susan J. Pharr, Harvard University, and Professor David P. Rapkin, University of Nebraska, all provided invaluable academic advice.

In Korea, professors Chung-Si Ahn, Seoul National University, Mikyung Chin, Ajou University, Sung-Don Hwang, Hankuk University of Foreign Studies, In-Young Kim, Hallym University, Junghyun Shin, Kyunghee University, Byung-Kook Kim, Korea University, Myungsoon Shin, Yonsei University, Jae-Kap Ryoo, Kyonggi University, Dukmin Yun, the Institute of Foreign Affairs and National Security, and Dr. Jong-Chun Baek, president of the Sejong Institute also read part or all of the manuscript and made helpful comments and suggestions. Professor Chung-in Moon of Yonsei University and Professor Sung Deuk Haham of Korea University provided valuable materials.

I would also like to thank Karla Fallon, Ph.D. candidate, University of British Columbia, and Daniel Kane, Ph.D. candidate, University of Hawaii at Manoa, for their comments and editorial advice, and Cynthia Yamane, for her secretarial support. I also express my appreciation to Dr. Marcia Craig, a professional editor in Alberta, Canada, who improved the text. It has also been a great pleasure to work with Doug Merwin of EastBridge.

Finally, this book could not have been written without the loving support and encouragement of my wife, Jaemyung Kim.

Choong Nam Kim
Honolulu, Hawaii

The Korean Presidents

Leadership for Nation Building

Chapter One
Introduction

> "Men make history and not the other way around. In periods where there is no leadership, society stands still. Progress occurs when courageous, skillful leaders seize the opportunity to change things for the better."
> —Harry S. Truman

The Blue House Blues[1]

South Korea's nation-building efforts succeeded in the midst of abject poverty and scarce resources and under the most trying circumstances—the legacy of Japanese rule, national division, civil war, the Korean War and continual confrontation with North Korea.[2] South Korea, with its thriving economy and dynamic democracy, oft referred to as "the miracle on the Han," has acquired a fascinating dual identity as "an East Asian model of economic prosperity and political democracy."[3] The Korean experience of building a modern state is indeed extraordinary, not only in the history of Korea, but also in comparison with many other third-world nations. In the 1950s the country was one of the poorest in the world, but by 2004 with its per capita income of $16,900 (increasing per capita income 125 times in 40 years) it had gained entry, as the tenth largest economy in the world, into the exclusive club of industrialized nations—the Organization for Economic Cooperation and Development (OECD). In early 1998, Korea also became the first third-wave democracy in East Asia to transfer power peacefully to an opposition party. Such swift national achievement has no parallel in history.

Yet despite such remarkable progress, South Korea continues to be regarded as a country of "missing leaders." Its first president, Syngman Rhee, the legendary leader of the independence movement and anti-Communist struggle, was driven from office by a student uprising. President Park Chung Hee, arguably the architect of South Korea's modernization, was murdered by one of his own associates. Presidents Chun Doo Hwan and Roh Tae Woo, who steered the nation through the difficult period of the 1980s and early 1990s, were jailed on charges of treason and corruption. Kim Young Sam, a courageous fighter for democracy, is now widely regarded as a failed president, especially in light of the 1997 economic crisis. And Kim Dae Jung, often called the Mandela of Asia, left office in disgrace amid a series of policy failures and corruption scandals. It is a great irony that South Korea's nation building is lauded while the leaders who largely

---

[1] The Blue House, known to Koreans as *Chong Wa Dae*, is the office and residence of the president of the Republic of Korea.
[2] It is fair to state that nation building is a higher level of national development than state building. An adequate level of nation building may be characterized by a stable society, an advanced economy and a high level of political institutionalization.
[3] *New York Times*, December 26, 1995, A14.

Introduction

engineered it are criticized and blamed for the failures and problems of the nation.

Does all this mean that South Korea has achieved its phenomenal success without leadership? Certainly not. South Korea's politics are leader-centric: the presidency has been the heart and mind of the country. Rather, South Korean presidents may be seen as victims of their country's turbulent modern history. The challenges facing post-1945 South Korea were formidable, with national partition and economic collapse exacerbated by the devastating Korean War. The nation was struggling for survival from the twin menaces of Communism and poverty. Extraordinary circumstances demanded extraordinary measures and, in its efforts to overcome threat and adversity, South Korean presidents made numerous trials and many mistakes, demanding the suffering and sacrifice of many. It is no wonder that protest and resistance became widespread. Even in Western societies, the most successful leaders of recent decades have been vilified.[4] Charles de Gaulle, who rescued France from anarchy in 1958, gave it stability, and laid the foundations of its present prosperity, was the object of intense hostility throughout his rule and was ignominiously turned out by popular vote in 1969. Margaret Thatcher, who performed similar services for Britain, was savagely axed by her colleagues in 1990. Abraham Lincoln, one of the greatest American presidents, was often regarded as a dictator.[5]

A leader in a developing nation, who must deal concurrently and under challenging circumstances, with many problems, becomes an easy target of criticism. Lee Kwan Yew of Singapore, perhaps the most resourceful of all postwar leaders, who transformed a city state with no natural resources and a per capita income of less than $100 into one of the richest states in the world, has been bitterly denounced as an autocrat by many in the world. Although there has been great progress, the South Korean people have remained largely frustrated by the many unresolved problems. In such cases, it is the leader who takes the blame. Former United States ambassador to South Korea Donald Gregg has noted, "Korean presidents fall victim to the expectation game that they are going to solve all the problems of the country. When they don't, people focus on what they haven't done, rather than what they have."[6] This is a common phenomenon in third world nations. Louis Fisher, a journalist and author of biographies of Gandhi and Sukarno, presents an insightful view of what people demand of their leaders:

> The new states of Asia and Africa were born in dreams and live on hope. Their people pine for a savior. They are hero-worshippers. They worship yet criticize. Imperfections in their idol make them bitter. He is a god who must produce miracles—or else. Asians are both impatient and impassive, and one can never know when impatience will take the upper hand... This one-man eminence may turn his head or break it. It is a tremendous responsibility, a great opportunity, and in the final analysis an impossibility. No single individual can achieve what a poor, underdeveloped country expects of him. He inevitably disappoints. His pink charm grows tarnished.[7]

---

[4] Paul Johnson, "A World without Leaders", *Commentary*, 98: 1 (July 1994), 21.
[5] Thomas J. Dilorenzo, *The Real Lincoln* (Roseville, CA: Prima, 2002).
[6] Quoted in Doug Struck, "For Kim, an Unhappy Ending", *Washington Post*, September 14, 2002.
[7] Louis Fischer, *The Story of Indonesia* (New York: Harper and Brothers, 1959), 296.

Introduction

What then were the roles of South Korean presidents during the post-1945 period of historical challenge and achievement? Over the last half century, South Korea has boasted some strong and domineering leaders who have made valuable contributions to the building of a modern nation. Yet, viewpoints of observers and historians conflict about the criteria by which these leaders should be judged and no consensus of opinion has emerged. Compared with other Asian democracies, South Korean distrust of their presidency and government is exceptionally high.[8] The negative view of South Koreans is not based on an objective evaluation and understanding of their presidencies. South Korean presidents are often criticized but seldom properly evaluated. Despite the central role of presidents in South Korean life, no systematic study of the nation's presidential leadership exists.[9] Indeed, the subject of South Korean political leadership as a whole has been surprisingly neglected.

The dominant trend in Korean social science, heavily influenced by Americans, has been a critique of government and president. The United States was born in a revolution against state authority. There are, therefore, constant differences separating America from everyone else: It is consistently more antistatist, individualistic, laissez-faire, and egalitarian than other democracies.[10] "When an American thinks about the problem of government-building," as Huntington puts it, "he directs himself not to the creation of authority and accumulation of power but rather to the limitation of authority and the division of power.... [He] is so fundamentally antigovernment that he identifies with restriction on government."[11] The antistatist academic trend led to a power-oriented approach in American political science; the dominant concept is politics as power. This approach equates politics with the pursuit of power and assumes that political leaders spend much of their energy prolonging or maximizing their power.[12] Blessed with economic plenty, social well-being, and political stability in the United States, American political science has thus been indifferent to political development and leadership, which handicaps the country in assisting political development of developing nations.[13]

Western (mainly American) influence had been far stronger in Korea than in any other new nation. During the three-year American occupation after liberation, Americans imposed their standards and institutions, including their presidential system. The Korean War and its legacy made South Korea dependent on continued American assistance and

---

[8] According to a 2004 World Economic Forum survey among sixty countries carried out by Gallup International, Koreans' criticism about the dishonesty of political leaders (85 percent) registers one of the highest percentages. Other countries higher than Korea were: Ecuador (96 percent), Mexico (93 percent), Nigeria (92 percent), Bolivia (91 percent), Peru (91 percent), India (91 percent), and Poland (90 percent), see <www.weforum.org/site/homepublic.nsf/Content/B205AC764B>.

[9] Despite the importance of political leaders in developing nations, serious works on the presidency or presidential system outside of the United States are limited. *Presidential Studies Quarterly* focuses exclusively on the United States.

[10] Seymour M. Lipset, *American Exceptionalism: A Double-Edged Sword* (New York: Norton, 1995).

[11] Huntington, *Political Order in Changing Societies*, 7.

[12] For a critique of this approach, see Tucker, *Politics as Leadership*. Some Korean scholars tend to blindly apply the approach to the study of Korean politics and leadership. For example, Kim Ho-chin, *Hanguk chongch'i chaeje ron* (Treatises on Korean Political System).

[13] Huntington, *op. cit.*, 5-7; and Paige, *Scientific Study of Political Leadership*, 11-40.

5

Introduction

advice. During this period, everything American was blindly accepted as a model in Korea. There was an enormous gap between Western ideals and Korean reality, but foreign scholars and journalists paid little attention to the difficulties South Korea faced, especially during the 1950s and 1960s. They wrote of Korean leaders in terms of biased stereotypes, reinforcing unfavorable images. As Jeanne J. Kirkpatrick, former United States ambassador to the United Nations, once said, "Most of the governments in the world are, by American standards, bad governments. Democracy has been rare in the world."[14]

Korean intellectuals tend to reflect these Western views and to evaluate and criticize their leaders using Western standards. It is no surprise that South Korean presidents fall short of expectations. There has been a tendency to define Korean politics in terms of a simple dichotomy between democracy and dictatorship. Thus, Korean presidents of earlier decades were likely to be regarded as "dictators" or at best "developmental dictators." However, leaders alone were not responsible for the failure of Korean democracy. Clinton L. Rossiter suggests three types of threats to democracy—war, economic catastrophe, and social unrest.[15] In fact, inexperienced and incompetent South Korean governments struggled with all those threats during the early period of the Republic. No government anywhere in the world could deal adequately with such a set of compounded problems. The trial and error of democracy in Korea is not unique; it is a phenomenon seen among most new democracies. Until the mid-1980s the failures of democracy was more the rule than the exception among developing nations.[16] Until the late 1980s Asia was hardly a lodestar of democracy. Japan and India stood as the sole exceptions in the region. Furthermore, the transplantation of the American presidential system rarely produced lasting political stability in most new democracies. Western democracy, itself, took centuries to take root and develop, and its path was not straight. Therefore, it makes little sense to compare Korean democracy with Western democracies.

Under the leadership of life-long democratic crusaders such as Kim Young Sam and Kim Dae Jung, serious tensions arose between democratic means and ends, as the country worked to cope with economic crisis while attempting to carry out democratic reforms. The task of simultaneously pursuing democratic reform and economic restructuring has proven difficult. These two democratically elected presidents indeed turned out to be authoritarian leaders similar to their predecessors.[17]

The outbreak of the 1997 Korean economic crisis and the continuation of ineffective leadership have rekindled nostalgia for the "good old days" of the authoritarian governments that contributed so much to economic prosperity. In the wake of the economic crisis, it was a popular belief that another Park Chung Hee was needed to revive the Korean miracle.[18] According to a 2001 survey, a sizeable majority (82 percent)

---

[14] Quoted in Richard M. Nixon, *Leaders* (New York: Warner Books, 1982), 340.

[15] Rossiter, *op. cit.*, 6.

[16] Linz and Stephan, eds., *The Breakdown of Democratic Regimes*. Of 93 cases, there are thirty-seven cases of stable democracy and fifty-five cases of democratic breakdown. See Alan Siaroff, "Premature Democracies: the Promotion of Development and Political-Cultural Factors", *Third World Quarterly*, 20:2 (1999): 405-419.

[17] For a discussion of this problem, see Fareed Zakaria, "The Rise of Illiberal Democracy", *Foreign Affairs* 76:6 (1997): 22-43.

[18] Doh C. Shin, *Mass Politics and Culture in Democratizing Korea*, 263.

of South Koreans believed Korean democracy to be in crisis, while a plurality of the respondents rated the Kim Dae Jung government more negatively than the authoritarian government of Chun Doo Hwan.[19] In South Korea there is a growing perception that the recent "democratic governments" have been neither very democratic nor very effective. Such crises of leadership and political instability have continued under President Roh Moo Hyun; there seems to be no easy solution in sight.

LEADERSHIP FOR NATION BUILDING

Not surprisingly, there has been a tendency to apply the standards of leadership—mostly American—of developed countries to the study of Korean leaders, without due consideration of the historical, economic, social and security realities in which their governments operated.[20] It seems that post-1945 South Korea has been regarded as a "normal" state—not much different from a Western democracy, which is generally socially stable, economically prosperous, and politically institutionalized and mature. It may be argued that South Korea during the early decades of its history was located at the other end of the extreme—highly vulnerable in terms of security, socially chaotic, economically poor, and politically underdeveloped. Nevertheless, scholars and writers of leadership in South Korea and other third world nations tend to remove leaders from their particular contexts. To evaluate leaders in such isolation is to see only part of the picture. Existing studies of South Korean presidents also reveal a methodological weakness: writers typically apply a trait or institutional approach which limits the scope of the study.

The trait approach focuses on the personalities of individual leaders.[21] A fault in this approach is an emphasis on the "individual" rather than on the individual as a factor in a unique social and political milieu. Another problem with this approach is a tendency to blame the leader for the failures and ailments of the nation, without understanding the circumstances in which the leader operates. In an institutional approach, it is assumed that the nature of a leader's role is determined in large part by the constitution and laws that define it, and by a well-established political process.[22] This approach focuses on interactions between the chief executive and other political institutions such as the legislature, political parties, and other politically relevant organizations. However, institutions are only one aspect of the leadership environment. The underdevelopment of political institutions among third world nations poses a major challenge to applying the institutional approach. It was Montesquieu's dictum that "at the birth of societies, it is the leaders of the commonwealth who create the institutions; afterwards it is the institutions that shape the leaders."[23] In the same context, Benjamin and Duvall argue

---

[19] Doh C. Shin, "Mass Politics, Public Opinion, and Democracy in Korea", in Samuel S. Kim, ed., *Korea's Democratization*, 65.

[20] Gunar Myrdal writes, "social science 'models', more or less appropriate to Western experience, are uncritically applied to non-Western developmental situations." *Asian Drama*, vol. 1 (New York: Pantheon Books, 1971), 73.

[21] Barber, *Presidential Character*; and Koo Kwangmo, *Daetongryongron* (A Study of Presidents).

[22] Pfiffner, *Modern Presidency*; and Hess, *Organizing the Presidency*.

[23] Rustow, *A World of Nations*, 135.

that in an advanced society political leaders are "constrained by the institutional-legal order," while in a developing society they are "the shaper of the emerging institutional-legal order."[24]

Leadership is a function of its situation; it is contingent on the interaction between the leader and the environment in which the leader operates.[25] Different historical, social and political contexts make different demands on leaders; what may be effective or advantageous leadership for one society may be disadvantageous for another. In other words, leadership tasks in developing nations are quite different from those encountered in Western democracies; consequently, leadership strategies and styles must differ.[26] In order to understand and evaluate third-world leaders, we need to pay more attention to their extraordinary leadership environments—formidable obstacles and challenges, difficult national tasks, and limited governmental capacity.

In a developing nation, therefore, situational factors tend to have more influence on a leader's behavior than the leader's personality or political institution. Therefore, a "situational approach" is more appropriate in leadership studies of developing nations.[27] The most popular situational approach is the contingency theory of leadership effectiveness developed by Fred E. Fiedler. According to Fiedler, leadership effectiveness is the result of interactions between the style of the leader and the characteristics of the environment in which the leader works.[28] He argues that a task-oriented and authoritarian style of leadership is more effective than a relationship-oriented (democratic) style under uncertain or difficult situations. In an uncertain situation where leader-follower relations are poor, the task is unstructured, or the legitimacy of the leader is weak, the task-oriented leader who gets things accomplished proves to be the most successful.

The nature and process of nation building are not well understood. Nation building is creating something where once was nothing. As Machiavelli noted, "There is nothing more difficult to arrange, more doubtful of success, and more dangerous to carry through, than to initiate a new order of things."[29] Emerging nations may be destined to pass through a period of turmoil, violence, and radical political experimentation on the road to social and political maturity. Even under the best of conditions, nation building is a difficult task. Thus, only a few states have succeeded in nation building while many others have failed, even collapsed.[30] Since the early 1990s, we have witnessed serious crises in Somalia, Haiti, Cambodia, Bosnia, Kosovo, Rwanda, Liberia, Sierra Leone, Congo, and Afghanistan. There are many failed leaders and even today many nations are experiencing a leadership crisis. In those nations, weak, incompetent, or nonexistent

---

[24] Roger Benjamin and Raymond Duvall, "The Capitalist State in Context", in Benjamin and Elkin, eds., *The Democratic State*, 42-45.
[25] Elgie, *Political Leadership in Liberal Democracies*, 7-8.
[26] Jones, *Leadership and Politics*, 89.
[27] Albert J. Murphy, "A Study of the Leadership Process", *American Sociological Review* 6 (1941): 647-687.
[28] Elcock, *Political Leadership*, 92-93; Jerry L. Gray and Frederick A. Starke, *Organizational Behavior* (Columbus, OH: Merrill, 1988), 264; and Robert T. Justice, "Leadership Effectiveness: A Contingency Approach", *Academy of Management Journal*, 18:1 (March 1975), 160-166.
[29] Niccolo Machiavelli, translated by George Bull, *The Prince* (Baltimore: Penguin Books, 1961), 51.
[30] Rotberg, *State Failure and State Weakness in a Time of Terror*.

government is the source of the crisis. However, the problems of nation building have not been restricted to third world states. The European state-building experience was much more violent and top-down than is commonly acknowledged.[31] Therefore, the ability to create missing state capabilities and institutions is critical to nation building.[32]

In order to evaluate political leaders in developing nations, it is crucial to understand the challenges and problems leaders of third world nations generally face.[33] First, there are the crises of identity and legitimacy.[34] Leaders of new nations face agonizing obstacles in winning the full commitment of their citizenry, something which is taken for granted in most Western societies. In the case of South Korea, identity and legitimacy have been the most serious political problems. A sense of national identity was fatally damaged by colonial rule. Then, the artificial division of the country and the establishment of an independent government in the southern half of the peninsula created a legitimacy crisis. No Koreans accepted the division of the country and therefore not only leftists but also moderates boycotted the 1948 election for the establishment of the Republic. Since then North Korea has been an enemy as well as a partner in reunification for South Koreans. Leftists and pro-unification groups have always questioned the legitimacy of the South Korean government and its anti-Communist policies. Political and administrative appointments of former colonial officials have also weakened the legitimacy of the government.

Second, there is a high degree of internal and/or external threat.[35] Public order is taken for granted in the industrial world, but such is often far from the case in third world nations. As Huntington puts it, "developing nations must expect a fairly high level of civil unrest for some time."[36] Furthermore, fledgling states are often under threat of aggression from neighboring countries. Aside from the importance of achieving economic development before worrying about democracy, transitional societies may fall into a state of disorder in which all progress becomes impossible. Under these circumstances, the problem of survival dominates other considerations. Even in Western democracies war government tends to concentrate power in the hands of the executive.[37] Third, a devastating combination of war and revolution, at times associated with massive migration, has been the most common sort of social dislocation to rock existing social and political structures of developing countries. Fourth, poverty is the most common problem facing developing societies. Economic underdevelopment and crisis degrade national morale and precipitate social unrest, triggering a legitimacy crisis. Nations that suffer from scarce resources and low governmental capacity are particularly prone to these factors. Finally, the time required to successfully complete nation building is

---

[31] Charles Tilly, ed., *The Formation of National States in Western Europe* (Princeton, NJ: Princeton University Press, 1975), 71.
[32] Francis Fukuyama, *State-Building*; and Joel S. Migdal, *Strong Societies, Weak States*.
[33] Anderson et al., *Issues of Political Development*, 8-11.
[34] Leonard Binder et al., *Crises and Sequences in Political Development*.
[35] See Job, ed., *Insecurity Dilemma*; Ayoob, *Third World Security Predicament*; and Azar and Moon, eds., *National Security in the Third World*.
[36] Huntington, *Political Order*, 42.
[37] Clinton L. Rossiter, *Constitutional Dictatorship: Crisis Government in Modern Democracies* (Princeton: Princeton University Press, 1948), 293-294.

Introduction

fundamentally different between the West and the third world. The tasks of nation building, which in the West were accomplished over long stretches of time in an evolutionary manner, in the third world must be completed in a revolutionary way, within a few decades, and under more complex and difficult circumstances.[38]

Thus, students of the third world posit the centrality of state building in the political life of their own states.[39] To this end, three primary functions of state building are emphasized: to protect people and property (law and order and national defense), to establish government institutions and formulate policy (policy capacity), and to extract resources to support governmental activities and provide public services (taxation or extraction). In other words, state building includes creating political institutions and political legitimacy and providing basic services such as security, law and order, and education. A good government is one that provides peace, security, minimal levels of material and psychic satisfaction, and that makes progressive efforts to solve existing and emergent problems.[40] We therefore find three major tasks of leadership for nation building in general[41]:

- *national security* (internal and external security)
- *economic welfare* (economic development and public services such as education)
- *political development* (political freedom and individual rights)

The political capacities of new states, which struggle to promote these tasks of nation building, are overloaded by the conjunction of many problems and challenges. These problems include the highly disruptive colonial inheritance, lack of policy capacity, underdevelopment of political and administrative institutions, and explosive demands for political participation, economic redistribution, and social justice.[42] Introduction of a democratic system will either decrease state capacity or generate demands for new types of state capabilities that are weak or nonexistent.[43] How to promote governance of new states thus becomes crucial. An ordinary approach is usually inappropriate in such extraordinary circumstances. In established Western democracies, what James McGregor Burns called "transactional" (managerial) leadership is appropriate. In third world countries where circumstances are uncertain and unfavorable and radical change is required, "transformational" or charismatic leadership may be of great importance.[44]

There is a hierarchy or priority among these three tasks of nation building.[45] The relative importance of these factors differs by time (within a society) and place (among

---

[38] Mohammed Ayoob, "The Security Predicament of the Third World State: Reflections on State Making in a Comparative Perspective", in Job, *op. cit.*, 63-80.

[39] Ayoob, *Third World Security Predicament*, 22-23.

[40] Tsurutani, Taketsugu, *Politics of National Development*, 175-179.

[41] Thomas considers military security, economic development, and political democracy as the three essential pillars of a nation. For detailed analysis of their relationship in India, see Raju G. C. Thomas, *Democracy, Security, and Development in India*.

[42] Ayoob, *Third World Security Predicament*, 41.

[43] Fukuyama, *op. cit.*, 15.

[44] Burns, *Leadership*, 5.

[45] Rotberg, *op. cit.*, 3.

Introduction

societies at the same time). In their study of the challenges faced by Japan and Turkey in achieving nation building, Ward and Rustow suggest that these nations faced four sequential crises: a crisis of national identity, the critical need for self-defense against external enemies, the need for economic development, and the need for political development.[46] Thus, in transitional societies priority setting is much more important than it is in Western democracies.

Post-1945 South Korean circumstances could not have been less favorable. Therefore, interactions and competition among the three crucial national goals (national security and stability, economic growth, and democracy) have dominated Korean politics. Like Israel, South Korea has been a state under siege: the country has remained locked in conflict with North Korea that entirely denies South Korea's authority or even its right to exist at all. Until the early 1960s, therefore, survival and security had been the main concerns of the country. When the mutual defense treaty with the United States improved the security of the peninsula, economic hardship became another major concern of South Korea. Of course, national security and social stability are interrelated with economic conditions.[47] Without security and social order, a stable and viable economy cannot develop; acute insecurity and sociopolitical turmoil discourages foreign investment and impairs economic growth. At the same time, without a solid economic foundation, security and social order cannot be guaranteed. After considerable economic growth, democratic development becomes a dominant national agenda.[48]

In South Korea, the emphasis shifted from the achievement of security and stability to that of economic prosperity, and finally to an extension of political liberty. This sequence of policy priorities allows development to be completed in stages—conditions for the success of each stage being built in an earlier stage. U.S. objectives in Korea have also been in priority order: security, economic growth, and democracy.[49] Until the mid-1970s, Washington believed that totalitarian Communist systems were more oppressive and a greater threat to the rest of the world than other types of authoritarian political systems, and supported anti-Communist authoritarian governments. After the Communist takeover of Cuba and the Communist expansion in Southeast Asia and other part of the world in the early 1960s, the Kennedy administration realized that economic prosperity would prevent Communist revolutions in developing countries, and supported economic growth in Korea. Finally, during the 1987 mass demonstration against the Chun Doo Hwan government, the United States influenced Korean political process, contributing to the transition to full democracy.

---

[46] Ward and Rostow, eds., *Political Modernization in Japan and Turkey*, 465-466. Burns also posits that people begin with the need for security and physical survival, and once those needs are met they concern themselves with "higher" needs like democracy and human rights. See Burns, *Leadership*, chapter 2. Psychologist Abraham Maslow suggests a hierarchy of needs: survival, security, social, esteem, and then once those are assured, self-actualization. See Abraham H. Maslow, *Motivation and Personality* (New York: Harper, 1954).

[47] Ethan B. Kapstein, "Economic Development and National Security", in Azar and Moon, eds., *op. cit.*, 136-151.

[48] Priority among security, economic growth and democracy is debatable. See Thomas, *op. cit.*, 28-30.

[49] David I. Steinberg, "U.S. Policy and Human Rights in the Republic of Korea: The Influence of Policy or the Policy of Influence", in Debra Liang-Fenton, ed., *Implementing U.S. Human Rights Policy* (Washington, DC: U.S. Institute of Peace, 2004), 176-179; and Huntington, *Political Order*, 5-7.

Introduction

An understanding of the interplay among issues of security, economic growth, and political development is necessary before an analysis of Korean leadership can be informative.

Nothing is as critical as the provision of national security. A government's prime function is to provide social and national security—to prevent cross-border invasions and infiltrations, to eliminate domestic threats, and to prevent crime and related dangers to domestic human security. If a considerable number of people question the legitimacy of their government, and if external or internal forces threaten the fledgling nation, its survival and stability become primary concerns of leadership. South Korea, Taiwan, Pakistan, and Israel are good examples. Without security, neither a functioning democracy nor a functioning economy can be guaranteed. In an April 2004 poll by the Coalition Provisional Authority in Iraq, 70 percent of Iraqis cited security as their single most important priority.[50]

Acute security pressures tend to compromise and erode democratic process, however. New democracies are sometimes faced with the prospect of either authoritarian encroachment or collapse as they attempt to address severe internal and external security problems. Governments often call upon their citizens to make sacrifices in order to preserve the security, sovereignty, and stability of the state, and their demand for personal and financial sacrifices often leads to the denial of the individual's basic rights and freedoms. Thus, attempts to establish democracies in Asia—Pakistan, Bangladesh, Myanmar, Thailand, Indonesia, Singapore, the Philippines, Taiwan, and South Korea—have been stymied at various times over the last few decades, usually in the name of national security or political and economic stability. During its first decade and a half, Israeli democracy was also paternalistic, personalistic, and top-heavy. The country's father figure, David Ben-Gurion, qualified for the dubious title of "democratic dictator," and Israel was portrayed as "a most imperfect democracy."[51] Whereas Western democracies perceive human rights as absolute and universal, developing nations often see their internal security problems and resultant human rights violations as part of a continuing process of state building. Western democracies are not entirely immune to security pressures that threaten to undermine the democratic system. In the United States, the internment of about 120,000 Japanese-Americans during World War II was undertaken on the grounds of national security. Approximately 22,000 Japanese-Canadians were similarly interned during that war. In 1988, the British passed legislation that limited democracy in troubled Northern Ireland, and the Thatcher government barred British radio and television from broadcasting interviews with the Irish Republican Army or its affiliated organizations.

Insecurity has been a perpetual feature of South Korea; the world has better realized the seriousness of South Korean security dilemma since the North Korean nuclear crisis in recent years. The condition of a divided Korea has presented a unique and extraordinary situation, a kind of acute security crisis. Two politically incompatible and mutually hostile regimes were established across the 38th parallel, each claiming jurisdiction over the entire country. From

---

[50] Fareed Zakaria, "No Security, No Democracy", *Newsweek*, May 24, 2004; and Ji Hermes, "Iraq Prefers Security to Democracy", <http://www.uwire.com/content/topops072104002.html>.

[51] Avner Yaniv, ed., *National Security and Democracy in Israel*, 3 and 9. For Taiwan, see Martin L. Lasater, *Taiwan: Facing Mounting Threats* (Washington, DC: Heritage Foundation, 1984). In the case of India, see Thomas, *op. cit.*, 20ff.

Introduction

the beginning, North Korea declared the elimination of the South Korean government to be its primary national goal. South Korea fought a bloody war, has remained technically at war, and has lived with the possibility of renewed and total war since the armistice in July 1953. In the period following the war, confrontation between the two Koreas prevailed.[52] The list of North Korean threats, provocations, clashes, and hostile acts is endless, making Pyongyang more provocative than any other government in the world. It reaches into the present day. The peninsula is one of the most heavily armed spots in the world. Besides preparing for reunification by force, the North Korean regime has aimed to bring the South under its rule by a strategy of "socialist revolution in the South."[53] Most student demonstrations in South Korea have historically been at least influenced by Pyongyang. Hwang Jang-yop, a defected top-level North Korean leader, said, "Practically all the student demonstrations in South Korea can be said to have been orchestrated by agents of the North."[54] Insurgence and social unrest threatened the newly installed government. Violence since the liberation until the Korean War claimed over 100,000 South Korean lives.[55] Thus, policy goals adopted by South Korean governments were heavily security-oriented. The security situation made the role of the military more important than in other developing nations.[56] It is difficult to make sense of South Korea without understanding the impact of the Korean War and consequent security problems. Earlier Korean governments and the United States oftentimes put security and stability considerations ahead of human rights concerns in South Korea.[57]

The internal situation of South Korea was also unstable in the early years of the republic.[58] It was a revolutionary situation, often termed a "powder keg," ready to explode at the application of a spark. The massive migration and social dislocation before and during the Korean War and unprecedented social and economic changes during the following decades resulted in serious social and political instability. During the colonial period, the established Korean social and political order was fundamentally disrupted, and all forms of authority weakened. After liberation, about 4 million Koreans, who had been forced to move to Japan, Manchuria, and Sakhalin during World War II, returned to South Korea and settled down, mostly in the cities. After the division, another one million North Korean refugees came to the South. During the Korean War, more than 1.3 million South Korean civilians and soldiers were killed and more than 2 million wounded; and almost 8 million, or 40 percent of the population, wandered the country as refugees. Unable to meet basic needs, Koreans, especially urbanites, often resorted to violent means. Starting in the 1960s, rapid urbanization, industrialization and mass education became new causes of social instability.

In studies of South Korean politics and presidential leadership, however, few

---

[52] For example, see Yong-Pyo Hong, *State Security and Regime Security*.

[53] Martin, *Under the Loving Care of the Fatherly Leader*, ch. 8.

[54] "Hwang Jang-Yop: North Will Nuke Japan and S. Korea", available at <http://www.kimsoft.com/korea/hwang1.htm>.

[55] Merrill, *Korea: Peninsula Origin of the War*, 181.

[56] Henderson, *Korea: Politics of the Vortex*, 355-357.

[57] William M. Drennan, "The Tipping Point: Kwangju, May 1980", in Steinberg, ed., *Korean Attitudes toward the United States*, 295.

[58] For details, see Henderson, *op. cit.*, chs. 4-6.

scholars explicitly and appropriately address national security issues.[59] Not one Korean college textbook of Korean politics contains a chapter (or even a section) dedicated to a discussion of Korean security issues. It is astonishing that security has been almost totally neglected in the study of Korean leadership, even in assessments of Syngman Rhee, who struggled against a Communist-led insurgency and the Korean War throughout his presidency. By contrast, in Israel, whose security situation is similar to Korea's, security has been considered an integral aspect of studies of Israeli politics and leadership.[60]

Wars have been the worst enemies of democracy, even in Western countries, and the Korean War and subsequent insecurity drastically curtailed the democratic aspirations of Koreans living in a "garrison state." Nevertheless, there is an antimilitary bias in South Korea, especially among students and intellectuals.[61] In the tradition of Buddhism and Confucianism, the man of arms was considered inferior to the man of letters—the *yangban* (landed gentry)—whose role was often seen as that of a moral critic and who paid little attention to security.[62] During and after the Korean War, however, the rapidly expanded South Korean military was established as a modern and resource-rich institution in an otherwise underdeveloped country. In the wake of the 1961 military coup, there emerged a struggle for legitimacy between civilian and military sectors. Park Chung Hee and other former military leaders who were proud of the efficiency, advanced technology and discipline of the military, despised the civilian mentality of the old order. However, intellectuals (scholars, journalists, students and the like) and the opposition regarded rule by generals-turned-presidents, even if legitimately elected, as not only illegitimate but unqualified and equated the ascendancy of the man on horseback with national degeneration. In this context, Cumings writes: "Sons of peasants [military leaders] now rode herd on the sons of aristocrats; young students infused with the idea that they had the mandate of heaven, the moral right to rule, often found themselves on the short end of a baton."[63]

The military has played an important role in many developing countries.[64] Considering South Korea's unique security challenges, a leader with a military background may seem natural. In Israel, former military leaders such as Yitzhak Rabin and Ezer Weizman played important roles in national politics.[65] In Pakistan and Bangladesh before 1990, the military was the dominant political actor. It is also interesting to note that twelve of the forty-two American presidents were former military

---

[59] Victor Cha, "Security and Democracy in South Korean Development", in Samuel S. Kim, ed., *Korea's Democratization*, 201.

[60] For details, see Yaniv, ed., *op. cit.*; and Daniel Shimshoni, *Israeli Democracy* (New York: Free Press, 1982), ch. 4.

[61] For examples, see Se-jin Kim, *Politics of Military Revolution*, ch. IV; and Henderson, *op. cit.*, 334-338.

[62] At the time of Korea's annexation by Japan in 1910, only 5,000 ill-equipped, poorly trained soldiers tried vainly to defend the country against the Japanese military takeover.

[63] Cumings, *Korea's Place in the Sun*, 349.

[64] See Johnson, ed., *Role of the Military in Underdeveloped Countries*; and Janowitz, *The Military in the Political Development of New Nations*.

[65] Yoram Peri, *Between Battles and Ballots: Israeli Military in Politics* (Cambridge, UK: Cambridge University Press, 1983).

generals. In the first hundred years of the United States, nearly every war produced a general who later became president.[66]

Once a nation is secure, it needs to develop an economy strong enough to provide for the basic needs and welfare of its people. Third world economic security is a life-or-death matter: economic growth, development, and capital accumulation are more important than issues of social equality and distributive justice—major concerns of democracy. As Benjamin and Duvall point out, in developing nations "social inequality is a necessary and hence acceptable byproduct of development: turmoil with respect to social inequality is a fully unacceptable threat to social order, to be met with the full force of the state."[67] Less democracy has thus been justified for the sake of economic growth.[68] Authoritarian regimes consider "too much democracy" unsuitable for developing countries because democracy handicaps the ability of political leaders to implement harsh but necessary economic measures. Thus, "the right to vote does not necessarily guarantee people the right to food, shelter, and the basic necessities of life."[69] Freedom from want may be more important for the poor than the freedom to vote. One careful analysis of ninety-eight countries came to the conclusion that "among the poor nations, an authoritarian political system increases the rate of economic development, while a democratic political system does appear to be a luxury which hinders development."[70] A majority of western development theorists thus seem to accept the seeming inevitability of development to be accompanied by authoritarian government.[71]

In Korea, economic growth has more important implications than in other developing countries. Economic performance is seen as a barometer in gauging the superiority of the two competing ideologies of the North and the South. In 1960, per capita income in the South was 60 dollars, while the North's figure was 208 dollars.[72] Blessed with abundant resources and Stalinist mobilization, North Korea was growing far more rapidly than South Korea. The barriers to economic improvements in South Korea—especially the unnatural division of the country, the ruinous Korean War, and the massive influx of refugees from the North—could not be surmounted easily. In the early 1960s, an American reporter characterized the country as "a divided country, war, devastation, too many people on too little land, not enough jobs, and not enough

---

[66] The Revolutionary War gave the young United States George Washington; the War of 1812 and associated Indian Wars, William Henry Harrison and Andrew Jackson; the Mexican-American War, Zachary Taylor and Franklin Pierce; and the Civil War, Ulysses S. Grant, Rutherford B. Hayes, James Garfield, and Benjamin Harrison. World War II yielded Dwight Eisenhower. Philip B. Kunhardt, Jr., Philip B. Kunhardt III, and Peter W. Kunhardt, *The American President* (New York: Riverhead, 1999), 2-5.

[67] Benjamin and Duvall, *op. cit.*, 39-40.

[68] See Thomas S. Axworthy, "Democracy and Development: Luxury or Necessity", in Bauzon, ed., *Development and Democratization in the Third World*, 111-118.

[69] Thomas, *op. cit.*, 5.

[70] Robert M. Marsh, "Does Democracy Hider Economic Development in the Latecomer Developing Nations?" *Comparative Social Research* 2 (1979): 244.

[71] Samuel P. Huntington, "The Goals of Development", in Weiner and Huntington, eds., *op. cit.*, 15; and Gersenkron, *Economic Backwardness in Historical Perspective*.

[72] Byoung-Lo Philo Kim, *Two Koreas in Development*, 66.

Introduction

resources to create enough industry to sop up the unemployed."[73] South Korea had to move fast to deal with its poverty, unemployment, inflation, overpopulation, and underdevelopment. It also had to strengthen economic foundation of its huge military. Without strong action to halt the economic stagnation and lingering social, political unrest, unification of the peninsula might well occur on terms favorable to the North. The survival and legitimacy of the Republic depended upon decreasing the widening South-North economic gap. Chiang Kai-shek's and Lee Kwan Yew's developmental strategies were derived from the motivation of regime survival and national security. Similarly, South Korean leaders had to demonstrate the effectiveness of a non-Communist path to economic development and military security.[74]

Political development, a long-term, gradual process, is the third requirement of a modern nation. It enables citizens to participate freely, openly, and fully in politics. It encompasses the essential freedoms: fundamental civil and human rights, the right to compete for office, respect and support for national and regional political institutions, and tolerance of dissent and difference. However, introducing democratic institutions in developing countries is difficult, and when such institutions are established, it is difficult to sustain them. Undoubtedly, security pressure is not the only force that prevents democracy from taking root. Poverty, illiteracy, the lack of political maturity and experience, or the tradition of authoritarian rule contributes to the difficulties of establishing and sustaining democracies.

Western-style democracy was hurriedly transplanted in 1948 onto a debilitated and inhospitable Korean political soil that had known no self-government for thirty-six years. Militaristic colonial rule had replaced an incompetent and tottering Confucian feudal dynasty. The influence of Confucianism on political understanding, culture and behavior remained pervasive. Confucian values of benevolent paternalistic authority are assumed to promote respect for government and its leaders.[75] The newly introduced democratic principles were nearly the opposite of the premises upon which life had been built for most Koreans up to the moment of independence. As one Korean scholar said, "Korea operates on Western hardware and Confucian software."[76] Therefore, Korean trials and errors in democracy were perhaps inevitable.

Koreans accepted democratic principles enthusiastically without knowing what they meant or implied. Nor were they fully aware of how imperfectly these ideas had been carried out in Western democracies. They did not recognize that a stable democracy is not a function of ideas alone, but of ideas that have, through long, disappointing, and often bitter experience become embedded in the lives of the people. Deviation from the ideal model of democracy has often been blamed on flaws of government and its leaders. In practice, the principles were frequently interpreted and used to legitimate opposition

---

[73] *New York Times*, March 21, 1961.

[74] Hilton L. Root, *Small Countries, Big Lessons*, 149.

[75] Yu Jeong Hwan, "Hanguk munhwawa jeongchi: yukyojeok jeongchi jilseoae daehan munhwaronjeok haesok" (Korean Culture and Politics: a Cultural Analysis of Confucian Political Order), *Hanguk jeongchi hakhaebo* (Korean Political Science Review), 29 (1995): 57-66; and Young Whan Kihl, "The Legacy of Confucian Culture and South Korean Politics", *Korea Journal*, 34(1994), 37-53.

[76] Quoted in David I. Steinberg, *Stone Mirror* (Norwalk, CT: EastBridge, 2002), 186.

to government. In post-1945 Korea, political participation was growing much more rapidly than government capability. Rapid social change—urbanization, increase in education and literacy, and mass media expansion—extended political consciousness, multiplied political demands, and broadened political participation, overloading the government and sometimes leading to breakdown and chaos. James Madison warned in *The Federalist*, No. 51, "you must first enable the government to control the governed; and in the next place it to control itself."[77] In Korea and other developing nations, governments have been unable to perform the first function, much less the second.

Owing to Confucian values and an aggressive promotion of mass education, the education level of South Korea was exceptionally high compared with other developing countries. Students and intellectuals exposed to the modern world, and in particular to the United States, perceived two great gaps. One gap was between the principles of modernity—equality, justice, individual freedom, economic well-being—and their realization in their own society. The second gap was between the existing conditions in advanced nations and those prevailing in South Korea. Thus, the more educated and informed they became, the more frustrated South Koreans grew with their leaders and government.[78] Owing to limited job opportunities, the education explosion led to increasing dissatisfaction with existing conditions, resulting in social unrest and political instability. Korean students protested against authoritarian as well as democratic governments.[79] Student opposition in Korea has been virtually independent of the nature of the government and of the nature of the policies which the government pursues.[80]

Democracy presupposes the presence of minimal economic autonomy to exercise political rights: the higher the socioeconomic level of a country, the greater the chance that it will be able to sustain a democracy.[81] When a society reaches a degree of economic development where the majority of the populace enjoys a comfortable life, democracy becomes a major concern. The priority of economic growth and social order comes under challenge when subordinate citizens and groups demand social equality and distributive justice. In addition, if authoritarian leaders succeed in overcoming insecurity and poverty, it becomes more difficult for them to justify their rule. South Korea's continuous and rapid economic growth at the sacrifice of democratic principles produced a seriously unbalanced society, one that was economically developed but politically immature, generating powerful

---

[77] Quoted in Huntington, *Political Order*, 7.

[78] Choong Nam Kim, Political Socialization: A Rational-Choice Perspective, the Case of Korea, Ph.D. Thesis, University of Minnesota, 1978; and Choong Nam Kim, "Political Socialization in Korea: External Factors and the Problem of National Identity", *Korea and World Affairs*, 5: 1 (1981), 107-119.

[79] Huntington, *Political Order*, 369-372.

[80] Seymour M. Lipset, "University Students and Politics in Underdeveloped Countries", in S. M. Lipset, ed., Special Issue on Student Politics, *Comparative Education Review*, 10 (June 1966): 132ff.

[81] Seymour M. Lipset, "Some Social Requisites of Democracy: Economic Development and Political Legitimacy", *American Political Science Review*, 53:1 (1959): 75; and Rose E. Burkhart and Michael Lewis-Beck, "Comparative Democracy: the Economic Development Thesis", *American Political Science Review*, 88 (1994): 903-910.

Introduction

pressures for democratization.[82] This imbalance led to serious tensions, ultimately attaining a crisis of legitimacy which led to a transition to full democracy. In 1988, the first year of the Roh Tae Woo administration, South Korea's per capita income reached $4,000—the level at which Adam Przeworski and his colleagues suggest, "Democracy is almost certain to survive."[83] In the late 1980s, South Koreans also witnessed the demise of Communism in Eastern Europe, weakening and strategically isolating North Korea and reducing that country's security threat toward South Korea. It was at this time that democracy became the most pressing national goal, a goal that could no longer be delayed in the name of national security and economic development.

The sequential priority among the goals of security, economics, and democracy may give an impression of insensitivity to human rights, the most fundamental and important feature of democracy. The three goals listed above may invoke incompatible values. Security is a state-centered concept. The term democracy, by contrast, puts the individual human being at the center of everything. Furthermore, in Confucian Korea individual sacrifice for family and state has often been regarded as a virtue. In South Korea under the acute and continuous threat of North Korea, the preoccupation with security and economic survival resulted in frequent violations of human rights and great sacrifices were made by many people.[84] Although security and economic growth were promoted in order to enhance the well-being of the people, violations of human rights were unjustifiable. However, given the terrible suffering and blatant human rights violations in North Korea and the constant threat to the South, it was understandable, if not inevitable, that South Korea would give priority in its national goals first to security, second to economics, and finally to democracy. We must also be careful not to judge South Korea's human rights record in the earlier decades through the prism of today's standards.

With this background, I have evaluated Korean presidencies in terms of the following criteria.[85] First, a leader of a new nation needs to provide a vision for the future of that nation. A good vision serves to strengthen national unity and galvanize popular support for, and participation in, nation building. Second, with limited political and economic resources, major tasks of nation building cannot be solved concurrently.

---

[82] Larry Diamond, "Economic Development and Democracy Reconsidered", in Gary Marks and Larry Diamond, eds., *Reexamining Democracy* (Newbury Park, CA: Sage, 1992), 93-139.

[83] Przeworski et al., *Democracy and Development*, 273.

[84] For details on human rights problems in Korea and related U.S. policy, see David I. Steinberg, "U.S. Policy and Human Rights in the Republic of Korea", in Liang-Fenton, ed., *op. cit.*, 167-213.

[85] For literature on evaluating American presidents, see Neustadt, *Presidential Power and Modern Presidents*; Gary Maranell, "The Evaluation of Presidents: An Extension of the Schlesinger Polls", *Journal of American History* 57 (1970), 104-113; and Simonton, *Why Presidents Succeed*. Greenstein suggests six qualities of an effective president: communication to the public; organizational capacity, political skill, policy vision, cognitive style, and emotional intelligence. See Fred I. Greenstein, "The Qualities of Effective Presidents: An Overview from FDR to Bill Clinton", *Presidential Studies Quarterly* 30:1 (March 2000): 178-185. Based on American criteria, Hahm uses such items as leadership quality, personality, intelligence, morality, democratic leadership, vision, appointments, crisis management, and achievement. See Hahm, Sung-Deuk, *Daetongryonghak* (The Korean Presidency).

Introduction

Therefore, agenda setting is crucial to successful leadership. In particular, security is a prerequisite for economic and political development, and adequate economic development is favorable to stable democracy. Third, managerial skill is very important in leadership for nation building. It includes the ability to make sound, informed appointments, effective organizational skills, and effective policymaking and implementation. The people of developing nations are preoccupied with the basic needs of everyday life. A political leader must be effective in improving their living conditions. In addition, nation building, which in the West was accomplished over centuries, must be completed in a few decades under more difficult circumstances. To overcome the inertia and resistance of existing institutions, a successful leader has to be highly motivated and forceful, one who can mobilize and concentrate resources to effectively implement his policies. Fourth, skill in crisis management is a critical quality, as internal and external threats to stability can be sudden and lethal. Finally, in developing nations where legitimacy and loyalty are not deeply rooted, integrity can cement popular trust and support for the leader.

In nation building, leadership style and managerial skills are two of the most important elements. A leader must produce results, especially in a developing country. A leader must be proactive, determined and task-oriented in order to overcome obstacles and tackle the difficult tasks that are certain to arise. In order to become an effective leader, managerial talent is also crucial. In terms of leadership style and managerial skill, we may divide leadership into four general types—inactive, operational, frustrated, and effective (Table 1).[86] In a developing country like South Korea, an active and achievement-oriented leader would likely be more successful.

Table 1. **Types of Leadership for Nation Building**

Leadership Style	*Low Managerial Skill*	*High Managerial Skill*
Passive	Inactive Leadership	Operational Leadership
Active	Frustrated Leadership	Effective Leadership

This book offers an empirical-historical study of seven full-term Korean presidents (from the first president Syngman Rhee to the current president Roh Moo Hyun) and their administrations. The subjects are examined in terms of changing security conditions, economic development, and political evolution. The relationship between security, economic growth, and democracy is important in understanding Korea's historical and developmental processes and presidential leadership. The book's general outline is chronological, covering the period between 1945 and early 2007.

I have addressed the following questions regarding each South Korean president: What was the context (historical, security, social, economic and political) he faced? What particular and pressing goals did he pursue and what policies did he formulate to do so? Were such goals appropriate in terms of the priority of nation building, international

---

[86] For types of American presidential leadership, see Richard Rose, "Evaluating Presidents", in George C. Edwards III, John H. Kessel, and Bert A. Rockman, eds., *Researching the Presidency* (Pittsburgh, PA: University of Pittsburgh Press, 1993), 453-484; Whicker and Moore, *When Presidents Are Great*; and Choong Nam Kim (1998), 206-219.

Introduction

relations, public support, and governmental capability? How did he implement his policies, and what were the effects of those implementations? How did his leadership style (charismatic, authoritarian, or democratic) measure up to the goals and challenges of the time? Finally, what contributions did he make to the nation, and to nation building in particular?

In order to answer these questions, I adopted a comprehensive approach — historical, comparative and analytical. In addition, I reviewed existing literature and materials on Korean political leadership, politics, economic development, security, and foreign policy. Primary and secondary sources were explored by checking the Blue House library, the National Assembly library and the National Archives of the United States and by conducting interviews with those who had participated in decision-making during each presidency. In order to enhance the objectivity of this study, I carefully considered views of domestic and foreign observers. This may be a pioneering study of the South Korean presidency, as there are very few such studies, and very limited materials, on this topic. It is also an insider's view of the modern South Korean presidency, democracy and nation building, since I am a Korean national who served as a member of the South Korean presidential staff from 1984 to 1996. In such a study of Korean presidents, one runs the risk of partiality for or against a particular leader but, having served both authoritarian and democratic presidents, I disavow any interest in making a case for or against a particular president; I have selected existing materials known to me at the time of this writing with the intention of maintaining scholarly objectivity and a balanced and comprehensive perspective.

Before discussing the South Korean presidencies, in Chapter Two I examine the initial conditions under which the Republic of Korea was established. In Chapters Three to Nine I analyze the presidencies in chronological order and in the final chapter I discuss lessons and implications.

My evaluations of Korean presidents differ from many existing views. For instance, critics blame Syngman Rhee, Park Chung Hee and Chun Doo Hwan for their authoritarian rule. This study explains how and why Rhee succeeded in saving his country from Communist rule. It also describes how Park and Chun made great strides in security and economic growth—two tasks of nation building. This work explains why former democratic crusaders, Kim Young Sam and Kim Dae Jung, turned out to be "failed presidents" and/or "imperial presidents." Their failures suggest that authoritarian leaders (Syngman Rhee, Park Chung Hee and Chun Doo Hwan) perhaps cannot be fully blamed for the trials and errors of pre-1987 Korean democracy. The book highlights the struggle for national survival during the Rhee administration, the struggle for economic development under Park Chung Hee and Chun Doo Hwan, the turbulent process of democratic transition under Roh Tae Woo and Kim Young Sam, the precipitation and management of the 1997-98 Korean financial crisis, and the controversial "sunshine" policy during the Kim Dae Jung presidency.

South Korea—a formerly war-ravaged country, a divided polity with its geostrategic location and security-scarce environment—is often regarded as an East Asian model of nation building. The study of Korean presidential leadership is both interesting and challenging, not only for Korean politics but also for comparative analysis. Since serious works on presidencies and presidential systems outside of the United States are limited, it is hoped that this study will be a valuable new addition to the literature of leadership and politics of the non-Western world.

Chapter Two
South Korea after Liberation

Upon liberation in 1945, Korea would have posed a challenge to even the most talented and determined of leaders. Thirty-five years of Japanese colonial rule had resulted in formidable socioeconomic, political, and ideological problems for Korea. The subsequent three-year American military government administration in southern Korea would leave its own mark. It is impossible to understand the problems and events faced by the establishment of the Republic of Korea (South Korea) in 1948 without reference to the legacies of Japanese colonial rule (1910-1945) and the American military government (1945-1948).

The Legacy of Japanese Rule

Japanese colonial rule in Korea was long and bitter. The Japanese rulers were militaristic, oppressive, and arbitrary, "the most despotic in the history of the Korean people."[1] Indeed, Japanese colonialism was arguably much crueler and harsher than its European counterpart. The colonial experience was intense and bitter, leaving deep fissures and conflicts with which the new Korean government had to struggle. Louise Yim, Korea's first minister of commerce and industry expressed her anger as follows:

> During forty years, you Japanese have done nothing but suck our blood. You have been trying to make us your eternal slave. You have no sense of justice or human dignity. You kill people as though they were cats or dogs. Korean people as a whole...think of the Japanese as a savage, not a civilized, people. Koreans will not yield one inch to the Japanese.[2]

When Japan annexed Korea in 1910, it established a military dictatorship. The new governor-general had absolute power over the new colony's affairs. Only generals and admirals were eligible for this position. Of the eight governors-general who successively controlled Korea, seven were army generals and one was an admiral. In Korea, the Japanese deployed two permanent army divisions, assisted by 13,000 military and regular policemen. Japan's colonial administration was sustained by its large constabulary force, which was given jurisdiction over the civilian police. The military police soon became the most dreaded enforcers of colonial directives, and their brutal oppression was a conspicuous source of grievance by the Korean people throughout the colonial period.[3]

Japanese colonial rule in Korea was unique owing to the geographic proximity of the

---

[1] See Dae-yeol Ku, *Korea under Colonialism* (Seoul: Seoul Computer Press, 1985); Andrew C. Nahm, ed., *Korea under Japanese Colonial Rule* (Kalamazoo, MI: Michigan State University, 1973); and Bruce Cumings, "The Legacy of Japanese Colonialism in Korea", in Ramon H. Myers and Mark R. Peattie, eds., *The Japanese Colonial Empire* (Princeton: Princeton University Press, 1984).
[2] Louise Yim, *My Forty Year Fight for Korea* (Seoul: Chungang University Press, 1951), 23.
[3] Dae-yeol Ku, *Korea*, 13.

colony to the colonial power and the extent of immigration between colonizer and colonized. The attempt at total administrative absorption was unprecedented in the history of imperial enterprise. Such a colonial experience differed greatly from that of any other colony in Asia. Whereas Westerners ruled in their colonies in relatively small numbers and left open the possibility of autonomous development, Japanese control and exploitation of its Korean colony was much more extensive, thorough and systematic, and included a massive bureaucratic presence. By 1937 more than 52,000 Japanese officials were posted to Korea. This can be compared to Indochina (Vietnam, Laos and Cambodia) where the French ruled a colony about the size of Korea with some 3,000 officials.[4] By the early 1940s, the number of Japanese (civilians, police, public officials and teachers) in Korea, a county with only 21 million inhabitants, was 704,000.[5] Japanese occupied 95 percent of higher civil service posts in Korea. Even among clerical posts, two-thirds of the senior clerkships were reserved for Japanese.

Japan held Korea tightly, watched it closely, and suppressed resistance ruthlessly. Koreans were denied civil rights: no political parties were allowed and public assemblies were limited and supervised. The criminal code was applied more severely to Koreans and prison conditions for Koreans were different than for Japanese. Learning opportunities for Koreans, particularly in higher education, were prohibitively limited. There were curbs on freedom of information: schools were strictly regulated in what they could teach, writers in what they could write, and publishers in what they could print. Newspapers critical of Japan were abruptly suspended.

Anti-Japanese sentiment was harshly suppressed from its inception. Suspected anti-Japanese activists were imprisoned and tortured during intermittent reigns of terror that culminated in the bloody repression of a nationwide peaceful movement for independence in March 1919, in which two million Koreans participated. Colonial rulers responded to the protests with indiscriminate slaughter, killing more than 7,500 unarmed Korean citizens and injuring 46,000 others over a period of twelve months. Following this, many Koreans continued to fall victim to torture, insults, and humiliation. As Japanese repression in Korea intensified, the size of the police force increased from about 6,000 in 1911 to some 60,000 in 1941—that is, one policeman for every 400 Koreans.[6]

As Japan moved toward domestic autocracy and external aggression in the mid-1930s, colonial policies became even more extreme. The Japanese formulated policies designed to fully assimilate Korea culturally and economically. In effect, Japan sought to eliminate the independent cultural identity of the Korean people. Koreans were ordered to change their Korean names to Japanese ones; students had to make ritual obeisance to the Japanese Emperor. Exclusive use of the Japanese language was ordered in 1938. All Koreans, even Christians, were forced to attend a daily service at a Shinto shrine.

After its attack on Pearl Harbor in 1941, Japan became desperate. The colonial government issued a national mobilization order to recruit Korean men and women for its growing war. Koreans were drafted to help the Japanese war effort in huge numbers. By 1944, 4 million men and women, 16 percent of the population, were forced to serve the

---

[4] Eckert et al., *Korea: Old and New*, 256-257.
[5] Steinberg, *Republic of Korea*, 42.
[6] Henderson, *Korea*, 79-80.

Japanese war effort; some were employed as fighters and others as laborers in Japanese factories, mines, and construction sites in Japan, Manchuria and on Sakhalin. Here the Korean laborers were "essentially slaves, huddled into what amounted to concentration camps guarded constantly by Japanese men and dogs."[7]

An especially appalling feature of this time was the rounding up of unsuspecting young Korean women to "comfort" Japanese soldiers in military brothels. Many of these establishments were in front-line combat zones, and women were required to endure large numbers of soldiers. It is estimated that 150,000 Korean women and 50,000 Thais, Filipinas and other nationalities served in the brothels. For modern Koreans, there is no more powerful image for the barbarous experience of Japanese colonial rule of their country.[8]

It is no surprise that Japanese rule produced "the profoundest sense of humiliation and outrage" on the part of the Korean people.[9] Japanese colonial rule over Korea led to the development of a culture in which the relationship between colonial officials and Korean people was "that of mutual distrust and contempt, manifested in the arrogant and aggressive attitude of officials toward the people and in the people's subservience in front of officials and contempt behind their backs and in the breaking and evading of laws and taxes."[10] Harsh treatment at the hands of the Japanese created an almost fanatical desire for independence among Koreans. Nationalism burned fiercely and was combined with an ingrained hatred of all governing authority. Disrespect for law and authority became so deeply entrenched that it persisted well after liberation. Thirty-five years of brutal Japanese rule would have serious repercussions in the years to come.

Japan appropriated its economic interests with as much ardor as it controlled its social and political policies. The colonial economic policy was directed toward strengthening the economic and strategic position of Japan. Under the aegis of the governor-general, Japanese residents in Korea came to monopolize commercial and industrial interests. Control over the Korean currency and the introduction of Japanese banking into Korea gave more affluent colonists the economic means to fully exploit and manipulate Korea economically.

The Japanese abolished traditional land relations and initiated an eight-year land survey from 1910. The survey forced registration of all land holdings. Many ignorant farmers were unable to meet all the requirements to establish their rightful ownership. Since the Japanese duly expropriated all land unregistered under the terms of the new system, many Koreans were suddenly stripped of land their families had farmed for generations. In 1910 Japanese owned about three percent of the arable land in Korea, by 1930 this figure was about sixty percent. More than half of Korea's total rice production was expropriated by the colonial administration to feed the expanding population of the Japanese islands.[11]

Concentration of landownership increased throughout the colonial period, creating a tenancy situation that had "few parallels in the world."[12] Rents averaged fifty percent of the

---

[7] Chong Sik Lee, *Japan and Korea: The Political Dimension* (Stanford: Stanford University, 1985), 15.

[8] For details, see Keith Howard, ed., *True Stories of the Korean Comfort Women* (London: Cassell Academic, 1996).

[9] Henderson, *Korea*, 74.

[10] Kwan Bong Kim, *Korea-Japan Treaty Crisis*, 9.

[11] Cho Kijun, *Hanguk Chabonjuui Songnipsaron* (History of Korean Capitalism) (Seoul, 1973); and Hart-Landsberg, *Rush to Development*, 104-105.

[12] Korea Land Economics Research Center, *A Study of Land Tenure* (Seoul, 1966), 45.

harvest and tenancy rates approached eighty percent in the main rice-producing regions of the southwest. Through Japanese policies of exploitation, Korean peasants were transformed from semi-cultivators to semi-tenants, to tenants, or to slash-and-burn field peasants. Korean peasants, who accounted for 75 to 85 percent of the population, struggled simply to maintain a subsistence level. Millions of farmers were forced to migrate to the cities in a desperate search for wages. Others left the country entirely, for Japan, Manchuria, or Siberia. According to a period census, by 1944 about 48 percent of farm households were tenant while about 37 percent were semi-tenant. When the Japanese left, Korean landlords were widely viewed as treacherous collaborators with the Japanese, and strong demands emerged for them to dole out their land to the tenants. This land situation was one of the most significant legacies of Japanese rule in Korea.[13]

Japan's systematic exploitation was not limited to agriculture; various mineral resources were also heavily appropriated to feed the burgeoning Japanese military-industrial machine. Colonial laws favored the Japanese and made it virtually impossible for Koreans to set up new businesses. No Korean was permitted to start a factory without permission and permission was almost always denied; Korean businesses were charged interest rates 25 percent higher than Japanese firms.[14] According to 1938 data, Japanese companies owned 90 to 95 percent, respectively, of all manufacturing and mining industry in Korea. Among employed Koreans in 1944, about 96.6 percent were unskilled labor; this left post-1945 Korea without the requisite personnel to manage the economy.

Industrial investment in Korea increased rapidly following Japan's conquest of Manchuria in the early 1930s. The newly established puppet state of Manchukuo (formerly Manchuria) was a rich source of raw materials, and Korea became a strategic base for Japan's continued military and economic expansion in the region, including northern China. As a result, hydroelectric power plants, heavy and chemical industries and mining operations were established in the northern part of the Korean peninsula. The fact that Korea was geographically close to Japan meant that economic activity in Korea could be tightly integrated into the core activities of the Japanese economy.[15] The Korean economy became totally dependent upon Japan: by 1931, 95 percent of Korean exports were sold to Japan and 80 percent of Korean imports came from Japan.

During World War II, the Japanese drew heavily on Korean resources. They also turned the printing presses loose and caused wild inflation by printing billions of new yen. The 380 million yen in circulation in Korea in late 1944 had increased to nine billion by August 1945. In the final weeks, when surrender seemed imminent, the Japanese gave their workers a year's salary in advance and paid savings deposits and insurance policies in full, flooding the currency market and creating galloping inflation. During the two or three months before Japan's surrender, prices in Korea increased twenty to twenty-five times. As Japan faced defeat and began to retreat, it destroyed everything it could not take to Japan.[16]

In August 1945, 90 percent of total capital and 80 percent of skilled labor in Korea's

---

[13] Gi-wook Shin, *Peasant Protest and Social Change in Colonial Korea* (Seattle: University of Washington Press, 1996), ch. 3.
[14] Ibid., 107.
[15] Hart-Landberg, *Rush*, 106-108.
[16] Lewis, *Reconstruction and Development*, 17.

manufacturing sector were Japanese. The departure of the Japanese removed almost all the country's technical and managerial skills as well as its industrial capital resources. Most of the industrial plants existing in Korea at war's end were "incapable of independent existence."[17] After liberation, the Korean economy stood on the brink of collapse: By the end of 1946, manufacturing plants had dropped by 44 percent, manufacturing employees by 59 percent; mining operations had dropped by 96 percent and mining employees by 97 percent.[18]

AMERICAN MILITARY RULE

On August 15, 1945, Koreans heard the Japanese emperor's voice for the first time as it came over the radio to announce the unconditional Japanese surrender. Suddenly, Korean flags that had been kept hidden for decades appeared on the streets and crowds went wild in a jubilant celebration of liberation. Japanese citizens, and the collaborators who could, fled retribution. Koreans finally got their country back, but in two parts.

In August 1945, as result of breaking Japanese diplomatic codes, the Soviet Union was the first to learn of the impending Japanese surrender. The USSR was quick to declare entry into the Pacific War. Within a week, Soviet armies swept into Manchuria and northern Korea. It had been forty years earlier that the Russians had lost the 1904 Russo-Japanese War and with it their influence on the Korean peninsula. At this point it seemed that little could stop a complete Soviet occupation of the Korean peninsula; American troops could not be deployed quickly enough to prevent it. The Americans, aware of the difficulties they had already encountered in Europe with the Soviets, were fearful of a complete Soviet occupation of the peninsula and decided to prevent it. They proposed a division of Korea into mutual zones of occupation. Surprisingly, the Soviets accepted. The decision to divide Korea along the 38th parallel was a hasty and arbitrary one. The Americans did not plan this to be a permanent division; it was a demarcation of convenience.

The act of national partition was perhaps more devastating than any other event in Korean history. The division was a "tragic act," a "most serious blunder": it became the very source of future difficulties, pain and suffering. On September 24, 1945, only two weeks after his arrival in Korea, General John R. Hodge, commander of U.S. forces in Korea, wrote, "The Allied Powers, by this division, have created a situation impossible of peaceful correction."[19] It is not too much to say that almost every aspect of life in South Korea has been dominated by national division and by the existence of two hostile regimes on the peninsula. It resulted in the severing of two complementary economies (North and South), a tragic Korean War, dependence upon American military and economic aid, the burden of supporting a huge military by a small, impoverished country, and a legacy of continuous inter-Korean confrontation.[20]

National division also dealt a mortal blow to an already collapsed economy. The effects

---

[17] McCune, *Korea Today*, 140.
[18] Ibid.
[19] Memorandum of Hodge to MacArthur, September 24, 1945, *Foreign Relations of the United States (FRUS), 1945*, 6:1055.
[20] Channing Liem, "United States Rule in Korea", *Far Eastern Survey*, 19:4 (April 1949): 77-80; and Kim, Hakjoon, "The American Military Government in South Korea, 1945-1948: Its Formation, Policies, and Legacies", *Asian Perspective*, 10:1 (spring-summer 1988).

of partition were more lethal in the South than the North: it virtually paralyzed the economy of the South by severing "the head from the body, the nerves from the muscle" of the economy. South Korea inherited an area that was cut off from necessary raw materials and power sources and was thus depleted and deprived of workable facilities.[21] The South was agriculturally rich while most natural resources were concentrated in the North (see Table 2). Most heavy industries and chemical plants were also located in the North. Most existing factories in South Korea were not operating; in the summer of 1947, industrial production amounted to only 20 percent of its prewar level.

Moreover, two-thirds of Korea's population was in the South. Within months after liberation, some 2.5 million Koreans who had migrated to Manchuria and Siberia, or who had been forced to work in Japanese mines and factories, returned to South Korea. South Korea's population, estimated at just over 16 million in 1945, grew by 21 percent the following year.[22] Mass starvation was averted only by large quantities of wheat shipped in from the United States.

Table 2. **Mining and Manufacturing in South and North Korea**
(% of Output Value)

Manufacturing (1940)	South	North	Mining (1936)	South	North
Electric Power	8.0	92.0	Gold (Sand Gold)	29.3	70.7
Metal	9.9	90.1	Gold and Silver Ore	27.3	72.7
Chemical	17.9	82.1	Iron Ore	0.1	99.9
Ceramics	20.3	79.7	Pig-iron	0.0	100.0
Machine	72.2	27.8	Wolframite & Molybdenite	21.5	78.5
Wooden Articles	65.3	34.7	Graphite Coal	29.0	71.0
Book Binding	65.1	34.9	Bituminous Coal	0.5	99.5
Printing	89.1	10.9	Anthracite	2.3	97.7
Foods	65.1	34.9			
Spinning	84.9	15.1			

Source: *The Bank of Chosun Chosun Economic Yearbook, 1948*

The division also brought about grave and largely unexpected political difficulties. One of these was the widening and increasingly bitter split between the political left and right, notably Communists and anti-Communists. In the midst of abject poverty and social and political confusion, Communists rapidly expanded their influence. The Communists blamed the people's troubles on evil acts of landlords, the Japanese, and Japanese

---

[21] McCune, *Korea Today*, 22-40 and 52-60.
[22] In 1945 South Korea was comprised of about 37,000 square miles with a population of 16 million (or 430 per square mile), whereas North Korea was about 48,000 square miles with a population of 9 million (or 190 per square mile).

collaborators. Communism's revolutionary ideas were well suited to a milieu in which most of the country's property was abruptly made ownerless by Japanese withdrawal.

With the departure of the Japanese overlords, national administration virtually collapsed and all that had been routine vanished overnight, plunging the nation into a state of anarchy. [23] When the Americans arrived on the Korean peninsula on September 8, 1945, they found great confusion and disorder: all government departments were in near total disarray, public services were suspended; in the bureaucratic workforce absenteeism approached 90 percent; Korean police officers had fled in droves and those that remained were afraid to carry out their duties.[24] American soldiers, largely a combat-oriented force, filled this vacuum of authority.

From the very start the American military authorities made serious blunders. On September 9, General Hodge announced that Japanese Governor-General Abe Nobuguki and other high-ranking Japanese officials would be temporarily retained in office in order to facilitate the administration of the military government and the orderly takeover of the Korean government. The announcement angered Koreans. One newspaper editorial wrote that Koreans would rather be governed by "some chief from Borneo" than by Abe.[25] Faced with this hostile reaction, Hodge replaced Abe, and all Japanese bureau chiefs were removed from office, though they continued to be used as unofficial advisers. The American military authorities also retained the old Japanese bureaucratic machinery, including the national police, in order to maintain law and order.[26]

Another serious American mistake had been the trusteeship plan for Korea. In Moscow on December 28, 1945, the United States, Great Britain, and the Soviet Union (later joined by China) formally decided to place Korea under a five-year trusteeship. They also agreed to establish a Soviet-American Joint Commission to work toward the establishment of a unified provisional Korean government.[27] When news of the Moscow Agreement reached Korea, the trusteeship plan was greeted with fierce opposition.[28] To Koreans, any trusteeship, no matter how temporary, would mean a postponement of independence.

The Soviets must have felt that the trusteeship would be a useful avenue to reach their ultimate ambition of a unified Korea under their influence. It is clear from the record that the Soviet Union would accept nothing less than a Communist government in Korea. On May 8, 1946, General Terenti Shtykov, head of the Soviet delegation to the Joint Commission, called on General Hodge and abruptly informed him that on orders from Moscow he was suspending negotiations and returning to North Korea. "The main reason," he told Hodge, "is that Russia is a close neighbor to Korea and, because of this, is interested in establishing in Korea a provisional democratic government which would be loyal to the Soviet Union."[29]

---

[23] Benninghoff to State Department, September 15, 1945, in FRUS 1945, 1049

[24] See the reports of team no. 3, the American military government, September 11-November 30, 1945, which is a daily journal of American activities in Seoul in United States Army, RG, 407, "World War II Operations Reports", entry no. 427.

[25] *Seoul Times*, September 10, 1945

[26] Meade, *American Military Government*, 76.

[27] *United States Department of State Bulletin*, December 30, 1945, 1030.

[28] *Seoul Shinmun*, December 30, 1945.

[29] Quoted in Carl Berger, *The Korean Knot* (Philadelphia: University of Pennsylvania Press, 1957), 69.

The Soviet Union tried to win American agreement for reuniting Korea under a coalition that would have been controlled by Communists. As for the United States, it had no concrete Korea policy save for the vague notion of trusteeship.[30]

The Americans were completely unprepared to handle the chaotic situation that met them in post-colonial Korea. They had no directives, no plans, no personnel trained in government duties, and less than a month to prepare for the Korean landing.[31] Furthermore, responsibility for setting policy was divided among U.S. authorities in Washington, Tokyo, and Seoul: a lack of coordination among them caused confusion, indecision, and inconsistency. Throughout the period of the American military government, the United States had no firm policy toward Korea.[32] This lack of preparation resulted in "frequent policy changes, deviations, mistakes and lack of coordination."[33]

Upon landing in Korea, the Americans had found a collapsed economy, an economy the U.S. troops knew nothing about and were unequipped to operate. The United States showed little interest in the economic development of Korea: the basic directive of the American military government was to "prevent hunger, disease, and unrest." Imports into South Korea consisted of food, fertilizer, coal, oil, blankets, clothing and textiles. In February 1948, General Charles Helmick, who had served as deputy military governor in the American military government, later attested that he had predicted: "after the U.S. forces withdraw, within two months South Korea will become nothing but a 'bull cart' economy, and nine million nonfood producers will face starvation." Without the present supplies of coal, food, oil, and gasoline from the United States, he had argued, the South Korean transportation system would cease to function within a week or ten days.[34]

The Americans were naïve politically. Generally guided by vague and lofty principles of democracy, they introduced all the features of a free and democratic system to the Korean people. The result of this policy was a proliferation of political parties (three hundred by August 1946) and of private armies of various ideological beliefs ranging from the extreme left to the extreme right and all vying for control of the government.[35] The South Korean Workers' Party—a Communist Party in the South—and other leftist organizations made full use of the political freedoms then existing in South Korea. Under such favorable conditions the membership of the Communist party increased rapidly, boasting 370,000 members at the height of its strength in 1947. The party established front organizations, primarily among workers, peasants, and students. Either in cooperation with or under the direction of the North Korean Communists, a large

---

[30] Oliver, *A History of the Korean People*, 163; and Cumings, *Korea's Place*, 187-190.

[31] Carl J. Friedrich and Associates, *American Experience in Military Government in World War II* (New York: Rinehart, 1948), 355-356. According to American historian Richard Whelan, about 2,000 civil affairs officers had been trained for military government duty in Japan, and elaborate plans had been drawn up for the country, but no one had been trained and no plans had been made for Korea (Richard Whelan, *Drawing the Line* (Boston: Little, Brown, 1990), 27).

[32] Soon Sung Cho, *Korea in World Politics*, 61-62 and 110-113.

[33] Ibid., 91.

[34] Memorandum of conversation by John G. Williams with Major General Charles G. Helmick, February 4, 1948, *FRUS 1948*, 1092.

[35] Kim Chin-Hak and Han Chol-Yong, *Chaehon Kukhoesa* [A History of the Constituent National Assembly] (Seoul: Shinjo, 1954).

number of Communists infiltrated the military, police, and government.[36] Since the Americans were searching for an agreement with the Soviet Union that would be a mutually acceptable solution to Korean trusteeship, they permitted the enlistment of Communists and their supporters in the constabulary and the police, on the principle that the security forces must be "strictly nonpolitical." It permitted Communist ownership of newspapers, magazines and motion picture theaters through which Communists could propagandize and agitate.

The leftists and Communists organized and mobilized massive uprisings throughout South Korea. The trouble started in September 1946 when 36,000 railway workers went on strike. Workers in all major industries joined in and the situation quickly developed into a general strike, involving 330,000 workers. On October 1, 1946, nearly three hundred demonstrators marched through Taegu, the third largest city in the nation, and occupied the central police station in support of the general strikes. The International News Service reported, "twenty-four hours of bloody rioting occurred with thirty-eight police officers and an undetermined number of civilians killed; the city looks like a veritable battlefield."[37] The Americans called out tanks and declared martial law in the city. The next day, however, a mob estimated at ten thousand overran the police station of Youngchun, a neighboring county, killing the county chief and many other officials and policemen. The riots spread like a prairie fire throughout North Kyongsang Province. The upheaval was such that on October 14, Hodge found it necessary to send the U.S. Sixth Infantry Division in full battle order to the region.[38] During the September-December 1946 uprisings, the riots developed into a massive rebellion that spread to forty counties in four provinces, more than one-third of South Korea's counties. The country was on the brink of a major rebellion.[39] The Russians in North Korea supported the rioters, giving them advice and money.[40]

The American occupation authorities had no interest in making long-range plans for South Korea because they believed it would be "only a matter of months—six months, perhaps—before American troops are withdrawn."[41] At the time Harry Truman was under strong pressure to "bring the boys back home" and to make drastic cuts in the military budget. In 1945 the United States had spent $50 billion on defense; in 1950 it spent only $5 billion. In 1945 there had been 8.25 million men on active duty; in 1950 there were less than 630,000, and no one had been drafted since March 1947.[42] The U.S.

---

[36] Kim Chong-bom and Kim Tong-un (1945), 62-66.

[37] Cited in Hakwon Harold Sunoo, *America's Dilemma in Asia: The Case of South Korea* (Chicago: Nelson-Hall, 1979), 56.

[38] Bruce Cumings, "Political Participation in Liberated Korea: Mobilization and Revolt in the Kyongsang Provinces, 1945-1950", *Journal of Korean Studies*, 1 (1979), 191.

[39] *FRUS 1947*, 802. Estimates suggest that 2.3 million staged the riots, with 1,000 rioters and 200 policemen killed, and some 30,000 protesters arrested. See Chŏng Haegu, *10 wŏl inmin hangjaeng yŏn'gu* (A Study of the October People's Uprisings) (Seoul: Yŏlŭmsa, 1988),148.

[40] Hyun Su Jeon and Gyoo Kahng, "The Shtykov Diaries: New Evidence on Soviet Policy in Korea", in *Cold War International History Project Bulletin* 6-7 (winter 1995-96).

[41] Soon-Sung Cho, "Hodge's Dilemma", *Korean Affairs*, IV: 1 (1965), 58-74; and Lew Young Ick (2000), 639-666.

[42] James L. Stokesbury, *A Short History of the Korean War* (New York: William Morrow, 1988), 40.

South Korea after Liberation

army had four divisions in Japan, five divisions in Europe, and another five divisions in the United States. The U.S. military had become too weak to meet the emerging challenges around the world. Europe was high on the list. As the Chiang Kai-shek government began to falter in China, Washington believed that forty thousand American troops in Korea offered more potential for embarrassment than for strategic advantage.

Korea was not of great strategic importance to the United States. In the spring of 1947, Korea was fifteenth among sixteen nations ranked by the U.S. Defense Department in terms of strategic priority. Also, the United States was pessimistic about the future of South Korea.[43] It believed that the Soviet Union was likely to obtain control of the Korean peninsula. The U.S. Joint Chiefs of Staff believed that "in the event of hostilities ... our present forces in Korea will be a military liability"[44] and in September 1947 announced that Korea was not essential to U.S. security.[45] The Joint Chiefs of Staff concluded: (1) the withdrawal of U.S. forces should be completed by the end of 1948; (2) the equipping and training of the South Korean armed forces should be left at a minimal level; and (3) future military aid should be granted to South Korea only after higher priority needs were met.[46]

In stark contrast, the Russians arrived in Korea with a wealth of background knowledge and well-formulated plans which they systematically carried out. From the beginning they sought to expand Communism on the Korean peninsula and strongly supported Kim Il Sung in his attempts to establish a Soviet-style system in the North. On June 3, 1946, *Pravda*, a newspaper of the Soviet Communist Party, stated that the Soviet Union had special interests in the Korean peninsula and the Soviet Union would not allow an independent Korean government that was not a Soviet satellite government.[47] The creation of a separate state was started in the North: In February 1946 the Provisional People's Committee led by Kim Il Sung became the first central government.[48] Land reform followed, and the Korea Communist Party merged with other political forces to create the Korean Workers' Party in August 1946. During next two years, purging non-Communists, Kim consolidated his power and became the preeminent figure in the North. The People's Committee in late 1947 began to draw various defense and security forces into a full-scale military force, a North Korean People's Army that was officially born in February 1948.[49] The Russians also sealed off the border at the 38th parallel and severely restricted traffic into and out of North Korea, effectively creating two Korean states.

---

[43] Chay, *Unequal Partners in Peace and War*, 40.
[44] Henderson, *Korea*, 149.
[45] John W. Spanier, *The Truman-MacArthur Controversy and the Korean War* (New York: Norton, 1965), 120.
[46] U.S. Joint Chiefs of Staff 1483/50, RG 218, JCS Records.
[47] Hagiwara Ryo, *The Korean War* (Tokyo: Bunkei Shunshu, 2004), 35.
[48] Charles K. Armstrong, *The North Korean Revolution, 1945-1950* (Ithaca: Cornell University Press, 2003), chapter 2.
[49] Ibid., 216-217.

Syngman Rhee

CHAPTER THREE
SYNGMAN RHEE
FOUNDER OF THE REPUBLIC

"Communism is akin to cholera; it is impossible to compromise or cooperate with it; the only choices are to surrender to Communist totalitarian control or oppose it."

"We can rebuild our economy and everything else; but if security is gone, what good is our having anything at all?"

—Syngman Rhee

"Those republics which in time of danger cannot resort to a dictatorship will generally be ruined when grave occasions occur."

—Machiavelli

Syngman Rhee (1875-1965) was a leading crusader for Korean independence from Japan and the first president of the Republic of Korea. He was arguably one of the most prominent Korean leaders of his time and in Korean history. He lived through the crucial decades stretching from the decline of the Choson dynasty, Japanese colonization, division of the Korean peninsula, and the Korean War. He played a pivotal role in liberating Korea, and in founding and defending the Republic of Korea. For many of his contemporaries, therefore, he symbolized the Korean struggle against the Japanese colonialists and against the Communists.

At the same time, Rhee is a historically misunderstood figure. Because of his inept handling of politics during a volatile period in Korean history, Korean scholars have largely neglected, and in some cases downright avoided, his record, a subject that deserves a thorough scholarly treatment. Studies done on Syngman Rhee by foreign academics have often been culturally biased.

For the young, post-Korean War generations, which now make up four-fifths of the South Korean population, Rhee is viewed as the primary figure responsible for national division, democratic failure, and the inefficiency and corruption of the government in the 1950s. To many foreign observers, Rhee was an Asian dictator, infamous for his stubborn opposition to the Korean War armistice and for his Machiavellian political style. I have diligently tried to avoid these generalizations and instead make a fresh reexamination of his presidency.

It is important to remember that Syngman Rhee was elected to lead a nation of confused, disillusioned, divided, and pessimistic people. He faced the nearly impossible task of rebuilding a nation ravaged by thirty-five years of Japanese colonial rule and a bloody, destructive war. No account of South Korean history would be complete without a careful study of his role in shaping it.

LIFE AND CHARACTER OF A GREAT PATRIOT

Syngman Rhee was born in a rural village in the western central province of Hwanghae on March 26, 1875, to a devout Buddhist family which had an aristocratic background but little wealth.[1] When he was two years old, his impoverished family moved to Seoul. Because it was customary at the time, his early education was in the Chinese classics. In his late teens, the young Rhee matriculated at Paejae Methodist School, an American missionary institution, where he became a Christian, learned English, and absorbed Western ideas on freedom, justice, and equality.

At the time, the Russians and the Japanese were competing to gain control of Korea. On October 9, 1895, Korea's Queen Min, who openly opposed Japan's influence, was brutally murdered by Japanese in her Seoul palace. On February 11, 1896, Emperor Kojong and the crown prince sought refuge in the Russian legation, where they remained for a year. Against this backdrop of rising foreign dominance in Korea, American-educated Suh Chae-pil (he also adopted an American name, Philip Jaisohn) founded the Independence Club in 1896 to spearhead a sociopolitical reform movement and prevent foreign intrusion into Korean affairs. Syngman Rhee took an active role in Independence Club meetings. On January 9, 1899, he led a group of eight thousand men in a sit-down demonstration at the gates of the emperor's palace, protesting against foreign dominance and demanding governmental and social reforms. He was arrested, subjected to seven months of brutal torture, and sentenced to life imprisonment.

While in prison he recorded his fundamental political beliefs in a work later published in San Francisco in 1906 entitled *The Spirit of Independence*. This became the "bible" of the Korean independence movement.[2] Because prison regulations prohibited access to reference materials and possession of paper and pen, Rhee wrote the manuscript in secrecy. The fact that he wrote at all under such difficult conditions is testimony to his determination and tenacity. The primary targets of criticism in the book were corrupt officials and the *yangban* (the traditional Korean ruling class). He attributed the weaknesses of the Korean people to the nation's traditional social and political order that oppressed common citizens and denied them the education he saw as key to saving both the people and the country. He also castigated China's arrogant and arbitrary decisions regarding Korea and warned of Russia's expansionist policies.

Following the outbreak of the Russo-Japanese War in 1904, which caused yet another realignment in the Korean government, Rhee was suddenly paroled after serving seven years in prison.[3] Within a few months he was on his way to the United States. The trip was putatively arranged with the blessing of two high court officials. They sent him in secret to a peace conference that had been convened to end the Russo-Japanese War. His mission was to seek the good offices of the United States in safeguarding Korea's independence. Arriving in Washington, D.C. in December 1904, he was able to meet Secretary of State John Hay and President Theodore Roosevelt with the help of his American friends. But the hoped-for

---

[1] For materials on Syngman Rhee's life, thoughts and activities, see Lew Young-Ick (1996 and 2000); Ho Chong (1970); Yi Won-sun (1965); So Chong-ju (1995); Yi Han-u (1995); Unam Chongi Pyonchan Wiwonhoe, *Unam noson* (1958); Oliver, *Syngman Rhee*; and Allen, *Korea's Syngman Rhee*.

[2] See Syngman Rhee, *Spirit of Independence*.

[3] After the war, the Japanese became dominant and Korean reformists took control of the government.

American intervention to prevent the Japanese annexation of Korea did not materialize.

Rhee stayed on in the United States, where in six years he earned a B.A. degree from George Washington University, an M.A. in European history from Harvard, and a Ph.D. in political science from Princeton. His academic achievements far surpassed those of his contemporaries in Korea. At Princeton he became personally acquainted with Woodrow Wilson, then president of that university, and whose later thoughts on national self-determination Rhee would often cite. Rhee attracted the attention of Wilson, who provided him with a letter of recommendation for a speaking engagement. The letter referred to Rhee as "a man of strong patriotic feeling and of great enthusiasm for his people."[4] This association later had a great impact on Rhee's legitimacy as a leader of the independence movement.

In the winter of 1910, less than three months after Japan's annexation of Korea, Rhee returned to Korea to begin work as chief secretary of the Seoul YMCA. There he secretly propagated independence views among Koreans. When the Japanese suppressed the Korean Christians, arresting hundreds of their leaders on charges of "conspiracy" to assassinate the Japanese governor-general of Korea, Rhee feared he might be next. With his nomination in 1912 as a Korean delegate to a Methodist convention to be held in Minneapolis, Rhee again left Korea. The following year he accepted a position as principal of a Hawaiian Methodist school for children of Korean immigrants, most of whom had gone to work on sugar plantations. He also established a Korean Christian church and became deeply involved in other organizations of the Korean community.

In late 1919, when the Korean provisional government was organized in China, Rhee was chosen as the first president of this shadow government. Thus began his career as a primary leader in the Korean overseas independence movement. The Korean provisional government's first cabinet meeting was held in Shanghai in 1920. Upon his arrival in Shanghai he found it difficult to work with the selected members of the cabinet, all of whom held varying political beliefs. The cabinet members came from Hawaii, the U.S. mainland, China, Manchuria, Korea and Russia. Many Korean patriots living in exile in Manchuria, Russia, and China had become Communists. When Rhee realized it would be impossible to work harmoniously with such leaders, he opted to return to the United States.[5]

In July 1919 in Washington, D.C., Rhee established a "shadow" Korean legation: the Korean Commission in the United States of the Korean provisional government.[6] Believing that Korea's independence would be made possible by appealing to the newly established League of Nations and the United States, he concentrated his efforts on publicity campaigns and diplomatic activity aimed at denouncing Japanese colonial rule over Korea. During a visit to Geneva in the spring of 1932 to make an appeal to the League of Nations for Korea's independence, he became acquainted with Miss Francesca Donner, an Austrian girl who was to become both his devoted wife and a dedicated

---

[4] Quoted in Oliver, *Syngman Rhee*, 111.

[5] Walter Jhung, "Korean Independence Activities of Overseas Koreans", *Korean Survey*, 1:4 (December 1952): 7-10.

[6] Its personnel consisted of Ben C. Limb [Limb Byung-jik] and Robert T. Oliver on a full time basis, with volunteer assistance and occasional counsel from Rhee's old time friends—especially John Staggers, busy with his own law practice, and Jay J. Williams, retired from his news-reporting job.

champion of Korean independence. He published *Japan Inside Out: the Challenge of Today* in 1941, in which he warned Japan would wage war against the United States sooner or later. Only a few months later, Japan attacked Pearl Harbor.

When World War II was coming to a close, Rhee, still in the United States, turned his attention to the Soviet Union. Predicting that the Soviet Union would apply the same expansionist policy to East Asia as it did to Eastern Europe, he called on America never to compromise with the Soviets. He warned that a new conflict was on the horizon—between Communism and democracy: "The only possibility of avoiding the ultimate conflict between the United States and the Soviet Union is to build up all democratic, not Communistic, elements wherever possible." He urged recognition of the Korean provisional government "to eliminate the possibility of civil war in Korea."[7] He also told the Americans that he had reports indicating that the Soviet Union intended to establish a Soviet republic in Korea and that an independent Korea could serve as a "bulwark" against Communism in the Orient.[8] He had spoken with foresight, but considering him a hindrance to its basic policy of cooperation with the Soviet Union, Washington at first did not endorse his return to Korea.

ESTABLISHMENT OF THE REPUBLIC

On October 16, 1945, two months after liberation, seventy-one-year-old Syngman Rhee returned to Korea from his forty-one year American exile. Most Koreans welcomed him as a national hero. His popularity and prestige were so high that almost all of the political parties, both left and right, wished to have him as their leader.

At a welcome meeting held for him on October 20, Rhee attacked the Soviet Union and the establishment of a border at the 38th parallel. He called for an end to a situation that most Koreans heavily opposed—the division of the country and the occupations of South and North Korea by American and Soviet troops. He appealed for the unity of the Korean people, echoing the idea of Abraham Lincoln: "United we live, divided we die."[9] On October 23, he held a meeting with 200 representatives of more than fifty political parties and social organizations and appealed for national unity. Explaining why they must all stand together, he told the participants: "When I met with General Douglas MacArthur in Tokyo, he told me bluntly that Koreans are not capable of self-government.... We must all unite together...to demonstrate to the world that we are capable of self-government."[10]

The announcement of a U.S.-Soviet agreement for Korean trusteeship on December 28, 1945, brought forth an angry reaction from the Korean people. Crowds of impassioned Koreans filled the streets; over a million marched in the streets of Seoul and other major cities. Syngman Rhee issued an immediate denunciation of the plan for trusteeship, calling on all Korean workers and Korean officials working in the American military government

---

[7] Rhee to State Department, June 5, 1944; quoted in *FRUS 1945*, 1,023; also Rhee to State Department, July 21, 1945; quoted on 1,031.

[8] The Assistant Secretary of State for Occupied Areas (Salzman) to the Comptroller General of the United States (Warren), April 6, 1948, *FRUS 1948*, 1174.

[9] *Chosun Ilbo*, October 21, 1945.

[10] Quoted in Joungwon Kim, *Divided Korea*, 58.

to go on a general strike. However, the South Korea Workers Party, a Communist political organization, reversed its original antitrusteeship stance. On January 2, 1946, after receiving instructions from North Korea, the party announced that it would support the trusteeship. Most Koreans condemned the Communists residing in South Korea as traitors.

Syngman Rhee warned of the dangers of Korean trusteeship. He believed that the Soviet-American Joint Commission would form a "coalition government," which would make it impossible for the Koreans to prevent Communization of the Korean peninsula.[11] He remembered that Russia had harbored imperialist ambitions toward Korea since the 1890s. While he was in the United States, he was astonished to learn that more than six million were killed and many more sent to Siberia to engage in forced labor by the Russian Communist regime. Now the Soviet Union occupied the northern part of the country and was busy establishing a Soviet Communist system there. The North Korean Communists and the Soviets in the North were supporting Communist activities in the South as well. Rhee believed that the Russians wanted nothing other than a Communist government subordinate to the Soviet Union in the peninsula.[12] He pointed out what had happened and was about to happen to other small nations enmeshed in the coils of the Soviet empire—Estonia, Latvia, Lithuania, Poland, Rumania, Bulgaria, Czechoslovakia, and Outer Mongolia. A Communist takeover of the South became a distinct possibility if the trusteeship were to materialize.

Antitrusteeship had become a rallying point for most South Koreans. Synman Rhee created an organization called "the National Society for the Rapid Realization of Korean Independence" and began to expand it into the provinces. In the spring of 1946 Rhee began an antitrusteeship campaign, traveling throughout the whole country giving daily speeches to large crowds. He promoted the twin themes of antitrusteeship and anti-Communism: "We must forget all partisan differences and join together to oppose trusteeship and support national independence…. Communism is akin to cholera; it is impossible to compromise or cooperate with it; the only choice is to surrender to Communist totalitarian control or oppose it."[13] He said the only salvation for Korea was to reject Communism and the trusteeship completely. In each area, he left a local chapter of the National Society, making the society the largest organization in the South. In order to support trusteeship, the Communists, with other leftist groups, formed a "People's Democratic Front" and attacked the rightists who rejected trusteeship. Thus, the conflict between the left and the right was intensified.

With the end of World War II and the establishment of the United Nations, the United States hoped to maintain friendly relations with the Soviet Union, its wartime ally. However, Rhee argued that Korean independence was unattainable without first checking the Communist expansion led by the Soviet Union.[14] He attacked U.S. policymakers, who he believed were ignorant of the Soviets' true nature and were leading U.S. policy in the direction of the Sovietization of Korea. He rejected cooperation with

---

[11] Oliver, *Syngman Rhee and American Involvement*, 83.
[12] *Donga Ilbo*, November 19, 1945.
[13] Ibid., 31.
[14] See Henry Chung, *The Russians Came to Korea* (Washington, DC: Korean Pacific Press, 1947); David J. Dallin, *The Rise of Russia in Asia* (New Haven: Yale University Press, 1949); and George A. Lensen, ed., *Korea and Manchuria between Russia and Japan* (Tallahassee, FL: Diplomatic Press, 1966).

the Communists, insisting that "to admit Russia in any guise into Korea would merely be to surrender the independence of the nation."[15]

The Communists in South Korea were an organized and violent political group. Members of the South Korean Workers' Party (a Communist party in the South) never exceeded 40,000, but it had vast numbers of sympathizers and supporters. It maintained command of the labor unions and dominated both farmers' organizations and student-intellectual groups. No group rivaled the Communists in discipline and hierarchy.

The breakdown of the Soviet-American Joint Commission was followed by an expansion of violence and political extremism instigated by the leftists in the South. As the American military government suppressed the Communists in the South, the South Korean Workers' Party relied on violence to advance its goals; this included demonstrations, strikes, riots, and a campaign to vilify the police. The social unrest caused by the Communists was almost out of control. Roy Roberts of the Associated Press in August 1947 reported that U.S. intelligence got an average of five police reports a day, "telling of fights in villages, fights between villages, beatings of rightists, beatings of leftists, burning of granaries, attacks on village officials, attacks on police, stoning of political meetings."[16]

The tide turned Rhee's way in early 1947 with the announcement of the Truman Doctrine, in which the United States proclaimed it would resolutely confront Soviet expansionism. What this meant to Korea was no less than an advance notice that the United States would give up the Moscow Agreement of Korean trusteeship in favor of a separate government in the South. The United States concluded that any agreement with the Soviet Union was impossible, and that a continuation of its military government in the South was inadvisable. The situation forced those involved to choose between negotiating with the Communists or accepting the reality of a divided Korea.[17] As a realist, Rhee believed that a mutually acceptable agreement between the Communists and the anti-Communists was a quixotic dream. He had campaigned actively within South Korea and the United States for the immediate and complete independence of Korea, even if this was first applied only to the southern half of the peninsula.

The Soviet-American Joint Commission reached a final deadlock in August 1947 and Washington found itself under pressure, in Korea and at home, to keep American soldiers in the South. Therefore, the United States sought assistance from the newly established United Nations. On November 14, 1947, the UN General Assembly passed a resolution recognizing Korea's "urgent and rightful claims to independence," and called for countrywide elections for a national assembly.[18] The UN General Assembly set up a United Nations Temporary Commission on Korea and sent it to Korea to supervise the general elections. The Soviets in the North refused the UN Commission's entry into the North. It was the same policy the Russians adopted in Germany and which led to division of that country into two competing states. Conservatives supported the general elections, while leftist groups vehemently opposed them.

---

[15] Oliver, *Syngman Rhee*, 220.

[16] Cumings, *Origins of Korean War*, vol. II, 351-79

[17] Allen, *Korea's Syngman Rhee*, 87.

[18] Miriam S. Farley, "Crisis in Korea", *Far Eastern Survey*, XIX:8 (August 1950): 149-150.

On March 12, 1948, several prominent leaders, such as Kim Ku and Kim Kyu-shik, issued a joint statement that pledged their commitment to a unified Korean government and vowed that they would not participate in any South Korean election. In April, Kim Il Sung invited 15 South Korean leaders, including Kim Ku and Kim Kyu-shik, to a "unity meeting" in Pyongyang.[19] The invitation was a last-ditch effort by the Soviet Union and the North Korean communists to block the UN-supervised elections in the South. In the North, Kim Ku and others became propaganda showpieces for the North Korean audiences. Some 695 representatives attended the political conference in Pyongyang. All the resolutions were passed without discussion.[20] The Pyongyang conference had the effect of polarizing the political situation in South Korea to an astonishing degree.

On May 10, 1948, under the supervision of the UN Commission, general elections were held in the South. About twenty parties and independents competed for 200 available seats in the National Assembly.[21] The results of the elections foreshadowed the highly uncertain future of the new nation (Table 3).

Table 3. **Results of the 1948 General Elections**

Party or Organization	Leader	Seats Elected
National Society	Syngman Rhee	55
Korean Democratic Party	Kim Sung-soo	29
Korea Independence Party	Kim Ku	12
National Youth Corps	Lee Bum-suk	6
Other parties		11
Independents		85

Source: *The National Assembly, Kukhoe sipnyonji, 85.*

None of the parties captured a majority of seats. Rhee's National Society emerged as the largest group, but still won only fifty-five seats. What's more, the National Society was no more than a coalition of many different organizations, lacking the dynamics of a true political party. Although the Korea Democratic Party (KDP), whose base was the landed class and former Japanese collaborators, secured only twenty-nine seats, it was the only cohesive political group capable of exerting political power in the assembly. Many of the KDP members ran as independents: it was estimated that between seventy and eighty of the eighty-five independents elected were associated in some way with the KDP. Therefore, the KDP became the dominant group in the National Assembly. The National Assembly held its first session on May 31, 1948. Rhee was elected chairman by a vote of 189 to 8, with the understanding that he would be elected as the first president of a Republic of Korea.

As the American military government had planned on vesting the new government with

---

[19] Seol Kook-hwan, the only reporter who accompanied the two leaders, said, "They knew it was impossible to establish a coalition government with the Communists. They only wanted to prevent Syngman Rhee assuming power." (Personal conversation in Honolulu on August 5, 2003.)
[20] George M. McCune, "The Korean Situation", *Far Eastern Survey*, September 8, 1948, 201.
[21] The 1948 constitution left 100 seats vacant in the assembly to be filled by North Korean representatives.

its powers on August 15, the assembly pushed ahead to form an official government with great haste. A draft constitution was prepared on July 12, and on July 17 Chairman Rhee signed the constitution as adopted by the National Assembly. The constitution was thus drawn up in a mere forty-two days under circumstances of minimal reflection. The constitution authorized the powers of presidential and cabinet systems. The president was given strong, independent powers, including broad emergency powers. At the same time, the National Assembly was also given considerable powers, including the right to elect the president and vice-president. There was also a provision for a prime minister, who would be subject to confirmation by the assembly.

On July 20, the seventy-three-year-old Syngman Rhee was elected president by a vote of 180, with sixteen of the members voting for Kim Ku. Perhaps Rhee's election resulted from the fact that he was virtually the only Korean of any national stature. Only Kim Ku could rival the consistency and forthrightness of his record. Kim Kyu-shik, Lyuh Un-hyong, and other leaders were all junior statesmen compared to Rhee.

Critics have blamed Syngman Rhee for the failure to establish a unified government. But the establishment of a unified government that was acceptable to the Soviets was impossible. If Rhee had agreed to a trusteeship or a coalition government with the Communists in North Korea, the results would have been far from what some idealists have dreamed. The Communists were so good not only at overthrowing governments but also at creating Communist governments.[22] The Communists controlled all of Eastern Europe and had expanded their influence through much of Asia. In March 1947, President Truman launched a "containment" policy to deter Communist expansion. In the fall of 1947, the East-West tension was high as the Soviet Union blockaded the city of Berlin. The establishment of the Republic of Korea might not have been possible without the determinant leadership of Syngman Rhee. As things were, there was not a better solution to the Korean problem.

In terms of initial nation building, a Communist strategy appeared to be superior to a liberal democratic approach. Communists in South Korea had an ideology, networks of organization, well-developed propaganda and were adept at subversive tactics. In contrast, liberal democrats introduced Western political and economic institutions to an alien soil and patiently waited for these institutions to take root. In other words, Communist nation building was well planned, aggressive, and militant, while liberal democratic nation building was less prepared, passive, and peaceful. In South Korea, the Americans emphasized that democracy would prevail over Communism in the long run but they failed to provide practical means for survival and nation building.

TASKS AND CHALLENGES OF STATE BUILDING

In July 1948, shortly after the presidential election, Rhee began the task of forming his cabinet. The KDP asked the president to appoint Kim Sung-soo, the KDP leader, as prime minister and to award the KDP eight out of twelve cabinet posts. Rhee, however, was determined to be a national leader on a nonpartisan basis and for this reason he attempted to build his own power base. Rhee also believed that the KDP had alienated

---

[22] Huntington, *Political Order*, 8.

the public and was losing popular support because of its former ties with the Japanese and the American military government.[23]

Rhee's first choice for prime minister was Lee Yoon-yung, a young Methodist minister from North Korea and acting chairman of the Chosun Democratic Party. Lee was rejected by the National Assembly. A compromise was reached in the selection of General Lee Bum-suk, who had graduated from the Whampoa Military Academy in China and later became a friend of Chiang Kai-shek. General Lee had been head of the military unit that had operated under the Korean provisional government in China. Rhee hoped that General Lee would be able to secure international support for his government.

Most of Rhee's cabinet appointments were leading figures associated with the independence movement, and all of them had been educated abroad: four in the United States, two in Europe, two in Japan, one in China, and one in the Soviet Union. All had good educational backgrounds, and their qualifications seemed to fit the posts to which they had been appointed.[24] His cabinet appointments also appeared to be designed to consolidate internal and external support for the new government. To solidify domestic support, he appointed leaders of the National Youth Corps, the Korean Labor Union, and the Women's Democratic Party. The first two of these groups were politically more powerful than any of the political parties at that time. The appointment of a former Communist (Cho Bong-am) as agriculture minister and the attempt to appoint a North Korean nationalist to the post of prime minister were also made with an eye toward international endorsement.

Only one ministerial position was given to the KDP. This defied the expectations of the KDP, which intended to grab all of the political power to itself, leaving the president as a mere figurehead. The KDP denounced Rhee's cabinet appointments. The daily *Donga Ilbo*, representing the KDP, criticized Rhee for having "gathered around him a weak, poorly suited group."[25] There was no doubt that most of the appointees lacked administrative experience. However, Rhee had virtually no reservoir of human resources from which to draw upon; the Koreans who had administrative experience from the colonial period had served largely as low-level clerks.

On August 15, 1948, Syngman Rhee was sworn in as the first president of the Republic of Korea. But the great goal of his life—restoration of the Korean state—was quite literally only half-achieved. The president was seventy-three years old, an age that made him ripe for retirement, not leadership. Yet President Rhee maintained high hopes for the Korean democracy. In his inaugural address, he declared:

> We ought to have a firm belief in democracy. Some people stress that a certain form of authoritarianism or dictatorship is more efficient in dealing with the many difficult problems arising from the process of state building in Korea, especially [the] destructive behavior of Communists, but this is a grave mistake because only

---

[23] In a letter to Robert Oliver, Rhee explained why he rejected Kim Sung Soo: "[I am] opposed to the machinery of North Korea and of the Democratic Party. The last one is as vicious as it can be because money speaks. In the country the people are through with them, and hope there will be a change to the other side." See Oliver, *Syngman Rhee and American Involvement*, 184.
[24] For a short biography of cabinet members, see McCune, *Korea Today*, 238-240.
[25] *Donga Ilbo*, August 7, 1948

democracy can bring welfare in the long run. History is full of instances where dictatorship has not contributed to freedom and development. However inefficient and time-consuming democracy may be in solving problems, the final victory will belong to it, since justice, after all, prevails over inequity.[26]

Despite the chaotic circumstances at the time, the coming of independence had a salutary and calming effect. Newspapers reported the ceremony with eloquence: "The Korean people in every village and hamlet enjoyed fully the glorious celebration of the fifteenth of August in an atmosphere filled with the auspicious signs permanently promising the future of the nation."[27]

As the Jewish people had once looked to Moses, so now the Korean people looked to their new president for miracles. However, Syngman Rhee inherited a nation unmanageable even for an experienced and capable government. It is unlikely that any government could have adequately dealt with such a set of complex problems. State building in Korea was much more difficult than in other new nations, primarily owing to territorial partition and the consequential ideological confrontation. It was a nearly impossible task for the new and inexperienced government to build a nation out of chaos and dire poverty while at the same time giving "on-the-job-training" to twenty million independent-minded, frustrated, and war-impoverished people.

President Rhee lacked the institutions, manpower, and resources to meet these challenges. The colonial institutions had been destroyed or discredited. He had to create new political and administrative institutions. Laws had to be enacted and administrative procedures developed. There was no established tradition to serve as a guide for planning, no precedent for administrative procedure. There were a very limited number of trained Koreans who knew how to manage the government and economy of a country. At that time no more than 25,000 Koreans had received any education beyond middle school. The president could not even secure his own assistants. As newcomers to government, leaders had to sort out their responsibilities and working relationships. Although high-level administrative structures were established, ministers and directors-general did not know how to manage their duties.

The Rhee administration, in the process of establishing an independent state, was faced with a serious security problem. Two hostile governments faced each other across the 38th parallel, each claiming to represent all of Korea and each dedicated to the other's destruction. The conditions were consequently ripe for civil war. Both sides initiated border raids, some of them quite bloody. North Korean guerrillas also infiltrated into the South and staged terrorist raids. Instigated by the Communists, South Korea was plagued by strikes, demonstrations, riots and armed insurrections.[28] Thus, strengthening the armed forces and maintaining social stability became the most urgent tasks of the new government. In the spring of 1948 the South Korean constabulary was limited to 18,000-20,000 men. At that time, General Hodge had estimated the strength of the North Korean army to be 120,000 to 150,000 soldiers.[29]

---

[26] Park Sung-Ha (1958), 110-113
[27] *Seoul Shinmun*, August 16, 1948.
[28] See Merrill, *op. cit.*, chapters 2 and 4.
[29] Soon Sung Cho, *Korea*, 249.

Syngman Rhee firmly believed that his nation had to have military forces sufficient to defend itself against the Soviet-trained North Korean forces. This became more critical as the United States began withdrawing its troops from South Korea. Since the United States was the only source from which South Korea could get needed training and equipment, Rhee exerted all the pressure he could to retain American military supplies. However, the Americans removed most of their military stockpile from Korea. Armaments transferred from the withdrawing American forces to the forces of South Korea were not only insufficient but, more importantly, consisted mainly of small arms.

Rhee's immediate focus was on the establishment of a defense infrastructure. On November 30, 1948, the Law for the Organization of the National Army was passed, the Korea constabulary was reorganized as the Army of the Republic of Korea, and the Coast Guard became the Navy. Rhee established and presided over the Military Security Committee, in which the defense minister, army chiefs of staff, and the chief of the U.S. Military Advisory Group in Korea participated. The committee met every week and Rhee received reports on security matters and provided additional direction.[30] As the North Korean threat appeared to grow, and as the situation in China deteriorated, the Rhee government began promptly to strengthen the new armed forces by recruiting tens of thousands of men with military backgrounds.[31] In August 1949, Rhee wrote a letter to the American president Harry Truman requesting equipment for a 100,000-man military. Truman rejected the appeal. Thus, the South Korean forces had no heavy artillery, no tanks, no anti-tank weapons, no military aircraft as well as no training. In the opinion of one American military adviser, the Korean army in June 1949 "could have been the American army in 1775."[32] By June 1950, the South Korean army had exhausted all of its spare parts. American military advisers in Korea estimated that 15 percent of the army's weapons and 35 percent of its vehicles were unserviceable.[33]

South Korea inherited a bankrupt economy. After nearly half a century of exploitive colonial economic policies, eight years of war as part of Japan, and three years of American occupation, the Korean economy in the late 1940s was in tatters. The division of the country had dealt an additional blow to the economy; the South lost heavy industries, major coal deposits, and almost all power capacity. Mines, factories, and farms were in disorder and disrepair, lacking equipment and technicians. At the time the total power-generating capacity of South Korea was some 80,000 KW, enough to supply electricity to one large factory. There was virtually no industrial activity,[34] and the farmlands were without fertilizer. During the first half of 1948, industrial production stood at about 20 percent of its prewar level. Only about half of the ten-million strong labor force was employed. The threat of inflation was pervasive. Seoul's wholesale prices rose about sixteen times from July to December 1945, and eighteen times from the day of liberation in 1945

---

[30] James H. Hausman and Il-wha Jung, *A U.S. Captain Who Influenced Korean Presidents: Hausman Memoir* (Seoul: Hankook Munwon, 1995), 163-169.

[31] Kyung-Cho Chung, *New Korea*, 102 ff.

[32] U.S. Department of the Army, *Military Advisers in Korea: KMAG in Peace and War* (Washington, DC: Office of the Chief of Military History, 1962), 69.

[33] "Improvement of Korean Army Logistical Situation", Telegram from Muccio to the Secretary of Sate, *FRUS 1950, VII*, 93.

[34] Interview with Shin Hyun Hwak on April 21, 2002.

to the end of 1949.[35]

The government had to supply necessities for about 30 percent of its population: three and a half million Koreans, returning from Japan, China, Siberia, or fleeing from the North, were without food, clothing, or shelter. In addition, more than 2.4 million people were in need of assistance in maintaining their livelihoods as of March 1949.[36] Since rural areas were inhospitable to newcomers, most refugees settled in urban areas, with Seoul receiving about a third of them. Thus, in the cities, shortages of housing and food and widespread unemployment became epidemic. The very survival of millions of people was at risk.

So many things needed immediate attention: roads, railways, and communication facilities had fallen into grievous disrepair; coalmines had to be brought back to production mode in order to supply fuel. The nation had to import food, fertilizer, coal, and petroleum, but it had little to export. The ratio between imports and exports in 1948 was 11 to 1. The fiscal and financial conditions were likewise very serious. The added demands of public security and national defense became unbearable.

Amidst the economic turmoil, the Rhee government embarked on the establishment of economic institutions. There were debates over whether to adopt a free market economy or a planned one, how to implement land reform, and how to strike a balance between state-owned enterprises and private firms. President Rhee, who had lived in the United States for more than forty years, strongly preferred a free market system.[37] Many laws were enacted to lay down the institutional groundwork of a free market economy. They included the Bank of Korea Law, the Banking Law, laws on the establishment of state-run enterprises, tax laws, and capital market laws.[38] The basic stance of the Rhee administration's economic policy was to eventually minimize government intervention and to pursue a free market economy.[39]

Among the policies that the Rhee government promoted was land reform, which had crucial economic, social, and political implications. A land reform bill was one of the first pieces of legislation to be introduced in the National Assembly. Rhee was determined to change the age-old land tenure system and appointed Cho Bong-am, who was popular among the leftists and peasants, as his first minister of agriculture. The peasants had suffered so long, especially under Japanese rule, that their frustrations had reached a boiling point. Communists were advocating the free redistribution of farmland to peasants. Land reform was urgent if social unrest was to be defused.

Rhee was enthusiastic about land reform because it would preempt the KDP and independent assemblymen's base of power. Redistribution of landholdings would undercut their power base in rural areas where they had the most clout. Conservative landowners, who preferred a president too weak to work against their interests, controlled the National Assembly and were unlikely to support a land reform bill.

---

[35] Kwang Suk Kim and Joon-Kyung Kim, "Korean Economic Development: An Overview", in Dong-Se Cha et al., eds. (1997), 5-9.

[36] *Korean Report*, I: 1 (1948-1952), 32.

[37] Seong Min Yoo and Sung Soon Lee, "Evolution of Industrial Organization and Policy Response in Korea: 1945-1995", in Dong-Se Cha et al., eds. (1997), 428-430.

[38] Kyung-Cho Chung, *Korea Tomorrow*, 25-26.

[39] Seong Min Yoo and Sung Soon Lee, *op. cit.*

Nonetheless, the broad-based popular support for land reform virtually eliminated vocal opposition to it.[40] The Rhee government cleverly offered landlords the opportunity to convert their farmlands into lucrative industrial holdings. Because the bill was financially attractive, the KDP and the independents supported it and the Land Redistribution Law was passed and promulgated on June 22, 1949. Land reform radically reshaped the South Korean countryside.[41] With landownership capped at 3 *chongbo* (7.5 acres), large landlords virtually disappeared. In 1944, the richest 3 percent owned 64 percent of all the farmland; by 1956, the top 6 percent owned only 18 percent. As a result, tenancy dropped from 49 to 7 percent among farming households.

Many peasants achieved their age-old dream of owning the land they tilled. These small farmers became independent and were no longer persuaded by the propaganda of the Communists. Land reform generated support for Rhee, and the government was able to avert social unrest and succeed in its anti-Communist campaign before the onset of the Korean War. Had the land remained in the hands of a limited number of landlords— who were considered collaborators with the Japanese—and the majority of the population remained as tenant farmers, the social and political stability of South Korea could not have been guaranteed. Like South Vietnam and the Philippines, without land reform, South Korea probably could not have won the military campaigns against the Communist guerrillas and the leftists before the Korean War.[42]

The Rhee government also attached a high priority to education. Rhee had emphasized the importance of education since the early 1910s when he was inculcating a national spirit among Korean youths in Hawaii. He believed that a lack of education was one of the main causes for the loss of Korean sovereignty. Under Japanese rule only a small percentage of Korean children were able to attend schools. In 1945, 78 percent of the Korean populace was illiterate because schoolrooms and teachers were available for only a fraction of school-age youngsters.[43]

The 1948 constitution provided that "every citizen has an equal right to seek an education appropriate to him." The Education Law, which stipulated free and universal education up to the sixth grade, was enacted in 1949, and a compulsory education system was installed for the primary level in the very first year of the Republic. Adoption of compulsory education was one of the crucial reforms of the Rhee government. However, resources for compulsory education were extremely scarce. There were "too few teachers, too few books, and too few school buildings."[44] Thousands of school buildings had to be constructed, hundreds of textbooks had to be written, and tens of thousands of teachers had to be recruited and trained. In order to offer learning opportunities for eligible children, a rotation system with students receiving only three months of schooling a year was used. The government mobilized all available means, established the basic structure of the Korean educational system, and expanded opportunities at nearly

---

[40] C. Clyde Mitchell, "Land Reform in South Korea", *Pacific Affairs*, 22:2 (June 1949): 144-154.

[41] Lie, *Han Unbound*, 11-12.

[42] One major objective of the Communist revolution in China and other Asian countries after WWII was to liberate peasants and tenant farmers from exploitation by landlords.

[43] Oliver, *Syngman Rhee and American Involvement*, 228.

[44] Robert T. Oliver, "Korea: A Progress Report (I)", *Current History* (September 1949): 136.

all levels of education. Considering the difficult circumstances of the time, it would have been almost impossible for South Korea to expand its educational system without the strong and active commitment of the president.

To meet these multiple challenges, the new government required enormous financial resources. But when most businesses were closed and people were barely surviving, paying taxes was the lowest of priorities. During the colonial period, tax evasion had been considered a patriotic act. Furthermore, thanks to land reform, taxes from the agricultural sector were reduced significantly. Before the reform, landlords had paid a substantial land tax, but after reform, millions of subsistence-level farmers could not afford to pay anything. With such a background, the new government found it very difficult to collect taxes.

A high-ranking official in the finance ministry at the time recalled that there was virtually no economic base from which tax could be collected.[45] For instance, out of a government budget of 211 billion won for fiscal year 1949-50 only 11 billion won (5 percent) was generated through taxation. As the North Korean regime built up its military and South Korean Communists intensified their subversive activities, the Rhee government was forced to provide urgent funding for the military and the national police. During the first eight months of the 1949-1950 fiscal year, deficit expenditure by the government exceeded the entire annual budget. Since American officials in Seoul had recommended drastic measures for inflation control, including the balancing of the national budget, the Rhee government could not print money to fill the budget gap. Without enough money, the government resorted to doling out rice as salary to public officials. Managing a country without significant financial resources was one of the serious difficulties in the early phase of South Korea's state building. Nevertheless, President Rhee had faced some critical internal and external challenges.

STRUGGLE FOR POLITICAL SURVIVAL.

Without its own political base, the Rhee administration had experienced serious difficulties in dealing with the opposition-controlled National Assembly. The constitution, a hybrid of parliamentary and presidential systems, proved to be a continuing source of tension and discord between the president and the National Assembly. The power of the president collided with that of the National Assembly on virtually every issue. Even as the nation was threatened by Communists from within and without, and in the face of mounting public dissatisfaction, the bitter struggle between the president and the prerogative-conscious assembly for political supremacy persisted.

Challenges from the National Assembly came quite early. On August 20, 1948, only five days after the inauguration of the government, a group of young assemblymen introduced a National Traitors' Law to punish Japanese collaborators (even though many KDP members were also vulnerable to such charges) in order to weaken Rhee's power base. News that the infant National Assembly had already begun to purge pro-Japanese elements spread like wildfire, and the reaction of the people was enthusiastic. Rhee, however, protested the bill, believing that if enacted it would result in serious internal disturbances, and that its timing could not be worse. Despite his

---

[45] Interview with In-Sang Song on April 21, 2002.

words of caution, on September 7, 1948, the National Assembly passed the bill by a vote of 103 to 6. Realizing that the National Assembly would probably pass the bill over his veto, and that the bill enjoyed overwhelming support from the people, Rhee had little choice but to sign it into law.

The National Traitors' Law empowered the National Assembly to arrest, prosecute, and bring to trial pro-Japanese Koreans. The National Assembly established its own courts, investigators, prosecutors, and even a special police force to implement the law. As the Special Investigation Committee of the National Assembly accelerated its investigation, many high-ranking police officers were brought to trial. In response, the National Police accused the assemblymen who endorsed the bill of being Communists. The police promoted mass demonstrations, made secret plans to assassinate those who were spearheading the purge campaign, and even arrested three assemblymen for their putative Communist connections and violations of the National Security Law.

On June 6, 1949, the Seoul Metropolitan Police sent a petition to President Rhee protesting the unlawful intervention of the National Assembly's Special Investigation Committee and threatening to resign en masse. Rhee believed it was time for action. On June 8, Rhee exercised the emergency powers granted to him by the constitution, with an executive order exempting the police force from the activities of the Special Investigation Committee. The opposition's attempt to purge the police and bureaucracy came to an end. At the time, national security was the president's top priority, and the police were the main institution on which the Rhee administration depended for its fight against Communist guerrillas and to quell civil disturbance. Almost all Koreans who had any government experience had gained it by working with the Japanese. There simply was not enough time and resources to train their replacements.

By passing no confidence resolutions, the opposition continued to undermine the government. Within months of the establishment of the government, several ministers were forced to resign. In December 1948, when the police arrested a labor leader, the National Assembly quickly passed a no-confidence resolution against the minister of home affairs who controlled the police. Although the resolution did not demand resignation, the minister voluntarily resigned. The foreign minister, who was accused as a Japanese collaborator by the Assembly, also resigned. The defense minister, pressed in October 1948 to accept responsibility for the Yosu mutiny[46] over which he had not yet established full control was forced to resign. The National Assembly held the minister of transportation responsible for the sinking of a ship that had been in poor condition, while the minister of commerce was accused of misuse of funds, and they resigned in late 1948 and early 1949, respectively.[47] In February 1949, the minister of agriculture accepted responsibility for the government's failure to collect the grain harvest and resigned. In June 1949, two resolutions for the resignation of the entire cabinet were passed in the Assembly. It was clear to Rhee that his government was threatened. As political pressure picked off the cabinet one-by-one, the authority of the Rhee government grew increasingly weak. Rhee was simply unable to find competent men to take on the ministerial posts; consequently, individuals with relatively unknown backgrounds and

---

[46] See below: the section entitled *The Anti-Communist Struggle*.
[47] *Chosun Ilbo*, December 29, 1948, and February 22, March 22, and May 28, 1949.

lesser capabilities moved into the cabinet.[48] It was nearly impossible for Rhee to get his cabinet to carry out his policies.

The second round of political battles between the president and the opposition erupted on January 27, 1950, when opposition members and some independents introduced a bill for a constitutional amendment creating a cabinet system.[49] It was a clear move to oust Rhee when his presidential term expired in 1952. The Rhee administration was determined to block the amendment's passage. Facing mobilized popular demonstrations against the proposed constitutional change, the National Assembly voted on the bill on March 14. Receiving only seventy-nine of the 123 votes, the bill was defeated.

As partisan conflicts between pro- and anti-Rhee groups intensified, the significance of the general elections in May 1950 became very high. The elections would determine whether the opposition could renew its challenge to Rhee, and more importantly, whether Rhee's re-election as president in the National Assembly was even possible. The president himself campaigned against his opponents. But the results of the election disappointed President Rhee. Pro-Rhee groups won only fifty-seven seats. One consolation was that other major parties also lost much of their strength as the main opposition party (KDP) fell to 24 seats from 68.[50]

At the time, the Western media depicted President Rhee as "irresponsible," "demagogic," and "domineering." But Rhee saw things differently: "To tell the truth, I am afraid there is more democracy here than in America.... Our National Assembly is more democratic than any other body of representatives I know of."[51] In fact, South Korean politics during the Rhee regime essentially revolved around Rhee's struggle to remain in power and the opposition's efforts to unseat him. As the president of a minority government, Rhee's power was very limited. Moreover, his government was still dependent on American aid. With a lack of resources and administrative capability, and laden with enormous political pressures from within and without, strong determination was perhaps the only political resource Rhee had left.

THE STRUGGLE FOR EXTERNAL ASSISTANCE.

The new Republic could not sustain itself economically or militarily; its survival depended greatly upon the continued availability of economic and military assistance from the United States. On June 7, 1949, President Truman sent a message to Congress requesting $150 million in South Korean aid for the 1949-1950 fiscal year. Congress was reluctant to provide economic aid to Korea, prompting Secretary of State Dean Acheson to warn that South Korea would collapse "within three months" if economic assistance were not provided. Undersecretary of State James Webb chimed in, alerting Congress that "without a continuation of outside assistance, the Korean economy will suffer a rapid, inevitable

---

[48] Dispatch from the Ambassador in Korea (Muccio) to the Secretary of State, *FRUS 1950*, VII, 9.
[49] In February 1949, the two parties (the KDP and the KIP) formed an opposition party, the Democratic Nationalist Party. The strong opposition party now controlled more than a majority of assembly seats.
[50] Quee-Young Kim, *Fall of Syngman Rhee*, 13-14.
[51] Oliver, *Syngman Rhee and American Involvement*, 220.

collapse. Under such circumstances, only the Communists will win."[52] The following February, despite continued requests by the Truman administration for the appropriation of Korean aid, Congress approved only $60 million, less than half of what was requested in the previous year.[53]

Rhee regarded the withdrawal of U.S. troops as a serious blow to his nation's security. Without American support, Rhee believed South Korea too weak to defend itself. In May 1949, Rhee sent a letter to Truman asking for the retention of U.S. forces until the defense forces of South Korea were capable of dealing with the Communist threat. And, if American forces were to leave, he suggested the United States should provide South Korean forces with sufficient military means to deter any possible aggression from the North. In June 1949, Rhee fretted over the imminent withdrawal of the remaining American forces: "The American forces will be out of Korea by the end of this month. What do we do for our defense? Most of our army men are without rifles and so are our police and navy. Our defense minister reports that we have ammunition, which will last for only three days of actual fighting.... From our own point of view at present, sufficient supplies of adequate weapons of war for our own defense seems more urgent than economic recovery. We can rebuild our economy and everything else; but if security is gone, what good is our having anything at all?"[54]

Realizing America's determination to withdraw its troops, Rhee became more interested in procuring a guarantee from the United States that it would solidly stand by South Korea in the face of any outside aggression. In May 1949, just one month before the completion of troop withdrawal, Rhee remarked: "Whether American soldiers go or stay does not matter very much. What is important is the policy of the United States toward the security of Korea. What I want is a statement by President Truman that the United States would consider an attack against South Korea to be the same as an attack against itself."[55] Rhee sent a letter to Truman requesting one of the following commitments in exchange for the withdrawal: (1) the formation of a Pacific pact along the lines of NATO; (2) a mutual defense agreement between the United States and South Korea; or, (3) a public pledge by the United States to defend South Korea in case of external threat.[56]

However, some policymakers in Washington believed, "The prospects for South Korean survival are not great even with military assistance; hence the United States should not waste expensive aid on a country likely to fall under Soviet domination."[57] The U.S. policy set out in the National Security Council documents produced in 1948 and 1949 holds that while some limited economic and military aid should be given to South Korea "the United States should not become so irrevocably involved in the

---

[52] Department of State *Bulletin*, June 19, 1949, 785.

[53] *Donga Ilbo*, April 12, 1950.

[54] Oliver, *Syngman Rhee and American Involvement*, 248-249.

[55] Oliver, *Syngman Rhee*, 295.

[56] *FRUS 1949*, VI, 1023-1024.

[57] Chull Baum Kim, "U.S. Policy on the Eve of the Korean War", in Phil Williams, Donald M. Goldstein, and Henry L. Andrews, Jr., eds., *Security in Korea* (Boulder, CO: Westview, 1994), 93.

Syngman Rhee

Korean situation."[58] Thus, on January 12, 1950, U.S. Secretary of State Dean Acheson announced that South Korea was outside the defined American defense perimeter. In May, U.S. Senator Tom Connally, chairman of the Senate Foreign Relations Committee, remarked that the United States did not intend to support South Korea militarily in case of war.[59] Even General MacArthur in Japan agreed with them, believing the United States lacked "the capability to train and equip Korean troops...[or] to cope with a full-scale invasion," and that if "a serious threat develops, the United States will have to give up active military support of the ROK forces."[60]

Though Rhee was slowly surmounting threats to domestic calm, he was fighting a losing battle in the search for external support. By 1950 the writing was clearly on the wall: the United States did not intend to defend South Korea. The young Republic stood alone.

THE ANTI-COMMUNIST STRUGGLE.

The most serious threat was the Communist. As Rhee struggled for state building, the Communist threat in the North and the South was rapidly increasing. In response to the establishment of the Republic of Korea, the North promptly held its own elections on August 25, 1948, and established the Democratic People's Republic of Korea (DPRK). DPRK claimed to be the sole legitimate government on the peninsula and proclaimed Kim Il Sung as its premier on September 9, 1948. Pyongyang made no secret of its intent to "liberate" the South by whatever means necessary. It waged a coordinated campaign of political pressure within South Korea, including assassination, violence, demonstrations, strikes, and propaganda. It even allied itself with elements in the South Korean National Assembly.[61] Through subversion, armed revolts and guerrilla warfare, it also created a civil war in the South.[62] The impoverished and unprepared South was vulnerable to the Communist activities. Communist revolts began to block elections for the establishment of the Republic scheduled for early May 1948. During the spring of 1948, anti-election violence was rampant throughout the nation, especially in the traditional Communist strongholds of South Cholla, Taegu, and the southern island of Cheju. The violence was greatest on Cheju. There, in the early morning of April 3, 3,000 to 4,000 Communist guerrillas and their supporters assaulted more than half of the island's twenty-four police stations, killing thirty police and youth group members while losing only four of their own. The guerrilla attacks succeeded in disrupting elections on the island. By early June, almost all of Cheju Island was under Communist control.[63] At the time of Rhee's inauguration, fighting between Communist guerrillas and South Korean constabulary forces on Cheju continued.

---

[58] NSC 8 is reproduced in *FRUS 1948, VI*, 1164-1169.
[59] *U.S. News and World Report*, June 5, 1950.
[60] Sawyer, *Military Advisers*, 98.
[61] Cumings writes (*Origins*, vol. II, 671) during North Korean occupation of Seoul "About sixty members of the National Assembly remained in Seoul, and...forty-eight of them held a meeting expressing their allegiance to the DPRK." Their decision to remain in Seoul, Cumings says (495), "has a retrospective eloquence" regarding Northern efforts to woo them.
[62] See Scalapino and Lee, *Communism*, vol. I, 298-311; and Merrill, *Korea*.
[63] For details of the Cheju rebellion, see Merrill, *Korea*, 63-70, 84-87 and 122-126; John Merrill, "Internal Warfare", in Cumings, *Child of Conflict*, 141.

On the night of October 18, 1948, only two months after the establishment of the Republic, the Fourteenth Regiment (one of the young republic's 10 regiments), which was being dispatched to Cheju to subjugate the Communist guerrillas, revolted in the southern port city of Yosu.[64] The revolt was instigated by young officers who had associated themselves with a major Communist conspiracy, possibly ordered by the Communists in the North, and was soon joined by many local leftists and their sympathizers.[65] The rebels killed twenty officers, including three battalion commanders. Rebel leaders told followers that the 38th parallel had been done away with and that unification with the North would soon follow. They distributed rifles and ammunition to local Communists, and quickly subdued the two hundred-member Yosu police force and took control of the entire city. The next morning, the rebels captured the neighboring city of Sunch'on. The 2,000 or so rebels proceeded to expand their perimeter of control out into the countryside. They established people's committees and "people's courts," which tried and executed about 900 people, including 400 police officers (Table 4).

Table 4. **Estimates of Casualties from the Yosu Rebellion**[66]

Loyalist soldiers & police killed	141	Rebels killed	821
Loyalist soldiers & police missing	263	Rebels captured	2,860
Civilians killed	1,000+	Guerrillas at large	1,000+

Source: The National Archives of the United States

The Rhee administration responded swiftly. It saw the revolts as the result of a Communist conspiracy to overthrow the South Korean government by fomenting a civil war.[67] Within a few hours of the outbreak of the rebellion, the government ordered the Fourth Regiment, stationed in the provincial capital of Kwangju, to launch an attack against the rebels. It also declared martial law in the southern region: a strict 11 p.m. curfew was enforced; police and troops patrolled the streets; people vulnerable to guerrilla attack were moved to safer regions; and activities deemed "subversive" were forbidden.[68] South Korean troops recaptured Yosu and Sunch'on on October 26, but several hundred rebels escaped to the nearby Chiri mountain region, where they became guerrilla forces. Although revolts were quickly suppressed, maintenance of law and order became extremely difficult as many civilian leftists joined the Communist-led guerrilla forces. In many rural areas, the government ruled during the day but guerrillas ruled at night.

At the time, a tremendous wave of anxiety swept the country. Fear and insecurity spread within the army, the police, and the public. The rebellion undermined confidence in the army,

---

[64] For details of the Yosu rebellion, see Merrill, *Korea*, 98-122.
[65] Citing former Soviet Colonel General Terenti Shtykov's recent *Memoirs*, Lee Ki-bong asserts that the Yosu-Sunchon rebellion was ordered by the Communist authorities in North Korea and the Soviet Union, possibly by Stalin himself. Lee also wrote that Shytykov established a guerrilla warfare command in the north in 1947. Lee Ki-bong, "Bukhan chumnyong soryongun sunoeui hoego: Yo-sun kunbanran sakon Stalin chisi yotta" (Recollections of a Soviet Occupation Army Chief in North Korea: Stalin Ordered the Army Mutinies in Yo-sun), *Sin Dong-A* (July 1995): 380-394.
[66] National Archives, 895.00 file, box 7127, Drumwright to State, December 10, 1948.
[67] Cumings, *Origins*, vol. II, 259-267.
[68] *Seoul Shinmun*, November 2-8, 1948.

and increased fear that the United States was about to abandon the country. A political collapse in South Korea was possible if the situation did not improve quickly. It was in this tense atmosphere that the government hurriedly passed the National Security Law in December 1948. The law outlawed Communism and gave the police almost unlimited powers to investigate, arrest, and detain suspected Communists. All major organizations in South Korea, including the military, the police, the press, schools, labor unions, and the government itself were subjected to careful scrutiny and massive purges. The police rounded up thousands of leftists. At the same time the government began a major buildup of its security forces: the number of soldiers was rapidly increased to 100,000, although only 50,000 of them were equipped with American infantry weaponry.[69] It also introduced compulsory military training in the schools, consolidated right-wing youth groups into a nationwide paramilitary organization, set up a centralized intelligence system.[70]

The South Korean army was heavily infiltrated by the Communists and their supporters. The Rhee government launched an investigation and a purge campaign of the military. Within weeks, more than ten majors and colonels, one hundred lieutenants and captains, and a thousand enlisted men were taken into custody, ultimately liquidating some 4,750 commissioned and noncommissioned officers, about 10 percent of the army at the time. The purge uprooted the Communist organizations and forced other leftist officers into hibernation, allowing the government to consolidate control over the army. If it had not been for the purge, it is highly likely the subsequent North Korean invasion would have precipitated widespread uprisings in the South Korean army, preventing American intervention and ensuring a Northern victory.[71]

The purge touched off further mutinies: The first and the second by the Sixth Regiment at Taegu in November and December 1948, and a third in January 1949 by a unit of the Sixth Regiment stationed in Pohang. Then in May 1949, two South Korean battalions stationed at the 38th parallel defected to North Korea. The defections were the most serious instance of disaffection within the South Korean army since the Yosu rebellion of the previous year and dealt a heavy blow to South Korean morale.

The purge campaign met with an exceedingly unfavorable reaction abroad. South Korea was often described as "an oppressive police state." Without question, the police often applied the National Security Law arbitrarily. The Rhee government asserted that forceful measures were necessary to combat the threat of Communist subversion. Communists commonly disguised themselves as pro-democracy demonstrators. It was often difficult to discriminate between Communist and democratic activists, and civil rights were often abused. The primacy of security over democracy may be justified on the ground that there will be no democracy to preserve if the security of the state is compromised. Fighting subversive Communists through democratic means can mean the death of democracy because using democratic methods alone might be a handicap when

---

[69] Kyung-Cho Chung, *New Korea*, 102 ff.

[70] Merrill, *Korea*, 115.

[71] Harutaka Sasaki, *Hankukchon pisa, sangwon: kongun kwa siryon* (Secret History of the Korean War, vol. 1: The Establishment of the Army and Its Trials) (Seoul: Pyonghak-sa, 1977), 408-416; and Dae-Sook Suh, *Kim Il Sung: The North Korean Leader* (New York: Columbia University Press, 1988), 121. According to Scalapino and Lee, some 80 percent of the 1947 graduates of the South Korean Military Academy were Communists or Communist sympathizers. (Scalapino and Lee, *op. cit.*, fn310.)

fighting against Communists who place no restrictions on their methods. In the end, the fledgling Republic was saved and as it emerged from under the dire Communist uprising, the majority of the population in the South rallied to its support. In hindsight, the Yosu rebellion and the resulting enactment of the National Security Law were critical events in the new and anti-Communist Rhee government. If the Yosu revolt had not taken place, South Korea likely would have succumbed to Communism.[72]

The military campaign to exterminate guerrillas in Cheju came to a virtual end in the early spring of 1949. 15,000 to 20,000 islanders died in the conflict. Three-quarters of the island's four hundred villages lay in ruins. More than twenty thousand houses, thirty-four schools, and fourteen local office buildings had burned down. In April 1949, President Rhee visited the island to assess the situation and encourage the inhabitants and troops. In his May 1949 report, U.S. Ambassador Muccio considered the restoration of public peace after the Yosu rebellion the most noteworthy achievement of the Rhee government during the spring of 1949.[73]

Communists meanwhile prepared for a military showdown with the new Rhee government by establishing guerrilla bases in alpine areas and training cadres for guerrilla operations at the Kangdong Political Institute in North Korea. In 1949, Communist guerrilla troops were active in at least six distinct mountain areas in the South—Mt. Chiri, Mt. Paegam, Mt. Songni, Mt. Kaya, Mt. Odae, and Mt. Yongmun. Pyongyang pinned its hopes for unification on a socialist revolution in the South with the goal of final victory by August 15, 1949. Thus, the internal security situation steadily descended toward anarchy; by mid-1949 the government faced rebellion in five of eight provinces. During the anti-guerrilla campaigns from October 20, 1948, to August 15, 1949, some 9,536 rebels were killed, wounded, or captured; 504 soldiers and policemen were killed and 345 wounded.[74] In addition to these internal troubles, the government was also confronted with increasing numbers of border clashes along the 38th parallel.[75] During the entire twenty-two-month period from the inauguration of President Rhee until the outbreak of the Korean War, a continuous state of civil war existed in the South: about one hundred thousand persons were killed in subversion, armed revolts, guerrilla warfare, and border clashes before the outbreak of the Korean War.[76]

The fall of the Nationalist government in China caused widespread and profound anxiety in South Korea. Western news media reported that Syngman Rhee would suffer the same fate as Chiang Kai-shek. Rhee, far from being a "little Chiang Kai-shek," reacted firmly to restore security, and unlike Chiang Kai-shek, he largely succeeded. In fact, the Rhee government waged a very successful campaign against the guerrillas; most were soon killed or captured, though some escaped across the 38th parallel. Thereafter, Communist activity gradually subsided and the most dangerous period faced by South Korea from the viewpoint of internal unrest was surmounted.

---

[72] Allen, *Korea's Syngman Rhee*, 78.
[73] Muccio to the Secretary of State, May 1, 1949, National Archives, RG, Numerical File 1945-1949, 895.00/4-1849, 895.00/5-1749.
[74] Cumings, *Origins*, vol. II, 144.
[75] Michael Hickey, *The Korean War* (Woodstock, NY: Overlook Press, 1999), 19.
[76] Merrill, *Korea*, 181.

Syngman Rhee

On the other hand, North Korea's military build-up had progressed rapidly with the full support and supervision of the Soviet Union. Since 1946, North Korea had dispatched to the Soviet Union over 10,000 soldiers to train as pilots, aircraft mechanics, and experts in tank warfare and maintenance. When the Soviet troops withdrew from the North in the late 1948, they transferred their weapons and equipment to the North Korean troops. Under the terms of an aid agreement concluded on March 17, 1949, the Soviet Union supplied North Korea with ten reconnaissance aircraft, 100 Yak fighter planes, 70 attack bombers, and 100 Russian T-34 and T-70 tanks and heavy artillery between the summer of 1949 and the next spring.[77]

After a successful Communist revolution, Red China was eager to support Kim Il Sung's takeover of South Korea. Between the summer of 1949 and the next spring the Chinese People's Liberation Army released some 30,000 ethnic Korean soldiers, all battle-hardened veterans during the war against the Japanese and the Nationalists, to return to the North with their military equipment. In the North they were reorganized as the Fifth, the Sixth and the Seventh Division of the North Korean Liberation Army and become the main forces advancing toward the South in June 1950. At the time, the North Korean military was regarded as the strongest in Asia.[78]

WARTIME LEADERSHIP

On Sunday morning, June 25, 1950, President Rhee received an urgent phone call from the defense minister, Shin Sung-mo: "North Korean puppet troops have launched attacks along the 38th parallel." It was the attack so long feared and anticipated.

A few hours later, four Yak fighters swept over the treetops of Seoul delivering bursts of fire into the Blue House, the official residence of the South Korean president. The president escaped physical injury, but he was deeply shocked and dismayed. Rhee was a man of courage but he was also an old man, past seventy now, and though he could boast a long list of hardships, war was not one of them. Within an hour, the defense minister dashed into the Blue House. In his initial report of the battle situation, he conceded initial losses but predicted victory within a few days.[79] A bit relieved of his anxiety, Rhee ordered the defense minister to convene a strategy meeting with military leaders. In the afternoon, Foreign Minister Lim Pyong-jik called on the president. The president ordered Lim to make an urgent appeal for U.S. military support to repel the aggressors and signed Presidential Emergency Order No. 1 on special procedure for the treatment of crimes under national emergency.

Late on the night of June 25, Rhee called General MacArthur at his Tokyo headquarters, asking for immediate assistance. MacArthur promised as much as he could. Rhee then called Ambassador Chang Myon in Washington instructing him to "call on President Truman at once and tell him that the enemy is at our threshold. Please ask him for supplies of arms, for help of any kind."[80] The president also cabled a plea to

---

[77] The development of North Korean forces may be found in Sawyer, *Military Adviser*, 104-109.

[78] Chen Jian, "The Sino-Soviet Alliance and China's Entry into the Korean War", Cold War International History Project, Working Paper No. 1, 1992, http://seas.gwu.edu/nsarchive/cwihp; and Hagiwara Ryo, *op. cit.*, 162-74.

[79] For details during the early phase of the Korean War, see Noble, *Embassy at War*.

[80] Harry S. Truman, *Memoirs: Years of Trial and Hope*, vol. II (Garden City, NY: Doubleday, 1956), 336.

President Truman: "As we face this national crisis, we appeal for your increasing support and ask that you at the same time extend effective and timely aid in order to prevent this act of destruction of world peace."[81]

Late on the night of June 26, President Rhee presided over an emergency cabinet meeting convened at the Blue House. General Lee Bum-suk, former defense minister, was also invited to the meeting. Lee strongly urged the government to retreat south of the Han River. He also suggested the Han River bridges be blown up, not only to deny the enemy an easy crossing but to ensure South Korean troops fought to the end. Because of the general's long military experience, the cabinet generally agreed to his proposals. Defense Minister Shin agreed, saying, "The government must move to the south of the Han River. Then we can continue to fight."[82]

Enemy planes darted from the sky to strafe targets in Seoul. Roaring guns reverberated steadily through the city of Seoul and its environs. The government was in turmoil; an incapable cabinet, an ineffective defense minister, no general staff, and no war plans—these were the inadequacies that now challenged Rhee as his government faced its darkest hour. Public officials rushed to their offices but no one could give them direction. Hundreds of thousands of panicked Seoulites flooded out of the city by any means possible, all bound for the south ahead of advancing North Korean troops. As *The New York Times* reported, the South Korean government was on the brink of a "complete collapse."[83]

At dawn on June 27, the defense minister knocked on Rhee's bedroom door and pleaded with him to leave the capital as the enemy troops approached. Rhee refused to depart, saying, "I must defend Seoul to the last."[84] Soon after, his security chief reported that enemy tanks had reached the outskirts of Seoul. It was a critical moment for the government. The safety and leadership of President Rhee were crucial for the morale of the fighting forces and the general public. If Rhee were killed or captured by the enemy, it would likely mean the death of the Republic of Korea as well. At 7 A.M. President Rhee and his party headed south on a special train. Rhee established himself at the provincial government office in Taejon. On the afternoon of June 27, he was informed that Truman had ordered General MacArthur to provide air and naval support to Korea. Rhee was relieved and greatly moved.

On June 28, U.S. Ambassador John Muccio called on President Rhee and delivered a secret message from General MacArthur: MacArthur would be in Suwon the next morning to observe the war situation, and to devise a war strategy. MacArthur asked Rhee to meet him there. The next morning, on June 29, MacArthur's plane touched down on Suwon's airstrip where Rhee greeted the general. They proceeded to a field office and received briefings on the military situation. Afterward, President Rhee, General MacArthur, and others went up the road toward the front at the south bank of the Han River, to visually assess the situation. They found the capital city in flames. Enemy forces were crossing the Han River. As soon as MacArthur's plane with its

---

[81] Ibid.
[82] Noble, *op. cit.*, 31.
[83] *New York Times*, June 28, 1950
[84] Shinn, *Forgotten War*, 65.

protection of jet fighters departed for Tokyo, Rhee and Muccio began to board a small plane to return to Taejon. Suddenly several enemy planes emerged from behind a cloudbank and began strafing the airfield. At first the pilot attempted to take off but then opted to spin the plane around in a half circle to avoid the attack. The door of the plane opened and the president and Muccio were helped out. Rhee was hurried to the cover of a nearby rice field. Once the enemy planes had flown away, Rhee and Muccio continued their journey to Taejon by car.[85]

The North Korean forces were far superior to their South Korean counterparts in training, firepower, and equipment. The South Korean army lost over 44,000 men (out of 98,000) in the first three days of conflict. Even though the South Korean army was only slightly smaller than the North Korean in number, there was no comparing the fighting capacity of the two forces. The South Koreans lacked tanks, medium range artillery, heavy mortars, and fighter planes. By June 28, the North Koreans had already occupied the capital city of Seoul. The invaders marched rapidly south, and at first their progress seemed unstoppable.

In Taejon, President Rhee organized a war cabinet and met with its members almost daily to evaluate the war situation and to decide on war measures, including mobilization of manpower and resources.[86] As the North Korean tanks approached Suwon, the South Korean army headquarters and the American embassy also moved to Taejon. If the enemy reached as far as Suwon, the fledgling South Korean forces would be unable to stop it. American air and naval support appeared to have no effect in slowing the enemy. Strongly urged by government and military leaders, the president established himself in the governor's residence in Taegu on July 8. Thus, for a period Taegu became the South Korean wartime capital.

The Korean army and the U.S. 24th Division commanded by General William Dean were fighting desperately to stall the enemy advance in the Taejon area in early July.[87] The anticipated early victory upon the arrival of the first American troops had been followed by defeat after defeat. Rhee had believed the American troops were invincible, and the continuing defeats were a terrible shock. His ardent hopes for victory, his confidence in American support, and his will to continue the fight waned. Chaos is not too strong a term to characterize the South Korean situation in the early weeks of the war. The American soldiers were poorly trained and equipped, and almost none of them could speak Korean. They were unable to distinguish between North Korean guerrillas and South Korean civilians. There was no tactical cooperation between Korean and American troops. To improve U.S.-Korean military cooperation during the war, President Rhee granted the United Nations command full control over South Korean troops in his July 15 letter to MacArthur:

> In view of the joint military effort of the United Nations on behalf of the Republic of Korea…in which you have been designated Supreme Commander of

---

[85] Noble, *op. cit.*, 91-92.
[86] The War Cabinet was composed of the president, prime minister, defense minister, home minister, finance minister, commerce minister, and transportation minister.
[87] Major General William Dean became North Korea's prisoner of war in Taejon. For details, see William P. Dean, *General Dean's Story* (New York: Viking Press, 1954.)

the United Nations forces, I am happy to assign to you command authority over all land, sea and air forces of the Republic of Korea during the period of the continuation of the present state of hostilities.[88]

By placing his military under General MacArthur, the president actually improved the position of the Rhee government to influence American policy. Without the unified command structure, there might have been serious strategic and tactical problems in managing the war, as the United States would later experience in Vietnam. Rhee's decision also demonstrated in an unambiguous way that South Korea and the United States were striving in unison to repel Communist aggression.

By late July and early August 1950, South Korean and UN forces had fallen back to a defensive line called the Pusan Perimeter encompassing both Taegu and Pusan, which were now under direct threat by advancing North Korean troops. At times the battlefront was only five to six miles from Taegu. Muccio urged Rhee to transfer the government to the island of Cheju, which, Muccio argued, was remote from enemy attack, and where a government-in-exile could be maintained even if all of Korea was seized by the Communists. Rhee pulled a pistol from his pocket to show the ambassador and told him: "This is for me to use on my wife and myself if the Communists surround us. We do not intend to move the government away from the peninsula. We will all stand and fight. We will not leave."[89] Rhee urged his people to defend themselves. On July 29, he described how he galvanized the nation:

> The cities and towns were captured one by one without resistance on the part of the people themselves. Now we have come to the last city, Taegu, only a short distance from Pusan.... It was reported this morning that the Communists are moving toward Taegu.... This city is profoundly stirred up and has asked us what to do. I am telling them to get up and arm themselves with sticks, bamboo spears, or any kind of home-made bombs, and get ready to fight. I tell them not to run away from their homes, for there is no place to go when this city falls. We must stand together in defense of our homes and our city, and our friends will do all they can to assist us.[90]

On August 27, the North Koreans launched their final offensive against the massive redoubt of the Pusan Perimeter. North Korean troops were now threatening Masan, a city within 30 miles of Pusan. In the midst of fierce fighting, in which key terrain changed hands thirteen times, General Walton Walker, U.S. Eighth Army commander, visited the U.S. 25th Infantry Division and issued what amounted to a "stand or die" order: "There will be no more retreating, withdrawal, or readjustment of the lines.... There is no line behind us to which we can retreat.... A retreat to Pusan would be one of the greatest butcheries in history."[91]

The North Korean military was far superior to its southern counterpart. The enemy forces had 210 fighter planes and 280 tanks, and thousands of heavy artillery pieces; even the American forces had great difficulty in confronting the enemy. The imbalance of

---

[88] Courtney Whitney, *MacArthur: His Rendezvous with History* (New York: Alfred A. Knopf, 1956), 338.
[89] Oliver, *Syngman Rhee and American Involvement*, 295.
[90] Ibid., 305.
[91] Clay Blair, *The Forgotten War: America in Korea, 1950-1953* (New York: Times Books, 1987), 168.

Syngman Rhee

military strength between South and North reflected a contrast in policies between Russians and Americans in Korea rather than a policy failure of the Rhee government; the Soviet Union was pursuing an aggressive expansion policy while the United States was taking a passive containment policy that excluded Korea from its defense perimeter. Rhee showed a firm will to build a strong military but had no means to do so; his government had no foreign reserves to purchase weapons, and the United States refused to supply them. In addition, Rhee had only one and a half years to build up the army while Kim Il Sung had more than four years to prepare for the war with full support from the Soviets.

Rhee was perhaps better qualified than any other Korean leader at the time to help the combined military operations of Korean and UN forces. Rhee was able to converse about America and the American decision-making process and felt quite at home with the English language.[92] During the war he had very close contacts with General Walker and Ambassador Muccio. Rhee's key advisers (Defense Minister Shin Sung-mo, Home Affairs Minister Cho Pyung-ok, and army chief of staff General Chung Il-kwon) also spoke English relatively well. President Rhee, Defense Minister Shin, and General Chung were invited to attend the daily Eighth Army briefings. Before and after the briefings, key leaders of the two allies consulted with one another on combat operations and other war-related matters. On occasion, Rhee and other Korean leaders attended the daily U.S. 5th Air Force briefings. Smooth communication and an amiable relationship between Korean leaders and American generals and diplomats were crucial for the successful operation of the war. Rhee also visited American army and marine divisions to encourage them and to express Korea's appreciation for their heroism and sacrifice.

The war situation for the South changed dramatically after the successful landing of UN forces at Inchon on September 15, 1950, and their retaking of Seoul on September 28, just three months after it had fallen to North Korean troops. Rhee and his government immediately returned to Seoul. The battered streets were lined by hundreds of thousands of citizens, holding national flags and cheering as President Rhee and his long cavalcade drove by. As UN and Korean forces advanced toward the north, the United Nations had not yet decided on military objectives north of the 38th parallel. On June 29, Secretary of State Acheson had stated that American policy was designed "for the purpose of restoring the Republic of Korea to its status prior to the invasion and of re-establishing the peace broken by that aggression."[93] In a September 1 broadcast, President Truman remarked, "we don't want the fighting in Korea to expand into a general war."[94]

However, sensing an opportunity to unify the country, Rhee decided to continue the northward advance. He believed it was in the vital interest of the Republic of Korea to press on to the Yalu River. Rhee, who had devoted his life to Korean independence,

---

[92] Western views on Rhee during the war are mostly negative. He was characterized as senile, unpredictable, obstinate, etc. But he opposed American war policies including armistice talks because he was determined to defend the survival of South Korea. See Stephen Jin-Woo Kim, *Master of Manipulation: Syngman Rhee and the Seoul-Washington Alliance 1953-1960* (Seoul: Yonsei University Press, 2001), Introduction.

[93] Dean Acheson, *Present at the Creation* (New York: Norton, 1969), 450-452.

[94] *Washington Post*, September 2, 1950.

could never accept anything else.⁹⁵ On September 29, President Rhee ordered General Chung Il-kwon, army chief of staff, to continue the push north, and at 11:30 P.M., October 1, an advance unit of the South Korean 3rd Division crossed the 38th parallel into North Korea. Rhee told the Korean people, "We have to advance as far as the Manchurian border until not a single enemy soldier is left in our country."⁹⁶ Six days later, on October 7, the UN General Assembly adopted a resolution approving military action north of the 38th parallel. The resolution called for steps "to ensure conditions of stability throughout Korea," and defined the UN objective as "the establishment of a unified, independent and democratic government" in Korea.

On October 19, Pyongyang, the North Korean capital, was taken. Rhee saw that his dream of a unified Korea was near. Exultant, Rhee flew to Pyongyang on October 30. Upon arriving in Pyongyang, he was greeted by a rejoicing crowd of some 50,000 citizens at the City Hall plaza waving Korean flags, and crying, "*mansei* (long life) for the president!" and "*mansei* for the Republic of Korea!" Rhee stood waving his hat to the cheering crowd, his face wet with tears of joy. At the ceremony in Pyongyang, President Rhee delivered an emotional speech:

> As the same lineage of Tangoon [legendary founding father of Korea], we must unify our nation and preserve freedom and peace forever in this beautiful land of ours by expelling the Communists.... You, the citizens of Pyongyang who have assembled here today, should go along with our march to the Yalu.⁹⁷

The citizens of Pyongyang were deeply moved by his speech. Afterward, Rhee walked into the crowd and embraced elderly citizens. For a brief moment, in the fall of 1950, it seemed as if Korea would achieve both freedom and unity. But in late 1950, half a million Communist Chinese troops entered the conflict on the side of North Korea. In a few stunning weeks, South Korean and UN forces were driven from the Yalu River on the Sino-Korean border back to the 38th parallel. In the United States, a heavy wave of pessimism gripped the nation and a thickening, post-Pearl Harbor atmosphere spread. President Truman declared a state of national emergency on December 15, 1950. "Our homes, our nation, all the things we believe in are in great danger," he said.⁹⁸ *The New York Times* wrote of a "Korean Dunkirk" and an "irretrievable situation." On December 29, the U.S. Joint Chiefs of Staff sent a directive to MacArthur, approved by Truman, stating, "Korea is not the place to fight a major war." The directive instructed MacArthur, if necessary, "to commence a withdrawal to Japan."⁹⁹ MacArthur had already given his staff instructions to continue plans for the evacuation of Korea.¹⁰⁰ Rumors spread that UN forces would be pulled out by February 15. A ranking officer at

---

⁹⁵ Shinn, *op. cit.*, 142-143.
⁹⁶ Ibid., 143.
⁹⁷ Shinn, *op. cit.*, 147-148.
⁹⁸ *New York Times*, December 15, 1950, 1.
⁹⁹ Quoted in Bevin R. Alexander, *Korea: The First War We Lost* (New York: Hippocrene, 1987), 377.
¹⁰⁰ Roy E. Appleman, *Ridgway Duels for Korea* (College Station, TX: Texas A & M University Press, 1990), 92.

MacArthur's Tokyo headquarters was quoted, "We should pull out, bring everybody and everything back to Japan."[101]

The situation was grim and desperate. Defeatism and despair were widespread. On a cold day in January 1951, yet another exodus from Seoul began. The Rhee government, which had returned from Pusan only three months before, joined thousands of soldiers and hundreds of thousands of refugees in flight across the frozen Han River. The loss of Seoul for the second time seriously damaged the morale and spirit of South Koreans, both civilian and military. The Rhee government was stunned by the Chinese intervention and plagued by constant fears of abandonment by the United States and the United Nations.

The qualities that make a man a great leader in war are not necessarily those that people desire in peace. Rhee did not spend the war indoors reading battle reports and receiving briefings from his ministers and generals. Against all odds and constraints, he provided great leadership during the struggle with the Communists. He did everything he could to win the war short of getting into uniform himself. Many of the young soldiers that were facing death on a daily basis wished to see their great leader before their ultimate sacrifice to the nation. Commanders of every division appealed to the president to visit their units.[102] Although now in his mid-seventies, Rhee regularly visited command posts and soldiers in combat zones to motivate and restore their fighting spirit. This was done when roads were largely unpaved, destroyed, and often nearly impassable.

General James Van Fleet, who for two years worked closely with President Rhee during the Korean War, wrote, "For almost two years he went out with me to the front lines and to training areas on an average of about once a week, under all kinds of conditions. When we had to travel by jeep in cold weather, he would shrug away my apologies and smile at my expressions of concern. Then he would climb up into the jeep, and ride there with his fine face and his fringe of white hair standing up out of his parka like a sun shining from above a dark cloud."[103] Rhee reviewed the troops, encouraged commanders in person, offered encouragement to officers and men and urged them all to persevere. The president's visits inspired the soldiers; General Paik Sun-yup, who was the commander of the South Korean First Division at the time, remembers:

> Defense Minister Shin was known as "Minister Tear Drop" from his reputed habit of crying around President Rhee. And sure enough, the minister's eyes brimmed with tears during the president's exhortative speech to the men and officers of the ROK First Division. But the effect was startling. The fact was that the officers and men of the division were touched by his tears and either cried along with him or at least suffered serious cases of blurry vision. His speech went a long, long way toward helping the ROK First Division team regain its fighting spirit, pull ourselves together, and get on with the war.[104]

Rhee was able to rally the disheartened people. As soon as any city was liberated from the Communists, Rhee rushed there to encourage its people. He visited military

---

[101] Quoted in Phil Williams et al., eds., *Security in Korea*, xvii.
[102] Author interview with Song In Sang, April 22, 2002.
[103] Quoted in Oliver, *Syngman Rhee*, 310-312.
[104] Sun Yup Paik, *From Pusan*, 120.

hospitals, schools, refugee camps and orphanages, passionately encouraging Koreans to maintain the anti-communist struggle. In Pusan on August 15, 1951, Rhee spoke to a gathering of Korean leaders and citizens at a celebration marking the third anniversary of the founding of the Republic of Korea,

> Liberty is worth saving, even at the risk of our lives. We must stand together to protect democracy or we shall all become victims of Communism.... We are caught in a gigantic global struggle between Communism and democracy. Coexistence of these two ideologies is impossible. Either one or the other must go.[105]

At their wartime capital in Pusan, Rhee and his ministers carried out their functions by any means possible. Offices were somehow found—often partly roofless and windowless—hastily refurnished with odds and ends of boards, packing cases, and cardboard, so that ministries and bureaus were able to function.[106] The UN Commission on the Unification and Rehabilitation of Korea (UNCURK), presented the UN General Assembly with a report on the conduct of the Korean government during the war:

> Before it was properly established, the young State was struck by war and devastation. Continuous emergency conditions have existed. Most of the country has been a battlefield one time or another.... Twice the Government of the Republic had to evacuate its capital and five times the central administration had to be moved and re-established in a different place. Serious problems in administration and internal security had to be faced as they arose, without previous planning or experience. It is therefore not surprising that deficiencies exist today in the Korean government, that abuse of power has sometimes occurred or that corruption and inefficiency can be found in some places. But they must be seen in perspective.

> The Republic of Korea has stood up to the strains of war remarkably well. The government apparatus did not disintegrate, despite difficulties, confusion, and danger. As districts were liberated,... the civil administration...was quickly re-established."[107]

With the outbreak of the Korean War, Rhee saw the reemergence of an opportunity last seen in the heady post-liberation days of 1945: a chance to realize his dream of national unification. Rhee's overriding concern and interest was unification of the divided country. As early as July 19, 1950, he made his goal in the war clear. In a message sent to President Truman, Rhee wrote:

> It would be utter folly to attempt to restore the *status quo ante*, and then await the enemy's pleasure for further attack.... The government and people of the Republic of Korea consider this is the time to unify Korea, and for anything less than reunification to come out of these great sacrifices of Koreans and their powerful allies would be unthinkable.[108]

---

[105] Ibid., 194.
[106] Oliver, *History*, 232.
[107] *UNCURK Report 1950-1*, UN General Assembly, 6th session, supplement 12, 20.
[108] Quoted in Oliver, *Syngman Rhee*, 306-307.

Rhee viewed the conflict as both a challenge and, more importantly, an opportunity—the possibility of unification under his control. He opposed any plan that fell short of unification. However, with its allies screaming for an end to the war, Washington was seeking any means out of the Korean conflict. The total defeat of North Korea was not a prerequisite for the achievement of American objectives. Washington's position partly reflected the growing discontent of its European allies, who feared that the Korean conflict might evolve into a worldwide military confrontation between the East and the West.[109] MacArthur, like Rhee, viewed the war in terms of a total victory, and he demanded authorization from Washington to bomb Chinese installations in Manchuria.[110] However, the U.S. Joint Chiefs of Staff sent MacArthur a message stating, "Korea is not the place to fight a major war." On April 11, 1951, Truman relieved MacArthur of his command. Shocked by the news, Rhee exclaimed, "Truman has killed our hopes."[111]

The UN command and the Communists agreed to a preliminary meeting for peaceful settlement on July 10, 1951. The Rhee government said in a statement that the Korean people would accept no peace terms until the South and the North were completely united. Going into negotiations, South Korean distrust of the United States ran deep. At the time, many Koreans believed that the United States had sold Korea out initially by agreeing with the Soviet Union to divide the peninsula in 1945. They now believed that the United States was once again brokering a deal with the Communists to divide the peninsula along roughly the same ante-bellum 38th parallel. Rhee, deeply disappointed, opposed any negotiation with the Communists, saying, "Freedom and Communism are opposite; they cannot be combined. Compromise with Communism is impossible; it is like mixing oil and water. The truce being sought at Panmunjom is inherently wrong."[112]

To end the war after such horrendous sacrifice and damage with nothing but the unsettled *status quo* was much more than the Koreans or Rhee could bear. During meetings with his ministers and other visitors, Rhee made his anti-truce position clear: "As a result of the sacrifice of our and allies' soldiers, we are in a favorable position in the war. Why do they try to negotiate in such a critical situation? Look at the free China! What would be the result of truce agreement? Not only the unification but also the very survival of all our people would be in danger. We must oppose the truce negotiations."[113] Koreans strongly supported their president and tens of thousands of demonstrators marched in the streets of Pusan and other major cities to protest against the truce negotiations.

The Western press repeatedly blamed Rhee for blocking an armistice. He was described more and more often as the "obstinate leader" of South Korea. Truman and Churchill came to dislike Rhee for stubbornly insisting on Korean reunification. But Rhee was determined to

---

[109] Burton I. Kaufman, *The Korean War: Challenges in Crisis, Credibility, and Command* (Philadelphia: Temple University Press, 1986), 110.

[110] The U.S. military establishment was also surprised and disconcerted. The generals thought the "only proper end of war was military victory, and they could not understand why it should be denied them." (Samuel P. Huntington, *The Soldier and the State: The Theory and Politics of Civil-Military Relations* (Cambridge, MA: Harvard University Press, 1957), 389.

[111] *Donga Ilbo*, April 12, 1951.

[112] Oliver, *Syngman Rhee and American Involvement*, 391.

[113] Paik Tu-jin (1976), 148.

protect what he saw as his nation's vital interests. In July 1951, Rhee sent a personal letter to General Matthew Ridgeway, U.S. Eighth Army Commander:

> We cannot maintain our nation in half. A divided Korea is a ruined Korea, unstable economically, politically, and militarily.... In every Korean heart and in every Korean mind the fact is clear that our nation would be plunged into irrevocable disaster by any acceptance of a continued dividing-line.... There is no need to settle short of the goal of reunification and free election.[114]

DIPLOMACY FOR NATIONAL SURVIVAL

> Truman lost his temper, MacArthur lost his job, Acheson lost his war, a million and a half lost their lives, and Stalin didn't even lose a night's sleep.—Clark Lee and Richard Henschel, *Douglas MacArthur*[115]

Alliance-Making. When negotiations for a cease-fire began at Kaesong in July 1951, President Rhee remained seriously concerned over how post-truce security could be guaranteed.[116] Rhee and the Korean people feared that a possible arrangement leading to an armistice and withdrawal of UN troops would leave South Korea undefended and unsupported. He never forgot the fact that North Korea had invaded the year following the withdrawal of American troops. He worried that history might be repeated and was determined to obtain a mutual security pact with the United States as the ultimate guarantee of national security.

As the president of a weak and dependent country, Rhee tried to maximize his bargaining position in order to obtain a security treaty from the United States. For this purpose, he strongly opposed the truce talks and repeatedly threatened that South Korean forces would withdraw from the UN command and go it alone against the Communists. Rhee probably realized the impossibility of opposing any U.S. government decision to enter into an armistice, yet he hoped to use his opposition to an armistice to obtain a bilateral defense pact, to obtain more military and economic aid, and to make his people feel he had a real voice in the armistice negotiations.

On March 21, 1952, Rhee sent a letter to Truman insisting, "A mutual security pact between our two nations, I sincerely believe, is an essential thing. Since your desire has been to defend Korea against red aggression, there can be no reason for objecting to such a pact which alone would give the Korean people the supporting assurance they would badly need during a hazardous armistice."[117] The Truman administration consistently refused to enter into a bilateral security relationship with South Korea. Secretary of State Acheson advised Truman that making such a security pact with South Korea would go against American interests.[118] The U.S. Defense Department strongly

---

[114] Shinn, *op. cit.*, 190.
[115] Clark Lee and Richard Henschel, *Douglas MacArthur* (New York: Henry Holt & Co., 1952), 206.
[116] For details of South Korea-U.S. relations during and after the Korean War, see Im Pyong-jik (1956) and Han Pyo-uk (1996).
[117] President Rhee to President Truman, March 21, 1952, *FRUS 1952-1954*, XV, Part. 11, 114-116.
[118] *Chosun Ilbo*, January 16, 1953; Memorandum by the Secretary of State to the President, April 30, 1953, *FRUS 1953*, 15, Part 1: 185-186.

opposed such a pact in the light of the fact that their general war plans did not call for the defense of Korea.

The new Eisenhower administration was determined to end the war as soon as possible. In May 1953, the United States countered by offering alternative measures: instead of a security treaty option, in return for Rhee's compliance with an armistice the United States would build up the South Korean army to twenty divisions and provide the equivalent of a billion dollars for rehabilitating South Korea. Rhee rejected the offer out of hand. Without a formal American commitment to preserve the security of the Republic, he believed that the security of South Korea would be in serious jeopardy.[119] During his meeting with General Mark Clark, UN forces commander, Rhee stated that he failed to understand how the United States could make security agreements with Japan, New Zealand, and Australia and at the same time not make a similar agreement with South Korea, which was doing most of the fighting and was the principal ally of the United States in battle.[120] Rhee again sent a letter to Eisenhower, reiterating his position:

> We are fearfully aware...that to accept any armistice would mean to the Korean Nation...an acceptance of a death sentence without protest.
>
> We propose a simultaneous withdrawal of both the Communist and United Nations forces from Korea, on the condition that a mutual defense pact between our two governments precedes it. The Communist puppet regime in North Korea has a military pact, I understand, with Red China, while the latter has another with [the] Soviet Union. Korea has nothing to counteract the formidable impact of this series of Communist military copulations.
>
> The Mutual Defense Pact will...cover the following points. The United States will agree to come to our military aid and assistance immediately.... The Security Pact should include the United States' help in the increase of the ROK armed forces.... Adequate supplies of arms, ammunition and general logistic materials will be given Korea.... The United States' air and naval forces will remain....[121]

In the face of Rhee's recalcitrance, the Americans prepared an action-plan to prevent Rhee from sabotaging a looming armistice agreement. By May 27, 1953, the scheme, code-named "Plan Eveready," was completed and was approved by Washington. The idea was to get Rhee away from Pusan. As soon as Rhee left for Seoul, U.S. troops in Pusan would seize ten top Korean government officials and take control of South Korea by martial law declared by the South Korea army chief of staff. If the Korean general balked, General Maxwell Taylor, Eighth Army commander, would declare martial law himself. If Rhee did not agree to accept UN armistice terms after these steps had been taken, he would be taken into custody by American troops, and General Clark would try to establish a government led by former prime minister Chang Myon.[122]

---

[119] *FRUS 1952-1954*, XV, 1086-1090.

[120] Telegram from the Commander in Chief, Far East (Clark) to the Joint Chiefs of Staff, May 13, 1953, *FRUS 1952-1954*, XV, 1011.

[121] President Rhee to President Eisenhower, May 30, 1953, *FRUS 1952-1954*, 1124-1126.

[122] Breuer, *Shadow Warriors*, 229; and *New York Times*, August 3, 1975.

Finally, the Eisenhower administration agreed that the United States would negotiate with South Korea over a bilateral defense treaty "*after* the conclusion and acceptance of an armistice." But Rhee must have realized that once the United States achieved a ceasefire, he would lose his bargaining power. He argued that Korea's security had to be assured *before*, not *after* the signing of the armistice.

Rhee also had one more trump card he could use for Korea's bargaining position. There were 34,000 anti-Communist North Korean prisoners of war (POW) who wanted to be freed in South Korea. Rhee believed that the agreement on the repatriation of prisoners of war signed at Panmunjom on June 8 made too many concessions. The United States and the United Nations had retreated from their former position of freeing the anti-Communist POWs. Rhee was dismayed and irate. He ordered his provost marshal to release those anti-Communist North Korean POWs who were held in POW camps guarded by South Korean military police under his command. Just after 2 A.M. on June 18, 1953, some 20,000 POWs were freed in a dramatic, well-planned operation.[123] At 9:00 A.M., Rhee took to the radio: "According to the Geneva Convention, and also to the principle of human rights, the anti-Communist Korean prisoners should have been released much earlier."[124] He said that he ordered their release on his own responsibility.

Rhee's action was hailed as an act of great statesmanship in South Korea. The South Korean people expressed great pride in the audacious gesture. Tens of thousands of people took to the streets and shouted "unification or death." Even opposition lawmakers, who had tended to be very critical of the president, had no choice but to side with him on this particular issue because of the popularity his bold decision had with the general public. It is no exaggeration to say that in this dramatic moment, Rhee was fighting for virtually every crumb necessary for Korea's future well being.[125]

Abroad, Rhee's unilateral action shocked the world, and criticism of Rhee poured in. Rhee was seen as "highly emotional," "unpredictable," or "obstinate." He was also depicted as a fanatic, capable of leading his country into a national suicide. Eisenhower was furious; he sent an indignant message to Rhee protesting that his action had created "an impossible situation for the UN command." Churchill called it "treachery," and Dulles told the Korean ambassador that Rhee's action was "a stab in the back."[126] When James Reston of *The New York Times* interviewed President Rhee at the Blue House in the summer of 1953, he gently informed the president, "Mr. President, your rejection of the truce is making you very unpopular in the United States." Rhee shot back, "I am not in a popularity contest."[127]

Nevertheless, Eisenhower was eager to end the "unpopular" war as soon as possible and dispatched a special envoy, Assistant Secretary of State Walter S. Robertson, to Seoul to persuade President Rhee to accept an armistice. Rhee set about driving as hard a bargain as he could with the American emissary. For over two weeks, Rhee and

---

[123] Of 27,000, 20,000 were released on June 18. However, some 7,000 other North Korean prisoners at camps guarded by American troops could not be freed.

[124] Oliver, *Syngman Rhee and American Involvement*, 409.

[125] Paik, *op. cit.*, 231.

[126] Allen, *Korea's Syngman Rhee*, 161-162.

[127] Oliver, *Syngman Rhee and American Involvement*, 389.

Robertson held almost daily bargaining sessions. After heated arguments and negotiations, often attended by Prime Minister Paik Tu-jin, Foreign Minister Pyun Yung-tai, General Clark, and Ambassador Ellis O. Briggs, the United States and the Republic of Korea reached an agreement. President Rhee promised the United States in writing that although he could not sign the armistice, "we shall not disturb the armistice while a political conference attempts to solve peacefully the problem of the liberation and re-unification of Korea."[128] In return, the United States promised President Rhee the following:

- A U.S.-ROK mutual security pact following the armistice

- Agreement to expand the South Korean army to twenty divisions

- Long-term economic aid, with an initial installment of $200 million for a total appropriation by the U.S. Congress of $1 billion, and $9.5 million in food to the Korean people immediately after the signing of the armistice

- Agreement that if the post-armistice political conference produced no results within ninety days, the U.S. and the Republic of Korea would withdraw to discuss plans of their own for unifying the country

- Agreement to hold high-level U.S.-ROK talks prior to the political conference

Securing a Mutual Defense Treaty with the United States was a great diplomatic coup for Rhee, and he was delighted with the achievement. A day after its initialization, the president made a public statement: "…Now that a defense treaty has been signed between Korea and the United States our posterity will enjoy the benefits accruing from the treaty for generations to come. Our united efforts in this field will assure our security, protecting us from alien aggressors."[129] It was Rhee's determined and desperate efforts to secure a bilateral security treaty with the United States that brought a reversal in the Eisenhower administration's earlier stance on the issue. The treaty was crucial because the presence of American forces under the treaty was the main factor in deterring a North Korean invasion. It would also guarantee the stability needed for rapid economic growth and democratic development of South Korea in the coming decades. Thanks to Rhee's diplomacy, Washington's Korea policy changed from a "minimum commitment" to a "maximum commitment" to the security of South Korea.

The United States was the most powerful country in the world. South Korea was a small and weak state whose survival was almost totally dependent on the military and economic assistance of the United States. What were Rhee's options in dealing with the United States? He appeared to have only two—bluffing and brinkmanship or absolute submission. He was a man

---

[128] Ibid., 431.

[129] Office of Public Information, the Republic of Korea, *Korea Flaming High*, vol. 1, 91-92. The importance of the mutual defense treaty can be more clearly realized when the South Korean case is compared with that of South Vietnam. Twenty years after the end of the Korean War, in 1973 the United States and North Vietnam signed a peace agreement in Paris ostensibly to end the Vietnam War. Only two years later, North Vietnam initiated a final military offensive that brought all of Vietnam under Communist control.

of strong ego and deep loyalties to his cause and his nation. Intent upon maximizing the national interests of Korea, he never accepted American proposals that appeared to violate Korean national interests. Facing unacceptable demands from the United States, he often resorted to the tactics of bluffing and brinkmanship and as a result Korea-U.S. relations experienced frequent friction. Though American officials and the American press often disliked him, Rhee succeeded in satisfying the conditions he viewed as critical to Korean security.[130]

Anti-Japan Policy. Like his anti-Communism (also anti-Russianism), Rhee's antipathy toward Japan was deep-rooted. Memories of Japanese cruelty remained vivid in the late 1940s and 1950s, and the vast majority of the Korean people harbored deep and strong anti-Japan sentiments.[131] Rhee thus spearheaded not only anti-communist movements but also anti-Japanese sentiment, increasing his popularity and firming up his image as "father of the nation."[132] Rhee's anti-Japanism began in the late nineteenth century, when as a young man in his twenties he watched as Japan and Russia contended for control of Korea. Ever since, Rhee hated not only Japan but Russia.

During World War II, China had been a crucial American ally in Asia. After Nationalist China's collapse in 1949, the fundamental Asian policy of the United States was to rebuild and restore Japan as the keystone of Asian stability. The United States encouraged the normalization of relations between South Korea and Japan to ensure a protective flank for Japan on the peninsula and to facilitate Japanese investments and develop South Korea as a major market for Japanese products. Rhee had been seriously frustrated by the persistent American tendency to treat Korea as a subsidiary factor in American relations with Japan. During a press conference on June 10, 1949, Rhee said, "Japanese imperialism is now growing under the protection of the United States."[133]

Anti-Japan sentiments were further generated by the Korean War. Rhee believed that Japan had profited economically from the tragedy to such a point that it was the key to Japan's postwar recovery, but without contributing any direct support or making any sacrifice in the conflict. The Korean War produced a large American demand for Japanese goods and services, and a sudden spur in the Japanese economy resulted. U.S. procurement in Japan during the Korean War totaled some $5 billion.[134] With the help and protection of the United States, Japan was reemerging as a viable economic and political force. Koreans were frustrated and fearful that a divided, devastated Korea was too vulnerable to economic penetration by Japan. Fear of Japanese economic and political domination was a source of great public concern in the 1950s. According to the foreign minister at the time, Rhee believed that his country "could not afford to fall into the Japanese lap economically without perpetuating the division of Korea…. Our national survival requires that we do not get mixed up with the Japanese spending and

---

[130] For a detailed analysis of Rhee's diplomacy toward the United States, see Chang Jin Park, "The Influence of Small States upon the Superpowers: United States-South Korean Relations as a Case Study, 1950-53", *World Politics*, 28:1 (October 1975), 97-117.

[131] Sung-Hwa Cheong, *Politics of Anti-Japanese Sentiment.*

[132] Im Pyong-jik, *op. cit.*, 340ff.

[133] *Chosun Ilbo*, June 11, 1949.

[134] Gavan McCormick, "Japan and South Korea, 1965-1975: Ten Years of 'Normalization'", in Gavan McCormack and Mark Selden, eds., *Korea, North and South: The Deepening Crisis* (New York: Monthly Review Press, 1978), 173.

our unification."[135]

MacArthur sought to initiate closer Korea-Japan ties through a personal invitation to President Rhee to visit Japan. Hoping to restart economic relations with Japan on a cooperative basis, Rhee visited Tokyo for the first time in October 1948 and again in February 1950. Each time, he met with Japanese leaders, but found the Japanese uninterested, and the prospects of obtaining reparations bleak.[136] Rhee was aware that Japan would enjoy a better bargaining position after the ratification of U.S.-Japan peace treaty in San Francisco by the U.S. Congress, and believed it would be best to resolve some outstanding Korean issues with Japan while the United States still had some leverage there. Thus, Rhee decided to hold talks with Japan. In November 1951, two months after the signing of the San Francisco peace treaty, Korea and Japan opened a preliminary dialogue. The Rhee government demanded at least $2 billion in compensation from Japan for colonial exploitation and war damages. But Japan not only refused to consider any obligation whatsoever, but even called for the return of Japanese property abandoned in Korea in 1945.[137]

Realizing that the Korean bargaining position was weakening in the wake of the upcoming negotiations, President Rhee proclaimed the "Peace Line" (also known as the "Rhee Line") on January 18, 1952, which extended the marine sovereignty of the Republic of Korea to 200 miles off the Korean coast, roughly corresponding to the MacArthur Line that was to be abolished with the end of the American occupation of Japan. Although the pronounced goal of the Peace Line was to protect marine resources, it was clear that the primary purpose was to gain an advantage in the coming conference with Japan. Rhee ordered his chief of naval operations to seize any non-UN vessels in the zone and bring them to Pusan. South Korea continued to patrol up to the Peace Line with its navy and seize Japanese vessels—sixty-three in less than a month. In response, Japan established its own patrols, and the risk of Korean-Japanese clashes grew in the midst of the ongoing Korean War.

On February 15, 1952, the first conference for the normalization of relations between South Korea and Japan commenced, but due to very different priorities and the uncompromising positions of both Korea and Japan, it failed to bring about any resolution of outstanding issues between the two nations. The Japanese showed little contrition for their occupation of Korea. On the contrary, they often insisted that Korea should be grateful to Japan for developing the peninsula. The Rhee government demanded that Japan renounce all of its property claims. Within a few months the talks reached an impasse.

In January 1953, UN commander General Clark sent President Rhee a personal invitation to visit him in Tokyo. Though an informal one, his visit to Japan was a historic occasion. President Rhee and Prime Minister Yoshida Shigeru held talks at Clark's residence. The following exchange at their initial meeting is well known. When Yoshida

---

[135] Yung-tai Pyun [Rhee's foreign minister (1953-55)]'s remarks quoted in Selig S. Harrison, *Korean Endgame: A Strategy for Reunification and U.S. Disengagement* (Princeton, NJ: Princeton University Press, 2002), 295.

[136] Kwan Bong Kim, *op. cit.*, 44.

[137] Oliver, *Syngman Rhee and American Involvement*, 462.

asked Rhee, "Aren't tigers still living in Korea?" Rhee replied "No, Kato Kiyomasa [Toyotomi Hideyoshi's frontline commander during Japan's invasion of Korea (1592-96)] caught them all and carted them off to Japan." [138] The meeting was chilly. Nevertheless, the atmosphere for renewed talks had improved.

Normalization talks resumed in April 1953 but came to an explosive end in October when the Japanese chief negotiator, Kubota Kanichiro, humiliated the Korean delegates by saying that the repatriation of Japanese from Korea, the disposition of the Japanese property by the American military government, and the establishment of an independent Korean state before the peace treaty with Japan, were all in violation of international law, and further, that the description in the Cairo Declaration of Korean "enslavement" was wartime hysteria, and that "Japan's compulsory occupation of Korea for 36 years was beneficial to the Korean people." The Koreans became furious. The Rhee government led an all-out campaign against the Japanese.[139]

Rhee had maintained an anti-Japan position throughout his presidency. At the time, Japan's persistence in rationalizing its colonial rule over Korea, and Korea's strong nationalism and anti-Japanese feelings were not conducive to restoring diplomatic ties. Japan was also reluctant to pay reparations to Korea, because Japan was still struggling to recover from the destruction of the Pacific War.

Post-War Reconstruction

After three years of war, South Korea lay in ruins. American planes dropped more bombs on tiny Korea than on all of Europe during World War II. Seoul changed hands four times during the war and was left almost completely destroyed. Fifty-two out of fifty-five South Korean cities were nearly decimated. The only cities that had not fallen into Communist hands were Pusan, Taegu, and Masan. Some 3,000 villages were destroyed, 600,000 houses—nearly one out of every six homes—had been demolished, and 75 percent of all mines and textile factories had suffered severe damage. Most public buildings and manufacturing facilities lay in ruins. Public utility services were at a virtual standstill; railways, bridges, harbors and irrigation works were also inoperable.[140] Shannon McCune described postwar South Korea as "rubble, shells of factories, large empty holes where buildings once stood, mangled railroad locomotives, all overlaid with dirt and dust." She concluded, "The future for Korea cannot with fairness be pictured in rosy hues. Life for the Koreans will be difficult."[141] The Neutral Nations Inspection Committee reported: "The country is dead…there is no activity."[142]

The physical damage defies reliable estimation, but one held that the physical destruction in South Korea amounted to $3 billion in an economy whose total GNP was about $1.7

---

[138] Im Pyong-jik (1964), 344-345.
[139] The U.S. Embassy Tokyo telegram 1441, December 10, 1953, 694.95B/12-1053.
[140] For the details of rehabilitation and reconstruction, see Paik Tu-jin (1975); Reeve, *Republic of Korea*, 36; and Lewis, *op. cit.*, 17.
[141] Shannon McCune, *Korea's Heritage: A Regional and Social Geography* (Tokyo: Tuttle, 1956), 191-192.
[142] Quoted in Woronoff, *Korea's Economy*, 18.

billion in 1953.[143] Nearly half of the manufacturing facilities (43 percent) were destroyed or damaged, industrial output declined to around 50 percent and agricultural production dropped 27 percent. At fighting's end the power generation capacity of all of South Korea was less than that of the battleship USS Missouri.[144]

The people had withstood extraordinary suffering. More than one million South Korean civilians and 136,859 soldiers had lost their lives and more than two million were wounded. Among the casualties were 500,000 war widows, 15,000 amputees, and 100,000 orphans. American casualties were 33,629 killed and 103,284 wounded. Non-American casualties were 17,000; among them, 1,000 British and 4,000 other nationalities were killed. Millions of Koreans had lost everything but the clothes they were wearing. About six million people, or 30 percent of the population, wandered the country as refugees during the war: they found shelter in shacks in the towns and cities; they suffered from disease, hunger, and lack of shelter; many starved. These homeless refugees depended in whole or in part on relief to stay alive. A new wave of one and a half million refugees from North Korea added to the chaos and confusion. Almost no family was untouched by the war. Reduction in production led to a rapid rise in prices. Rampant inflation, which had been out of control since liberation, had become a chronic social condition by the end of the war.[145] The retail price index (1947=100) rose from 331 in 1950 to 4, 329 in 1953.[146]

There was an extreme dearth of food, raw materials, equipment, and skilled labor. To deal with this situation, the Rhee government needed an astronomical amount of resources. Yet the wartime destruction was so vast that the tax base was greatly reduced at the very time when expenditures necessary to repair the devastation were at their highest. The government found it difficult to collect taxes, achieving only 20 percent of its original projections. Few citizens were in a position to pay taxes. The tax receipts were barely enough to cover the minimum expenses of the government.[147] In addition to devastation and mass shortages, the country had the burden of maintaining a 20-division army. The proposed Korean defense budget was two and a half times the annual revenues of the government. During the postwar period of 1954-57, South Korea's defense expenditures accounted for an astounding 53 percent of the government budget, the highest defense apportionment in the world at that time.[148] The gap between resources available and resources required was enormous.[149] The government had to

---

[143] Lawrence B. Krause, "The Political Economy of South Korea", in Dong-se Cha et al., eds. (1997), 109.

[144] Tasca Mission Report on Strengthening the Korean Economy, June 15, 1953, *FRUS 1952-1954*, XV, 1248-1249.

[145] Before that, from the American occupation in September 1945 to June 1950, retail prices increased 25-fold and wholesale prices 29-fold. And in the two or three-month period before the Japanese surrender, prices increased 20 to 25 times over. See Lewis, *op. cit.*, 17-18.

[146] Nam, *Korea*, 482.

[147] Tu-jin Paik (1976), 116-117.

[148] Tasca Report, *FRUS 1952-1954*, 1249.

[149] In 1955, for example, the government collected only 22,900 million *won* in taxes, about 38 percent of its budget. For the Special War Account, the government budgeted and spent 79,300 million *won* but was able to collect only 26,100 million *won* (less than 33 percent of the budget).

print money to meet the costs of the military and other necessities.

The restoration of schools and teachers was another urgent task facing the Rhee government. During the war, two-thirds of the schools were destroyed. Many of the remaining school buildings were taken over by the military and used either as hospitals or camps. Many teachers volunteered or were drafted into the army. Many others were killed. During the war, education continued without a break in makeshift barracks and outdoor classrooms. Children carried blackboards every day back and forth from somebody's home to their classrooms. At the entrance of one school, an archway had been erected covered with cloth banners, which read: "This is our battlefield. It is here we learn how to keep ourselves and our nation free." The foreign press described Korea as an "education hungry country."[150] Despite all the difficulties it faced, the Rhee government put strong emphasis on education, promulgating the Wartime Emergency Education Act in 1951. For Rhee, education was the key to winning the struggle against the Communists and securing future prosperity.

Soon after the Korean War, as part of a rehabilitation program, the government prepared and carried out the Six-Year Accomplishment Plan of Compulsory Education (1954-1959). The plan aimed at achieving a 96 percent level of enrollment of school-age children by the end of the plan's period, to be accomplished by building an additional 30,000 classrooms.[151] The draft law was revised to exempt schoolteachers from military service. In 1955, still in the miserable aftermath of the war, the enrollment level at elementary schools was already 95 percent—nearly universal enrolment. The portion allotted to education in the national budget was second only to defense. Although school enrollment increased at all levels over time, the growth spurt in the elementary and secondary school levels was the most pronounced during the 1950s. In the late fifties, the education level of Korea was exceptionally high compared with other underdeveloped countries.[152] Without such a rapid development in education, the economic growth of the sixties and seventies would have been impossible.

Devastated Korea presented a formidable task of relief and rehabilitation, a burden that the country could ill afford to bear alone. Foreign aid was critical for reconstruction. During the war, the UN command established the UN Civil Assistance Command in Korea (UNCACK) and managed the relief programs. Aid necessary to prevent hunger and disease was provided through military channels. General Clark, the UN forces commander, said that "in order to execute the war effectively, it was necessary to make certain that unrest, disease, and starvation were eliminated or at least minimized in South Korea…[We] couldn't afford to let a group of UN economists decide to rehabilitate textile factories, for instance, with money we sorely needed to dredge a harbor or a channel to make way for our supply ships."[153]

In November 1951, President Rhee issued a statement of principles and procedures governing reconstruction. He announced a schedule of priorities, calling for restoration

---

[150] Oliver, *Syngman Rhee and American Involvement*, 357 and 385.
[151] Ministry of Education, *Six-Year Accomplishment Plan of Compulsory Education, 1954-1959* (Seoul, 1954).
[152] In late 1950s the combined portion of defense and education expenses in the national budget was more than 50 percent. See Song In-sang (1993), 224.
[153] Clark, *Danube to the Yellow*, 143-144.

of six hundred thousand destroyed homes; the reopening of coal and tungsten mines; the development of electric power plants; the restoration of damaged textile and rubber shoe plants; and the establishment of new fertilizer, rayon, and cement factories, fish canneries, and shipbuilding yards. Long-range rehabilitation, he urged, should concentrate on the development of heavy industries and machine-tool plants and on the restoration of "thousands of square blocks of wrecked buildings in our cities, including schools, government buildings, office buildings, and apartment houses."[154] The reconstruction of roads and bridges and the dredging of rivers and harbors were also placed on the urgent list. He emphasized again and again that with all the outside aid being donated, the immediate needs of his people could be met with just one-third outlay of the provided funds. He wanted the other two-thirds to go into plants that could provide permanent wealth to South Korea.

Given Rhee's priorities, serious disagreements were quick to emerge with the UN command over the allocation of aid funds. While Rhee emphasized South Korean fiscal sovereignty, American officials insisted that those who provided the money should decide how it would be spent. Bilateral negotiations broke off in November 1951 over Korean protests that the command's control over Korea's foreign exchange was unacceptable.[155] After months of negotiations, in May 1952 South Korea and the United States signed an Economic Coordination Agreement which provided for the creation of a Combined Economic Board, a channel for regular policy consultations between the two sides, and joint decision-making. The agreement gave the UN command a say over Korea's use of foreign exchange, but it also gave the Korean government a say over the American aid program, a concession for which Rhee had long been fighting.[156]

The chief American representative on the board was the commanding general of the Korean Communications Zone, a component of the UN command, who took charge of all the command's civil functions in Korea. The American economic coordinator on the board (C. Tyler Wood) assumed his role, not as representative of the U.S. government, but as an agent of the UN command. Therefore, American efforts focused on relief efforts as part of military activities. After prolonged and difficult negotiations, the Agreement for a Program of Economic Reconstruction and Financial Stabilization was signed on December 14, 1953, by Korean and U.S. representatives on the Combined Economic Board.[157] Nevertheless, there had been no close consultation with the Korean government, which began complaining it did not know what was being brought into the country until the supplies arrived. The large and uncoordinated influx of aid in the form of goods had succeeded in keeping the Korean economy alive, but it also kept it dependent. A U.S. embassy report at the time commented, "It is possible that [aid in the form of goods] have damaged reserves of recuperative energy the Korean industry may have possessed within itself.... Activating stagnant manufacturing capacity at the grass-roots level has been disregarded."[158]

Foreign aid, which constituted a third of the South Korean national budget in 1954, rose to

---

[154] Oliver, *History*, 245-248.
[155] Song In-Sang, *op. cit.*
[156] Lyons, *Military Policy*, 114-123.
[157] Chu, Sok-Kyun, "Why American Aid Failed", *Koreanna Quarterly*, 4: 1 (autumn 1962): 81-93.
[158] Macdonald, *U.S.-Korea Relations*, 259.

58.4 percent in 1956.[159] But the United States placed its policy priority on checking inflation and providing a minimum standard of living for the Korean people. It emphasized increasing the supply of final products such as consumer goods and some intermediate goods that did not require much additional processing within Korea. In 1953, consumer goods accounted for 98.5 percent of foreign aid. Though the share of consumer goods gradually decreased to 69.4 percent by 1959, the proportion was still high. In addition, the large influx of grain products from the United States, which accounted for as much as 20 percent of South Korea's grain production in 1957, dealt a devastating blow to the country's rural economy.[160] The U.S. aid program dominated South Korea's economy, creating large imports without comparable exports. U.S. aid shipments accounted for 86 percent of all Korean imports, and Korea's imports in 1958 were approximately 23 percent of its GNP, placing its dependency on imports among the highest in the world.[161]

The psychology that had guided U.S. aid programs in Korea emphasized stopgaps. Famine relief was provided, but the Americans didn't look beyond to permanently solving the food problem.[162] American economic aid could not but fail to reconstruct the Korean economy (see Table 5).[163]

Table 5. **Foreign Aid Received** ($M)
(1953-1960)

Project Aid 1954-60		Non-Project Aid 1953-60	
Transportation	176	Fertilizer	304
Railways	151	Raw Cotton	167
Industry & Mining	136	Petroleum, Coal & Other Fuels	150
Power Plants	45	Wheat, Barley & Other Foodstuffs	111
Fertilizer Plants	39	All Other	511
Small Industries	23		
Agriculture & Natural Resources	28		
Social Services	80		
Other	24		
Total Project Aid	444	Total Non-Project Aid	1,143

Source: Bank of Korea Monthly Statistical Review November 1961

---

[159] During the late 1950s and the early 1960s, American aid accounted for about 75 percent of the South Korea's defense budget and 50 percent of the civil budget (James W. Morley, *Japan and Korea: America's Allies in the Pacific* (New York: Walker, 1965), 48-49.
[160] Dong-Se Cha et al., eds. (1997), 147-148; and *Handbook of Korea* (New York: Pageant Press, 1958), 379-384.
[161] *Korean Survey*, III:6 (June/July 1954): 3-4. Paek Tu-jin, Korean finance minister, was Korean co-chairman of the board.
[162] This point was mentioned by Robert Johnson, a National Security Council staffer, in his memorandum to Deputy National Security Adviser Walter Rostow in April 3, 1961. See *FRUS 1961-1963*, XXII, 208.
[163] Sock Kyun Chu, *op. cit.*, 93.

Because of its budgetary austerity, the U.S. government tried to buy two things—extraordinary South Korean military strength and economic reconstruction—for little more than the price of one thing in Korea. The South Korean army had more than twenty divisions, which Korea and the United States were determined to maintain. The United States tended to submerge heavy military support in a limited "relief and rehabilitation" effort. For instance, in 1954 the United States provided $450 million for military aid and $250 million for relief and rehabilitation.[164] The Korean War marked a critical juncture in U.S. foreign assistance programs. Prior to the war, the ratio of economic to military aid was about four to one; by the end of 1950, that ratio had been reversed. This trend continued, although to a lesser degree, throughout the 1950s as the ratio of military to economic aid averaged about two to one.

A June 12, 1961, memorandum sent from a staff member of the U.S. National Security Council to McGeorge Bundy, President Kennedy's national security adviser, pointed out that one of the basic reasons why the Korean economy had remained stagnant was the United States' predominantly military focus. American policy was based largely on the notion that a fragile truce hung like a Damocles' sword over the peninsula, and that hostilities might be renewed at any time. As a result, American aid did little more than keep the Korean economy afloat, as the United States focused its efforts on maintaining the sizable Korean military forces.[165]

After the Korean War, the viability of the Japanese economy was questionable. The Japanese conducted intense lobbying to get the United States to spend its Korean aid money to purchase goods from Japan.[166] The Eisenhower administration had tried to coordinate its economic assistance policies through recycling aid resources in East Asia. The American policy meant linking a subordinate Korean economy to the revival of Japan; Korea had to be a market for Japanese goods and a state economically dependent on Japan. Rhee was adamantly opposed to the American policy of granting huge sums of aid money to build Japanese industries while aid to Korea was restricted to the import of consumer goods. Rhee insisted that the money be used entirely in Korea to build up the Korean economy. He expressed his fear that "if Japan is built up with the money to be used for Korea, and if the other countries in Asia, including Korea, remain as buyers, the others will become 'slaves' to Japan."[167]

In 1955, Rhee established the Ministry of Reconstruction in order to promote systematic reconstruction. In 1956, the Rhee government inaugurated a fiscal stabilization program to bring a halt to the inflation spiral.[168] The stabilization plan contributed significantly to the stabilization of the national economy. Wholesale prices showed only a modest annual increase rate of 5.8 percent during 1957-1960, and even

---

[164] Lewis, *op. cit.*, 39-43.

[165] "Relative Priority of Military vs. Reconstruction Focus in Korea" (Memorandum from Robert W. Komer of the National Security Council Staff to the President's Special Assistant for National Security Affairs), *FRUS 1961-1963*, XXII, no. 226.

[166] Woo, *Race*, 56.

[167] Ibid.

[168] Marshall D. Wattles, "South Korea's Balance of Payments Problems", *Far Eastern Survey*, XXIX:9 (September 1960): 132-137.

recorded a decline of 6.1 percent in 1958.[169] In March 1958, the Economic Development Council was formed as a consulting and research agency for the Ministry of Reconstruction and was given the responsibility of developing a long-term economic plan. In April 1959 the council drafted a Three-Year Plan, but the plan still had not been implemented as the Rhee government stood on the verge of collapse.

It has been widely believed that Rhee failed in his economic policies. His failures—inflation, stagnation, and corruption—draw much attention, while the success remained largely unnoticed. South Korea recorded an average annual growth of 4.4 percent during 1954-1959; this was impressive in comparison to other countries at the time. The annual average growth rate for Korean industry in the 1950s was 10.8 percent, far greater than that in the primary sector of 2.5 percent and for the service sector at 3.9 percent.[170] In fact, the Rhee era is not synonymous with economic degeneration and stagnation. But it is also true that the record is meager when compared with the spectacular performance during the coming decades. An expert believes that "the reason had less to do with wrong policy choices than inauspicious beginnings and unquestionable calamities" of the Korean War.[171]

DEMOCRACY ON TRIAL

The Korean War was a defining event for contemporary Korea. The war set the state agenda for all subsequent Korean regimes. The war killed and maimed millions of Koreans, but it also scarred an entire generation of survivors; it left a legacy of fear and insecurity that continues today. It is difficult to imagine the suffering of those who experienced the war, such as the terror of occupying Communist armies and incendiary bombings, the separation of families, the frantic flight to refugee camps up and down the peninsula, the subsequent struggle for survival in a swirling mass of similarly displaced and desperate people, and the fear of reprisal from one side or the other.

Nevertheless, as a Western scholar of the Korean War wrote, the war "gave Rhee what the South Korean president could never have gained on his own in a thousand years—a just cause and a banner of moral legitimacy."[172] Before the war, many questioned the survival of the Rhee government. However, the war had helped consolidate the strident anti-Communist leader's position as the supreme leader and key spokesman for the nation.[173] The war shaped the visceral character of South Korean anti-Communism. During the war, more than one million South Korean civilians and 320,000 soldiers had lost their lives and more than two million were wounded. The Communist occupation of the South lasted only four months. Nevertheless, it was long enough to allow the South Korean people to discover the cruel nature of Communism. Communist "purification" efforts were no more than the elimination of individuals associated with any activities defined as objectionable to Communism. It was estimated that 129,000 civilians were executed without trial during the North Korean

---

[169] Joe-Won Lee, "Planning Efforts for Economic Development", in Joseph S. Chung, ed., *Patterns of Economic Development: Korea* (Kalamazoo, MI: Korea Research and Publications, 1966), 111.
[170] Woo, *Race*, 59.
[171] Ibid.
[172] Max Hastings, *The Korean War* (New York: Simon & Schuster, 1991), 57.
[173] Kim Hakjoon, *Hankuk jeonjaeng* (The Korean War) (Seoul: Pakyoungsa, 1989), 357-365.

occupation of the South, 84,000 were kidnapped, and 200,000 South Koreans were press-ganged into the northern military.[174] The brutal persecution and needless killings the invaders inflicted quickly persuaded the South Koreans that their own system, in spite of its many faults, was far preferable to Communism. Many had fled North Korea before and during the war and became fervent anti-Communists, which further strengthened Rhee's anti-Communist position.

Many South Koreans who had been either sympathetic or indifferent to Communism before the war became avowed anti-Communists afterward. The tragic war had left most Southerners implacably anti-Communist, and it was perhaps inevitable that any South Korean government in the future would be militantly anti-Communist.[175] Rhee's uncompromising anti-Communism became a long-standing principle in South Korea's domestic and foreign policy. His anti-Communist rhetoric supplied the populace with a feeling of solidarity and provided a strong motivation for the people to fight against the Communists. Thus, anti-Communism came to be seen not merely as an ideological choice but as a necessity for survival. A strong centralized state was needed to tackle the twin challenges of national security and economic reconstruction. Leading a country that lacked democratic traditions, under poor conditions for democracy, and requiring emergency powers to face an unprecedented national crisis, Rhee's determination to be a strong leader was completely rational.

In Pusan, the wartime capital, the conduct of the war had never been an issue of oppositional politics: the opposition continued to attack the government. In September 1950, the most critical period of the war, in a move to prevent governmental violation of human rights, the National Assembly passed a law providing for the abolition of capital punishment, a law for the treatment of Communist collaborators, and a law introducing a review procedure in the case of capital punishment. Believing these laws would disrupt operation of the war, Rhee vetoed them, but the Assembly overruled him. Conflict between Rhee and his political opponents thus increased in intensity. With Rhee's term due to expire in August 1952, oppositions, which dominated the National Assembly, were determined to drive Rhee out in the coming presidential election. The 1948 constitution had given the right to elect the president to the National Assembly. When it became evident that Rhee had little chance of re-election in the National Assembly under the existing system, a constitutional amendment for direct election of the president by the people became essential to his political survival. But such a constitutional amendment would not be possible without a political battle against the anti-Rhee groups in the National Assembly. The overriding necessity of maintaining at least a façade of national unity during wartime would argue against ousting the chief executive in the midst of the war. Although Rhee was unpopular with the more educated sector of the population because of his heavy-handed style of leadership, he was recognized by the people as the rallying point of anti-Communist struggle. As a man with a clear sense of mission, Rhee was confident that Korea needed his leadership at this critical time.

---

[174] Breen, *Koreans*, 124. The North Koreans committed awful mass murders, of which the 5,000 bodies discovered in Taejon alone were only a example. Hastings, *Korean War*, 90.
[175] Scalapino and Lee write that, as the war came to an end, South Korea was "one of the most staunchly anti-Communist societies in the world." Scalapino and Lee, *Communism in Korea*, vol. 1, 462.

On November 30, 1951, Rhee submitted a constitutional amendment to the National Assembly calling for the popular election of the president. As expected, the amendment was rejected by a substantial majority. Although blocked by the assembly, Rhee was determined to stay in office and lead the nation that was fighting a fateful war with the Communists. To wage such a political war, he organized the Liberal Party in late 1951, departing from his previous no-party position, and in early 1952 ninety-three lawmakers were persuaded to join this newly established political party.[176] On April 17, 1952, the opposition party lost little time in introducing its own constitutional amendment providing for a cabinet system. The move failed. Rhee blasted the lawmakers as "selfish minorities." He said the assembly's action no longer reflected "the will of the people," and argued that, "The real struggle for power is between the entire nation and a group of assemblymen. There is no one more anxious than I am to see this country firmly established as a truly independent and democratic state. This has been the sole objective of my lifelong struggle."[177] He insisted that the Korean people be allowed to pick the president directly. In May 1952, as the expiration date of his term of office was rapidly approaching, he re-introduced his amendment, with a number of concessions to the parliamentary advocates.

At first, people did not understand what the issue was, but when they learned that President Rhee wanted the people to have the right to elect their own president whereas the National Assembly insisted on retaining the right of election, an overwhelming majority favored the amendment. The Liberal Party then began to mobilize pro-government groups to intimidate the opposition. Pro-government groups staged massive demonstrations against the opposition demanding the recall of legislation that disregarded "the will of the people." Pro-government demonstrations were stirred up in Pusan. The demonstrators surrounded the building where the National Assembly was meeting and demanded that it grant the people the right to select their president.[178]

On May 25, after reshuffling his cabinet, Rhee proclaimed martial law in Pusan on the grounds of national security. Several assemblymen were arrested and charged with being North Korean spies. On May 30, Lee Bum-suk, the new minister of home affairs, announced that two dozen assemblymen had been jailed for conspiring to assassinate President Rhee and other leaders in an attempt to unify the South under Communist rule. Rhee's tenure would expire on August 15 and therefore the next president should be elected within sixty days. The succession crisis reached a breaking point. The government intensified its pressure on the assembly. Rhee threatened to dissolve the National Assembly if it did not approve the amendment. With public demonstrations outside and physical intimidation inside the assembly, the opposition finally capitulated on July 7, 1952, and by a vote of 163 to zero (out of 166 present), the National Assembly passed the amendment for the direct election of the president. Rhee had "won" the political war against the opposition and was now unchallengeable. He had restored both the actual and symbolic powers of the chief executive. The balance of power had shifted from the National Assembly to the president.

His single-minded concentration on the highest priority of national survival brought about some excesses. There was no doubt that the war power of the president was

---

[176] Quee-Young Kim, *Fall of Syngman Rhee*, 22.
[177] Quoted in Sunoo, *20th Century Korea*, 256.
[178] *Youngnam Ilbo*, May 23 and 24, 1952 and *Pusan Ilbo*, June 27, 1952.

utilized to the fullest extent to bolster the political position of President Rhee. Yet none dared question these powers because the country was in the midst of war. [179] Rhee was determined to save the nation by any means. During the Civil War Lincoln wondered whether it is "possible to lose the nation and yet preserve the Constitution," and took some unconstitutional measures. [180] Perceptions of the 1952 constitutional amendment were mixed. More than anything else, it painted a picture of Rhee as a self-serving autocrat. On the other hand, his supporters pointed out that the amendment secured Korean democracy on the tenable foundation of the vote of the people. An American editorial commented: "It may be that the sounder—yes, the more democratic cause—is stand clear and let Rhee, with his solid backing by the people and the army, revise the constitution in his own way, even though his means appear to comprise the very antithesis of the democratic process."[181] The UN command was far from dismayed, because the re-election of Rhee was a guarantee that the Koreans would remain anti-Communist and disruption behind the lines would not occur. Colonel Harry L. Mayfield, then commander of the Seoul Civil Assistance Team of the U.S. Eighth Army, remarked on the event:

> When President Rhee was forcing through the amendment, we were all against him. But we have changed our minds. We admire him for the courage and skill with which he won his fight. Moreover, we have had time for a second thought about what would have happened if he had yielded to the foreign pressures and had dropped his plan for the amendment. The National Assembly would have elected someone besides Rhee and the people would have been divided and embittered. The whole of South Korea would probably have fallen into chaos. That would have made an impossible situation for our troops. We've got to admit the old man was right.[182]

In the first popular presidential election on August 5, the Koreans voted overwhelmingly for Syngman Rhee, electing him with the largest percentage (74.6 percent) of the popular vote in the history of the Republic of Korea even to this day. The opposition party did not even attempt to field an opposition candidate. His only challenger was his first agriculture minister, Cho Bong-am, who received only 797,000 votes, as opposed to 5,238,000 for Syngman Rhee. *The New York Times* described the power that Rhee exerted over the electorate:

> Without speeches, without campaigning and without acknowledging the party that nominated him, President Syngman Rhee swept South Korea this week in its first presidential election by direct popular vote.
>
> The most important fact for South Korean voters is that even today, seven years after the country obtained its freedom from the Japanese, only one name and one face is known in every bamboo backyard and paddy clearing—Syngman Rhee's.

---

[179] Oh, *Korea: Democracy on Trial*, 47.
[180] Quoted in James MacGregor Burns, *Presidential Government* (Boston: Houghton Mifflin, 1965), 36.
[181] *San Francisco Chronicle*, June 18, 1952.
[182] Oliver, *Syngman Rhee*, 289.

No one was surprised at the enormous vote given to President Rhee—"That is the way it must be." Nobody knows who is "the government" anyhow, except, of course for President Syngman Rhee.[183]

With the landslide victory, Rhee became more and more convinced of his authoritarian leadership. He believed that he alone was qualified to manage national policy and to lead the nation. This was also the beginning of his downfall. Following his re-election, Rhee's attention turned toward parliamentary elections in 1954, when for the first time the Liberal Party would contest for seats in the assembly. The aim of the ruling Liberal Party in the 1954 elections was to win a two-thirds majority of the assembly, making new amendments to the constitution that would abolish all vestiges of the parliamentary system. The ruling party won an overwhelming victory by securing 114 seats (short of two-thirds majority) against fifteen for the Democratic Nationalist Party and sixty-seven for assorted independents. Within days, enough independents had been gathered into the Liberal Party to give it the required two-thirds majority.

With this comfortable majority in the Assembly, the Rhee administration introduced another constitutional amendment on November 29, 1954. The amendment included the abolition of the position of prime minister as well as the abolition of all other elements of a parliamentary system. The most publicized of the new amendments was a provision stating that the first president, Syngman Rhee, was not limited to two terms of office. The amendment received only 135 of the 203 votes. The speaker of the National Assembly, assuming 136 votes were required for it to pass, at first declared the amendment defeated. But at the next session the speaker reversed his decision, declaring that by rounding off to the nearest whole number only 135 votes were needed for passage. Thus, the amendment passed the National Assembly, enabling Rhee to be president for life.

There was no doubt that Rhee would be re-elected for a third term in the 1956 presidential election. He was eighty-one years of age and the normally ceremonial position of vice president assumed critical importance. If Rhee died in office during his term, an event generally expected, he would be succeeded by the vice president. The amended constitution failed to introduce a provision for jointly electing the president and vice-president from the same ticket. Thus, the election of the vice-president became a crucial issue in the 1956 election. Rhee endorsed Lee Ki-poong, the chairman of the ruling Liberal Party, as his vice-presidential candidate. Lee had served as Rhee's private secretary and chief of staff during 1947-1949. Lee had been mayor of Seoul, defense minister, and then speaker of the National Assembly. Moreover, his wife, Park Maria, was a good friend of the first lady and a woman of great charm, social poise, and high intellectual ability, evidenced by her position as dean of Ewha Women's University. After four decades in exile in the United States, the first family had no close relatives and friends in Korea. The Lees were almost the only Korean couple with whom the president and the first lady socialized.

The Democratic Party nominated the "old faction" leader, Shin Ik-hui, as its candidate for president and the "new faction" leader, Chang Myon, for vice president. Even though the opposition candidate Shin died before election day, Rhee, who had

---

[183] *New York Times*, August 10, 1952.

received 74.6 percent of the total vote four years before, polled at only 55.6 percent. One of the most significant results of the election was not the re-election of Rhee, but the surprising election of opposition leader Chang Myon as vice-president, seriously damaging Rhee's prestige. Chang's victory introduced considerable uncertainty into presidential succession. It not only strengthened the political base of the opposition, but it created a situation in which the Liberal Party could be left out in the cold should Rhee die prior to the 1960 presidential election.

The 1956 presidential election revealed considerably more popular dissatisfaction with the Rhee regime than had been evident up to that time. During the 1950s Seoul became "one of the largest education centers of the world." It law schools produced about eighteen times as many graduates in 1960 as the field could absorb. At the lower levels of education, the expansion was even more striking, with the literacy rate increasing from about 20 percent to over 60 percent in the early 1960s.[184] Forty to fifty percent of college graduates were believed to be unemployed or underemployed. Economic difficulties were the main source of the frustration. The economy recovered to a certain extent with American economic aid after the armistice, but soon the growth rate had begun a new descent (5.2 percent in 1954, 4.0 percent in 1955, and 0.3 percent in 1956). The economic troubles were felt most keenly by the urban population. Intellectuals, students, and the mass media were concentrated in Seoul and a few other major cities. The mood was aptly summed up in the popular slogan of the opposition party in the late 1950s: "We can't live like this any longer. Let's have a change."

Unfortunately, by 1956, eighty-one-year-old Rhee was becoming too old to control the ruling party or pay attention to the difficulties of the people. He was no longer mentally alert and physically active. He made few public appearances, was inattentive in the day-to-day running of his government, and seemed disengaged during cabinet meetings. Rhee turned over the major responsibilities of government administration to his ministers. Unable to obtain detailed and balanced information about the nation, the president was not capable of understanding the widespread discontent among the people.[185] For fear that Rhee's health might be impaired, he was carefully shielded from all information that might upset him. Thus, the aged and secluded president became a captive of the system he had built, rather than its master.[186]

The election of Chang as vice president emboldened the opposition and put them in a better position to contest the Liberal Party's control of the government. In the 1958 parliamentary elections the opposition made a considerably stronger showing by winning more than three times the number of previously held seats (see Table 6). While the proportion of ruling party seats suffered a decrease, support for the opposition party in the major cities was strong.

---

[184] Henderson, *Korea: Politics of Vortex*, 170.
[185] Quee-Young Kim, *op. cit.*, 17.
[186] Telegram from the Embassy in Korea to the Department of State, August 15, 1959, *FRUS 1958-1960*, XVIII, 580-581.

Table 6. **Party Membership of the National Assembly**

Session	Party			Total Seats
	Liberal	Democratic	Independents	
1948-50	75	38	85	198
1950-54	57	26	127	210
1954-58	114	21	68	203
1958-60	126	79	28	233

Source: *Central Election Management Committee, National Assembly Election Results 1971.*

Moreover, economic conditions deteriorated owing to rapidly decreasing American aid. Facing increasing taxpayer resistance to the heavy burden of foreign aid, Washington reduced its aid to South Korea substantially in the late 1950s.[187] Anxious to keep its aid burden to a minimum, the United States advised the Rhee government to adopt an economic stabilization program built around higher taxes, reduced government spending, and a lower exchange rate. Coupled with American aid cuts, however, the economic stabilization program (1957-1960) triggered a serious economic slowdown. The program was an all-out attack on government spending, but it also retarded new investment. In the absence of substantial domestic economic growth, a reduction in foreign aid resulted in a serious recession. Unemployment soared; in 1959 the Ministry of Reconstruction estimated that the unemployed and underemployed together totaled about 2 million workers, about 20 percent of the labor force.[188]

Anticipating the 1960 presidential election, the issue of Rhee's age and the goal of electing Lee Ki-poong became an obsession of the ruling circle. The Rhee administration became increasingly repressive as the Liberal Party leaders came to dominate the political area, including government operations. In 1960, Rhee was eighty-five-years old. His chief presidential opponent, Cho Pyong-ok, had died at the Walter Reed Hospital in the United States while undergoing surgery, leaving Rhee with no significant electoral opponent. Therefore, the focus of the 1960 presidential election again shifted to the vice presidency, a position that would likely lead to the presidency given Rhee's advanced age. Rhee's choice of a running mate was again Lee Ki-poong. Given the stakes, the ruling party was determined to win the vice presidency at any cost. Lee emerged as the winner with an overwhelming majority of 8,221,000 to 1,844,000 votes. It was obvious that the election had been rigged. On the day of the election, protests took place in several cities and the discovery of the body of a student killed during protests against election fraud in the southern city of Masan, sparked nationwide student protests. On April 19, thousands of students in Seoul marched in protest toward the presidential mansion. Police fired on the crowd, killing nearly a hundred.[189] The American government sent a message that "the demonstrations in Korea are a reflection of public dissatisfaction over the conduct

---

[187] Robert T. Oliver, "Economic Rehabilitation in Korea", *Korean Survey* (January 1957): 3-12.
[188] The UNCURK report to the UN General Assembly, September 15, 1960, quoted in David M. Earl, "Korea: The Meaning of the Second Republic", *Far Eastern Survey*, XXIX: 11 (1960), 169-170.
[189] For an analysis of the student uprising, see C. I. Eugene Kim and Ke-Soo Kim, "The April 1960 Korean Student Movement", *Western Political Quarterly*, 17:1 (March 1964): 83-92.

of the recent elections and repressive measures."[190]

Rhee was kept in the dark by his inner circle. He would not learn of the illegal March 15 elections until the evening of April 25. He was deeply disturbed to learn of the election fraud. On the morning of April 26, the Blue House released a presidential statement, stating that if people wished him to resign he would.[191] On April 27 President Rhee submitted his resignation to the National Assembly: "I, Syngman Rhee, respect the resolution of the National Assembly, and resign from the office of the presidency. Henceforth, I will devote myself for the rest of my life, to my country and its people as a citizen of this country."[192] After resigning from the presidency, Rhee and his wife moved to their private quarters. Tens of thousands of citizens poured into the streets, standing several lines deep on either side of the road to catch a last glimpse of the old leader. They all stood in silence with profound reverence, many eyes brimming with tears, as if bidding final farewell to a national hero. In fact, many Koreans still revere Syngman Rhee as a great national leader.[193] On May 9, 1960, twelve days after Rhee's resignation from office, U.S. President Eisenhower sent him the following letter:

> With your voluntary withdrawal from political life, I am reminded ever more strongly of how much your country will remain in your debt. The rebirth of Korea in 1945 was the fruition of your long years of patient and arduous labor. Your tenacity and indomitable courage at a time when the Republic was the prey of Communist armies won the admiration of the entire free world as well as the gratitude of all Koreans. Since then, under your guidance, Korea has recovered from the deepest wounds of that conflict and is today a monument to your life-long work.
>
> I cannot but feel that your decision, momentous as it is, is yet another example of wisdom as well as selfless service.[194]

On May 29, Syngman and Francesca Rhee left Korea. Many wept as they saw the back of the old patriot who had witnessed the most difficult period of Korean history. Later Syngman Rhee died in Hawaii as a lonely exile. During the three-month period of interim government, the constitution was revised from a presidential system into a cabinet system. After general elections, the former opposition Democratic Party organized the government (known as the Second Republic), with Chang Myon as prime minister and Yoon Po-sun as president.

---

[190] U.S. Department of State, Historical Office, *American Foreign Policy: Current Documents 1960* (Washington, DC: Government Printing Office, 1964), 680.

[191] Quee-Young Kim, *Fall of Syngman Rhee*, 195-198.

[192] *Chosun Ilbo*, April 28, 1960.

[193] Chong Lim Kim, "Potential for Democratic Change in a Divided Nation", in Kim and Kihl (1988), 59-60. A study of students after the student uprising shows that Rhee had not been a primary target of the uprisings. As much as 84.5 percent of the respondents indicated that they opposed the Liberal Party, only 11.3 percent indicated opposition to Syngman Rhee (Eugene Kim and Ke-Soo Kim, *op cit.*, 83-92).

[194] Quoted in Kyung Cho Chung, *New Korea*, 68.

LEADERSHIP FOR NATIONAL SURVIVAL

Context of the Presidency. South Korea's nation building was significantly different from that of most new states born after World War II. During the initial stage of nation building, the Korean peninsula was divided into two hostile states. In addition, the South Korean economy had nearly collapsed. Liberation had severed functional linkages with Japan, and an arbitrary division at the thirty-eighth parallel rendered critical intra-Korea economic cooperation impossible. Moreover, the country did not inherit a working political and economic system. Chaos had ruled in post-colonial and divided South Korea. Even the American military government with its power, abundant resources and modern equipment, had failed to manage the situation. Many Americans believed at the time that the chances of South Korea's survival were extremely low at best.

Newly independent nations often struggle because of problems with regime legitimacy. This situation was even more serious in the case of South Korea. Both South and North Korea claimed the sovereignty of the whole peninsula and denied the legitimacy of the other. When the Republic of Korea was established, the North Korean Communists immediately declared that they would destroy the South Korean government by any means. To topple the Rhee government and unify the whole country, Pyongyang had embarked on an all-out subversive campaign, leading to a civil war in the South. Only one and a half years after the Republic was born, it experienced an all-out invasion from the North. During the three years of the Korean War, society was completely devastated—new problems were added to the many already confronted.

Under the circumstances, Syngman Rhee was the hope and symbol of his nation and people. Revered as a founding father of an independent Korea, he was "regarded by large segments of the Korean population as a Moses or a messianic leader."[195] The people had great expectations of his leadership. Their expectations by far exceeded the capability of the new government, which confronted awesome difficulties. Rhee, who lacked experience in government, had to assume the extremely difficult tasks of state building. His power and resources were considerably constrained, however. Owing to his life-long exile, the septuagenarian president had no political base and a limited understanding of the realities of Korean society and people.[196] Moreover, there was no political or administrative infrastructure, no capable manpower to manage the government. The government also suffered from poor resources; tax collection was almost impossible in the ailing economy. The survival of the nation was greatly dependent on foreign aid. Therefore, Rhee's power was further constrained by the influence of the United States, Korea's primary aid provider. It was a situation that even an experienced and capable government would find difficult to overcome.

The suddenly imported democratic institutions suffered from many drawbacks. They were incongruent with existing political traditions and the socioeconomic foundations of a country just freed from colonial rule. The political system was a mixture of parliamentary and presidential systems. The constitution was supposed to have created a government of separate powers. It did nothing of the sort. Rather, it created a government of separate institutions struggling for power. The clash between President Rhee and the National Assembly, which

---

[195] Chan Kwon, "Leadership of Syngman Rhee", *Koreana Quarterly*, 13: 1-2 (1971), 41.
[196] Henderson, *Korea*, 151-152.

the opposition controlled, was inevitable. At no other time has the National Assembly (i.e., the opposition) enjoyed such high prestige and power vis-à-vis the government as in the period of the Rhee administration. In terms of historical perspective, the assembly was most active during the Rhee presidency (see Figure 1).[197]

Figure 1. **Days in Floor Sessions**
(1948-1996)

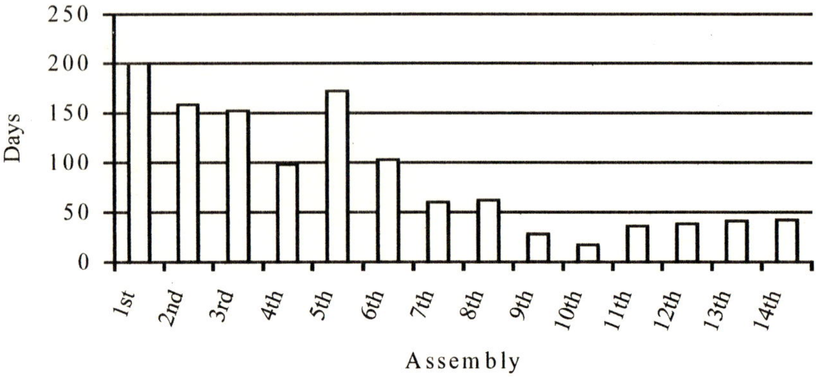

Source: National assembly, Statistical Data on Legislative Activities (1996)

Agenda Setting. Even before the inauguration of its government, South Korea had been threatened by the Communists. The very existence of the Republic was of urgent concern from the beginning. The security situation became so critical during and after the Korean War that national security had become Rhee's top priority. Even after the war, Rhee continued to believe that unification was a panacea for other national problems and was obsessed with unification. He saw the futility of economic growth and prosperity in the absence of military security: "We do not intend to restore Korea to economic strength only to be forced to give it all to the Communists and put on the shackles of slavery."[198]

However, the Korean people were driven to despair by deteriorating social and economic conditions. Millions of refugees wandered aimlessly seeking shelter, food and other necessities. Half of the workforce was unemployed. Most people were preoccupied with physical and economic survival. Economist Paul Kuznets, speaking of this period, noted, "It was not an issue of supporting or promoting democracy. It was an issue of keeping people alive. It was as simple as that."[199]

A nation cannot achieve all the major tasks of nation building at the same time. In

---

[197] The Rhee administration covers from the first to fourth assembly, and the Chang Myon administration covers the fifth assembly. The data are based on *Statistical Data on Legislative Activities* (1996) published by the National Assembly.
[198] Office of Public Information, Republic of Korea, *Korea Flaming High*, Seoul, 1956, 239.
[199] Quoted in Clifford, *Troubled Tiger*, 303.

South Korea in the late 1940s and the 1950s, security would come before proper economics and democracy. The nation had an enormous defense burden. Although Rhee had emphasized the importance of building an industrial economy, he lacked the means of achieving the goal (resources, technology and manpower). The government had also no authority to pursue an independent economic policy; every policy was imposed or constrained by the "patron" superpower. American aid policy was flawed because American officials lacked experience of the needs of a developing economy and, incredibly, were opposed to national economic planning.[200]

Rhee's knowledge of and confidence in foreign affairs had a significant influence on his emphasis on security matters. As he poured most of his time and energy into foreign policy, domestic policies were generally neglected, precisely at a time when domestic problems were mounting. His preoccupation with security and reunification distracted his government from tackling the difficulties of the people, and he consequently became alienated by turning outward to other nations instead of inward toward the serious domestic socioeconomic problems. Preoccupied with the anti-communist struggle, the government also sacrificed principles of democracy. Rhee could not have cold-war state building and a political system with checks and balances at the same time.

Rhee had good reasons to worry about the security situation of his nation. It is clear that Rhee, who lived in the United States for more than forty years, was less sensitive than other Korean leaders to the pressing needs of the people, and he had no economic vision. For the common people after the war, however, issues that directly affected their lives were of main concern. As domestic demands went unmet, public support for the government and its foreign and security policies inevitably declined. A leader who does not pay enough attention to the pressing needs of his people cannot be successful. As the nation became safer after signing the mutual security treaty with the United States, Rhee should have paid more attention to the management of the economy and the welfare and demands of the people.

Appointments and Leadership Style. Syngman Rhee had to create a government from scratch. His appointments to government were crucial not only to establishing the government but also to its operation. But the president had virtually no reservoir of qualified manpower from which to draw. To add to this difficulty was the fact that those who had some experience in government had worked for the colonial government of Japan and were thus labeled Japanese collaborators. Rhee, therefore, resorted to cabinet appointments based on proven personal loyalty to him rather than on qualifications or experience.[201] Most of his ministers, however, proved unable to handle their responsibilities successfully and were accused (in rumor and by the press) of corruption. Within a few months of his inauguration, under pressure from the opposition and the media, Rhee began the first of what would be frequent cabinet shake-ups. However,

---

[200] Macdonald, *Koreans*, 199.

[201] Han Sung-jo, "*Hanguk chongch'I ui kwolloyk elite* (The Power Elite in Korean Politics), in Kim Wun-tae et al., eds., *Hanguk chongch'i ron* (Treaties on Korean Politics), 2nd ed. (Seoul: Pakyoungsa, 1989), 405-7.

compared with cabinet members of Korea's later presidents, the tenure of Rhee's ministers is not so different.[202]

There is a noticeable pattern in his cabinet reshuffles. Rhee changed the prime minister, home affairs minister, and agriculture minister more frequently than other ministers. This may reflect the continuous social, political turmoil during the Rhee government. The tenures of foreign minister, defense minister and education minister were relatively longer, reflecting his emphasis on those fields. Considering the extremely turbulent circumstances in the 1950s, such cabinet instability is not surprising or unusual. For example, during the American Civil War, Lincoln had two different secretaries of state, three different secretaries of war, five different secretaries of the treasury, three attorney generals, two secretaries of the navy, and three different secretaries of the interior.

Rhee had no experience in managing a large, complex organization such as a government. The Blue House was so un-bureaucratized that the term "organization" may not be applicable; there was no brain trust to put his ideas into form and to carry out important tasks. Rhee conducted business with the aid of a senior staff and six clerical staffers. He himself drafted and typed most of the important political messages and speeches, official letters, and diplomatic documents. Although Rhee was an authoritarian leader, he lacked any policy staff and thus had no adequate grip on the government. The old man concentrated his time and energy on national security and foreign affairs and wished to delegate power and authority for domestic matters to his ministers.[203] Most of the ministers, particularly during early years of his rule, had been educated in the West and had more experience abroad than at home. In addition, there was no workable bureaucracy; ministers were not confident in their decision-making and tended to ask for final approval from the president.

Only an immensely powerful leader could have held the nation together during these critical years. The circumstances themselves required strong personal leadership. Rhee's charisma was further strengthened during the Korean War. He was convinced that he was indispensable to the security of the Republic and attempted to ensure his continued rule by revising the constitution. One of the economic consultants appointed to the UN Korean Reconstruction Agency explained the context of the Rhee presidency:

> Whatever its shortcomings, the Rhee regime is not an unrepresentative clique which has willfully and cunningly imposed a regimen of venal inefficiency and autocracy on a protesting citizenry. More nearly, it is a fair expression of the present degree of Korean political maturity. Syngman Rhee, somewhat like Winston Churchill, is too extraordinary a personal phenomenon for one to leave this appraisal unqualified. If he should suddenly depart from the scene, the Koreans could hardly find a successor who could bargain so astutely with the West, or could hold his government together so firmly.... A structured, systematic alternative to the present regime is not just suppressed; it presently is nonexistent.

---

[202] The average tenure of Rhee's ministers is 16.5 months, while those of his successors are: the Park government, 24.3 months; the Chun government, 18.3 months; the Roh government, 13.7 months; the Kim Young Sam government, 12.5 months; and the Kim Dae Jung government, 10.5 months.

[203] Song In-Sang (1993), 161.

> Moreover, the government included a good part of the talented, progressive, dedicated Koreans upon which any reconstruction effort must depend.[204]

Rhee was accused of being inflexible and stubborn. He rejected compromise both on principle and on its incompatibility with his personality. During his life-long struggle, he was without influential friends, or financial resources. His principal resources were his own personality and characteristics—unswerving determination and a deep devotion to his people. Without his sense of conviction, he would have given up in the face of the many discouraging failures he experienced through five decades, beginning with his struggle against the Yi monarch in late nineteenth century. He remained insistent upon protecting and promoting what he saw as vital Korean interests. In his dealing with the United States and other nations, he stubbornly made the point that even while Korea was a very weak country it was unyielding in maintaining its sovereignty.

Like Sukarno of Indonesia, the hero of independence was ill-suited by temperament to manage a government. He lacked the quality of temperament that an effective leader of a developing country needs. Also, he never understood the technical and administrative complexity that was required for solving Korea's immense problems. His charismatic leadership, based on his compelling personality which served him well during the years of national crisis, failed to work when faced with the technical, administrative tasks of government in later years. Sukarno, also an immensely charismatic leader who led a successful struggle for independence, proved to be a disaster once independence was secured.[205]

Charismatic leadership is more likely to emerge in a crisis. When the crisis ends, the leader may have to take on a different role. But Rhee failed to do so. He never learned to delegate authority and operate through a bureaucratic system, but tried to oversee the entire governmental process personally. Relying instead on his charismatic appeals to the people, he failed to create effective institutions and the necessary administrative capacity to carry out his policies.[206]

Achievements and Legacy. Syngman Rhee is an underestimated figure. He is perhaps the most important figure in contemporary Korean history. He played a pivotal role in the founding of the Republic and subsequent state building. Without his vision and determined leadership, the establishment of the Republic of Korea might have remained a dream rather than becoming a reality. Without his uncompromising anti-Communism and his courageous diplomacy, the nation's survival would have been highly questionable. During his presidency, the government established the legal and administrative infrastructure of the nation, and it kept stability in the state through revolt, guerilla action, invasion, war, and lost of most of the country. It set the basis for national security through a mutual defense treaty with the United States and a strong military buildup, and it created the conditions (such as land reform and educational development) for national development in the coming decades.[207] With his ideology of anti-colonial and

---

[204] Lewis, *Reconstruction*, 32.

[205] See Fischer, *Story of Indonesia*.

[206] Allen, *Korea's Syngman Rhee*, 213.

[207] Princeton Lyman, "Economic Development in South Korea: Prospects and Problems", *Asian Survey*, VI:7 (July 1966): 385.

anti-communist nationalism, Rhee consolidated the loyalty of the Korean people to the new government of the Republic of Korea.

In the emerging cold war environment, where one Eastern European government after another was being taken over by the Communists, and the North Korean Communists were a growing threat, Rhee was able to succeed where other leaders failed. His contribution to the survival of the Republic becomes evident when one compares South Korea with South Vietnam. Looking back on the truce negotiations during the Korean War, and comparing this situation with the fall of Saigon after the negotiated "peace," we realize that Rhee's policies were courageous and farsighted. The United States intervened in the Korean War with unprepared forces, while it went into Vietnam with a strong army and full logistical support. Despite the differences, South Korea survived the Communist aggression while South Vietnam could not.[208]

Why did South Korea succeed where South Vietnam failed? One of the crucial differences was the strong leadership in South Korea. Syngman Rhee was a strident anti-Communist leader who had consistently warned of the danger of Communism and pursued an uncompromising anti-Communist policy. In the very early stage of his government, in response to the Yosu rebellion, the Rhee government enacted the National Security Law and eliminated most of the Communist elements in South Korea. The Rhee government was very effective in fighting against the Communist insurgency. In contrast, there was no such strong anti-Communist leader in South Vietnam. The government in Saigon never succeeded in cracking down on the Communists and mobilizing support for the government.

Despite his constraints as head of a weak nation, Rhee was a great strategist and diplomat. He parlayed Korea's status as a victim of global Communist aggression into support from the United States. Rhee's success in identifying the defense of his country with U.S. interests is remarkable. In 1950, South Korea's general economic poverty, lack of natural resources, and extreme strategic vulnerability were doubtless factors which contributed to its exclusion from the Truman administration's proclaimed defense perimeter in the Pacific. Three years later, with all these drawbacks multiplied tenfold, Rhee's domain was bound to the United States through a mutual security pact.[209]

Without the stubborn "Oriental bargainer,"[210] it is doubtful whether Washington would have agreed to such a treaty or to the continued defense of South Korea after the war. An armistice agreement with the Communists has often proven to be meaningless. Only two years after a peace agreement between the United States and North Vietnam, Saigon fell into the hands of the Communists. The security and stability provided by the U.S.-South Korea alliance enabled South Korea to become an economic powerhouse and to develop a dynamic democracy despite the hostile presence of the Communists across the DMZ. Syngman Rhee was very different from Chiang Kai-shek of Nationalist China and the leaders of South Vietnam, and this may have been the crucial difference in

---

[208] Ronald H. Spector, "The Korean War through the Lens of Vietnam", in Andrews et al., eds., *op. cit*, 151-153.

[209] Allen, *Korea's Syngman Rhee*, 239.

[210] John Foster Dulles, NSC Meeting, August 8, 1957, NSC Series, Box 9, AW File, Eisenhower Library.

the fates of these countries.[211] Unfortunately, Rhee's stubborn anti-Communist stance had some negative ramifications. In embracing whoever opposed Communism, he failed to liquidate collaborators with the Japanese and other vestiges of Japan's colonial rule. Using anti-Communism as a major political and ideological weapon, he also extended his presidential term two times by amending the constitution.

Although Rhee had vast experience in democratic countries, he failed to institute the basic tradition of democracy. Whether motivated by desires for personal power or not, he bypassed the law and set himself up as the sole interpreter of what was best for Korea. While his role as the stern symbol of the Republic during the darkest period of the Korean War should not be underestimated, he crassly took advantage of the crisis of Communist aggression to make himself an undisputed ruler. However, he is not solely responsible for the failure of Korean democracy at the time. Western-style democracy was hurriedly transplanted in 1948 onto a debilitated and inhospitable Korean political soil that had known no self-government for thirty-six years. The influence of Confucianism on political understanding, culture and behavior remained pervasive. Confucian values of benevolent paternalistic authority are assumed to promote respect for government and its leaders.[212] The newly introduced democratic principles were nearly the opposite of the premises upon which life had been built for most Koreans up to the moment of independence. Korean trials and errors in democracy were perhaps inevitable.

The security, social and economic conditions were also extremely unfavorable. Rhee was driven by circumstances to the use of more arbitrary power than perhaps any other president had seized. Clinton L. Rossiter believes that there are three types of crisis or threat in the life of a democratic nation—war, rebellion, and economic crisis.[213] Korean democracy during the Rhee government faced all three of these crises at once. In crises that affect society as a whole—threats of war, economic catastrophes, social unrest—the nation looks to its leader as a rescuer; the people are likely to rally around a leader and to give him power.[214] The Korean circumstances demanded a strong executive. Given the underdevelopment of political institutions, Rhee became a dominant figure in South Korea.

We find similar instances of strong presidents in American history. During the Civil War Abraham Lincoln overrode constitutional liberties. The right of habeas corpus was suspended wholesale. All persons "discouraging enlistments, resisting military drafts, or persons discouraging military drafts or guilty of any disloyal practice affording aid and comfort to the rebels" were subject to martial law and liable to trial and punishment by

---

[211] *FRUS 1955-1957*, XXIII, 485.

[212] Yu Jeong Hwan, "Hanguk munhwawa jeongchi: yukyojeok jeongchi jilseoae daehan munhwaronjeok haesok" (Korean Culture and Politics: a Cultural Analysis of Confucian Political Order), *Hanguk jeongchi hakhaebo* (Korean Political Science Review), 29 (1995): 57-66; and Young Whan Kihl, "The Legacy of Confucian Culture and South Korean Politics", *Korea Journal*, 34(1994): 37-53.

[213] Rossiter, *Constitutional Dictatorship*, 6.

[214] When a nation faces so many challenges, people seem willing to grant extraordinary power and give away their freedom. See S. N. Eisenstadt, ed., Max Weber, *On Charisma and Institution Building* (Chicago: University of Chicago Press, 1968), 18. In a historical study of thirty-five dictatorships, all of them emerged during times of social distress. See J. O. Hertzler, "Crisis and Dictatorship", *American Sociological Review*, 5 (1940), 157-169.

court martial or military tribunal.[215] He allowed his subordinates to indulge in sporadic efforts to censor the mails and even arrest and detain editors. There were thousands of arbitrary arrests, many followed by long drawn out trials. Lincoln believed that "measures otherwise unconstitutional might become lawful by becoming indispensable to the preservation of the Constitution through the preservation of the nation."[216] As a result, at various times during his presidency, the press labeled Lincoln a despot, tyrant, monster, ape, buffoon, traitor, idiot, or lunatic.[217]

A week before the United States entered World War I Woodrow Wilson declared, "To fight you must be brutal and ruthless and the spirit of ruthless brutality will enter into the very fiber of our national life, infecting Congress, the courts, the policeman on the beat, the man in the street."[218] Wilson thought that the constitution would not survive the war; that free speech and the right of assembly would go; that a nation could not put its strength into a war and keep its head level. During the World War I the federal government indicted almost two thousand persons under the extraordinary Espionage Act of 1917, almost half of whom were convicted. Although President Franklin D. Roosevelt had planned to retire after two terms, the threat of war seemed to render that impossible. Even though no American president had ever run for a third term, Roosevelt maneuvered to gain his nomination. As he had in the fight against the Great Depression, he assumed many extraordinary powers in the war against the Axis nations. Rigid control was placed on prices and wages, hundreds of billions of dollars were appropriated, and millions of fighting men were drafted. Censorship was imposed, and more than a hundred thousand Japanese Americans were taken from their west coast homes and interned for the duration of the war.[219] Clinton Rossiter writes that the Americans had accepted those actions that "would have been looked upon as unconstitutional, undemocratic, and downright dictatorial in time of peace."[220] In Britain during and after the World War II, parliamentary elections were suspended for ten years.

Syngman Rhee had dreamed of being the George Washington of Korea. The circumstances which he faced were unfavorable. He did establish some bad precedents which have left their blot upon Korean constitutional history, notably forcing through not one but two amendments to the constitution. If he had retired at the end of his third term, he would likely be remembered as a great leader, and his reputation secured. However, under the South Korean circumstances in the 1950s, it was difficult to replace the aged leader as the Korean society was so disorganized and its institutions so new that the country was not politically consolidated.

General Clark, the UN commander who worked closely with President Rhee during the later phase of the Korean War, praised him:

---

[215] James D. Richardson, *Messages and Papers of the Presidents, 1789-1897* (Washington, DC: Bureau of National Literature, 1897), vol. VI, 98-99.

[216] John G. Nicolay and John Hay, *Complete Works of Abraham Lincoln* (New York: Francis D. Tandy Co., 1905), vol. X, 66.

[217] Thomas J. Dilorenzo, *The Real Lincoln* (Roseville, CA: Forum, 2002), 108.

[218] Quoted in Burns, *Presidential Government*, 284.

[219] See Joseph Gies, *Franklin D. Roosevelt: Portrait of a President* (Garden City, NY: Doubleday, 1971).

[220] Rossiter, 4.

> Through the Korean War Rhee had attained a stature in Asia that ranked him with Chiang Kai-shek and Nehru. He had developed into the leader of anti-communist and many non-Communist Asians. He became a leader not only through the fight against Communism but also through the fact that he was not afraid to stand up against even the United States of America on occasion. Rhee was no puppet. Rhee was an Asian. Rhee was a strong leader.... For many Asians, Rhee brought dignity and pride to the Far East by the struggles, right or wrong, which he made to shape the war in his country to his will rather than to the will of the more powerful nations that were his allies.... His eyes were beyond Korea to the day when he might be the man or one of a handful of men to lead the free Asians against the Communist Asians in a tremendous struggle for survival.[221]

In an article in *Life* magazine, General Van Fleet, who commanded the ground forces in the final months of the war, described Rhee as "one of the greatest thinkers, scholars, statesmen and patriots of our time."[222] Admiral Arthur W. Radford, chairman of the Joint Chiefs of Staff during the Eisenhower administration, paid a great tribute to Rhee, whom he believed more of an asset to the United States than a liability. "For all his faults," Radford said, "Rhee was the George Washington of Korea, and the people of Korea strongly supported him. There was no alternative to his forceful control of the country."[223]

Historians have increasingly acknowledged that Syngman Rhee's contribution to Korea's nation building was immense. Korean historian Lew Young-ick remarked: "He was the architect of modern Korea. He was the best-prepared man to lead Korea through the war and into the new era of peace."[224] His mistakes and ignoble end notwithstanding, Syngman Rhee will be remembered as one of the greatest leaders in Korean history.

---

[221] Clark, *Danube to the Yellow*, 160.
[222] Quoted in Oliver, *Syngman Rhee*, 310.
[223] *FRUS 1955-1957*, XXIII, 219.
[224] Quoted in Donald Kirk, "Korean Crisis: Pride and Identity in the IMF Era", *Journal of East Asian Affairs*, XIII:2 (1999): 338.

Park Chung Hee

CHAPTER FOUR
PARK CHUNG HEE
ARCHITECT OF MODERN KOREA

"This revolution is the turning point in the history of modern Korea.... Spiritually, this revolution must establish our self-respect. Socially, it is to modernize our society. It is to revive our people, reconstruct our nation and reform us. This is a revolution of national reform."

"With a strong enemy across the 38th parallel, this economic struggle takes precedence over combat or politics. We have to accomplish, as quickly as possible, the goal of an independent economy. We must defeat Communist North Korea in economic battle."

—Park Chung Hee

"There would be no Republic of Korea as we know it today, if President Park Chung Hee were engrossed only with the immediate present."[1]

—Lee Kwan Yew

At 3:30 A.M. on May 16, 1961, Park Chung Hee (1917-1979), small and wiry with a sharp face and a narrow nose, and sporting dark sunglasses, made his abrupt entrance onto the center stage of Korean history. While the Korean people slept that spring night, a small elite force of some 1,600 troops, led by the forty-three-year-old Major General Park, crossed the Han River Bridge into Seoul. He saw the military coup as the "only means to save the nation and the people, who are driven to the extreme."[2] It was the belief of South Korean military leaders that if they failed to act on what they perceived as an extreme national emergency, a different and irreversible revolution, probably Communist-directed, would be inevitable.[3] Before the coup, most Koreans had never heard the name Park Chung Hee; no one knew what to make of this physically diminutive man.

There was virtually no resistance as elements of the South Korean military seized control of the country. Popular reaction to the unprecedented military coup was somewhat fatalistic; the inevitable had finally arrived. Upon meeting the coup leaders, even President Yoon Po-sun, a figurehead in the Chang Myon administration, reportedly said, "I had believed revolution inevitable."[4] In the view of General James A. Van Fleet, commander of

---

[1] *Korea News Review*, 8: 44 (November 3, 1979): 8.
[2] Park's letter to General Chang Toyoung, chief of staff of the army at the time of the coup, quoted in Chung Chae-Kyong (1983), 158.
[3] Chung Kyung Cho, *New Korea*, 119.
[4] Walter Briggs, "The Military Revolution in Korea: On Its Leader and Achievements", *Koreana Quarterly*, V:2 (summer, 1963): 28.

the U.S. Eighth Army during the Korean War, "the military revolution, under such circumstances, was unavoidable. Had there not been such resoluteness on the part of those patriotic officers, Korea's existence would have long since vanished under Communist pressure... The May revolution was an act of self-defense by and for the Korean people and was the finest thing that has happened to Korea in a thousand years."[5]

Park Chung Hee and his associates took over Korea, promising to do away with the "evil legacies" of Korean history, end corruption, rebuild national pride, and spur economic development. From the very first day of the coup, this dour military man engineered an extraordinary economic and social revolution with remarkable thoroughness, transforming his country, its people, and history. However, he is still regarded as a man of contradiction at home and abroad. To critics, he is known as a heavy-handed dictator. But to his supporters, he is remembered as a brilliant leader. A proper understanding of Park Chung Hee will surely contribute to a better understanding of contemporary South Korean history.

Failures Of The Chang Regime

After the collapse of the Rhee government, Koreans enjoyed a short period of euphoria not seen since Korea's liberation. However, the new ruling party had neither the experience nor the capability to lead the nation. The constitution was hastily revised to change the presidential system to a parliamentary system, giving decisive powers to a new bicameral National Assembly. In the general election of June 29, 1960, the former opposition Democratic Party won control of both houses of the National Assembly, with more than a two-thirds majority in the House of Representatives and with a clear majority in the House of Councilors.[6]

The ruling party was almost evenly split into two rival factions.[7] Chang Myon was barely elected prime minister. He organized a "coalition" cabinet that included seven new faction members, six old faction members, and two independents. Responding to the demands of different factions, Chang had to make a cabinet reshuffle as early as two weeks after the formation of his first cabinet and as often as three times over a period of six months. The coalition government was fragile; the prime minister barely kept his cabinet from disintegration. Bickering between the competing factions continued during the regime.[8]

The high hopes and unrealistic expectations that followed the student revolution soon turned to despair and frustration. The Chang government was staffed by men with the same background, attitudes, and programs as their predecessors in the Rhee administration. The failing administration of the Chang regime convinced many Koreans that changing the government from one headed by the Liberal Party to one led by the

---

[5] James A. Van Fleet, "Emergence of New Leadership in Korea", *Koreana Quarterly*, 4:1 (autumn 1962): 14.
[6] For details of the Chang regime, see Sungjoo Han, *The Failure of Democracy in South Korea*.
[7] John M. Barr, "The Second Republic of Korea", *Far Eastern Survey*, XXIX:9 (September 1960): 129-132; and David M. Earl, "Korea: The Meaning of the Second Republic, *Far Eastern Survey*, XXIX:11 (November 1960): 169-175.
[8] Om Kihyong, "*Hanguk chongchiindul ui chongundaesong*" (Pre-modern Characteristics of Korean Politicians), *Sasanggye*, IX:3 (March 1961): 131.

Democratic Party would achieve nothing. Democracy seemed merely a struggle for power and spoils, yielding nothing of benefit for the common people.[9] A Korean observer wrote: The Liberal Party could sustain itself in one way or another, thanks to a central figure, President Syngman Rhee, who was once looked up to by the Korean people as a great leader as well as a courageous anti-Japanese fighter. Unfortunately, there was no such leader during the Chang administration.[10] Prime Minister Chang was perhaps too gentle to be a chief executive at such a difficult time. He lacked all the leadership qualities the situation demanded. The Chang government was unable to cope with mounting popular dissatisfaction and unrest, stop corruption, and openly confront the pro-Communist, anti-American forces within South Korea.[11]

Disappointed with a government that was appallingly weak and incompetent, students and citizens again took to the streets to express their discontent and frustration. During the nine-month period following the demise of the Rhee regime there were some 2,000 demonstrations with roughly 900,000 participants. The Chang government became popularly known as the "government by demonstrations." The government was again in danger of being overthrown by the extreme left.[12]

On October 11, 1960, radical students occupied the rostrum of the National Assembly and demanded stiffer penalties for ousted officials of the Rhee regime. The following day the National Assembly gave in and passed a law legalizing the retrial of those officials. As self-righteous guardians of the nation's morals and politics, the students seemed out of control.[13] Pressured by the students, the Chang government discharged 17,000 policemen, including eighty-one police chiefs. The police force, which had supported the Rhee regime, became so discredited and demoralized that it often showed itself either unwilling or unable to control crime, preserve public order, or investigate Communist activities.[14]

Under such unstable social and political conditions, the economic situation went from bad to worse.[15] In April 1961 more than four million city dwellers representing 35 percent of the total labor force were unemployed or only partially employed. The economy was on the verge of collapse. The U.S. ambassador in Seoul sent a classified cable to Washington. In it he lamented that the "stark, bleak facts of economic life" were behind South Koreans' "widespread feelings of hopelessness."[16] Newspapers were filled with reports of pervasive

---

[9] Soon–Il Hong, "On Current Political Phenomena", *Korean Affairs*, II:1 (1963): 96.

[10] Chung, *New Korea*, 125.

[11] According to a survey of 3,000 college students conducted in December 1960, less than 4 percent indicated strong support of the Chang government. A majority of them would wait and see. See Oh, *Korea: Democracy on Trial*, 82.

[12] According to a survey of Korean students, less than 4 percent of the respondents gave their full support to the Chang government. See Henderson, *Korea: Politics of Vortex*, 181.

[13] William A. Douglas, "Korean Students and Politics", *Asian Survey*, 3:12 (December 1963):584-595.

[14] *Hapdong yongam* (Hapdong Annual), 1961 (Seoul: Hapdong Tongsinsa, 1962), 152-53.

[15] When survey groups asked 3,000 South Koreans about "their most urgent requests to the government", over 70 percent named the solution of various economic problems. *Donga Ilbo*, December 28, 1960.

[16] Ambassador Walter P. McConaughy, "Telegram from the Embassy in Korea to the Department of State", April 11, 1961, Document No. 210 in *FRUS 1961-1963, XXII*. See also Wattles,

economic and social ills, including chronic food shortages, skyrocketing inflation, high unemployment, and serious rural poverty. On May 3, 1961, less than two weeks before the Park-led coup, an editorial in an independent daily, *Hanguk Ilbo*, described the prevailing gloomy social and economic conditions:

> The streets are filled with the unemployed and beggars, while the farmers and laborers are suffering from starvation and privation. The price of goods is on the rise, while production is on the decline to the point of a shutdown. Robbery and thievery run rampant everywhere, while the efficiency of law enforcement is vitiated.... Everyone is complaining and bemoaning. Life has certainly become more unbearable than before.[17]

The impoverished, war-devastated South remained vulnerable to Communist infiltration and subversion. The North was quick to see in the chaotic situation an opportunity for socialist revolution in the South. Radio Pyongyang announced a seven-point message. The message proclaimed "free elections" throughout all parts of the country without UN supervision and the immediate reduction of the military to 100,000. The North Korean regime was sending increasing numbers of agents and saboteurs to the South. Student groups supported North Korea's proposal of unification. A group of radical students called for U.S. troop withdrawal from South Korea and a South-North student unification conference. They planned to march *en masse* to Panmunjom to hold discussions with North Korean students on May 20, 1961. The rampancy of pro-unification (and pro-Communist) and anti-American sentiments represented a radical departure from the ideological legacies of the Rhee presidency.[18]

Despite the mounting threat to national security, the Chang government attempted to reduce the size of the military. Chang campaigned during the June 1960 general election on a platform of reducing the Korean military by 200,000 men, or a third of the army.[19] Army morale sagged dangerously at a time when North Korean Communists, and their sympathizers in South Korea, were making every attempt to foment chaos. The prolonged political paralysis caused many citizens to begin to fear that the situation would become a fatal invitation for North Korea to launch another military adventure. Such apprehension was particularly strong in the military.

After Fidel Castro's takeover of Cuba in 1959, Washington was seriously concerned with the unstable situation in Korea and Southeast Asia. A Special National Intelligence Estimate prepared by the CIA and other intelligence organizations of the United States detailed the explosive situation of South Korea:

> ...the seven months of Prime Minister Chang Myon's government have been expended largely in customary Korean politicking, and the government's position is none too strong.... The deep divisions within the [ruling] party showed up almost immediately and led to a prolonged struggle for party control....

Marshall D. "South Korea's Balance of Payments Problems", *Far Eastern Survey*, 29:9 (September 1960): 132-139.

[17] *Hankuk Ilbo*, May 3, 1961.

[18] Han, *Failure of Democracy*, 181-82.

[19] After assuming power, Chang attempted to press a 100,000-man cut, but the United States opposed and agreed only to cut 30,000. See Cary Report on ROK Force Levels, *FRUS 1961-1963*, XXII, 259.

> The Communists have increased their efforts to subvert the ROK. North Korean broadcasts aimed at the South have increased in number and intensity, and there has been a greater North Korean effort of late to increase the influx of subversive literature and support in the ROK.... The national police and security services were a primary target of the popular revulsion that led to last April's revolution. Since that time, purges and reorganizations have gone on repeatedly, causing a serious drop in the capabilities and morale of the police.
>
> Underlying the political unrest is the weak and uncertain state of an economy.... The situation has already produced strikes, demonstrations, and petitions among the laboring groups. There has been no improvement in the employment situation, and unemployment and serious underemployment continue to affect about 20 percent of the labor force.[20]

Chang Myon had no vision and was extremely subservient to the United States, hurting his credibility among Koreans as well as Americans.[21] Americans began to seriously question internally the survival of the Chang regime. In February 1961, Hugh Farley of the International Cooperation Administration in Seoul reported to Walter Rostow, President Kennedy's deputy special assistant for national security affairs, that the South Korean situation was "dangerously deteriorating," but that the Chang government was "increasingly powerless to take the necessary actions."[22] As Kornhauser says, "Rapid and violent displacement of that [autocratic] authority by a democratic regime is highly favorable to the emergence of extremist mass movement that tend to transform the new democracy in antidemocratic directions."[23]

The survival of the representative government was in jeopardy as it faced simultaneously domestic unrest, economic crisis, and a threat to national security.[24] The nation reached a point where social disorder and political impotence were threatening the nation's cardinal concern, the very survival of the Republic. The country needed a far more resolute leadership if disaster were to be averted.[25] Several months after the coup, General Park recollected: "We are certainly at the crossroads in terms of whether [South Korea] is revolutionized by Communism or whether its democratic system will be protected [by us, the military coup leaders], or whether [South Koreans] will die or live. For this reason, I led May 16 [military coup]."[26] He also stated that to believe that democracy would arise from "past confusion" was tantamount to believing that "a rose could blossom in a garbage can."[27]

---

[20] "Short-Range Outlook in the Republic of Korea: Special National Intelligence Estimate", NSF, Countries Series, Korea, General, 1/61-3/61, JFK Library.

[21] U.S. Embassy in Seoul to the Secretary of State, March 11, 1961, NSF, Box 127, JFK Library.

[22] Hugh D. Farley, "The Situation in Korea, February 1961", Kennedy Library, President's Office Files, Countries Series, Korea, Security 1961-1963.

[23] Quoted in Huntington, *Political Order*, 82.

[24] For an analysis of the failure of democracy, see Stamps, *Why Democracies Fail*.

[25] William A. Douglas, "South Korea's Search for Leadership", *Pacific Affairs*, 37:1 (spring 1964): 20-36.

[26] Park Sanggil, "*30 nyon mane tasi ponun kukka wa hyongmyong kwa na*" (Reexamining 'The Country, the Revolution and I after 30 years') in Chosun Ilbosa (1993), 195.

[27] *Time*, May 25, 1962, 38.

THE ROOTS OF A GREAT REVOLUTIONARY

Park Chung Hee was born on November 14, 1917, in a small village, about sixty miles northwest of Taegu.[28] He was the youngest of five boys and two girls of an impoverished farming family living in a small, mud-walled, thatch-roofed house. He walked to school in straw shoes, often in drenching rains or knee-deep snow, over a rugged mountain path, covering a distance of about five miles a day, for six years.

Park excelled in school, and at the age of fifteen he was awarded one of ninety openings at the very competitive Taegu Normal School, one of three such schools in Japanese-controlled Korea. The school was free and included accommodation, allowing him to continue his higher education. Here, however, Park was far from a satisfactory student. As a recalcitrant adolescent, he was obviously frustrated with the Japanese colonial rule in general and school life in particular. He was characterized as "moody, frustrated, inactive and lacking in determination."[29] Frustrated by the fate of Korea, Park gradually developed a strong sense of national consciousness.

After graduation in 1937, he was posted as a teacher to a primary school in a remote village near Moonkyung. That lasted little more than two years. Frustrated with his teaching career, in 1940 Park made a fateful decision; he went to Manchuria and volunteered for the military academy in Manchukuo, the puppet state that imperial Japan had set up in Northeast China (Manchuria) in the 1930s. Training at a military academy was for some ambitious young Koreans a sure path to success. This would be so for the young cadet Park as well. Smart and hard-working, Park was sent to continue his training at the Japanese military academy near Tokyo after graduating from the military school in Manchuria in 1942. After being commissioned as a second lieutenant in the Japanese army in April 1944, he was assigned to the Japanese Kwantung army in Manchuria. At the time of Japan's unconditional surrender on August 15, 1945, he was stationed in Manchuria as a first lieutenant.[30]

After liberation, Park returned to Korea in May 1946, and in September of that year joined the officer's training school of the South Korean constabulary. After eighty days of training, he graduated on December 14, 1946. Owing to his previous experience, he was commissioned with the rank of captain. On November 11, 1948, Park Chung Hee, now a major, was arrested on charges of engaging in Communist activities in the army, including involvement in the Yosu mutiny. A court martial sentenced him to death. Reportedly, after volunteering intelligence about Communist cells in the Korean army, his sentence was rescinded and he was allowed to continue his duties as a civilian in the intelligence division of the South Korean army headquarters.[31]

When the Korean War broke out, Park was quickly recommissioned as a major. The war provided him with not only the opportunity to salvage his military career but also to rise in the ranks from major to colonel in little less than a year. Owing to his record of Communist activities, his promotions came slower than those of his classmates and, in

---

[28] For Park's biographies, see Paik Nam-ju (1961); "Biographical Sketch of General Chung Hee Park", *Korean Observer*, August 1963; and Gab-je Cho (1998), vol. 1 and 2.
[29] Gap-je Cho (1992), 70.
[30] See Cho Gab-je (1998), vol. 2, chapter 6.
[31] Merrill, *Korea*, 204-205.

some cases, even of his juniors. Still, by 1953, the last year of the Korean War, he had advanced to the rank of brigadier general. In the same year he went to the United States to undertake an advanced course at the U.S. army artillery school at Fort Sill, Oklahoma. He returned to Korea in June 1954, and was posted as commandant of the army artillery school, followed by promotion to deputy commander of the Sixth Corps, commanding general of the Fifth and Seventh Divisions (1955-57), then First Army chief of staff (1958-59). In 1959 he was promoted to major general. From July 1959 to the time of the coup, he filled five different assignments.

Park was known as a thrifty, clean, and unusually able officer. He built an indisputable reputation as a stubborn and incorruptible general. His command effectiveness and personal popularity was well known in the military. A man of few words, with an intense interest in national affairs, an indefatigable and talented organizer with a reputation for integrity, General Park was the kind of officer that many Korean military officers aspired to be. He became a natural leader of the army's reformists. The group instigated anti-corruption campaigns in the military during the Chang administration.

Park was a frustrated nationalist. He wrote: "[We] have been mauled by the big powers, assimilated by foreign cultures, impeded by primitive forms of industry, indulged in fratricidal squabbles. Ours has been a history of stagnation, idleness, complacency, accommodation and feudalism."[32] Soon after the military revolution, Park elaborated the larger purpose of the military revolution:

> This revolution was not simply a change of regimes. It was a new and vigorous debut of the nation which represented...the closure of the entire record of [Korea's] division strife...and...the closure of five hundred years of stagnation of the Yi Dynasty, the 36 years of tyranny of Japanese rule and various diseases spread by the foreign systems after liberation.
>
> It is a national debut, inspired with the courage and self-confidence of people determined never again to be poor, weak, or dumb. This revolution is the turning point in the history of modern Korea.... This is a revolution of national reform.[33]

THE MILITARY GOVERNMENT (1961-63)

On the morning of May 16, 1961, the revolutionary forces controlling the capital city of Seoul announced over public radio that "military authorities" had taken over "the executive, legislative, and judicial branches of the state" and organized a "Military Revolutionary Committee."

The same morning, coup leader General Park Chung Hee paid a visit to President Yoon Po-sun seeking his personal support for the coup and the presidential sanction for martial law. While refusing to approve the martial law already declared, Yoon agreed to write personal letters to all army corps commanders urging them to resolve the national crisis without bloodshed. The revolutionary forces had secured the crucial support of the president, the constitutional head of the state.

---

[32] Park Chung Hee, *The Country, the Revolution and I*, 166.
[33] Ibid., 22-23.

On May 19, the Military Revolutionary Committee was renamed the Supreme Council for National Reconstruction (SCNR). On June 6, the council, made up of thirty-two military officers, promulgated the "Law Regarding Extraordinary Measures for National Reconstruction," which defined the functions and powers of the council. The Supreme Council dissolved the National Assembly and all political parties. About a third of the members of the Supreme Council were lieutenant colonels and colonels, mostly in their thirties. Before long, General Park Chung Hee became chairman of the Supreme Council. Thus, General Park emerged as a symbol of the new leadership.

Metaphorically speaking, Park Chung Hee believed the military revolution was a "surgical operation" to excise malignant social, political, and economic tumors. Park said, "The revolution was staged with the compassion of a benevolent surgeon who sometimes must cause pain in order to preserve life and restore health."[34] When a person becomes ill, a doctor may restrict and regulate the activities of the patient, may order his hospitalization, and may even force an operation. "A surgical operation is not a merry amusement but a sacrifice of a part in order to save the whole. It is, therefore, accepted as a necessary evil."[35]

As part of this surgical operation, during the period between May 16 and December 31, the military set about "purifying" Korea. By proclaiming "anti-Communism" to be the nation's foremost priority, the coup leaders effectively exploited public sentiment. Under a renewed anti-Communist frenzy, some 3,300 pro-Communists and their sympathizers were arrested and some 600 punished. The junta, with militaristic speed and method, adopted various measures designed to remedy the social and economic maladies. In the first six days following the coup, more than 4,000 hoodlums, smugglers, black marketers, and usurers were arrested. Within weeks, nearly 14,000 thugs and gangsters had been rounded up. Smuggled foreign goods such as cigarettes were confiscated, and smugglers were threatened with capital punishment. Demonstrations and strikes were prohibited. Thousands of traffic and curfew violators were retained at police stations.

In March 1962, the much-debated Political Purification Law was put into effect. The law barred some 4,367 persons, mostly former politicians and former high-ranking officials, from political activity for six years unless they underwent a screening by the military government. The screening process cleared all but seventy-four politicians,[36] all top leaders of the Democratic Party or other progressives. The junta was also determined to reform the corrupt and inactive bureaucracy. Some 6,900 public officials were dismissed or arrested on various charges ranging from "evasion of military service" and "irregularities" to "violation of rules" and "peddling political influence." The military was not immune from this purification drive. By July 1962, 2,000 military officers were forcibly retired, including some forty generals.

A poor farm boy himself by birth and upbringing, Park was deeply concerned with the nation's poverty. At the time, South Korea was one of the poorest states of the

---

[34] Park Chung Hee, *Our Nation's Path*, 198.
[35] Park Chung Hee, *Jidojado* (Leadership) (Seoul: Kukka chaekon choego hoeui, 1961), 26.
[36] Supreme Council for National Reconstruction, Republic of Korea, *Military Revolution in South Korea* (Seoul, 1961), 652-653.

world. Nearly three out of every five Koreans lived on a tiny farm plot, eking out a subsistence living. The country sorely lacked industrial facilities or natural resources. Its survival was entirely dependent on foreign aid, assistance that was itself insufficient and consistently declining. Without building a solid economic base, there could be no future for the country. For a people with overwhelming economic problems, Park believed, "democracy is a species of social luxury, at best a precarious venture."[37] During a dinner meeting with journalists, he reemphasized his conviction in his "economy first" policy: "Sometimes I feel like crying when I think that our people are so poor... There is no other way but to tighten our belts and start an all-out production in every sector."[38] He repeatedly emphasized that the primary objective of the military revolution was to liberate the Korean people from poverty.

Park was very concerned about the superiority of North Korea's military and its economy. Blessed with abundant supplies of electric power and most of the peninsula's raw material resources, as well as its industrial facilities inherited from the Japanese, the North Korean economy was far superior to that of the South. In late 1960, *Time* magazine reported the impressive industrial progress in the North:

> By rigid regimentation and the help of technicians from Eastern Europe, Communist North Korea has made impressive economic progress of a sort. Ninety-five percent of the peasants are herded into Soviet-style communes. Factory workers toil 12 to 14 hours a day for wages that average $21 a month in plants that often operate round the clock ...The North Koreans proudly contrast their achievements with South Korea. The North has less than half the South's population, but the Communists fell heir to 70% of undivided Korea's heavy industry, 90% of the electric power, 70% of the coal.... They claim that last year the North produced ten times as much steel as South Korea, five times more cement, just as much grain.[39]

Two ideologically incompatible regimes were competing for legitimacy throughout the peninsula. Economic performance was seen as a barometer in gauging the superiority of the two competing ideologies. In 1960, per capita income in the South was 60 dollars, while the North's figure was 208 dollars.[40] As a result, during 1959-1962 some 75,000 of Korean residents in Japan joined in an exodus to North Korea.[41] A Western academic's 1965 article entitled "Korean Miracle" referred not to the South Korean but to the North Korean economy.[42] Park believed that the survival and legitimacy of the Republic depended upon decreasing the widening South-North economic gap. South Korea had to move fast to deal with its poverty and underdevelopment.

Park firmly believed only one road led to eventual unification and victory over Communism. It was neither negotiation nor invasion. "With a strong enemy across the

---

[37] Park's interview with *Korean Journal* (September 1961): 13.
[38] Cho Gab-je, "Spit on My Grave", *Chosun Ilbo*, July 19, 1999.
[39] "Korea", *Time*, November 14, 1960.
[40] Byoung-Lo Philo Kim, *Two Koreas in Development* (New Brunswick, N.J.: Transaction Publishers, 1992), 66.
[41] Martin, *op. cit.*, 101.
[42] Joan Robinson, "Korean Miracle", *Monthly Review* (January 1965): 545-548, quoted in Joseph Sang-hoon Chung, *The North Korean Economy* (Stanford: Hoover Institution Press, 1974), 151.

38th parallel, this economic struggle takes precedence over combat or politics. We have to accomplish, as quickly as possible, the goal of an independent economy.... We must defeat Communist North Korea in economic battle," he emphasized.[43] In other words, Park perceived the South-North problem in terms of political and economic competition, rather than an ideological and military struggle.

From the beginning, Park showed a strong sense of nationalism, as captured in his slogan, "modernization of the fatherland." Modernization became his main political mantra and was used to justify policies and popular mobilization for the attainment of national goals.[44] He was fond of identifying his modernization drive with four other revolutions of recent history, namely, Sun Yat-sen's modernization of China; the Meiji Restoration in Japan; Kemal Atatürk's Turkish Revolution; and Gamal Abdel Nasser's Egyptian Revolution.[45] Of these, Park compared his revolution more particularly to the Turkish Revolution and the Meiji reform. In regard to the former, he highlighted the sufferings of Turkey as an oppressed nation and the positive outcomes of the revolution. In regard to the latter, he lauded the Meiji Restoration as a great nation building effort: the elimination of feudalism, the fostering of national patriotism, and the promotion of national capitalism. He stated that "the case of the Meiji imperial restoration will be of great help to the performance of our own revolution," and "my interest in this direction remains strong and constant."[46] As advisers, Park invited Rupert Emerson of Harvard University and Gilbert Plantz of New York University, both experts on emerging nations. They recommended the Japanese developmental model: "For Korea, the compressed Japanese modernization style is better than the standard Western model that took several hundred years."[47] Park saw Japan as a close neighbor of Korea with similar cultural traditions. If Japan had succeeded in modernization, he believed, there was no reason Korea could not do the same.

As indicated in the "Construct and Fight at the Same Time" slogan, anti-Communism and economic development were the twin goals of the military regime. On June 10, Chairman Park established the Korean Central Intelligence Agency (KCIA) "in order to supervise and coordinate both international and domestic intelligence activities."[48] In order to give teeth to the strong anti-Communist policy, the military government not only strengthened the National Security Law but also promulgated an even more prohibitive Anti-Communist Law in July 1961.[49] More importantly, in July 1961, only two months after the coup, the junta established the Economic Planning Board (EPB). Park Chung Hee planned economic policies like a professional soldier using plans, strategies, and commands. The idea of organizing and running an economy made perfect military sense. The EPB was given not only the responsibility to direct

---

[43] Park Chung Hee, *Country*, 26.

[44] Sung Chul Yang, "Political Ideology in Korean Politics: Its Elements and Roles", in Kim and Cho, eds., *Government and Politics of Korea*, 25-42.

[45] Park,Chung Hee *Country*, 109-142.

[46] Amsden, *Asia's Next Giant: South Korea*, 52.

[47] Cho Gab-je, "*Spit on My Grave*", *Chosun Ilbo*, March 24, 1999.

[48] *Hankuk Ilbo*, June 21, 1961.

[49] *Dong-A Ilbo*, July 17, 1961.

planning but also, by virtue of the fact that it controlled the national budget and thus government spending priorities, the ability to implement plans. The EPB was also given the power, unprecedented in Korean history, to regulate foreign borrowing. The EPB and the KCIA became the command centers for economic development and national security. They were highly centralized organizations, second only in power to the office of the president. Park Chung Hee was at the top, directly commanding the twin engines of development and security. On January 1, 1962, barely six months after the military takeover, Park announced with great fanfare the first five-year economic development plan (1962-1966), newly prepared by the EPB.

South Korea was heavily dependent on American military and economic assistance, and that remained true in the days following the coup. The Kennedy administration had been deeply concerned with the chaotic Korean situation during the Chang administration. After the coup in Korea the White House immediately formed a task force on Korea and reviewed its Korea policy. Its new Korea policy focused not on the coup itself but on the best means to restore Korean stability. The task force report suggested that the United States required a long-term developmental strategy behind its Korean aid program and asked the Korean junta to begin serious economic planning.[50] In a memorandum sent on June 12, 1961, from a staff member of the National Security Council to McGeorge Bundy, Kennedy's national security adviser, it was pointed out that one of the basic reasons the Korean economy had remained stagnant had been America's predominantly military focus.[51] The Kennedy administration now realized that the risk of another North Korean invasion was far less than that of an internal political subversion by the Communist elements in South Korea. Thus, the task force recommended a shift in U.S. emphasis to economic development in South Korea.[52]

At the National Security Council meeting held on June 13, 1961, Secretary of State Dean Rusk pointed out that the greatest hindrance to Korean economic development was the continued animosity between Japan and South Korea and the failure to re-establish their formal relations. President Kennedy decided to take up the subject of improving relations between the two nations in an upcoming meeting with the Japanese prime minister, Ikeda Hayato, and directed Ambassador Samuel Berger to concentrate on the issue.[53] On the same day, Kennedy approved the actions of the meeting. They included: a plan to invite General Park Chung Hee to Washington, an offer of technical

---

[50] The Task Force Report on Korea, Memorandum by Robert H. Johnson of the National Security Council staff, June 5, 1961, in FRUS 1961-1963, XXII, 555-556.

[51] Relative Priority of Military vs. Reconstruction Focus in Korea, Memorandum from Robert W. Komer of the National Security Council Staff to the President's Special Assistant for National Security Affairs, in FRUS 1961-1963, XXII, no. 226.

[52] The Task Force Report on Korea, Memorandum by Robert H. Johnson of the National Security Council staff, June 13, FRUS 1961-1963, XXII, no. 227. Walter W. Rostow, Kennedy's deputy security adviser and former economic professor at Massachusetts Institute of Technology, had stimulated an enormous debate with his 1960 book, *The Stages of Economic Growth*, which inaugurated the new, Kennedy-style concern with "nation building" and economic development (Macdonald, *U.S.-Korea Relations*, 26-27).

[53] Notes of the 485th Meeting of the National Security Council, June 13, 1961, in FRUS 1961-1963, XXII, no. 229.

experts to assist the Korean government in preparation of its five-year development plan, and the provision of resources to help carry out the development plan.[54] Thus, at the Kennedy administration's first National Security Council meeting following the coup, it was decided to support the Korean junta.

The increasingly tense Soviet-American rivalry was a factor in prompting this decision. At that time the Kennedy administration was facing some extremely volatile foreign policy issues related to the Sino-Soviet bloc, including security concerns in Berlin, Cuba and other Latin American countries, the Middle East, Southeast Asia, and other points of immediate friction. The last thing the Kennedy administration wanted was an unstable Korea, which might precipitate a general conflict in the Far East. Washington also wanted to use Park's visit to Washington as an opportunity to encourage diplomatic normalization with Japan. Facing unprecedented challenges from the Communist bloc, Kennedy believed it was essential that Korean-Japanese relations be normalized to assure peace and security in the Far East.

American officials in Seoul recognized that the South Korean government had made some constructive reforms. For example, on October 28, 1961, U.S. Ambassador Samuel Berger sent a very positive telegram to Washington describing the ability of the military government:

> [The] military government has now been in power five months. It has taken hold with energy, earnestness, determination and imagination, albeit with certain authoritarian and military characteristics.... It is nonetheless a genuine revolution from the top trying to introduce sweeping reforms of a most fundamental kind.
>
> [The] military government's efforts to deal with wholesale graft, bribery and corruption...are genuine and are producing results.... [The] majority of cabinet ministers...have impressed us with their competence and effectiveness for administration...[The] military government has its enemies, but it is not without support. If it has little positive support, it can claim with justice that it has considerable mass good will on the part of many who fear a return to instability and drifting....
>
> [It] seems inescapable that we must be prepared accept either Pak Chong-hui [Park Chung Hee] or a man selected by him as Korea's leader, subject to the provision that this leadership must be legitimated by the people through processes sufficiently free and fair to be acceptable in Korea and the world. *Pak is the only figure now in sight who seems to possess sufficient intelligence, vision, breadth of contact, forcefulness, personal reputation, and access to power (especially over military) to fulfill present leadership requirements.*[55] (Italics added)

Only six months after the military revolution, General Park came to Washington to meet President Kennedy. During the White House meeting between Kennedy and Park on November 14, 1961, the two young leaders—they were in fact the same age—spoke candidly on matters of mutual concern, including Korea-Japan relations, Vietnam, and American aid to

---

[54] Record of National Security Council Action No. 2430, June 13, 1961-1963, in FRUS XXII, 482-486.
[55] Telegram from the Embassy in Korea to the Department of State, October 28, 1961, in FRUS 1961-1963, XXII, 522-526.

Korea. On December 4, 1961, U.S. Secretary of State Dean Rusk sent a cable to Ambassador Berger in Seoul, praising Park Chung Hee's recent visit to Washington: "Park Chung Hee left a good impression with the high-ranking officials he met. Park was seen as a confident intelligent leader, well aware of the problems facing his country."[56]

Park and his junta government confronted an arresting mix of problems as they began to think about implementing the ambitious goals of the military revolution. He did not separate the question of his aims from that of the practical issue of means. He immediately followed his question of "what is it we want to do?" with another query, "how is it to be done?" The second question proved to be far more troublesome and divisive than the first. How did he set about achieving his ambitious goals? The answer lies in the revolutionary reorganization of the South Korean state that Park began to undertake after the coup.

The muscle needed to transform society had to come from somewhere. Existing governmental institutions were flaccid, and many of the high-ranking officials were ambivalent, if not downright opposed, to the challenge. Where, then, could Park find the muscle necessary to transform Korean society? His answer included two steps. First, as a stopgap solution, he relied heavily on the military. Military men were regarded as action- and goal-oriented, modern, managerial, organizationally effective, and with clear concepts of national development. Second, he tried to reform the state agencies and related institutions. The stopgap solution drew on former army officers to fill important public positions. The military government launched a massive placement of former military officers in the traditionally exclusive civil service. The infusion of a great number of disciplined, relatively well-trained, young former officers into the static and corrupted bureaucracy changed the whole operational culture of the bureaucracy.[57] Modern techniques of organizational management, called the "Fort Leavenworth style," named after the army fort in Kansas where most of the Korean officers were trained, were introduced at all levels of government administration.

In the long run, however, the military alone could not undertake the enormous tasks of nation building. Park concluded early that only an effective bureaucracy could ensure the success of the revolution. The military government launched a number of reforms designed to improve bureaucratic performance and implementation.[58] Park, who had read widely on the Meiji Restoration, had a keen interest in how Japan had modernized so rapidly and successfully. He concluded that the solid bureaucratic system of Japan was one of the most important factors in its successful modernization. After being elected president, Park created the Ministry of Government Administration and appointed Lee Suk-jae, a highly motivated retired general and a core member of the coup, as its minister. During a meeting just after his appointment, Park said to the new minister:

> To modernize the country we should create a good civil service system. It is often said there are three pillars of a nation. First, the military must be strong enough to defend the nation. Second, the bureaucrats must fulfill their duties. Finally, the

---

[56] See Letter from Ambassador Berger to Secretary of State Rusk, December 15, 1961, in *FRUS 1961-1963*, XXII, 542-548.
[57] Hahn-Been Lee, *Korea*, 145-152; and Chang-Hyun Cho, "Bureaucracy and Local Government in South Korea", in Kim and Cho, eds., *Government*, 98.
[58] Kyung Cho Chung, *New Korea*, 144-145.

business firms must become the cornerstone of the economy. Minister Lee, you take care of the civil service, one of the three pillars. Reorganize it to encompass professionals and guarantee their positions in spite of government changes so that they will dedicate their lives to their work.[59]

During the six years and nine months of his tenure, Lee doggedly led the revolutionary transformation of the bureaucracy and administrative system. In the spring of 1964, he visited the United States, France, West Germany, Italy, Taiwan, and the Philippines to study their civil service systems. In the United States he interviewed twelve federal government directors. He made a careful study of the organization, recruitment methods, salaries, promotion, and retirement systems of the American civil service system. Returning home, he realized how outdated the Korean civil service was. There was no table of organization, and ministers could appoint as many or as few civil servants as desired. There was an examination system, but it was based on favoritism.[60]

The Park government consistently pursued administrative development. For fourteen years of Park's eighteen-year rule, administrative reform was led by three former generals who were appointed ministers of government administration.[61] These ministers not only introduced a modern military administrative system for governance, but also modernized the administrative bureaucracy. As a result, Korean bureaucrats became active vanguards of Korea's modernization for the first time.

THE THIRD REPUBLIC (1963-1972)

In its first year the military government functioned effectively. But beginning in early 1962, a series of difficulties surfaced owing to the economic problems the junta had inherited. Industries were hamstrung by power shortages and inadequate management and financing. Farmers were burdened with debt and high interest rates. The military government was trying to go too far too fast, resulting in a huge budget deficit, inflation, and a foreign exchange crisis. In addition, crop failures in 1962 and 1963 brought on a food crisis and aggravated the rising inflation.

In December of 1962, the military government drew up a new constitution and put it to a popular referendum, where it received 78.8 percent of the vote. Under this constitution, the president was to be elected by direct popular vote and have strong powers, including the authority to appoint the prime minister and cabinet members without legislative consent and to order emergency financial and economic measures.[62] On New Year's Day 1963, the government lifted the ban on political activity in preparation for the upcoming elections. In the spring of 1963, Park Chung Hee and his associates established the Democratic Republican Party (DRP).

On August 30, in a military ceremony, General Park ended his seventeen-year military

---

[59] Lee Suk-jae (1995), 217-218.

[60] Interview with Lee Suk-jae, March 22, 2002.

[61] The first minister (Lee Suk-jae) of the Third Republic served 5 years 10 months (1963. 12~1969. 10); the second minister (Suh Il-gyo) 4 years 2 months (1969.10~1973.12); and the third minister (Shim Heung-sun) 4 years and one month (1973.12~1977.12). Before Lee Suk-jae was appointed, he was the minister of cabinet administration in the military government.

[62] Ki-bum Kim, "Certain Features of the Constitution", *Korean Affairs*, III:1 (April, 1964).

career in order to prepare for the upcoming presidential election, scheduled on October 15. Park's retirement set the tempo of the election campaign at full speed. Against Park, former president Yoon Po-sun emerged as a serious challenger. The forty-five-year old Park faced strong competition in sixty-five-year old Yoon, a well-known political leader at the time. In terms of reputation and image, Park, who had emerged as the junta leader only two years before, fell far short of Yoon, who had been a political leader since liberation.[63]

Park and Yoon represented two different political generations. Yoon was a political figure that had dominated Korean politics since 1948—a leader who gathered followers on a personal basis. He had been born into a *yangban* family of considerable wealth and social status; his life was shaped by traditional Korean thought, values, and mores. Park represented a new generation. He had been heavily exposed to the ways and ideas of the outside world and had experienced the implications of modern science and technology. Park came from a poor peasant family. Thus, some viewed the election as a contest between a conservative aristocrat and a young reformist. Yoon waged a vigorous campaign, hitting on two main themes aimed at discrediting Park: his Communist past and allegations that he was unable to command the support and confidence of the United States.[64] Park got people's attention by emphasizing his commitment to reform and with hard-hitting attacks against the conservatives. He criticized Yoon and his party as the feudalistic remnants of the Yi dynasty, an old guard that cared little for the people, primarily respected the greatness of external powers, and indulged in factionalism. In contrast, Park defined his revolutionary forces as the modern nationalists, dedicated to building an independent and economically and militarily self-sufficient country.[65]

Following a bitter and intensive two-month campaign, elections were held on October 15, 1963, in an atmosphere later described by a UN observer as "the most honest and peaceful election in fifteen years of South Korean history." The balloting and counting were fair, which set a precedent.[66] After a heated race, Park defeated Yoon by a margin of 156,000 votes, 42.6 percent to 41.2 percent. It was clear that Park did not achieve the decisive victory he expected. Park won decisively in the five southern provinces, while Yoon carried the northern provinces as well as Seoul, where anti-Communism was strong. Park won 51 percent of the rural votes, while Yoon received 57 percent of the urban votes.[67] Contrary to predictions of an opposition majority, in subsequent parliamentary elections held in November 1963, the DRP won a smashing victory, winning 110 of the 175 seats.[68] The Park government had now become an elected and legitimate government.

---

[63] Myong-whai Kim, "The Presidential Election in Korea, 1963", *Korean Affairs*, III:3-4 (October 1963): 372-378.

[64] Telegram from the Embassy in Korea to the Department of State, October 9, 1963, in *FRUS 1961-1963*, XXII, 661-664; and *Korea Times*, September 29, 1963.

[65] For the general background of Park's election, see William A. Douglas, "South Korea's Search for Leadership", *Pacific Affairs*, 37:1 (spring 1964): 20-36.

[66] Telegram from the Embassy in Korea to the Department of State, October 16, 1963, *FRUS 1961-1963*, XXII, 665-666; and *New York Times*, October 19, 1963, 24.

[67] Eugene Kim, "Significance of the 1963 Korean Election", *Asian Survey*, XVII:1 (March 1964): 765-773.

[68] Hong-bin Yim, "An Analysis of the General Election in 1963", *Korean Affairs*, III:1 (April, 1964): 120-128.

When Park Chung Hee was sworn in as president on December 17, 1963, he declared the beginning of what he called the Third Republic. In his inaugural address, Park swore to dedicate his body and mind to achieving the historical task of national modernization. He revealed his strong conviction to accomplish this goal by saying:

> In human societies, progress and prosperity are achieved only at the cost of sweat, blood and work. If we of this generation do not put forward our most devoted efforts to throw off the yoke of backwardness in this era of tumultuous change, the black clouds of past generations will veil our country, our people and our history forever.[69]

As soon as Park assumed power, he turned his energies to strengthening the presidency.[70] He created a military-style executive staff—a functionally diversified, modern staff system. It was meant to transform the duties of presidential staff from simple clerical to policy-related. He introduced a chief of staff and delegated considerable power to that office. It was Park's belief that a centralized, strong, and effective Blue House staff was necessary to plan, coordinate, and monitor governmental policies.[71] Park's presidency marked the transformation of the presidential staff from a small, personalized office to a systematic, policy-oriented one with hundreds of professional staffers.

As Park began to focus on the solution of economic problems, the need for expertise and managerial skills both at the cabinet level and in the bureaucracy became clearer to the new president. He placed emphasis on managerial skills in his appointments. His first cabinet included seven ex-military men who had demonstrated administrative or technical ability, as well as political loyalty to Park during the military government. The eight nonmilitary members of the cabinet represented a variety of professional skills and signaled the first real infusion of civilian experts into the government.[72] There were bankers, bureaucrats, journalists, lawyers, professors, engineers, and physicians. The economic difficulties of the 1962-63 period caused Park to turn more to professional civilian experts in the cabinet and the bureaucracy for the management of economic affairs.

In May 1964, under the pressure of student protests against normalization talks with Japan, Park reshuffled his cabinet after only five months in office. The second cabinet included some prominent figures. The new prime minister was Chung Il-kwon, who held the office until the end of 1970. Chung had risen to the position of army chief of staff during the Korean War, and then gone on to become chairman of the Joint Chiefs of Staff. After retirement from the army, Chung held various ambassadorial appointments

---

[69] Bum Shik Shin, 286.

[70] See Sung Deuk Hahm, "The Institutional Development of Blue House in the Park Chung Hee Presidency", *Asian Perspective*, 26:2 (2002), 101-130.

[71] Even in America, a strong White House staff was believed to be essential. As one of President Kennedy's aides said, "Everybody believes in democracy until he gets to the White House and then you begin to believe in dictatorship, because it is so hard to get things done." Quoted in Thomas Cronin, *The State of the Presidency* (Boston: Little, Brown, 1980), 223.

[72] The cabinet positions held by ex-military from 1964-1967 were prime minister, and ministers of defense, home affairs, communications, health and social affairs (by a former military physician), government administration, public information, and commerce and industry.

from 1959 to 1963. Chung brought to the cabinet close ties with, and the confidence of, the senior officers as well as national recognition for his role in the war, experience abroad including familiarity with the United States, strong but relatively quiet and uncontroversial administrative leadership, and loyalty to Park. Some of the most important civilian members in the cabinet were the deputy prime minister and EPB minister Chang Key-young, former vice president of the Bank of Korea, and the foreign minister, Lee Dong-won, a Ph.D. from Oxford University who took the normalization talks with Japan out of the hands of Kim Jong-pil, director of the KCIA.

Before accepting the position, Chang requested the position of the EPB minister be raised to deputy prime minister so that he could coordinate economic policies. Park agreed. Thus, economic and fiscal policies came under the very firm direction of the deputy prime minister. The organization and coordination of economic programs under one cabinet minister represented an important institutional change. Chang aggressively promoted an economic stabilization program, which included substantial cuts in farm subsidies, earning him the nickname "bulldozer." Lawmakers, including those of the ruling party, were angered and tried to drive him out of the office. But Chang's assertiveness, ability, and self-confidence had won the support of the president. Park defended the highly centralized and aggressive direction of economic policy under Chang and twice intervened personally—in 1965 and 1966—to prevent an attempt within the ruling party to obtain a vote of no confidence against Chang.

The Park government concentrated almost single-mindedly on economic growth and began to gain confidence in its ability to achieve economic growth and exports. By the end of 1964, progress was evident in several areas. Exports were up as much as 50 percent that year. The government's emphasis on exports began to play a dominant role in economic policy. The government had also succeeded in controlling inflation. The issue of economic development had grown in importance in Korean politics for the first time in its history. Instead of large nationalistic programs, concrete economic performance, as shown by the targets of annual growth rate and exports, became the touchstone of governmental performance and national progress.[73]

The First Five-Year Plan was completed in 1966 with remarkable success. The results far outpaced the plan, with annual GNP growth from 1962 through 1966 averaging 8.3 percent, compared with a planned 7.1 percent. The government thus succeeded in bringing about rapid economic development, the utmost concern of the people. Park began to gain confidence as a national leader. With confidence and pride, the government announced the Second Five-Year Plan (1967-1971). The target growth rate of the plan was again set at 7 percent, but because the realized growth rate of the first plan had been higher than the target, the government raised the target to 10 percent. The government appeared to gain legitimacy through economic performance, and cities could no longer be viewed as a stronghold of the opposition. Even intellectuals who had generally been anti-government now believed that democracy would have to be sacrificed somewhat to achieve economic development, and gave the highest priority to economic

---

[73] Cole and Lyman, *Korean Development*, 78-97.

growth as a national goal.[74] Park had succeeded in making economic development the most important issue on the national agenda.

During the four years of his first term Park succeeded in establishing an effective and stable government; his emphasis on program achievement, professionalism, and Western methods of administration began to take root in the government. His presidency, based on a combination of concentrated presidential power and determined leadership, represented a fundamental shift in Korean outlook and policies: a step back from a chronic economic dependence on the United States and a generally pessimistic attitude toward the Republic itself, and a step toward an aggressive policy of economic development, active international diplomacy, and enhancement of national confidence.

In 1967, fifty-year old Park embarked on his re-election campaign almost entirely on the development record of his first term and the developmental potential in the Second Five-Year Plan. In the opening statement of his presidential campaign, he proclaimed that, "the establishment of a self-supporting Korea is my supreme goal."[75] His theme was the modernization of the country and the prestige and position of Korea in the world. Yoon Po-sun, the presidential candidate of the opposition party, argued that the Park administration's economic policies had benefited only a few and proposed alternative economic policies which he claimed would benefit the masses.

The election results were more decisive than those of 1963, reflecting the remarkable achievements of Park's first term.[76] Park won 51.4 percent of the total votes, as opposed to only 41 percent for Yoon Po-sun, and 8 percent for other candidates. Park's victory margin was slightly more than one million votes out of more than eleven million votes cast. Park's support in the cities increased dramatically: he carried 50.4 percent, as compared with only 30.2 percent in 1963. In Seoul, the traditional stronghold of the opposition, Park had lost by more than two to one in 1963, whereas in 1967 he drew 47 percent against Yoon's 49 percent. Park also carried the second largest city, Pusan. In the city of Ulsan, the country's major industrial center at the time, Park won by a nine to one margin. Nationwide voting patterns had also changed. In 1963, Park won the southern provinces and lost the northern ones. In 1967, he won those along the east coast and lost those along the west coast.[77] In the parliamentary elections held on June 8, the ruling party took 130 out of 175 seats, an increase of 19, against 45 seats for the opposition party. The DRP's margin of victory was unexpectedly large, better than a two-thirds majority in the assembly, sufficient to enable it to pass constitutional amendments. As a result, Park was able to enjoy political legitimacy and a strong mandate to resume his mission of nation building.

Park's second term was expected to expire in 1971. It seems that Park himself initiated a series of moves to remain president. The ruling party promoted a constitutional amendment that would eliminate the constitutional limitation on the presidency to two terms.[78] Park's

---

[74] See Song Chick Hong, *The Intellectuals and Modernization: A Study of Korean Attitudes* (Seoul: Korea University, 1967). Hong conducted a survey of 1515 professors and journalists in late 1966.
[75] *Korea Times*, April 16, 1967.
[76] Central Election Management Committee, *Taehan Minguk Sunko-sa* (History of Election in the Republic of Korea), Seoul, 1967.
[77] Central Election Management Committee (1967), 583.
[78] See Y. C. Han, "The 1969 Constitutional Revision and Party Politics in South Korea", *Pacific Affairs*, 44:2 (summer 1971): 242-258.

loyalists were convinced that Park was the only leader who could maintain the momentum of high economic growth and strengthen national security. At the time, South Korea's security conditions were deteriorating: encouraged by the success of the Communist guerrilla war in Vietnam, North Korean military and political offensives were escalating; at the same time, after declaration of the 1969 Nixon Doctrine, the United States was withdrawing its forces from South Korea.

On September 14, 1969, with the opposition occupying the rostrum to block the passage of the constitutional amendment bill, the ruling party, supported by eleven members of a minor party and four independents, passed the amendment, which was approved in an October referendum by 65 percent of the votes cast. Park was at the peak of his power following the impressive vote of confidence he received in the constitutional referendum. He received full credit for economic progress and for the political and social stability created during his tenure. He had also won a reputation for hard work and personal honesty. In the 1971 presidential election, Park's victory was unquestioned. In seeking re-election, Park pointed to a solid record of achievement, particularly in the area of economic growth. He emphasized three economic objectives—growth, equitable distribution of income, and price stability—during the Third Five-Year Plan. Park and his party stressed that his continued rule was essential for "uninterrupted economic development and political stability."

Against this powerful and increasingly popular incumbent, Kim Dae Jung, then forty-six, emerged as the opposition candidate of the New Democratic Party. He had been one of the two young leaders (the other being Kim Young Sam) who had advocated democratic reforms during the 1960s. Kim's anti-Park and populist rhetoric generated a ground swell of support among students, progressives, and socially alienated citizens. In order to appeal to young voters, Kim pledged that he would abolish the KCIA, the homeland reserve forces, and the military training program for students.[79] Kim also proposed to accelerate unification by utilizing more conciliatory approaches to reduce tensions between the two Koreas. Park and his party condemned Kim as "irresponsible" and "careless" in his political ambition. Considering the increasingly aggressive provocations of North Korea, the Nixon Doctrine, and consequent partial withdrawal of U.S. forces from Korea, many were concerned about the security situation. When the votes were tallied, Park received 51.2 percent of the votes and Kim received 45.2 percent. The margin of 947,000 votes out of about twelve million votes cast indicated that Park had maintained the support level he had received in the 1967 presidential election. Kim received support similar to that of Yoon Po-sun in that election.[80] Kim enjoyed strong support from his home region, the Cholla provinces, where Kim's candidacy stirred unusual excitement.

What worried President Park was the poor performance of the ruling DRP in the general elections held one month later. The DRP won only 113 seats of the total 204-member assembly while the opposition (the NDP) captured eighty-nine, doubling the number of its seats. The opposition party won a sweeping victory in urban areas (forty-six seats vs. nineteen seats). The election was a major defeat for the ruling party.

---

[79] *Chosun Ilbo*, October 25, 1970.
[80] Central Election Management Committee, *Results of the 1971 Presidential Election*, Seoul, 1971.

Park Chung Hee

MODERNIZATION OF THE FATHERLAND

> In human life, economics precedes politics or culture.[81]

Immediately after taking over the government, declaring that the key factor of the military revolution was "to affect an industrial revolution in Korea," Park Chung Hee had wasted no time in committing himself to economic growth, making it his top national priority. A self-reliant economy was an integral part of his nationalistic vision of a prosperous and independent Korea: the "modernization of the fatherland."[82] Park believed that chronic poverty was the most urgent problem facing the nation, thus he emphasized the importance of economic development. He projected the government's commitment to economic growth in public speeches, meetings on economic matters, and on-site visits to review the progress of state development projects. Looking back after a decade in power, he wrote: "In May 1961, when I took over power, I honestly felt as if I had been given a pilfered household or bankrupt firm to manage. Around me I could find little hope of encouragement. The outlook was bleak."[83] His flexible thinking allowed him to learn the essence of economics within a short period of time.

In the early 1960s, the economy was so underdeveloped that the guiding idea of economic policy was "to make something out of nothing." The government had to mobilize capital and other resources, build up industrial infrastructure—including factories—and train manpower. Park created the means by which to achieve his goals. In July 1961, he established the EPB, which would be responsible for creating and managing an industrialization strategy. In addition, the government also created the Ministry of Construction (MOC), charged with national physical planning and construction. With the government dedicated to industrialization, the power of the Ministry of Commerce and Industry (MCI) was greatly strengthened. The nationalization of the banks and the centralization of the financial system also made the Ministry of Finance (MOF) extremely powerful. If the EPB was the brains of economic policy, the MCI, the MOF and the MOC were the brawn.

The First Five-Year Plan of 1961 aimed to create an economic base for industrialization of self-sustained growth and was geared toward attaining a 41 percent increase in gross national product during 1962-66. The projected growth rate was seen as "almost impossible"—unprecedented not only in Korea, but in any developing country. Not surprisingly, pessimism and skepticism about economic development were widespread. The government formally launched the plan in January 1962. Park wrote a succinct introduction to the plan as an indication of his personal commitment to economic development. Such an action by a chief executive was unprecedented in Korean history. He made his strategy for economic growth clear: "The economic system will be a form of guided capitalism, in which the principle of free enterprise and respect

---

[81] Park Chung Hee, *Country*, 26.

[82] For materials on the economic development of the Park period, see Mason et al., *Economic and Social Modernization*; Jones and Sakong, *Government, Business, and Entrepreneurship*; Huer, *Marching Orders*; Cole and Lyman, *Korean Development*; Cho and Kim, *Economic Development*; and Amsden, *Asia's Next Giant*.

[83] Park Chung Hee, *To Build a Nation*, 105.

for the freedom and initiative of free enterprise will be observed, but in which the government will directly participate or indirectly render guidance to the basic industries and other important fields."[84] As a part of the First Five-Year Plan, the construction of the Ulsan Industrial Complex was commenced on January 27, 1962. Park went to Ulsan himself to cut the inaugural tape. He declared that Ulsan, a small city on the southeastern coast, would become a special industrial zone. "As the Aswan Dam stands for Nasser's revolution, so must the Ulsan Industrial Complex and the First Five-Year Plan for economic development stand for our May revolution," he proclaimed.[85] The area became the site of Korea's first petrochemical complex and later the location of the Hyundai Group's huge shipyard and auto factory.

The First Five-Year Plan required two and a half billion dollars. The government nationalized all five commercial banks, all six special banks, and two of the country's three major nonbank financial institutions. Directed by the government, the nationalized banks provided low-interest loans to selected industries in excess of their net worth. Tax concessions were also granted to approved industries. The ambitious development plan required enormous amounts of foreign capital. Financial and technological support from abroad was critical. Without a significant reduction of its military aid to Korea, the United States could not support such an ambitious development plan. As the amount of American aid was reduced over the years, the Park government turned to "financial diplomacy" with other countries, such as Japan and West Germany.

Park wasted no time in implementing his plans for economic development. He ran his economy like a military operation.[86] If the Japanese high-growth era was primarily the work of bureaucrats, Korea's economic success was the work of the military. The young officers contrasted sharply with what the term "military government" would normally imply. Yes, they had been trained as soldiers in a harsh war, but they had learned progressively more about high technology. Many had undergone additional professional training in the United States. They provided a pool of relatively skilled talent that was well-accustomed to systematic planning and staff work. Park also gathered around him a new group of technocrats (economists and engineers) to act as a general staff for the management of economic development.

Park committed the full weight of his power and that of his government in support of the unprecedented economic development plan, which became his "marching orders." The political commitment was quickly matched with concrete executive actions, as he proceeded methodically to create the machinery needed to achieve his ambitious economic goals. His appointment of tough-minded technocrats to the post of the EPB minister revealed his single-minded commitment to the mantra of economic growth. His commitment was also evident in his appointments of economy-related ministers. He appointed people with specialized professional knowledge or experience in economic fields, rather than those with military backgrounds, to ministries such as industry, finance, and agriculture.

The First Five-Year Plan initially put an emphasis on rural development and import-

---

[84] Quoted in Clifford, *Troubled Tiger*, 49-50.
[85] Park Chung Hee, *Country*, 177.
[86] Huer, *Marching Orders*.

substitution industries. Exports were merely a means of raising foreign currency to pay for imports. In the first two years (1962-63) of the plan, the results in the priority areas fell far short of targets, and exports rose far above expectations, increasing 34 percent in 1962 and 58 percent in 1963. The government revised the plan by the end of 1963, changing the priority from import-substitution to export-oriented industrialization.[87] In order to develop, it was essential to build manufacturing facilities and to import a large amount of intermediate goods and raw materials. Park recognized that in order to acquire the foreign currency reserves needed for imports, manufacture of exportable goods was essential. Park and his associates also agreed that the Korean domestic market was too small for industry to grow quickly and the economy required foreign markets. In dramatic contrast to Kim Il Sung's inward-oriented development strategy of self-reliance (*Juche*), the Park government adopted an outward-looking developmental strategy, with confidence in the prospects of large scale exports. This represented an extraordinary change for a country still known as the "hermit kingdom," whose people were still terribly suspicious of the Japanese and uncomfortable with American influence.

Thus, Park put a strong emphasis on export promotion. Beginning in 1964, the government took decisive actions to make the economy suitable for export-oriented industrialization: it devalued the Korean currency to cheapen exports, and adopted comprehensive measures for export promotion, consistent with the new exchange rate system. Export-oriented firms were given preferential credits and tax benefits. The government borrowed heavily and invested the money in export industries and the national infrastructure to support them. Conglomerates were given export targets by the government. Park and his government were almost "religiously" committed to fulfilling the nation's annual export target. During his regional tour to see newly established factories, Park had the chance to speak with the minister of commerce and industry, Park Choong-hoon. The minister said that the traditional hierarchy of Korean society (scholar, farmer, industrialist, and merchant) had to be changed to place industrialists first. Park Chung Hee, however, wanted to reverse the hierarchy completely, saying that it did not matter how good your product was if you had nobody to whom to export it. This idea was alien to Korean thinking and raised the wrath of scholars, students, journalists and other intellectuals. Park Chung Hee's thinking was progressive and internationally oriented.[88]

On November 30, 1964, Korea celebrated annual exports of $100 million for the first time in its history (and that date has been known in South Korea ever since as Export Day). Every year on November 30, celebrations were held to mark the achievement of export targets, at which Park would decorate businesses and individuals who had exceeded their export targets. The remarkable expansion of exports gave government and business self-confidence and pride. The expansion of exports resulted in corresponding increases in production, and therefore the government framed export promotion and industrialization into a coherent strategy of export-led industrialization.

Encouraged by the success, Park strengthened economic institutions to support his export drive. Korea had little experience in dealing with large-scale exports. A convenient

---

[87] Kwang Suk Kim, "Outward-Looking Industrialization Strategy: The Case of Korea", in Wontack Hong and Anne O. Kruger, eds., *Trade and Development in Korea*, Seoul: KDI, 1975.
[88] Cho Gab-je, "*Spit on My Grave*", *Chosun Ilbo*, February 22, 1999.

model for Korea was provided by Japan's Ministry of Commerce and Industry (later transformed into the Ministry of International Trade and Industry, or MITI). In 1965, the Park government reorganized the Ministry of Commerce and Industry to create an export component in each of its industrial bureaus, supplementing the existing Bureau of Foreign Trade. The main function of each export component was to set annual export targets by commodity, as well as by region and country of destination, and to monitor the export performance of firms that were under the oversight of each bureau.

The government adopted two other administrative instruments to promote exports.[89] The first was the government-owned Korea Trade Promotion Corporation (KOTRA), concerned with the overseas marketing activities of Korean exporters. Twenty-two trade centers were established in various nations to promote trade. The second was the Monthly Export Promotion Meeting. The meeting was chaired by the president himself and attended by economic ministers and vice ministers, ruling party representatives, representatives of the National Assembly, conglomerates, trade associations, and labor leaders of export-oriented industries. The gathering was a very effective means for the implementation of export promotion policies. It reviewed progress, discussed necessary measures for reaching export targets, provided current information to ministries and firms on export performance by product and region, and noted discrepancies between targets and achievements. It also provided appropriate guidelines for action from both the government and exporting firms. Areas of disagreement between government and business were openly addressed. Naturally, consensus was built and the distortion and inefficiency of the bureaucratic process were reduced.

The export-oriented industrialization policy achieved spectacular success (see Figure 2).[90] Between 1961 and 1972, total exports expanded more than 40 times, manufactured exports expanded 170 times, and the rate of export growth averaged more than 60 percent annually. With poorly developed capital markets, infrastructure, and exporting experience, the advent of export-led industrialization was remarkable. The economic structure also changed radically. While agriculture's share of total domestic production dropped from 45.2 percent to 29.5 percent, the manufacturing sector's share increased from 17.1 percent to 35.2 percent during this period. South Korea was rapidly transforming itself from an agricultural dwarf to an industrial giant.[91] When exports exceeded $1 billion for the first time in 1970, Park declared a national holiday to mark the event.

One reason South Korea differed from other developing countries was its president's personal involvement. Park Chung Hee chaired monthly export meetings, monthly economic reviews, and quarterly science and technology promotion meetings. He also had a regular system of visiting ministries. His background as the commanding general of the Logistics Base Command gave him the confidence and organizational abilities needed to manage a small economy like South Korea's. He could easily familiarize himself with details and find ways to reduce bottlenecks. He drew on plenty of sources of information and advice. If President Park was the supreme commander in the national drive for

---

[89] Hinton, *Small Countries*, 25-26.
[90] The figure is based on the Economic Planning Board, *Major Statistics of Korean Economy* (various years).
[91] Charles R. Frank, Jr. et al., *South Korea*, 77-78.

Park Chung Hee

economic growth, his economic ministers were his field commanders, his vice ministers acted as deputy commanders, and his directors-general of industrial planning were the main troop leaders. Park made the Blue House the supreme headquarters for the drive toward economic development. He established an economic situation room adjacent to his Blue House office and frequently checked on the progress of each project.

Figure 2. Export Growth ($10M)
(1961-1979)

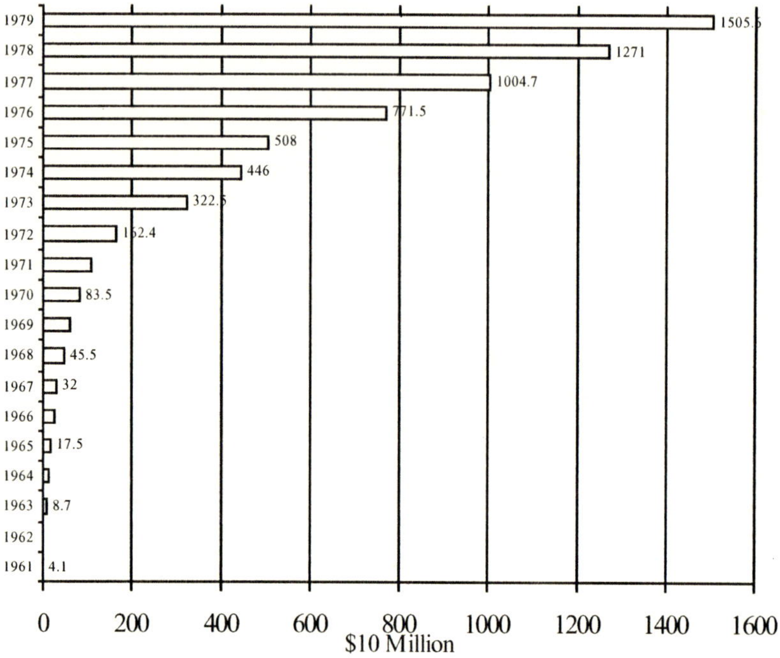

Year	Value
1979	1505.5
1978	1271
1977	1004.7
1976	771.5
1975	508
1974	446
1973	322.5
1972	162.4
1971	
1970	83.5
1969	
1968	45.5
1967	32
1966	
1965	17.5
1964	
1963	8.7
1962	
1961	4.1

$10 Million

In the autumn of 1965, President Park invited reporters to the Blue House for a tea party. One of them asked the president if they could see his newly established situation room. Park led them there. The reporters were surprised to find that the walls were covered with diagrams and statistics, including the trends of trade, tax collection and the status of the construction of industrial facilities. Perhaps what most impressed them was the number of chimneys on a map of Korea, indicating completed factories, those under construction and those still in the planning stages. He picked up a pointer and from memory explained the economic statistics to the reporters without making a mistake. He asserted confidently that if current trends continued, by the late 1970s Korea would have a self-sufficient economy, free from American dominance.

Every January and February, Park visited every ministry and provincial government to be briefed on programs and strategies for the current year and on the preceding year's performance. At this annual "New Year's briefing session," attendants included all the ministers, presidential advisers, governors, leaders of the ruling party and the National Assembly, as well as most bureau directors and section chiefs of the ministry or the province. National development programs were examined and revised every year, with each ministry doing its best to achieve its assigned annual target. Park surprised bureaucrats with his knowledge of their work. His presence was felt not only in terms of general policy but in a very specific directional push. He returned the following year to each ministry and went through the promised target sentence by sentence. He set, and dramatized in public, a clear, cold-blooded, and very consistent criteria for reward and punishment: only those who achieved 100 percent or more of the planned target could be promoted. Those ministers who achieved less than 80 percent of what they promised over two or three evaluation periods were fired without exception.

The First Five-Year Plan was completed in 1966 with remarkable success. The net result was a GNP growth of 43.9 percent in the plan period, averaging 8.3 percent annually as opposed to the planned 7.1 percent. Industrial production rose from 18 percent of GNP in 1960 to 28 percent in 1967. The average value of exports expanded 40 percent annually during the five years. The income in nonfarming sectors was almost doubled. Industrial workers increased from 390,000 in 1962 to 1.3 million in 1967. The Korean "economic miracle" had just begun. Park's drive to convince Koreans that they could stand tall was paying off more quickly than he could have hoped.

Encouraged by the success of the First Five-Year Plan, the Park government launched the Second Five-Year Plan (1967-1971) with a heavy emphasis on the promotion of export-oriented industries. Annual GNP growth was set at 7 percent in the second development plan period despite the World Bank's protest that it was too high to be realistic. The actual result of the second development plan was 11.4 percent, with the 1969 growth rate reaching an astonishing 13.8 percent. Economic planners boasted, "The successful completion of the first two plans has instilled new hope in the minds of the people whose attitude has been plagued by negativism and pessimism...It has given them the courage to say, 'We, too, can be rich and strong.'"[92] The highly focused and integrated economic policies and the single-mindedness of Park's leadership brought tremendous results.

As the Korean economy expanded rapidly, Park was increasingly concerned that an inadequate transportation system would create serious hurdles to economic growth. There were not enough roads and bridges or ports and dams, and those that existed often had to be rehabilitated. It was necessary to build many more to keep up with rapid expansion of the economy. This was not an easy task, given the underdevelopment of infrastructure and its devastation during the Korean War. Park had a special interest in the construction of expressways. In 1953, when he trained at an artillery school in the United States, he saw freeways for the first time. He realized that highways were an essential element in the infrastructure of a modern industrial state. During his visit to West Germany in 1964, he heard from German Chancellor Erhard that the autobahn was the symbol of German economic reconstruction. Park was deeply impressed by the autobahns and was determined to build modern highways in Korea.[93]

In 1966 Park ordered one of his senior staffers to prepare a special memorandum on expressway construction. In April 1967, as part of his presidential election

---

[92] Quoted in Jones and Sakong, *Government*, 51.
[93] Chung–Yum Kim, *Policymaking*, 114-115.

campaign, he revealed his comprehensive plan for building expressways and ports and developing river routes. In November the construction minister reported on a long-term road development plan during a meeting at the Blue House. Park directed him to build the Seoul-Pusan expressway in order to facilitate long-term transportation needs and to coordinate the development of widely disparate regions. The attitude inside and outside the country was predominantly pessimistic about the project because of its sheer technical difficulties and for economic reasons. No one but Park believed it could be done; even his own party thought it would bankrupt the country. Opposition to the project escalated when the plan was publicly announced. The opposition ridiculed the idea, "Why do we waste money to build such a highway when the people have no cars?" The media, big business, intellectuals, all spoke out loudly against it. The World Bank also believed that the road made no economic sense. Yet, Park repeated his firm belief in the necessity of the project in order to jump up to a higher stage of industrialization, emphasizing that domestic funds, skills, and efforts would be invested in the construction because the expressway would symbolize Korea's modernization.

In January 1968 the construction of the Seoul-Pusan expressway began. The government mobilized all available resources to accomplish construction of the 428-kilometer route within three years. Park decided to take advantage of army engineering officers to construct those sections of the road that required specialized civil engineering skills and to train college graduates in civil engineering as supervisors. He appointed as new minister of construction, a highway specialist (Chu Won) with whom he conferred frequently. Park also met several times with the chairman of the Hyundai Construction Company (Chung Ju-yung) to check on the possibility of cost reduction.

The president supervised every aspect of the construction, even inspecting by helicopter all possible routes of the superhighway.[94] He made field visits to the construction site by helicopter every other day in order to check on progress and help solve problems. He usually invited ministers in charge of finance, construction, transportation, or anybody related to the task to join his field trips, and discussed with them its progress and problems.[95] An engineer on the project recalled that "after a while, I found myself thinking of him [Park], of all things, as a sort of a conductor of an orchestra—with his helicopter as his baton. Up and down he would go, this time with a team of geologists to determine what was wrong with some mountainside that had crumbled on our tunnel-makers, the next time with a couple of United Nations hydrologists to figure out how our own surveyors had got some water table wrong. If he didn't know the answer on Tuesday, President Park was back with it on Thursday or Saturday."[96]

The construction of the expressway was finished on July 7, 1970, two years and five months from the start of construction. It was "the largest civil engineering project ever launched in Korea's history," wrote Park. The successful construction of the expressway "gave the Korean people a new confidence that they can do whatever they want to do."[97] It

---

[94] Chung Kil Chung, "Policymaking in the Executive Branch", in Bun Woong Kim et al., *Administrative Dynamics and Development*, 125.

[95] Dong-Kyu Choi (1991), 50.

[96] Keon, *Korean Phoenix*, 79.

[97] Park Chung Hee, *To Build a Nation*, 121.

transformed Korea's entire socioeconomic structure and was one of the key factors in what is called the Korean economic miracle. The Seoul-Pusan expressway became, as Park envisioned, the bloodline of the Korean transportation system, as well as a key in the development of higher-level industries like steel and automobiles. Such a project, daring in scope and staggering in technical obstacles, also served Park's symbolic purpose in demonstrating his government's intentions as well as its abilities. In December 1970, the Honam expressway, running through the southwestern Cholla region, was also opened for service. At a time when South Korea's main roads were still unpaved, a network of expressways was a dream-come-true. Today the construction of the Seoul-Pusan expressway is regarded as the third greatest achievement in the history of the Republic.[98]

Diplomacy for Economic Growth

Normalization with Japan. In the early 1960s it was important that South Korea improve its relations with the free world. Its relations had long been largely confined to the United States, the Philippines, Taiwan, and South Vietnam. The Park administration's first and most urgent diplomatic priority was Japan. Unlike the emotional Syngman Rhee, Park knew how to apply pragmatism to foreign policy and approached the task of normalizing diplomatic ties with Japan by a realistic assessment of South Korea's overall strategic requirements. One of the most compelling reasons behind Korea-Japan diplomatic normalization was the strong political pressure exerted by the United States. Washington had long wished to see normal diplomatic ties established between its two principal East Asian allies. As South Korea remained far from economic self-sufficiency, Washington was eager to share its burden with an increasingly prosperous Japan. Normalization was also critical to South Korea's breakthrough in economic development.[99]

Despite the plentiful justifications for normalization, the majority of South Koreans rejected Park's diplomatic initiative. Hatred of Japan ran both deep and wide among Koreans. Normalization with Japan soon became the most explosive issue, and negotiations with Japan proved socially painful and politically precarious. Nevertheless, Park was determined to normalize relations with Japan. To Park, it was irrational and counterproductive that Korea and Japan, with their geographical proximity and mutual participation in the alliance of free nations against Communism, had no diplomatic relations. He was also a pragmatic leader. To promote his ambitious development program, the development of major new sources of investment capital was seen as more necessary than ever. U.S. economic assistance began its downward spiral at a time when South Korea's need to build its economic infrastructure was rapidly rising. The American people had become weary of foreign aid, and the U.S. Congress was pushing for a sharp reduction.[100] For these reasons, South Korea's settlement of relations

---

[98] According to a Gallup Korea survey, the construction of the expressway was ranked third among the ten greatest achievements in the fifty-year history of post-1945 Korea. *Chosun Ilbo,* July 15, 1998.

[99] For the details of Korea-Japan negotiations, see Office of Public Information, Republic of Korea, Hanil hoedam paekso (White Paper on the Korea-Japan Talks), Seoul, 1966; and Kwan-bong Kim, Korea-Japan Treaty Crisis.

[100] U.S. grant-aid to South Korea was declining rapidly: from $165 million in 1962, to $119 million in 1963, $88 million in 1964, and $71 million in 1965. By contrast, grant-aid to the Second Republic in 1960 was $225 million. See *Korea Annual 1967,* 165.

with Japan had become more pressing. Yook In-soo, Park's brother-in-law, related Park's thinking on the normalization of ties with Japan:

> The [military] revolution launched on Park's initiative aimed at two targets. One was military: the North Korean menace. The other was Korea's economic reconstruction, i.e., to break out of the country's poverty.... Nothing was needed by Korea more than funds. The U.S. supported Korea, but could not double its aid and could therefore not be relied on. If Korea-Japan relations could be successfully normalized, Korea might be in a position to make a straightforward request for official development assistance funds from Japan. It was, after all, an irreparable loss for Korea to break off Korea-Japan talks on account of anti-Japanese feelings or Korea's sense of national humiliation.[101]

Negotiations between Korea and Japan began in Tokyo on October 20, 1961. A visit by Chairman Park Chung Hee to Japan was arranged in preparation for his visit to the United States. On November 11 in Tokyo, Park held a ninety-minute personal meeting with Prime Minister Ikeda Hayato—at Ikeda's own invitation—and agreed that Korea-Japan negotiations should be rapidly initiated. This meeting was a major breakthrough in the normalization of Korea-Japan relations. In Washington, Park discussed the normalization issue with Kennedy and other American leaders.

The Korea-Japan negotiations began after a brief recess during the Japanese election season in the first half of 1962. Fully cognizant of the importance of normalizing ties with Japan, Park asked Kim Jong-pil, director of the KCIA, to take charge of the Korean negotiation team. On October 24, Kim flew to Tokyo for secret independent negotiations; on November 12 he made a secret agreement with Japanese Foreign Minister Ohira Masayoshi outlining the basis for an agreement to restore diplomatic relations. As the 1963 presidential election approached, the military government became the target of constant, bitter attacks by the opposition, which made the Korea-Japan negotiations one of the major issues in the presidential election. The Park administration resumed normalization talks with Japan almost immediately after the 1963 Korean presidential election. President Park sent Kim Jong-pil as a presidential envoy to Japan to work out the final arrangements for a treaty. On March 23, Kim, having already negotiated the preliminary arrangements in secret a year before, announced in Tokyo that a final agreement would be concluded by the end of March and a treaty signed by May.

The response was angry reactions from anti-government groups. The following day, some 80,000 students poured into the streets of major cities in protest, demanding Kim Jong-pil's immediate recall from Tokyo. The demonstrations continued for five days, despite the application of military force in an effort to restore order. On March 28, under intense student and opposition pressure, Park recalled Kim from Tokyo. But Park was not to be dissuaded. Determined to conclude the negotiations as soon as possible, in May the Park administration announced its intention of renewing normalization talks. As expected, the students and opposition took to the streets again. Throughout May a serious crisis moved to a head, threatening the very existence of the Park government. The chaotic situation was reminiscent of the 1960 student uprisings, with all Seoul streets

---

[101] Quoted in Wakamiya Yoshibumi, *The Postwar Conservative View of Asia* (Tokyo: LTCB International Library Foundation, 1999), 190.

leading from the National Assembly to the Blue House occupied by demonstrators. On June 3, 15,000 students attacked government buildings, demanding the resignation of Park. Demonstrations soon turned to rioting: police boxes were destroyed, government trucks and jeeps were seized, a police armory was robbed, and the police suffered many casualties.[102] Park believed that the student movement had exceeded its rightful boundaries and needed to be curbed. He declared martial law and deployed military forces in Seoul. Park possessed the political will and determination to subdue the strong opposition and doggedly pursued that aim. He was not doing what the anti-government elements wanted, but he was doing what he believed had to be done. At the time, the U.S. government strongly supported Park's measures.[103]

As 1965 dawned, the anti-treaty movement was renewed with increased vigor. In April 1965, the two countries agreed on a Treaty on Basic Relations. As Korea withdrew its demand for reparations (which President Rhee had so vigorously demanded), Japan offered to provide a direct grant of some $300 million and loans of $200 million to Korea, along with a promise of private investments amounting to an additional $300 million. This was at a time when Korea's total exports were $200 million. The South Korean public was outraged when they learned about the paltry settlement and also about not obtaining a formal apology from the Japanese government. By June, the streets and campuses were once more filled daily with protesting students, and demonstrations were occurring in every major city in South Korea.

On June 21, 1965, the government closed South Korea's thirteen universities, and the following day the normalization treaty was signed while the major opposition leaders went on a hunger strike.[104] Pending ratification, protests continued. On July 1, Christian leaders issued a statement protesting the treaty. On July 12, hundreds of professors appealed to the assembly not to ratify it. Aware they lacked the votes to block passage of the treaty, opposition members tried instead to find ways to kill the bill through filibusters and other delaying tactics. On August 14, the ruling party rammed the ratification of the treaty through the National Assembly in a wild session punctuated by fistfights.

Korea-Japan diplomatic normalization was undoubtedly the most serious crisis the Park regime faced.[105] The crisis inspired nearly three million people, on both sides of the issue, to participate in open demonstrations. The treaty crisis proved a great political opportunity for the opposition, as well as a severe test of survival for the government. But for the Park government, normalization represented a major turning point. The negative legacies of the past—anti-Japanese sentiment and a sense of dependency on the U.S.—eventually dissipated. The government could now concentrate its time and energies on economic growth and exports.

---

[102] *Chosun Ilbo*, June 3, 1964.

[103] Robert W. Komer of the U.S. National Security Council staff criticized the anti-government forces of Korea: "It is regrettable that the irresponsibility of a minority of the students, egged on by an irresponsible opposition, is undermining the ROK's real future hopes. This country is not ready for democracy yet, any more than it was for the Rhee-style dictatorship in the 50s." See Memorandum for the President's Special Assistant for National Security Affairs, June 3, 1964, *FRUS 1964-1968*, XXIX, 25.

[104] *Donga Ilbo*, June 23, 1965.

[105] Kwan-bong Kim, *Korea-Japan Treaty Crisis*; and Chong-sik Lee, "Korea: Troubles in a Divided State", *Asian Survey*, 5:1 (January 1965): 25.

Within several years after normalization, there were dramatic changes in Korea-Japan relations. The improvement was regarded as far greater than either side would have predicted. South Korea adopted tested Japanese technologies. Thousands of managers, engineers, bureaucrats, and company executives were sent to Japan to learn about modern Japanese technology and management style. Within little more than a year after normalization, Japan surpassed the United States as South Korea's most important trading partner, a position it maintained throughout the 1960s and 1970s. About 51 percent of technology transfer cases were from Japan while 27 percent were from the United States during 1962-1991. The foreign direct investment from Japan increased tenfold after 1965. For the total foreign direct investment during 1962-1991, 43 percent came from Japan; the United States was a distant second, with 28 percent.[106] It is now apparent that Japanese capital and technology were essential to Korea's remarkable economic growth in the years that followed normalization.[107]

Participation in the Vietnam War. While the Park government was engaging in a major struggle to normalize relations with Japan, it also initiated another important foreign policy campaign—Korea's participation in the Vietnam War.[108] When Park Chung Hee visited Washington in November 1961, he offered President Kennedy South Korean troops to assist U.S. troops in Vietnam. It was a proposal Park had coolly calculated. During a meeting in a southern port (Jinhae) in July 1963, Park informed military leaders, "If we leave Vietnam as it is, it will be taken over by the Communists. A domino effect could sweep the region, which would endanger Thailand, Malaysia and even the Philippines. This would be a danger to our national security."[109]

In August 1964, a North Vietnamese patrol boat fired a torpedo at the USS *Maddox* in Tonkin Bay in North Vietnam. Based on the Gulf of Tonkin Resolution passed by the U.S. Congress, President Lynden Johnson decided to send combat troops to Vietnam on his own initiative. On December 19, 1964, Johnson sent a message to President Park proposing South Korea contribute combat engineers and a transportation company to the growing effort in Vietnam. Park responded positively to the request, saying that the countries of the free world would share the burden. After contentious objection by the opposition, on January 26, 1965, the National Assembly approved, by an overwhelming majority, sending a contingency of 2,000 South Korean troops to Vietnam.[110] This was the first time in Korea's modern history that it dispatched a military force to another country.

By mid-April, the Vietnam situation was rapidly deteriorating, and Washington indicated a strong desire to accelerate troop deployment. In late April, Henry Cabot Lodge, the U.S. ambassador to Vietnam, came to Seoul with Johnson's message to President Park requesting Korean combat troops. Johnson also dispatched special envoy Averell Harriman to Korea to negotiate Korea's participation in the Vietnam War. Harriman suggested to Park the dispatch of Korea's first combat division to

---

[106] Sakong, *Korea in the World Economy*, 268 and 276.
[107] See Robert Castley, *Korea's Economic Miracle: The Crucial Role of Japan* (London: Macmillan, 1997).
[108] Joungwon A. Kim, "Korean Participation in the Vietnam War", *World Politics* (April 1966): 28-35.
[109] Gab-je Cho, "Spit on My Grave", *Chosun Ilbo*, August 25, 1999.
[110] *Chosun Ilbo*, January 27, 1965.

South Vietnam and also asked him to visit the United States for further consultations.[111]

Park apparently saw the American request as an opportunity to increase Korea's leverage with the United States in terms of economic and military assistance as well as American commitments to South Korean security. Moreover, he saw an opportunity for gaining battlefield experience for the Korean army and for earning substantial amounts of American dollars. In contrast to the common belief that Park sent troops to Vietnam only for economic gain, recently declassified sources reveal his main agenda. Korean involvement in the Vietnam War was intended to strengthen the U.S. security commitment to Korea. Park foresaw that if Korea refused to assist the United States in Vietnam, Washington might withdraw its troops from Korea and send them to Vietnam. The two U.S. army divisions in Korea were the only available troops Washington could mobilize. Reduction or total withdrawal of the American ground troops from Korea would have a serious and detrimental impact on South Korean security and economic development. According to an aide to U.S. Secretary of Defense Robert S. McNamara, the United States was considering troop reductions in South Korea in 1963 and 1966, but these plans were not carried out because of Johnson's overriding interest in enlisting allies for combat in Vietnam.[112] Park's decision to deploy troops to Vietnam was intended primarily to induce the United States to maintain its force level in Korea. During the negotiations, the United States repeated many times its commitment that "no U.S. troops will be withdrawn from Korea without prior consultation with the Republic of Korea."[113]

On May 16, 1965, Park again visited Washington. One reason behind President Johnson's invitation was to assure Park that the United States would not abandon South Korea to Japanese control in the wake of the Korea-Japan settlement. Johnson assured Park of the maintenance of American force levels in the South and a strong commitment to continued U.S. assistance. During the summit meeting, Johnson asked Park whether Korea could send one combat division to Vietnam. Park replied that his people would be worrying about Korea's defense by sending too many troops to Vietnam. Johnson guaranteed Korean security and promised economic and military assistance to ensure it.

On August 18, the ruling party passed a bill authorizing the government to dispatch 20,000 troops to Vietnam, while opposition members boycotted the National Assembly session. In October, the so-called "Tiger Division" departed for Vietnam. In a sending-off ceremony for the Korean troops in Seoul, President Park declared, "The history of Korea is at a turning point. In the past, we have depended on foreign assistance, but we are about to embark on a new age in which we can lend help to others."[114] Park was making the point that South Korea was a worthy ally, willing to take risks and to suffer

---

[111] Telegram from U.S. Embassy in Korea to the Department of State, April 27, 1965, *FRUS 1964-1968*, XXIX, 79-80.

[112] U.S. House of Representatives, *Investigation of Korean-American Relations* (Washington, DC: U.S. Government Printing Office, 1978), 61.

[113] Stanley R. Larson and James L. Collins, Jr., *Allied Participation in Vietnam* (Washington, DC: Department of the Army, 1975), 95; Seoul Embassy Telegram 1238, 9 September 1967, NSF, Box 91, LBJ Library; and Princeton N. Lyman, "Korea's Involvement in Vietnam", *Orbis*, 12:2 (summer 1967).

[114] Bum Shik Shin, *Major Speeches*, 281.

for the interests of the non-Communist world.

In early 1966, through the visit of American Vice President Hubert Humphrey and other diplomatic channels, the United States asked South Korea to send an additional division to Vietnam, and South Korea and the United States soon began talks on the dispatching of additional Korean troops. On March 7, after several weeks of negotiations between the two countries, Foreign Minister Lee Dong-won and U.S. Ambassador Harold Brown announced a fourteen-point agreement known as the Brown Memorandum, which would go on to form the basis for U.S. aid to Korea in exchange for the commitment of additional troops.[115]

Among the American promises were compensation for the total cost of sending the additional troops to Vietnam; the seventeen army divisions and one marine division of the Korean armed forces would be brought up to date with modern equipment; the United States would equip three additional reserve divisions in Korea to replace the troops being sent to Vietnam; the Military Assistance Program to Korea would cease to purchase American goods and replace them with purchases of Korean goods paid for by dollars; the United States would improve anti-infiltration measures in Korea, and increased production of ammunition and material in Korea would be promoted.

Because of his shrewd negotiations, Park not only delayed the U.S. planned reduction in military and economic aid, but also maximized U.S. support for Korea's economic development and military modernization plans. Under the Brown Memorandum, about $1 billion in American payments went to Korea in the period between 1965 and 1970. The United States also paid vast sums to supply new military equipment, and provide assistance to South Korean civilian workers in Vietnam. It is estimated that this arrangement annually accounted for between 7 and 8 percent of Korea's GDP in the period between 1966 and 1969 and for as much as 19 percent of its total foreign earnings.[116]

While some 50,000 Korean soldiers were fighting in Vietnam, some 16,000 Korean technicians, business people, and workers were busy there as well. Korean firms won lucrative contracts to market their products, and the Korean service sector provided services to both American and Korean troops stationed there. Korean construction companies took advantage of construction projects in Vietnam. Those projects accounted for 94 percent of Korea's total steel exports and 52 percent of its exports of transportation equipment.[117] The exports of South Korean cement and fertilizer also amounted to 70 percent and 75 percents of its total exports respectively in 1970.[118] If the normalization of relations with Japan was a critical component in Park's ambitious plans for modernization, the Vietnam War was a fortuitous economic bonanza for Korea. The Vietnam War boom, like the Korea-Japan normalization treaty, gave the economy an important lift during its critical take-off period—similar to what the Korean War did for Japan in the 1950s.

---

[115] Joungwon A. Kim, "Korean Participation in the Vietnam War", *World Affairs* (spring 1966): 34.
[116] Macdonald, *U.S.-Korea Relations*, 110. In 1966 the war accounted for 40 percent of Korea's crucial foreign exchange receipts. It was estimated that the overall total was about $10 billion. See Frank Baldwin, *Without Parallel: the American-Korean Relationship Since 1945*, 30.
[117] Woo, *Race*, 95-96.
[118] Lie, *Han Unbound*, 64-65.

Visit to West Germany. From the beginning, Park Chung Hee had been interested in the successful economic recovery of West Germany after the devastation of World War II. West Germany shared with South Korea the misfortune of national division. Park repeatedly pointed to the economic miracle of West Germany as a model for Korean national development. In his 1963 book, *The Country, the Revolution and I*, Park paid special attention to German economic success, dedicating an entire chapter to its postwar reconstruction.

Park visited West Germany during the first year of his term. At the ceremony marking his departure for Europe, he remarked, "I will examine the details of that country's recovery and prosperity, its great economic reconstruction accomplished while confronting the Communists."[119] On the way to West Germany, Park questioned his translator, the German-educated economics professor Paik Young-hoon, on the German economy: "Can you tell me about the West German economy? They say that the country's success is the 'miracle on the Rhine.' What generated this miracle? What are the key industries of Germany?" After explaining some details on the German economy, Dr. Paik said, "I would say that it was the successful economic policy pursued by German Chancellor Ludwig Erhard."[120]

When President Park met with German Chancellor Erhard, the man who, as the West German economic minister, had achieved the "miracle on the Rhine," he asked numerous questions about the revival of the German economy. Erhard summarized the major factors that contributed to the German success: the expansion of social overhead capital, such as highways and harbors, investment in basic industries, early recovery of a market economy, and promotion of small and medium firms. Erhard emphasized that the only way to beat the Communists as a divided nation was to build a strong economy, then he explained how the autobahns had contributed to the German economy.[121]

Park traveled on the autobahn from Bonn to Köln. He was informed that the Germans were very proud of having built the expressway because it was a symbol of German economic revival. During the 160-kilometer per hour trip, Park stopped the car twice so that he could study the center divider, the road surface, and the crossing facilities. He asked his German guide, the chief of protocol to the German president, many questions: "How did you construct an expressway? How much did construction cost? How did you raise the money? How do you maintain them?"[122]

During his visit to Germany, Park visited a coalmine in the Ruhr region where Korean coal miners were working. Some 300 Korean coal miners and fifty Korean nurses welcomed their president at the mine. Park walked to the pithead and embraced some of the Korean workers, whose faces were black with coal dust. Inside a hall of the coalmine company, a Korean coalminer brass band played the Korean national anthem and all the Koreans sang along. Many of the Korean workers began to cry and could not finish the national anthem. The president and the first lady also cried. Then Park tried to deliver a prepared speech but he was so deeply touched the speech became impromptu: "My beloved young men and women, I know you really miss your family and hometown.

---

[119] *Chosun Ilbo*, December 7, 1964.
[120] Gab-je Cho (1998), vol. 6, 180.
[121] Chung–Yum Kim, *Policymaking*, 114-115.
[122] Cho Gab-je, *Naemudome*, vol. 6, 186-197.

Even if we may not achieve while we are alive, we must build the foundation of prosperity for next generations..."[123] The participants were weeping silently, and Park could not finish his speech. Most of the Korean workers at the German mines were college graduates in Korea, but were working in the German mines because of the lack of jobs in South Korea. On his return to Bonn, Park appeared very gloomy, at times teary-eyed. It was a moving experience, which strengthened Park's determination to make Korea prosperous and independent.[124]

After returning to Seoul, Park wrote of his impressions of West Germany, including the reasons for and lessons of the German economic miracle. He noted, "As Korea and Germany are each a nation of one race, we should each be reunited as one country, and that unification should be achieved through peaceful means, and to this end freedom and economic prosperity are the first tasks to solve."[125] Park's visit to Germany had a considerable impact on his subsequent strategies and policies toward Korean modernization.

In fact, Park wisely maneuvered his foreign policy to support his primary goal of economic development. Along with the normalization of relations with Japan and Korea's participation in the Vietnam War, the Park administration opened a radically different diplomatic front. In its new foreign policy outlook, the government drastically altered the Rhee government's emphasis on ideology and nationalism as criteria in foreign policy, pursuing instead flexible and pragmatic goals. Before the 1961 military revolution, Korea had maintained diplomatic relations with only twenty-two nations. From 1961, the Park government began an aggressive campaign to open diplomatic relations in order to extend Korea's export markets to nations there, regardless of their ideological positions, sending goodwill missions to the nations of South and Southeast Asia, the Middle East, and Africa.[126] By 1972, the number of embassies had increased to eighty-four, the consulates to thirty-one.

THE FOURTH REPUBLIC (1972-79)

> "When a national survival is at stake, politics, economy, culture, and everything should be organized and mobilized for that single purpose."
>
> —Park Chung Hee

Until 1971 South Korea operated under the political framework it adopted in 1963. Even though Park imposed some restrictions on members of the press, intellectuals, and opposition politicians, these groups were permitted considerable latitude to criticize the government and to engage in anti-government activities. But from the late 1960s the Park government faced a number of internal and external challenges simultaneously. A sense of crisis over national security ultimately led Park to adopt a system of rigid authoritarianism and to build heavy and chemical industries, including defense industries.

---

[123] Ibid., 202-205.
[124] Author interview with Kim Chung Yum, August 23, 2001.
[125] Park Chung Hee, "Impressions of Visits to West Germany", in Bum Shik Shin, *Major Speeches*, 19-21.
[126] Seung K. Ko, "South Korea's Policy toward the Non-Aligned Countries", *Asian Forum*, 3:2 (1971): 111-117.

Emerging Crises from Within and Without. In the mid-1960s, while South Korean forces were fighting in the jungles of Vietnam, North Korea stepped up its infiltration and provocation activities. Encouraged by the success of Communist guerrilla warfare in Vietnam, Kim Il Sung was determined to liberate the southern half of Korea in his own lifetime.[127] A special force of North Korea's 25,000-strong well-trained commandos and guerrillas was already infiltrating the South. In 1967, North Korea's provocations escalated to an alarming extent, with 784 guerrilla-related incidents. The raids continued in 1968, when more than 600 infiltrations were reported.[128]

On January 21, 1968, thirty-one well-trained commandos of the North Korean 124th Unit (special forces) made a daring incursion across the truce line to raid the Blue House. Around ten o'clock in the evening, just 600 yards from the Blue House compound, the infiltrators, who wore civilian clothes and topcoats and were armed with submachine guns and hand grenades, were halted by the police. In the ensuing gunfight in the central part of Seoul, and the subsequent two-week long search for those commandos who escaped, twenty-nine North Korean infiltrators were killed, one (Kim Shin-jo) was captured, and one escaped. Twenty-six South Korean soldiers, two U.S. soldiers, one police officer, and six civilians were killed, while fifty-six others were wounded. According to an excerpt from the interrogation of Kim Shin-jo, the mission was to "chop off Park Chung Hee's head." On January 23, less than 48 hours after the raid, North Korean forces seized an unarmed U.S. intelligence-gathering vessel, the USS *Pueblo* with its crew of 83, in international waters off Wonsan, North Korea. President Park now considered his country to be in a state of security crisis.[129]

Faced with these military provocations, Park concluded that efforts for a peaceful solution would not stem, and might even accelerate, North Korean infiltrations and raids. In a letter to President Johnson on February 5, Park stated, "The Communists should be taught a lesson that any aggressive action cannot escape due punitive action."[130] Replying to Park, Johnson expressed concern about North Korea's provocative acts but rejected his request: "the seizure of the *Pueblo*...must be dealt with promptly and decisively.... The security of the Republic of Korea...is a continuing problem."[131] The Johnson administration had apparently decided to avoid the risk of

---

[127] See Kim Il Sung, Let Us Embody More Thoroughly the Revolutionary Spirit of Independence, Self-Sustenance and Self-Defense in All Fields of State Activity (Pyongyang: Foreign Languages Publishing House, 1967), 20-29.

[128] "Security Conditions in South Korea", Report Prepared by the Office of National Estimates of the Central Intelligence Agency, June 23, 1967, FRUS *1964-1968*, XXIX, 257-259; and Soon-sung Cho, "North and South Korea: Stepped-up Aggression and the Search for New Security", *Asian Survey*, 9:1 (January 1969): 29-39. Among 3,693 armed infiltrations from the North since 1950, about 20 percent occurred during 1967-68 (Rinn S. Shinn, *North Korea: Chronology of Provocations, 1950-2000, Congressional Research Service Reports,* January 22, 2001).

[129] In a telegram sent to the chairman of the Joint Chiefs of Staff, General Wheeler, on January 24, 1968, General Bonesteel reported that Kim Il Sung believed that the U.S. military effort was so extended in support of Vietnam that the United States was unable to adequately assist South Korea. See FRUS *1964-1968*, XXIX, 313-315.

[130] Letter from President Park to President Johnson, FRUS *1964-1968*, XXIX, no. 155

[131] Letter from President Johnson to President Park, FRUS *1964-1968*, XXIX, no. 159.

opening a second Asian front. Subsequently, Washington engaged directly in secret negotiations with North Korea at Panmunjom. There was a strong feeling at all levels in South Korea that the U.S. government had not responded adequately to the North Korean assault on the Blue House—the national symbol of the Republic. If the North Korean commandos had succeeded in hitting the Blue House there would have been an all-out war. The U.S.-North Korean negotiations created suspicion among South Koreans and a loss of confidence in the United States. Koreans felt that Washington placed higher priority on the *Pueblo* incident than on that of the Korean presidential office. They demanded that negotiations at Panmunjom should not be limited to the *Pueblo* but should also address the raid on the Blue House.

Park, confirmed in his conviction that his country should strengthen its capability to defend against aggression from the North, acted immediately. On February 7, 1968, he announced that the government would establish a homeland reserve force of 2.5 million men. In 1969, the government introduced military training programs for high schools and colleges. Two factors appear to have motivated Park. First, he saw the need to be fully prepared for a total showdown with North Korea. Second, Park aimed to rely on Korean resources for national survival. It was in this spirit that Park introduced national slogans such as "Our Fatherland with Our Own Strength" and "National Defense on the One Hand, Construction on the Other."

North Korea's provocations intensified during 1968. Several North Korean commando landings on South Korea's east coast were intercepted and repelled. For example, in November 1968, 130 sea-borne commandos infiltrated the eastern mountains in an attempt to organize a Vietnamese-type guerrilla war, attacking villages intermittently for more than a month. In March 1969, six North Korean commandos killed a South Korean policeman in an eastern coastal area.[132] In April, an EC-121 American reconnaissance plane flying over the East Sea some ninety miles off the North Korean coast, was shot down by a North Korean air patrol, and three of its four crew members were killed. Park's anxieties over Korean security and over American commitment to it increased when the United States once again refused to retaliate when North Korea shot down the American reconnaissance plane.

A sudden shift in U.S. Asian policy further increased South Korea's sense of security crisis. On July 25, 1969, President Nixon announced his new Asian policy, the "Nixon Doctrine," which ruled out direct involvement by American forces in any possible war in Asia, including Korea. The doctrine signaled a U.S. withdrawal from Vietnam without victory, virtually abandoning Seoul's counterpart regime in Saigon. For South Korea, whose security rested greatly upon the United States, the doctrine represented a potentially dangerous shift in America's security commitment, coming at a time when North Korean provocations were intensifying. The Nixon administration wanted to get out of South Vietnam as soon as possible. To the Nixon administration, South Korea seemed the best possibility for implementing the doctrine outside of Vietnam. The sudden announcement of American troop withdrawal from Korea in July 1970 touched a sensitive nerve among South Korean leaders. Without prior consultation with the Park government, the Nixon administration decided to remove 20,000 of the 62,000 American troops stationed in South Korea, with the

---

[132] In 1969, over 150 infiltrations were attempted, involving almost 400 agents.

rest to be phased out over the next five years.[133] Park and his government were appalled by the withdrawal plan and publicly showed their disappointment, anger, and feelings of betrayal. Many Koreans believed their country would be the next domino to fall in Asia.

Park desperately sought to reverse the withdrawal decision. During a meeting with U.S. Ambassador William Porter, Park insisted that the United States had no right to withdraw its troops and that he would not allow it. Faced with strong Korean resistance, Nixon sent Vice President Spiro Agnew to Seoul in late August. Agnew failed to persuade Park that the withdrawal did not mean the United States was abandoning its commitment to defend Korea. In a meeting scheduled to last one hour, Park and Agnew went at it for a full six hours. There were no breaks for coffee, lunch, or even to go to the toilet.[134] In March 1971, over Park's vehement objections, the United States completed the withdrawal of almost a third of its total forces in Korea. The withdrawal was one of the most significant changes in U.S. policy toward Korea since the Korean War.[135]

In February 1971, in his annual foreign policy message to the Congress, Nixon declared: "The post-war order in international relations is gone. With it are gone the conditions which have determined the assumptions and practices of United States foreign policy since 1945."[136] In February 1972, Nixon made his historic visit to China and declared in the Shanghai joint communiqué that "there is but one China and that Taiwan is a part of China." The announcement meant an effective end to American support for Taiwan, South Korea's close anti-Communist ally. Park worried that South Korea would be a scapegoat for the big powers. In other words, Nixon's historic détente with China became a security nightmare for Park and his government. The Nixon Doctrine led the Park government to conclude that it would be unrealistic to rely heavily on U.S. commitment for its security.

Sino-American détente had immediate and direct influences on inter-Korean relations. For both Koreas, the détente meant that traditional cold war ideologies became largely untenable. They were compelled to search for new identities and roles in the rapidly changing international environment. In August 1971, within a month of the announcement of Nixon's China visit, the two Koreas agreed to hold Red Cross talks to arrange a reunion among members of separated families. In the wake of some ten months of Red Cross talks came a more dramatic opening of direct "political" talks between Seoul and Pyongyang. On July 4, 1972, South and North Korea surprised the world by publicly issuing a Joint Communiqué, in which the two Koreas agreed on three principles of unification—through independent efforts, peaceful means, and national

---

[133] U.S. Secretary of Defense Melvin Laird had planned for a phased withdrawal of all U.S. forces from South Korea. When Vice President Spiro Agnew visited Seoul to negotiate with President Park the first troop withdrawals, he confirmed that all U.S. forces in Korea were to be withdrawn within five years. See *The Washington Post*, August 27, 1970; and Ambassadors William Porter and Winthrop Brown in their joint congressional testimony in 1970: U.S. Congress Report, *U.S. Security Agreements and Commitments Abroad*, 1970, 1530-1533.

[134] Boettcher, *Gifts of Deceit*, 89-91.

[135] Robert A. Scalapino, "Korea and Vietnam", in Wayne Wilcox et al., eds., *Asia and the International System* (Cambridge, MA: Winthrop, 1972), 153.

[136] Richard M. Nixon, U.S. Foreign Policy for the 1970s: Building for Peace, A Report to the Congress, February 25, 1971 (Washington, D.C.: U.S. Government Printing Office, 1971).

unity. It was the first meaningful South-North dialogue since the signing of the armistice nearly two decades before.

In the South-North dialogue (from December 1972), Seoul started, on the one hand, with the easiest, nonpolitical tasks, such as economic and cultural exchanges, and then gradually proceeded to political and security issues. On the other hand, Pyongyang primarily focused on political and military issues. The North argued that the South should first sign a peace treaty formally ending the Korean War and U.S. forces should be withdrawn. It also called for a mutual reduction in armed forces on both sides to 100,000. Seoul found Pyongyang's proposals unrealistic and dangerous considering the history and reality of North Korea's military threat. It quickly became obvious that there was a fundamental disagreement between the two sides. The inter-Korean dialogue reached a stalemate during the first part of 1973.

As expected, neither the South nor the North was ready to negotiate anything of substantial value. Park planned to strengthen South Korea's economic and defense capabilities while avoiding direct confrontation with North Korea. He had no interest in rapprochement with North Korea, as he did not believe it was truly possible.[137] On the other hand, Kim Il Sung began to see certain advantages in the U.S.-China rapprochement. He saw the inter-Korean dialogue as a way of separating South Korea from the United States and bringing about the withdrawal of U.S. troops from the South. While the secret meetings between Seoul and Pyongyang were going on, Kim Il Sung, in an interview with *The New York Times*, urged the United States to withdraw troops from South Korea to improve U.S.-North Korean relations.[138] Then, in April 1973, North Korea's legislature, the Supreme People's Assembly, sent a telegram to the U.S. Congress referring to the developments on the peninsula and asking U.S. lawmakers for help in withdrawing American troops from the South, just as they had been removed from South Vietnam.[139]

On the economic front, the Park government also faced serious challenges. Economic growth declined continuously from 1969. External factors dealt a blow to the economy: with the partial withdrawal of American troops in Korea, foreign investor confidence in the Korean economy plummeted—a serious matter for a country that had financed more than a quarter of its total imports with foreign credit.[140] The economic situation deteriorated even more as most industrial countries, the destination of Korea's exports, went into recession, triggering an increase in protectionism. The IMF stepped in with a stabilization program. However, the IMF austerity program further intensified the financial troubles of business. Unable to get subsidized state loans, businesses were forced into bankruptcies. To stave off massive bankruptcies and to stimulate the economy, President Park issued, on August 3, 1972, the Emergency Decree on Economic Stabilization and Growth. Under the decree, all outstanding "private loans" already extended to firms were frozen for three years; after a three-year grace period, the borrowers could pay them back over the following five years at a monthly interest rate of

---

[137] Interview with Kim Chung-yum.
[138] *New York Times*, May 31, 1972.
[139] Oberdorfer, *Two Koreas*, 45.
[140] Woo, *Race*, 124.

1.35 percent.[141]

Encouraged by the results of the 1971 presidential and parliamentary elections, opposition forces became more visible and active, and the Park regime was plagued by persistent and increasingly militant demonstrations. Student demonstrations during 1971 reportedly involved hundreds of thousands of participants in 225 rallies. By autumn 1971, social disorder in Seoul, caused by massive anti-government movements, reached dangerous levels. Facing multiple external and domestic challenges at the same time, Park concluded, "The Republic of Korea at the moment is faced with a critical situation in terms of its national security,"[142] and declared a state of national emergency in December 1971. Then the ruling party passed a bill granting the president complete power to control, regulate, and mobilize the people, the economy, the press, and everything else in the public domain. Despite the special measures, anti-government demonstrations, now joined by professionals and intellectuals, intensified in 1972. In April, major press associations banded together and issued a joint declaration asserting freedom of the press. In July, a judicial crisis ensued when a substantial number of judges tendered their resignations en masse in protest against government interference in the judicial process. In August, university professors adopted resolutions calling for a guarantee of academic freedom.

The Yushin System. October 17, 1972, in a special declaration, "October Yushin," often dubbed as a "coup in office," President Park abruptly proclaimed martial law, suspending the constitution which he himself had promulgated in 1962 and amended in 1969. Under the decree, he dissolved the National Assembly, outlawed all political activities, imposed tight press censorship, and temporarily closed all universities. These measures were necessary, as Park's spokesman put it, because "we must have unity in order to have a dialogue with the North" and because South Korea "cannot afford to risk political unity when North Koreas have complete control over everything their people say and do."[143] Park stated later, on January 12, 1973, that the constitutional revision was necessary to cope with the "great changes" on the international scene, which according to him included such events as the Sino-U.S. rapprochement, the Sino-Japanese diplomatic normalization, the severing of Japan's official ties with Taiwan, the deteriorating situation in Vietnam, and uncertainty in the South-North Korean dialogue.[144] Although Park did not state it outright at the time, his action was probably also motivated by insecurity over the withdrawal of some 20,000 American soldiers, the U.S. Seventh Division, in March 1971.

From the early days of his regime, Park made his intention clear to put modernization and national security ahead of democracy. After the successful completion of the two five-year development plans, Park's push for modernization seemed to be elevated almost to the level of zealotry. He expressed a strong distaste for what in his view was the irresponsible and unproductive nature of "democratic" politics. Ironically, South Koreans' exposure to North Koreans made Park nervous about South

---

[141] The real cost of capital from 1966 to 1970 averaged 39.6 percent for curb market loans, 9.8 percent for domestic loans, and minus 3.1 percent for foreign loans (Amsden, *Asia's Next Giant*, 76).

[142] *Korea Annual* 1972, 21.

[143] *Hankook Ilbo*, October 18, 1972.

[144] *Donga Ilbo*, January 12, 1973.

Korea's internal weakness. Kim Il Sung had built a strong one-man system and ruthlessly suppressed dissidents. Such unity gave the impression of total strength. Park believed Kim Il Sung was no ordinary man. Park stated: "As long as Kim Il Sung is alive, the Republic of Korea is never safe. I am the only man who can deal with Kim Il Sung."[145] In Park's opinion, none of the other potential South Korean leaders—Kim Jong-pil, Kim Young Sam, or Kim Dae Jung—was any match for Kim Il Sung. The social unrest in the South gave an impression of fragility. Park believed that "less politics" would be more conducive to guarantee national security and to bring about rapid economic growth. Park's primacy of security and development over democracy was based on his strategic choice between economic prosperity, which was perceived as leading to general levels of security, on the one hand, and individual rights and political freedom, which were perceived as not necessarily providing decent living standards, on the other.

The State Council, which acted with the authority of the National Assembly, promulgated a new *Yushin* Constitution. The new constitution did not abandon democratic ideals, but sidelined them for the sake of security, stability, and economic development. The constitution, which borrowed some elements from the Fifth Republic constitution of France and the Sukarno constitution of Indonesia, gave Park unprecedented power.[146] It established the president above the three branches of government. The president's term of office was set at six years, but with an unlimited right to re-election, thereby legitimizing a lifetime presidency for Park. The president was to be elected indirectly by the newly created National Conference for Unification consisting of 2,560 members, half appointed by the president, the other half elected from a personally approved list of candidates. The president was empowered to nominate one-third of the National Assembly members, to dissolve the National Assembly at will, and to take emergency measures in cases of national emergency and threats to national security. At the same time, the new constitution severely restricted the basic rights of the people.

The *Yushin* constitution was approved by 91.5 percent in a national referendum held on November 21, 1972. In December, Park was reelected president by the newly created electoral college, and he was re-inaugurated as president for a six-year term (1972-1978). The Fourth Republic was abruptly established, and Park emerged as an undisputed, powerful dictator. *Yushin*, meaning "revitalizing reforms," was borrowed from a Japanese term describing the period following the Japanese Meiji Restoration of 1868 (called in Japanese, Meiji *Yishin*), a time of aggressive industrial and military growth in Japan. Park wanted to complete the task of modernizing Korea in the way Japan had modernized during the Meiji era (1868-1912). It took more than four decades for the Meiji government to modernize Japan. Park's ten years in office would be insufficient to build a modern Korea.

To accomplish his goals, Park was now playing a desperate game, gambling that he could both speed up the revolution of "national restoration" and control its direction. He was virtually fighting against the tide of history: he had reversed the course of political

---

[145] Lee Suk-jae, *op. cit.*, 46.
[146] Interview with Kim Chung-yum on March 20, 2001.

development by establishing the *Yushin* system.[147] Through the transition from the Third to the Fourth Republic, Park and his cohorts had shown their inherent political limitations. The institutional development of democracy, which Park and his associates had pledged to pursue in the early 1960s, had been discarded. The establishment of a one-man authoritarian regime, a retrogressive step, was more complex than a simple palace coup. Nevertheless, Park could take comfort in the examples of Asia's other long-term authoritarian leaders, such as Chiang Kai-shek, Lee Kwan Yew, Ferdinand Marcos, and Mohamed Suharto. As soon as Park had consolidated and prolonged his power, he initiated some aggressive policy measures, such as the "Big Push" in heavy and defense industries, the New Village Movement, and an attempt to promote a secret nuclear program.

The Big Push. The export-oriented industrialization policies had created light industries, which depended on the import of capital and intermediate goods for production and export. In order to build a self-sustaining "independent" economy, it was necessary for the Park government to establish domestic production bases for materials, intermediate goods, and capital goods. To Park, economic development was synonymous with heavy industries such as steel, auto, and machinery. It was always his dream to make heavy industries, and not shoes or wigs, the symbol of his industrialization drive. As late as 1970, plywood was the second-largest export, trailing textiles; wigs were third. The huge export gains in light industries were beginning to level off. Other developing countries were now playing the same game, pushing exports of labor-intensive products. A World Bank study pointed out that "unless new exports are vigorously developed, Korea cannot hope to capture an increasing share of the world market of manufacturing goods."[148] It was time for the Park government to switch its emphasis toward heavy and chemical industries.

Park was a nationalistic leader. He wanted to build up an economically and militarily self-reliant nation, independent from both Japan and the United States. After the Nixon Doctrine, refuge could no longer be found in the indulgence of a mutual defense treaty with the United States. Heavy industries were considered essential to constructing the nation's self-defense capabilities. The development of heavy industries held the promise of a vibrant defense industry that could provide the means for long-term defense against North Korea and end the reliance on American largess in weaponry, thus avoiding its various attendant political inconveniences. Park's ultimate goal was to catch up with Japan—to build a strong economy and a modern society. But Korea still had a long way to go.

During his New Year's press conference in January 1973, Park announced a bold new economic initiative: his government would promote the heavy and chemical industries (HCI) so that by 1980 Korea could be one of the leading developing countries, with a per capita income of $1,000 and exports of $10 billion.[149] Designed to both upgrade and diversify Korean exports, as well as reduce the country's import dependence, the plan targeted the development of six new industries: iron and steel, petrochemicals, electronics, machinery, shipbuilding, and transport equipment. The ambition was to turn the country from a final

---

[147] Hak-Kyu Son, *Authoritarianism and Opposition in South Korea*; and C. I. Eugene Kim, "Korea at the Crossroads: The Birth of the Fourth Republic", *Pacific Affairs*, 46: 2 (summer 1973), 218-231.

[148] Parvej Hasan and D.C. Rao, *Korea: Policy Issues for Long Term Development* (Baltimore: Johns Hopkins University press, 1979), 79.

[149] Economic Planning Board, *Long-Term Perspective Plan (1972-1981)*, 1973.

processor of export goods to one of the world's major exporters of steel, ships, autos and other manufactured goods. The goals looked overly optimistic. Exports in 1972 were only $1.6 billion and per capita income just $318. Exports would have to be increased six times and per capita income three times in eight years. Most Western advisers and American-educated Korean economists had strong reservations about the program. They believed that since labor was cheap in Korea, the country should stay in labor-intensive industries.[150]

In order to develop heavy industries, Park further centralized economic decision-making in the Blue House. He appointed a second senior secretary for economic affairs to take charge of the heavy and chemical industries and the defense industry. He also established a special Blue House task force, called the Corps for Planning and Management of Heavy and Chemical Industries. The task force drew up a ten-year master plan for five industries—shipbuilding, machinery, chemicals, steel, and nonferrous metals, envisioning a total investment of approximately $9.6 billion. The Heavy and Chemical Industries Promotion Act was enacted to support these industries and the National Investment Fund was set up to fund the plan. The president and his advisers decided where plants would be built, what their capacity would be, and which companies would build them. The president himself asked the conglomerates to carry out each project, thereby contributing to the creation and strengthening of the big *chaebol* (conglomerates, or *zaibatsu*). The government provided astronomical "policy loans" to fund heavy industries.

The *chaebol* established heavy industries such as shipbuilding, petrochemicals, automobiles, and electronics. These were all businesses with big economies of scale, so concentration on them encouraged the growth of big conglomerates like Samsung, Hyundai, Daewoo and Lucky-Goldstar. Development of these new industries was combined with an overall national development plan. The government created a large industrial complex for each of the targeted heavy and chemical industries. By the end of the Fourth Five-Year Plan (1977-1981), the Yosu industrial complex had been built for petrochemicals, the Changwon complex for machinery, the Pohang complex for steel, the Okpo complex for shipbuilding, the Kumi complex for electronics, and the Onsan complex for a nonferrous metal industry.[151]

The results of the big push were impressive.[152] The economy grew by an average of 11 percent from 1973 to 1978, with heavy industry accounting for 70 percent of total manufacturing investment. The share of heavy and chemical industries in manufacturing output increased from 39.7 percent in 1972 to 54.9 percent in 1979. Moreover, the percentage of heavy and chemical exports in total exports increased from 13.7 percent in 1971 to 37.7 percent in 1979. By the end of 1977 Korea had reached the goal of $10

---

[150] For details on the heavy and chemical industry drive, see Suk-chae Lee, "The Heavy and Chemical Industries Promotion Plan (1973-1979)", in Cho and Kim, eds., *Economic Development*, 431-471.

[151] Changwon was the largest. It became the center of steel, machine, automobile, and shipbuilding industries. The Park government estimated that about half of the nation's total industrial production would take place in Changwon by the early 1980s. Two hundred and twenty companies with about 100,000 workers were scheduled to operate.

[152] Woo, *Race*, 155.

billion in annual exports.[153] The government held a large celebration at the Jangchoong Gymnasium in Seoul. At the party, President Park proudly declared:

> We have finally achieved the target of $10 billion in annual exports. Korea's exports in the beginning year (1962) of the first five-year plan amounted to $55 million. Fifteen years later, we have reached the target, that is, 4 years earlier than originally planned. It took West Germany, a major economic power, 11 years to reach an annual export of $10 billion from $1 billion, and it took Japan 16 years. Korea has done it in only 7 years. And we have made this great achievement under the most difficult conditions: that is, we have achieved it amid constant threat from the most belligerent North Korea, and despite a worldwide recession. The achievement of $10 billion has a great significance for us, for it represents the unlimited ability and potential of our nation.[154]

By the end of the 1970s, South Korea had become the number-one third-world exporter of manufactured goods to developed countries. Its efficient steel industry, its modern shipyards, its production of advanced electronics all bespoke a successful economic transformation. To most observers, it was obvious that South Korea had become a major industrial power and a model for third-world countries. It was a grand success and a declaration of Korean industrial sovereignty.[155] But just as importantly, Park was prevailing in the economic contest with Kim Il Sung. In 1974, South Korea surpassed the North in per capita income for the first time since the division of the country. During the decade after the Korean War, the centrally controlled economy of North Korea had grown more rapidly than market-oriented South Korea's. But by 1977 the balance of economic power on the peninsula was shifting decisively in favor of the South.

The New Village Movement. One of Park's pledges in the October 1972 special declaration was to give priority to the *Saemaul* (New Village) Movement in national policy. Park frequently emphasized the close relation between the *Yushin* reform and the New Village Movement by saying, "The October reforms is another way of saying the *saemaul* movement." Thus, the movement became an important part of his new leadership strategy, and it was initiated with the full support of the president and his government.[156]

During his first ten years, Park concentrated most of his resources and efforts on industrialization. As a result, the income gap between urban and rural areas was widening. Park was acutely conscious of the problems farmers faced and had a strong commitment to eradicating the poverty in rural areas. In order to modernize the whole country, the poor rural areas had to be changed as well. Thus, Park called for a rural development strategy based on cooperative village self-reliance.

Park remained the driving force of the movement. He wrote both the words and

---

[153] Roy Rowan, "There Is Also Some Good News About South Korea", *Fortune*, September 1977.
[154] *Chosun Ilbo*, December 23, 1977.
[155] In 1970 Korea had a remarkable 86 percent rate of dependency on foreign imports in machine tools. By 1977, domestic parts made up 90 percent of Korean autos.
[156] For details on the New Village Movement, see Ban, Sung Hwan et al., *Rural Development* (Cambridge, MA: Council on East Asian Studies, Harvard University Press, 1980); and In-Joung Whang, *Management of Rural Change in Korea: the Saemaul Undong* (Seoul: Seoul National University Press, 1981).

music for the *saemaul* song, and designed the *saemaul* flag by himself, making it clear that he was strongly committed to the success of the movement. *Saemaul* leaders were invited to talk about their villages' successes at the monthly economic meetings chaired by the president. The leaders were awarded with *saemaul* medals during the meeting. He frequently visited "new villages" all over the country, dressed in plain clothes and sporting a straw hat. He tried to identify himself with farmers by working alongside them in the rice paddies, sharing Korean rice wine (*maggoli*), embracing elderly farmwomen, and lecturing their husbands. His rural-oriented attitudes and behavior motivated the farmers to participate enthusiastically in the movement.

The launch of the New Village Movement was an important milestone in the modernization of Korea. Korea had been an agriculturally oriented society. In order to help peasants out of their enduring poverty, the movement aimed to enlighten the rural populace, improve their living conditions, and increase their income. Each rural village was encouraged to devise its own developmental programs in order to secure aid from the government. Numerous small-scale projects to improve the rural living environment were undertaken with the voluntary participation of local people. Bridges, access roads to farms, washing facilities, wells, irrigation canals, dikes, and small reservoirs were built as part of the self-help programs, with the government lending support in the form of cement and other required materials and equipment.

For thousands of years the Korean countryside had remained quite literally the "land of morning calm." With *saemaul*, the villages were no longer calm in the morning. At 6:00 a.m., all village loudspeakers played the *saemaul* song: "The dawn bell rang already, let you and I get up and turn our efforts to building our *saemaul*. Let us make a prosperous *saemaul* with our own hands!" Then came a *saemaul* pledge in the form of loud speeches. The green-and-yellow *saemaul* flag flew over villages throughout the country. A great social revolution was taking place in rural Korea.

Park termed the movement a "spiritual revolution," emphasizing "self-reliance, self-help, and mutual cooperation." It aimed to reform the farmers' way of thinking and living, through their own enlightenment, but also by enhancing their spirit of self-help and cooperation through educational campaigns. The role of leadership was important. A village movement leader and a women's leader were selected by villagers. Thousands of village movement leaders received leadership training at the *Saemaul* Leaders' Training Institute at Suwon, as well as at 15 provincial institutes. The movement helped to cultivate a "can do" spirit and restore confidence among rural dwellers.

Park believed the thatched roof was the symbol of Korea's poverty and underdevelopment. The government decided to replace thatched roofs, which had dotted the countryside for centuries, with metal roofs and concrete tiles. Between 1972 and 1979, about 2.5 million houses, almost half of all the houses in rural areas, had their thatched roofs replaced, and nearly 2.8 million homes were electrified. Farmers could install televisions, which would bring them into contact with the modern world. The degree of government support for villages was based on the success of self-help programs. If a village was successful, the government provided more support for it than to less successful villages. This incentive policy encouraged a competitive spirit in the villages, soliciting the enthusiastic participation of farmers in the movement.

The movement contributed remarkably to the improvement of the rural infrastructure and environment, and consequently to a better income for farmers. By the mid-1970s, the average rural household income had increased so dramatically that it had caught up with, and in one year even surpassed, the average urban household income. The farm household income increased ninefold over the ten-year period 1970-79, as compared to a sevenfold increase in its urban counterpart.[157] The movement helped raise poor farmers out of a situation of abject poverty and low morale and inspired them with a development-oriented mentality. It helped to transform almost every aspect of rural Korea, becoming one of the most successful rural development movements in the world. Koreans believe that the New Village Movement is a monumental achievement in Korean history. According to a Gallup Korea survey in July 1998, the movement was regarded as the most successful among the 10 historical achievements of post-1945 Korea.[158]

A Self-reliant Defense. While Park was pushing heavy industry build-up, challenges from North Korea were mounting. In November 1974, the South Korean army discovered a huge underground tunnel, excavated by the North Korean military, reaching to the southern side of the demilitarized zone. Its intended discharge point would have been well behind South Korean forward defense lines, which could jeopardize the forward defense positions of the South. The tunnel was large enough to permit North Korea to send an entire light infantry division through the tunnel in a single hour. If North Korean soldiers could capture strategic positions behind the forward defense line, they could completely isolate the advance defense contingent. In addition, the tunnel would have been highly useful in infiltrating North Korean commandos and agents into the South. Suddenly South Korea faced the threat of a surprise attack from below the earth, and behind its forward defense lines. The discovery caused a considerable shock among South Korean leaders and the populace. The South Korean military subsequently made every effort to locate other tunnels and, in February 1975, they discovered a second one, even larger than the first.

In the spring of 1975, the conclusive Communist victories in Vietnam and the helter-skelter flight of South Vietnamese refugees were fresh in the minds of many South Koreans. South Korea was often depicted as the next domino to fall. The sense of crisis weighed so heavily on the public that some citizens were preparing baked rice-powder as emergency food. Park was deeply shocked by the U.S. failure in Indochina and especially by the catastrophic fall of Saigon. The plight of South Vietnam, another divided country supported by the United States, bore an uncomfortable resemblance to the situation in South Korea. American military withdrawal from Vietnam, and more especially the betrayal of South Vietnam after the Paris peace agreement with the Communists, raised agonizing doubts about the reliability of American security commitments to South Korea. As matter of fact, in the United States, public support for the U.S. security commitment to South Korea was very low. In April 1975, the month Saigon fell, only 14 percent of Americans in a Harris public opinion poll favored U.S. involvement if North Korea attacked South Korea, while 65 percent said they would oppose it.[159] In Paris in January 1973, the United States, North Vietnam, South Vietnam, and representatives of the Communist Viet Cong had put their signatures to a peace accord. Although Nixon

---

[157] In-Joung Whang, *Management*, 178-180.
[158] *Chosun Ilbo*, July 15, 1998.
[159] Oberdorfer, *Two Koreas*, 87.

described the agreement as "peace with honor," the Communists had merely used it for the Communization of the south. The United States, true to the terms of the accord, removed its forces from Indochina. Park's concern was serious. In his diary on 30 April 1975, the day of the fall of Saigon, he wrote:

> Now the Republic of Vietnam has surrendered unconditionally to the Communist Army.... The name, Republic of Vietnam, has been erased from the earth. We saw the inevitable and cruel reality, and the truth that any country without the national determination and strength to guard its own existence for itself will not survive. We witnessed with our own eyes the tragedy of this national ruin simply because one nation relied on another's help only, without being equipped with a will to guard the nation for oneself.[160]

After the fall of South Vietnam, the Park administration became preoccupied with the security crisis. On May 10, a huge anti-communist rally, which attracted one and a half million participants, was held in Seoul. Within two weeks of the fall of Saigon, President Park issued an emergency decree on May 13, which made criticism of the constitution and the president a criminal act. It was the ninth emergency decree in less than a year and a half. In mid-1975 he pushed security-related laws, intended to put the nation on a wartime footing, through the National Assembly: a tightened National Security Law and a Civil Defense Law creating "combat reserve forces," including the "student national defense corps." The government doubled defense spending in the 1976 budget.[161]

In an interview with Time magazine in June 1975, Park said the fall of Saigon "produced a tremendous shock in Korea." Among the lessons the country had to learn from Indochina was that "when a nation is split at a time of crisis, it cannot function properly and [must] suffer defeat no matter how superior its weapons and troops may be." Responding to foreign critics regarding the repression of dissidents, he said that "people who criticize what we do in Korea measure the situation with the same yardstick that they use in the U.S. Here the situation is much more desperate. Only 25 miles from Seoul, an enemy is bent on destroying us. We cannot allow disorder. I am at a loss to understand criticism of us when we are faced with questions of survival."[162] He believed that freedom, without the state's ability to preserve it against a security threat, had no meaning, simply because "it will disappear instantly."[163]

North Korean provocations had become more bold and brutal. On the morning of August 18, 1976, a group of North Korean soldiers, wielding axes and metal pikes, attacked a U.S.-South Korean tree-trimming work team in a neutral area at Panmunjom, killing Captain Arthur Bonifas and Lieutenant Mark Barrett and wounding four American enlisted men and five South Korean soldiers. Bonifas was so badly beaten with the blunt end of an ax that his face was no longer recognizable. It was a deliberate

---

[160] Chung Chae-kyung, *Park Chung Hee silgi* (Real Records of Park Chung Hee), 472.
[161] John K.C. Oh, "South Korea 1975: A Permanent Emergency", *Asian Survey*, 16: 1 (January 1976), 72-75.
[162] *Time*, June 30, 1975.
[163] *Donga Ilbo*, October 5, 1974.

provocation.[164] President Park was privately furious at the killings, writing in his diary "I cannot tolerate this barbaric act by crazy Kim Il Sung's gangs…. You stupid, cruel, violent gangs—you should know there is a limit to our patience. Mad dogs deserve clubs."[165] During his meeting with General Richard Stilwell, commander of the U.S. forces in Korea, to discuss the military response, Park advocated "the strongest possible protest," including demands for an apology, reparations, guarantees against repetition, and "appropriate counteraction" by military force to teach North Korea a lesson, but without the use of firearms.[166] The United States condemned the North Korean act as a "vicious and unprovoked murder" and deployed a naval task force from Hawaii, F-4 jet fighters from Okinawa, B-52s from Guam and F-111 warplanes from Idaho. In response, North Korea placed its entire army and reserve forces into "full combat readiness." South Korean and American front-line forces were prepared for battle.

The Ford administration decided to cut down the poplar tree at Panmunjom, instead of retaliating militarily. When Stilwell reported the American plan, Park expressed a firm belief that a military response should be limited to the removal of the tree, believing military retaliation might lead to an all-out war that Kim Il Sung was probably trying to trigger. At 7 A.M., August 21, three days after the killings, a convoy of twenty-three American and South Korean vehicles rolled into the joint security area of Panmunjom to begin what was named Operation Paul Bunyan. Aboard was a sixteen-member engineering team with chain saws and axes, who immediately began cutting down the tree. They were accompanied by a thirty-man security platoon and sixty-four South Korean special forces soldiers. This small special task force was backed by a mighty array of forces appropriate for the initiation of World War III. Hovering overhead with a noisy whirl of rotors was a U.S. infantry company in twenty utility helicopters, accompanied by seven Cobra attack helicopters. Behind them on the horizon were the B-52 bombers, escorted by the U.S. F-4 fighters and South Korean F-5 fighters. Waiting on the runway at Osan Air Base, some sixty miles to the south, were nuclear-capable F-111 fighter-bombers. The *Midway* aircraft-carrier task force was stationed offshore. On the ground at the border of the DMZ were heavily armed Korean and American infantry, armor, and artillery backup forces. The operation ended successfully without North Korean resistance. Kim Il Sung sent the UN command a personal message in which he declared the incident "regrettable." The Korean peninsula was on the brink of another war.

Park Chung Hee believed that the most dependable road to a self-reliant defense was to build a defense industry; he became determined to accelerate his defense program. The establishment of a "self-reliant defense" became the catchword for South Korean security efforts at the time. The Park administration initiated an aggressive military modernization program, the Force Improvement Plan (1975-1981), or what was called the Yulgok Plan. The goal of the plan was to acquire a military capability sufficient to defend against North

---

[164] Wayne A. Kirkbride, *DMZ: A Story of the Panmunjom Axe Murder* (Elizabeth, NJ: Hollym, 1984). U.S.-South Korean soldiers attempted to cut branches off a poplar tree which obstructs the view of a southern guard post.
[165] Park Chung Hee, "Blue House Diary", *Minju Ilbo*, November 24, 1989.
[166] Oberdorfer, *Two Koreas*, 80.

Korean aggression without taking Korean alliance support into account.[167]

North Korea was militarily superior to South Korea. Kim Il Sung had dedicated most of the North's resources to enhancing its military capability. From the mid-1960s to the mid-1970s, North Korea allocated about 15 to 20 percent of its national income to the military while South Korea spent an average of only 5 percent.[168] By the end of the 1960s North Korea was producing large quantities of its own field artillery pieces, rocket launchers, armored personnel carriers, main battle tanks, and surface-to-air missiles. Its navy had twenty submarines; South Korea had none. Pyongyang continued to build up its armed forces in the 1970s. A U.S. military analysis concluded that 1972-77 was a time of "remarkable North Korean army growth," surpassing any other period since the Korean War.[169]

In order to finance a military modernization program that called for a total allotment of $7.6 billion for the first phase, the Park government adopted a number of legislative bills to impose a new income tax surcharge of 10 percent. Defense spending rapidly increased to $3.2 billion in 1979 from $382 million in 1974.[170] As a result, the government was able to set about acquiring missiles, patrol boats, aircraft, artillery, and advanced weapons systems that could not be produced domestically. In addition, it sought and obtained advice and assistance from abroad in expanding its industrial capacity to produce military hardware and munitions. By the late 1970s, already manufacturing rifles, machine guns, and tactical radios, South Korea moved to rebuild older tanks; produce artillery and air defense weapons; and co-produce light helicopters, infantry weapons, and some patrol craft. The government also created a mechanized army division and five special forces brigades, doubled the size of the navy, purchasing U.S. ships and missiles, and modernized its air force with faster, deadlier U.S. jets and missiles.

In conjunction with the nation's defense programs in conventional arms, Park also pursued nuclear capability. When the Nixon Doctrine raised the possibility of pulling all U.S. ground forces and tactical nuclear weapons out of South Korea, the Park administration became convinced that the country's future security ultimately rested on nuclear weapons, and launched a secret and serious effort to develop a nuclear bomb. In 1972 the Park government tried to acquire reprocessing equipment and technology from

---

[167] *Donga Ilbo*, July 12, 1975. Park adopted Yulgok, a pen name of Yi I, a well-known scholar and official of the Yi dynasty, who insisted on building a 100,000-man army right before Japan's invasion of Korea in 1592.

[168] Central Intelligence Agency, *The Economic Race between the North and the South* (Washington, D.C.: CIA, 1978), 6-8. The portion of North Korea's military expenditure soared sharply from 5.6 percent of its GNP during 1955-65 to the staggering rate of 31.2 percent during 1967-70. South Korea's total defense expenditure during 1965-74 was $1.2 billion while North Korea was estimated to have spent $3.2 billion. See Walter C. Clemens, "GRIT at Panmunjom: Conflict and Cooperation in Divided Korea", *Asian Survey*, 12:1 (January 1973): 535.

[169] Oberdorfer, *Two Koreas*, 59.

[170] The defense budget increased consistently to $914 million in 1975, $1.45 billion in 1976, $1.96 billion in 1977, $2.66 billion in 1978.

France to manufacture plutonium.[171] Recognizing the gravity of the situation, the Ford administration strongly warned the Park government that a South Korean nuclear weapons program "could endanger U.S.-Korea relations." Faced with adamant U.S. opposition, Park reluctantly canceled the contract with France. When President Carter announced the withdrawal of all U.S. ground forces from Korea in 1977, the Park government once again began discussions with France regarding reprocessing facilities. Once again Washington blocked the deal. Park had not decided to actually produce a nuclear bomb but was determined to acquire the technology and capability to do so. During his interview with Washington Post columnist Robert Novak in early June 1975, Park commented, "We have the capability," though he denied that his government was using it. In a plea for continuing U.S. military support, Park added, "If the U.S. nuclear umbrella were to be removed, we have to start developing our nuclear capability to save ourselves."[172]

Decline of the Park Regime. The establishment of the *Yushin* system and the subsequent series of developments put the whole nation in a state of shock—the response of Park's opponents ranged from disbelief to outrage. The *Yushin* constitution, they protested, was undemocratic in both content and structure. Park's opponents argued that he was using external circumstances as an excuse to establish a life-long dictatorship. In fact, the declaration of the *Yushin* system seriously weakened Park's moral legitimacy, which he had earned through economic growth.

An all-out confrontation between the Park regime and the anti-government forces was inevitable. The government believed that the only way to maintain order and stability and effectively promote ambitious national policies was to suppress anti-government activities. Park replaced martial law, which was proclaimed as part of the Yushin declaration, with rule by emergency decrees, prohibiting criticism of the constitution and the president and severely curbing such rights as freedom of assembly and of the press. The decrees were especially hard on anti-government elements. Numerous dissidents were arrested and imprisoned, the press was severely censored, and strikes were banned. The heavy-handed measures of the Park regime alienated a large number of the populace.[173]

At the time, the most well known dissident was Kim Dae Jung. After his defeat in the 1971 presidential election, Kim went to the United States. Unlike his political colleagues who were under the strong hand of the government, Kim, living abroad, was free to attack the Park government. Immediately after the inauguration of the Yushin system, Kim condemned Park's actions as dictatorial, unconstitutional, and unjustified; one time he disgraced Park as "an Asian version of Hitler."[174] While his activities drew the attention of the foreign press, they angered the Park administration. During his dissident activities in Tokyo in August 1973, Kim was kidnapped, brought back to Seoul, and abandoned on the street near his home five days later. American intelligence officers discovered that KCIA

---

[171] On Park's reprocessing effort, see Gab-je Cho, "Nuclear Game on the Korean Peninsula", *Monthly Chosun* (June 1993); and "Korea Close to N-bomb Development in Late 1970s", *Korea Herald*, October 6, 1995.
[172] Rowland Evans and Robert Novak, "Korea: Park's Inflexibility", *Washington Post*, June 12, 1975.
[173] See Sohn, *Authoritarianism and Opposition*; and George E. Ogle, *South Korea: Dissent within the Economic Miracle* (Atlantic Highlands, NJ: Zed Books, 1990).
[174] *Time*, August 30, 1973.

agents were involved in the abduction and Washington pressured Seoul to release Kim, who might be killed.[175] When Park realized that KCIA director Lee Hu-rak (Park's former chief of staff) had ordered the abduction, the president became enraged and fired Lee. Kim's abduction became sensational news in Japan and around the world. Because of the incident, Park Chung Hee and the KCIA became notorious abroad.

The abduction turned out to be an irrecoverable misstep for Park. It dealt a serious blow to the moral authority and legitimacy of Park Chung Hee. In the eyes of the world Park became known as a heavy-handed dictator, even while a majority of South Koreans regarded him as a sincere, hard-working, respected leader. On the other hand, Kim Dae Jung enjoyed a degree of popularity both at home and abroad. The media in the United States and Japan praised Kim as a great democratic crusader while they became increasingly critical of the Park regime. Encouraged by reports in the foreign press, students and intellectuals conducted a national campaign to revise the 1972 constitution in the fall of 1973. As tens of thousands of students and other activists held mass rallies and demonstrations nationwide demanding revision of the constitution, other democratic reforms, and the release of "political prisoners," the president issued his first emergency decree in January 1974, outlawing all such activities. Successive emergency measures imposed further restrictions on the society.

On August 15, 1974, Park Chung Hee suffered a personal tragedy. During a ceremony, an agent of a pro-North Korean group in Japan (Moon Se-kwang) fired several shots at President Park and First Lady Yook Young-soo. The first lady was killed.[176] She had been Park's constant source of emotional support, his confidante, his sounding board, and in many ways his source of strength. After the incident, Park became gloomy and more sensitive, and he no longer showed the strong determination and confidence that he had shown in the past. He became more reclusive and came to rely more and more on Cha Chi-chol, chief of the presidential security force, alienating other government leaders as well as the public.

The inauguration of Jimmy Carter immediately complicated Korean–American relations and created additional difficulties for Park's leadership. In the wake of the Vietnam disaster, Americans feared that U.S. forces might become involved in another Asian conflict, perhaps in Korea. The post-Vietnam aversion to military involvement abroad was at a high point in the United States. During the 1976 presidential campaign, Carter pledged, if elected, to withdraw all combat troops from South Korea. When Carter took over the White House in January 1977, there was a fundamental shift in U.S. foreign policy.[177] At a press conference on May 26, 1977, President Carter formally announced he would withdraw all U.S. ground forces from Korea over a five-year period. To South Korea, this represented a serious problem because without American security guarantees South Korea's security and economic development would be in grave peril. Foreign investors simply would not invest in Korea and might indeed withdraw investments already made. The decision was perceived by the South Koreans as abandonment, or at least a serious weakening of the U.S. commitment to South Korean security.

---

[175] Oberdorfer, *Two Koreas*, 44.
[176] Korean women keep their maiden names after marriage.
[177] *Congressional Weekly Report*, vol. 35 (Washington, DC: Congressional Quarterly Inc., 1977), 1108.

In addition to the troop withdrawal issue, the violation of human rights by the Park government and Korea's lobbying activities in Washington, which began just after Nixon's 1970 announcement of U.S. troop withdrawals from Korea, became contentious topics in the United States. The arrest and conviction of eighteen Christian leaders in April 1976 for issuing an anti-government manifesto provoked especially strong reactions from American churches and the public. In October 1976, *The Washington Post* reported that a Korean agent, Park Tong-sun, had distributed as much as $1 million per year in bribes to as many as ninety members of Congress and other officials. The lobbying activities became an influence-peddling scandal that was given the name Koreagate.[178] By the end of 1977, with full cooperation from the Carter administration, four full-scale congressional investigations on South Korean lobbying activities were under way, and governmental agencies had launched additional investigations. Investigations received significant press coverage and weakened American support for South Korea. Eventually, only one member of Congress was convicted. But with the charges of bribery and a series of investigations filling the news, the Park government had become an easy target of criticism in the United States, and nobody on Capitol Hill wanted to vote for military aid to compensate for the withdrawal of U.S. ground forces from Korea. In May 1978, U.S.–South Korea relations reached their nadir when the U.S. House of Representatives voted on a bill to cut off military sales credits and grain aid to South Korea under U.S. Public Law 480, if former South Korean ambassador Kim Dong-jo refused to provide the information necessary for investigation of the influence-peddling scandal. The open pressure of the United States on the Park regime greatly encouraged anti-government elements in Korea.

Park Chung Hee's strongest defense against his critics was rapid economic growth. But two rounds of a world oil crisis seriously damaged the Korean economy. South Korea, which imported all of its petroleum from abroad, was one of the countries most severely hit by skyrocketing oil prices. The decline of export markets, and a sharp rise in world interest rates exacerbated the problem. South Korea, which was a substantial borrower with an enormous debt burden of $18 billion in 1978, tried unsuccessfully to invite foreign loans. With the onset of the oil crisis and subsequent worldwide recession, South Korea's growth rate shrank considerably. In spite of the tightening money supply, Park continued to pour a large amount of funds into heavy industry build-up. In 1978, policy loans for heavy industries accounted for about 75 percent of total bank loans, and light industries were struggling.[179] A second oil shock in 1979 dealt a more devastating blow to the economy. Its effects were compounded by overinvestment in heavy industry and by rising demands for higher wages. Exports were beginning to deteriorate, and at the same time export profitability declined continuously. Export-led growth became export-led recession; growth was faltering, the balance of payments was deteriorating, and foreign debts were mounting rapidly.

Inflation was also a serious problem: between 1974 and 1980, wholesale prices nearly tripled, rising at an average of 23 percent annually; consumer prices rose just as quickly.[180] But wages

---

[178] See Robert Boettcher and Gordon L. Freeman, *Gifts of Deceit: Sun Myung Moon, Tongsun Park, and the Korea Scandal* (New York: Rinehart, 1980).

[179] Amsden, *Asia's Next Giant*, 60.

[180] Kihwan Kim, *Korean Economy*, 44-45.

failed to keep pace with rising prices. Workers were disillusioned and angry. Layoffs, low pay, and tough working conditions fostered both worker solidarity and militancy. To address economic ills, Park replaced his economic team in the cabinet in December 1978, and in April 1979 the government belatedly announced an economic stabilization program to cool down the economy.[181] But the plan caused a serious recession leading to a succession of bankruptcies and increased unemployment.[182]

As the economy started to slow, Park's political base began to fray. The opposition party (NDP) outpolled the ruling party (DRP) by a margin of 32.8 to 31.7 percent in the December 1978 parliamentary elections. Independent candidates won 27.2 percent of the vote and twenty-two seats in the National Assembly; fifteen of them subsequently joined the opposition party.[183] Encouraged by the election results, the opposition became more outspoken in its attacks on President Park and the Yushin regime.[184] The opposition party, influenced by the results of the elections, elected a courageous leader named Kim Young Sam as its president. Taking over the party, Kim immediately and directly challenged the authority of Park Chung Hee. On June 23, Kim delivered a keynote speech in the National Assembly bitterly accusing President Park of staying in power too long. The government's reaction was harsh. When the opposition party's organ Minju Chosun (Democratic Front) printed the speech, the government retaliated by seizing all of the copies and arresting its editor. Kim Young Sam angrily reacted to the Park regime by declaring that he would start a public campaign to "overthrow the Park regime." On September 16, in an interview with The New York Times, Kim Young Sam publicly appealed to the United States to end its support for Park's "dictatorial regime." Kim said that the "minority dictatorial regime" of Park Chung Hee, which he compared with that of the Shah of Iran, was "on its last legs" and said, "The time has come for the United States to make a clear choice between a basically dictatorial regime...and the majority who aspire to democracy."[185]

Confronted by increasing unrest and challenges, the government declared that it would return to the strict enforcement of restrictions on dissidents and the opposition. On October 4, Kim Young Sam was expelled from the National Assembly by a two-thirds majority vote in line with the constitution. As part of a protest against the regime, the lawmakers of the opposition resigned *en masse*, plunging the country into in a political crisis. Kim's ouster sparked violent demonstrations in the southern industrial cities of Pusan and Masan, Kim's home ground, which involved not only increasingly militant students but also disenchanted workers. The government declared a garrison decree in both cities and cracked down on the demonstrators with a heavy hand, moving in with tanks and armored vehicles.

Kim Jae-kyu (director of the KCIA) had been embroiled in an argument with Cha Chi-chol, head of presidential security guard, over how to respond to the riots in Pusan

---

[181] For the background and contents of the program, see Sang-Woo Nam, "The Comprehensive Stabilization Program", in Cho and Kim, eds., *Economic Development*, 207-244.
[182] Cha et al., eds., *Korean Economy*, 117-119.
[183] For details, see C. I. Eugene Kim, "Significance of Korea's 10th National Assembly election", *Asian Survey*, XIX:5 (May 1979): 523-532.
[184] For a general overview of Korean politics in 1979, see Chong-Sik Lee, "South Korea 1979: Confrontation, Assassination, and Transition", *Asian Survey*, 20:1 (January 1980): 63-76.
[185] *New York Times*, September 16, 1979.

and Masan. Kim believed that the government should pursue a policy of conciliation, while Cha argued that it was time to crack down. On the evening of October 26, the nation's most powerful figures, President Park, Kim Jae-kyu, Kim Kye-won (Blue House chief of staff), and Cha Chi-chol, met in a KCIA safe house near the Blue House for dinner to discuss, among other things, the Pusan situation. President Park proceeded to criticize the KCIA director for failing to control the massive social unrest.[186] In the sharply divided argument that followed, Kim, supported by his agents, suddenly gunned down the president, Cha, and their bodyguards. It was a tragic end to the heroic leader. Just as abruptly as it had begun on a spring morning in May 1961, the era of Park Chung Hee came to a tragic end on a fall evening in 1979.

The death of Park Chung Hee shocked the country. Revered, respected, or hated, his rule had been a fact of life for a whole generation. At his funeral, more than nine million Koreans, one of every four people in Korea, paid their respects to the slain president. Two million people turned out in the streets of Seoul to watch the journey of his coffin to the national cemetery and wonder about the future of their country. The acting president Choi Kyu-ha lamented, "The heavens trembled and the earth shook, nature seemed to wither and the people were stricken by fright and grief."[187]

LEADERSHIP FOR MODERNIZATION

Context of the Presidency. Park Chung Hee took over a nation with painful problems. South Korea faced a serious national crisis, which the Chang regime exacerbated and had been incapable of solving. The crisis, which threatened the very survival of the Republic, had its origins in colonial rule, national partition, and the Korean War. There were no easy solutions. By the eve of the military coup, the country had descended into near total chaos, economically, politically and socially. If disaster was to be averted, South Korea needed a resolute leader.

External challenges were as serious as domestic ones. At the time, North Korea was far superior militarily and economically. Following the 1960 student uprisings, North Korean Communists, eyeing their chance for a socialist revolution in the South, were quick to take advantage of the South Korean situation. The political dissension, economic stagnation, and social unrest rendered South Korea increasingly vulnerable to North Korean efforts. Only seven years after the end of the bloody Korean War, pro-Communist and anti-American sentiments were rampant in South Korea, engendering security and ideological crises. Since the mid-1960s, encouraged by the success of the Communist guerrilla warfare in Vietnam, North Korea had stepped up its infiltration and military provocations in the South. Beaten and fatigued by the Vietnam War, the United States began reducing its military presence in Asia, including South Korea.

Park Chung Hee had no leadership legitimacy in the South Korean social order. Having been in the Japanese army, he lacked the anti-colonial credentials of Syngman Rhee. The Korean military at that time suffered from a stigma stemming from a Confucian tradition that the sword is inferior to the pen. It was inevitable that intellectuals and college students

---

[186] Kim Jae-kyu, a retired three-star army general, was Park's classmate at Korean officer training school in 1946 and one of Park's old friend.
[187] *Korea Herald*, November 3, 1979.

would challenge the military-dominant regime sooner or later. Despite all the problems and challenges, he did enjoy some advantages. Park and his military associates organized a military junta after the 1961 coup, and monopolized political power for two and a half years. During that period, he purged many of his political opponents and challengers and established his power base without serious resistance. With firm control over the military, he was free to mobilize the military, the most effective and modern institution of the country at the time, to promote national development.

Agenda Setting. A truly successful leader possesses a keen sense of history. Having a sense of history involves the ability to separate the transient from the permanent, the secondary from the primary. It includes the ability to grasp the whole. It means shunning short-term political successes in order to tackle the more serious and controversial problems.[188] Park Chung Hee possessed an unusually strong sense of history. He defined the essence of his revolution as the "modernization of the fatherland and national restoration" through spiritual, social and economic modernization. His vision, his willingness to see in Japan what Korea could one day become, was probably one of his best and most surprising qualities.

National leaders of developing nations have to place relative priorities on national goals—security, economic development, and political development. Park realized the difficulty of trying to simultaneously achieve those three national goals. He believed progress on one front is far better than failure on all the three fronts. Since the 1961 military coup, he had repeatedly stated that his first priority was to drive poverty away from his chronically impoverished country, and that this was the only way to prevail in the struggle against Communism.[189] His primary goal was to surpass the economic and military strength of North Korea.

He was a pragmatic leader, committed to what was possible (economic development) rather than what was desirable (democratic development). It was his firm belief and his priority as a leader to concentrate on economic development. He asserted that "unless we can establish 'economy first' consciousness, our dream of building a strong national state will end in a dream and nothing more."[190] He believed that his country lacked the fundamental requirements for democracy, and that democracy in South Korea should be fostered, step-by-step, through constant training and practice, so that eventually it might take root firmly in Korean soil. He was willing to let history be the final judge of his service.

Park's national priorities contrasted with those of his predecessor Syngman Rhee. Rhee was obsessed with national defense and reunification. Park was a realist and a pragmatist. He believed that without a solid economic foundation, national security could not be guaranteed. While Prime Minister Chang stayed focused on the pure ideals of democracy, Park believed that democracy could only prosper and grow on a healthy social and economic foundation.[191] Economic growth was central to his nation building.

Although both Rhee and Park were nationalists, their nationalism was contrasting. Rhee's nationalism was basically reactive to negative forces; he used anti-colonialism and

---

[188] Murray and Blessing, *Greatness in the White House: Rating the Presidents*, 88-89.
[189] Lee Dong Won (1992), 181-185; and Lee Byong Joo (1991), 134-137.
[190] Park Chung Hee, *Our Nation's Path*, 172-173.
[191] Chung-yum Kim, *Policymaking*, 116.

anti-Communism (also anti-Russianism) as means of consolidating his people. To Rhee, Japan was a target for hatred. In contrast, Park's nationalism was positive. He tried to transform the rather unfocused and counterproductive anti-Japan sentiment of Koreans into a more focused resolve of catching up with Japan.[192] Rhee believed the regime in Pyongyang was an evil regime that had to be eliminated. To Park, North Korea was seen more as a competitor in national development.

Appointments and Leadership Style. The military revolution, according to Park, was to form "a new force for the age." Retired military officers were conspicuous in important positions in government and public enterprise.[193] The military elite who were young, dedicated, and possessed managerial skills became the driving force of Park's modernization.[194]

The military leadership of the 1960's sharply contrasted with the civilian leadership of previous administrations. Under Rhee and Chang, the ruling elites were generally urban, educated abroad, and Christian. They represented the middle or upper classes—landlords, rich families, or colonial bureaucrats. The new elites after the 1961 military revolution represented the lower-middle or low classes as characterized by their humble rural background and Buddhism. They were mostly educated in Korea after 1945 and trained by the Americans or the American-oriented Korean military. Whereas the civilian elites were conservative and imbued with factionalism, the military elites were more professional and reform-oriented. In short, a generational change implied significant differences in the ruling elites.[195] The age distribution of the political leaders graphically shows how different the Park regime was from the Rhee and Chang regimes (see Figure 3).[196] During the Rhee administration, about 74 percent of political leaders were over age fifty. Under the Chang regime, the trend was similar—64 percent were older than fifty. In contrast, under the Park regime, an astonishing 95 percent of political elites were below age forty-nine. Park and his cohorts represented a new generation in Korea. When Park took power, he was only 43-years old and his associates, such as Kim Jong-pil, were in their thirties. This new generation was future-oriented, dynamic and action-oriented.

Park had no expertise in economics and therefore relied heavily on technocrats. For instance, he appointed career bureaucrats and experts as vice-ministers and ministers of

---

[192] Woo, *Race*, 98.

[193] By the late 1960s, former military officers occupied one-fifth to one-half of all cabinet posts and headed three-fourths of the large, government-owned corporations. They also dominated the National Assembly and filled the majority of influential ambassadorial posts. See Se-jin Kim, *Government and Politics*, 162-163.

[194] During the early 1950s-1987, some 36,000 officers received short-term training and long-term education under the Military Assistance Program, most of them in the United States (Jeon Chong-sup, "*Chonmungga yokwhal kwa yunrijok chaekim*" (The Role and Ethical Responsibilities of Experts), in Hankuk haengjeong hakhoe, ed., *Hanguk minju haengjeongron* (On Democratic Administration) (Seoul: Koshiwon, 1988), 452. For the military as reformers, see Huntington, *Political Order*, 201-207.

[195] Huer, *Marching Orders*, 61-62. While Syngman Rhee, Chang Myon, Kim Young Sam and Kim Dae Jung are Christians, the generals-turned-leaders (Park Chung Hee, Chun Doo Hwan and Roh Tae Woo) are Buddhists.

[196] Bae-ho Hahn and Kyu-taik Kim, "Korean Political Leaders (1952-1962): Their Social Origins and Skills", *Asian Survey*, 3:7 (July 1963): 29.

the EPB and finance ministry and as his economic advisers. On the other hand, Park appointed ex-military generals as ministers of other economy-related ministries, such as the construction, transportation and communications ministries. During the sixteen years (1964-79) of the Park government, only seven (14.9 percent) of forty-seven economic ministers were former military officers, compared to forty-six (38.3 percent) of 120 noneconomic ministers.[197] In the 1960s and 1970s, the economy was so underdeveloped that the goal of economic policy was to make "something out of nothing." The government itself mobilized resources, and built up industrial infrastructure, including factories. The generals-turned-ministers provided strong leadership in building highways, railroads, dams, harbors, communication networks, and industrial parks.[198]

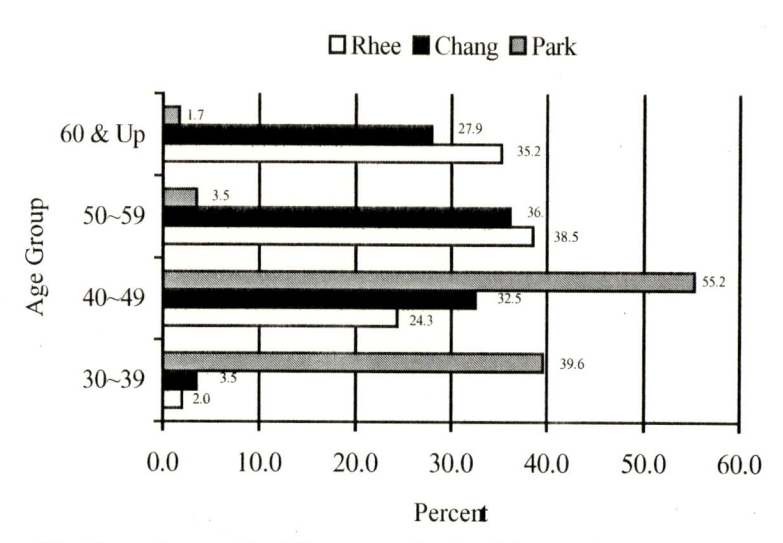

Figure 3. **Age Distribution of Political Leaders**(%)

☐ Rhee ■ Chang ▨ Park

Age Group	Rhee	Chang	Park
60 & Up	35.2	27.9	1.7
50~59	38.5	36	3.5
40~49	24.3	32.5	55.2
30~39	2.0	3.5	39.6

Percent

One of Park's merits was his ability to appoint the right people to the right positions at the right time. He was regarded as "a genius in personnel management."[199] He was a good judge of people and their usefulness, and he was very cautious in selecting his ministers and advisers. He took competence and compatibility as important criteria in his appointments, especially at the cabinet level. His appointment policy was characterized not only by the selection of well-qualified persons but also by the long duration of their

---

[197] Chung Kil Chung, "The Ideology of Economic Development and Its Impact on Policy Process", *Korean Journal of Policy Studies*, vol.1 (Seoul, 1986), 38.
[198] Chung-Kil Chung, "Presidential Decision-Making and Bureaucratic Expertise in Korea", *Governance*, 2 (July 1989), 3.
[199] According to a survey of 320 opinion leaders on the personnel management of Korean Presidents, Park is ranked first with 69 points followed by Chun Doo Hwan with 65 points. See Hankuk daetongryong pyongga wiwonhoe, ed., *Hankukui yokdae daetongryong pyongga* (Evaluation of Korean Presidents) (Seoul: Chosun Ilbosa, 2002), 81.

tenures, especially those in important government positions. For example, Nam Duck-woo worked for more than ten years in the Park government—first as finance minister and then minister of the Economic Planning Board. Kim Chung-yum served more than sixteen years during the eighteen-year period of Park's presidency—as vice-minister and minister of finance (1962-66), minister of commerce and industry (1966-69), and Blue House chief of staff (1969-1978). As Table 7 shows, Park's government, the economic team in particular, was extraordinarily stable. As a result, the government was able to maintain a high level of teamwork and policy consistency.

Table 7. **Stability of Park's Economic Team**

Prime Minister	Term	Trade & Industry Minister	Term
I. K. Chung (64.5-70.12):	6 yr 8 mo	C. H. Park (64.5-67.10):	3 yr 5 mo
J. P. Kim (71.6-75.12):	4 yr 7 mo	C. Y. Kim (67.10-69.10):	2 yr 1 mo
K. H. Choi (75.12-79.12):	3 yr 11 mo	N. S. Lee (69.10-73.12):	4 yr 1 mo
		Y. J. Chang (73.12-77.12):	4 yr 1 mo
Chief of Staff			
H. R. Lee (63.12-69.10):	5 yr 11 mo	*Finance Minister*	
C. Y. Kim (69.10-78.12):	9 yr 3 mo	D.W. Nam (69.10-74.9):	4 yr 11 mo
		Y. H. Kim (74.9-78.12):	4 yr 3 mo
EPB Minister			
K. Y. Chang (64.5-67.10):	3 yr 5 mo	*Science & Technology Minister*	
H. R. Kim (69.6-72.1):	2 yr 7 mo	H. S. Choi (71.6-78.12):	7 yr 7 mo
W.S. Tae (72.1-74.9):	2 yr 8 mo		
D. W. Nam (74.9-78.12):	4 yr 3 mo		

Source: *Civil Service Commission*

Park understood the need for institutions to make leadership accountable in the pursuit of his vision. He created institutions and administrative capacity that could carry out the objectives of policy independently of the president's personal actions. He was known as an institutional builder. During his eighteen-year rule, Park crafted the foundation upon which modern Korea was built.[200] Important among the new institutions were the presidential secretariat and the Economic Planning Board, among others. Park established a strong system of professional staff in the Blue House—a functionally diversified, modern presidential staff system—to effectively manage his policies.[201] He also created a modern bureaucracy and administrative structure so that policy implementation would depend not on presidential or party involvement, but on the actions and competence of rank and file bureaucrats.

Park was very strong in organizational leadership. He made the best use of

---

[200] Root, *Small Countries*, 18.
[201] Choong Nam Kim, *Sunggonghan Daetongryong, silpaehan daetongryong* (Successful Presidents, Unsuccessful Presidents), 82-87; Sung Deuk Hahm, "Institutional Development of the Blue House in the Park Chung Hee Presidency", *Asian Perspective* 20:2 (1998): 34-56. The total number of presidential staff members increased from around ten to around 137 in the early 1960s.

governmental institutions with emphasis on delegation, teamwork, and coordination. He presided over monthly export promotion meetings and other regular governmental meetings. A major function of these meetings was general policy clarification. His government and cabinet became a truly functioning collegial body. His longstanding use of meetings was a useful means of exercising his authority. His style was highly reminiscent of the leadership of President Eisenhower, who introduced a military-style management system to the White House and exercised a systematic command.[202]

Park aimed to achieve maximum managerial effectiveness. His goals of national development were translated into performance standards at the level of the firms receiving government support. The government targeted specific projects for promotion in addition to broad industry-specific goals. The goals were clear and expressed in numbers. The policy choices of the Park regime were efficient, consistent, and coherent, and its policy implementation was highly effective—a single-minded concentration of efforts, mobilization of all available resources, and the determined removal of obstacles. The careful specification of performance standards allowed monitoring by the Blue House. He checked projects in progress and emphasized results. He studied and checked every problem in detail, took notes, and asked searching questions.

Park's personal convictions were a source of his strength. He administered to the needs of the country rather than to his personal popularity. Difficulties, obstacles, and constraints were removed or suppressed: he was not reluctant to use the power at his disposal. His strong commitment and iron determination were the source of his driving force and they proved to be indispensable elements of his success. Despite strong protests and other difficulties, he pushed through historical decisions—the normalization of diplomatic relations with Japan, the dispatch of troops to Vietnam, construction of the Seoul–Pusan expressway, and the development of heavy industry.[203] He frequently said, "The only useful judgments of a public man are the judgments of history."[204] Like Machiavelli's Prince, Park Chung Hee had a definite purpose: to turn his vision into a reality. Park belongs to a category of leaders who believe that it is within their power to change the course of national history. Throughout the eighteen years of his presidency, he showed a firm grasp of the complexities involved in the goals he set for the nation, and he did not deviate from the discipline that he believed was necessary to attain these goals. What was needed in Korea was leadership that was authoritative, but also exemplary, rational, predictable, and accountable. He provided just that kind of leadership.

In his eighteen years in power, Park had been obsessed with ushering the country into the ranks of developed nations, had pursued his goal relentlessly. He emphasized the virtues of cooperation and national harmony. It was in the name of promoting national harmony that he suppressed political dissension and opposition. He despised partisan bickering and inter-party disputes. It was in the name of injecting a new spirit of the *Yushin* system in October 1972. Having been trained under the Japanese, he closely

---

[202] Francis H. Heller, "The Eisenhower White House", *Presidential Studies Quarterly*, 23:3 (summer 1993): 509-517; Stephen E. Ambrose, *Eisenhower, Vol. Two: The President* (New York: Simon and Schuster, 1984); and Fred I. Greenstein, *The Hidden-hand Presidency: Eisenhower as Leader* (New York: Basic Books, 1982), 104-108.

[203] Cole and Lyman, *Korean Development*, 37.

[204] Keon, *Korean Phoenix*, 214.

patterned his development strategies after Japan's, where a feudal society had been turned into a modern nation between the 1860s and 1930s. The Japanese leaders of the Meiji era, however, possessed two advantages over Park. First, they had operated in a period when the masses were less politically conscious and authoritarian control was more easily accepted. This was not the situation in South Korea, where students had already toppled a government in 1960. Second, Meiji Japan had enjoyed sovereignty, but the Park government had been under considerable pressure from the United States.

For all his sins as a heavy-handed authoritarian ruler, he was a brilliant man with strategic vision. He not only understood what Korea could become but also had the intelligence, skill, and drive to achieve his country's modernization with stunning speed. He lived simply, empathized with the common people, and hewed to the priorities and values of most Koreans.

Achievements and Legacies. Every great achievement is a dream before it becomes reality; and Park Chung Hee's vision was of a state that would not simply survive but prosper. Park took over South Korea vowing to do away with the "evil legacies" of Korean history, end corruption, rebuild national pride, and spur economic development. During the eighteen years of his rule, Park converted most of these vague revolutionary slogans into reality with remarkable thoroughness. Under his leadership, South Korea made giant strides toward stability, economic viability, and international acceptance.

Korea reached nearly the top of the world's growth charts. Korea's per-capita income increased tenfold during Park's tenure. In 1961, Korea's per capita income placed the country below Ghana, Senegal, Liberia, Zambia, Honduras, Nicaragua, El Salvador, and Peru. After eighteen years, its per capita income was raised to a level three times the average of the above-mentioned four African countries and more than two times that of the four Latin American countries. Except in neighboring Taiwan, this sustained boom has no parallel in history—neither in the United States nor in Europe during their high-growth stages, not even in postwar Japan.

South Korea's phenomenal growth from the 1960s is the heritage that Park Chung Hee bequeathed the Korean people. The Park administration successfully completed three five-year economic development plans. The annual economic growth rate averaged 9.6 percent during the period between 1962 and 1979. It is fair to say that without Park Chung Hee this extraordinary growth era would never have happened (see Figure 4).[205] The World Bank calculates that gross domestic product (GDP) in Korea grew an average of 9.9 percent from 1965 to 1980 and its manufacturing sector grew even more rapidly—18.7 percent per year during the same period.[206] Korea's GNP grew twenty-seven times, from $2.3 billion in 1962 to $62.7 billion by 1979, pushing up the per capita income nineteen times, from $87 to $1,640 over the same period.

It took Korea only 11 years (1966-76) to double its real income per person, whereas it took Japan 34 years (1885-1919). The United States took 47 years (1839-86) and Britain took 58 years (1780-1838).[207] Led by a marvelous export performance with an average

---

[205] The GNP data are based on the Bank of Korea, *Korea Statistical Yearbook, 1965-1980*.

[206] World Bank, *East Asia and the Pacific Regional Development Review: Sustaining Rapid Development* (Washington, DC, 1993).

[207] *Economist*, October 16, 1993.

annual growth rate of 37.8 percent, exports increased from $40.9 million in 1961 to $15 billion in 1979, making Korea a rapidly growing trading nation.[208]

The big push for the development of heavy and chemical industries became the basis for the comprehensive development of a self-reliant economic structure that ultimately made Korea competitive with Japan and other advanced countries. It was a grand success and a declaration of Korean industrial sovereignty. Despite the economic side effects and social and political sacrifices, Park's drive for heavy industries transformed the economy and laid a solid foundation for continuous economic growth in the succeeding decades. By the end of the 1970s, South Korea had become the number one third world exporter of manufactured goods to developed countries. Its efficient steel industry, modern shipyards, and production of advanced electronics all bespoke a

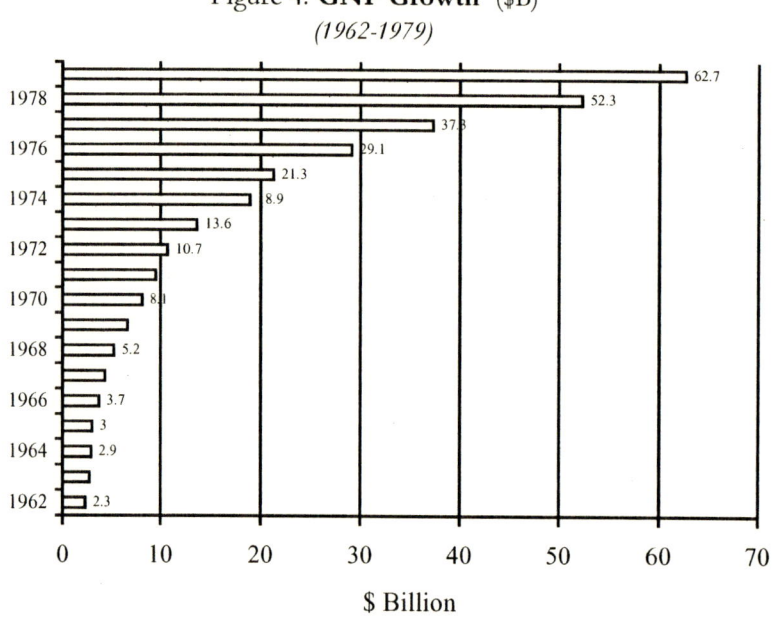

Figure 4. **GNP Growth** ($B)
(1962-1979)

Year	$ Billion
1978	62.7
	52.3
1976	37.8
	29.1
1974	21.3
	8.9
1972	13.6
	10.7
1970	8.1
1968	5.2
1966	3.7
	3
1964	2.9
1962	2.3

successful economic transformation. Despite its initial opposition to Park's policies, even the World Bank eventually declared South Korea's industrial transformation a success. Park restored the confidence of the Korean people, transforming the national ethos from chronic nihilism into a "can-do" spirit. Perhaps that was his greatest achievement.

Park's other lasting accomplishment, one not widely recognized, was the inculcation of South Korean confidence in dealing with North Korea. Until the early 1960s North

---

[208] According to a survey of 320 opinion leaders on the achievements of Korean Presidents, Park is ranked first in economic policy with 85 points (100 points is the maximum) followed by Chun Doo Hwan with 70 points, and in education, science and technology policy Park is again ranked first with 72.6 points followed by Chun Doo Hwan with 56.4 points. See Hankuk daetongryong pyongga wiwonhoe, *Hankukui yokdae daetongryong pyongga* (Evaluation of Korean Presidents), 88-89.

Korea asserted that it was the legitimate spokesman for Korean nationalism. At that time, the North was far superior to South Korea militarily and economically. Pyongyang stridently championed the values of self-reliance and unification. Over and over again Pyongyang conducted diplomatic and propaganda offensives. South Korea was always on the defensive. But Park decisively won the economic competition with Kim Il Sung. As South Korea's economy became stronger, it became more confident in dealing with the North.[209] Thanks to South Korea's strong economy, Park's military modernization program also recorded phenomenal success, and it provided South Korea with the means for long-term defense against North Korea and ended the dependency on American military equipment. Military modernization is perhaps his most profound contribution to South Korea's nation building.

Although Park initially criticized the existing political system, he failed to establish a durable and stable democracy. Modernization was not enough. What was required was a more positive effort to shape a new political order.[210] He tried to practice democracy during the 1960s, but as domestic and external challenges intensified he became more and more obsessed with the achievement of his ambitious developmental goals even at the cost of democracy. He established the *Yushin* system, but frequently had to resort to oppressive measures to hold this system together. For seven years from 1972 until his assassination, He ruled South Korea by emergency decrees. Park failed to learn the political lessons of his predecessor Syngman Rhee, who had revised the constitution twice and was forced to resign after twelve years of rule. Park also revised the constitution twice and ruled the country for eighteen years. A life-long presidency could not be justified or tolerated in South Korea. In his final years, he suffered from faulty judgment and paranoia and could no longer control the country even through draconian measures, alienating the people as well as some of his own advisers. In the end, he became a victim of his failure to build durable democratic institutions. There was still no peaceful method for transition of power. He did not even have a successor.

Nevertheless, Park's historic accomplishments overshadowed his political shortcomings. According to a Gallup Korea survey in July 1998, the New Village Movement (1st), the construction of the Seoul-Pusan expressway (3rd), the launching of the five-year development plan (7th), and the administrative reform in the early 1960s (9th) are regarded as among the ten greatest achievements in the fifty-year history of the Republic.[211] He lived simply but dreamed grandly, and he maintained a firm grip on reality. His sense of mission remained strong; but dedication gave way to self-righteousness. If Park Chung Hee can be said to belong to history, this is no accident. Park willed it that way. He directed his life toward shaping history to the pattern of his own vision. For Park, politics was not primarily the art of the possible; it was the art of the willed. Great leaders invite great controversy. They acquire strong friends and bitter enemies.

The Greek poet Sophocles once said, "One must wait until the evening to see how splendid the day has been." Park was not popular in his final days, but the passage of

---

[209] Fuji Kamiya, "The Korean Peninsula after Park Chung Hee", *Asian Survey*, 20: 7 (July 1980), 745-746.

[210] Huntington, *Political Order*, 262.

[211] *Chosun Ilbo*, July 15, 1998.

Park Chung Hee

time has brought a growing appreciation for his many achievements. Park often said he would stand or fall, not by any measurement of him in his lifetime, but by the judgment of history. In politics as well as history, the only test is the test of time. When President Kim Young Sam's approval rating hit 90 percent during the early months of his term, Park Chung Hee appeared to be forgotten. When Kim's leadership was tumbling and his people were struggling in the midst of the 1997-1998 financial crisis, a wave of nostalgia for Park Chung Hee swept the nation. Park's achievements inspired many to place him on a pedestal and to proclaim him as Korea's "savior from poverty."[212] He is now remembered less for his authoritarian rule than as the father of Korea's modernization and the greatest president of the nation. In numerous annual surveys conducted over the last fifteen years, Park Chung Hee has been number one among all past Korean leaders, always receiving the votes of more than two-thirds of the respondents, cutting across age and gender.[213]

Park led a nation that surpassed all other developing nations in what may be called the United Nations development decades—the 1960s and 1970s. His modernization program started almost a decade before that of Lee Kwan Yew, who transformed Singapore "from third world to first" within two decades. Deng Xiaoping, who engineered China's reform and opening, was also impressed by Park's rapid industrialization. Almost all the nations of Asia, especially the Philippines under Ferdinand Marcos, Indonesia under Suharto, and Malaysia under Mohamed Mahathir, have carefully studied Park's leadership and policies. Post-Soviet Russia also turned its attention to Park's economic successes. Even the North Korean dictator Kim Il Sung and his son Kim Jong Il, who both hated Park Chung Hee and were determined to destroy his regime, have paid attention to the merits of Park's developmental strategy. Park may have been one of the most intelligent and capable third world state leaders of the post-World War II era. It is not surprising that *Time* magazine designated Park Chung Hee as one of the great Asian leaders of the twentieth century.[214]

In many ways, Park Chung Hee was the right leader for South Korea during the period when its national foundation had to be laid. He was a nation-builder with few peers in the modern world. None of the better-known national architects of the 20th century—Kemal Atatürk, Gamal Abdel Nasser, and Vladimir I. Lenin—have built a more durable and prosperous country than Park. Park's strategy of modernization became a model for development among other developing nations. Park Chung Hee was only five-and-a-half-feet tall, but he is a giant in Korean history, and probably in the history of the world. He will be remembered as one of the greatest leaders in the long history of Korea.

---

[212] On nostalgia for Park, see Shim Jae Hoon, "Rose-tinted Glasses", *Far Eastern Economic Review*, July 17, 1997; "The Park Chung Hee Memorial", *Korea Herald*, July 31, 1999.
[213] *Chosun Ilbo*, March 5, 1995. According to a Gallup Korea Poll conducted in early 1993, 83.5 percent of respondents listed Park Chung Hee as "the best president" since 1948.
[214] *Time*, August 30, 1999.

Chun Doo Hwan

Chapter Five
Chun Doo Hwan
Pushing Korea Toward the First World

> "A Korean president has to work in a harsh environment. The country is divided, and the Republic confronts a notoriously warlike adversary [North Korea] who constantly wishes us ill. We have to work to defend the peace of the country, achieve sustained economic growth, and maintain social and political stability. The Korean president must pursue these three objectives simultaneously."
>
> "I would like the history books to write that I was the first Korean President who handed over power by legal and constitutional means."
>
> —Chun Doo Hwan

Chun Doo Hwan burst into the forefront of Korean history. His rise as the top leader of South Korea was a consequence of national crisis following the assassination of long-time president and strongman Park Chung Hee. Owing to the turbulent nature of the transition, perhaps no president has been the subject of more controversy during the past twenty years than has Chun. He inherited a nation with formidable problems and challenges. South Koreans soon realized just how quickly their economy faltered when the country lacked political stability and decisive leadership, as was the case after Park's sudden death. Under the circumstances, Chun Doo Hwan came on the scene as a crisis manager.

After their long struggle against the Park regime, pro-democracy forces—the opposition, the students, intellectuals, and other antigovernment activists—expected an immediate democratic transition with Park's passing. For several months in late 1979 and early 1980 it seemed that such a dream might come true. But Korea experienced social and political turmoil owing to the power vacuum, which Major General Chun Doo Hwan and his followers filled, by arresting army chief of staff, General Chun Seung Hwa, and commanders loyal to him on the night of December 12, 1979. President Kim Young Sam later called the nighttime takeover of the military a "coup-like incident." Many Koreans believed that Chun Doo Hwan and his regime had stolen the golden opportunity for democratization, to which they aspired after eighteen years of Park's iron-fisted rule.

The legacy of the Kwangju uprising was serious for the Chun government. When the foreign media reported on South Korea, Chun was frequently criticized for the brutal crackdown at Kwangju, though the tragedy occurred before his assumption of power. He could not avoid accusations of his direct or indirect involvement, because he was one of the leading military figures at the time. Chun Doo Hwan was not a well-known figure, and the boots of the charismatic Park Chung Hee, who had dominated the country for eighteen years, proved too big for him to fill. In addition, South Korean society had grown so diversified, specialized, and democratically oriented that a former general could no longer dominate it.

Chun Doo Hwan

Chun Doo Hwan proved a controversial figure from the beginning. He was the target of hatred and vilification at home and was infamous abroad owing to his authoritarian rule and alleged implication in the Kwangju uprising. However, there exists a contrasting view of Chun—that of a very effective national leader. These two conflicting images of Chun continue to confuse objective observers. Fifteen years after the end of his rule, he remains an enigma, misrepresented and misunderstood. In such a complex political scene as South Korea, it is an extremely difficult, if not dangerous, task to evaluate the man objectively, yet still worth the effort. Before discussing the Chun presidency, it is important to review the events of the transition period that followed upon the death of Park Chung Hee.

A TURBULENT TRANSITION

When Park Chung Hee was assassinated, the army chief of staff, General Chung Seung-hwa, was enjoying dinner with the assistant director of the KCIA in a nearby room in the same house.[1] After shooting Park, the assassin, KCIA director Kim Jae-kyu, went immediately to General Chung. The general was shocked, since he heard the wild shooting only several yards away from where the president had been dining. Kim hastily explained that a tragedy had befallen the president and asked Chung to accompany him immediately to KCIA headquarters. General Chung, who knew his martial law responsibilities, insisted they proceed to army headquarters in Yongsan, about five miles away from the Blue House. So Kim and Chung went to Yongsan. During the fateful encounter between the two, who were intimate friends, Kim allegedly attempted without success to persuade Chung to declare martial law and to assume full presidential authority, placing the two of them in a position to run the country.[2]

At approximately 9 P.M. in a conference room in the National Defense Ministry in Yongsan, a tense meeting began that lasted until dawn. Present were Prime Minister Choi Kyu-ha, Defense Minister Roh Jae-hyun, Kim Jae-kyu, General Chung Seung-hwa, Blue House chief of staff Kim Kye-won, and other government and military leaders. Kim Jae-kyu informed the assembly that President Park was "incapacitated" and strongly argued that this was a propitious opportunity for the military to take over the government. At the meeting, the Blue House chief of staff acknowledged that he had been present at the assassination, but refused to reveal any details or reveal who had done the shooting. Just before midnight, the Blue House chief of staff pulled the defense minister and the army chief of staff aside and informed them that Kim Jae-kyu was the assassin. Kim Jae-kyu was arrested immediately by the military police. As prescribed by the constitution, Prime Minister Choi became acting president. Martial law was declared and General Chung was designated martial-law commander. The proclamation of martial law put the military leadership at the center of Korean politics.

Major General Chun Doo Hwan, commander of the Defense Security Command (DSC), had also been present at the overnight meeting. He was designated head of the newly established Joint Investigation Headquarters for the purposes of investigating Park's assassination. The DSC functioned within the military as a counterintelligence and

---

[1] For details, see Cho Gab-je (1998), vol. 1; and Gleysteen, *Massive Entanglement*, 53-76.
[2] Wickham, *Korea on the Brink*, 16; and Gleysteen, *op. cit.*, 56.

internal security organization. Because of the sensitivity of the position, Park Chung Hee had personally approved the assignment of General Chun to head the DSC. General Chun had become commander of the DSC in February 1979, seven months before Park's death.

Park's assassination deeply shocked the Carter administration, still reeling from the Iranian hostage crisis and growing tensions with the Soviet Union. In late 1978, the Pahlevi regime was overthrown and in November 1979 militant revolutionaries seized the U.S. Embassy in Teheran and held sixty-nine diplomats and others hostage. In December the Soviet Union invaded Afghanistan. The death of Park created a sense of panic in Washington. A political confrontation in South Korea could spark an explosion and precipitate a third crisis point in the world. The Carter administration set up a secret taskforce to follow Korean events that set one of top priorities as preventing "another Iran" in South Korea.[3] It also sent an aircraft carrier battle group to Korean waters and bluntly warned North Korea it would face attack if it intervened in the South.

Investigation of the assassination was a dangerous task. At that time no one knew if a coup was still in process. The KCIA was a powerful, secretive, and feared organization. The director of the KCIA and his men had assassinated the president. The assassination broached the possibility of an antigovernment alliance between elements in the Blue House, the military, and the KCIA. The fact that General Chung Seung-hwa had been near the scene of the assassination raised serious concerns about his role, if any, in the death of Park. As the army chief of staff with responsibility for defending the nation and its president, General Chung had failed to check the incident although it had occurred only several yards away from him. It was also widely speculated that the North Koreans might have been behind the president's death.[4]

The DSC, in the course of its investigation, uncovered sufficient evidence to indicate the possible complicity of some senior army officers in a conspiracy to kill Park. As the chief investigator, General Chun Doo Hwan wondered why the assassin had not been arrested immediately after the president's murder and thought the delay very suspicious.[5] Although investigators had interrogated all those directly and indirectly involved in the assassination, they had not been able to arrange for the questioning of the army chief of staff. Now the powerful martial law commander, General Chung deftly evaded interrogation.

At the same time, Chun was informed of rumors concerning the imminent reassignment of certain senior military officers, including himself. As martial law commander, General Chung was in the unassailable position of being able to control all military assignments and promotions. The rumors indicated that Chun Doo Hwan would likely not be retired, but rather reassigned to the East Coast Security Command, tantamount to being put out to pasture. If Chun were removed as commander of the DSC and replaced by one of Chung's associates, there would be no interrogation of Chung and the martial law commander would be free to further consolidate his military power. Chun determined he must act quickly.

In the late afternoon of December 12, 1979, at the headquarters of the 30th Brigade located inside the Kyongbok Palace compound, a stone's throw from the Blue House, a

---

[3] Tim Shorrock, "The U.S. Role in Korea in 1979 and 1980", <http://www.kimsoft.com/korea/kwangju3.htm>
[4] Wickham, *Korea*, 18.
[5] Ibid., 32-33.

secret meeting was held. Several influential generals were in attendance.[6] General Chun Doo Hwan reportedly began the meeting by sharing his deep concerns about the national situation and the army chief of staff and martial law commander General Chung Seung-hwa in particular. Chun also told the participants that General Chung was planning to retire or reassign a number of generals, clear indication that he was laying the groundwork to seize power himself. The generals decided to arrest General Chung Seung Hwa by accusing him of having played a role in the assassination. They accused their boss of being a suspect because during the murder, he was close to the scene of the crime and because he opposed the investigation of his possible involvement. The generals recognized that these actions might be regarded as highly irregular, but they believed that the defense minister and President Choi could be persuaded to approve the arrest. Thus, Chun ordered the DSC team to move on Chung's residence.[7]

At General Chung's residence at 6:30 P.M., Chung's bodyguards opened fire, and the DSC team responded. One man was killed and several others injured. General Chung was arrested. When commanders, who were loyal to the army chief of staff, mobilized troops, General Chun and his cohorts also mobilized units they commanded. Crashes in front of the Army headquarters and other places occurred, resulting in a few casualties. At the same time, General Chun went to the president's residence to seek President Choi's approval for the arrest. Choi said he would refuse unless the defense minister concurred. After the defense minister reluctantly approved, the president formally acquiesced as well. Thus, Chun and his followers took control of the military.

What happened on the night of December 12, 1979—called the December 12 incident—was more than a conflict within the military; it was a mutiny. Subordinate officers removed the army chief of staff without endorsement of the civilian leadership. According to a 1994 Seoul District Prosecutor's Office report, Chun Doo Hwan and Roh Tae Woo met on December 7 and decided to make the twelfth their "D-Day." On December 12, Chun and Roh mobilized parts of the Ninth Division, Seoul's capital garrison, and special forces to prepare for a possible reaction against the arrest of General Chung. Clearly these troop movements were made against the regular Korean army command.

Subsequently, the DSC's investigation uncovered "significant evidence" to indicate the possible complicity of General Chung and other senior officers in a conspiracy to kill President Park. The Joint Investigation Headquarters officially concluded that Kim Jae-kyu assassinated President Park in order to seize power, with the explicit or implicit consent and support of General Chung Sung-hwa. Kim Jae-kyu was tried, found guilty of the assassination, and executed, and Chung was sentenced to ten years in prison, but later released on grounds of ill health.

Given the enormous power that Park Chung Hee held under the *Yushin* system, his sudden death came like an earthquake that shook the very foundations of the country; economic downturn, social unrest, political uncertainty, and renewed tension with North Korea combined to cause a serious national crisis. Park's death came at the worst possible time. After almost two decades of phenomenal economic success, growth had

---

[6] *Hankook Ilbo*, December 2, 1995.
[7] Ibid., 54-55.

turned sour toward the end of 1979.[8] In 1980 the Korean economy was on the brink of bankruptcy; the nation experienced a 5.7 percent decline in its gross national product for the first time since the end of the Korean War.

In addition to shrinking exports after the second oil shock in 1979, Korea's price of crude oil imports jumped from $2.2 billion in 1979 to $5.6 billion in 1980. Thus, foreign debt increased rapidly: foreign loans amounted to only $10 billion in 1978, but had soared to $27 billion by 1980. As a result, payment on foreign debt became a serious burden. In 1979 these payments amounted to $3 billion, but by 1981 they were $5 billion. Adding to the $3 billion spent on oil imports, in 1981 South Korea required an additional $8 billion in loans.[9] The nation desperately needed foreign loans to span the widening gap between imports and exports as well as to pay the interest on existing loans. However, the economic and sociopolitical crisis in Korea rang financial alarm bells around the world. Foreign lenders were reluctant to provide new loans to South Korea. On January 25, 1980, at a meeting of major U.S. bankers, the U.S. Federal Reserve Board singled out South Korea as a country where bankers should tread cautiously. It cited the country's account deficit, dim prospects for exports, and the risk of increased domestic political instability as reasons bankers should be wary of making new loans.[10]

If there had been an economic downturn and Park Chung Hee had still been running the country it might have been different, but the country was experiencing political turmoil and economic downturn at the same time. The political instability threatened to undo the gains of almost two decades of hard-earned economic growth. An unprecedented wave of bankruptcies swept the country. Inflation was also serious: consumer prices soared 34.6 percent, and wholesale prices leaped an alarming 44 percent in 1980.[11] With the government in disarray, workers turned to direct action to improve their situation. Thus, labor activities became more frequent and more radical. The Korea Times reported that there were 897 labor disputes in the first five months of 1980 alone, more than had taken place in the entire Yushin period (1973-79).[12] The most radical labor protest was the four-day miners' riot at Tongwon Coal Mine in a town near the east coast. There, in April 1980, nearly 4,000 miners rioted and stormed into town, seizing a police station for several days. Armed with rifles and dynamite, they proceeded to fight off attacks by riot police. Police reinforcements and army units had to be dispatched to restore order.

Park's death created a political vacuum. His powerful political machine crumbled immediately. The *Yushin* constitution had been widely discredited. The National

---

[8] The number of companies unable to meet their payrolls rose by four times compared to the previous year. The 1979 economic performance was dismal—24 percent overall inflation but 50 percent rise in food prices; and a $4.3 billion balance-of-payments deficit. See *Donga Ilbo*, December 5, 1979; and *Fortune*, April 21, 1980

[9] Korea's total foreign debt rose from 30 percent of GNP in 1978 to 53 percent of GNP in 1982. The rate of principal and interest payments burden surpassed the "dangerous level" of 20 percent in 1982. The U.S. weekly *Time* revealed that South Korea's outstanding foreign loans reached 49 percent of the governmental budget. The OECD and other international economic organizations declared South Korea a defaulter. See Sunoo, *20th Century Korea*, 276-277.

[10] Clifford, *Troubled Tiger*, 171.

[11] Krause, "Political Economy of South Korea", in Cha et al., eds. (1997), 119.

[12] Hart-Landsberg, *Rush*, 215.

Assembly, with one-third of its members appointed by Park, had long been rendered impotent. The ruling party (DRP) was adrift after losing its captain. Dissident Kim Dae Jung was engulfed in factional strife with the opposition NDP leader, Kim Young Sam, and it was widely believed that the opposition party lacked the experience and capability to run the government. Meanwhile, the interim Choi government was proving too weak to manage the mounting chaos. There was no succession plan, no heir apparent, and no sufficient political standing to assume leadership. More importantly, there was no solid institutional foundation upon which to construct a successor administration. In a power vacuum, the students, a traditional moral force, and the military were competing to control the nation. Koreans remembered the dominance of the students in politics after the student uprising of April 1960. Pentagon sources told reporters that the best idea was to rely on the Korean military, which they thought was the only institution with effective power after Park's murder.[13]

In the spring of 1980, while politicians engaged in the struggle for realignment, college students were restless for action. Chun Doo Hwan's ambitious move aggravated the situation. In April, Chun, the Defense Security commander, was also named as acting director of the KCIA, putting him in charge of civilian and military intelligence. Therefore, student demonstrations grew more aggressive. As labor unrest flared up and student protest intensified, the United States approved the Korean contingency plans to use the military because South Korea would have faced total chaos without it. Shortly before his meeting with South Korean leaders, U.S. Ambassador Gleysteen reported to Washington in a cable on May 7: "In none of our discussion will we in any way suggest that the USG [U.S. government] oppose ROKG [Republic of Korea Government] contingency plans to maintain law and order."[14] "We agree that we should not oppose ROK contingency plans to maintain law and order," Warren Christopher, Deputy Secretary of State, cabled back the next day.[15] U.S. officials also became convinced that the military was a safer alternative to the chaos the protesters represented.[16]

The student demonstrations peaked on May 15, when an estimated 100,000 people packed the central part of downtown Seoul. In the afternoon, the demonstration became considerably rougher as the students pushed their way north toward government buildings. Students trapped and burned several armored police vehicles that were spraying tear gas. A policeman was killed and a number of others seriously injured. Events were quickly getting out of control.[17] Student leaders issued an ultimatum demanding the government lift martial law by May 20, complete the political transition by the end of 1980, publicly schedule the resignation of the "remnant of the *Yushin* system," including Prime Minister Shin Hyun-hwack and General Chun Doo Hwa.

Student demonstrations paralyzed the nation. The Choi government and the military leaders saw that absolutely no more concessions could be made as the government was already teetering on the edge of an abyss. During a May 17 cabinet debate over the

---

[13] *New York Times*, December 15, 1979.
[14] Gleysteen to Christopher on May 7, 1980.
[15] Christopher to Gleysteen on May 8, 1980.
[16] Tim Shorrock, "Debacle in Kwangju", <http://base21.org/show/show.php?p_docnbr=20986>
[17] "Tens of Thousands of Students Demonstrate in Nation's Streets", *Korea Herald*, May 16, 1980.

imposition of full martial law, the ministers concluded that student demands could never be satisfied, as it would essentially mean a total overthrow of the government. Obviously pressured by the military the cabinet unanimously recommended the imposition of full martial law, the arrests of opposition political leaders and radicals, and closure of the National Assembly. The intent was to deal firmly and swiftly with "an anarchic situation."[18] As a direct result, on May 17 President Choi issued an extraordinary national emergency declaration, imposing full martial law and setting the stage for the armed forces to suppress demonstrations and prevent them from spreading throughout the nation.

Under full martial law, the military replaced the civilian counterpart. Military authorities arrested some 100 student leaders from various campuses. Under martial law decree number 10, all forms of political activity and labor strikes were banned, censorship was imposed, and universities and colleges were closed "for the time being." The next day (May 18) the leading figures of the Park era, including Kim Jong-pil, were arrested on charges of corruption. Also, Kim Dae Jung was arrested on charges of sedition and Kim Young Sam was placed under house arrest. The National Assembly was closed, as were the headquarters of the political parties.[19]

While troops quickly imposed a stern order in Seoul and other major cities, the arrest of Kim Dae Jung touched off passionate protests in Kwangju, the capital of South Cholla province and the political stronghold of opposition leader Kim.[20] Unable to control the growing unrest, and fearing that rioting could spread to other cities, lead to anarchy, and even invite an invasion from North Korea, the martial law command dispatched special forces to Kwangju. This proved a costly mistake: the military was not equipped or trained to deal with civil uprising, and its ability to make sense of and deal with the civil riots was severely limited. The troops used excessive and brutal force, which was said to have been deliberately provoked by radicals to incite a riot. News that demonstrators were being roughly handled by the military troops spread quickly throughout the city. Angry citizens joined in, driven by alleged rumors that the "soldiers of Kyongsang province origin came to exterminate the seeds of the Cholla people."

After suffering some initial casualties, the protesters quickly militarized themselves by commandeering hundreds of military vehicles and seizing weapons and ammunition from the armories and explosive storage bunkers of the homeland reserve forces and the police. The rioters were in possession of more than 4,000 military weapons and a supply of demolitions; they possessed machine-gun-equipped trucks and were using walkie-talkies to coordinate their moves. Some radicals set up a machine gun on the roof of a local hospital and fired on government troops and police below. They occupied most of government buildings and emptied a local prison, which contained some 2,000 leftists. Out of a population of 750,000, it was believed that more than 200,000 had joined the

---

[18] *Korea Annual* 1980, 104.

[19] *Korea Annual* 1981, 8.

[20] The Kwangju uprising was later called as "the Kwangju democratic movement" under the Kim Dae Jung government. The Cholla region had a long anti-establishment and antigovernment tradition. Kwangju was the center of the Tonghak peasant uprisings of the late nineteenth century and the 1927 student uprising against Japanese colonial rule. Cholla people had long believed themselves the victims of discrimination by both the central government and other regions, particularly neighboring Kyongsang province to the east.

uprising. By May 21 the military and police had been driven from the city, which was then controlled by citizens' councils for the next five days. The rebellion spread from Kwangju to surrounding areas showing the potential of a civil war. There was now imminent danger that the uprising could spread to other areas, including Seoul.[21]

It was the worst crisis South Korea had faced since the end of the Korean War. As one informed U.S. official noted, "The situation is dangerous almost beyond words. It is the most dangerous situation to confront a U.S. ally in Asia since the fall of Saigon in 1975."[22] In a cable to Washington, U.S. Ambassador William Gleysteen called the Kwangju events "a massive insurrection" that is "out of control and poses an alarming situation for the ROK military."[23] The United States warned North Korea against attempting to exploit the situation. AWACS surveillance planes and a naval task force headed by the aircraft carrier *Coral Sea* were moved to the area as a warning to North Korea not to intervene.

In the National Security Council meeting at the White House on May 22, American leaders reached agreement that "the first priority is the restoration of order in Kwangju." President Carter then told an American television audience forthrightly that "human rights issues had to be subordinate to security concerns" in Korea.[24] And then, on May 27 the U.S. State Department stated: "We recognize that a situation of total disorder and disruption in a major city cannot be allowed to go on indefinitely."[25] General John Wickham thus released Korean troops from the U.S.-Korea Combined Forces Command to end the uprising. Donald Gregg, one of the participants in the White House meeting, said that their real concern was that North Korea might use the chaos as a pretext for intervention.[26]

The nine days of bloody civil uprising in Kwangju ended with a predawn military maneuver. The casualties amounted to 191 people killed (164 civilians, 23 soldiers and 4 policemen).[27] It was the worst domestic tragedy in modern Korean history. Roh Tae Woo, one of the military leaders at the time, later recollected: "If Kwangju type upheavals were to have occurred in Taegu, Pusan and other major cities, the very existence of Korea as we know it would have been imperiled. South Korea was unlike the United States in size and stage of political development; hence, internal difficulties required different solutions."[28] Although there are still debates about who was responsible for the tragedy, Chun Doo Hwan

---

[21] Wickham, *Korea*, 133; Gleysteen, *Massive Entanglement*, 130. There are some detailed reports of the Kwangju tragedy, but mostly by persons representing Kwangju. For example, see Chung Sang-yong Rhyu Simin et al., *Kwangju minju hangjeng* (The People's Struggle for Democracy) Seoul: Tolbege, 1990); *Kwangju Mail Daily, Cheongsa 5.18* (The Correct History of May 18) (Seoul: Sahwoe Pyongnon, 1995); 5.18 Kwangju minjung hangjeng yujokhwoe (*The Survivors' Association of the May 18 Kwangju People's Struggle for Democracy*), ed., Kwangju minju hangjeng pimangnok (*A Memorandum on the Kwangju People's Struggle for Democracy*) (Kwangju: Mipung, 1995).

[22] *Washington Post*, May 27, 1980.

[23] Embassy cable, "The Kwangju Crisis", May 21, 1980, quoted in Oberdorfer, *Two Koreas*, 128.

[24] Gleysteen, *Massive Entanglement*, 65.

[25] Quoted in Donald N. Clark, ed., *The Kwangju Uprising: Shadows over the Regime in South Korea* (Boulder, CO: Westview, 1988), 14.

[26] Shorrock, *op. cit.*, 3.

[27] *Korea Herald*, June 8, 1985.

[28] Quoted in Wickham, *Korea*, 167.

and his military colleagues cannot avoid the responsibilities of the tragedy, because they at the time dominated the military and the government. The Kwangju uprising shocked the entire nation and left a bitter memory that damaged the image of the army and its leaders. The specter of Kwangju was to haunt the soon-to-be new government for years to come.

The Choi government failed to manage the potentially disastrous national crisis. Nobody was sure what would happen next. The worst scenario would be another North Korean military attack. In a crisis situation, formal rules and procedures give way to informal processes and provisions and extraordinary measures are inevitable. Under the pressure of circumstances, official authorities may be overruled by situational leaders. For making critical decisions, official qualifications and jurisdictions are less important than the capacity for a resolute and rapid response to the crisis.[29] The dominant trend after the death of Park Chung Hee was the rapid growth in the power of the army. Military leaders who had served in combat in the Vietnam War vividly remembered the fall of South Vietnam. They were determined not to allow such a tragedy to be repeated in their country.

On May 30, probably urged by impatient military leaders, President Choi summoned a National Security Council meeting to deal with the crisis. Participants concluded that the current situation was the most dangerous and difficult that the nation had faced since the Korean War. The next day Choi announced the formation of a twenty-five member Special Committee for National Security Affairs to facilitate "cooperation" between the cabinet and the martial law command. The special committee, consisting of key cabinet members and senior military leaders, would function with a standing committee. President Choi was the titular chair of the special committee and General Chun Doo Hwan was in charge of the standing committee. The junta-like standing committee, consisting of eighteen field-level officers and twelve high-level government officials, was to operate through fourteen functional subcommittees, which for all practical purposes constituted a government within the government. Although the committees were operating "totally within the constitution,"[30] they completely took over political and economic administration, weakening the cabinet and martial law authorities.

The committees were determined to clean out perceived sources of sociopolitical disruption. The tool employed to carry out the task was a sweeping purge in the name of social purification. By the end of July some 3,000 public employees had been dismissed or held for trial on grounds of corruption, inefficiency, or irregularities. In addition, Kim Dae Jung and twenty-three of his followers were indicted in July on sedition and other charges. Formally accused of plotting the insurrection in Kwangju, Kim was put on trial by court-martial, found guilty and, on September 17, sentenced to death. Civilian sectors were also targets of the purification campaign. Crackdowns on "riffraff, racketeers, gangsters, and gamblers" netted a reported 30,000 "troublemakers," of whom 1,000 were subsequently tried by court-martial. Eight thousand others were released after questioning, and the rest were sentenced to a four-week re-education program. In July

---

[29] Uriel Rosenthal, Michael T. Charles, and Paul T. Hart, ed., *Coping with Crisis: The Management of Disasters, Riots and Terrorism* (Springfield, IL: Charles C. Thomas, 1989), 18.
[30] R. Richardson, "South Korea: The Chon [Chun] Brigade Takes Over", *Far Eastern Economic Review*, 108:24 (June 6, 1980): 12.

and August, the government banned 172 periodicals on the grounds that they contributed to social decay. In addition, several hundred journalists were dismissed from newspapers and broadcasting stations.

Among the reform measures, corporate restructuring was a top priority.[31] The first target was the troubled heavy industrial sector. Many of the heavy industry plants remained almost idle or operated at low rates of capacity. For example, electric generating manufacture was operating at 10 percent capacity, the marine diesel industry at 7 percent, and the fledgling auto industry was running at about 30 percent.[32] During the summer of 1980, the government, advised by the special committee, ordered twenty-two companies in six strategic industries to merge or consolidate operations. These reform measures infuriated some people, but the sincere effort to eradicate "social evils" and punish wrongdoers also generated substantial amount of public approval.

After Park's death, Prime Minister Choi Kyu-ha was unexpectedly elevated to national leadership at a time when the country faced major crises. Choi was a career diplomat, a political lightweight who lacked the character and political power base to manage the turbulent transition.[33] During the critical transition, he demonstrated no leadership ability in managing the political vacuum left by the assassination of Park.[34] There was almost universal agreement in the Korean hierarchy that Choi could not govern the nation effectively. It was felt that in order to preclude another potentially dangerous incident, such as that in Kwangju, he should retire in August, just prior to the reopening of the universities."[35]

At the crucial moment, General Wickham, commander of U.S. forces in Korea, made a statement supporting the rise of Chun Doo Hwan to power. During an interview with The Los Angeles Times on August 8, when asked "whether the United States would support Chun as president," Wickham replied "Yes, provided he comes to power legitimately and demonstrates, over time, a broad base of support, and does not jeopardize the security situation on the peninsula." By stating that Chun would have to come to power "legitimately," Wickham made it clear that the United States was asking that constitutional requirements be observed in form but not in substance.[36] In the same interview, Wickham was quoted as saying, "Peace and stability are important to the United States here, and national security and internal stability surely come before political liberalization.... I'm not sure democracy the way we understand it is ready for Korea or the Koreans ready for it.... Korea seems to need a strong leader. For a variety of reasons, Chun seems to have emerged as a leader, an unnatural one—but nonetheless a leader."[37] Wickham made the remark in the crucial period when such comments aided Chun's takeover of governmental power.

---

[31] Clifford, *Troubled Tiger*, 185-190.

[32] *Institutional Investor* (May 1981), 90-91.

[33] Kihl, *Politics and Policies*, 77.

[34] Gleysteen was so pessimistic about Choi's ability to run the government that he began to focus on other men within the government such as Prime Minister Shin Hyun-hwack. See telegrams from Gleysteen to Vance, "Discussion of Military Grab with President Choi", December 13, 1979; and "Korea Focus: My Meeting with Prime Minister, December 18", December 18, 1979.

[35] Quoted in Wickham, *Korea*, 164.

[36] Sam Jameson, "U.S. Support Claimed for S. Korea's Chon", *Los Angeles Times*, August 8, 1980.

[37] *Los Angeles Times*, August 11, 1980.

On August 16, President Choi announced his resignation because, in his words, he had "failed to fulfill satisfactorily the presidential duties, and because several political decisions have been made where results had a destabilizing influence on the nation." He took responsibility for the Kwangju incident, which he called "a grave mistake" by the government. At the same time, Choi praised General Chun as "an unselfish man full of confidence and ability to put theory into practice. In a country like South Korea, which faces a special security situation, the national leader should be a man who is widely supported by the military."[38] As a result of Choi's surprise resignation, Chun retired from the military in order to succeed to the presidency. His retirement was a necessary precondition, as the Korean constitution required that the president be a civilian. Ending a twenty-nine-year military career, he announced his candidacy for the presidency, to which he was duly elected on August 27, 1980, by the electoral college, as stipulated by the existing constitution.[39]

Since then, Chun and his cohorts have steadfastly maintained that they had been motivated by their "patriotic fervor" in the wake of President Park's assassination, lest it should lead to internal chaos and invite another North Korean invasion. To Chun's opponents, however, his stepwise rise to power was seen as a "carefully premeditated plan" to seize control of the military and ultimately to capture the government.[40]

THE MAN AND HIS CHARACTER

Chun Doo Hwan was born on January 18, 1931, the seventh child of a poor family in a little farming village located thirty miles southwest of Taegu.[41] In late 1939, when Chun Doo Hwan was eight years old, his father hurled a Japanese policeman who had insulted him down an embankment, nearly killing him. Immediately after this incident the Chun family fled to Manchuria, where poverty was the order of the day for most Korean migrants in Manchuria, as it was for the Chun family. There the boy enrolled in an elementary school under Japanese control.

Realizing there was no future for them in Manchuria, in March 1941 the Chun family returned to Korea and settled in Taegu, at that time a city with a population of 130,000. They lived in a small hut-like shelter on the outskirts of the city. Life was hard for the large family. Schools within walking distance had no extra room for Doo Hwan. Nevertheless, he obtained the second grade textbooks and studied on his own. He then enrolled in the third grade at an alternative school open to children who could not attend a regular school. While attending the alternative school, he earned some money for his family by delivering newspapers. After skipping two grades he entered Hido Elementary School in the fourth grade. After graduation from the school in the summer of 1947, he entered Taegu Technical High School.

In December 1951, in the midst of the Korean War, Chun was admitted into the Korea Military Academy as a member in the first class of a rigorous four-year program modeled after the United States Military Academy. Cadet Chun had a hard time taking so many courses in mathematics, physics, and engineering. Most days, he slept only for five

---

[38] *Joongang Ilbo*, August 16, 1980.
[39] *Donga Ilbo*, August 27, 1980.
[40] Oh, *Korean Politics*, 175-177.
[41] For a biography of Chun Doo Hwan, see Kum Sung Cheon, *Chun Doo Hwan*.

hours, going to bed at 10 P.M. and rising at 3 A.M. At that early hour he would steal out of the sleeping quarters and go into an empty barracks building where he prepared for the day's classes. While his academic performance at the academy was below average, he excelled in athletics. He became the captain and goalkeeper of the academy soccer team. He was always ready to lend a hand to classmates who were ill or weak, often carrying two rifles during the monthly 14-kilometer running marches in full gear. Among his friends and colleagues he was always the leader.

He graduated in September 1955 and was commissioned to a division near the demilitarized zone. As the first graduates of the military academy, Chun and his classmates were very proud of themselves and maintained thereafter a special bond. As an army captain, in 1959-60 Chun went to the United States to acquire ranger training and study psychological warfare. During his stay in the United States, he bought a used car, obtained a driver's license, and often traveled on weekends. Unlike Park Chung Hee, who was educated under Japanese rule and was never at ease with Americans, Chun Doo Hwan felt he knew Americans and could deal with them without feeling uncomfortable.

On the day following Park Chung Hee's coup in 1961, then Captain Chun allegedly demanded to meet General Park to confirm he was not just another corrupt general. According to the account of a later biography, Park explained to the young captain that he was opposed to the corruption and incompetence of the government and that he planned to develop a nationalistic democracy. Satisfied, Chun supported Park's coup and went on to serve as his secretary for civil affairs during the junta government. After serving as Park's secretary for a year, he turned down Park's suggestion that he embark on a political career and returned to the army. President Park continued to pay special attention to Chun, and Chun in turn kept his loyalty to the Park government.

After promotion to colonel, Chun commanded a regiment of the White Horse Division in Vietnam. In South Vietnam, another divided country that faced the same Communist threat as South Korea, Colonel Chun vividly witnessed why South Vietnam was unable to defend itself despite sophisticated weaponry and abundant supplies provided by the United States. He thought internal strife was the real source of South Vietnam's vulnerability. He believed that South Korea should learn stern lessons from the Vietnamese failure.[42] Chun became a brigadier general in 1971 and was given command of the First Airborne Special Forces. In June 1976, Chun was reassigned as an assistant director for operations of the presidential security force at the Blue House, where he had frequent personal contact with Park. In early 1977 Chun was promoted to major general, the first in his military academy class of 156 to achieve the rank. In early 1978 he was appointed commander of the key First Division, the authority of which included the traditional invasion corridor north of Seoul. His command oversaw the construction of a strategic defense wall near the DMZ and the discovery of a third North Korean invasion tunnel under the DMZ.

In March 1979, only seven months before Park's assassination, Chun became commanding general of the Defense Security Command, a military intelligence agency. Chun owed his appointment to President Park and was generally regarded as his confidant. The assignment was crucial not only for Chun but also for South Korea. If

---

[42] Ibid., 82.

Chun had not been appointed to the position, the history of South Korea in the 1980s might have been different. Because of his special relationship with Park, Chun would later attempt to continue Park's program of nation building.

THE FIFTH REPUBLIC (1981-1987)

On September 1, 1980, forty-nine-year old Chun Doo Hwan was sworn in as president. His sudden assumption of power was not the result of a coup but of what President Kim Young Sam would later call "a coup-like incident." During his interview with Don Oberdorfer, a Northeast Asia correspondent for *The Washington Post*, Chun said, "I have never run away from problems since the sudden death of the president." He insisted that he had not planned what had happened to him since the death of Park, but attributed it largely to "divine providence," which had given him few choices about his course of action.[43] In the 1961 coup, Park Chung Hee and his associates had carefully studied and prepared how to lead the nation. After the coup, Park had brought thousands of military officers into the government.[44] Chun had no such plans because they had never planned a coup. After assuming the presidency, he brought only a dozen military officers into the government and the ruling party. Most of the military officers he brought in were technocrats with Ph.D.s in economics, science, engineering, and other fields.

Ahead of the new president would be the task of leading a nation in a serious economic depression beset by social and political unrest. It was a nation without hope and with no destination. To many, Chun Doo Hwan seemed too ordinary a man to step into the shoes of such a great leader as Park Chung Hee. During the late 1970s, Park Chung Hee had been under great pressure, and the pressure ultimately led to the fall of his regime. But the pressure on Chun was much worse. The president inherited a nation in dire straits; he was under pressure to come up with strong measures—measures that would only make him unpopular.

Chun came to power without any experience in government. There were grave doubts concerning his competency for the office. As soon as he entered the Blue House, therefore, he tried to create a strong and effective government. He appointed first-rate technocrats to his staff and to the ministries. The most important was his chief of staff Kim Kyung-won, a political scientist and Harvard Ph.D., who had served as senior adviser to former presidents Park and Choi. Among other such appointments was Chun's chief economist (and his tutor), Kim Jae-ik, who held a doctorate from Stanford. As his prime minister, President Chun chose Nam Duck-woo, a U.S.–trained economist who for a decade had served as Park's minister of the Economic Planning Board and minister of finance. He named Shin Byung-hyun, former president of the Bank of Korea, as minister of the Economic Planning Board, and a capable diplomat, Lho Shin-yong, as foreign minister. Only two retired generals were included in his twenty-two-member cabinet.[45]

As soon as the new president had made his top cabinet appointments, he moved immediately to repair the containing vessel that had been weakened by Park's assassination. In an effort to restore public trust in the government, Chun renewed his

---

[43] Oberdorfer, *Two Koreas*, 132.
[44] Lee Suk-jae (1995), 13-88.
[45] *Joongang Ilbo*, September 2.

strong determination to root out corruption. The government introduced various antigraft measures to "purify" the public service. For example, high-ranking officials were required to register their assets as an institutional device to prevent them from gaining illegal wealth by taking advantage of their positions. It also introduced a system of notification of proposals and requests for political or administrative favors made to politicians and high-ranking officials. Both the giver and the taker were held equally responsible and accountable for any improprieties. In April 1981, the entire cabinet, led by the prime minister, took an oath of service in front of President Chun, and all public officials had to swear that they would shun requests for personal favors and refrain from engaging in influence peddling. Finally, the government established an ethics law for public officials to reward "clean and exemplary officials," and to improve legal and systematic structures designed to clean up the bureaucracy.[46]

Given the tight governmental control of the economy under the Park administration, many of the economic difficulties that Korea experienced after Park's death were caused by political instability. Therefore, Chun was determined to maintain social and political stability for the sake of economic recovery. He stressed the importance of social and political stability: "Political and social stability is an essential precondition to the resumption of sustained economic growth. Only sustained economic growth will make possible the strengthening of national security which is indispensable to the survival of our country and our people."[47] The threat posed by North Korean forces deployed in attack formation just twenty-five miles north of Seoul was a source of constant concern. The danger of renewed hostilities remained high, particularly during crises in South Korea.[48] Pyongyang had tried every possible means to destabilize and topple the South Korean government. Like Park Chung Hee, Chun believed that Korea's condition for mature democracy was not at hand:

> The task of accumulating truly democratic strength lies before us. Democracy is now regarded as a universal good; however, it is not indigenous to Korea, but was introduced only after liberation. Therefore, despite this nation's various efforts to practice democratic politics, we have repeatedly paid the price of trial-and-error in the absence of a foundation on which democracy could materialize. The democratic system is a complex and elaborate political institution, one that can hardly function satisfactorily until, and unless, the conditions of maturity it requires are at hand.[49]

Chun saw that the most serious problem for Korean democracy was the fact that the country lacked experience in the peaceful transfer of power. After twelve years of rule, Syngman Rhee had been forced to resign by a student uprising. Park Chung Hee's eighteen years of rule had ended with an assassin's bullet. Chun believed that the tendency of a life-long presidency during the past three decades not only weakened the legitimacy of the government but also became the major cause of frequent political turmoil. He believed that former presidents

---

[46] Jong Sup Jun, "The Paradoxes of Development: Problems of Korea's Transformation", in Bung Woong Kim et al., eds., *Administrative Dynamics and Development*, 66.

[47] The President Secretariat (1981), vol. 1, 16.

[48] Wickham, *Korea*, 169.

[49] The President Secretariat (1981), vol. 1, 5.

Rhee and Park had made great contributions to the nation, but they had tried to remain in power indefinitely. He saw that "democratization could become virtually an empty slogan if one individual were permitted to hold the reigns of government for an overly long period."[50]

On September 19, 1980, the Chun government presented to the nation the official draft of a new constitution. The new constitution was considerably different from the *Yushin* constitution, although it maintained the provision that the president was to be elected indirectly by a popularly elected electoral college.[51] The president was authorized to take emergency measures, but only with the concurrence of the National Assembly (Article 51), rather than simply on his own authority as under the *Yushin* constitution. The *Yushin* constitution placed no restrictions on the president's power to dissolve the National Assembly, whereas the new constitution (Article 57) limited the exercise of this power to the period beginning one year after the "formation" of the National Assembly, and stipulated that no National Assembly could be dissolved twice for the same reason.

Most important, the president was limited to a single seven-year term in office (Article 45). Further, if the new constitution were amended, the change would not apply to the president in office at that time (Article 129). This restriction was obviously designed to guarantee that Chun would not try to imitate presidents Rhee and Park by prolonging his tenure in office even if, contrary to his promise, he should feel tempted to try. Chun believed that there was a national consensus that there should be no more protracted personal rule. Despite the provisions that limited the excessive power of the president, maintenance of the indirect election of the president suggested to critics that the new constitution resembled the *Yushin* constitution. The new constitution was approved in a referendum on October 22, 1980, by an overwhelming mandate of 91.6 percent, with 95.5 percent eligible voter participation. Under the new constitution, all political parties and the National Assembly were automatically dissolved.

As Chun promised, martial law was lifted on January 24, 1981. A group of pro-Chun elements soon set up the Democratic Justice Party (DJP) that became the ruling party in 1981. Following this, the Democratic Korea Party and the Korean National Party emerged as opposition parties.[52] When the electoral college was elected on February 11, candidates of the DJP gained 69.6 percent of the seats. On February 25, the electoral college elected Chun Doo Hwan as president for a seven-year term. On March 3, in his inaugural address, Chun pledged his determination to attain "the freedoms all Koreans have yearned for and sought for so long"—these being "freedom from the threat of war, freedom from poverty, and freedom from political repression and abuses of power." Then he declared emphatically, "I will not fail to establish the tradition of peaceful transfer of power, a long-delayed national task."[53] He believed that repeated constitutional revisions by questionable means "left deep scars on the legal and moral authority of the constitution." He stated that "the peaceful transfer of political power is the core of the process to firmly root democracy" and pledged that he would never

---

[50] Ibid., 6.

[51] Hinton, *Korea*, 62.

[52] For details of Chun's first year, see Dae-Sook Suh, "South Korea in 1981: The First Year of the Fifth Republic", *Asian Survey*, 22:1 (January 1982): 109-115.

[53] Chun Doo Hwan, "Inaugural Address", in the Presidential Secretariat (1981), vol. 1, 28-31.

commit the mistakes of his predecessors in trying to hang on to power.[54]

In a national survey conducted in March 1981, popular reactions to Chun's often-stated intention to peacefully transfer power were mixed. Forty-five percent of the respondents said that the transfer of power "may change depending on the development of the situation," but thirty-two percent believed "it will be realized by all means." Skepticism was not completely unwarranted: during the thirty-three-year history of the Republic, the terms of incumbents were extended five times by means of constitutional amendments. As one foreign reporter aptly observed: "Many Koreans, naturally, are skeptical… But if [Chun] brings the country a measure of order and progress, and then quits on schedule, he will have done something unprecedented for South Korea."[55] The same survey asked respondents what they believed the priority of the Fifth Republic ought to be. The largest number of respondents (41.5 percent) pointed to economic stability as the government's most pressing task. Other critical concerns indicated were: social stability (19.5 percent), national security (13.8petrcent), expansion of welfare facilities (12 percent), political development (8.7 percent), and the promotion of foreign relations (3.1 percent). Thus, unlike the opposition and students who demanded rapid democratization, the absolute majority of the people were preoccupied with their own welfare and national stability.

Under the provisions of the new constitution, elections for the National Assembly were scheduled for March 1981. Under the terms of the electoral law, half of the 184 seats of the National Assembly were to be elected directly. The remaining half were to be allocated on the basis of proportional representation: the party winning a plurality or majority of the elected seats would be allotted two-thirds of the proportional seats; the balance of the latter would be divided proportionally among the other parties winning at least five seats each. It was a system of proportional representation aimed to guarantee political stability. In the general election held on March 25, the ruling DJP won 35 percent of the votes, but through the proportional representation system, it was able to control 55 percent of the seats in the National Assembly (151 of the 276 seats), a comfortable majority for President Chun. The Democratic Korea Party won eighty-one seats and the Korean National Party won twenty-five seats.[56]

The Chun administration benefited from a changing and favorable international environment. In particular, the inauguration of the Reagan administration in January 1981 came as a blessing for Chun Doo Hwan. Ronald Reagan came to power with a clear idea of reversing the course of American foreign policy. Reagan made it clear during his presidential campaign that he would abandon Carter's human rights policies and make a major effort to mend relations with South Korea. Immediately after his inauguration, Reagan, who pursued a strong anti-Communist policy—most clearly manifested in his designation of the Soviet Union as an "evil empire"—supported the new Chun regime.[57]

---

[54] Ibid.
[55] "Koreans, Weary of Turmoil, Are Ready to Tolerate Chun", *Asian Wall Street Journal*, April 14, 1981.
[56] *Donga Ilbo*, March 28, 1981; and Jae Hoon Shim, "Chun Wins Another One", *Far Eastern Economic Review* (April 3, 1981): 18-19.
[57] At President Jimmy Carter's first transition meeting with president-elect Ronald Reagan in late 1980, Reagan expressed enthusiasm for the authority that Korean President Park Chung Hee had exercised during the time of campus unrest, when he had closed the universities and drafted the

Ensuring that political instability in South Korea did not trigger another crisis point for the United States had become Reagan's overriding policy goal in Korea throughout the Chun administration. Chun Doo Hwan was the first head of state invited to the White House under the new American administration.

The summit was also part of a tradeoff that was negotiated to prevent the execution of Kim Dae Jung. After assuming power, Chun was anxious to be invited to Washington "not only to signify full regularization of U.S.-Korean relations but to give an aura of legitimacy to his new government."[58] As a *quid pro quo* for a Reagan invitation, Chun promised to commute Kim Dae Jung's death sentence.[59]

At their summit of February 2, 1981, Reagan assured his South Korean counterpart that the United States harbored "no plans to withdraw its ground combat forces from the Korean peninsula"[60] and promised full diplomatic, military and economic cooperation. Reagan's policy of strengthening the defense capabilities of his allies against Communist countries and his strong commitment to security virtually wiped out Korean anxieties over Washington's Korea policy.

The U.S.-Korea summit strengthened the legitimacy of Chun during the early months of his presidency and also helped in early stabilization of the social and economic situation in Korea.[61] The matter of overseas credit guarantees, which were so desired, was solved in the summit talks. In addition, the two leaders agreed to hold the first annual Korean-U.S. Economic Consultation Meeting. The most difficult problem faced by the Korean economy at the time was a deficit in the international balance of payments. The acquisition of foreign loans was difficult, as Korea's credibility could not be guaranteed abroad. U.S. security, political, and economic guarantees of South Korea sent a green light to international monetary organizations, Japan, and Western European countries. Stability—political, social, and economic—was important not only to business but also to South Korea's image in the world. In spite of the dismal economic situation, international bankers decided to provide more loans to South Korea because the political climate had calmed considerably with Chun's consolidation of power, and with his demonstrated willingness to take tough measures to fight inflation and other economic woes.[62]

As Chun stabilized the social and political situation, he embarked on programs to improve government efficiency and rationality. First, the Chun government made efforts to reduce red tape as a way of reducing corruption. Another change introduced was the emphasis on interchange of officials among ministries and agencies. The most unprecedented movement toward efficiency in government was the restructuring of the government bureaucracy in October 1981, an effort to cut redundant and wasteful functions of government. The elimination of 531 positions held by officials with a fourth

---

demonstrators." Jimmy Carter, *Keeping Faith: Memoirs of a President* (New York: Bantam Books, 1982), 578.

[58] Gleysteen, *op. cit.*, 182-189.

[59] William H. Gleysteen, Jr. "Korea: A Special Target of American Concern", in *The Diplomacy of Human Rights*, ed. David D. Newsom (Lanham, MD: University Press of America, 1986), 98.

[60] "ROK-U.S. Joint Communiqué" (The White House, February 2, 1981), in *Forging A New Era: The Republic of Korea* (Seoul: Korean Overseas Information Service, 1981), 63.

[61] *Korea Herald*, February 3, 1981.

[62] "Are Bankers Kidding Themselves about South Korea?" *Institutional Investor* (May 1981): 89.

grade rank and higher (ranks higher than middle management) was the largest administrative reduction in Korean history. The government reorganization reduced three agencies, forty-one bureaus and 135 divisions and branches. Four advisory agencies established during the Park administration were also abolished.[63] Another important administrative reform was the introduction of a zero-based budgeting system, which aimed to maximize efficiency, reduce waste, improve priority setting, and thereby economize the overall budget.

As Chun was able to bring social stability earlier than most had predicted, he took some social liberalization measures. On January 5, 1982, Chun announced that the midnight to 4 A.M. curfew, instituted by the U.S. military government more than thirty years before, would be lifted.[64] The curfew had long been a symbol of the government's strong social control. The government also removed the requirement for school uniforms, which had formerly been enforced by the colonial government. Millions of middle and high school students were now liberated from their black uniforms. In addition, the government eased restrictions on foreign travel and study abroad.[65] These measures were welcomed by the public. Although it is difficult to measure the effects of the social liberalization policy, it appears to have stimulated significant social, economic, and political development. In addition, on March 2, 1982, Kim Dae Jung's sentence was reduced to twenty years, and the terms of 2,862 other prisoners were also reduced or canceled altogether.[66]

Unfortunately, a curbside loan scandal, often dubbed the "Lady Chang scandal," broke out in the spring of 1982, and the Chun government's slogan of a "just society" rang hollow. A woman named Chang Young-ja, a curbside money market operator, induced a number of companies to give her letters of credit for discount usage (estimated at about $361 million) as collateral for bank loans which she promised to give them at low interest rates under a favorable repayment schedule. She and her husband offered these letters of credit at curbside market rates to mobilize funds. They poured these funds into stock market investments, in which they suffered massive losses.[67] The scandal led to the bankruptcy of two major companies—Kong Yung Construction and Ilshin Steel—and several other medium-sized companies. Many believed that Chang's operation would have been impossible without powerful political connections. Chang was related to the South Korean first lady, Lee Soon-ja, through the latter's uncle, Lee Kyu-kwang, who was Chang's former brother-in-law. Lee Kyu-kwang, president of the government-operated Korea Mining Promotion Corporation, was alleged to have taken tens of thousands dollars in bribes from Chang, and it was also alleged that he was instrumental in putting pressure on banks to extend large loans to troubled companies. Chun ordered a complete and thorough investigation of the scandal, which resulted in the arrest of 32 persons, including the main culprits, Chang and her husband, as well as

---

[63] *Donga Ilbo,* October 16, 1981.
[64] *Joongang Ilbo,* January 5, 1982.
[65] Interview with Lee Hak-bong.
[66] *New York Times,* March 4, 1982.
[67] Won-be Yoon, *Kum-yoong shil-myung-je* (Real-name Financial Transaction System) (Seoul: Bibong, 1992), 176ff.

several bank executives. At the trial Chang and her husband received fifteen-year sentences and heavy fines, Lee Kyu-kwang received a four-year sentence, and twenty-two other defendants were given prison terms. The fraudulent loan scandal dealt a blow to the moral authority of the Chun regime.[68] In order to restore public confidence in the government, Chun replaced eleven members of the twenty-four-member cabinet and the secretary-general of the ruling party in May 1982.

In order to restructure the financial sector, in July the Chun government announced a financial reform measure called the "7.3 Measure." Its stated goals were the promotion of "regularity in financial transactions by establishing the practice of using real names" and the "eradication of the underground economy and improvement of fairness in the tax code by applying progressive income taxes to incomes from financial assets."[69] As parts of the measure, the government slashed lending interest rates to 10 percent from a 13.5 percent bank prime rate and cut corporate taxes to 20 percent from the existing level of 33 to 38 percent. These measures expanded credit, taking the heat off thousands of companies that were in danger of going under. In December 1983, the National Assembly enacted the Act on Real Name Financial Transactions, a significantly watered-down version of the 7.3 Measure, which stated that implementation of the real-name system would begin at a time to be determined by presidential decree after January 1, 1986.[70]

After three years in office Chun had become quite confident in running the country both in economic and political terms. Through enforcement of the economic stabilization policy, the government successfully managed to improve the economic growth rate from minus 5.7 percent in 1980 to 11.9 percent in 1983, while also shrinking inflation from 28.7 percent in 1980 to 3.4 percent in 1983. The government improved relations with both the United States and Japan, which had been considerably strained during the 1970s. Chun was confident enough about the stability of his rule to be willing to further relax social, political control. Thus, the government decided to expand its liberalization policy into the political arena. In late December 1982, Chun ordered the release of Kim Dae Jung from prison and allowed him to go to the United States for medical treatment. In the spring of 1983, police forces were removed from university campuses and students and professors who had been expelled for antigovernment activities were restored to their original positions. The ban on political activities for some opposition politicians was also removed.

Politics of Olympics. Most observers neglect the importance of the 1988 Seoul Olympics in the Chun Doo Hwan presidency. But the Seoul Olympics were a historical turning point in South Korea's nation building.[71] Under the galvanizing slogan of "successful hosting of the 1988 Olympics," Korea was able to accelerate economic and social development in order to make the international event a success. The successful preparation and hosting of the international games became a common national objective. Had it not been

---

[68] *Washington Post*, August 9, 1982.
[69] Lee Jang-kyu (1992), 173-174.
[70] Jongsoo Lee, "The Real Name Financial System and the Politics of Economic Reform in the Republic of Korea", *Pacific Focus*, 10:1 (spring 1995): 109-110.
[71] For the impact of the Seoul Olympics, see Larson and Park, *Global Television*, and Jong-gie Kim et al. (1989).

awarded the 1988 Olympics, South Korea's course in the 1980s and 1990s might very well have been different.

At the time, most government officials were opposed to the plan to bid for the 1988 Olympics for economic reasons. As one South Korean official put it, "It is impossible for Korea to host the Olympics even if the right to do so is awarded, we cannot afford the enormous financial burden necessary for preparing for the event."[72] The general public was also skeptical. They believed Korea was not yet ready for the Olympics and feared that the international community would never consider Korea up to the task. However, Chun believed that Seoul's hosting of the Olympics would demonstrate South Korea's graduation from third-world adolescence to international maturity and allow it to join the ranks of advanced nations, and he strongly supported the bid. Since the modern rejuvenation of the Olympics in 1896, the hosts had been almost exclusively advanced nations.[73] In other words, he aimed to inculcate the effort with a sense of nationalism—to build an advanced country, to enhance national pride, and to improve Korea's image in the world.

In early 1981, Chun established the Ministry of State, a cabinet post without portfolio. Considering the importance of the mission, he appointed his close friend Roh Tae Woo as its first minister. Roh's responsibility was the high-profile task of bringing the 1988 Olympics to Seoul. Four months before the IOC voting, Chung Ju-yung, chairman of the Hyundai Group, was named chairman of the committee for bringing the Olympics to Seoul. Roh and Chung and other higher-ranking delegates traveled widely to mobilize support for the bid. The task was not an easy one. At that time, Korea was not well known internationally. Also, the Korean peninsula was regarded as one of the most dangerous places in the world. With memories of the terror during the 1972 Munich Olympics still fairly fresh, some seriously questioned whether a potential Asian flashpoint was a wise choice for Olympic host. The Korean delegation persuaded the IOC members that "Korea must host the Olympics in order to bring peace to the Korean peninsula."[74] It also tried to win the support of developing nations. It played for their sympathy by arguing, "The Olympic Games must not be the monopoly of advanced nations. The games must also be awarded to a developing nation."[75]

After a fierce competition, South Korean efforts were rewarded with success. On September 30, 1981, the 84th International Olympic Committee session held in Baden-Baden, West Germany, awarded Seoul the right to host the 1988 Olympics. The decision was so unexpected that most Koreans were overcome with an emotional mixture of great surprise, joy, and pride, especially because the only other competitor for the games had been Japan, an economic superpower and the target of much Korean animosity. The Koreans had defeated the Japanese by a 52-27 margin. The decision was a crucial victory for the new Chun administration, and the Olympics would have a profound historical significance on his presidency, his people, and the nation.

---

[72] Vincent J. Ricquart, *The Games Within the Games: The Story Behind the 1988 Seoul Olympics* (Seoul: Hantong Books, 1988), 15.
[73] Young Ho Lee, "The Seoul Olympics: What They Mean to the Korean People", *Korea and World Affairs*, 12:2 (summer 1988): 253-269.
[74] Roh Tae Woo, "The Reminiscences of Roh Tae Woo, Part 1", *Wolgan Chosun* (May 1999).
[75] Ibid.

In a country where targets and goals are typical forms of popular motivation, the Olympics provided South Koreans just such a tangible goal to work toward. As soon as the Olympics were awarded, the Chun government embarked on intense efforts to prepare for the international event. The Seoul Olympics became a pan-national project for the government. The massive effort could be explained by Korea's status as a developing nation. Under the scrutiny of the rest of the world, South Koreans were extremely self-conscious. Impression management was at work everywhere. The government and corporations spent huge sums to beautify the country and South Korean products. The government launched a comprehensive program of construction and national development. Olympic preparations and national development plans were coordinated. The government worked hard to prepare for the staging of the games, through massive infrastructure development projects, including elaborate sports facilities, throughout the country.

The Han River Development Project was one of the most important and successful of the Olympic projects. The Han River is legendary as the lifeline of the Korean capital and the Korean nation. However, as the city of Seoul burgeoned around the Han River during the 1960s and 1970s, the water became foul and polluted to the extent that fish could no longer live in the river's lower reaches that flowed through the capital. Chun was strongly motivated to clean up the river, a desire made more critical by the fact that most of the Olympic facilities would be located on or near the river. A clean-flowing river would become the location for the opening ceremony of the games with the Han River boat parade. It would also be the site of the Han River festival accompanying the games. Highways that would run along the banks of the river would become the Olympic marathon course. Thus, the Han River would be one of the most frequently televised backdrops as Seoul presented itself to the world.

But the project required at least a billion dollars. The government could not afford such a huge investment. Chun, however, had an economic idea to develop the project.[76] The government and the city of Seoul decided to award the nation's ten major construction companies the right to dredge the river in return for their free participation in the project. Owing to the construction boom, sand and gravel were very expensive materials for the construction industry. There was plenty of sand and gravel beneath the water. Thus, the Han River Development Project could be completed on a minimum budget. The project involved drainage work, dredging, and the construction of raised embankments on both sides of the river within the city. These embankments were developed into public parks, gardens and athletic fields. A new, 37-kilometer Olympic Expressway, connecting Kimpo International Airport and the Olympic Park, was built on the south bank of the river. The historical project changed the face of Seoul completely. The Han became a clean and beautiful river, commensurate with "the miracle on the Han."

Transportation was regarded as an essential element for the successful hosting of the Olympics. Thus, in addition to completion of the Olympic Expressway, the government pushed for the construction of a complex network to enhance the Seoul subway system. In 1985, one year before the Asian Games, the three newest lines of the Seoul subway system were completed simultaneously. Before the Olympics, a circle line was finished

---

[76] See Kim Sung-ik (1992), 355-356.

Chun Doo Hwan

and the metropolitan subway and railway system networks were completed. Consequently, Seoul was able to utilize one of the most modern subway systems in the world for both the Asian Games and the Seoul Olympics.

The government also engaged in a massive public campaign aimed at ensuring success in hosting the Olympics. The government tried to use the national campaigns to promote social modernization. One of the campaigns was a movement to "make public order, kindness and cleanness a part of daily life." The campaign emphasized public order in the streets, in sports venues, and in commercial transactions. The government required businesses to post price tags. Millions of merchants participated in seminars, education programs, and talks to promote commercial ethics. Foreign-language programs were also encouraged in the service sector. Since almost everyone wanted the Olympics to be successful, many people enthusiastically participated.[77]

The Seoul Asian Games in 1986 were widely viewed as a dress rehearsal for the 1988 Olympics. Virtually all the Olympic venues had been completed by that time and were used for the sports activities. The Asian Games were very successful. The Seoul Olympic Games were prepared through well-planned, well-implemented programs pushed by Chun's strong commitment and dedication, and sustained by the enthusiastic support and participation of the South Korean people. They were held only seven months after Chun's retirement and turned out to be the most successful Olympics ever held.[78]

THE SECOND ECONOMIC TAKEOFF

Market-Oriented Reform. Park Chung Hee had been an effective leader, especially when it came to economic policy. But before his inauguration Chun Doo Hwan knew nothing about economics. Many observers, in South Korea and elsewhere, doubted his capacity for economic management. Before moving to the center of national power, his priorities were national security and social stability. Assuming power, he soon realized that economic malaise was a major cause of the national crisis. The growth rate plunged to negative 5.7 percent, current account deficits recorded $5.5 billion, foreign debts reached $34 billion, and inflation was well over 30 percent in 1980. Moreover, a series of economic tutoring sessions convinced him that if he failed to sustain Park's legacy of economic growth he would not be a successful president. Chun learned on the job and he learned quickly.

Such a grave situation demanded decisive leadership. As capable as they might be, on their own, the technocrats could not make the difficult decisions and take the tough actions required. But Chun was a take-charge sort of leader. Although he brought a group of bright, articulate, Western-trained economists into the economic policymaking team, he himself was determined to learn about economics and economic policy. He recalled the Korean saying, "Even a rural mayor can do his job when he knows what to do and how." Three or four mornings a week Chun had tutoring sessions in economic issues with prominent technocrats. Kim Jae-ik, who soon became his chief economic adviser, was the principal tutor, but later,

---

[77] Larson and Park, *Global Television*, 152-156.
[78] This will be discussed further in the chapter on the Roh Tae Woo presidency.

several other brilliant technocrats joined the team of economic coaches.[79] Chun was sincere, sometimes naïve, and always straightforward. He was willing to admit that he had much to learn, particularly in the field of economics. During the first year of his term, large cardboard charts were propped up against the wall in the corner of his office. They were the instruction charts for his daily economic lessons with his economic advisers.

Through his yearlong lessons in economics, Chun became familiar not only with economic issues but also with the technocrats themselves. He succeeded in organizing a capable body of economic policymakers who became important members of his economic team. He gave his advisers and cabinet members considerable freedom of action. Because they benefited from the president's full support and from no effective opposition, the technocrats could act as they saw fit. After he became president, Chun offered Kim Jae-ik the chief economic adviser position. Accustomed to a military staff system, Chun knew the crucial role advisers and experts played in decision-making. The president was willing to trust his advisers to a degree that would have been unimaginable under Park Chung Hee. When Kim once asked the president if he would lend his full support to policy positions that would face serious resistance, Chun replied simply, "You are the president of economic affairs."[80]

As seen through his private economic lessons, Chun attached great importance to technocrats and think tanks. He received reports on major policy-related studies directly from researchers. For example, Sakong Il, then a senior fellow at the Korea Development Institute (KDI), reported to the president the results of a 'public corporations reform' study. It was unprecedented for a researcher to report directly to the president. Chun did not listen passively to the reports; he interjected here and there, asking questions and expressing his opinions. Other participants were also asked to make comments. A one-hour meeting was extended to two or more hours of detailed and lively discussion. Through such meetings, Chun tried to learn and solve the problems of his policy agenda.[81]

After Kim Jae-ik was killed in a North Korean terrorist attack in Rangoon in October 1983, Sakong Il, then president of the Korea Institute for Economics and Technology (KIET), was appointed Chun's chief economic adviser. On a Sunday morning, Sakong was preparing for his job with his staff in the Blue House when the president unexpectedly invited him for lunch. During a two-hour lunch, Chun explained his economic policy and Kim Jae-ik's efforts, and said: "You will have so many things to do that you will not have enough time to review all policy issues on your own. You must use the resources of the think tanks such as the KDI and the KIET. You may nominate the new presidents of these institutes, persons who will cooperate with you."[82] Around the same time, Kim Man-jae, president of the KDI, had been named minister of the

---

[79] Others included Sakong Il (who became chief economic adviser after Kim's death in Rangoon), Park Bong-hwan (later commerce and industry minister), Kim Ki-hwan (later deputy minister of the Economic Planning Board), and Suh Sang-chul (later energy minister).
[80] Lee Jang-kyu (1992), 8.
[81] Interview with Sakong Il on April 19, 2002.
[82] Ibid.

Economic Planning Board, thus, the KDI presidency was open.[83] Chun's delegation of such a task to an adviser was unprecedented. Chun fully trusted his new economic adviser and apparently believed Sakong could organize the best working team. Kim Man-jae and Sakong Il cooperated closely in leading the economic team. This example illustrates that Chun recognized the importance of think tanks, delegation, and teamwork. During an interview with the author, Sakong explained: "Like President Park, President Chun made the best use of the think tanks. A good government is one that can develop policies based on ideas from the best brains available."[84]

What made the South Korean economic miracle possible between 1962 and 1979 was, in part, the government-guided strategy for economic development. Chun's economic advisers persuaded the new president to stabilize and restructure the economy. They believed that the economy faced five serious challenges: high inflation, a structural imbalance between heavy and light industry, a high trade deficit caused by the loss of international competitiveness, a slowdown in economic growth, and the deterioration of income distribution. The government had to solve those problems and lay the foundations for a second take-off. They agreed that there was a need for fundamental change in the government's role in the national economy. As the economy became more complex and sophisticated, it was believed that it was desirable to gradually relax government interference in it.[85]

Seeing himself as the torch carrier of Park's economic legacy, Chun was more anxious than anyone to get the economy moving and determined to make economic success a cornerstone of his presidency. He was a reform-oriented, decisive leader who was willing and ready to administer whatever bitter medicine was called for. During an interview with a foreign magazine in late 1981, Chun summarized his economic policy as follows:

> I intend to build, first of all, a solid foundation for economic stability and seek growth on that basis.... The force of inflation in Korea was such that wholesale prices jumped 44 percent in 1980. The government pledged itself to reduce the inflation rate to 20 or 25 percent this year. As matters stand now, I anticipate the price increase rate to remain below the 20 percent level for the entire year of 1981. It should be noted that such a reduction in inflation is being achieved in spite of the fact that the bulk of price controls were removed this year. Only by maintaining stability in that manner will it be possible to reinforce the market mechanism and let the economy be operated primarily on private initiative. This will insure more efficient and effective allocation of resources and improved productivity throughout the Korean economy.
>
> The present administration is especially concerned about satisfying the basic needs of the people and achieving more equitable income distribution.... In my

---

[83] Kim Man-jae was a leading technocrat during the 1970s and 1980s. President Park appointed Kim as the first president of the KDI. Kim led the economic think tank for more than eleven years.

[84] Interview with Sakong Il.

[85] Sang-Mok Suh, "The Economy in Historical Perspective" and In-Joung Whang, "Economic Management for Structural Adjustment in the 1980s", in Corbo and Suh, eds., *Structural Adjustment*, 6-34 and 305-327.

definition of basic needs I include price stability, greater opportunities for education at all levels, better housing and more and better medical care.

> Lastly, I must add that I will see to it that our economic policies are not distorted by extraneous factors, such as political pressures, as is often the case in many developing countries. It is my unwavering conviction that the economy must be operated according to economic consideration and judgment and not otherwise.[86]

Chun took immediate steps toward restructuring and redirecting the economy. He aimed to achieve high growth with stability and equity. He believed that the goal could be accomplished through private initiative and a competitive market system. He had very difficult choices, however. He needed to stimulate economic activity, but curb inflation and promote the general welfare without incurring an unmanageable budget deficit. But his immediate goal was to promote economic stability, rather than the high growth that had been the consistent objective of his predecessor.

Chun's blueprint for achieving a "second economic miracle in Korea" was contained in his ambitious Fifth Five-Year Economic and Social Development Plan (1982-1986), which was announced in August 1981. The plan represented the direction and contents of Chun's economic policy for the 1980s. The plan included three key measures: maintaining price stability, liberalizing the economy through lessened government control, and increasing social development benefits. It was unlike previous plans in that it did not set an annual investment target. It focused on institutional reform in order to solve structural problems. In addition, the term "economic and social development" was used for the first time. This emphasis on "economic development" as well as "social development" indicated a change in development strategy, from a quantity-centered growth strategy to a quality-centered one.[87] The plan envisaged an annual growth of 7 to 8 percent in national income, while holding the inflation rate to single digits. It forecast a welfare investment ratio of 28.5 percent and set a goal of a 20 percent annual increase in exports. To finance the plan, the government announced plans to hike the rate of domestic savings from 21.2 percent in 1980 to 29.6 percent by 1986 and to reduce dependency on foreign loans from 9.8 percent in 1980 to as low as 2.9 percent by 1986. The plan was intended to concentrate on restructuring the economy during the first two years and to launch the "second takeoff" of the economy by 1983.[88]

Stability First. Through intensive consultations, Chun realized that inflation was a cancer eating away at the body politic, and radical treatment was necessary to eliminate it. He was likewise convinced that stabilization was the only way to revitalize the economy, and for this he was willing to pay the price. In his 1981 New Year's address to the nation, he declared: "Stability is the key to economic progress," promising the country that under his administration the permanent economic crisis state of the 1970s would be avoided. In his 1982 budget proposal to the National Assembly in September 1981, President Chun stated, "Price stability should be our foremost policy priority, to provide a stable living environment for the general public

---

[86] *Institutional Investor* (February 1982), 74-75.
[87] See Economic Planning Board, *The Fifth Five-Year Economic and Social Development Plan, 1982-1986* (Seoul, 1981), 11.
[88] *Korea News Review*, August 29, 1981.

and to strengthen the international competitiveness of our industries." From then, the president was briefed on price movements every 10 days.[89]

The principle of "economic stability first" represented a sharp departure from the principle of "economic growth first," the guiding policy of the 1960s and 1970s.[90] In order to promote the stability-first policy, the government tried to cut back on government spending and tighten the monetary supply. It drastically reduced governmental investment, infrastructure development, and subsidies to business. Chun approved of whatever the technocrats suggested in order to curb inflation. In 1982, the government tried to set an example through disciplined fiscal management. It introduced a zero-based budgeting system to optimize government expenditure. In 1983 the government took drastic and unpopular measures: it froze the budget, civil servant salaries, and rice-purchase prices to help reduce the budgetary deficit. The three freezes in the year before the crucial general elections made the government's intention and commitment more credible.[91]

In order to promote the international competitiveness of Korean products, both import duties and subsidies for exports were reduced. In addition, monetary policy was tightened and interest rates were raised. Companies that had depended on easy credit howled in pain. Big corporations became preoccupied with their own survival rather than expansion, and the Federation of Korean Industries, the main umbrella organization of the big corporations, protested the policies. The government also slammed the brakes on wage growth. The government set up wage guidelines for the private sector. Wages were growing more than 34 percent a year from 1976 to 1978. But the wage growth rate decelerated quickly under the Chun government. From 1984 through 1986 wages rose less than 10 percent a year, the only three years of single-digit wage growth since Park Chung Hee had taken power in 1961. Farmers were also alienated by the policies of reduced subsidy and import liberalization for foreign farm products.[92]

The "stabilization first" policy was socio-economically unpopular and politically dangerous. Despite the general benefit of price stability, businesses, labor, white-color workers, farmers, and even public officials disliked the anti-inflation policies. Political opposition was therefore very strong. Lawmakers, including ruling party members, the press, and even powerful political advisers to the president, strongly argued against the stabilization measures. It was a politically critical period for the president but he was determined to continue the stabilization policy. He was often quoted as saying, "Since I will retire after my term, I do not care about my own popularity." His strong support of anti-inflation measures made the technocrats implement the unpopular policy without worrying too much about political resistance.

Chun tried to sell his policy to as many people as possible and made full use of meetings to do so. He met with the chairmen of big conglomerates and urged them to reduce or stabilize the prices of consumer products. He sometimes forced businesses to

---

[89] Sakong, *Korea*, 68.
[90] Jang Kyu Lee (1992), 220-231.
[91] A budget freeze succeeded in cutting the total government deficit as a percentage of GNP from 4.7 percent in 1981 to 1.4 percent in 1984.
[92] Sakong, *Korea*, 66-71.

reduce prices by mentioning the possibility of import liberalization of certain items as an alternative to price stabilization. The president also met labor leaders and leaders of farmers' organizations to persuade them not to demand higher wages or more farm subsidies. To enhance popular understanding of the difficult economic situation, and to build a broad consensus behind the painful anti-inflation policy, an economic education program was initiated toward the end of 1980 on Chun's initiative. The education program targeted all classes of people, and the educational media was diversified to include lectures, slides, videotapes, newspapers, booklets, radio, and television. The newly established Economic Education Bureau formulated an annual education program, supported education in other organizations by preparing educational materials and appointing education officers, and sent materials on major economic policies to about 5,000 public opinion leaders.[93] Chun personally evaluated the education program and often sat in on economic education briefing sessions led by working-level government officials. This reflected his strong determination to fight inflation.[94]

The anti-inflation policy was very successful. In fact, remarkable results came much faster than expected. Wholesale price increases, which had reached 42.3 percent in 1980, dropped to 11.3 percent in 1981, 2.4 percent in 1982, and 0.2 percent in 1983. Consumer price increases, which had risen to 38.2 percent in 1980, were brought down to 13.8 percent in 1981, 4.7 percent in 1982, and 3.4 percent in 1983. This was the first time Korean inflation had dropped to the one-digit level since 1965. The Chun government had achieved what had been considered impossible.

Liberalization. Together with the stabilization efforts, the government introduced various liberalizing measures. The heart of the liberalization program was the privatization and deregulation of the financial system.[95] The essential component of Park Chung Hee's government-led development strategy was geared toward government control of the financial sector. In the early 1980s, the Chun government either abolished or simplified hundreds of financial regulations and directives. Another important liberalization measure was the privatization of commercial banks. Between 1981 and 1983, four existing national commercial banks and ten regional banks were privatized. Moreover, entry into the financial industry was relaxed when the government allowed a number of new financial institutions to be established. Between 1982 and 1983, two commercial banks, 12 investment and finance companies, and 58 mutual savings and finance companies were established.

As part of economic liberalization, the government introduced measures to curtail the influence of big conglomerates and to increase the international competitiveness of Korean firms. It enacted the Monopoly Regulation and Fair Trade Act in April 1981, and the Fair Trade Administration was established under the EPB to oversee the activities of big business groups and promote fair competition. The enactment was an important turning point in the history of interaction between market and government in South Korea. It is interesting to observe that South Korea adopted a competition law as early as 1981, when most other

---

[93] In-Joung Whang, "Economic Management", Corbo and Suh, eds., *op. cit.*, 317-321.
[94] Sakong, *Korea*, 67.
[95] See Alice H. Amsden and Y. D. Euh, "South Korea's 1980s Financial Reform", *World Development*, 21: 3 (1993).

developing nations, and even some advanced ones, did not have one. This demonstrates the urgent need for a competition law at a time when the high growth of the 1960s and 1970s had resulted in a serious concentration of economic resources in the hands of large conglomerates. The enactment of the law is regarded as one of Chun's most significant legislative achievements.[96]

The government also opened Korean markets by liberalizing imports and foreign direct investment. During the early weeks of the Chun regime, the government announced it would "liberalize the economy to accelerate the inflow of foreign capital and technology."[97] The government liberalized markets for technology and foreign direct investment. Effective from July 1981, a new policy on direct foreign investment also allowed an equity share by foreign investors of up to 100 percent in more than fifty-six industries.[98] The external liberalization was based on the belief that to increase international competitiveness, import liberalization was inevitable. By introducing foreign competition at a steadily increasing pace, import liberalization was expected to pressure South Korean companies into raising both productivity and quality. If Korean products could not compete with imported goods in the domestic market, where foreign goods were handicapped by tariffs and transportation costs, the government believed they would not compete effectively overseas. To offset rapidly expanding imports owing to import liberalization, the government launched programs of export promotion and export diversification. It targeted the cash-rich Middle East. In 1981 South Korean exports to the Middle East equaled 73 percent of the total South Korean trade deficit and 38 percent of its foreign currency earnings. In addition, trade with other parts of the world grew; in 1981, for example, one third of export growth was in Latin American and African countries.[99]

Rapidly rising income, financial liberalization, policies of stable but higher interest rates, and anti-inflation measures helped raise the level of private and corporate savings. The government also encouraged savings. By the mid-eighties, the national savings rate had climbed to almost 35 percent of the GNP, in contrast to the low 20 percent level maintained during the previous decade.[100] At this point, without dependence on foreign loans, South Korea was able to support the huge investment economic development demanded.

Industrial Restructuring. The negative legacies of Park's heavy industry drive were serious. Headlong investment in heavy industry had produced duplication, wastage, and excess capacity. Owing to rising energy costs, overcapitalization, and shrinking markets, many factories had become economic disaster areas. Also, there were a large number of unfinished projects in Park's heavy industrialization plan that required constant huge capital input. Most of the big companies in heavy industry were losing money every day. Meanwhile, small and medium-sized firms, which had been Korea's main exporters, suffered from a lack of financial assistance and too little investment. From the onset of the Chun government,

---

[96] Ibid., 450-51.
[97] *Korean Newsletter*, October 1980.
[98] *Far Eastern Economic Review*, November 25, 1981.
[99] Tony Michell, *From a Developing to a Newly Industrialized Country: The Republic of Korea, 1962-82* (Paris: International Labour Office, 1988), 15.
[100] The figure is based on Korea Statistical Yearbooks.

therefore, the second focus of economic reform was placed on achieving balanced growth between heavy and light industry and between large and small businesses.

The Chun administration pushed anti-*chaebol* measures hard.[101] The newly enacted fair trade law included a broad array of *chaebol* reforms: anticompetitive mergers were prohibited, and unfair and deceptive advertising was forbidden. The government ordered conglomerates to dispose of affiliated companies in excess of management capabilities. The targets of the reform measures were giant *chaebol* that had become top-heavy and uneconomical, thanks largely to cheap credit, defense contracts, and tax concessions. In order to eliminate wasteful competition, the government adopted strong measures of corporate restructuring. It tightened credit, even though this forced some companies into bankruptcy or reorganization, and restricted cross-equity sharing among *chaebol* subsidiaries.[102] In addition, the government announced a new policy wherein companies were forced to disclose landholdings, sell idle lands, and repay loans. The aim was to reduce government support and control, thereby making industry freer but more beholden to the market situation.[103]

In 1984, as the economy stabilized and began to revitalize, the government embarked on the most difficult part of industrial restructuring—reform of the construction and shipping sectors. Each major *chaebol* owned at least one construction and shipping company. Since the Middle East construction boom of the 1970s, as many as eight-three Korean construction companies had established themselves in the area, sixty-nine in Saudi Arabia alone. But by the early 1980s the construction boom in the Middle East had turned to bust. Excessive competition among the Korean firms had driven them all to a state just short of bankruptcy. Major shipping companies were also in serious trouble. Owing to rising oil prices, sluggish world trade, and falling shipping charges, in the late 1970s the worldwide marine transportation business was suffering. Despite this, the Park government had allowed shipping companies to buy some 530 cargo carriers. Because of declining exports in the late 1970s and early 1980s owing to two rounds of oil crisis, these companies had accumulated huge debts. There was danger of massive bankruptcies among these financially stricken firms and possibly of the commercial banks involved. In order to avoid widespread bankruptcies, in 1984 and 1985 the government implemented "rationalization" programs for construction and shipping industries. After the restructuring, about one-third of the construction companies had merged and only seventeen of sixty-seven shipping firms remained.[104] The restructuring evoked predictable hardships and complaints, but in the end this policy resulted in a greatly improved competitive efficiency of the economy.

Stabilization and reform had a quickening if unpleasantly medicinal effect on the economy. Restructuring policies laid the foundation for the sharp recovery and

---

[101] *Forbes* (February 11, 1985): 40; and Ha Joon Chang, "The Political Economy of Industry Policy in Korea", *Cambridge Journal of Economics*, 17:2 (1993): 131-157.

[102] Sakong, *Korea*, 62-63.

[103] Forced corporate restructuring resulted in a series of bankruptcies such as those of the Dongmyung Timber Co. and Hwashin Group in 1980, Myungsung Group in 1983, and Kukje Group in 1985.

[104] Sakong, *Korea*, 75-79; and Clifford, *Troubled Tiger*, 215-216.

subsequent economic boom of the mid-1980s.[105]

Telecommunications Revolution. The Chun government also promoted an aggressive science and technology policy. Just as Park Chung Hee had promoted the export-oriented drive in the 1970s, Chun Doo Hwan promoted a technology drive in the 1980s.[106] One of the most serious problems facing the Korean economy was its heavy dependence on foreign technologies.[107] In the 1960s and 1970s, Korea was competing against Japanese and American companies largely on the basis of its low labor costs. The Korean economy required an urgent upgrade; therefore, technological development became imperative.

Chun's understanding of science and engineering was better than his grasp of economics. He was a graduate of a technical high school and of the Korea Military Academy, which places great importance on science and engineering. From the beginning he paid close attention to the nation's science and technology policy and repeatedly emphasized, "We should make utmost efforts to develop technology ourselves." Top-notch technocrats, many of them with Ph.D.s in science and engineering from American universities, were appointed as advisers in this area. The government pumped money into research and development as fast as it could. Under the Chun government, there was a remarkable increase in research and development investments; under the "technology drive" policy, investment in science and technology increased from 0.8 percent of GNP in 1981 to 2.2 percent in 1987 (see Figure 5).[108]

A long-term master plan for the development of science and technology through the year 2000 was launched. The primary emphasis of the plan, which called for increasing investment in science and technology to up to 3.1 percent of GNP by the year 2000, was on the development and mobilization of manpower. As a foundation for advancing to the next stage of economic development, the government aimed to create a scientific research infrastructure and highly trained manpower. It placed great emphasis on "catching up" with more advanced countries at the cutting edge of modern technology.[109] As part of the technology promotion plan, in 1986 the government launched an ambitious plan that would double its increase of new engineers within five years.[110] To promote research and development in the private sector, the government offered tax and financial incentives and revised the commercial tax law. Through these incentives, the government encouraged the private sector's investment in technological development, including the creation of research institutes and research teams. As a result, the number of research centers in the private sector multiplied almost six fold, from fifty-three in 1981 to 290 in 1987.

In order to push his science and technology programs, President Chun established the Science and Technology Promotion Meeting. The meeting was chaired by the president himself and attended by the minister of science and technology and other

---

[105] See IMF, *A Case of Successful Adjustment: Korea's Experience During 1980-84*; and Corbo and Suh, eds., *op. cit.*, 336-345.

[106] Ministry of Science and Technology, *Twenty Years' History of Science and Technology and Technology Administration* (Seoul, 1987).

[107] This section is based on the author's interview with Oh Myung on April 13, 2002.

[108] The figure is based on data provided by the Ministry of Science and Technology, Korea.

[109] Ministry of Science and Technology, *op. cit.*

[110] *Business Week*, December 23, 1985.

science-related ministers, and by representatives from the science and engineering research institutes, science-related organizations, and business. The meeting reviewed the progress and problems of the major projects and discussed necessary measures for the government and the private sector. The meeting was an effective means for promoting the science and technology policy.

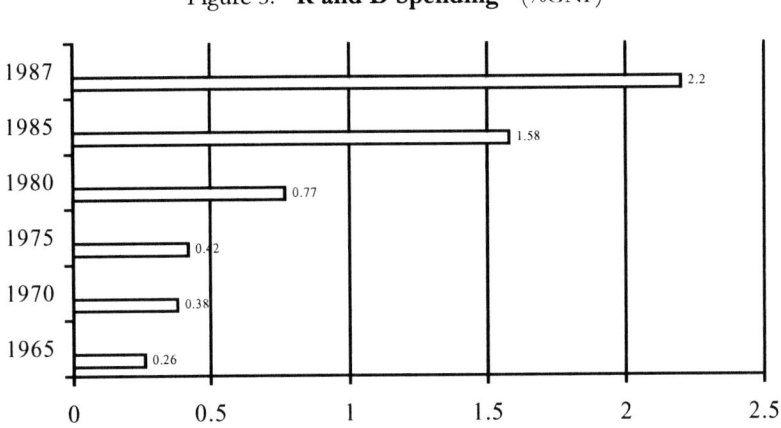

Figure 5. **R and D Spending** (%GNP)

Year	% GNP
1987	2.2
1985	1.58
1980	0.77
1975	0.42
1970	0.38
1965	0.26

The telecommunications sector was the key contributor to technological development during the Chun administration. This sector had become one of the fastest growing in the world in the 1980s.[111] In late 1980, Chun established a Blue House task force of twenty-eight persons, composed of related officials and private experts, to formulate an electronic industry promotion plan. After three months of intensive efforts, the Blue House announced an ambitious blue print for electronic industry development in the 1980s. The plan designated semiconductors, computers, and electronic switching systems as three strategic industries that the government would promote, with the aim of increasing their production and export by three times over five years. Many, including government officials, regarded the plan as sheer folly. They were accustomed to the importance of the heavy and chemical industries that former president Park had promoted. The electronic sector lagged far behind.[112]

Following the blue print for electronic development, the government vigorously promoted two ambitious collaborative public and private projects—the TDX electronic switching system project and the 4-megabit DRAM semiconductor project. The digital switching system is a key component of modern telephone and communications networks, while semiconductors are building blocks of all modern computers and electronic products. At that time, only advanced countries produced electronic switching systems.

After four years of intensive effort, South Korea acquired the capability to produce

---

[111] Kim Jungsoo, *Hankukui jungbotongsin hyukmyung* (Korea's Telecommunications Revolution) (Seoul: Nanam, 2000); and James F. Larson, *The Telecommunications Revolution in Korea* (New York: Oxford University Press, 1995).
[112] Lee Jang-kyu (1992), 265.

electronic switching systems, mini-computers, and 4-megabit DRAM chips. The joint government-industry effort to develop the TDX electronic switching system was of special importance. It allowed Korea to increase rapidly the proportion of electronic switches in its telephone network. It also instilled a confidence that carried over to ensuing technology transfer and development projects. The TDX project, which both India and Brazil had tried and failed, would not have been possible without President Chun's strong personal commitment and full support. He provided a research fund of 24 billion *won* (about $35 million) at a time when there was no research project over 1 billon *won*. Chun also emphasized the importance of memory-chips: he said, "The memory chip is the 'rice' of the electronic industry. Without it, we cannot develop a computer and other high-tech products." The successful memory-chip project, initiated and supported by the government, allowed Korean manufacturers to gain a large share of the world market for DRAM chips in the coming decades.[113]

Thanks to the indigenous development of the electronic switching system, the Chun administration embarked on a comprehensive and ambitious program to modernize its telecommunications infrastructure. For all of the phenomenal economic growth of the 1970s, South Korean telecommunications remained highly underdeveloped. In 1974, the price of a telephone was more than $2,000, when Korean per capita income was only $400. Moreover, there was a $700 application fee for the phone's installation, followed by months of waiting. Ownership of a telephone remained a status symbol of the rich. Yet even after installation, people suffered through poor audio quality and equally lamentable service. By 1980, 87 percent of all South Korean households possessed television sets, while only 24 percent had telephones.[114]

With the lack of a modern nationwide telephone network, and in spite of the political turmoil of 1979-1980, in 1981 the Chun government announced the goal of achieving "one telephone, one household" in Korea. The policy was extremely ambitious. It required the confidence and leadership to finance the infrastructure buildup, which primarily centered on electronic switching systems. By the end of 1987, the last year of Chun's term, Korea had more than 10 million telephone subscribers and had achieved a penetration rate of one phone per household. Even more striking was the arrival of "same-day service"—telephone customers were now offered installation within a single working day.[115]

During his recent interview, Oh Myung, the architect of Korea's telecommunications revolution, confidently asserted: "In terms of information technology, Korea today is one of the most advanced countries in the world. Korea's installation of telephone service is the fastest in the world. Its telecommunications service has the narrowest gap between the rural and urban areas. Its per capita capacity of broadband telecommunications networks is ten times as much as the United States. *The Wall Street Journal* reported that Korea began to run with an IT [information and technology] engine. Korea's IT industry is five years ahead of Japan's. These are the results of the continuous implementations of the basic plans that began to be promoted during the Chun

---

[113] Interview with Oh Myung on April 15, 2002.
[114] Larson, *Telecommunications Revolution*, 15.
[115] Kim Jungsoo, *op. cit.*, 33-35.

administration."[116] During the 1980s the character of the Korean economy changed in fundamental ways. In that decade the information and communication sector grew an average of 28.6 percent annually, more than twice the rate of overall economic growth.[117] As a consequence, in 1986 the electronics and telecommunications sector caught and surpassed the textile industry as Korea's leading export industry. By the end of the 1980s, the Korean economy revolved around the manufacture and sale, both domestically and in export markets, of communication-related products.[118]

"*Koreans Are Coming.*" The Chun administration's policies of economic stabilization and restructuring proved highly successful.[119] The Korean economy had weathered the economic crises of the late 1970s and the early 1980s and was back on its high-growth track. Fueled by the improvement in international competitiveness and an intensive exports promotion effort, exports had nearly doubled in the first half of the decade, growing from $17.5 billion in 1980 to $30.3 billion in 1985. By the standards of most economies, this was a very impressive performance. Yet in the next three years, exports doubled yet again to $60.7 billion. Strenuous stabilization efforts, combined with the favorable international economic environment of the time—such as low oil prices, a weak dollar against the Japanese yen, and low international interest rates—resulted in a boom of unprecedented magnitude, with the economy growing more than 12 percent a year between 1986 and 1988.[120] The economic boom, which was capped by the 1988 Seoul Olympics, erased much of the self-doubt and feelings of inferiority that had traditionally influenced Korean minds. At last the long-awaited "second take-off" had arrived.

The increase in exports ($13.4 billion) in 1988 alone was nearly equal to the total exports ($14.7 billion) of 1979. By 1987, Korea was a larger exporter than many European countries, including Spain, Ireland, Norway, Finland, Denmark, and Austria. Korea moved into the ranks of the top twelve trading nations in the world. As a result, the nation's international balance of payments situation improved remarkably. In 1987, the last year of the Chun presidency, economic expansion was led by the heavy industry sector, which had been the major trouble spot of the economy in the late 1970s and the early 1980s. During this period, South Korea emerged as the most powerful of the Asian developing economies. Founded by Park and restructured by Chun, the strength of South Korea's heavy industry—shipbuilding, chemicals, autos—differentiated the country from the other tigers. During the second half of the 1980s, South Korea was the second-largest shipbuilder in the non-Communist world, trailing only Japan. In autos, South Korea emerged as the only developing nation capable of designing and producing its own cars for export. South Korea was also emerging as one of the world's largest suppliers of semiconductor chips, as well as one of the world's largest petrochemical suppliers. South Korea now assumed the role of the world's key new manufacturing

---

[116] Ibid. Oh served as vice minister and minister of telecommunications for seven and a half years.
[117] "Economy and Industry Trends", *Korea Trade & Business* (October 1992): 11.
[118] Young-Kon Kim and Chang-Bun Yoo, "Country Strategy for Developing the Information and Communication Technology and Its Infrastructure: Korea", *Korean Journal of Information Society*, 3:1 (spring 1991): 140.
[119] Clifford, *Troubled Tiger*, 236-52.
[120] The figure is based on *Korea Statistical Yearbook*, various years.

center, a status that none of its Asian rivals enjoyed.

After running a chronic trade deficit for forty years, South Korea quickly began generating large surpluses. These were significant amounts of money—a total of $23 billion between 1986 and 1988. It was an extraordinary turnaround for a country that had never before had a trade surplus. The surplus was used to pay off foreign debt. Korea's 1979-1980 economic crisis had forced the nation to engage in massive foreign borrowing. The country's foreign debt grew from $20 billion in 1979 to $51 billion in 1985. In fact, as of 1985, Korea's foreign debt was more than 50 percent of its gross national product. But, owing to the successful economic policy of the Chun administration, the amount of foreign debt began to decrease rapidly (see Figure 6).[121]

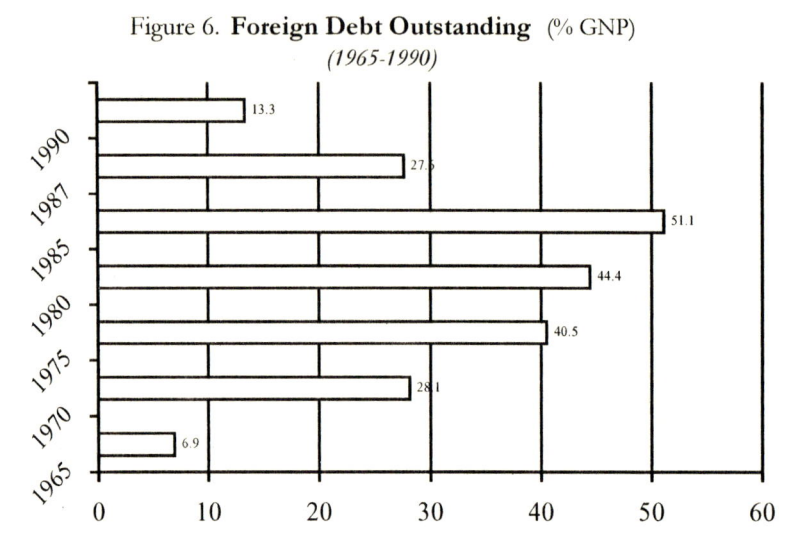

Figure 6. **Foreign Debt Outstanding** (% GNP) *(1965-1990)*

Year	% GNP
1990	13.3
1987	27.6
1985	51.1
1980	44.4
1975	40.5
1970	28.1
1965	6.9

Korea's per capita income had risen from $80 in the early 1960s to more than $3,200 in 1987, higher than that of Portugal. Its GNP of $136 billion was already larger than that of half of the members of the Organization for Economic Cooperation and Development (OECD), a club of twenty-four advanced nations. South Korea's industrial muscle had pushed it ahead of such OECD members as Austria, Belgium, Greece, Norway, and Sweden. The South Koreans now sensed a historic opportunity. As one official told an American reporter: "This is the first time in our 5,000-year history that we have a chance to become an economically advanced country. We have to do it."[122] Park Chung Hee had created the foundation with his ambitious industrialization drive, but his goals remained half-finished. Chun Doo Hwan inherited and successfully completed Park's ambitious

---

[121] Gibney, *Korea's Quiet Revolution*, 78-82; and *Time*, September 10, 1984. Figure 7 is based on data in Ho-Youn Kwon, *Contemporary Korea* (Chicago: Center for Korean Studies, North Park College, 1997), 90.

[122] Quoted in "The Koreans Are Coming", *Business Week*, December 23, 1985.

projects. The "miracle on the Han" was no longer a dream but a reality. It was really a "man-made miracle."[123] No one could deny that Park had succeeded in the rapid industrialization of Korea. But at the time of his death Park's economic modernization was incomplete and rather shaky. If there had been no successful adjustment and painful restructuring of the economy in the 1980s under the determined leadership of Chun Doo Hwan, the Korean economy probably could not have grown to the point that it was able to compete on equal footing with the world's leading economies.

DIPLOMACY FOR SECURITY AND THE OLYMPICS

Closer Ties with Washington and Tokyo. In the late 1970s Seoul-Washington relations were strained—a natural outcome of Park Chung Hee's repressive measures mixed with Jimmy Carter's Korea policies of troop withdrawal and human rights concerns. However, as the United States faced renewed Communist challenges around the world Carter's "human rights" diplomacy encountered criticism. During 1979-1980, the United States faced security crises worldwide.[124] In January 1979, fundamentalist Moslems overthrew the Pahlavi regime in Iran. On November 4, Iranian militants seized the U.S. embassy in Teheran, trapping ninety hostages. As 1979 drew to a close, the Soviet Union invaded Afghanistan in support of a Communist regime unable to sustain itself. In Southeast Asia, Vietnam invaded Cambodia and completed its occupation in January 1979. In Latin America, the Somoza regime of Nicaragua was overthrown by left-wing Sandinista guerrillas in July 1979, and the leftist revolution soon raised fears that unrest would spread to other Central American countries.

When Ronald Reagan assumed the presidency in January 1981, the dark clouds hanging over Seoul-Washington relations began to disappear. Reagan's views stood in stark contrast to those of his predecessor. The priorities of Reagan's Korea policy were security and stability. Indeed, the Reagan era began auspiciously for the Chun government. Chun was the first Korean president to visit the United States in twelve years and the first head of any state to meet with the newly inaugurated American president. The Chun-Reagan summit symbolized the normalization of U.S.-Korea relations after a period of prolonged strain. The strong security commitment and support for strengthening South Korean defense capabilities helped relieve South Korea's concerns over national security that had steadily intensified after the 1975 fall of Saigon.

After restoring close relations with Washington, Chun moved to improve relations with Tokyo. Seoul-Tokyo relations had also experienced strain in the 1970s due to the kidnapping of Kim Dae Jung from Japan and an assassination attempt on President Park by a Korean-Japanese terrorist who, in the process, killed the first lady. During his meeting with Japanese Prime Minister Suzuki Zenko at the Blue House on March 2, 1981, President Chun emphasized the importance of closer Korea-Japan cooperation and an increased role for Japan in regional security: "Korea spends 6 percent of its $60-billion GNP for defense, while Japan spends only 0.9 percent of its huge GNP—one trillion, 160 billion dollars. Thanks to Korea's heavy burden of security, Japan now enjoys prosperity. Therefore, Japan

---

[123] For overall evaluation of the Korean economy in early 1988, see "South Korea Survey: a Man-Made Miracle", *Economist*, May 21, 1988.
[124] See Robert D. Schulzinger, *U. S. Diplomacy since 1900* (New York: Oxford University Press, 1998), 328-334.

should provide some economic support for the compensation of South Korea's defense spending."[125] In this regard, in April 1981, the Korean government requested a $6 billion government loan and a $4 billion bank loan from Japan over a five-year period.

When Nakasone Yasuhiro was elected Japan's prime minister in late 1982, Seoul-Tokyo relations quickly improved. In January 1983, on his first official foreign tour, Nakasone visited South Korea, becoming the first postwar Japanese prime minister to pay a state visit to the country. At a party with Chun, Nakasone even sang a Korean song to solidify the newfound friendship. Following their cordial summit, Chun and Nakasone agreed to open a "new era of friendship and cooperation as genuine partners," reaffirmed the concept that South Korea's security was essential to that of Japan, and stressed the importance of their respective military ties with the United States. As a concrete manifestation of Japan's cooperation, Nakasone promised to provide a $4 billion economic cooperation package to South Korea. The funds were expected to finance some of the projects of Korea's Fifth Five-Year Plan.[126]

The following year, Chun made a return visit to Japan. In Japan, his visit was regarded differently from visits of Syngman Rhee and Park Chung Hee, because his was the first official state visit by the president of the Republic of Korea. It was heralded as an epoch-making event—even in the light of the long and intense history of Korea-Japan relations—owing to Chun's meeting with Japanese Emperor Hirohito and a dinner banquet hosted by the emperor in Chun's honor.[127] To Koreans, Hirohito was the most prominent symbol of Japanese colonialism. A great deal of attention was given to Chun's meeting with Hirohito, who had presided over the last twenty-four years of Japan's colonial rule in Korea. At the state banquet, Hirohito stated, "I feel great regret that there was an unhappy phase in relations between our two countries in a certain period of this century despite the close ties between us. I believe that such things should not be repeated."[128] Nakasone offered a more direct apology. He told the Korean President, "Japan brought to bear great sufferings upon your country and its people." He continued, "The Japanese government and people express a deep regret for the wrongs done to you and your people and are determined to strictly caution themselves against repeating them in the future." Through his summit diplomacy, Chun was able to cultivate the personal friendship and confidence of Reagan and Nakasone.

Olympic Diplomacy. From the time the Olympics were awarded to Seoul, the Chun government initiated an aggressive diplomatic outreach campaign never before seen in the history of the international games. The fact that South Korea was not only a developing nation but a divided one proved a major challenge for the successful hosting of the games. Diplomatic efforts were essential for the Olympics' success, especially considering the backdrop of the U.S.–led boycott of the 1980 Moscow Olympics and the Soviet Union-led boycott of the 1984 Los Angeles Olympics.

Chun's foreign policy was pragmatic. He was well aware of the value of enhancing his

---

[125] Lho (2000), 243-244.
[126] *Korea Herald*, January 13, 1983.
[127] Wakamiya Yoshibumi, *The Postwar Conservative View of Asia* (Tokyo: LTCB International Library Foundation, 1999), 243.
[128] *Korea Herald*, September 8, 1984.

nation's prestige and exploring new market opportunities wherever he could. Through Olympic diplomacy, he attempted to explore new markets for South Korean exports. His diplomacy was sometimes called "economic diplomacy." Thus, the foreign policy of the Chun government may be described as having had two prongs: Olympic diplomacy and economic diplomacy. Thus, the government moved in the early 1980s to improve relations with third world countries in Asia and Africa.

In late June and early July 1981, Chun Doo Hwan ventured into a regional diplomatic effort with the aim of establishing comprehensive cooperation with the countries in Southeast Asia that had until then been generally neglected as viable economic partners.[129] He asked prominent business leaders to join his trip and twenty-nine accompanied him. In so doing, he set the precedent of having South Korean business leaders participate in executive diplomacy. His diplomacy on behalf of the Seoul Olympics and export market even reached the continent of Africa. It was the first time a South Korean president had visited that continent. Aiming to expand South Korea's relations throughout the third world, in August 1982 he made official visits to Nigeria, Kenya, Gabon, and Senegal. His visits became a turning point in South Korea's relations with the African continent.[130]

Chun saw the Olympic Games as a door through which South Korea might finally reach out to the socialist countries from which it had been secluded for the past forty years. The Chun administration believed that in order to promote peace and stability on the Korean peninsula and to host the Seoul Olympics successfully, South Korea needed open channels of dialogue with the Soviet Union and China. At the same time, it hoped to broaden its export market into the socialist bloc countries. In an effort to create an atmosphere conducive to improving relations with socialist countries, the Chun government had already repealed the Anti-Communist Law to promote exchanges with nonhostile Communist nations for economic and diplomatic reasons.[131] The most important but unpublicized initiative of the Chun government was its attempt to open channels with the Soviet Union. In mid-October, 1981, just three weeks after the IOC decision on the 1988 Summer Olympics, Chun secretly dispatched Hahm Pyong-choon, former Korean ambassador to Washington and a leading foreign policy intellectual, to Moscow. In Moscow, Hahm met Mikhail Kapitsa, director of the Institute of Oriental Studies, and the two exchanged views on Northeast Asia. Kapitsa, who subsequently became vice minister of foreign affairs, was a leading expert on Northeast Asian affairs in the Soviet government. Hahm and Kapitsa agreed to organize a conference on South Korea-USSR relations. Thus, was a seed of Seoul's northern diplomacy sown.[132]

Given the lack of South Korean contact with socialist countries, the Seoul Olympics served as a large, multifaceted vehicle for communication, helping to establish sound relations with those nations. Sports authorities from all participating nations had to deal directly with the South Koreans regarding the many details of their Olympic participation. As the Seoul Olympic Games approached, the Chun government expanded relations and

---

[129] Lho (2000), 256-261.
[130] Ibid., 306-308.
[131] *Korea Herald*, December 28, 1980.
[132] Park Bo-kyun (1994), 396-404.

contacts, including an exchange of sports teams, with East European countries as well as with China, largely in anticipation of their participation in the Olympics.

In May 1983 the Chun government had a dramatic and fortuitous opportunity to melt its frozen relations with China when Chinese hijackers forced a Chinese airplane with passengers and crew of 105 people to land at a South Korean airport. The Chinese government dispatched a thirty-three-member negotiating team to Seoul. These were the first direct negotiations between the Republic of Korea and the People's Republic of China. Both sides signed a memorandum by which South Korea allowed the return of the Chinese passengers and crew along with the aircraft. Both parties also agreed to maintain a spirit of cooperation "in future cases of emergency." After the incident, South Koreans were admitted to China for the purpose of participating in international conferences. The Chun government hoped that this precedent would pave the way for China's eventual participation in the 1986 Asian Games and the 1988 Olympic Games.[133]

Regarding relations with North Korea, Chun tried to balance the need for maintaining an appropriate defense posture with the necessity for dialogue. From the beginning of his term, he tried to promote dialogue with North Korea. In his New Year policy speech of January 12, 1981, he proposed exchange visits between the highest authorities in the South and the North to provide momentum toward a resumption of the suspended dialogue, as well as to address the unification question. Specifically, he announced: "I invite President Kim Il Sung of North Korea to visit Seoul without any condition... I also want to make it clear that I am prepared, at any time, to visit North Korea if he invites me."[134] On January 22, 1982, before the National Assembly, he announced a comprehensive and specific "peaceful unification formula." [135] As expected, Pyongyang rejected the proposals.

The Rangoon Bombing. In sharp contrast to its improving relations with China, Seoul's relations with Moscow took a turn for the worse on September 1, 1983. Korean Air Lines (KAL) flight 007, on its way from New York through Anchorage to Seoul, strayed into Soviet airspace near Sakhalin Island and was shot down by a Soviet fighter. All 269 persons aboard the Boeing 747 jumbo jet were killed.[136] The anti-Soviet sentiment resulting from the tragedy poured cold water over the tentative steps that the Chun government had been making to open unofficial diplomatic channels with Moscow.

On October 9, 1983, little more than a month after the incident of KAL 007, a second shock interrupted President Chun's state visit to Burma, the first leg of an eighteen-day, six-nation trip that would include visits to India, Sri Lanka, Brunei, Australia, and New Zealand. At the Martyrs' Mausoleum in Rangoon, high-ranking South Korean delegates were waiting for President Chun's arrival for a wreath-laying ceremony. The Korean ambassador to Rangoon arrived ahead of President Chun and the first lady, whereupon the Burmese band immediately began to practice for the president's arrival. At that moment, terrorists, mistaking the ambassador's arrival and the band

---

[133] Chae-Jin Lee, "South Korea in 1983: Crisis Management and Political Legitimacy", *Asian Survey*, 24:1 (January 1984): 113-114.
[134] The Presidential Secretariat (1981), vol. 1, 20.
[135] *Chosun Ilbo*, January 22, 1982.
[136] *Korea Herald*, September 1 and 2, 1983.

practice for the start of the ceremony, detonated several powerful bombs.[137] The center of the building took the full brunt of the blast. In the tragic explosion, seventeen top-level Korean officials, including four members of the South Korean cabinet, two senior presidential advisers, and the Korean ambassador to Burma were killed instantly. Forty-seven others were wounded, some seriously. Only four members of the sixteen-man official delegation survived the bombing.[138]

At the moment the bombs went off, President Chun was about a mile from the mausoleum. When the president and Mrs. Chun heard the explosion, their motorcade immediately turned around. There was great danger of additional attacks. Chun proved to be a courageous leader in crisis. As most of his closest advisers and assistants were among the killed or wounded, he had to do everything himself under very dangerous circumstances in a foreign environment. He rushed to the military hospital to check on the treatment of the victims. He discovered that the Burmese military facilities and medical staff were in a dismal state, short of even the most basic medicines. He immediately ordered his cabinet in Seoul to dispatch a special charter plane equipped with an emergency medical team and supplies in order to retrieve the dead and wounded as soon as possible. He demanded as well that a team of South Korean experts come to Burma and conduct their own investigation.

Chun immediately canceled the rest of his trip. Arriving haggard at Kimpo International Airport in Seoul, he rushed directly to an emergency Blue House meeting of the surviving members of his cabinet and the national security team at 5:10 A.M., October 10. At the meeting, Defense Minister Yoon Song-min proposed that the Korean Air Force bomb North Korea in retaliation, but Chun, concerned with the possibility of full-scale war, rejected the proposal out of hand. In a statement following the meeting Chun announced, "We will not be the only ones to point to the North Korean Communists, the most inhumane group of people on earth, as the perpetrators of the brutal crime to harm me as the head of state of the Republic"[139] The South Korean armed forces, along with U.S. forces stationed in Korea, were placed on full alert. The Reagan government ordered the aircraft carrier USS *Carl Vinson* and its battle group to stay in Korean waters beyond their scheduled departure date.

Just after the state funeral for the Rangoon victims, which more than one million mourners attended, Chun drastically reshuffled fourteen positions in his twenty-four-member cabinet. He tried to find new ministers of stature equal to those lost in Rangoon. Shin Byong-hyun, chairman of the Korea Traders Association, returned to his old post as the EPB minister. Other appointments included Lee Won-kyong (former

---

[137] *Korea Herald*, October 9-13, 183. North Korean army major Zin Mo and two captains (Kang Min-chul and Shin Ki-chul) had planted themselves two days before on the roof of the mausoleum.

[138] Among the victims were Deputy Prime Minister and Minister of the Economic Planning Board Suh Sok-jun, Minister of Foreign Affairs Lee Bum-suk, Presidential Chief of Staff and former Ambassador to Washington Hahm Pyong-choon, Minister of Energy Suh Sang-chul, Minister of Commerce and Industry Kim Dong-whie, and senior economic adviser Kim Jae-ik. There were three known previous assassination attempts against South Korean presidents: a commando raid on the Blue House in 1968; a bomb at the National Cemetery in 1970 detonated as it was being planted the day before President Park was due to visit; and an assassin in 1974 missed Park, but killed his wife.

[139] *Joongang Ilbo*, October 10, 1983.

minister of sports) as minister of foreign affairs and Kim Man-jae (former president of the Korean-American Bank) as minister of finance. The current finance minister, Kang Kyong-sik, was promoted to chief of staff and Sakong Il became chief economic adviser. The caliber and qualifications of Chun's new appointees were as high as those of the outgoing members or of those killed in Rangoon.[140]

A Burmese inquiry found that three North Korean terrorist commandos had slipped off a North Korean cargo ship anchored in Rangoon in late September 1983. They stayed at a North Korean diplomatic residence, where they received bomb material, including liquid incendiary bombs, TNT powder, and liquid fuel. Two days before the blast, the commandos installed two remote controlled Claymore mines. The three North Korean terrorists tried to escape arrest by blowing themselves up with hand grenades. One of the commandos was killed; another killed three Burmese soldiers before being arrested.[141] Burma, which maintained close relations with North Korea, quickly broke off relations with Pyongyang. A few weeks later, South Korean intelligence authorities charged that Pyongyang had planned to launch commando raids against South Korea after Chun's expected assassination in Rangoon. Hwang Jang-yop, former secretary of North Korean Communist party who defected to the South in 1997, wrote that Kim Jong Il, son of North Korean dictator Kim Il Sung, had ordered the attack.[142] Kang Myung-do, a well-connected North Korean who defected in 1994, told South Korean authorities that a mass insurrection on the order of the 1980 Kwangju uprising was anticipated if Chun had been killed.[143] The Rangoon bombing reminded South Koreans that Pyongyang would do anything to achieve its goal of unification.

Since Seoul was awarded the Olympics, the Chun government was eager to minimize the possibility of a North Korean attempt to disrupt the Olympics as well as the risk of a boycott of the games by Communist bloc nations. The North Korean terrorist attack in Burma dampened South Korea's efforts for improved relations with the North. Despite the incident, however, and beginning in 1984, a co-hosting arrangement was negotiated between the South and the North. The Soviet Union played a key role by suggesting to South Korea that its own participation might be made more difficult if North Korea continued to object and that it would be advisable for Seoul to share several events with Pyongyang. By late 1984, an agreement had been reached for direct talks between North and South Korea under the supervision of the IOC. Subsequently, several meetings and a series of negotiations were held.

Against this background, in September 1984 the Chun government accepted North Korea's offer of relief goods for South Korean flood victims.[144] Even though President Chun and other Korean leaders were fully aware of the possibility that Pyongyang would

---

[140] Chae-Jin Lee, "South Korea in 1983", *Asian Survey*, 24:1 (January 1984): 116-117.
[141] Clifford, *Troubled Tiger*, 205, 2n.
[142] "Kim Jong Il has a morbid interest in terrorism and personally controls all terrorist attacks initiated by North." Hwang wrote. "The Myanmar bombing may have been orchestrated as part of the so-called 'Class struggle' to assassinate important figures of the South Korean ruling class." Hwang Jang-yop, *The Problems of Human Rights in North Korea (3)*, trans. Network for North Korean Democracy and Human Rights (Seoul Nknet, 2002), http:/nknet.org/en/keys/lastkeys/2002/9/04.php.
[143] Oberdorfer, *Two Koreas*, 143.
[144] *Choongang Ilbo*, September 14, 1984.

gain substantial dividends in psychological warfare and international prestige, they boldly seized upon this new opportunity, in part because they were confident of South Korea's economic and technological superiority over their northern neighbor.[145] The Chun government wanted to seize the event as an opportunity for South-North rapprochement, including North Korean participation in the Olympics. Also, tension reduction was necessary in order to further attract foreign investment and develop new export markets in China and other socialist nations. Seoul's acceptance of Pyongyang's offer and the actual delivery of supplies opened a fresh and promising page in the mostly negative history of inter-Korean relations. In September 1985, through arrangements worked out by the Red Cross societies of the two sides, about thirty persons from the South and a similar number from the North crossed the DMZ to meet in Pyongyang and Seoul with members of families that had been separated by hostile confrontation for thirty-five years or more. Performing arts troupes from each side put on shows. Media representatives also went along to report on the unprecedented softening in the normally rigid South-North standoff. At that time, North Korean Foreign Minister Ho Dam secretly met with President Chun in Seoul, paving the way for a softened policy toward the North in the coming years.[146]

In January 1986, however, Pyongyang broke off all channels of communication, charging that the annual joint "Team Spirit" military exercise of South Korean and American forces had poisoned the atmosphere for dialogue. Pyongyang was appalled at the possibility that the Soviet Union and the East European states would take part in the Seoul Olympics and thus indicate their acceptance of South Korea's legitimacy. Pyongyang was unable to prevent the Chinese from sending a 500-member delegation to participate in the 1986 Asian Games in Seoul or to dissuade the Soviets and East Europeans from competing in a variety of sports events in Seoul in 1985 and 1986. Pyongyang was desperate to block the Seoul Olympics by any means and repeatedly threatened: "If Seoul hosts the Olympics, a war will break out. It is absolutely impossible for Seoul to host the Olympic Games."[147] In November 1987, less than a year before the opening of the games, North Korean terrorists, including Kim Hyun-hee, bombed Korean Air flight 858, killing all 115 persons aboard. Under South Korean questionings Kim said she had been told by her superior in Pyongyang that her orders came directly from Kim Jong Il. Hwang Jang-yop, former secretary of North Korean Communist party, has blamed Kim Jong Il for the incident.[148]

---

[145] According to Bradley Martin, Pyongyang assumed that Seoul would reject the offer. The North Korean official in charge was exiled. Owing to the aid, North Korea experienced severe food shortages. Martin, *op. cit.*, 342 and 392.
[146] Chun supported a secret, back-channel dialogue between the South and the North. During 1984 and 1985 officials of the two governments met several times to discuss economic cooperation and other exchanges.
[147] Roh Tae Woo, "Reminiscences", *Wolgan Chosun* (May 1999).
[148] Kim Hyun-hee later wrote a book, *The Tears of My Soul* (New York: William Morrow, 1993), which provides details of their operation. "The bombing of the Korean commercial plane is evidence of the perverted character of Kim Jong Il, who has little respect for human life and loves to terrorize people." Hwang wrote. Hwang, *Problems of Human Rights* (3).

Toward Democratic Transition

There was no question about the essentially authoritarian nature of the Chun government. But, unlike the diehard rulers of other authoritarian regimes, Chun made repeated promises to step down once his initial term expired. Even bitter critics privately acknowledged that the government was administratively competent, that the country was prospering, and that there had been noticeable, if limited, expansion of political and press freedoms.[149] Unfortunately, Chun never achieved full political legitimacy. Despite considerable success in economy and diplomacy, his government failed to win public trust. Many regarded him as a usurper of power who had deprived South Korea of its opportunity to restore democracy. Although the constitution and laws of the Fifth Republic were significantly improved from those of the *Yushin* regime, many believed that the regime fell far short of full democracy. Even though he tried to dissociate himself from Park Chung Hee's *Yushin* system, in practice his strong-arm tactics of harassing and persecuting opposition politicians and critics were seen as little more than an extension of Park's authoritarianism.

In an effort to solve the perennial dilemma of student demonstrations, in the spring of 1984 the government removed direct police surveillance from campuses, released hundreds of student dissidents from prisons, and permitted academic reinstatement of more than 1,000 expelled students. This liberalization policy was a great miscalculation on the part of the Chun government. The direct consequence of the liberalization was a resurrection of militant student activism. In the two years following the liberalization measures, there were feverish organizational activities by those dissidents freed from prisons or legal restrictions. From the beginning of the Chun administration, time-honored dissidents—a loose coalition of opposition politicians, students, religious leaders, radical laborers, and alienated intellectuals—that had increased their numbers and strengthened their methods during the Park regime, continued to challenge the government. They simply believed that Chun was responsible for the brutal crackdown of the 1980 Kwangju uprising and that his administration was the continuation of the dictatorial Park regime under a different name. Thus they tried continuously to topple the Chun government. The ghosts of Kwangju haunted Chun throughout his tenure. Every year in May, violent memorial rallies were staged in the city and on campuses nationwide.

This generation of student activists was different from preceding ones. [150] During the 1970s, young intellectuals had struggled for freedom, democracy and human rights. In the 1980s, a small number of radicals led the student movement. They argued that the basic cause for the political and social malaise in South Korea was "American imperialism," which they believed had dominated the country since 1945. In their view, "American imperialism" buttressed the military dictatorship and the exploitative capitalist system; the struggle against the military dictatorship and American imperialism was inseparable. This position was the same argument that North Korea had been advancing since 1945. To these activists, the state and the government were now simply considered the enemy, to be

---

[149] William H. Gleysteen, Jr. and Alan D. Romberg, "Korea: Asian Paradox", *Foreign Affairs* 65:5 (summer 1987): 1039.

[150] Kenneth M. Wells, ed., *South Korea's Minjung Movement: The Culture and Politics of Dissidence*, Honolulu: University of Hawaii Press, 1995.

destroyed and replaced with a populist regime. Those radicals called for a new "people's constitution" with a leading political role for "minjung (people)." Student activists maintained that their eventual goal was to establish a unified "independent" state where the minjung forces would take the initiative, and that this could only be realized when labor, farmers and progressive intellectuals together ousted the ruling system through popular struggle. They strongly advocated unification. The continued confrontation of South and North Korea meant not only a wasteful arms race but also an increasing dependency on the United States. Thus, the radicals were generally sympathetic with the policies of North Korea on many issues, including unification.[151] They openly advocated U.S. troop withdrawal from South Korea and condemned American support of the Chun regime.

Student demonstrations increased rapidly during 1985. Thousands of students marched on the street; throwing stones and Molotov cocktails at the riot police. They occupied university buildings, attacked police stations, and set fire to police buses. According to a report by the Ministry of Home Affairs, 1,371 demonstrations and 448 sit-ins, in which 650,000 students participated, occurred in the first ten months of 1985.[152] Radical students attacked American installations—the American Chamber of Commerce (May 21, 1985), the U.S. Cultural Center in Seoul (May 23, 1985), the U.S. Cultural Center in Kwangju (December 2, 1985), and the U.S. Cultural Center in Pusan (May 21, 1986).

The labor movement also went through radical changes during this period. The development of heavy industries resulted in the rapid increase and concentration of labor, which made massive and violent strikes easy. large-scale militant strikes were frequent in the major industrial zones. For example, some 30,000 workers participated in the 1986 strikes at Hyundai Heavy Industries in Ulsan. Activist organizations placed priority on strengthening the labor movement, and concentrated on organizing workers and supporting strikes. During the first half of the 1980s, hundreds of student activists, who were either expelled from school or voluntarily gave up study, became "disguised workers" to organize labor. Soon the labor movement had become quite organically meshed with the student movement.[153]

Encouraged by the widespread antigovernment movement, opposition leaders intensified their struggle against the government. In May and June 1983, opposition leader Kim Young Sam, who had been under house arrest since 1980, went on a twenty-three-day hunger strike to oppose the government. A few months later, he and Kim Dae Jung, who had been in the United States since December 1982, issued a joint political message in which they pledged to cooperate in their struggle for the restoration of democracy in South Korea.

The National Assembly elections, expected to be held in February 1985, were crucial not only for the ruling party but the opposition as well.[154] The winner in the elections would likely prevail in the upcoming power succession. The ruling party was eager to do

---

[151] Oh, *Korean Politics*, 87-91; and Young Whan Kihl, "South Korea's Search for a New Order: An Overview", in Kim and Kihl, eds. (1988), 12.

[152] Quoted in Kleiner, *Korea*, 209.

[153] Hart-Landsberg, *Rush to Development*, 288-290.

[154] For an analysis of the 1985 elections, see B. C. Koh, "The 1985 Parliamentary Election in South Korea", *Asian Survey*, 30:9 (September 1985), 883-897.

better in order to show popular approval of the Chun administration. It was confident that its record of solid national achievement could draw more votes in 1985 than it had in 1981. Indeed, the Chun administration had much to support its claims of achievement. With his decisive leadership in crisis management, Chun had restored social and political stability, reduced inflation significantly, and revived the momentum of the growth-oriented economy. Chun and his party became confident and pledged, time and again, to conduct a fair and clean election. Before his April 1985 visit to the United States, Chun wanted to project an image of moderation abroad. On November 30, 1984, the government lifted a ban on political activities for eighty-four ex-politicians.

These newly liberated politicians became the nucleus of the New Korea Democratic Party (NKDP), which was hastily organized in January 1985. Although Kim Young Sam and Kim Dae Jung were still barred from political activity, they were behind the new party. Entry of the hard-line opposition into the election, however, changed the complexion of the campaigns. The NKDP candidates made frontal assaults on Chun's rule, assailing the Chun government as "unjust and immoral," "corrupt and illegal," and "military controlled and dictatorial."[155] They also advocated a constitutional amendment to allow a direct popular vote for president. Not only was Chun's legitimacy challenged but topics that had long been considered taboo were openly discussed—allegedly Chun's handling of the 1980 Kwangju uprising and his wife's ties to financial scandals. By challenging the legitimacy of the regime, the election became a referendum on the legitimacy of the regime itself. The audacious attacks of the NKDP candidates aroused the interest of the electorate and boosted support for the new opposition party. Kim Dae Jung's return to Seoul, just four days before the election, also helped to mobilize support for the new opposition party.

Surprisingly, the election was a turning point for the political development of the coming years. The ruling party failed to receive a popular mandate. It undoubtedly retained a majority status in the assembly, winning 148 seats (54 percent) of the 276-member National Assembly. What really surprised observers was the emergence of the hard-line NKDP as the main opposition party, largely at the expense of the more mainstream opposition, the Democratic Korea Party. The NKDP captured sixty-seven seats and 29 percent of the national vote. Absorbing some members of other opposition parties, the NKDP formed a strong parliamentary group of 103 members.[156] Although Chun's uncompromising economic reforms were successful, their political effect appeared deadly. The economic policies turned laborers and farmers against the Chun regime.[157]

The full-scale struggle for the presidential succession began in February 1986, when the opposition leadership decided to mobilize popular support by launching a nationwide petition campaign to push for a constitutional amendment incorporating provisions for direct election of the president. The 1980 constitution that provided for an electoral college system was an important target of the opposition's attack, and revision of the constitution became a critical rallying point. The opposition groups were convinced that potential presidential candidates, such as Kim Young Sam and Kim Dae Jung, had mass

---

[155] For example, *Hankuk Ilbo*, February 5-15, 1985.
[156] *Chosun Ilbo*, February 14, 1985.
[157] Larry Diamond and Byung-Kook Kim, "Introduction: Consolidating Democracy in South Korea", in Diamond and Kim, eds. (2000), 22-23.

followings and stood a good chance of being popularly elected. The opposition forces brought to mind the "people power" phenomenon in the Philippines, when massive demonstrations swept Ferdinand Marcos out of office in the spring of 1986.

The United States played some role in removing Marcos from power.[158] But the U.S. government refused to draw an analogy between conditions in the Philippines and those in South Korea, thereby strongly dissuading the Korean opposition from pushing such a risky strategy. U.S. Secretary of State George Shultz paid a visit to Seoul in May 1986 and made an unexpected statement that praised the efforts of the Chun government to bring peaceful political change, instead of admonishing the government as the opposition leaders had desired. Nevertheless, Chun had, inevitably but absurdly, been compared with Marcos. For all its considerable imperfections as a democratic state, Korea was not the Philippines. Not even his enemies had accused the austere and hardworking Chun of Marcos-like cronyism and corruption.[159] Unlike Marcos, who prolonged his power over two decades, Chun had made repeated promises to step down upon the completion of his seven-year single term. Unlike the bankrupt Philippines, South Korea would soon be labeled "a second Japan." The economic crisis in the Philippines had increased pressure on Marcos, which eventually contributed to his downfall. At that time, the Philippine economy was characterized by poverty, stagnation and foreign debt, while its South Korean counterpart was enjoying an unprecedented boom.[160] To put it more bluntly, the Philippines was a case of failure, while South Korea was a model of success.[161]

In order to seek a negotiated solution, in April 1986 Chun announced that he would support any constitutional change endorsed by the National Assembly. In June a special constitution revision committee was set up in the National Assembly. The predominant debate became whether the new system would provide for the direct election of a president, upon which the opposition insisted, or a parliamentary system, which the ruling party favored. Negotiations made no progress. On April 13, 1987, Chun announced an end to negotiations, thus returning to his earlier position that constitutional change should come after the 1988 Olympics. His decision only fueled antigovernment demonstrations.

The Seoul Olympics had important political ramifications. Thanks to the Olympics, Korea—especially its student demonstrations—received a great deal of international media attention. The antigovernment groups and the opposition possessed a powerful hostage in the form of the Olympics. By threatening to disrupt the games, they saw great advantages for their antigovernment struggle. With steady and frequent foreign exposure, antigovernment demonstrations became increasingly bold and radical. Clashes between

---

[158] T. C. Rivera, "The State, Civil Society and Foreign Actors: The Politics of Philippine Industrialization", *Contemporary Southeast Asia*, 16:2 (February 1994): 171-172.

[159] "The Tide Keeps Rising", *Time*, April 14, 1986.

[160] June Kronholz, "Marcos' Weak Spot: Philippines' Economy", *Wall Street Journal*, February 5, 1986. During the Marcos rule, the Philippines could only manage an average growth rate of 1.6 percent. See T. C. Rivera, *op. cit.*, 157.

[161] Robert S. Greenberger, "Cooling of the Korean Political Scene Could Be a Fortuitous Plus for Reagan", *Wall Street Journal*, August 4, 1986.

riot-geared police and demonstrators were almost daily events in Seoul.[162] On June 10, 1987, when the ruling party formally nominated Roh Tae Woo as the party's presidential candidate, the country erupted in violent street demonstrations. The confrontations between demonstrators and riot police continued for almost three weeks. A considerable number of middle class citizens joined the protests. The central districts of Seoul were quickly turning into a "war zone." The endless demonstrations were smudging the reputation of South Korea as an appropriate site for the 1988 Olympics. Chun was acutely aware that an unsuccessful Olympics would inflict a grave political, economic, and diplomatic blow on the country as well as on the legacy of his presidency. Yet unlike President Park, who had declared martial law several times during his eighteen-year rule, Chun moved with exceeding care. The government never declared martial law but relied on the riot police to maintain law and order.

There were two reasons why Chun had been cautious to mobilize troops to crush the demonstrators at the time. Chun and his advisers were determined to avoid another bloody incident like Kwangju. He also could not ignore the advice of Washington whose support was crucial not only for the security of his country but also for a successful hosting of the Olympics. Through a special envoy, Gaston Sigur, assistant secretary of State for East Asian and Pacific Affairs, the U.S. government warned Chun on June 23 against the use of the military for political purposes.[163]

South Korea had achieved an "economic miracle" under successive authoritarian governments, but with this phenomenal rise in the standard of living there appeared more vocal popular calls for full democracy. The public was no longer satisfied with mere economic success. Proud of their economic prowess, Koreans did not want to be looked upon as politically backward. Many believed, as Chun himself had said, that the time had come to modernize their political system. Many South Koreans harbored no support for the opposition per se but wished simply for the opportunity to choose the national leader on their own. On the morning of June 22, Chun Doo Hwan called in Roh Tae Woo, presidential candidate of the ruling party, and discussed a broad range of measures aimed at defusing the political crisis. He also met top national leaders, including opposition leader Kim Young Sam.[164] On the evening of June 24, Chun called Roh to the Blue House and abruptly asked him, "Don't you think you can win even if it is a popular election?" Taken off guard, Roh replied, "What are you talking about? No, I don't think so." Roh wanted to ascertain Chun's exact intentions. If Chun again changed his mind, Roh believed, the nation would face a grave crisis. Chun attempted to persuade Roh:

> "Since you have built up a good image among the people, I think you will win even if Kim Dae Jung is pardoned and he runs for president."
>
> "Are you serious?" Roh countered incredulously.

---

[162] On student activism during this period, see Wonmo Dong, "Student Activism and the Presidential Politics of 1987 in South Korea", in Kim and Kihl, eds. (1988), 169-188.
[163] William Steuck, "Democratization in Korea: The United States Role, 1980 and 1987", *International Journal of Korean Studies*, 2, no. 1 (fall-winter 1998).
[164] "Brinkmanship in South Korea", *Newsweek*, July 6, 1987, 26-27; and Chalmers Johnson, "South Korean Democratization: The Role of Economic Development", in Cotton, ed., *Korea Under Roh Tae-Woo*, 104-107.

Chun's answer was simple, "There is no alternative."[165]

What was significant was Chun's willingness to transfer power to an opposition leader. His predecessors had not relinquished their power so willingly. Chun later revealed his mindset during his discussions with Roh over direct presidential elections:

> In view of the mounting demand for a direct presidential election, accepting such a demand would be the most popular move. I concluded that candidate Roh should announce an acceptance of a direct election as his own decision. This single act should enable Roh to win over the two Kims. Thus I told Roh to accept the direct election system. Greatly surprised, Roh said it could not be done...the main reason being that he was not confident of a victory in an election contest against the Kims.... I told him that his acceptance of a direct election would make him a hero.[166]

On June 29, Roh Tae Woo surprised the nation by announcing a democratic reform package that embodied the wholesale acceptance of the opposition demands. Roh's eight-point proposal pledged "the speedy amendment" of the constitution to allow direct presidential elections, as well as amnesty for Kim Dae Jung and the restoration of his civil rights, allowing to him run for president. Two days later, President Chun endorsed the proposal by saying: "Our politics must now cast aside its old shabby ways, which are incongruous with our level of economic development, and thus achieve an advanced form of democracy that we can proudly show to the world."[167] A transition to full democracy had finally begun.

In agreeing to a direct presidential election, there was a rational calculation in the ruling circle that the chances of victory were not as slim as earlier thought. The economy was booming and this meant that perhaps the middle class vote could be counted on. With an economic miracle, the hosting of the Olympics, and two opposition presidential candidates (i.e., Kim Young Sam and Kim Dae Jung), the probability of Roh's victory was reasonably good. The democratization initiative of the ruling camp improved the legitimacy and image of the government and ruling party. According to the facts revealed in an interview with Chun in 1992, it was Chun who constructed the image of Roh as a reformer, and Chun himself as a hardliner, with the double objective of making Roh's June declaration more effective and the Roh candidacy more palatable to the public.[168] Roh's declaration is often wrongly interpreted as a "political coup" against Chun. Dissidents hated Chun, and indeed he was fairly unpopular nationwide. Therefore, many have tended to underestimate his strengths. However, Chun successfully weathered several earlier crises. He was confident in his ability to manage the imminent one. The general-turned-leader believed that, as is often the case in real warfare, a frontal attack is sometimes the best strategy to win a political war. The political process that led to the transition to full democracy and the election of Roh was the result of a political master

---

[165] "The Reminiscences of Roh Tae Woo, Part 2", *Wolgan Chosun* (June 1999): 214-215.
[166] Lee Pyong-do, "*Hidae ui kongjak: 6.29 sonon*" (The Extraordinary Scheme: The 6.29 Declaration), *Chukan Hankuk* (August 23, 1993): 3.
[167] William R. Doerner, "Suddenly, A New Day", *Time*, July 13, 1987.
[168] Sung-Ik Kim, "Chun Doo Hwan's Live Testimony for History", *Wolgan Chosun* (January 1992).

plan engineered by the Chun regime.[169]

The National Assembly established a special committee on constitutional revision. After nineteen rounds of intensive negotiations between ruling and opposition parties, they managed to reach an agreement concerning the constitutional amendment and the timetable for presidential elections. On October 12, 1987, the National Assembly approved a new constitution by a margin of 254-4. On October 28, the new constitution was ratified by 93 percent of voters in a national referendum. The constitution provides that the president be elected directly by a plurality of voters every five years for a single term. The constitutional amendment was very important for Korean democracy in that it was agreed upon by both ruling and opposition parties. Never before was a constitutional revision made through political deals between opposing camps.

The December 1987 presidential election was a three-way contest between Roh Tae Woo, Kim Young Sam, and Kim Dae Jung. With the platform of stability and continued economic growth, Roh Tae Woo was elected president in a free and competitive election. As *The Washington Times* correspondent Michael Breen believed, the opposition parties were known as protest groups rather than capable alternatives to the ruling party. He said, "It would be a great distortion to portray the struggle for democracy as a battle waged by noble civilian democrats against a corrupt and brutal military regime.... Although Chun was personally unpopular, this dislike did not translate into support for the opposition. People had accepted that Chun had overcome his predecessors' weakness for perpetual rule and would actually step down. The government in general had significant support. It was seen capable of managing the economy and the defense against North Korea."[170]

The victory of Roh Tae Woo symbolized the overall success of the Chun presidency. It demonstrated broad middle class support for the development strategy the government had pursued, and skepticism toward the economic and social claims of the opposition. Considering the strong aspirations for democracy, victory of the ruling party candidate would have been very difficult, if not impossible, without the impressive achievements of the Chun administration.

LEADERSHIP FOR NATIONAL REVITALIZATION

Context of the Presidency. In the late 1970s South Korea experienced considerable social and political instability marked by frequent labor protests and student demonstrations. After a long period of rapid growth, the Korean economy was afflicted by global economic trends of inflation and recession, brought on by the second oil crisis. The assassination of Park Chung Hee added political turmoil to the social instability and economic downturn. The result was a critical national crisis. The country began to drift aimlessly like a kite cut off from its string.

The shadow of Park was too great for the new leader. Chun was unknown to many of his countrymen and much of the world when he became president. To many, surprised by his sudden rise, he seemed to be too ordinary a man to fill the shoes of the charismatic Park Chung Hee. Chun might be compared to Truman who inherited the

---

[169] I was Chun's assistant for political affairs since the summer of 1986.
[170] Breen, *Koreans*, 217.

presidency upon the sudden death of the charismatic President Roosevelt. When Truman became president, he was seen as a nonentity—a shallow, visionless man attempting to function far beyond his capabilities.[171] Park's charisma, both as the center of effective power and source of legitimacy, produced the effect of belittling the prestige, status and competence of the new leader, and of dwarfing his role to the point where he was unable to quickly acquire the kind of authority that was vital for effective governance. Chun also suffered from some handicaps as a national leader. First of all, he had come to office not through the collective will of the people but through illegitimate means: the legitimacy of the Chun regime was questioned from its inception. Thus, the antigovernment forces tenaciously and persistently attacked the Chun government.

Another legacy of the Park era was the unrealistic expectations the people had of the presidency. The more concentrated the power in the person of the leader, the more his absence is felt, and the greater the likelihood of national crisis in his absence. So strong and controlling was Park's leadership that the state could not function properly without him. Chun, as the new leader, was now expected to perform as effectively as Park. But Chun inherited a nation in turmoil and was obliged to find strong and effective countermeasures. Fortunately, most South Koreans in late 1980 seemed to welcome the end of the political uncertainty that followed the assassination of Park Chung Hee. They looked forward to a resumption of political calm and economic expansion.

Agenda Setting. Upon assuming the presidency, Chun inherited a ship of state suffering from a series of social, economic and political woes, and moved decisively to repair the troubled vessel. He acted to reduce public disorientation and calm fears. The economy was on the brink of bankruptcy and, if left unchecked, could have rapidly deteriorated into full economic collapse with a concomitant security crisis. In order to avert this possibility, the economy required a massive influx of foreign loans. Without social and political stability, foreigners would not invest in South Korea. The restoration of social and political stability was critical to economic recovery and national security. In order to defuse the social and political crises, the Chun government adopted emergency measures.

Since Chun believed that the economic crisis was creating social and political crises which in turn endangered national security, stabilizing and revitalizing the economy became the most urgent tasks.[172] Before his retirement, he recalled South Korea's economic problems of the early 1980s:

> The economy was in a state of bankruptcy. In the early stages of my presidency, I did not know what I should do first or how I should lead the country. To make matters worse, the so-called second oil shock struck the world and international crude oil prices doubled from $18 per barrel to $36. Moreover, the rate of interest on international loans increased from an annual rate of about 7 percent to 14 to 15 percent. Despite this, obtaining loans from a foreign country was more difficult than picking a star from the sky. Nevertheless, we had to suffer from annual increases in foreign loans of more than $7 billion, and were unable to cope with this situation. Thus, the terms of redemption on the principal and interest for the

---

[171] Greenstein, *Leadership*, 53-56.
[172] For the discussion of determined leadership, see Chalmers Johnson, "South Korean Democratization: The Role of Economic Development", in Cotton, ed. (1993), 92-107.

> loans we induced from foreign countries were to expire all at once.... Most firms were reduced to a state just short of bankruptcy.... To make matters worse, the price of importing goods increased by 42 percent and the trade deficit was more than $5.3 billion in 1981.... One difficulty brought on another difficulty.[173]

Through his intensive consultations, Chun realized that the economy required painful emergency medicine and gave top priority to economic stability and growth. He stressed that economic stability was a necessary condition for revitalization and that only sustained economic growth would guarantee the strengthening of national security and the healthy development of democracy. The stability-first policy of the Chun government contrasted with Park's growth-first policy. Chun's anti-inflation measures were socially unpopular and politically dangerous. It is no surprise that his stabilization policy faced strong social and political opposition. But despite the resistance, his belief in the importance of economic stability held firm. In order to revitalize the economy and make it internationally competitive, the Chun government also pursued aggressive market-oriented economic reforms and undertook to free the economy from governmental controls.

Appointments and Leadership Style. Chun came to power without any formal government training or experience. There were grave doubts about how competent he was for the office. During an interview with a foreign correspondent, he reflected on his role as president:

> A Korean president has to work in a harsh environment. The country is divided, and the Republic confronts a notoriously warlike adversary [North Korea] who constantly wishes us ill. We have to work to defend the peace of the country, achieve sustained economic growth, and maintain social and political stability. The Korean president must pursue these three objectives simultaneously.... His convictions must be firm.... He must have a very strong sense of responsibility. And finally, he must inspire the confidence of the people, if not their respect.[174]

Chun recognized the problems of the Park regime's power structure—concentration of power, abuse of power, internal power struggles and the distortion of governmental management. He was determined not to repeat such mistakes. He believed that the concentration and abuse of power by his advisers would alienate ministers and bureaucrats, and thus frowned on the intervention of his staff in cabinet affairs. He warned himself of the danger of being manipulated by close subordinates.[175] He tried to boost the authority of ministers so that they might lead career bureaucrats.[176] Unlike Park, Chun assigned a more positive role to political parties. He also firmly believed that the KCIA had been too powerful and too abusive, and he reduced its size and powers, renaming it the National Security Planning Agency.

Chun wanted to restore the proper role of the Blue House staff. He abolished the offices of eight special advisers to the president, and consolidated the offices of two senior secretaries for economic affairs into one, integrating the coordination and control

---

[173] Foreign Broadcasting Information Service (FBIS), *East Asia*, February 22, 1988, 32-33.
[174] "The World according to Chun Doo Hwan" *Institutional Investor* (February 1982): 72-73.
[175] Chun Doo Hwan, "Advice for the Incoming President", *Wolgan Chosun* (February 1999): 120.
[176] Interview with Il Sakong.

of economic policy. He recognized the importance of advisers and experts. During an interview with a local newspaper ten weeks after his inauguration, he was quoted as saying, "The president is a human being with finite abilities. I am trying hard to supplement my limited abilities with the advisory functions of the Blue House staff and the cabinet."[177] He established an effective presidential staff and emphasized that its main role was assisting the president. Thus, staff activities focused on the planning, monitoring and coordinating of major policies.

When Chun was elected president, he knew little about governing or about how to solve complex economic and social problems. He was a quick study, though, a very successful case of presidential on-the-job training. His intelligence allowed him a tremendous capacity for growth. In his early fifties, he was vigorous, dynamic, and action-oriented. He knew that national issues were serious and complex and had the good sense to put them in the hands of capable technocrats. For instance, he knew he was comparatively weak in the area of economic policy, so he turned to experienced experts for economic advice. He appointed the brightest and the most capable technocrats to the Blue House staff. His choice of cabinet members was also impressive. His personnel management was evaluated to be as good as that of Park Chung Hee.[178] Sakong Il, who served as Chun's senior economic adviser for four years, remembers Chun's leadership style:

> President Park Chung Hee managed the government through his chief of staff, and the role of the senior secretaries was relatively limited. He also controlled the economy through the EPB minister. In contrast, President Chun gave more roles to his senior secretaries, but at the same time, he asked his staff be faceless and voiceless. He wanted to give more power and authority to ministers. During four years in the Blue House, I had no interviews with the media. I frequently but unnoticeably met the EPB minister and discussed policy issues. The president frequently called and asked how the major projects were proceeding. He was stern with his staff and demanded perfect performance. Through his control and monitoring of his staff, he was indirectly controlling the cabinet. Once he trusted an assistant, he delegated more power to that assistant and protected him from political pressure. Despite his occasional high-handedness, he had a reputation for listening carefully to experts and advisers before making a decision. He was not the sort whose stubbornness prevented him from changing his mind in the face of persuasive arguments.[179]

Under Chun's leadership, teamwork and policy consistency were stressed. He gave a relatively longer tenure to his ministers to ensure teamwork among policymakers and policy consistency.[180] Ministers and presidential aides were asked to share common goals

---

[177] Korea Overseas Information Service, *An Interview with President Chun Doo Hwan,* November 21, 1980, 6.

[178] According to a survey of 320 opinion leaders on the personnel management of Korean Presidents, Park is ranked first with 69 points followed by Chun Doo Hwan with 65 points. See *Hankuk daetongryong pyongga wiwonhoe* (2002), 81.

[179] Interview on April 19, 2002.

[180] Average ministerial tenure was 18.3 months. Owing to the North Korean terror attack against his cabinet members, Chun had to reshuffle his cabinet. Without the tragedy, the cabinet in the Chun government would have been even more stable.

and similar policy lines. Like Park Chung Hee, Chun met regularly with his cabinet through the monthly trade promotion meetings and other meetings. His reliance on official meetings seemed, like his use of the chief of staff and his extensive delegation of authority to ministers and advisers, to have military roots—in this case the planning conferences of top military commanders. The president was well aware of the importance of presidential decisions. He believed that wise presidential decisions were the product of accurate information and its proper analysis. He tried to avoid making a quick decision based on a written report prepared by his staff or a briefing by a particular minister. When being briefed by a minister, he would ask the minister to bring along other officials responsible for the policy in question. On some important policy issues, he asked to have a task force organized or a consultative meeting held, gathering together representatives of related ministries and other public and private organizations.[181] Before a policy was finalized, it would be subjected to vigorous discussion and consultation among private experts and concerned government departments.

Chun had a strong commitment to his major policies and maintained their consistency. He believed that the sacrifice of short-term desires was necessary to overcome the national crisis and ensure the achievement of long-term national goals. In order to rescue the failing economy, he administered bitter economic medicine, alienating almost every sector of society. He presided over many meetings, giving detailed information and persuasively explaining his policies to the participants. He mobilized all resources available for the successful implementation of policies. He protected technocrats from the pressure of politicians, labor unions and other pressure groups. He suppressed those elements that disturbed social and political stability and economic growth. Thus, he was often criticized at home and abroad as a heavy-handed dictator. But his determined leadership resulted in the fastest growing economy in the world.

The president viewed the presidency not as a position to "enjoy something" but as one to "do something." He firmly believed "the president should be the hardest-working citizen of this country, willing to work even when all of the people are taking a rest."[182] He was constantly aware that voters would mark their ballots for him on the basis of what he had accomplished rather than who he was. In his mind, hard work and high achievement were the only sure ways to get public approval. As a former general, he knew that successful implementation was as important as the order itself. He was a tireless traveler, frequently visiting ministries, agencies and local governments to examine how his policies were going. He visited the construction sites of major government projects. He maintained the military habit of midnight inspections, encouraging those who worked at night in military posts, police boxes and fire stations. He worked vigorously from early in the morning till late in the evening, often commenting wryly, "I am too busy to get sick."[183] Roh Tae Woo, Chun's close friend from their days at the military academy, said that he never met a person in national leadership who worked as

---

[181] Chun Doo Hwan, "Advice", 120.
[182] Korean Overseas Information Service, *An Interview with President Chun Doo Hwan*, November 21, 1980, 5-6.
[183] Ibid., 13.

hard as Chun.[184]

One of Chun's problems was that he did not calculate the political consequences of his actions. He was a strong character and always determined to succeed. The rigidity of his character and the firmness of his decision-making became apparent immediately. He did not want to appear weak under any circumstances. He was damaged by his willingness to face up squarely to difficult, unpopular, and politically damaging decisions. Ultimately, he paid a heavy price for his earlier heavy-handed measures. Then there was the legacy of the Park regime. If Park had not been assassinated, but had instead willingly retired, he would have subsequently faced insults and attempts at revenge from opposition and dissident groups. With Park's untimely death, Chun had to accept much of the blame and revenge that belonged to his predecessor.

Achievements and Legacies. When Chun assumed the presidency, serious questions were asked about the future of South Korea. After seven years of his leadership, most of these questions had received positive answers. During his term he succeeded in rescuing the Korean economy from the brink of collapse, converting it into one of the fastest growing economies in the world, and leading the country to the doorstep of advanced nationhood. Such a transformation would have been impossible without his determined leadership. By successfully preparing the Seoul Olympics, the Chun administration demonstrated Korea's remarkable economic and social development and enhanced the nation's prestige and status in the world. According to a Gallup Korea survey in July 1998, the hosting of the Seoul Olympics was regarded as the second greatest achievement of the nation in the fifty-year history of the Republic.[185] Without Chun Doo Hwan, "the miracle on the Han," which was started by Park Chung Hee, probably would not have been achieved. Without his resolute leadership, Koreans might have enjoyed more freedom but Korea's economic performance during the Chun administration was remarkable, especially in light of the economic legacy inherited from the Park era and despite social and political unrest during his term. The Korean economy successfully overcame its structural problems and was set on a firm foundation for a second takeoff. By all accounts, the economy had overcome the vicious cycle of over-investment, high inflation, wage hikes and mounting foreign debts that had begun during the 1970s. Given a myriad of failed episodes of stabilization and structural adjustment in the third world, the Korean case was remarkably successful. The effective management of the economic crisis in the early 1980s made Korea a textbook example of economic reforms in the third world.[186]

The economic stabilization policy successfully eradicated the chronic high inflation from which the country had suffered since the start of modernization, and which had seriously undermined the country's growth potential, particularly in the latter part of the 1970s. The rate of wholesale prices declined sharply, from 44 percent in 1980 to 4.6 percent in 1982, and remained at less than 1.0 percent for the years 1983-87. The rate of consumer prices fell from 34.6 percent in 1980 to 7 percent in 1982, and remained at about 3 percent during 1983-87. The average annual growth rate during his seven-year

---

[184] Roh Tae Woo, "Reminiscences", *Wolgan Chosun* (June 1999): 243.
[185] *Chosun Ilbo*, July 15, 1998.
[186] Corbo and Suh, eds., *Structural Adjustment.*

term was 9.5 percent, the highest in the world. During the three-year period of the turbulent democratic transition beginning in 1986, the economy underwent a boom of unprecedented magnitude, with the economy growing more than 12 percent a year and recording a sizable trade surplus during the same period for the first time in its modern history (see Figure 7).

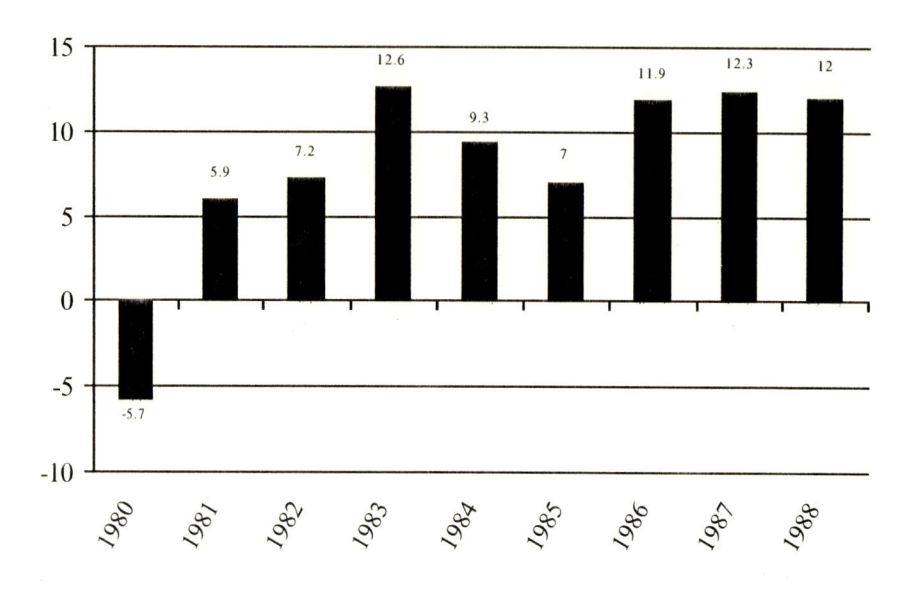

Figure 7. **Economic Growth** (% GDP)

Year	% GDP
1980	-5.7
1981	5.9
1982	7.2
1983	12.6
1984	9.3
1985	7
1986	11.9
1987	12.3
1988	12

Korea's GNP by the end of 1987, the last year of the Chun presidency, surpassed $136 billion, with a per capita income of $3,110. In 1980 Korea's GNP was only $63 billion and the per capita income was $1,600. The momentum of high growth continued in 1988, with a growth rate of 12 percent, propelling Korea's GNP to $180 billion and per capita income to $4,300. The balance of payments also improved greatly during the Chun administration, going from a deficit of $4.4 billion in 1981 to a record surplus of $10 billion in 1987, largely owing to a trade surplus (see Figure 8). This was the first trade surplus in the history of the Republic. It meant that Korean products had improved their international competitiveness. Trade deficits had been a chronic problem for the South Korean economy, one that Park Chung Hee, a genius in economic management, had been unable to overcome. The country began to pay off its foreign debt. In fact, Korea was the only third world country to begin to pay back its loans. With the achievements of price stability, high growth and trade surplus, the Chun government became known as "a government which caught three rabbits at the same time." Overall, the economic achievements of the Chun administration were highly evaluated, somewhat lower than those of Park Chung Hee, but much higher than those of Chun's successors.[187]

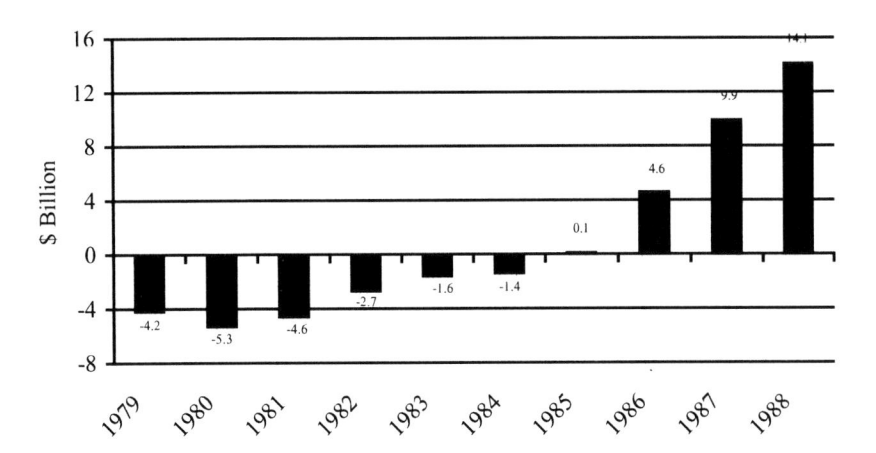

Figure 8. **Balance of Payments** ($B)

Year	$ Billion
1979	-4.2
1980	-5.3
1981	-4.6
1982	-2.7
1983	-1.6
1984	-1.4
1985	0.1
1986	4.6
1987	9.9
1988	14.1

Chun will always be our paradox. Both accomplishments and liabilities were clearly identified with regard to his presidency. His record is a paradoxical blend of competent rule and unpopularity. The legitimacy of his government was continuously challenged not only by the opposition but also by a variety of antigovernment forces. Riot police became a symbol of the Chun administration, which adopted some ironhanded measures against its opponents. However, unlike President Park who declared martial law several times during his rule, Chun never resorted to the military to maintain law and order. In the future, we will look back and see that despite the mistakes and scandals, he left the country far better off than he found it in the early 1980s. Economically, socially, and diplomatically, the nation made substantial progress under his leadership. There was, however, a dark side to his rule. Chun took power after the 1979 mutiny, trampled the opportunity for democratic transition, and ordered the violent crackdown of the 1980 Kwangju uprising.[188] In December 1995 under the Kim Young Sam administration, Chun was charged with corruption and also with crimes committed in relation to the military rebellion of December 1979 and the suppression of the citizens' uprising in Kwangju of May 1980. During the trial, Chun and codefendants steadfastly maintained that they had been motivated by their "patriotic fervor" in the wake of President Park's assassination, lest it should lead to internal chaos inviting another North Korean invasion. In August 1996, the South Korean court found Chun Doo Hwan guilty of

---

[187] According to a survey of opinion leaders on the economic achievements of Korean presidents, Chun is ranked second with 70 points, after Park Chung Hee with 85 points. See *Hankuk daetongryong pyongga wiwonhoe* (2002), 88.
[188] For an abridged version of the text of the court's judgment, see *Hankook Ilbo* (August 27, 1996): 1-10.

mutiny and of treason for the Kwangju massacre. In the course of the trial key questions surrounding the Kwangju tragedy, such as who actually issued the shoot-to-kill order and what was the level of involvement by Chun went unanswered. It was also found that he had spent $680 million in slush funds collected from conglomerates during his presidency from March 1981 to February 1988.

But it is worth asking what would have happened if one of the two Kims (Kim Young Sam and Kim Dae Jung) had become president in 1980. South Koreans might have come to enjoy democracy earlier, but they might not have succeeded in overcoming the economic crisis. The circumstances in the early 1980s demanded the restoration of law and order. Without social and political stability, no foreign lender would provide additional loans to debt-ridden South Korea. Chun succeeded in achieving social stability and rapid economic growth, which became a solid foundation for the 1988 transition to full democracy and made South Korea far superior to North Korea. The politics of the Chun regime were also somewhat of an improvement over Park Chung Hee's *Yushin* system. According to Donald S. Macdonald, a long-term observer of Korean politics, "The Fifth Republic, roughly similar in law and fact to the Third Republic, was a significant step toward more liberal politics."[189] Whereas the Park regime changed from the democratic and constitutional polity of the 1960s to the dictatorial *Yushin* system of the 1970s, the Chun regime evolved from the authoritarian polity of the early 1980s to a more democratic polity.

By the time Chun's term was over, South Koreans were enjoying full democracy. Chun confined his presidency to a single term and set a precedent for the peaceful transfer of power upon his departure. These were valuable contributions to South Korea's political development.[190] He believed that Syngman Rhee and Park Chung Hee would have been greater leaders if they had not prolonged their rules through constitutional revisions. He repeatedly stated, "I would like the history books to write that I was the first Korean President who handed over power by legal and constitutional means." Chun kept his promise to retire when his term was over, and his political departure established a significant milestone in Korean political history.

A serious problem with Chun's leadership was the fact that, although he was strict with others, he failed to be stern with himself and his relatives. He began his presidency on the strong platform of a "just society," one which is healthy and equitable, and tried to remove the "corrupt" or "unhealthy" elements from the nation, thereby creating many victims and political enemies. Unfortunately, the president and his relatives bore the full brunt of the assault on corruption—a boomerang effect of his "purification" drive. Corruption is a serious national issue. Although Chun's huge slush fund was mostly spent on political campaigns and other political activities and these practices were necessary in the past, such actions cannot be justified. Chun also failed to control the activities of his relatives.[191] Owing to his own "slush fund" and corruption scandals

---

[189] Macdonald, *Koreans*, 59.
[190] Woon-tae Kim, *Hankook jungchiron* (Korean Politics) (Seoul: Pakyoungsa, 1994), 416ff.
[191] It appears to be unfair for Chun that all the political contributions were regarded as his personal bribery. Compared with the influence peddling of his successors' family members and relatives, the level of corruption of Chun's relatives was minor. Readers will recognize this later.

implicating his relatives, his image as an effective leader was seriously tarnished.[192]

Chun's achievements were many and spectacular, but he also had some spectacular failures. He started badly but ended grandly: he turned out to be good for the nation and the people. He was never popular while in office, but after the poor performances of his successors, and especially after the 1997 financial crisis, Chun Doo Hwan's reputation has been reevaluated and in great part redeemed. Although politically much maligned, he may perhaps ultimately be considered to be the effective national manager the South Korean situation so demanded during the turbulent 1980s.

---

[192] Chun Doo Hwan was arrested mainly for the charge of mutiny and the suppression of the Kwangju uprising. But the charge was controversial and many believed it was prompted by political revenge. Thus, a corruption charge was added.

Roh Tae Woo

CHAPTER SIX
ROH TAE WOO
PRESIDENT OF DEMOCRATIC TRANSITION

"The days when freedom and human rights could be slighted in the name of economic growth and national security have ended.... The time has come for the government and all segments of society to strive in concert to achieve a just and fair distribution of income."

"Real courage means to be patient and to wait: this is my philosophy of practicing democracy. For democracy we must pay the appropriate price."

"Since I could not go directly to Pyongyang, I decided to get there through Moscow and Beijing."

—Roh Tae Woo

On February 25, 1988, history was made in the constitutional history of South Korea. On this day the first peaceful and orderly transition of power in the Republic's forty-year history took place between Chun Doo Hwan and Roh Tae Woo. If the basic criterion of democracy is free and fair elections leading to a peaceful change of government, South Korea had finally passed this test. Although a general-turned-politician, Roh was popularly elected and could claim full political legitimacy.[1] The inauguration brought jubilation and hope in part because the country had finally overcome its political crisis and in part because the voters had finally been able to elect fairly their own president.

South Korea now faced the dual challenge of implementing democratic reforms and delivering economic growth with equity. However, Roh did not have a strong mandate: he was a minority president, and his power base was limited to the party established by Chun Doo Hwan. Moreover, in pursuing democratic reform Roh was severely handicapped by his past. As a close friend and political protégé of Chun Doo Hwan, Roh had been deeply involved in the establishment and running of the Chun administration. Anti-government elements regarded the democratic transition as the fruit of their struggles and believed the Roh administration to be nothing more than an extension of the Chun regime.

In addition, the Korean economy was sure to face more difficulties. It was a matter of speculation whether the economy was healthy enough to sustain a turbulent democratic transition. Only time would tell whether the Roh government could satisfy both the middle class and the less advantaged, including labor. The former expected continuous growth while the latter demanded equity. Fortunately, Roh inherited two important political assets: a strong economy and the 1988 Seoul Olympics. But these

---

[1] For overall evaluations of the Roh presidency, see Gibney, *Korea's Quiet Revolution*; Cotton, ed. (1993); Bedeski (1994); Ahn and Chin, eds. (1994); and Kim and Yeom (1993).

blessings carried with them the risk of becoming political liabilities. If he failed to maintain the current state of the nation (i.e., economic boom and social stability), his presidency would be blamed for the results. How the gentlemanly Roh would manage the democratic transition while achieving his contradictory goals—democratic reform, economic growth, and political stability—was yet to be seen.

LIFE AND CHARACTER OF THE "ORDINARY MAN"

Roh Tae Woo was born on December 4, 1932, in a tiny farming village in Kongsan County near Taegu, a major city in southeastern Korea.[2] His father was killed in a traffic accident when Roh was seven years old. The boy was the older of two brothers raised by their mother, widowed at age thirty, with financial help from an uncle, a small manufacturer of stationery items in Taegu. The boy walked five miles each way along a mountain path to graduate from the Kongsan Elementary School with a perfect attendance record. In 1944 Roh entered the Taegu Technical High School, but three years later transferred to the Kyongbuk High School, hoping to become a medical doctor.

The outbreak of the Korean War in 1950 put an end to Roh's dreams of becoming a doctor. Still wearing his high school uniform, he volunteered for the army, beginning a military career at the age of eighteen. While serving as a military policeman, he was accepted as a cadet in the first class of the regular military academy in January 1952. Life at the academy included regular college courses as well as military training and sports. Like Chun Doo Hwan, Roh excelled at sports. At first he was a leader of field sports and later a leading member of the rugby team. Roh had a quieter and more refined side as well. In the midst of his busy life at the military academy, he indulged his love for reading poems and novels, and was particularly fond of Hermann Hesse and Leo Tolstoy. On Sunday he often visited a Seoul concert hall to enjoy the music of Tchaikovsky, Beethoven and Debussy.

When he graduated from the military academy in September 1955, Roh was assigned to the Fifth Infantry Division, where he met Brigadier General Park Chung Hee, the division commander. Roh Tae Woo, who was known as a hard-working, model officer, made a good impression on General Park. One day, Roh was invited to lunch by Park. It was an unusual invitation. After lunch, the general asked the young lieutenant to join him on a goose hunt, but Roh declined because he had something else to do. Curious about why a platoon leader would reject an invitation from the division commander, Park asked what kept him busy. The young lieutenant answered, "I am working on leveling a firing range."

Six years after his lunch with Roh, Park Chung Hee staged his successful military coup. At the time, Roh, now a captain, was an instructor at the ROTC unit of Seoul National University. Park soon transferred Roh to the intelligence section of the staff of the military junta. Park ordered Roh to secretly survey the country's agricultural situation. Roh reported that the mission gave Park a true grasp of the country's predicament: "I went to a village that was practicing slash and burn farming...and found that people were essentially hibernating. To save the scarce food, people would eat one or two potatoes a day and sleep all day long. I made a report to General Park, who was angry that food was still scarce, but curious about

---

[2] For a biography, see Lee Kyung-Nam (1987).

this human hibernation."[3]

In 1969, Roh served as battalion commander in the South Korean contingent in Vietnam. Roh rose steadily in the military, reaching the position of commander of the Ninth Division around the time President Park was assassinated in October 1979. When the showdown between Generals Chun Doo Hwan and Chung Seung-hwa took place on the night of December 12, 1979, it was General Roh who quickly dispatched a regiment from his division to support General Chun. After that General Roh was appointed commander of the Capital Garrison Command and then the Defense Security Command. He retired from the military in July 1981, a four-star general at the age of forty-nine.

After retiring from the military, Roh began his political career as minister of state for national security and foreign affairs, a cabinet post without portfolio in the Chun government. His main task, however, was to win the 1988 Summer Olympic Games for Seoul. Following South Korea's successful bid, he served briefly as the first minister of the newly established sports ministry, which was set up to organize and support the staging of the coming Seoul Olympics. Subsequently, he was named minister of home affairs. Then, in 1983 he was chosen chairman of the Seoul Olympic Organizing Committee. In that capacity he traveled abroad almost constantly, talking to a variety of people in an effort to ensure the success of the Seoul Olympics. These years of international travel, working out Korea's hosting of the Olympics, developed in Roh something of an international perspective.

In 1985 Roh became a member of the National Assembly, running on the ruling party's national ticket, and shortly afterward he was elected chairman of the government party. At the National Assembly, he gained experience in legislative activities—debate, dialogue, compromise, and confrontation. In contrast to Park Chung Hee and Chun Doo Hwan, both of whom assumed power without any experience in government, Roh had "civilianized" himself and had accumulated valuable experience in government, foreign affairs, and national politics for more than seven years previous to assuming the presidency.

In a country of politicians with notoriously short fuses, Roh was a thoughtful and patient leader, the type of man who waited patiently for the fruit to ripen and fall naturally from the tree. Whenever possible he took the role of conciliator among his colleagues.[4] After an interview with Roh before the 1987 presidential election, Karen Elliot House, foreign editor of The Wall Street Journal, gave her impression: "Mr. Roh does not fit the caricature of a third world general. He comes across in an interview as low-key, straight-talking and modest.... If one encountered Mr. Roh and the Messrs. Kim without knowing who was who, one would be inclined to label Kim Dae Jung as the power-seeking general, Kim Young Sam as a slick and shallow politician, and Mr. Roh as an earnest and intelligent alternative to the present leadership..."[5]

---

[3] Interview with Roh Tae Woo on December 22, 2001.
[4] Lee Kyung-Nam (1987), 75ff.
[5] Karen E. House, "U.S. Needs Patience in Korea", *Wall Street Journal*, June 9, 1987.

Turbulent Voyage to Full Democracy

About 9 o'clock in the morning on June 29, 1987, Roh Tae Woo, the presidential candidate of the ruling party, made an unexpected appearance on the nation's television screens. With solemn face he made an announcement that stunned the nation: "I have now come to a firm conviction about the future of our nation," Roh intoned. "The people are the nation's masters, and the people's will must come before everything else." He then announced an eight-point proposal for democratic reform that embodied a wholesale acceptance of opposition demands:

1. amendment of the constitution for the direct election of the president

2. revision of the presidential election laws to ensure fair elections

3. granting of amnesty to Kim Dae Jung and other political prisoners and allowing them to resume political activities

4. guaranteeing basic rights to all citizens

5. restoring freedom of the press by abolishing the repressive Basic Press Law

6. ensuring local self-government through the popular election of local assemblies and executive heads of local governments

7. creation of a new political climate for dialogue and compromise

8. carrying out bold social reforms to build a clean, honest society.[6]

His June 29 declaration was a turning point, not only in his political career, but in the history of Korea. His bold action dramatically altered the national mood, from one of political crisis to "stunning political miracle" that promised to lay the foundations of a genuine democracy.[7]

The weeks before his declaration had been a period of major crisis in Korean political history: street demonstrations in Seoul and other major cities continued for seventeen consecutive days, becoming unmanageable for the police. Many Korea observers believed that the country was headed for a social explosion. Immediately after his announcement, demonstrations ceased and the looming political crisis seemed to melt away. The public mood was suddenly upbeat, and Roh was called a hero. The daily *JoongAng Ilbo* exulted, "It is great news. Real democracy is coming. Again and again Koreans have been disappointed by their government. Now Koreans finally believe the government is listening to the people."[8] Restaurants, bars, and other amusement centers in downtown Seoul reveled in crowds of customers. Rejoicing over Roh's announcement, the owner of a coffee house in downtown Seoul posted a notice that read, "Today is a very joyous day and so whatever you drink here today will be free of charge." She went on to serve her patrons free tea and

---

[6] For a complete statement, see Roh Tae Woo, "Grand National Harmony and Progress Toward a Great Nation: Special Declaration on June 29, 1987", in Cotton, ed. (1993), 317-321.

[7] As assistant for political affairs, I personally experienced the dramatic political transition for both Presidents Chun and Roh.

[8] *Joonang Ilbo*, June 29, 1987.

coffee for nine hours.[9] The opposition, in a rare show of approval, welcomed Roh's proposal. He was also applauded by the international media.

For several months before his announcement, Roh had realized that dramatic measures of democratic reform were needed to break a stalemate and to avoid a crisis of confrontation between government and opposition forces. During an interview with a foreign correspondent at the time, Roh explained:

> Since the birth of this Republic, we have had to grapple with three fundamental tasks. Namely, to secure the survival of the country, to see the economy developed, and in doing all this to develop the country into a more mature democracy. In the initial stage, security was our main concern. In the next stage, we were able to make economic progress, based on national security. But now is the stage which people want us to have democratic development…What I had in mind at the time was that I had been given the role to make this country into a more mature, developed democracy.[10]

As the presidential election was scheduled for mid-December, national attention shifted to the electoral competition. As part of his election campaign, Roh Tae Woo tried to transform his image, from that of authoritarian to democracy's new hope. It was a task made especially challenging by a popular resentment built up through years of authoritarian rule. However, thanks to his June 29th proposals for democratic reforms, Roh was largely successful in his new image-shaping campaign. He was aware that a considerable body of voters, particularly in the new industrial areas of the southeast, as well as around Seoul, were prepared to support him because of the governmental success in handling such vital issues as national security and economic growth, or through fear of the chaos that might result from an opposition victory.

On the other hand, Kim Young Sam and his long-term archrival within the opposition, Kim Dae Jung, failed to agree on a single candidacy, and both decided to run for the allegiance of opposition-minded voters. The two Kims ran against each other as much as against Roh. The division of the opposition led to street battles between rival Kim supporters. As the campaign progressed, the people became increasingly disillusioned with the two Kims. Joining the three-way race was Kim Jong-pil, the chief architect of the 1961 coup and prime minister under President Park, who was expected to lure conservative votes away from Roh.

As the presidential race heated up, labor became more militant, staging over 3,500 strikes and demonstrations in the three months after Roh's June 29 announcement.[11] During this short period wages rose by 20 percent, and business feared an end to South Korea's rapid economic growth. Roh advanced himself as the only candidate who could guarantee stability and prosperity. Given the high stakes involved, opposition candidates, especially Kim Dae Jung, advocated populist policies. Roh Tae Woo promised short-term policy options, such as the construction of two million new housing units, to

---

[9] *Korea Herald*, July 1, 1987; and Nick B. Williams and Mark Fineman, "Chun Party Chief Agrees to Reforms; Roh Backs Korea Protest Demands, Including Direct Vote for President", *Los Angels Times*, June 29, 1987.

[10] Claudia Rosett, "Asia: Korea's Roh Tae-Woo Places His Bet", *Wall Street Journal*, July 27, 1987.

[11] *Far Eastern Economic Review*, September 24, 1987.

neutralize the appeal of the opposition. Thus, presidential candidates were outbidding each other for welfare spending, damaging the growth potential of the economy.[12]

After a fierce campaign, Roh Tae Woo was elected with 36.6 percent of the vote, followed by Kim Young Sam with 28 percent, and Kim Dae Jung with 27 percent. Despite predictions of a neck-and-neck race, Roh overwhelmed opposition leaders by a very comfortable margin of 2 million votes. Though Roh's percentage of support was the lowest among the winners of past direct presidential elections, his margin of victory was the largest in the history of the Republic. Rather than coming into office as the illegitimate handpicked successor of Chun, Roh assumed the presidency as a legitimately elected candidate.

The Roh victory revealed the ruling party to be far more resourceful and flexible than many had predicted. It apparently reflected Koreans' desire for the stability and gradual democratic change Roh had promised during the campaign. Some have argued that Roh's victory was a fluke, the result of the split between the main opposition candidates Kim Young Sam and Kim Dae Jung. Such a view overlooks the fact that Roh, a direct protégé of President Chun Doo Hwan, managed to secure 37 percent of the presidential vote and that a fourth candidate with direct ties to the Park Chung Hee regime, Kim Jong-pil, received another 8 percent. It is doubtful that either Kim Young Sam or Kim Dae Jung could have won even if only one of the two Kims had run, owing to the deep regional antagonism and rivalries that separated them.[13] The three major candidates were favored in their home regions (see Table 8): Roh in Taegu and North Kyungsang; Kim Young Sam in Pusan and South Kyungsang; and Kim Dae Jung in Kwangju and Cholla.

The popular presidential election put an end to the divisive controversy surrounding government legitimacy that had plagued the nation for decades. Most Koreans seemed to accept Roh Tae Woo as the legitimate winner. Even many people who voted for the opposition said they wanted to give Roh time to prove he would somehow be more democratic than his predecessor. At that time, however, four major tasks awaited the new president. First, he was compelled to fulfill the promises of democracy he had made the previous June. Second, he had to keep the economy growing as fast as people had come to expect. Growth of 6 percent was needed to accommodate a population boom if unemployment was not to rise or living conditions fall. Third, he had to maintain social and political stability in order to continue such economic growth. Finally, he had to reduce tensions between South and North Korea. These were not ordinary tasks that any government could reasonably handle. The South Korean people expected Roh Tae Woo to achieve such goals much better than the opposition leaders.

---

[12] Tun-jen Cheng and Lawrence B. Krause, "Democracy and Development: With Special Attention to Korea", *Journal of Northeast Asian Studies*, 10:2 (summer 1991): 7-8.
[13] See Young Whan Kihl and Ilpyong J. Kim",The Sixth Republic: Problems, Prospects, and the 1988 Olympiad", in Kim and Kihl, eds. (1988), 244.

Table 8. **Presidential Election Results by Region** (%)

Region	T. W. Roh	Y. S. Kim	D. J. Kim	J. P. Kim
Seoul	24.4	28.6	32.1	8.1
Inchon	38.7	29.4	20.9	9.1
Kyonggi	40.6	27.0	21.8	8.3
Kangwon	57.9	25.4	8.6	5.3
N. Chungchong	45.7	27.5	10.7	13.2
S. Chungchong	26.6	15.8	12.1	42.8
Cheju	48.6	26.1	18.1	4.4
Kwangju	4.5	0.4	93.3	0.2
N. Cholla	13.7	1.4	80.9	0.7
S. Cholla	7.9	1.1	87.9	0.3
Taegu	69.8	24.0	2.6	2.0
N. Kyongsang	64.8	27.5	2.3	2.5
Pusan	31.6	55.2	9.0	2.6
S. Kyongsang	40.4	50.3	4.4	26
Total	36.6	28.0	27.0	8.1

Source: *Choongang Ilbo*, December 18, 1987.

Roh's inauguration on February 25, 1988, marked the first peaceful transfer of power in Korea since 1948. In his inaugural address, Roh Tae Woo presented democratic reform and national conciliation as the two guidelines of his administration. He promised to push forward for full democracy and appealed for popular support to realize national reconciliation. The new president pronounced:

> We gather...to proclaim a new beginning.... The day when freedom and human rights could be slighted in the name of economic growth and national security has ended.... At the same time, the day when confusion was irresponsibly created on the pretext of freedom and participation must also come to an end. We will have an era of mature democracy, when human rights are inviolable and freedom with responsibility prevails, so that both economic development and national security are assured....
>
> Growing disparities between social strata and geographical regions have bred strife and schisms, seriously undermining national cohesion.... The time has come for the government and all segments of society to strive in concert to achieve a just and fair distribution of come.[14]

---

[14] Cotton, *Korea under Roh Tae Woo*, 322-325.

Entering the Blue House, Roh tried to bring a new style to the presidency. He made a good first impression. He proclaimed himself an ordinary man in a new "era of the ordinary people." He broke with precedent by refusing to be called "Excellency." He cut down on his personal security guards and opened the road fronting the Blue House to pedestrians. Roh smiled broadly at everyone. He called for national reconciliation and set about honing a distinctively populist image—a contrasting style with Chun's stern and uncompromising manner.

Despite his repeated pledge of change, Roh's first cabinet appointments provoked widespread criticism; he retained seven of Chun's ministers for the sake of policy consistency, significantly damaging his legitimacy as a democratically elected president. Critics contended the lineup was particularly disappointing because Roh appeared to have signaled an era of change with his earlier appointment of Lee Hyon-jae, a respected former president of Seoul National University, as prime minister. Even members of his own party believed that Roh's choices damaged his credibility. Roh also appointed four former professors to ministerial posts. In other words, the cabinet lacked focus and a sense of teamwork, and the lineup fell "short of broad expectations for change."[15]

In an effort to remove elements of authoritarian government, Roh reduced the size and role of the Blue House staff. At the same time he created two important offices in the Blue House—senior secretary for foreign affairs and national security and special assistant for policy affairs. Roh named Kim Chong-whi, a former professor at the National Defense University, as chief security adviser and Park Chul-un, Roh's nephew-in-law and former public prosecutor, as special assistant for policy affairs.[16] The establishment of the two offices forecast Roh's emphasis on foreign policy in his administration. However, his other appointments of Blue House staff once again disappointed the nation. To strengthen his image as a democratic reformer, Roh appointed fresh but inexperienced scholars and journalists as his top advisers. For instance, he named economics professor Park Seung as his chief economic adviser. Park was unable to gain the full support of the economic bureaucrats and, as a result, apparently had difficulty advising the president.[17] Choi Byung-ryol, former editor-in-chief of the daily *Chosun Ilbo*, was his senior secretary for political affairs. Later, Kim Hak-joon, a former political science professor, was appointed as his spokesman, and two former political science professors, Lee Hong-ku and Roh Jae-bong, were successively named as special assistants for political affairs. These civilian appointees were well known and popular but lacked administrative experience and managerial capability. In other words, Roh put more emphasis on creating a fresh image than on expertise. Although the Blue House staff appeared to be suitable for compromise and coordination among various groups, it lacked the will and capability to actively lead the country and meet the challenges the nation now faced.[18]

Unfortunately, the April 26 general elections brought an abrupt end to Roh's

---

[15] *Donga Ilbo*, March 25, 1988.

[16] Park Chul-un was assistant for legal affairs for President Chun, and then worked in the KCIA, engaging in secret contacts with North Korea.

[17] In less than ten months Roh replaced Park with Moon Hee-kap, a career bureaucrat and former deputy minister of the EPB.

[18] Duck-kyu Chin, "*Roh Tae Woo jeonghuui kwonryokkuchowa jeongchichaeje* (Power Structure and Political System of Roh Tae Woo Government), in Ahn and Chin, eds. (1994), 66-70.

honeymoon, if indeed he had ever had one.[19] The electoral upset undermined his ability to govern and threatened a period of stalemate and uncertainty in Korean politics. The misfortune was partly of the ruling party's own making. The elections were held just two months after Roh's inauguration. The elections were critical as the new constitution granted the National Assembly more power than it had previously held and they would now determine how strong a mandate President Roh could garner. They would also test whether Kim Young Sam and Kim Dae Jung could remain atop the opposition forces, or whether one would emerge as more powerful than the other. The opposition parties, therefore, had a big stake in the parliamentary elections as well.

It seemed as if Roh and his inexperienced team of advisers had made a fatal mistake.[20] After their victory in the presidential election, the president and his advisers had waxed optimistic about almost everything, too naive to foresee the imminent counterattacks by opposition forces. Rather than preparing for such attacks, Roh and his associates were more concerned with how to reduce the influence of former President Chun and his loyalists within the ruling party. The presidential election victory had made them overconfident, even arrogant. Roh and his party believed that the ruling party could win a landslide victory in the parliamentary elections, or at least a comfortable majority.[21] But they had underestimated the political potential of the resilient opposition leaders. During much darker hours in the past, the two Kims had never given up, and they certainly would not now. There were hundreds of thousands of activists and students still determined to challenge the Roh government. A combination of arrogance and lack of experience can lead to serious mistakes on the part of any new administration.

Initially, the ruling DJP wanted to hold elections in February. It believed it could benefit from the bandwagon effect of its victory in the presidential election and from the disarray among the demoralized opposition. But holding the election in February, before the retirement of President Chun, would enable Chun to nominate his loyal supporters as DJP candidates for assembly seats at the expense of President-elect Roh. Therefore, Roh opted for an April election, well after his assumption of the presidency. Following the announcement of the April election date, the DJP nominated its 224 candidates. Surprisingly, many influential lawmakers were denied re-nomination. The party dismissed twenty-eight of the eighty-six incumbent local chapter chairmen (32.6 percent), while nominating 125 new individuals as candidates. The nominations were apparently geared to consolidating the power of Roh Tae Woo within the ruling party.[22]

For Roh and the government party, the timing of the election was highly unfavorable. Every April, college students are active in commemorating the 1960 student uprising. Every May, students and anti-government forces protest the bloody crackdown of the 1980

---

[19] For details of the 1988 parliamentary elections, David Brady and Jongryn Mo, "Electoral Systems and Institutional Choice: A Case Study of the 1988 Korean Elections", *Comparative Political Studies*, 24:4 (January 1992): 405-429; and Hong-Nack Kim, "The 1988 Parliamentary election in South Korea", in Cotton, ed. (1993), 111-126

[20] For information on the danger in the early period of a government, see James P. Pfiffner, *The Strategic Presidency* (Chicago, IL: Dorsey, 1988), 7-8.

[21] Roh Tae Woo, "*Roh Tae Woo ui yooksung hoegorok 2*" (Reminiscences of Roh Tae Woo 2), *Wolgan Chosun* (June 1999): 227-228.

[22] *Donga Ilbo*, March 22, 1988.

Kwangju uprising. Released from authoritarian control and stimulated by student demonstrations, the national mood was almost uncontrollable. While protests and other forms of challenges became widespread, existing public institutions were distrusted or discredited. The press, now free of government control, reported sensationally on the wrongdoings of the previous administration, feeding public opinion even more. In an effort to calm protests, on April 1 Roh publicly expressed regret over the Kwangju incident. This was the first time the government had admitted any possible wrongdoing. His statement redefined the uprising as "part of the efforts by students and citizens of Kwangju to democratize the nation," Included in Roh's statement were an apology and a promise of compensation for the victims.[23] Rather than mollifying the resentment many felt toward Roh and Chun, the measures only encouraged anti-government forces and intensified protests and demands.

In an effort to defuse the burgeoning social unrest, the Roh administration "scapegoated" Chun Doo Hwan and his associates for illicit activities of the Chun regime, as if to say a totally new era had dawned. The Roh government arrested Chun Doo Hwan's youngest brother, Chun Kyung-hwan, on charges of embezzlement and influence peddling while he had been chairman of the New Village Movement. But the governmental concession only encouraged the demands of the opposition groups. The highly publicized arrest of the younger Chun shortly before the election served as a public reminder that there were yet more scandals involving corruption and abuse of power that could not be separated from President Roh and the ruling DJP. In Korea it is a regrettable tradition to take revenge on the formerly powerful. All who were identified with the Chun regime were now assumed to be criminals. Rumors rather than evidence informed public opinion, and many gloated over the sufferings of the formerly powerful, chief among them the former president himself.

The April elections gave the opposition parties time to recuperate from their losses in December.[24] With the start of the campaign, the opposition parties launched massive political offensives against the ruling camp, making fierce charges about the 1980 Kwangju incident and the excesses of the Chun government. They also raised questions about the legitimacy of the Roh government, which they regarded as a mere extension of the Chun regime. The "three Kims", namely Kim Young Sam, Kim Dae Jung, and Kim Jong-pil, spearheaded the political offensive in exposing irregularities of the former government. Meanwhile, President Roh appealed to voters to support the DJP and provide him with the seats necessary to carry out his campaign promises of continued economic and political development amidst stability. Once again, the election became a fierce showdown between Roh and the three Kims. The election resulted in a stunning defeat for Roh and his party. The DJP failed to secure a majority, winning only 125 (42%) of the 299 seats in the National Assembly. President Roh and his party belatedly realized that their election timing and strategy had been wrong. The surge of regionalism was the most important aspect of the April 1988 elections (see Table 9).

Almost everyone deplored the regional antagonisms evident in the voting, with much of the support for the three opposition parties emerging from each party leader's home

---

[23] *Korea Herald*, April 2, 1988.
[24] Sung-Joo Han, "South Korea in 1988", *Asian Survey*, XXIX: 1 (January 1989), 29-31.

territory.[25] Observers saw troubling signs for Korean democratization. Again, Kim Dae Jung's party virtually swept the southwestern Cholla region, the party led by Kim Young Sam took the southeastern Pusan region, and followers of Kim Jong-pil drew support from his provincial base of Chungchong. The unexpected election results resurrected the political life of Kim Young Sam and Kim Dae Jung. This was the first time in forty years that the government party failed to win a majority in the National Assembly. The formation of a political configuration called *yoso yadae* (small government party, big opposition) in the National Assembly, together with the militant anti-government groups, effectively pushed the Roh administration into a corner.[26]

Table 9. **Regional Base of Support for Political Parties**

Party & Leader	Home Region	% Vote (in Home Region)	% Seats (in Home Region)	% Vote (National)	% Seats (National)
DJP & Roh TW	Taegu	48.4	100.0	34.0	38.8
	North Kyongsang	51.0	81.0	34.0	38.8
PPD & Kim DJ	Kwangju	88.6	100.0	19.3	24.1
	North Cholla	61.5	100.0	19.3	24.1
	South Cholla	67.9	94.4	19.3	24.1
RDP & Kim YS	Pusan	54.1	93.3	23.8	20.5
	South Kyongsang	36.9	40.9	23.8	20.5
NDRP & Kim JP	South Chungchong	46.5	72.2	15.6	12.1

Source: *Central Election Management Committee*

The new constitution ended the president's right to dissolve the National Assembly while enhancing the assembly's powers, including the right to investigate administration affairs. Many foresaw that confrontations in the assembly between ruling and opposition parties could now reach a critical point. In a political culture where a zero-sum notion of politics prevailed, it was difficult to expect cross-voting and compromise between ruling and opposition parties. President Roh had to deal with a fragmented multiparty system, often described by Western scholars as the "kiss of death" for presidential democracy.[27]

The three Kims triumphantly returned to the chamber of the National Assembly, and their combined power began to dominate the Roh administration. Roh had made efforts to replace confrontation and dispute with dialogue and negotiation. However, the opposition made it clear from the outset that it was intent on establishing its own political agenda. The National Assembly's rejection of Roh's nomination for chief justice was only the first bump on the difficult road ahead. Two weeks later, an opposition-sponsored bill, which would have given a special panel of the National Assembly the

---

[25] Urban C. Lehner, "Ruling Party Suffers an Upset in Korean Vote", *Wall Street Journal*, April 27, 1988.

[26] For an observation of the early stage of the Roh presidency, see "South Korea: Foursquare to the Future", *Economist*, May 21, 1988.

[27] The Roh government was often plagued by the predicament of "a difficult combination of presidentialism with multipartyism." (Scott Mainwaring, "Presidentialism, Multipartyism, and Democracy: The Difficult Combination", *Comparative Political Studies 26* (1993): 198-227.)

power to investigate alleged wrongdoings of the Chun administration, was passed by the National Assembly. Roh vetoed the bill to prevent the assembly from forcing his predecessor to testify on alleged abuses of power.[28] Roh could veto other opposition-sponsored bills, but he lacked the votes to put through new laws. As a result, Roh could not successfully pursue his agenda and had to resort to defending himself from the challenges of the opposition.

Nevertheless, Roh's immediate concern was the successful hosting of the Olympics, to be held in Seoul from September 17 to October 2, 1988. On the eve of the Seoul Olympics, however, North Korea continued to pressure its allies to boycott the Games. Further, there was a possibility of North Korean terror. In November of the previous year, North Korean terrorists had blown up a Korean passenger airplane in flight. Preventing North Korea terrorist attacks during the Olympics was a critical task facing the government. The government was eager to minimize the possibility of a North Korean attempt to disrupt the Olympics and to reduce the risk of a massive boycott by socialist countries. Negotiations were under way between the two Koreas, under the auspices of the International Olympic Committee (IOC), for North Korean participation in the Seoul Olympics. In response to Pyongyang's proposal that it co-host the Olympics with Seoul and that half of the events as well as the opening and closing ceremonies take place in Pyongyang, South Korea and the IOC offered to let the North host four events. But for Pyongyang the issue was "a strategic political fight against the South's regime and its imperialistic supporters,"[29] with considerations related to sports given second priority or even none at all.

On September 17, President Roh declared the opening of the Twenty-fourth Olympiad. The 1988 Olympics in Seoul were the best organized, and the largest in history in terms of the number of participating countries and athletes. The Olympic games brought the prestige of South Korea to a high point.

After a two-week political truce during the Olympics, the opposition parties again began to exercise their political clout. The opposition leaders, determined to have their revenge on the previous regime, vied with one another with demands the ruling party found difficult to satisfy. The opposition challenged the Roh administration by initiating a parliamentary investigation into the wrongdoings of the Chun regime, and established a special committee to investigate the Kwangju incident and other matters.

From October to December, the National Assembly held televised hearings on the wrongdoings of the previous government. Though hardly more than political show trials, the nationally televised proceedings plunged the country into tumult. For weeks millions of viewers were treated to a parade of witnesses, including former government officials, military leaders, top businessmen, and newspaper owners, who were subjected to long hours of grilling and scolding by lawmakers. Although critics found these hearings inconclusive and unsatisfactory, through them the opposition parties were able to exercise unprecedented power. Inspired by the hearings, thousands of radical students

---

[28] *Donga Ilbo*, July 18, 1988.
[29] Oberdorfer, *Two Koreas*, 182-183.

and dissidents marched every day for a month to Chun's private residence in the western part of Seoul, where they battled police guarding the former president's home.[30]

The legislative investigation led to the arrest of fourteen of Chun's relatives and forced the former president and his wife into self-imposed exile. Pressured by the National Assembly and public uproar, former president Chun, in a televised address broadcast on November 23, 1988, took full responsibility for what he acknowledged was a period of authoritarian irregularities. He said he would leave the capital for a "quiet period of repentance" at a remote temple near Mt. Sorak in the rugged northeastern part of the country not far from the DMZ, and that he would surrender all his private property to the state.[31] Some Koreans felt sorry for the man who had done so much for the nation. Others, though satisfied with the result, were still angry. After almost three decades of authoritarian rule, the political pendulum had swung to the other extreme resulting in deadlock-prone national politics. Roh was so distracted by the challenges of the opposition and dissident groups that he lost his momentum in leading the nation. The Roh administration experienced continued legislative deadlock and political stalemate. At a time when the government was called upon to work aggressively, it found itself to be a very "limited government."[32] In early December, only nine months after the inauguration of his first cabinet, Roh carried out a major reshuffle of the cabinet and the ruling party.

While politicians were fighting for political issues such as "liquidation of the Fifth Republic irregularities," the people expected something else from them. According to a survey conducted by *Chosun Ilbo* and Gallup Korea to identify the most urgent problems facing the nation, the elimination and punishment of irregularities and wrongdoings of previous governments came in third, behind political and social stability. Democratization, Roh's primary agenda, finished a distant ninth on the list. Social order and political stability were primary concerns for the public.[33]

As the government became weaker, public demands mushroomed.[34] Everybody wanted something they had not had before. Many groups selfishly sought to promote their own interests at the expense of others. Labor unions often struck illegally or used violence to gain their objectives, resulting in a slowdown in production. As part of democratic reform, the government released hundreds of dissidents, but the release only intensified their anti-establishment activities. On university campuses and at worksites nationwide, radicals took control of the anti-government movements. They were revolutionists rather than democratic reformers: they advocated a wholesale removal of the ruling system. As Molotov cocktail throwing students and workers confronted riot police virtually everywhere every day, industries and education came to a halt. Sometimes

---

[30] Susan Moffat, "Koreans Test Democratic Institutions by Pressing Demands in Chun Inquiry", *Asian Wall Street Journal Weekly*, November 21, 1988.
[31] *Chosun Ilbo*, November 24, 1988.
[32] Chin Duck-kyu, *op. cit.*, 45-47.
[33] Derek Davies and John McBeth, "Democracy by Degrees", *Far Eastern Economic Review*, March 2, 1989.
[34] Chin Duck-kyu, *op. cit.*, 48-52.

protesters overturned buses and set them afire. On May 3, 1989, six policemen were killed in a blaze set by radical students on a college campus in Pusan.[35]

Activists also intensified their unification movement. In the weeks preceding the opening of the Seoul Olympics, some 20,000 radical students, taking a pro-unification and anti-American stance, had attempted to march to Panmunjom on the DMZ. In March 1989, Reverend Moon Ik-hwan, a dissident leader, secretly traveled to North Korea to meet with the North Korean leader Kim Il Sung. In July 1989, a student activist organization, again in violation of the national security law, secretly sent its representative, Im Soo-kyung, to Pyongyang. Their trips and other unauthorized visits intensified ideological divisions in South Korea.[36]

Long accustomed to an active and strong president, the people looked to Roh to resolve the crisis. However, he was passive and indecisive and lacked political and economic direction. Unable to control the situation, the government drifted from crisis to crisis. During a press conference on the second anniversary of his June 29 Declaration, Roh stated he had intentionally refused to "impose democracy from the top" and would continue to refrain from exercising "public power" to create an orderly democracy. Democracy, he said, "is not something that can be forced upon the people" but must develop "through self-regulation and self-help" by people in all sectors of society.[37]

Roh's passive approach satisfied nobody. Those who expected stability and continuous economic growth were perhaps the most disappointed. Radicals were likewise unsatisfied and called for many more radical reforms. In the midst of chaos, Roh decided to cancel a national referendum on his leadership in March 1989. During his presidential campaign sixteen months earlier, the then-candidate Roh promised that if elected, he would give the voters a chance to assess his performance following the Seoul Olympics. His decision gave the anti-government forces another rallying cry—broken campaign promises. But ordinary people were not looking forward to having to go to the polls again so soon after the 1987 presidential and April 1988 parliamentary elections. They were also worried about the potential chaos that might result if Roh was forced to resign.[38] Cancellation of the referendum contributed to Roh's image as a man unable to make tough decisions and stick to them. The combination of student unrest and labor strife clearly alienated portions of the middle class. The confrontation on the streets coupled with continued deadlock in the National Assembly contributed to perceptions of government weakness. The perception of drift was heightened when economic growth slowed in the second half of 1989 and inflation increased. Public dissatisfaction steadily mounted. According to a public opinion survey, 92 percent of the respondents believed that the political situation was unstable. The public image of the opposition was also

---

[35] *Chosun Ilbo*, May 4, 1989.
[36] Young Whan Kihl, "South Korea in 1989", *Asian Survey* 30:1 (January 1990): 69-70.
[37] *Korea Herald*, June 30, 1989.
[38] Urban C. Lehner, "Roh's Decision to Postpone Referendum Gives Critics in South Korea Fresh Fuel", *Wall Street Journal*, March 21, 1989.

strongly negative: when asked how well opposition parties were dealing with political instability, 74 percent of the respondents viewed their performance as poor.[39]

Rapid liberalization of the South Korean political system demanded a huge price in terms of "state capacity" in two senses: first, the ability to get specific policies implemented and second, the ability to mobilize a national consensus around government goals. The loss of efficient and effective state capacities began to appear immediately after Roh took office. Roh obviously had no guidelines or programs to attain his national goals. The core members of the Roh administration were divided: those from academia and the media advocated more idealistic, reform-oriented policies while career bureaucrats preferred gradual and orderly change. This lack of coordination within the Blue House and among different government agencies drew the attention of the press from the early days of the government.

As Roh completed the second year of his five-year term, skeptics began to question the ability of this popularly elected yet politically enfeebled president to govern the nation. In dealing with a fragmented society, Roh characteristically let events take their own course until it became clear that the president had no alternative but to take action. During the early period of his presidency such a 'laissez faire' style worked, as there was little the government could do to either promote or hinder the historical process of turbulent democratic transition. However, this passive style of leadership would prove to be ineffective in the months and years to come. Rife with their own mutual antagonisms, even the opposition parties controlling the National Assembly could not push their legislative programs at will. The three Kims, heads of the major opposition parties, were already competing with each other as presumed candidates in the next presidential election. As such, the four-party structure aggravated regional antagonism. The public had become disgusted with the four-party confrontations and urged cooperation to address impending national issues.

In an effort to break the political stalemate, the four parties reached an accord called a "grand compromise," concerning the controversial issue of "liquidating the negative legacies of the Fifth Republic," an issue that had been a heated subject of political debate for nearly two years. On December 15, 1989, after a seven-hour meeting at the Blue House, President Roh and leaders of the three opposition parties (Kim Young Sam, Kim Dae Jung, and Kim Jong-pil) declared in a joint statement, "we agreed to render joint efforts to completely settle the Fifth Republic's problems within the year."[40] They agreed that former President Chun should testify before the National Assembly, while implicitly assuring that Chun's responsibility for the irregularities of the Fifth Republic would no longer be the subject of political inquest. Chun Doo Hwan testified before the National Assembly and a nationwide television audience on December 31, and on January 3, 1990, President Roh declared an end to inquiries concerning the Fifth Republic issues.

Only three weeks after Chun's testimony, on January 22, 1990, Roh Tae Woo and the two opposition leaders, Kim Young Sam (head of the Reunification and Democracy

---

[39] *Joongang Ilbo*, May 9, 1989. For the discussion of the pervading crisis, see Kyoung Eun Lee and June Hyoung Rhie, "An Anatomy of South Korea's 'Total Crisis' in the Spring of 1990", *Pacific Focus*, V:2 (fall 1990): 155-183.
[40] *Joongang Ilbo*, December 16, 1989.

Party) and Kim Jong-pil (head of the New Democratic Republican Party), surprised the nation by jointly announcing the creation of a "grand conservative coalition" party, the Democratic Liberal Party (DLP), which controlled 217 of 299 seats in the National Assembly, a more than two-thirds majority.[41] The three leaders announced that "to save the nation," they had agreed to end the problematic four-party system, thereby staging what was then termed "an honorable political revolution."[42] Their goal was to create a party akin to Japan's Liberal Democratic Party, which had guaranteed decades of political stability and economic growth. However, the three factions of the new party had different perspectives, goals, and policy lines. Nonetheless, implications of the merger were far-reaching. It ended the political stalemate which neither Roh nor the country could afford. Now the dominant ruling party could manage the pace of democratic transition and major national issues. Finally, the merger freed President Roh from the unbearable political gridlock that the opposition-dominated assembly had imposed on his administration.

As anticipated, the merger intensified political conflicts by radicalizing the remaining opposition party, the Cholla-region-based PPD led by Kim Dae Jung. The opposition resorted to sit-ins, walkouts, public denunciations, and even hunger strikes. The opposition spared no effort to block the passage of government bills. On July 17, 1990, after weeks of fruitless negotiations with the opposition, the ruling DLP unilaterally pushed twenty-six bills through the National Assembly in only thirty seconds. There were no formal hearings, debates, or votes. Denouncing the passage of the bills as legislative tyranny by the majority, seventy-six lawmakers of the opposition party immediately tendered their resignations en masse and refused to return to the National Assembly. For several months the legislative process was completely paralyzed.

THE ECONOMY DURING DEMOCRATIC TRANSITION

At the beginning of the Roh presidency, the economic situation in many respects was very favorable. Economic growth stood at 12.1 percent in 1988, the highest in the world, and exports, which exceeded imports by $9 billion, grew 27 percent.[43] However, the economy's excellent performance was reflecting the extension of an economic boom begun under the Chun administration. With an optimistic outlook, Roh Tae Woo and his advisers paid little attention to the economic consequences of democratic transition. As a result, the Roh administration had neither a clear vision of nor a strong commitment to the economy. Roh appointed an inexperienced economics professor, Park Seung, as his top economic adviser. Nine months later, he changed his economic adviser, appointing another economics professor, Cho Soon, as the EPB minister. The Roh administration was not well prepared to manage the economy during the turbulent period of democratic transition.

---

[41] For an analysis of the three-party merger, see Jin Park, "Political Change in South Korea: The Challenge of Conservative Alliance", *Asian Survey*, 30:12 (December 1990): 1154-1168. On the background and effects of the three-party merger, see Hak-Joon Kim, "New Political Development with a Vision", in Cotton, ed. (1993), 153-169.

[42] Roh Tae Woo, "Joint Declaration on Creating a New Era: Launching a New National Political Party", in The Presidential Secretariat (1990).

[43] Economic Planning Board, *Korea Statistical Yearbook* (Seoul, 1990).

In response to an extensive and strong public demand for economic democratization, Roh as well as other candidates in the 1987 presidential election pledged to achieve an "economic democracy". His inaugural address had set his economic tone: he emphasized distribution and equity over growth.[44] The government revised the ongoing Sixth Economic and Social Development Plan (1987-91), which it inherited from the Chun government. In the revised plan the government, acknowledging that "political democratization brought with it a strong demand for economic democratization," called for an "equitable distribution of the fruits of economic growth".[45] But the minority government either backtracked on its promises of reform or failed to carry out promised initiatives. The government had consistently encountered strong opposition in the National Assembly on the one side and demanding pressure groups on the other. Under the pressure from opposition and activist groups, welfare handouts replaced the sort of practical economic policies that had enabled South Korea to prosper. Within the National Assembly, the rice-pricing policy, social welfare expenditure, trade policy, and even defense expenditures became politicized in the fierce rivalry among the four political parties.

Farmers demanded a double-digit increase in rice subsidies. A compromise was reached, wherein prices of government-purchased rice rose in parity with civil service salaries: 14 percent. In reality, the one had nothing to do with the other, but the compromise was typical of the economic policymaking that characterized the late 1980s and early 1990s. These increases in turn stimulated wage hikes for workers. On top of this generous price increase, in early 1990 the government bailed out farmers with an expensive and indiscriminate loan package, at a cost of $6 billion over ten years—something that had been vigorously and consistently demanded by populist opposition leader Kim Dae Jung.[46] Thus, economic policies were based more on political contingency than economic necessity. As the political agenda dominated economic issues, the economic management team was pushed aside by the more aggressive political forces. The EPB minister and his economic policymaking team lacked the nerve to tackle the economy's structural problems and to deal with politicians and pressure groups. Unlike earlier EPB ministers who had enjoyed full presidential support during the Park and Chun governments, the minister found little presidential backing for his policies.

Before long the economy paid a painful price of democratic transition. While an insightful observer might have recognized the dilemma the Roh government faced, Korean labor had little patience for such insights. While the hand of the government was stayed, labor unions unleashed a wave of breathtaking wage demands which led to a series of violent strikes. Not surprisingly, major industrial zones were scenes of bitter labor warfare. For example, in December 1988 some 24,000 workers from Hyundai Heavy Industries shipyards in Ulsan began what turned into a 109-day strike. Demands for a 50 percent wage increase were commonplace. The wave of violent strikes extended far beyond industrial workers. Workers at insurance companies, banks, hospitals, and

---

[44] "Inaugural Address", Cotton, ed. (1993), 324.

[45] Economic Planning Board, The Revised Sixth Five-Year Socio-Economic Development Plan, 1987-1991 (Seoul, 1988), 82 and 123.

[46] The figure comes from Koo Bohn-young, Roh's assistant for economic affairs, in a commentary published in *the International Herald Tribune*, January 18, 1990.

newspapers all went out on strike demanding democratic unions, higher wages, and improved working conditions. The result was significant increases in both wages and inflation. Industrial wages doubled between 1988 and 1990—an average annual increase of 24 percent. In 1989 Korean aggregate wage levels were the second highest in Asia, second only to Japan. At the same time there was a sharp decline in labor productivity. Inflation, which had been checked at less than 3 percent during the Chun administration, soared to from 13 to 19 percent during 1990-92.[47]

In addition, the economy was acutely vulnerable to external shocks. As the country's current account surplus continued to increase, it was under constant pressure to liberalize its protected domestic market to allow greater imports. South Korea's trade surplus with the United States had grown through the 1980s, flooding the U.S. market with cars, computers, microwaves, and other consumer electronics, reaching some $10 billion of surplus in 1987. This trade surplus came at a time when the United States, a target for approximately 40 percent of South Korea's exports, was struggling with its own rapidly growing trade deficit. The United States demanded import liberalization and a revaluation of the Korean *won* against the U.S. dollar.[48] When he assumed office, Roh immediately appreciated the Korean currency by 15 percent and liberalized foreign trade. With Korea's trade surplus setting new records, he no doubt felt confident that these measures could be taken with little or no danger to the economy.

A booming economy and newly found political freedoms gave people a sense of comfort and power. Investments in stock and real estate markets were popular. Families of the rapidly expanding middle class accelerated the demand for homes. Losing competitiveness in the international market, firms diverted capital into real estate speculation, driving housing costs out of reach for many South Koreans while hobbling industrial growth. Land prices climbed 27.5 percent in 1988, 32 percent in 1989, and 21 percent in 1990.[49] Land speculation became a favorite *chaebol* investment activity. *Chaebol* speculation also meant that the economic gains of the 1986-1988 period were wasted rather than used to improve the country's international competitiveness.

The rapid rise of land prices was probably the single most contentious economic issue at the time. According to a government report, the total value of land in South Korea was equivalent to 70 percent of the entire U.S. land area.[50] Many people resented real estate speculation, which had helped to drive rents up by 50 to 100 percent in big cities. Manufacturing ventures went bankrupt, while the non-productive service sector grew with great speed. The rise in housing prices led to rising rents, angering workers who were unable to keep up with this additional living expense. Workers became frustrated and demanded higher and higher wages. With income inequality and real estate speculation fueling inflation, and conspicuous consumption by the wealthy, the frustrations of ordinary people rose above the tolerance level.

In fact, Roh's early confidence in the economy was not well founded. The higher value of Korean currency, labor unrest, rising wages, *chaebol* speculation, the

---

[47] Economic Planning Board, *Korea Statistical Yearbook*, various issues.
[48] *Far Eastern Economic Review*, November 19, 1987, 42.
[49] Karl Schoenberger, "Speculators Fuel Real Estate Fever in South Korea", *Los Angeles Times*, March 18, 1990.
[50] *Donga Ilbo*, October 28, 1991.

protectionism of foreign markets, and import liberalization all took their toll on the economy. In June 1989, Roh told his economic ministers that South Korea's "economic achievements of the past thirty years will burst like a bubble" if these negative trends were not reversed.[51] In 1989 South Korea's GNP growth rate fell to 6.4 percent, about half of the rate of the previous year. Exports, the engine of the country's economic growth, increased by only 2.6 percent in 1989, as compared with an increase of 28 percent in 1988 and 36 percent in 1987. In terms of real quantity, exports decreased 6 percent—the worst economic performance since the introduction of the export-oriented growth policy in 1962. On the other hand, the booming domestic economy drew in 15 percent more imports in 1990 than it had done in 1989. Furthermore, as the consumption of energy rose sharply, the bill for imported energy was up by 42 percent. As a result, the trade surplus disappeared in 1989, and by 1990 the trade balance was back in deficit by $5 billion.[52] In 1991 the South Korean economy was betraying many signs of structural limitation, as evidenced by the $10 billion trade deficit—the largest since the early 1960s.

After the three-party merger of the grand coalition, the new ruling party asserted that economic reform measures should be implemented gradually in consideration of the economic conditions and the effectiveness of implementation. The government was now shifting its main political energies toward economic growth in order to prevent a further downturn of the economy. In March 1990, President Roh replaced fifteen of his twenty-seven cabinet ministers, removing the three most important ministers, including the EPB minister Cho Soon who had been in office only fifteen months. The new EPB minister Lee Seung-yoon, known as the head of the "crisis management team," began to pursue a growth-first policy. On April 4, stating that weak economic performance dictated the primacy of economic recovery over economic reforms that might derail economic growth, the government announced a Comprehensive Policy for Economic Revitalization.[53]

Owing to the growth-first policy, real estate speculation and inflation became worse. Less than a year after reshuffling his economic team, Roh again replaced the EPB minister in February 1991. The new minister emphasized economic stability rather than growth. In an effort to control skyrocketing rents and real estate prices, in April 1991 the government tried once again to regain control over *chaebol* activity, declaring that the *chaebol* must select three core areas of industry in which to specialize. In those areas, the companies would be permitted to borrow as much money as banks could lend.

At the same time, the government tried to boost its popularity and the economy by raising social expenditures and building homes. In order to carry out Roh's election promise of providing two million units of new affordable apartments and to contain the skyrocketing real estate and housing-rent prices, the government embarked on an ambitious and economically controversial construction project. But building 2 million housing units within three years was beyond the economy's resource base. This government-financed program diverted much capital and labor away from the already weakened manufacturing sector. Shortages of labor, land and construction materials

---

[51] *Joongang Ilbo*, June 18, 1989.
[52] Hart-Landsberg, *Rush to Development*, 244-245.
[53] *Joongang Ilbo*, April 4, 1990.

drove up construction costs and accelerated inflation, pushing up interest rates and wages. Interest rates soared to an astonishing 20 percent per annum, sharply reducing profit margins in manufacturing. The *chaebol*, instead of upgrading their competitiveness by investing in new plants and technology, obtained artificial profits from land speculation and government-funded construction projects.

During the last year of his term, Roh announced a six-year infrastructure program, the fruit of a task force on infrastructure development working at the Blue House since 1989. The government planned to spend $50 billion to build high-profile projects such as a high-speed railway connecting Seoul and Pusan. The railway was regarded as portion of a once and future trans-Siberian railway connecting Korea, China, Siberia and Europe. The government also started to construct a new international airport at Inchon and a new expressway connecting major cities along the country's west coast.[54]

As a result of the massive construction projects, economic stability and future growth potential were sacrificed for short-term growth; the economy grew 8.4% in 1991, but the trade deficit was recorded at $8.7 billion. In order to reign in runaway inflation and land prices, the government adopted an economic stabilization program, including a tight money supply. Despite various efforts to sustain growth, the economic growth rate dropped sharply in 1992, and a record number of 10,769 medium and small firms went bankrupt. The Korean people seemed to lose the dynamism of previous decades. The "can do" attitude that had been widespread among the public turned to despair and cynicism. The foreign media that had criticized the low wages and bad working conditions now claimed that South Koreans had uncorked their champagne bottles too soon. It was a sharp turnaround within a short period of time, and the country entered a period of economic crisis.[55]

The economic downturn was partly a product of factors such as global recession, increasing protectionism abroad, fierce competition from other newly industrializing countries, and overconsumption. Democratization and leadership incompetence were also to blame for the decline. The new democratic landscape made the Roh administration's economic management increasingly erratic, severely reducing policy credibility. One Korean scholar, who analyzed the economic leadership of Korean presidents, concluded that economic policy was the weakest point of the Roh administration.[56] Upon his inauguration, Roh pledged to undertake extensive economic reforms such as the reduction of economic concentration and income redistribution. When the reform efforts, combined with a contractionary economic policy, began to produce a recession, Roh radically swung back to growth-first policies, encouraging rampant real estate and stock market speculations which overheated the economy. When inflation soared and social and political discontent heightened, the government again

---

[54] "Politics of Planning: South Korea Debates Infrastructure", *Far Eastern Economic Review*, September 10, 1992.

[55] *Asian Wall Street Journal*, February 26, 1990. According to the international competitiveness index of the manufacturing sector estimated by the Bank of Korea, Korea (8.6) surpassed Japan (7.0) during 1986-88. But during the period of 1989-90, Korea's index dropped to 3.8, thus lagging behind that of Japan (5.3) and Taiwan (13.8). *Wolgan Chosun* (July 1999), 434.

[56] Chung Jung-kil, *Deatongryung ui kyongje leadeoship* (Economic Leadership for Presidents) (Seoul: Hankuk Kyungje Sinmunsa, 1994), 250-254.

turned back to a contractionary policy. This policy inconsistency further weakened the economy and undermined the government's credibility.

Experts blame the erratic economic policy on Roh's frequent reshuffling of his economic advisers and failure to monitor economic bureaucracy.[57] The frequent policy swings reflected the difficulties of economic management during the democratic transition. Arguably what was needed to make the successful transition in the economy to a higher level of maturation was a more skillful and effective leadership that could consistently pursue effective economic policy, even when this policy was unpopular. The frequent shifts in economic teams and policy reflected a lack of vision and strategy in the Roh government. During the democratic transition, economic policy and the roles of government and business were in a state of uncertainty. Roh had limited the government's role in making hard decisions; as a result, there was confusion as to who had, or should, take control of the economy. It was a time that needed economic leadership.[58]

Chun Doo Hwan's remarkable economic revitalization was significantly jeopardized during the Roh administration. Economic growth plummeted from 12.9 percent in 1987 to 4.7 percent in 1992 (the last year of Roh's term), the worst growth rate in decades, except for 1980, the year after President Park's death. A record high current account surplus ($10 billion) in 1987 turned into net deficits starting in 1990 and culminated in a deficit of $8.7 billion in 1991. Inflation also increased from 2.7 percent in 1986 to 9.3 percent in 1991. The economic downturn, which started in 1988, the first year of the Roh administration, lasted more than sixty-two months, becoming the longest recession in Korean history. Despite his campaign pledge that he would guarantee stability and growth, Roh failed to achieve either. According to an opinion survey by Gallup Korea about two weeks before Roh's retirement, only 7.8 percent of the people believed that the government had done well in managing the economy, while 68.9 percent thought it had done poorly.[59]

THE NORTHERN POLICY

As noted previously, Roh Tae Woo's aggressive diplomatic initiative, which was dubbed the "northern policy," was closely linked with the hosting of the 1988 Seoul Olympics. It is meaningful to briefly review the implications of the international sports event for his northern policy as well as for South Korean nation building.

On September 17, 1988, at the impressive new Olympic Stadium in eastern Seoul, President Roh declared the opening of the Twenty-fourth Olympiad. The nations of east and west had finally overcome ideological differences, and joined together in Seoul "to share a celebration of harmony and progress."[60] With 161 participating nations, and 14,000 athletes and officials, the 1988 summer games proved to be the biggest Olympiad in history. In 1980 the United States and its allies had boycotted the Moscow Olympics,

---

[57] Ibid., 228-254.
[58] Chung-in Moon and Yong-cheol Kim, "A Circle of Paradox: Development and Democracy in South Korea", in Adrian Leftwich, ed., *Democracy and Development* (Cambridge, UK: Polity Press, 1996), 155-156.
[59] *Chosun Ilbo*, February 13, 1993.
[60] She Jik Park, *The Seoul Olympics* (London: Bellow, 1991).

and four years later the Soviet bloc did the same at the Los Angeles Olympics. Roh and his government breathed a collective sigh of relief as the entire Communist world—China, the Soviet Union, Eastern European nations—as well as the uncommitted third world nations participated despite the angry protests of Pyongyang.

The Olympics came to symbolize a high-water mark in Korean history—a clear symbol of successful national development. The success of the games was a remarkable feat for this newly industrialized country on a remote Northeast Asian peninsula; a country that that had survived the harsh repression of colonial rule and the ravages of the Korean War and was divided still. The country had long been known as a poor, underdeveloped, unstable and dependent nation. Many Koreans regarded the Olympics as a national *rite de passage*, the international coming of age of the nation. Pride and the prospect of enhanced international recognition were in the minds of many. The event had a great impact on the national psyche: the people, for the most part, felt great satisfaction with what they thought was proof of their country's emergence, after much suffering and hard work, as a developed nation. The Olympics ended the long sentence of national humiliation under the Japanese, the mendicant mentality of the Korean War, and the abuses that followed.[61] The national hype over the Olympics struck a teary chord for older people: "I used to beg for chocolate from GIs; now Americans come to Korea and they are impressed by our amazing progress." The Seoul Olympics proved that Koreans could do anything.

Thus, millions of proud Koreans welcomed their Olympic guests. Not the least part of that welcome was the modern city of Seoul itself, with an architecturally superb stadium, new subway and highway systems, a complex of spacious parks along the Han River, high-rise office buildings, and hundreds of luxurious condominium complexes. Considering the usual fare of publicity on Korea, which focused predominantly on student protests and labor unrest, the Seoul Olympics provided an opportunity for over three billion television viewers across the world to see the dynamic capabilities of South Korea. South Korea now proudly joined the community of nations. As the chairman of the Seoul Olympic Organizing Committee Park She-jik commented: "The world's view of Korea had been mostly formed by the dark days of war-torn Korea. The Seoul Olympic…wiped the image away."[62]

The Soviet Union and East European nations sent large contingents of athletes and officials to the Seoul Olympics. They sent trade and cultural delegations as well. For the four decades since the partition of Korea, Communist countries and many third world nations had refused contacts with South Korea. Arriving in the late summer of 1988, no foreign guest could have imagined that just over thirty years ago the city was a barren ruin, completely destroyed during the Korean War. Remarks by Soviet visitors during the games illustrate their amazement when they saw the South Korean capital. Vitaly Ignatenko, who served as leader of the Soviet press at the Seoul Olympics and later became President Mikhail Gorbachev's press secretary, said his first visit to Seoul was "a shock." He said, "Everything I had read before [about South Korea] turned out to be outdated; I arrived into the twenty-first century." *Pravda*, the Communist Party

---

[61] See Kim, Jong-gie et al., *Impact of the Seoul Olympic Games on National Development*.
[62] Larson and Park, *Global Television and the Politics of the Seoul Olympics*, 190.

newspaper in Moscow, summed up its impression after the games: "The sports facilities in Seoul are the best in the world, and the values of the Korean traditional smile and etiquette have been greatly underestimated."[63]

The success of the Seoul Olympics was in great part the result of South Korea's aggressive Olympic diplomacy of the 1980s. The confluence of high economic growth, democratic transition and a successful Olympics provided a timely boost for Roh Tae Woo's "northern policy," or *Nordpolitik*. This northern policy was reminiscent of Willy Brandt's "eastern policy" (*Ostpolitik*). West German chancellor Brandt had promoted *Ostpolitik*, a push for greater association with the socialist countries of East Europe, during his tenure in the late 1960s and 1970s (in the midst of which West Germany had also hosted the summer Olympics). In the minds of almost all South Koreans, the Olympics marked the moment of South Korea's ascendancy over North Korea. The contest was over in terms of which system would win. The enhancement of a sense of national self-esteem among South Koreans engendered a similar sense of mission, a desire to advance into the international community and make the dream of reunification a reality. This renewed national purpose was a driving force behind his northern policy.[64]

During a presidential campaign stop at Inchon, a major port city on the Yellow Sea, Roh declared the opening of the "era of the west coast," saying, "Across the sea there is the huge Chinese market waiting for us. We will cross the Yellow Sea to China in order to resume the historic relationship with Korea's giant neighbor and to bring new prosperity to the nation's west coast areas. We have to build airports, harbors and highways on the west coast."[65] From the beginning of his term, he made it clear that a "northern policy" would be a cornerstone of his foreign policy.

When he entered the Blue House, Roh established the office of senior secretary for foreign affairs and national security to promote this bold new foreign policy initiative. As a result, his national security adviser, Kim Chong-whi, integrated and coordinated foreign, security and unification policies. Until that time, foreign affairs had been coordinated by the senior secretary for political affairs, and national defense had been the bailiwick of the senior secretary for administrative affairs. Roh also created the position of senior adviser for policy affairs, appointing to the post his confidant Park Chul-un, who had enjoyed secret contacts with North Korean officials during the previous administration.[66] In addition, Roh established inter-ministerial organizations to provide policy coordination and to build a national consensus. The chief organs were: the Coordination and Consultation Committee on the Northern Policy, composed of fourteen cabinet-level ministers, which hammered out policies and guidelines; the

---

[63] Oberdorfer, *Two Koreas*, 200.

[64] For details, see Hak-joon Kim, "The Republic of Korea's Northern Policy: Origin, Development, and Prospects", in Cotton, ed. (1993), 245-266, and Sang-Seek Park, "Northern Diplomacy and Inter-Korean Relations", *Korea and World Affairs,* 12: 4 (winter 1988).

[65] Roh Tae Woo, "The Reminiscences of Roh Tae Woo, Part 2", *Wolgan Chosun* (June 1999), 224-225. Ten years after the Roh government began construction, the new international airport at Inchon and a new west coast superhighway connecting Inchon, Kunsan, Kwangju and Mokpo were completed.

[66] Park Chul-un, Roh's nephew-in-law and a close associate, was also known as a key player in the northern policy.

External Economic Cooperation Committee, which was presided over by the EPB minister and which dealt with economic exchanges with socialist countries; and the Economic Council of Korea, which included four major business organizations and served as a private-sector channel for economic exchange with socialist countries.[67]

For South Korea, improving relations with the Soviet Union and mainland China, traditional allies of North Korea, implied much more than normal diplomatic efforts. By promoting the northern policy, Roh and his advisers aimed to improve the security environment, create favorable conditions for unification and broaden export markets.[68] It was also the opening of a new diplomatic horizon. So far, Korean diplomatic relations were confined to the non-socialist nations and therefore its diplomacy was relatively constrained. If South Korea normalized relations with the socialist countries, it would mean overcoming the constraints of the Cold War structure and the opening of a vast diplomatic frontier. Later, Roh reflected on the rationale of his northern policy:

> "South-North Korean relations have limits. No matter how many dialogues we have at Panmunjom, the two sides only run parallel lines.... Any Communist country changes when it opens up. In order to change North Korea, we must create an international environment in which North Korea can open up.... Since we cannot directly open the door of Pyongyang, we decided to go to Pyongyang through Moscow and Beijing.... Thus, our first target was non-aligned nations and then we aimed to improve relations with the socialist nations, such as the Soviet Union, China and other Eastern European countries which have maintained close relations with North Korea.... If North Korea completely opens up, it is not far from reunification. This is the best and most realistic approach to unification. In short, the primary target of my northern policy is reunification, but the ultimate goal is to broaden Korea's life-space to the northern hemisphere."[69]

The Seoul Olympics stood out as a benchmark event in accelerating Korea's relations with socialist countries. Participants from the socialist nations were shocked by the material reality they witnessed in South Korea. After visiting Seoul, their image of South Korea changed dramatically, from that of an underdeveloped, reactionary puppet-nation to a very important and dynamic economic powerhouse in the Far East. After the Seoul Olympics, socialist nations began to see South Korea in an entirely new light, one that revealed neither a "colony of American imperialists" nor a nation economically dependent on "international capitalism." Visitors could confirm firsthand that South Korea was a prospering nation well on its way to democracy. It was high time for South Korea to promote a northern policy.[70]

The Roh government made the best use of the opportunity; before and during the Games authorities from socialist nations had to deal directly with Seoul regarding the details of their participation. Some of these official contacts were momentous because

---

[67] Park Chul-un, "Hankukui miraewa bukbangjeongchaek (Korea's Future and Its Northern Policy)", *Minjokjiseong* (April 1989): 188-191.

[68] Ibid.

[69] Roh Tae Woo, "The Reminiscences of Roh Tae Woo", *Wolgan Chosun* (May 1999), 86-87.

[70] For a Russian view on Korea, see Alexander Fedorovsky, "South Korea as a New Economic Power", in Vladimir Ivanov, ed., *USSR and the Pacific Region in the 21st Century* (New Delhi: Allied Publishers, 1989), 94-102.

hardly a word had ever been exchanged on an official level between South Korea and socialist countries. Talks on trade, investment, and other relations flourished. Trade offices, air routes, and new shipping and communication lines were opened with socialist countries. Major South Korean trading companies opened offices in major cities in China, the Soviet Union and other East European nations. Two weeks after the close of the Olympics, President Roh addressed the United Nations General Assembly. His message centered on the northern policy. He proposed a consultative conference attended by the two Koreas, the United States, the Soviet Union, China, and Japan aimed at paving the way for a permanent peace settlement as a step toward eventual reunification. The Soviet Union welcomed Roh's proposal.

Roh and his advisers had paid close attention to developments in international relations. There were several favorable international factors that boded well for the northern policy. Under the leadership of President Mikhail Gorbachev, the Soviet Union had been promoting a policy of reform and opening, *perestroika* and *glasnost*. The country was shifting the emphasis of foreign policy from ideology to pragmatism. As part of its new foreign policy, the Soviet Union withdrew its forces from Afghanistan and Vietnam, normalized relations with China, and tried to improve relations with Japan. On September 16, 1988, Gorbachev delivered a speech in Krasnoyarsk in which he stated: "If relations between South and North Korea improve, there might be an opportunity of improving economic relations between the Soviet Union and South Korea."[71]

After the fall of the Berlin Wall, hopes of an early unification rose rapidly in South Korea. The dawning of the post-Cold War era afforded the Roh government a new opportunity to accelerate its northern diplomacy. By riding skillfully on the waves of epochal changes in East-West relations, the government struggled not to be left behind as the lone Cold War island. As a result of its steadfast efforts to preserve a hard-won international reputation following the Seoul Olympics, the Roh administration began to reap diplomatic and economic benefits. On February 1, 1989, Hungary became the first Communist nation to formally open diplomatic relations with the Republic of Korea. Relations were normalized with Poland in November 1989, with Yugoslavia in December 1989, and with Czechoslovakia and Bulgaria in March 1990. The reasons behind the diplomatic normalization with South Korea were primarily economic. With the fall of the Eastern Bloc, these countries were in need of South Korean assistance and were eager to establish trade and investment ties with Seoul. The long and fierce diplomatic competition between the South and the North seemed to be over, decisively in favor of the South.

But the main targets of the northern policy were the Soviet Union and China. Contacts with the Soviet Union and China had long been a goal of the South Korean government, in the belief that such relationships would enhance the South's security, and potentially undercut the North. The logic of the northern policy closely paralleled the situation in Germany, where Bonn's improved relations with Moscow built up pressure on East Germany for economic and political reforms. Roh obviously wanted a similar

---

[71] Chan Young Bang, "Prospects of Korean-Soviet Economic Cooperation and Its Impact on Security and Stability of the Korean Peninsula", *Korean Journal of International Studies*, 21:3 (autumn 1990): 313.

situation to develop on the Korean peninsula, where he would use the new diplomatic leverage with socialist countries to moderate Pyongyang's behavior.

There were fierce debates in the Blue House over the decision to which country—the Soviet Union or China—South Korea should first make overtures. Some argued that the government should focus first on China as a close neighbor with historical and cultural affinities as well as a huge market. Also, the South Korean people maintained a certain animosity for the Soviet Union for its shooting down of Korean Air flight 007 in 1983. But Roh and his advisers preferred the Soviet Union. Moscow had strong motivations to improve its economic conditions and had been paying keen attention to South Korea's dynamic economy. Meanwhile, the Chinese economy was performing quite well and had no immediate economic need to improve relations with South Korea. Moreover, Moscow's main concern was Europe and the United States and it had no compelling reason to continue its support for North Korea. In contrast, Beijing had both political and security reasons for maintaining close ties with Pyongyang.

Roh concluded that the Soviet Union should be the first target and ordered his security adviser Kim Chong-whi to secretly visit Moscow in September 1988. Like Henry Kissinger in China, Kim brought Roh's message to Soviet President Gorbachev, laying a foundation for further development of Soviet-South Korean relations.[72] Like relations with other East European nations, South Korea's relations with the Soviet Union changed dramatically after the Olympics. At the end of 1988, Moscow lifted restrictions on entry to the Soviet Union by South Koreans. Shortly thereafter, the two nations opened postal and telecommunication links. In April 1989, both countries exchanged trade offices. In December of that same year the two countries agreed to establish *de facto* consular ties.

Moscow initially looked to Japanese assistance and investment to improve its economic situation, but the dispute over the Northern Territories interfered with these prospects. Booming South Korea was the logical alternative. Moscow began to regard South Korea as a potentially important economic partner. One Russian Korea specialist praised the South Korean economy: "South Korea has been establishing formidable credentials as a regional economic center.... The dynamism of South Korean economic development, the nature of the changes in its economic structure, and the extent of the country's involvement in the international division of labor show its growing role in global economic relations."[73] The high Soviet regard for South Korea's economic development made South Korea a desirable economic partner of the Soviet Union. An editorial in *The New Times*, an authoritative Moscow weekly, even suggested "South Korea may become for the USSR as important an economic partner as Japan was for China in the 1970s."[74] Moscow needed cheaper consumer goods as well as investment in resource development in the Soviet Far East. Russians saw that South Korea had more to offer in appropriate technology than Japan, whose products were too advanced and expensive. Having seen what South Korea had done economically, the Soviet leaders rapidly redefined South Korea as an economic partner, even an economic model, rather than a strategic client of the United States. Gorbachev initially wanted to limit

---

[72] Interview with Kim Chong-Whi on April 19, 2002.
[73] Quoted from Hakjoon Kim, Korea's Relations with Her Neighbors in a Changing World, 404.
[74] Ibid.

Moscow-Seoul links to the economic sphere, while preserving Moscow-Pyongyang political and military ties.

On the other hand, Roh's interest in the Soviet Union was primarily political, not economic. In the absence of diplomatic relations, South Korean firms were reluctant to do business in the Soviet Union. With a rapidly plunging national economy, and his *perestroika* in danger, Gorbachev was in dire straits, and eager for financial support wherever he could find it. In May 1990 Gorbachev allowed his top foreign policy adviser Anatoly Dobrynin to travel officially to Seoul. After his arrival on May 22, Dobrynin met secretly with President Roh and his security adviser at the Blue House. Dobrynin brought news that Gorbachev was willing to meet Roh Tae Woo. Dobrynin also requested from Roh a loan of billions of dollars. Roh's reply was that South Korea would provide major assistance to the Soviet Union if and only if full diplomatic relations were established between the two countries. To such ends, it was agreed to convene an historic meeting between Roh and Gorbachev two weeks later in San Francisco, a city the Soviet leader planned to visit after wrapping up his American summit with George Bush.[75]

On June 5, 1990, the increasing rapprochement in Seoul-Moscow relations came to a climax at the Fairmont Hotel summit in San Francisco between Presidents Roh and Gorbachev. As *The Christian Science Monitor* reported, this historic meeting, dramatizing "the breakthrough in its relations with the Soviet Union," was "a political coup for South Korea" as well as "a personal triumph for President Roh." It also meant *de facto* recognition of the Republic of Korea by the Soviet Union.[76] It was a dramatic diplomatic breakthrough of immense importance. It would deprive North Korea of the support of its primary sponsor, North Korea's most important source of economic and military assistance and an important security guarantor. The meeting also meant the legitimization of the South Korean government virtually everywhere, and the final defeat of North Korea's strenuous efforts to wall off the southern regime from Communist nations.

On August 2, two months after the San Francisco summit, a high-ranking delegation of South Korean officials led by Kim Chong-whi, senior secretary for diplomacy and national security, and Kim Chong-in, senior secretary for economic affairs, visited Moscow to meet with Soviet officials led by Yuri Maslyukov, first deputy prime minister and head of the State Planning Agency. These first-ever government-to-government negotiations between the Republic of Korea and the Soviet Union produced wide-ranging accords on industrial, scientific, and technological cooperation.[77] At that time the Soviets requested enormous loans before formal diplomatic normalization. Kim Chong-whi, however, rejected the Soviet proposal, arguing that if South Korea were to provide loans prior to normalization, "diplomatic normalization would likely be seen as Korea buying normalization and your country trading it for a loan. It will be better to delay normalization." Kim even upped the ante, "In Korea there are many people who oppose normalization with your country. When we provide economic assistance to your country, if your country continues supplying sophisticated weapon systems such as fighters, tanks and missiles and providing other military assistance to North Korea, I will also oppose

---

[75] Interview with Kim Chong Whi on April 19, 2002.
[76] John Hughes, "A Coup for South Korea and Mr. Roh", *Christian Science Monitor*, June 11, 1990.
[77] Hakjoon Kim, *Korea's Relations*, 412.

economic cooperation with your country."[78] The Soviet economic situation was desperate. The Soviet delegation agreed on early normalization, and Maslyukov also promised that if economic assistance were provided, the Soviet Union would end military cooperation with North Korea.

Although Gorbachev implied at the time of the San Francisco summit that full diplomatic relations were still very distant by saying, "Let the fruit grow ripe and when it grows ripe, we shall eat it,"[79] harvest time arrived only two months later, on September 30, 1990, when full diplomatic relations were established between the two countries. Gorbachev's decision to accelerate the development of Moscow-Seoul ties can be traced to Roh's refusal to provide significant economic aid and investment to the Soviet Union until Moscow normalized diplomatic relations. On December 13, President Roh left on a historic four-day official visit to Moscow, the first state visit to the Soviet Union ever made by a South Korean leader. During the summit, Roh received a Soviet pledge of peace and security for the Korean peninsula, promising South Korean economic assistance in turn. At the summit's conclusion, Roh and Gorbachev issued a joint Declaration on General Principles of Relations, which pledged "good-neighborly" relations, joint efforts toward ending the Cold War in Asia, a relaxation of tensions on the Korean peninsula, and eventual reunification of South and North Korea.[80]

Four months after normalization, on January 22, 1991, South Korea agreed to provide the Soviet Union with a $3 billion economic cooperation package, the largest aid package in Korea's history. In return, the Soviet Union gave a written commitment to support South Korea's admission to the United Nations, offered assurances that offensive weapons would no longer be supplied to North Korea, and guaranteed that assistance would no longer be given to the North's nuclear program. It was certainly a historic moment when South Korea was able to provide a large loan to the Soviet Union, the leader of the socialist world and one of the world's two superpowers.[81] In a gesture of reciprocity, Gorbachev visited South Korea's southernmost island of Cheju in April 1991, the first visit to Korea—South or North—by a Soviet head of state. As expected, Pyongyang's reaction to normalization was furious. An editorial in *The Pyongyang Times* characterized the Soviet decision as an act of betrayal, accusing the Soviets of having sold the dignity and honor of a socialist state, for South Korean economic aid.[82]

But Roh had his sights on another key element of his northern policy: Korea-China relations stretched back well over a millennium, and therefore it was very important to restore such historical relations at the dawn of the post-Cold War era. What's more, China, which shares a similar culture, promised great potential as a target of South Korean exports and investment. During his presidential campaign, Roh repeatedly emphasized his hope to improve relations with China, a hope he reiterated after his election victory. During an interview with The Washington Post, Roh said that he was "ready to go" to Beijing to work

---

[78] Interview with Kim Chong-Whi on April 22, 2002.

[79] *New York Times*, June 5, 1990, 1.

[80] *Korea Herald*, December 15, 1990.

[81] Hakjoon Kim, "The Process Leading to the Establishment of Diplomatic Relations Between South Korea and the Soviet Union", *Asian Survey*, 37:7 (July 1997): 637-651.

[82] *Pyongyang Times*, October 6, 1990.

for improved ties between his country and China, which he described as "almost a necessity" for both countries. "I think the People's Republic of China would like to have more developed relations with us, and they seem to have moved beyond thinking only of North Korea," he said.[83]

Immediately upon his inauguration, Roh mobilized his personal connections to pave the way for diplomatic relations with China. The 1990 Asian Games in Beijing provided a golden opportunity for the Roh government. As a the leader of the country that had successfully hosted the 1986 Asian Games and the 1988 Summer Olympics, Roh and his government were eager to render the necessary assistance, technical and financial, to make the Beijing Asian Games a success. South Korea dispatched athletic teams and sports officials, accompanied by large numbers of tourists and business representatives, to participate in the Beijing Asian Games. It was a warm gesture on the part of South Korea because at the time China found itself isolated by the sanctions imposed by Western countries after the 1989 Tiananmen massacre. Through the cooperative window of the games, both South Korea and China broadened unofficial relations. After the games the two nations exchanged semiofficial trade offices with consular functions in the two capitals.

China and Korea had already become important trading partners. In 1988, Sino-Korea trade stood at $3.1 billion a year, or a full 84 percent of South Korea's trade with Communist states. Bilateral trade relations increased by leaps and bounds: in 1990 two-way trade amounted to $5.6 billion, a 33.6 percent increase over 1989. However, China remained cautious in normalizing relations with Seoul, insisting on the clear-cut separation of politics from economics. In 1991 China shifted its foreign policy: in May it changed its economic relations with North Korea from concessionary and barter exchanges to trade based on convertible currency at international prices. In the same year, China, one of the permanent members of the UN Security Council, did not object to South Korea's entry into the world body. Ideological ties were pushed aside by economic priorities. China was trying to extract external resources of capital, markets, and technology for rapid economic growth. South Korea with its dynamic economy, situated across the Yellow Sea, was a natural economic partner for China.

While participating in a meeting of APEC (Asia Pacific Economic Cooperation) in Seoul On November 21, 1991, Chinese Foreign Minister Qian Qichen called on President Roh, a first for a high-ranking Chinese official. Roh observed that the "Korean relationship with China has a 5,000 year history, going back to ancient days of good neighbors, closer to each other than any other country" and that "the period of severed relations since 1945 is without precedent and cause for shame. I firmly believe that it is our great mission to normalize relations between the two countries." Recognizing China's concern with North Korea, Roh assured that "China, [South] Korea and North Korea can build a relationship without betraying that loyalty. As I have stated several times, we are not thinking, not even in dreams, of German-style unification by absorption, which North Korea is worried about."[84]

---

[83] *Washington Post*, December 23, 1987.

[84] Memorandum of conversation: "Dialogue with Foreign Minister Qian Qichen—11/12/91", (Korean) Ministry of Foreign Affairs, Republic of Korea.

Since then, Sino-Korean relations have improved rapidly. On April 13, 1992, in Beijing, when Korean Foreign Minister Lee Sang-ok was participating in a meeting of a UN agency, the Economic and Social Commission for Asia and the Pacific, his Chinese counterpart Qian Qichen confidentially informed him that China was ready to open negotiations leading to diplomatic normalization. After four months of negotiations, the two countries set up diplomatic relations on August 24, 1992. A month later, on September 28, Roh visited China. It was the first state visit by a South Korean president to a one-time enemy. On that day Roh announced, "After Moscow, we now have reached Beijing, which is the last gate leading to Pyongyang.... Normalization of relations between Korea and China will greatly contribute to the resolution of various pending issues between South and North Korea.... With this, we have become new friends of two nations neighboring North Korea."[85] In Beijing, Roh Tae Woo and Chinese President Yang Shang-kun had a summit meeting and discussed issues of mutual concern, such as North Korea and economic cooperation.

Roh firmly believed that inter-Korean relations and South Korea's relations with socialist nations were interrelated: with the normalization of ties with the Soviet Union and China, South and North Korean relations would likely improve as well. As part of the northern policy, he made efforts to improve the South's relations with the North from the early months of his term. Addressing the National Assembly on July 7, 1988, he offered North Korea a chance to improve its ties with Seoul and its allies. In this statement, he made it clear that South Korea would not regard North Korea as its adversary, but rather would seek to develop a partnership in the work for unification. He proceeded to unveil a six-point program, including promotion of trade, exchanges of visits at all levels, and humanitarian contacts between the two Koreas. He made it known that South Korea would not oppose nonmilitary merchandise trade between North Korea and South Korea's allies and friends. Finally, the statement called for an end to diplomatic confrontation between the two Koreas. In essence, the declaration meant Seoul would seek to ensure peace and stability on the Korean peninsula through a cross-recognition of the two Koreas by the outside powers.[86]

Addressing the UN General Assembly on October 18, 1988, President Roh now used the world forum to propose more specific proposals and measures for settling the Korean problem, including a six-power consultative conference on Korea, building a "city of peace" in the DMZ, a non-aggression declaration, and a North-South summit. A year later on September 11, 1989, he unveiled a new unification policy proposing the establishment of a Korean Commonwealth as an interim state toward eventual unification.[87] In July 1990, the South and the North began their first direct trade in forty-six years. A month later, the Special Act Governing Inter-Korean Exchanges and Cooperation was passed in the National Assembly and the South-North Korea Cooperation Fund was established.

---

[85] *Korea Herald*, September 19, 1992.
[86] Roh Tae Woo, "Special Declaration in the Interest of National Self-Respect, Unification and Prosperity, July 7, 1988", in Cotton, ed. (1993), 328-330.
[87] Roh Tae Woo, "A Choice for Unity: Special Address to the National Assembly Concerning National Unification", in the Presidential Secretariat (1990), 76-83.

With the dramatic change in Seoul-Moscow relations following the San Francisco Roh-Gorbachev summit of June 1990, Pyongyang began to modify its attitude toward the South, and Seoul and Pyongyang resumed an inter-Korea dialogue. Following a series of preliminary talks in Panmunjom, both sides agreed to hold "the highest level" ministerial talks. The first such conference took place in Seoul in September 1990, followed closely by a second in Pyongyang in October, and a third in Seoul in December. In the meantime, sports and cultural exchanges had occurred as well. During an official call on President Roh Tae Woo on September 6, 1990, North Korean Prime Minister Yon Hyong-muk, who was attending the inter-Korean dialogue in Seoul, was reportedly asked by Roh to convey to Kim Il Sung a three-point proposal aimed at breaking the impasse in the South-North dialogue. It included: (1) a summit meeting with Kim to produce a broad framework for working-level talks on a host of pending issues between the two sides; (2) an assurance of noninterference in North Korea's internal politics; and (3) the offer of an economic aid package, including trade and investment, if Pyongyang agreed to open its border for communications and travel with the outside.[88]

As Roh was preparing the final year of his term, his government was shifting toward a more conciliatory posture toward the North. The two sides thus agreed to set aside the nuclear issue. As a result, high-level talks proceeded at full speed. On December 13, 1991, at the end of the fifth round of South-North Korean prime minister talks in Seoul, an Agreement on Reconciliation, Non-aggression, Exchange and Cooperation between the South and the North was signed. It was a remarkable historical breakthrough in the forty-three-year history of inter-Korean relations. The agreement was by far the most important document adopted by the two Koreas since the South-North joint statement of July 4, 1972. The agreement upheld the principle of noninterference in the internal politics of the other and likewise renounced the use of military force against the other. Both sides also promised to "conduct economic exchanges and cooperation,...trade in goods as a kind of domestic commerce, and joint investment in industrial projects, in order to promote an integrated and balanced development of the national economy."[89] On December 31, 1991, the two Koreas also reached an agreement not to "test, produce, receive, possess, deploy or use nuclear weapons"—the Joint Declaration of a Non-nuclear Korean Peninsula.

On the other hand, the IAEA (International Atomic Energy Agency) inspections of North Korea's nuclear facilities rapidly augmented suspicions concerning Pyongyang's nuclear program. South Korea and its allies suspected that North Korea was processing plutonium to build a nuclear weapon. On June 29, 1992, Roh announced that he would not seek a summit meeting with Kim Il Sung unless North Korea ended its alleged nuclear program.[90]

The northern policy had important strategic and economic implications for South Korea. First of all, the policy effectively won over Pyongyang's two primary patrons and closed the circle in terms of isolating North Korea. South Korea could be confident that neither the Soviet Union nor China would support the use of force against it by the

---

[88] *Far Eastern Economic Review*, September 20, 1990, 24.
[89] *Korea Times*, December 14, 1991.
[90] Karen House and Damon Darlin, "Roh Says He Won't Seek Korean Summit", *Wall Street Journal*, July 1, 1992.

North. The Soviet Union also ended military and economic support to North Korea, and as a result the North Korean military threat was reduced significantly. In Seoul's eyes, this was the ultimate victory in the zero-sum competition between the two Koreas. Second, because of the northern policy South Korea was able to open diplomatic relations with 39 countries, including all the socialist nations whose population totaled 1.7 billion. Third, owing to South Korea's enhanced world stature and legitimacy and the weakened position of North Korea, North Korea could no longer refuse direct dialogue with South Korea. For the first time since national division, Seoul took the initiative against Pyongyang, resulting in an unprecedented breakthrough in inter-Korean relations.

Finally, thanks to Roh's bold diplomatic initiatives, South Korea was able to greatly expand its export markets; especially, economic relations with China were accelerated and South Korea-China trade began to expand some 35 percent annually. China has now become South Korea's major economic partner. Bilateral trade stood at $90 billion in 2004, making China South Korea's second largest trading partner and its largest export market. As of December 2003, South Koreans have set up 27,000 businesses with a total investment of $19.7 billion, positioning themselves as the second largest foreign direct investors in China.[91]

The northern policy stands as testament to the great success of modern South Korean diplomacy. Since 1945, Korea had been a virtual client state of the United States. By persuading just about all of the world's states to welcome it as a useful partner, South Korea was able to break out of its former isolation and assume an independent role in world affairs.

POLITICS OF PRESIDENTIAL SUCCESSION

After the three-party merger, Roh was never able to maintain a firm grip on the ruling party; his ambitious aim of securing political stability and economic growth through a three-party merger appeared to be leading nowhere. Rather than providing political stability as promised, the new mega-party itself dissolved into intra-party squabbles over who would succeed Roh in 1993.[92] From the beginning, the merger contained the seeds of factional strife that could lead to calamity. Even in uniting, each of the three leaders harbored different motivations: political stability for Roh Tae Woo, the presidency for Kim Young Sam, and constitutional revision to a cabinet system for Kim Jong-pil.[93] Rather than a happy union, the marriage of convenience had resulted only in "three parties under one roof." What's more, Roh's leadership was further tarnished by intra-party disputes. The passive president could not control an aggressive Kim Young Sam who often resorted to brinkmanship tactics. As Kim Young Sam's influence increased, Roh became a virtual lame duck.

Before the merger, the public widely attributed the cause of economic and political

---

[91] Song Jian, "Whole-hearted Cooperation for Common Development", a paper presented at the Northeast Asia Economic Forum held during February 2-3, 2004, Niigata, Japan.
[92] Manwoo Lee, "South Korea's Politics of Succession and the December 1992 Presidential Election", in Cotton, ed. (1995), 35-65.
[93] Kim Young Sam was known to say when he decided to merge, "Enter a tiger den to catch the tiger." Of course, for Kim the tiger was the presidency itself.

problems to student demonstrations, labor strikes, and irresponsible opposition parties. Now, the government, which controlled the absolute majority of the National Assembly, was unable to solve widespread national problems. The factional struggles for hegemony and succession in the ruling party made the Roh government and the party very ineffective in promoting their policy agenda. The public began to believe that the national crisis had been brought about by the president and his party.[94] With the slowing economy, strikes, demonstrations and political stalemate, Roh's approval rating plummeted from 60 percent in January 1990, when he crafted the seemingly brilliant three-party merger, to 14 percent in mid-May.[95] Emboldened by this sharp drop in public confidence, tens of thousands of students took to the streets of Seoul and other major cities with rocks and firebombs, staging the largest protests in nearly three years.

Soon after its formation, the new ruling party launched a trial effort at constitutional revision. The party platform called for full parliamentary democracy. The proposed change in the constitution was part of a plan to achieve intra-party consensus, especially in the post-Roh era. With his strong presidential ambitions, Kim Young Sam, executive chairman of the DLP, was distancing himself from the proposed constitutional amendment, stating that constitutional revision should come only with the support of the people.[96] Anti-Kim factions in the ruling party openly accused Kim of pursuing "hegemonic politics".[97]

The constitutional amendment issue soon developed into an intra-party crisis. On October 26, 1990, the *JoongAng Ilbo* daily disclosed a photocopy of a top-secret agreement that Roh Tae Woo, Kim Young Sam and Kim Jong-pil had signed on May 6, 1990, shortly before the two opposition leaders officially joined the DLP. The three leaders had supposedly agreed to introduce a parliamentary system promising Kim Young Sam the first chance to head the cabinet, and to share power among the three factions of the new party.[98] Kim Young Sam and his faction believed that the leak was the doing of Roh confidants, who had access to the document, to embarrass Kim Young Sam. Kim took this as an open attack on his leadership and blamed Roh and his faction for conspiring against him. Without notice Kim left for Masan, a city near Pusan, seriously considering a break with the party and the creation of his own. It was his second boycott. Public opinion was on Kim's side, however. Untainted by an authoritarian past, Kim's brand of conservative reformism found favor with a middle class wary of the pro-Roh faction. Roh was concerned that the intra-party dispute would end in political disaster—a party split and renewed political turmoil. When Roh promised that the ruling party would not promote a constitutional revision if the people did not wish it, Kim agreed to return to Seoul. But the constitutional revision controversy lingered on well into 1991.[99]

---

[94] Fifty-eight percent of respondents in a joint *Chosun Ilbo* and Gallup Korea poll thought the ruling party was doing less well than had been expected at the time of the merger (*Chosun Ilbo*, April 15, 1990).

[95] "A Crisis of Confidence", *Newsweek*, May 21, 1990.

[96] *Korea Herald*, June 20, 1990.

[97] *Hankuk Ilbo*, September 28, 1990.

[98] *Joongang Ilbo*, October 26, 1990.

[99] Roh Tae Woo, "Reminiscences of Roh Tae Woo 2", *Wolgan Chosun* (June 1999), 248-254.

Roh's diplomatic success came as a welcome relief from the domestic scandals that were encumbering his government. On February 15, 1991, the chairman of the Hanbo Group was arrested for bribery. The Hanbo Construction Company was accused of paying off politicians and officials to rezone land in Seoul's green belt for commercial use. The so-called "Susuh scandal" led to the arrest and imprisonment of a presidential aide and five lawmakers. The scandal was considered to be the largest corruption scandal of the Roh administration, which dealt a severe blow to its moral authority. The opposition and anti-government forces wanted to use the Susuh scandal to their advantage. Student demonstrations escalated into opposition party rallies and mass demonstrations organized by various opposition groups. Throughout the spring, massive and violent demonstrations continued, some demonstrators even resorting to self-immolation. In an effort to prevent further escalation of the scandal, Roh replaced his EPB minister, construction minister, the mayor of Seoul, and the presidential secretary for administrative affairs.[100]

In the midst of the corruption scandal, the first round of local elections was held on March 25, 1991. Council members of small cities, counties, and wards in big cities were chosen. The second round of local elections for provincial council members was held in June, and the ruling DLP declared landslide victories. Nearly three decades had passed since the military junta had abolished the system of local autonomy in 1961. Roh's 1987 declaration of democratic reform included local autonomy and local elections. The dominance of the ruling party in the local elections seemed to indicate that the middle class yearned for social stability over social justice, and economic growth over equality. The general populace was sick of the ongoing demonstrations.

At the same time, social discipline continued to erode. Student demonstrations and labor strikes frequently crippled universities and factories. Crimes were rampant owing to a demoralized police force. Traffic jams and water and air pollution were worsening, and the government was not effectively responding to these emerging issues. Political instability and serious economic downturn resulted in what was called "a total national crisis." When one poll asked respondents to evaluate the seriousness of a series of social and political issues facing the country, the majority of respondents believed that most issues mentioned were serious (see Table 10).

Instead of the anticipated easy victory in the March 1992 parliamentary elections, voters delivered a stunning defeat to the ruling party, which had 218 seats in the 299-seat assembly before the election. Now the DLP managed to secure only 149 seats, one vote shy of a simple majority. The Democratic Party (DP) led by Kim Dae Jung won ninety-seven seats. The new Unification National Party (UNP), which was formed a few months before the election by the former chairman of the Hyundai Group, Chung Ju-yung, won thirty-one seats.[101] Roh's ambitious plans for establishing a stable ruling party had failed.

Factional squabbles flared as to who should be blamed for the shocking election setback. Kim Young Sam demonstrated his political skill by transforming the political setback into a political offensive against his opponents; he immediately assigned

---

[100] *Yonhap News*, February 19, 1991.
[101] *Joongang Ilbo*, March 25, 1992.

responsibility to the incompetence of President Roh and the Blue House staff. But the anti-Kim Young Sam factions blamed him for the defeat.[102] On March 28, 1992, without consulting Roh, Kim Young Sam declared his presidential candidacy. Kim thus succeeded in shifting the public attention from who should be blamed for the defeat of the parliamentary elections to the issue of candidacy. Although Kim represented a minor faction in the ruling party, his faction believed him to be the natural presidential candidate for 1992. Thus, public attention shifted to the upcoming presidential election. Kim demanded an early selection of the DLP presidential candidate, to be designated by President Roh.

Table 10. **Seriousness of Current Issues**

Issue	Respondents consider "serious" (%)	Issue	Respondents consider "serious" (%)
Inflation	97.3	Corruption	91.4
Pollution	96.7	Political Instability	87.8
Traffic Jam	96.4	Unemployment	85.8
Security	94.5	Exports	73.0
Housing	94.0	Labor Disputes	68.4
Education	92.7	Regionalism	62.0

Source: *Donga Ilbo*, April 1, 1991

On the other hand, Kim's opponents within the party wanted the open, competitive nominating procedure of a party convention. The DJP faction was split over the post-Roh leadership. Many were dissatisfied with Kim Young Sam, especially the factions led by Park Tae-joon and Lee Jong-chan. Park Tae-joon was quite serious about his candidacy and asserted that Kim Young Sam had "no character, no knowledge, and no vision."[103] Park Tae-joon, formerly a close associate of Park Chung Hee, was the legendary founder of the POSCO Steel Company. Lee Jong-chan, grandson of a well-known independence fighter, was regarded as a reform-minded next-generation leader. He had been a long-term lawmaker and consequently enjoyed a broad support base in Seoul and the surrounding Kyunggi Province. He had served as a floor leader of the DJP, its secretary general, and then minister of political affairs under both Chun and Roh. He had stood against the three party merger of 1990 and was a constant critic of Kim Young Sam after the union.

Eventually, the various splinter groups selected Lee Jong-chan. Lee aimed to get rid of old-time politics: "Politics has lost people's trust…. Politics has to be conducted by the institution and not just by a handful of people. Our primary goal is to institutionalize the politics so that it may not be swayed by personal whims."[104] He called for termination

---

[102] *Korea Times*, March 27, 1992.
[103] Huh Nam-jin, "*Roh Taw-woo ei YS daekwon mandulki* (The Making of President Kim Young Sam by Roh Tae Woo), *Wolgan Joongang* (May 1992), 142.
[104] *Korea Times*, April 17, 1991.

of the confrontational era of the two Kims (Kim Young Sam and Kim Dae Jung) and argued that chronic regional antagonism would only end if the two Kims retired.[105] Some polls showed Lee in good standing and more and more people began to consider him as Roh's successor.[106] At the last minute Lee withdrew from the presidential candidate election at the party convention, stating that his candidacy was a sham designed to make the selection process appear competitive.[107] He accused the Blue House of engaging in "a free competition in disguise," Thus, Kim Young Sam managed to obtain the DLP candidacy for president. Kim had entered the DLP as leader of a minority faction, yet he had become the ruling party's presidential nominee two and a half years after his opposition party merged with the government party.

After winning the presidential candidacy, Kim Young Sam's relationship with President Roh became further strained. To boost his popularity, Kim intermittently criticized the Roh government and its policies. On September 16, 1992, Kim held a press conference and demanded a sweeping cabinet reshuffle that included replacing the prime minister, who at that time was involved in high-level talks in Pyongyang. The move angered President Roh, who felt that Kim had crossed the line and encroached on his exclusive domain with regard to cabinet change. On September 18, Roh announced that he was resigning from the position of president of the ruling party to remove himself, he claimed, from possible partisan entanglement.[108] He then appointed a new prime minister and a neutral cabinet to manage the presidential election that would decide his successor.

Kim Dae Jung, the presidential candidate of the main opposition party, hailed Roh's move as "a Copernican turning point in politics."[109] However, it was generally believed that Roh's decision was as much retaliation against Kim Young Sam as a move to ensure a fair presidential election. After retirement, Roh found cause to regret his erstwhile support for Kim Young Sam. "Kim lacks virtue," Roh said. "His goal was not democracy. He stopped at nothing to become president."[110]

The presidential elections, which elected the ruling party candidate Kim Young Sam, strengthened the process of democratic consolidation. Nevertheless, Roh failed to establish a stable dominant party and to change the political system into a parliamentary one. Instead, his grand political design ended in intra-party squabbles over presidential succession. As a result, the government and the ruling party became less effective in managing national affairs and Roh's leadership was greatly undermined.

---

[105] *Korea Times*, April 26, 1992.

[106] In a poll conducted by Korea Research and the *Ilyo Shinmun*, Lee Jong-Chan got 36.9 percent and Kim Young Sam 31.2 percent when respondents were asked whom they liked as a candidate. See Kim Hyun Jong, "*Roh Tae Woo e banki dun Lee Jong Chan ei gaesan* (The Calculation of Lee Jong-Chan's Revolt Against Roh Tae Woo)", *Wolgan Joongang* (June 1992), 242.

[107] Interview with Lee Jong-chan (August 10, 2001).

[108] *Korea Times*, September 19, 1992.

[109] *Korea Times*, September 22, 1992.

[110] Roh Tae Woo, "Reminiscences", *Wolgan Chosun* (June 1999): 272-275.

LEADERSHIP FOR DEMOCRATIC TRANSITION

Context of the Presidency. Roh Tae Woo seemed to mark a good beginning. It is not too much to assert that the first year of his term was the finest year in modern Korean history. The economy was booming and the world was coming to Seoul to participate in the Summer Olympics. The strong economy and the Seoul Olympics were two important political assets that Roh inherited. As the first popularly elected president since 1971, he enjoyed wide support. The beginning of the Roh presidency also coincided with a profound international transformation. The Cold War structure was rapidly dismantling. The disintegration of the Soviet Union and the breakdown of the socialist bloc provided opportunity as well as uncertainty for South Korea.

There is, however, a concealed danger in assuming office during a time of national prosperity. It is more likely that national fortunes will come down than continue rising. If the national situation worsens, the leader faces popular censure. Roh Tae Woo was swept into the presidency on a tide of violent anti-government protests. In addition, the political and economic bases of the Roh administration were unstable and subject to reversal. Though Roh was legitimately elected, his power base was still the party established by Chun Doo Hwan.

With strong regional support, the losers, especially Kim Young Sam and Kim Dae Jung, whose ultimate goals were also the presidency, were desperate and eager to challenge Roh. Moreover, as a result of the parliamentary elections only two months after Roh's inauguration, the ruling party almost immediately found itself a minority in the National Assembly. The electoral upset further undermined his ability to govern effectively. After the 1990 merger of the three parties, Roh was further challenged from within the ruling party by the stubborn and aggressive Kim Young Sam. Thus, throughout his five-year term, Roh was unable to consolidate his power.

The transition to full democracy was very volatile. Social conflicts and unrest increased as each sector attempted to promote its own interests, making it difficult for the government to mobilize a national consensus around its policies. Protests and other challenges were widespread, and existing public institutions were distrusted or discredited along with the former authoritarian government. Freed from governmental restrictions, anti-government forces called for drastic political and economic reforms, including the punishment of leaders from the previous government.

Agenda Setting. During the very competitive presidential election of 1987, Roh had promised almost everything for everybody. Perhaps this was inevitable in that the other candidates had made even more irresponsible promises. Making too many promises created problems for the presidency. As a candidate Roh had pledged democratic reform, economic growth, social and political stability, and social welfare. The wide disparity of these promises suggests that he failed to appreciate the difficulties involved. He had no clear political and economic plans for achieving all of these tasks simultaneously. In addition, his power was constrained by the opposition, which dominated the National Assembly.

There is no doubt that the historic democratic transition in South Korea had come about because of Roh Tae Woo's June 29 declaration of democratic reform and its subsequent implementation. Although both the opposition and anti-government forces regarded Roh as an extension of the past "military" regime, Roh himself wanted to go down in history as a great democratic reformer. It is clear that his primary agenda was democratic reform. Owing to the high priority he placed on democratic reform, he established a relatively strong political staff in the Blue House. But he had forgotten that the two Kims were lifelong democratic crusaders, reputations they would never allow the Johnny-come-lately Roh to appropriate. He also neglected the fact that democratic transition could be successful only when the economy was strong. Ordinary people were more concerned with economic realities than abstract political ideals.[111]

The successful hosting of the Seoul Olympics and the historic breakup of the world's Cold War structure provided a timely boost to Roh's "northern policy." There was also an increased possibility that a major change would take place in North Korea, and as a result a major shift was anticipated in inter-Korean relations. Although a skilled diplomat, Roh lacked understanding of, and commitment to, economic matters. He also lacked clear economic vision. The officials he appointed to manage the economy were neither as qualified nor as dynamic as those in charge of foreign affairs. Moreover, he changed his economic team frequently and, as a result, his economic policy was neither consistent nor effective. Like Mikhail Gorbachev, Roh Tae Woo became a leader better thought of abroad than at home. Koreans were less concerned about foreign policy than domestic issues. Although he seemed to relish diplomatic initiatives, he lacked the same fervor for tackling domestic issues. At one point, on his return from a visit to the United States in October 1989, he casually commented, "We need a president for domestic affairs."[112]

As Gallup Korea polls show, the South Korean public paid less attention to Roh's major agenda items than to more mundane issues. During his term, the economy and socio-political stability were the primary concerns of the people (see Figure 9).[113] Those who believed political issues and foreign policy issues were priorities represented a small minority, while the majority believed economic problems were the most serious issues facing the nation. In 1988 when the economy was in its best shape ever, the public did not pay much attention. But after massive strikes, rapid real estate price increases and a poor foreign trade performance, concerns over the economy increased dramatically. When the Roh administration failed to deliver on its campaign pledges of sustained economic growth and political stability, the people were naturally disappointed.[114]

---

[111] According to a survey conducted by *Donga Ilbo* in June 1990, some 61.2% of the respondents believed that "democracy should be realized gradually while minimizing confusion", and about 20.6% thought that "democracy should be realized promptly even at the cost of some confusion." *Donga Ilbo*, June 7, 1990.

[112] Interview with Kim Hak Joon. See also Gibney (1992), 94.

[113] Data are based on Gallup Korea surveys (1988~1992). Responses are combined as follows: **Economic Problem** = Inflation, Economic Stability & Growth, Rent & Real Estate Hikes, Labor Disputes, Rural Problems, and Rich-Poor Gap; **Political Problem** = Political Stability, Democratic Reform, and Elimination of Past Wrongdoings; **Social Problem** = Demonstration, Law and Order, and Traffic Jams; and **Foreign Policy Problem** = Unification. In a multiple-choice questionnaire, the ten most-mentioned issues were tabulated.

[114] According to a survey by *Chosun Ilbo* and Gallup Korea, the urgent need for democratic reform and the elimination of the legacy of the Chun regime ranked sixteenth (2.2 percent) and eighteenth on a list of eighteen priorities, after law and order (30.1 percent), economic stability (28.3 percent), housing (18.6 percent), traffic congestion (17.1 percent), political stability (14.2 percent) (*Chosun Ilbo*, March 6, 1990.)

Roh kept a black notebook to record the promises he had made as a presidential candidate. During a press conference in early 1992, the last year of his term, he stated in all earnestness: "I made a total of 459 promises during my campaigns. Of these, 448 have been taken up as of today. A total of 175 promises have been completed, and the remaining 273 are in the process of being worked out."[115] One wonders why he was so unpopular despite such meticulous attention to his campaign pledges. The problem was agenda setting and priority making. Concerned with the micromanagement of many minor issues, he neglected major agenda items.

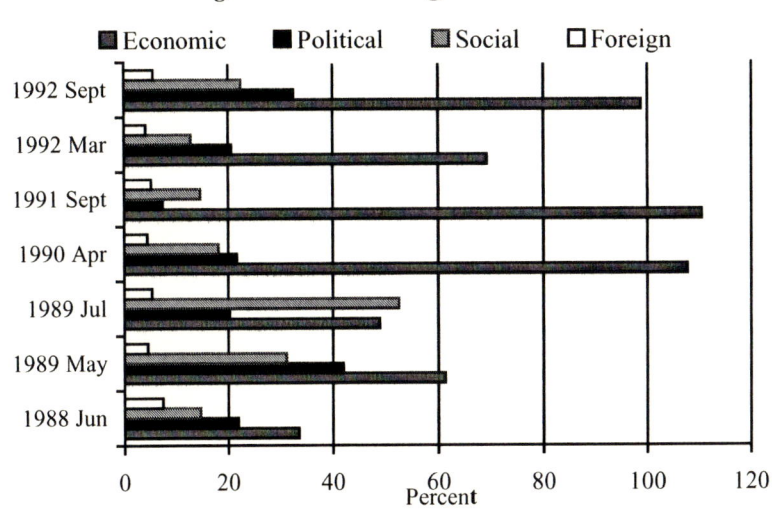

Figure 9. **Most Pressing Issues**

Appointments and Leadership Style. Roh's appointments reflected his top priorities—democratic reform and the northern policy. Upon becoming president, Roh created three important positions in the Blue House—special adviser for political affairs, senior secretary for security and foreign policy, and special assistant for policy affairs. These new offices aimed at promoting his two top priorities. He appointed former professors and journalists as his advisers for foreign policy and political affairs. As his preference for professors and journalists shows, image was more important than experience and ability in his appointments.

His northern policy was successful largely because he established a strong and stable foreign policy team. Considering his tendency to change ministers and advisers frequently, the foreign policy team was exceptionally stable: he had only two foreign ministers during his term, and the national security adviser served through his entire term. However, his economic policymakers were frequently changed: he had four

---

[115] *Korea Herald*, February 20, 1993.

different EPB ministers and four different economic advisers during his five-year term. As a result, teamwork in economic policymaking was weak and lacked coordination and consistency. The average tenure of his cabinet members was short—only 13.7 months. Poor performance of domestic policies and consequent distrust in the government were consequences of cabinet instability.

Roh tried to nurture an image of the "common man" president, reacting against the authoritarian or "imperial" presidency of his predecessors. At first, the public welcomed the new leadership style. But it seemed to go over less well as his term progressed. His sincere efforts to present himself as a common person rather than as a president seem ultimately to have backfired. Leaders are not common men. If they try to appear common, they come across as unnatural—not only phony, but also condescending. His opponents continuously challenged the president and considerably undermined the authority of his office. Style and rhetoric alone are insufficient for a top leader. The substance and results of his policies are what people are most concerned with.

Roh was a far more thoughtful and patient personality than Chun. However, he was passive and cautious. He has been likened to Tokugawa Ieyasu (1542-1616), the famous Japanese samurai ruler, who it is said patiently awaited for the ripening of an apple and its natural fall from the tree. Despite a semi-revolutionary social situation, there was no sense of tension or urgency in the Roh government; a "wait-and-see" attitude prevailed. Most Koreans, accustomed to strong and decisive leadership, were disappointed and frustrated with Roh's indecisive and seemingly weak leadership style. During his interview with the author, Kim Hakjoon, one of Roh's key advisers, said that "the main problem of President Roh's leadership was lack of commitment."[116]

Given a variety of problems and demands, Roh tried to avoid direct government interference as much as possible, while people worked off steam in protests, demonstrations, and strikes. A basic element of democratic government is to respect public opinion; but in a democratic society there is often no consensus, only conflicting views. He was often praised for conducting his presidency with restraint. Patience, however, is only one aspect of good leadership. A leader often needs to be decisive in order to make the difficult decisions and overcome the challenges necessary to achieving objectives.

Throughout his term, social unrest had been the most serious problem. Roh and his close advisers regarded protests, demonstrations and strikes as a natural phenomenon during democratic transition. He had a laissez-faire approach to disorder and lawlessness. He often said, "Real courage is to be patient and to wait: it is my philosophy of practicing democracy. If my government strictly applied the law to all cases of violation, Korea might have faced a situation where national order collapsed completely."[117] He believed that through chaotic experiences, the people would develop the self-regulation and self-protection which constitute the backbone of democratic order. His advisers argued that during a democratic transition the role of government should be passive. For example, Kim Hakjoon, former Blue House spokesman in the Roh administration, argued:

> "When the great deluge of systemic change flows, the government should just follow the flood. If the government attempts to keep the current from

---

[116] Interview with Kim Hakjoon on April 23, 2002.
[117] Roh Tae Woo, "Reminiscences, Part 2", *Wolgan Chosun* (June 1999), 236-237.

overflowing, not only the government but also the whole of society will collapse. Governmental intervention on the ground of maintaining law and order means nothing but the return to an authoritarian government. Therefore, we waited patiently. We had to pile up sandbags until the flood subsides."[118]

Such a view might be more appropriate in an academic conference than in real politics. It appeared highly uncertain whether these problems would solve themselves without effective leadership. Toleration was Roh's strength as well as his weakness: he could promote the fragile democracy by maintaining a proper balance between the two extreme forces; he could compromise with the opposition and moderate the activists' demands; but often, he couldn't solve anything and ended up disappointing both sides. In fact, he even failed to win the sympathies of people who had voted for him. In spite of his continuous efforts to respond to the exploding demands of various groups, he became increasingly unpopular throughout his term (see Figure 10). Only one year after his inauguration, he had already become a lame duck president.

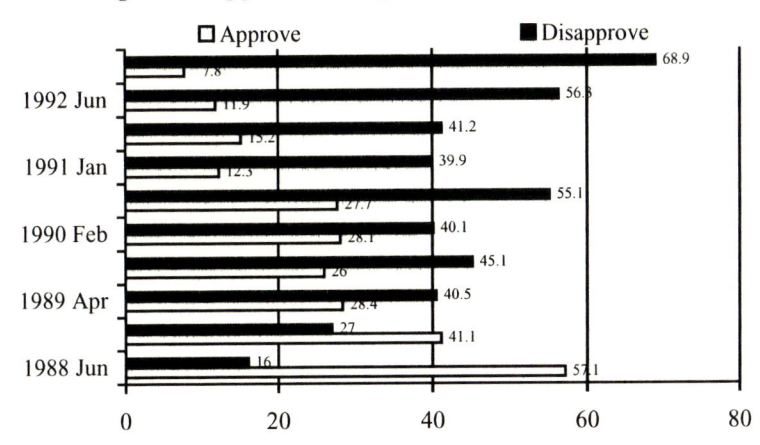

Figure 10. **Approval Rating of Roh Tae Woo** (%)

Date	Approve	Disapprove
1992 Jun	7.8	68.9
	11.9	56.8
	15.2	41.2
1991 Jan	12.3	39.9
	27.7	55.1
1990 Feb	28.1	40.1
	26	45.1
1989 Apr	28.4	40.5
	27	41.1
1988 Jun	16	57.1

Source: Gallup Korea Surveys, 1988-92.

Achievements and Legacies. Roh Tae Woo entered office with staggering problems. Considering the various constraints he faced, he tried hard and did reasonably well. He has been credited with three major accomplishments during his tenure: democratic reforms, the northern policy, and inter-Korean dialogue.

Roh may have been a reluctant democrat, but the considerable progress in democratic transition was made possible by his steadfast commitment to democracy and the character of the democratizing regime of the Sixth Republic.[119] During his presidency he consciously strengthened Korea's democratic system, and as a result, the democratization process made

---

[118] Kim Hak-Joon, "*Roh jeongbunun muljeongbuil su bake upsossa* (Inevitability of a Weak Government of the Roh Administration)", *Sindonga* (February 1993): 444-445.
[119] Leslie H. Gelb, editorial, *New York Times*, December 24, 1992, A-13.

great strides. The National Assembly regained legitimacy as the nation's lawmaking body. The Covenant on Civil and Political Rights was signed. The laws governing judicial proceedings were modified to make the judicial system more independent of executive control and less subject to political interference. The National Security Law was revised to protect the basic rights of the people, and laws of assembly and demonstration were enacted. Democratic reforms also brought local autonomy for the first time since 1961.[120] Freedom of the press was also realized: press censorship was abolished with the repeal of the Basic Press Law and new legal measures were established to ensure the independence and self-regulation of the mass media. As one journalist commented, "There certainly exists an unprecedented freedom of the press in contemporary South Korea."[121] In early 1990, the International Press Institution reported, "Visible and invisible restrictions imposed on the press have been abolished in favor of a greater freedom of information and the right of the people to know has been guaranteed."[122]

As president, Roh encouraged fair elections and the rule of law and respected the authority of the National Assembly. In the belief that democracy must take root through the self-regulation of people, he exercised maximum restraint in using public power in order to maintain law and order.[123] In retrospect, he appears to be the most democratic president in the history of the Republic. During the first two years of his presidency, the minority government and the majority opposition lived in a sort of perpetual stalemate. he tried to work with the opposition, pursuing a politics of dialogue and compromise in terms of the give-and-take principle. He was the only Korean president who did not intimidate or threaten opposition parties with governmental power.[124] Probably, Korea under Roh was more democratic than under the life-long democratic crusaders Kim Young Sam and Kim Dae Jung.

Among the accomplishments of President Roh, the northern policy was the most successful. He had a grand vision for South Korea's foreign policy and reunification and consistently and diligently pursued his policy goals. He broke through decades-old Korean fears and distrust of Communist nations to open unprecedented relations. He established diplomatic relations of immense strategic and economic importance to South Korea with the Soviet Union and China. After Seoul-Moscow normalization, the Soviet Union stopped supplying fighters and other sophisticated weapons systems to North Korea.[125] In addition, he significantly broadened Korea's export markets in Eastern Europe and Asia. Within a decade, China became South Korea's second largest trading partner. The success of the northern policy isolated North Korea from its allies and nudged it to the negotiating table. As a result, there was a breakthrough in inter-Korean relations: after a series of high-level talks, South and North Korea agreed on a basic

---

[120] Yeom Hong-Chul, "Roh Tae Woo: daese suneung hyong lideoship (Roh Tae Woo: A Passive Leader)", Korea Journal of Political Science Association 35 (2001): 268-276.
[121] Jae-Youl Kim, "Democratization in South Korea", in Cotton, ed., *Korea*, 49.
[122] Quoted in Kyu Ho Youm and Michael B. Salwen, "A Free Press in South Korea: Temporary Phenomenon or Permanent Fixture?" *Asian Survey*, 30: 3 (1990), 312.
[123] Bret L. Billet, "South Korea at the Crossroads: An Evolving Democracy or Authoritarian Rule Revisited?" *Asian Survey*, 30:3 (1990): 300-311.
[124] Gibney, *Korea*, 98-99.
[125] "South Korea: in Praise of Roh", *Economist*, November 21, 1992.

framework to improve their relations. It is inconceivable that this could have happened so quickly and successfully without his initiative and commitment.

However, Roh was widely regarded as a failed president in domestic terms, especially regarding the management of the economy. Many South Koreans were discontented with the slower growing economy, rising inflation, and sagging international competitiveness. People thought that since democracy had not yielded immediate improvements, and the country continued to experience strikes, uncertainty and disorder, Roh must be to blame. Nevertheless, survey results showed generally positive views on the Roh presidency. Asked how much their living conditions had improved since Roh had come to office, 58.4 percent responded "somewhat better," while 30 percent said "worse." On democratic reform, 58.6 percent said there was more democracy than five years before, while 22.5 percent said there was less. Regarding the northern policy, 66 percent recognized its success, and 82 percent believed that the basic inter-Korean accord was a great achievement.[126]

Unfortunately, Roh's secret "slush fund," disclosed by an opposition legislator in 1995, and the subsequent trial, not only ruined the legacy of his presidency but also that of his predecessor. The scandal gave opponents of Roh and Chun, including President Kim Young Sam, a golden opportunity for revenge. Thousands of students and dissidents demanded the arrest of the two former presidents. The two former leaders were arrested and charged with corruption and also with military mutiny in December 1979 and with the suppression of the citizens uprising in Kwangju in May 1980. They were sentenced to prison terms and later pardoned. However, the court found no one who actually ordered the shooting during the 1980 Kwangju uprising.[127] Whatever the motive behind Roh's maintainence of such a huge fund brooks no excuse. Some observers speculated at the time that the two former presidents were clandestinely planning to organize a new party, splitting the ruling party led by Kim Young Sam. The slush fund scandal also seriously damaged the authority of the Korean presidency itself.

The South Korean democratic transition began with the December 1987 presidential elections and climaxed with the presidential elections of December 1992, thereby completing the full electoral cycle of an orderly and peaceful transfer of power. Roh Tae Woo patiently managed the difficult democratic transition, laid the groundwork for inter-Korean reconciliation and cooperation, and normalized relations with the countries of the former socialist bloc. His achievements are, without question, important and enduring elements of South Korea's nation building.

---

[126] *Yonhap News*, February 24, 1993.
[127] For details of the court's judgment, see *Joongang Ilbo*, August 26, 1996. Although Chun was charged with corruption, the prosecutors could not locate the alleged slush fund by the time of this writing, late 2003. The background of the trial will be discussed in the next chapter.

Kim Young Sam

Chapter Seven
Kim Young Sam
President of Democratic Reform

"We are sick with what has been termed "Korean disease."

"When power comes into being by fraudulent means, the legitimacy of the state is infringed upon and law and order collapses."

"No foreign ally can be equal in importance to our ethnic brethren in the North. No ideology can bring greater happiness than national kinship."

—Kim Young Sam

The inauguration of Kim Young Sam in February 1993 as the country's first civilian president since 1961 was a watershed in South Korea's drive toward democracy. It symbolized the end of decades of political struggle for full democracy. It was also the crowning achievement of Kim's long political career. His image as a clean and decent politician had been engraved on the Korean consciousness over thirty years of relentless democratic activism. Thus, Kim entered office claiming both an electoral and a moral mandate to undertake wide-ranging reform.

Kim was known as a man of conviction, courage and determination, and yet he lacked a clear vision for Korea's future. He inherited a government with serious problems—a flagging economy, the menace of a North Korean nuclear program, and the emerging challenges of globalization. In addition, his leadership qualifications had been questioned. Until becoming president, he had done little but challenge the country's authoritarian governments. Therefore, he lacked a solid grasp of major issues. Once his lifelong presidential goal had been attained, the next question was, what goals would define his presidency? According to his close aides, the moment Kim was elected, he had one primary, if vague, ambition—to become "an outstanding president,"[1] one that would be remembered in history.

The Man and His Character

Kim Young Sam was born December 20, 1927, into a well-to-do family on the island of Koje, off Korea's southern coast, later the site of a prisoner-of-war camp during the Korean War. His father, a successful businessman in the fishing industry, owned two aquaculture farms and several fishing vessels. Kim Young Sam was the only son in a family

---

[1] Kim Hyon-Chong, "Kim Young Sam's Leadership Style Examined", *Wolgan Chosun* (March 1993): 148-165, trans. in *Foreign Broadcasting Iinformation Service, East Asia*, 23 April 1993, 25.

of five girls; he naturally became the center of attention among family members and relatives. He was an overprotected child, often self-centered, obstinate, and mischievous.[2]

Kim came from a Christian family. As a child he attended a nearby village school, but finished his last two years of elementary school some distance away from home. His grandfather wished that he attend a prestigious middle school, so Kim was sent to secondary school in Pusan—a major change for an overprotected island boy. As a student at what is today Kyungnam High School, he became an avid soccer player. Through soccer, he acquired an enduring habit of daily physical exercise. However, no biographies note any particular academic merit in the young Kim.

In September 1948 Kim entered the philosophy department of the newly reorganized Seoul National University, which has since become South Korea's premier university. A turning point in his life came in his sophomore year, when he entered a speech contest. He won second prize, which was given out by Foreign Minister Chang Taek-sang, an influential member of the Korea Democratic Party.[3] From that point Chang became mentor to the young Kim. Two years later, in May 1950, when Kim was still a college junior, Chang decided to run for a seat in the National Assembly. Kim became a campaign orator, contributing to Chang's successful bid. This cemented their relationship as patron and protégé. More importantly, it aroused Kim's political ambitions. Kim began writing numerous letters to locals on Koje Island in order to form an electoral base in his hometown.

Less than a month after the elections, the Korean War broke out. Most young men were drafted and many young students volunteered to fight the Communists. Kim participated in the war in a different way. According to his official curriculum vitae, he "joined the army...as a troop information and education specialist [and] worked as a writer of propaganda materials directed at North Korea."[4] In February 1951, only eight months after he had become what was termed a "student volunteer," Kim was able to rejoin Chang Taek-sang, now vice speaker of the National Assembly, as his secretary and to continue his study career on a part-time basis. He graduated from Seoul National University in 1952.

By the time the third National Assembly election was held in May 1954, Kim was old enough to be eligible for an assembly seat. He ran for the ruling Liberal Party as an assemblyman from Koje and was elected at the age of twenty-five. He was the youngest member of the National Assembly ever—a record that still stands. Soon after the 1954 elections, the ruling party passed a constitutional amendment making President Syngman Rhee eligible for a third term. In protest of the amendment—and just seven months after joining the ruling party in April 1955—Kim bolted along with eleven fellow members to become one of thirty-three charter members of the opposition Democratic Party. This began a lifelong advocacy of democracy.

---

[2] See Nam Hong-chin, trans. by Lee Sung-Kyu, *A Life Story of President Kim Young-Sam* (Seoul: Bansok, 1993); and Yonhap News Agency, *Crusader for Democracy: the Life and Times of Kim Young-Sam*. (Seoul, 1993).

[3] Chang was well known for his high-profile service as the decidedly right-wing director of the Metropolitan Police Bureau of Seoul during the American military government.

[4] "Biographical Sketch of Kim Young Sam", Ministry of Foreign Affairs, Republic of Korea, 1993.

Kim Young Sam switched his electoral district to Pusan—the second largest city in South Korea and its principal port, only to lose in the 1958 National Assembly elections. In 1960, Kim experienced both personal tragedy and political triumph. His mother was killed by a North Korean infiltrator, but after the sudden fall of the Rhee regime he found himself re-elected to the National Assembly seat in a district of Pusan. He represented the district for the next twenty years, making Pusan his political stronghold. This proved crucial to his political success.

After the 1961 military coup, Kim was stripped of his seat in the National Assembly when that body was dissolved. In the parliamentary elections of November 1963, after two and half years of a military government, Kim was again elected, and chosen as floor leader of an opposition party at the age of thirty-seven, another youthful record. From then on Kim's political career was marked by success after success: he became the most frequently elected lawmaker (nine times), a frequently elected leader of an opposition party (four times), the most frequent floor leader (five times), and was twice made spokesman for the opposition.

After the adoption of the 1972 Yushin constitution, Kim's criticisms of the Park Chung Hee regime intensified. During the 1970s Kim solidified his reputation as a politician of courage with an impeccable commitment to democracy. At a time when people were afraid of defying the Yushin system, he criticized it relentlessly: "The river of history sometimes flows upward, but it flows downward eventually. The Yushin system was not a policy for reform but one which led to the retrogression of history."[5] To emphasize his determination to fight for democracy, whatever the consequences, he was fond of saying, "Though the rooster is strangled, the dawn will arrive without fail."

After Chun Doo Hwan took power, Kim was forced to announce his resignation from all public positions. From October 1980, when the government banned him from all political activities, until 1982 Kim was under house arrest. On May 18, 1983, the third anniversary of the Kwangju uprising, Kim Young Sam went on a twenty-three-day hunger strike, demanding democratic reforms. He had once again made himself the focus of dissent. After the hunger strike, his political position was strengthened. The opposition forces were reinvigorated in their determination to fight for democracy, resulting in the formation of the New Korea Democratic Party (NKDP). The new party emerged as the largest opposition party in the 1985 parliamentary elections.

Kim Young Sam is a man of great will and courage. A close adviser once stated that Kim's heart was as strong and bold as a lion's. When confronting his enemies, he always exuded strength and confidence. He never relented: he fought against obstacles and enemies until he overcame them. Once he set a goal, his mind was dominated by strategic considerations on how to achieve it. He was a stubborn political fighter, completely dedicated to winning "the game" he had made his life's work.

Kim Young Sam—like Kim Dae Jung—claimed to be a fighter for democracy, but his real objective, so many suspected, was power, specifically the presidency. The two Kims were popularly said to be infected with the "presidential disease" (*daetongryong byong*), an overwhelming hunger for the highest office. Kim Young Sam had never really been interested in national issues, and South Korean elections, as well as legislative

---

[5] Hong-chin Nam, *op. cit.*, 74-75.

processes, were not often issue-oriented as is the case in advanced democracies. Though his pursuit of the country's highest office was naturally couched in the rhetoric of democracy and social justice, it involved acts of manipulation, conspiracy, maneuvering, and deception.

ASCENT TO THE PRESIDENCY

Kim Young Sam stood at a political turning point in early 1990 when he aligned himself with Roh Tae Woo and Kim Jong-pil to create a new ruling party. Previously, Kim Young Sam had fought bitterly against both these men. He characterized this political maneuver as a grave decision made "to save the nation" from governmental paralysis. However, perhaps his real motivation was revealed when he stated one had to "enter a tiger's lair to capture the tiger," in this case, the presidency. Factional disputes over post-Roh leadership emerged not long after the three party merger. Kim Young Sam played the succession game brilliantly. He was a master of brinkmanship, frequently threatening to leave the ruling party when he felt his position threatened. Eventually, he was selected as the ruling party's candidate for the 1992 presidential election.

Kim Young Sam, who had taken third after Roh Tae Woo and Kim Dae Jung in the 1987 presidential election, was now widely considered the front-runner. He consistently maintained his lead in major polls. Not surprisingly, Kim Dae Jung was nominated as the presidential candidate for the opposition Democratic Party. At the same time, seventy-seven-year-old Chung Ju-yung, founder of the Hyundai Group, one of the largest conglomerates in Korea, hurriedly organized his own political base, the United People's Party, in early 1992 and proclaimed his presidential candidacy.[6]

As a campaign strategy, Kim Young Sam made great efforts to distance himself from President Roh and harshly criticized his economic mismanagement. He relied on the strength of his record as a fighter for democracy rather than his position as candidate of the ruling party. He campaigned on the theme of "creating a new Korea" and "reform amidst stability." He asserted that the country suffered from the "Korean disease": rampant corruption, a withering work ethic, and weakening authority.

During the election, the most salient issue was the sluggish economy. The economic growth in 1992 was 4.7 percent, the lowest rate since 1981. All three candidates attacked President Roh's economic legacy, and all called for economic reforms. However, therein lay Kim Young Sam's real problem. Many people perceived a wide gap between his rhetoric and future performance. They believed he had few qualifications to manage the economy.

Kim Young Sam proved an indefatigable campaigner. He waxed stronger when attacking his opponents, as he had shown during the Park and Chun eras. He criticized his main rival, Kim Dae Jung, for forging links with left-wing political groups and for being soft on North Korea. By invoking "red scare" tactics, Kim Young Sam put Kim Dae Jung on the defensive. Kim Young Sam also criticized Chung Ju-yung for his attempt to "purchase" the presidency.

Kim Young Sam was the clear winner of the election by a margin of 41.4 percent to Kim Dae Jung's 33.4 percent and Chung Ju-yung's 16.1 percent. Kim Young Sam had

---

[6] For details of the 1992 presidential election, see Chan Wook Park, "Korean Voters' Candidate Choice in the 1992 Presidential Election", *Korea and World Affairs*, 18:3 (fall 1993): 432-458.

suffered a severe loss among his supporters during the election: only 44.5 percent of his 1987 supporters stayed with him. On the other hand, 66 percent of Roh Tae Woo's supporters from 1987 supported Kim Young Sam in 1992. In other words, Kim Young Sam won greater support from among former Roh supporters than from his own.[7]

Regionalism continued to be the most important factor in the election (see Figure 11). Kim Dae Jung received 88 percent of the vote in the Cholla provinces, and an amazing 95 percent of the vote in the city of Kwangju, thus failing to overcome his image as a regional candidate. In contrast, Kim Young Sam received 71.4 percent of the South Kyongsang Province vote, 60.4 percent from Pusan, and 58.8 percent from Taegu.

Apparently Kim Young Sam did not recognize the difficulty of the tasks ahead of him. He had only five years to create a "new Korea," a fundamental transformation of the country—obviously too ambitious a goal. He had no administrative experience, nor did most of his political confidantes. His organizational life was limited to small and traditional political parties which functioned in a rather informal way. During a lifelong struggle for democracy, his efforts were animated by broad and lofty slogans, such as democracy and human rights.

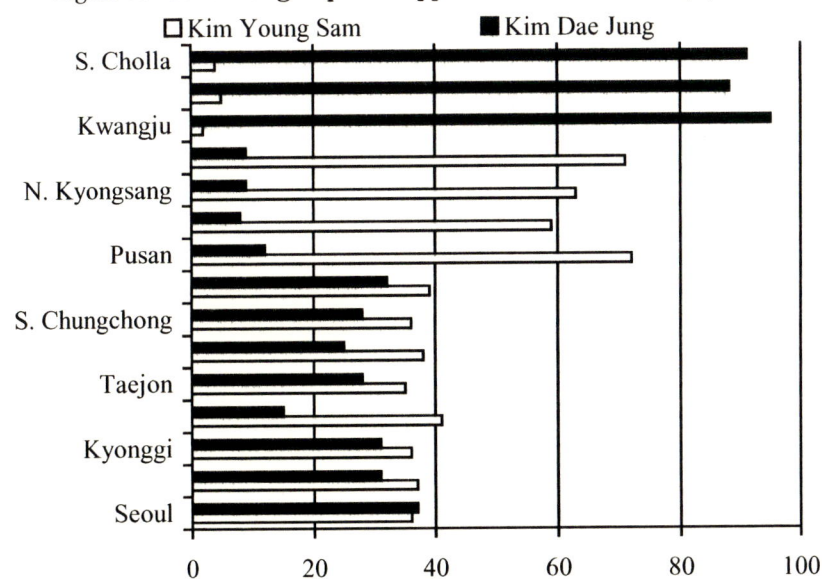

Figure 11. **Contrasting Popular Support for the Two Kims** (%)

Source: The Central Election Management Committee.

---

[7] Bae Sun-kwang, "Continuity or Change: The Voter's Choice in the 1992 Presidential Election", in Cotton, ed., *Politics and Policy*, 68-70.

Many worried how the new president would manage national affairs. By his own admission, Kim was more a politician than an intellectual, claiming that he would "borrow other people's brains." His loyalists argued that sound instincts and principles could suffice in the absence of a detailed knowledge of issues; a president, after all, could delegate to capable technocrats and advisers. When critics questioned his qualities of leadership, Kim responded, "Appointment is above everything," implying that he would pay special attention to personnel management. Many believed that the success or failure of his presidency would be greatly dependent on the appointments of staff and cabinet. His choices allowed a glimpse into the president's leadership style and personnel policy, the intent and direction of his policies, and the policy management capacity of his administration. But Kim was hobbled from the beginning. He made it clear that he had no intention of appointing anyone from an entrenched group of the past to a key position in his government. Because the president excluded those who had served under previous governments, in order to assure the "civilian" government's identity and commitment to reform, the new president had only a limited number of persons from which to choose.

Since Kim Young Sam could provide no direct guidance to his ministers owing to his limited expertise in national affairs, the role of the presidential staff appeared to be far more important than in previous administrations. Blue House staffs were selected for "reform-mindedness," and their competence in managing national affairs remained questionable. His appointees turned out to be mainly idealistic and "less-experienced outsiders," or Kim loyalists. Kim's chief of staff, Park Kwan-yong, a close associate from Kim's days in the opposition trenches, had no experience in government. The eight senior presidential secretaries included two professors, two journalists, two bureaucrats-turned-politicians, and two lifelong dissidents. The two most important presidential advisers, the senior secretary for economic affairs, Park Jae-yoon, and the senior secretary for foreign affairs and national security, Chung Chong-uk, hailed from academia. In particular, the appointment of Kim Jung-nam as senior secretary for social and cultural affairs drew wide attention. He was a lifelong left-oriented dissident, and a central figure in the anti-government demonstrations of the 1970s and 1980s. Many junior staff members were former activists who had helped to fight authoritarian governments and had worked on Kim's presidential campaign. It was evident that the Blue House under Kim Young Sam would have difficulty developing sound policies, not to mention coordinating and monitoring their implementation.[8]

Kim's choice of cabinet members was also not promising. For instance, despite the increasing danger of a North Korean nuclear program, and even a North Korean collapse, his foreign policy team seemed alarmingly inexperienced: Han Wan-sang, a well-known dissident and sociology professor from Seoul National University, was appointed the unification minister; Han Sung-joo, a political science professor from Korea University, was selected as foreign minister; Kim Deok, another professor, was named director of the National Security Planning Agency (NSPA), a South Korean

---

[8] Among members of his high-ranking staff, there were some with only high school degrees. In the Kim Young Sam Blue House, 100 out of a staff of 500 were political supporters with no governmental experience. Han Wan-sang, the new unification minister stated flatly, "We do not need the experiences and lessons of the old days."

version of the CIA. The ministers of economic affairs were relatively more experienced, although two professors were included among them: of the ten economy-related ministers, five had bureaucratic backgrounds; the remaining five had no administrative experience. In fact, the economic team lacked focus and was susceptible to manipulation by presidential aides and politicians.[9]

Kim selected many political appointees from the narrow manpower reservoir of his personal networks. It was widely suspected that high-level posts had been distributed as rewards for loyalty. When he rose to power, he compensated faithfulness and loyalty by appointing his supporters to public posts, helped them become lawmakers, or disbursed political funds in their direction.[10] Despite their fresh image, the "outsiders" were often targets of criticism for their lack of ability and practical experience, their idiosyncratic remarks and behavior, and their progressive values. A foreign correspondent noted that "President Kim runs the risk of creating a wobbly government that rests on rhetoric rather than substance.... It is a cabinet striking for its lack of administrators."[11]

The appointment procedure was also unusual. There was no systematic, open screening process; the president never discussed candidates for important positions openly with his advisers, including his chief of staff, concealing his selections until the last moment. Kim did not trust the filed information on potential appointees. One of the key elements of his appointments was secrecy. The list of his appointments was given to his press secretary just twenty minutes before public announcement. Such a procedure was fraught with danger, as his selections were not informed by consultation with others. The press and the general public did not respond favorably to his appointments. Critics commented that appointment, rather than being "everything," was in fact a "disaster," noting that high posts were filled with those who had questionable integrity, records of accumulation of personal fortunes, or had strong personal ties with the president.[12] In short, Kim built a one-man leadership structure. He repeatedly pledged a strong government, but what he really meant was a strong presidency.

AN ALL-OUT REFORM DRIVE

The goals Kim Young Sam pursued would be crucial, not only for his presidency but for the nation as well. By the early 1990s South Korea had achieved both industrialization and democratization. The country was entering into a post-industrial stage. The world too was rapidly changing: the Cold War had ended and there was an accelerating trend

---

[9] See "Major Officials Profiled", *Yonhap News*, February 26, 1993.
[10] Chong-Bum Lee, "Traits of President Kim Young-sam's Leadership and National Management Style", *Proceedings of the Korean Public Administration Association* (spring 1994), 5-31; and Kang-no Lee, "Style of Kim Young Sam's Leadership", *Korea Journal of Political Science Association* 27:2 (1993): 145-163.
[11] Jae Hoon Shim, "South Korea: The Outs Are In—Kim Young Sam Appoints a New Cabinet", *Far Eastern Economic Review*, March 11, 1993.
[12] For example, see Lee Chul, "Kim Young Sam's Favoritism in Appointment Is the Barrier to Reform", *Wolgan Chosun* (May 1993): 134-140; Oh Sok Hong, "Is Appointment Everything or a Disaster?" *Shindonga* (October 1994): 218-223; and Kyung-hyo Park, "Minister- and Vice-Minister Level Staffing of the Kim Young-sam Administration", *Korea Journal*, 39:2 (summer 1999): 133-161.

toward globalization. South Korea's new leader was expected to provide a new vision for the twenty-first century.[13]

During his presidential campaign, Kim had pledged to forge a "new Korea." It was never clear what this "new Korea" would look like, or how it was to be created. In the tradition of the British leader Margaret Thatcher, Kim argued that his country had been suffering from a "Korean disease," which would be cured in the "new Korea." During his presidential campaign, Kim had also emphasized, "reform amid stability," appealing to both those who expected reform and change and those who preferred stability and continued economic growth. Following the election, Kim declared: "Genuine stability is achievable only when there is reform." In other words, reform was his primary goal. During the presidential election Kim had won more votes from Roh supporters than from his own former supporters. This signified a desire for stability and continuity. Yet despite this, the new president opted for a policy of radical reform rather than the pledged "reform amid stability." In his inaugural address of February 25, 1993, Kim Young Sam made his intentions clear:

> "Corruption in our society is the dreadful enemy that destroys the country little by little from within. There will be no sanctuary in eradicating corruption. We will stamp out all manner of improprieties and graft.... We should re-establish the discipline of the state.... When power comes into being by fraudulent means, the legitimacy of the state is infringed upon and law and order collapses.... There must be an end to the dark political night..."[14]

It was an inaugural speech glowing with confidence and optimism. Kim was rightly proud of himself; he was South Korea's first civilian president in thirty-two years. He emphasized that he was "the first legitimately elected" head of a Korean government. The unusual emphasis on "legitimacy" greatly affected his perceived role as president.[15] Implying his rejection of legitimacy of all previous governments, Kim repeatedly claimed that his government had inherited the legitimacy of the Korean Provisional Government in China, formed in 1919 in the wake of Japanese colonization, the April 1960 student uprising against Syngman Rhee, the May 1980 Kwangju uprising, and the 1987 democratic movements. In this way, he equated the launching of his government with "the second founding of the Korean Republic," consequently negating or, at the very least discrediting, the legitimacy and achievements of his predecessors—Syngman Rhee, Park Chung Hee, Chun Doo Hwan, and Roh Tae Woo. Kim and his associates believed that they had nothing to learn from the past. This led to their out-of-hand dismissal of any proffered advice and to rejection of the methods, organizations, and policies of their predecessors who were deemed to have tainted associations with former administrations.[16]

---

[13] For details of Kim's reform drive, see Deog Ryong Kim, "Reform and National Development", *Korea and World Affairs*, 17:3 (fall 1993): 405-418, Soong-Hoom Kil, "Political Reforms of the Kim Young Sam Government", *Korea and World Affairs*, 17:3 (fall 1993): 419-31, and Young Jo Lee, "The Rise and Fall of Kim Young Sam's Embedded Reformism", in Diamond and Shin, eds., *Institutional Reform*, 97-125.

[14] "Inaugural Address", the Presidential Secretariat (1995), 7-8.

[15] Kim Jung Nam, "*Moonmin jeongbunun hankuksaeseo mueosinga*" (Meaning of Civilian Government in Korean History), in Ham, ed. (2001), 189-200.

[16] Pfiffner worries about this problem after a transition or a party turnover. Kim, who was the candidate of the ruling party, acted like an opposition leader. (Pfiffner, *Strategic Presidency*, 1-5.)

After the presidential election, being proud of their democratic legitimacy and moral superiority, Kim Young Sam and his followers acted like sacred warriors, firmly believing they held the moral authority to eradicate the remnants of authoritarian governments and to transform society.[17] They seemed to believe that their democratic legitimacy could solve all of Korea's problems. After his inauguration, Kim became even more evangelical and dogmatic. Rather than trying to persuade the people to participate in his reform drive, he seemed to order the public to follow, often using "must" or "should" in his speeches.[18] Koreans had high expectations that things would be different from previous governments—more democratic, reform-oriented, and less corrupt.

Thus, Kim pursued reform as an end in itself (something akin to a religion) rather than as a means to an end. Many wondered what the ultimate direction of his reforms would be. One of his close aides commented, "The creation of a new Korea presumes segregation from the past. What matters are the remnants of the 30-year long authoritarian regimes that have hardened just as the Soviet system bequeathed by Stalin did. The authority and entrenched interests accumulated in the era of the development-oriented dictatorship still endure, and they are precisely the targets President Kim must bring down to be a president worthy of his name."[19]

But despite the difficult task of governance, Kim surrounded himself by long-term loyalists. The new president and his inexperienced advisers were hopeful and jubilant, not recognizing that they now faced a period of crisis. As Napoleon once noted, the aftermath of victory is the most dangerous. Kim and his associates suffered from hope and ignorance. The ignorance was born of inexperience while the hopefulness invited arrogance. The combination of high expectations and lack of experience led to serious mistakes. Before long, such naiveté put the country at risk.[20]

Immediately after assuming office Kim launched an all-out anticorruption campaign and made frugality a fashion statement. He started with moralistic and symbolic actions: closing the presidential golf driving range and swearing off golf for the duration of his five-year term, replacing gourmet meals with plain noodles at Blue House luncheons, and tearing down the guest villa near the Blue House (where Park Chung Hee had been assassinated). He also opened streets near the Blue House to pedestrian traffic and allowed hikers to climb Mt. Inwang, which flanks the presidential residence to the west. He was trying to conform to an old Korean proverb: "If water in the upper stream is clean, the water downstream will also be clean."[21] Through these symbolic actions he tried to present himself as a moralistic *yangban* leader: he was preaching the gospel of honest, upright government.[22]

During his first cabinet meeting on February 27, two days after his inauguration, the

---

[17] Kim Jung Nam, Kim's political ideologue during the early phase of his term, argued that "democratic forces" are "moralistic forces." Kim Jung Nam, *op. cit.*, 186.

[18] Oh, *Korean Politics*, 130.

[19] Kim Hyon Chong, *op. cit.*, 27.

[20] A leading American scholar of presidential studies, Richard Neustadt, warns of the danger. See Neustadt, *Presidential Power*, 233.

[21] "South Korea: Whirlwind Honeymoon", *Far Eastern Economic Review*, June 24, 1993.

[22] Chaibong Hahm, "The Confucian Tradition and Economic Reform", in Mo and Moon, eds., *Democracy and the Korean Economy*, 35-54.

president told his ministers and advisers that he would lead the anticorruption drive by making his personal assets public and encouraged them, as well as other high-ranking administration officials and all ruling party members, to make public their family assets as well. Then, in his first press conference on March 4, Kim announced, "I will not receive any money by way of political contributions during my term." No reform measure was more supported by the people than the disclosure of personal assets by ranking public officials and ruling party lawmakers. Kim rode a wave of popularity and support larger than any president in the history of modern Korea.[23]

Unfortunately, the disclosure undermined, rather than strengthened, the squeaky clean image of the new administration. The media sensationalized its reports of real estate holdings. The disclosures revealed considerable personal fortunes and triggered a public uproar that led to the downfall of several ministers and lawmakers. Only two weeks after their appointments, the president dismissed three ministers, five deputy ministers, and the mayor of Seoul, for making fortunes through allegedly illegal means. The replacements destroyed much of the good will the new president experienced during the early days of his term and cast doubt on his judgment. It was especially embarrassing given that during the election campaign he had repeatedly told voters that his strength lay in selecting the best and most qualified persons for government positions.[24] Critical observers raised serious questions about Kim's leadership. A leading opposition lawmaker criticized Kim's appointments in harsh terms, "All this trouble is the inevitable outgrowth of the way he rewarded his followers."[25]

The asset disclosures shook the country to its political foundations. Among those tainted by allegations of cheating, tax evasion and under-reporting, were leading politicians. Park Joon-kyu, speaker of the National Assembly, and fourteen other leading lawmakers, as well as Kim Jae-soon (Park's predecessor as speaker), were forced to declare their retirement from politics. Park and Kim felt a strong sense of betrayal toward the new president because they had played crucial roles in his election. Kim Jai-soon denounced President Kim, citing the proverb "after catching the hare, the hunter kills his hunting dog." There were corruption charges against the president's political enemies as well. The lawmaker Park Chul-un, who spearheaded the attack against Kim Young Sam during the intra-party squabbles, was tried for bribery and jailed. President Kim also forced Park Tae-joon, his rival in the bid for the Democratic Liberal Party's presidential nomination, to resign as honorary chairman of the government-owned Pohang Iron & Steel Co. (POSCO). Park was the legendary founder of POSCO and former co-chairman of the ruling party along with Kim Young Sam. Park fled to Japan to avoid standing trial and suffered the ignominy of seeing his house seized to pay tax evasion fines. Chung Ju-young, founder of the Hyundai business group and contender in the presidential election of 1992, was indicted on the charge of embezzling company funds to aid his campaign and sentenced to three years in prison. However, the sentence was suspended because Chung was seventy-seven years old. The anti-corruption drive hit

---

[23] For a general review of Kim's first year, see Chong-Sik Lee and Hyuk-Sang Sohn, "South Korea in 1993: The Year of Great Reform", *Asian Survey*, 34:1 (January 1994): 1-9.
[24] Jae Hoon Shim, "South Korea: Out of Office, Again", *Far Eastern Economic Review*, March 18, 1993.
[25] Ibid.

mainly figures from the past. Thus, the drive eliminated many of Kim's political enemies. Some observers believed that his campaign was politically motivated.[26]

The prosecutor general and the chief justice of the Supreme Court, the highest officials in the judiciary, were also forced to step down as was the head of the National Police. The purge extended to every corner of central and local government. Within three months of Kim's inauguration, nearly 1,000 public officials had been arrested, fired, or reprimanded.[27]

The disclosures of assets revealed no hard evidence of wrongdoing under South Korean laws, drawing criticism that the president was running the country (in terms of personal property and privacy rights) according to the arbitrary rule of one man rather than the rule of law.[28] The steep sums involved had been largely accumulated by astronomical real estate appreciation during the three decades of rapid urbanization and economic growth. The combination of sensationalist media reporting and emotional public response exerted strong pressures on anyone with substantial assets. The circumstances under which the disclosures were carried out could be described almost as revolutionary. This led some observers to question whether reform-minded zealots in the administration had begun to equate wealth with guilt. "This is something akin to a revolution, a kangaroo court trial where being rich is looked at as a sin," complained a ruling party lawmaker. As matter of fact, President Kim said, "I will make suffer those who have big assets."[29] In May 1993, the National Assembly revised the Public Officials' Ethics Law to require cabinet members, legislators, and other high-ranking government officials to register and disclose their assets on an annual basis.

Confident of his legitimacy and popularity, Kim Young Sam then carried his anticorruption drive straight to the once sacrosanct South Korean military, purging senior officers, especially those closely linked to former presidents Chun and Roh.[30] On the morning of March 8, 1993, President Kim called in his defense minister for breakfast at the Blue House. The new president got to the point, "Now that I am finished with cabinet appointments, I would like to deal with military assignments." Kim then asked, "Don't military generals submit resignations when a president takes office?"

"No, Mr. President." the defense minister replied, and he explained the procedure followed in military assignments. After hearing the minister's explanation, Kim then directed him, "I want the army chief of staff, General Kim Jin-young, and the commander of the Defense Security Command (DSC), Lieutenant General Suh Wan-soo, replaced."[31]

It was the beginning of a military shake up. Although Kim had little knowledge of military affairs, and no clear idea of how to strengthen the armed forces, he was determined

---

[26] Clifford, *op cit.*, 334-338.
[27] Chong-Sik Lee and Hyuk-Sang Sohn, *op. cit.*, 3.
[28] Chu Don-Shik, *Munmin jeongbu chunyibaekil* (One Thousand Two Hundred Days of the Civilian Government) (Seoul: Saram kwa Chaek, 1997), 17.
[29] *Joongang Ilbo*, March 13, 1993.
[30] For details of Kim's purges in the military, see June Hyoung Rhie, "Civilianization of the Military under Kim's Rule: Performance and Prospects", *Pacific Focus*, X: 1 (spring 1995): 129-14.
[31] Donga Ilbosa (1999), vol. 1, 22-24.

to establish firm control over the military. The summary removal of two such important officers administered a tremendous shock to the military. But sudden and alarming personnel shifts and replacements, including the chiefs of staff of the other military branches, soon followed. One commentator equated it to a "great massacre."[32] In May 1993 President Kim declared that the incident of December 12, 1979, that ultimately led Chun Doo Hwan to power, had been illegal, and he removed four generals, including the chairman of the Joint Chiefs of Staff, for taking part in the incident. The government also disclosed a list of 142 army officers who were members of a private army clique called Hanahoe (One Society), and forced their retirement. The government in its first 100 days replaced five of eight top defense ministry officials, nine of eleven senior Joint Chiefs of Staff officials, eleven of fourteen senior army posts, five of eleven corps commanders, nine of twenty-two division commanders, seven of eleven navy senior officers, and four of the top ten air force officers. The government purged more than 1,000 military officers in its first year.[33]

Although the shake-up achieved civil supremacy over the military, it disrupted the command system and seriously damaged the morale and combat readiness of the troops. The timing of his move against the military leadership hardly appeared propitious in view of the mounting tension on the peninsula after Pyongyang had bolted from the nuclear nonproliferation treaty. In addition to concern over the North's nuclear development, the South Korean military were anxious about the semi-state of war alert in effect in the North, a state which now boasted the world's fourth-largest armed forces. North Korea's economic crisis, food shortages, and international isolation had made Pyongyang more desperate than ever. Observers worried that North Korea might lash out militarily because of its domestic crisis.

People in the street lauded Kim's anticorruption drives. The dissident-turned-president had become the most popular leader in Korean history. According to a joint poll by the *Chosun Ilbo* and Gallup Korea, Kim's approval rating was 90 percent in April 1993, 88 percent in May, and 79 percent in August. Kim became extremely confident, and seemed to believe there was nothing he could not reform. But lawmakers, policymakers and businessmen were unsettled. "Is this good for the country or is it another form of dictatorship?" asked an aide to Kim Dae Jung. "How far do you go in order to conduct reform, and what definition of corruption do you use?"[34] Although the public was enthusiastic about the massive purges, their cynicism and their distrust of government and politics had deepened.

While Kim indulged himself in purging South Korea of its "big shots," he failed to tackle more serious issues such as market-opening pressures under the Uruguay Round of trade negotiations and the North Korean nuclear challenge. Just a year earlier, candidate Kim had pledged to step down from office rather than open up the home market to imported rice. Before his departure for the trade negotiations in Geneva,

---

[32] *Chosun Ilbo*, March 9, 1993; and Victor D. Cha, "Politics and Democracy under the Kim Young Sam Government: Something Old, Something New", *Asian Survey* 33:9 (1993): 860.

[33] Donga Ilbosa (1999), vol. 1, 36-49; and Jung Kwan Cho, "Taming the Military to Consolidate Democracy: The South Korean Experience", *Pacific Focus*, 16 (spring 2001).

[34] Steve Glain, "South Korea's Corruption Crackdown Hinders Economy It Seeks to Clean Up", *Wall Street Journal*, September 17, 1993.

Agriculture Minister Huh Shin-haeng solemnly promised, "I will not allow a bushel of foreign rice in the Korean market."[35] However, Korea, already a major trading power, had to accept the Uruguay Round agreement that required broader opening of the South Korean market. In response, angry farmers and students stormed the streets of Seoul and other major cities. Openly declaring, "The only way for our country to prosper is through openness and reform," President Kim accepted the humiliation of apologizing to the nation.[36] As a result, the government faced a potential crisis of confidence. In order to thwart the crisis, on December 21, 1993, barely ten months after the inauguration of the first cabinet, Kim sacked fourteen of his twenty-two ministers.

In addition to the anti-corruption drive, institutional reforms were necessary to consolidate democracy. The appointment of a professor as director of the National Security Planning Agency (former KCIA), was the most significant signal of President Kim's determination for reform. The new director was given the task of depoliticizing the powerful agency. On his second day in office the director recalled NSPA agents operating inside social, political, or economic organizations throughout the nation and ordered them to adhere strictly to their legally defined activities. President Kim also ordered the Defense Security Command (DSC) not to meddle in activities unrelated to military affairs. In January 1994 President Kim asked the National Assembly to revise laws governing activities of the two security agencies, thereby forcing them to "leave politics" and return to their original missions. For the first time in more than three decades these two powerful agencies became subject to parliamentary oversight and were prohibited from conducting political surveillance over other branches of government, public officials, or private citizens. Those measures to depoliticize and downsize the security agencies established the unchallenged supremacy of civilian rule.[37]

The purification drive was backed up by a set of economic reforms that directly challenged the sources of corruption. In a nationally televised statement on August 12, 1993, President Kim, six months into office, issued an extraordinary presidential decree declaring: "From this time on, all financial transactions have to be made under real names to realize a clean and just society. Without real-name financial accounts, a sound democracy cannot flower."[38] The decree banned anonymous bank accounts and required the mandatory use of real names in all financial transactions. The "real-name" financial reform, subsequently approved by the National Assembly, aimed to dismantle the structure of political corruption by severing the collusive links between politics and business. Less attention was paid to its impact on the economy. Kim chose to exercise the decree power reserved for the president by 1983 legislation enacted during the Chun Doo Hwan administration. This legislation provided that the timing of a full-scale implementation of "the real-name system" was to be

---

[35] *Chosun Ilbo*, December 3, 1993.
[36] *Joongang Ilbo*, December 9, 1993.
[37] Larry Diamond and Doh Chull Shin, "Introduction", in Diamond and Shin, eds. (2000), 10-11. The new NSPA director promised he would boldly do away with political surveillance. However, important posts in the NSPA, equivalent to the cabinet vice minister level, were occupied by members of Kim's inner circle. See Uh Jong-chang, "Kim Loyalists Take High Posts in ANSP", *Wolgan Chosun* (March 1993): 30-32.
[38] *Joongang Ilbo*, August 12, 1993.

determined by presidential decree sometime after January 1986.[39] Kim's surprising decree was possible because his plan was kept secret right up to the moment of its announcement. Because many officials, including Kim's own economic adviser, were opposed to the plan, they were kept in the dark until the moment of its announcement.[40]

The early timing of Kim's decree took the nation by surprise. The economy had hardly begun to improve when the decree was announced, and the decree risked further weakening the economy. Nevertheless, the measure was hailed in both domestic and foreign media as a key to transparency in all economic transactions. It was expected that the policy would improve transparency in *chaebol* management and limit political financing and political kickbacks by the *chaebol*. The system also made it difficult to establish "slush funds" that were used as political kickbacks and bribes to government officials and politicians. In other words, the reform was regarded as a significant step toward achieving a clean political system. In March 1994 the National Assembly enacted the new Real-name Real Estate Registration Law. Building on the 1993 Real-name Financial Transaction Law, the new law required the use of real names in the registration of all real estate parcels. These two laws, together with the Public Officials' Ethics Law, represent perhaps the most important pieces of anticorruption legislation in any East Asian country.[41]

During the second year of his presidency, Kim extended his reform drive to the political arena.[42] In March 1994 the National Assembly revised existing laws on elections, campaign financing, and local autonomy. To ensure freer, cleaner, and more frugal elections, the new Comprehensive Election Law increased government subsidies to campaigns and fixed allowances for politicians with strict upper limits on what politicians could spend. When coupled with the "real-name" financial reforms, the government appeared to have made it substantially harder to exceed spending limits.

REFORMS FOR A "NEW ECONOMY"

The most salient issue during the 1992 presidential campaign was the sluggish economy. Kim Young Sam promised that if elected he would make economic revitalization one of his top priorities. His experience, however, was basically limited to that of a dissident leader; he had little, if any, experience in economic issues. Throughout his career he had shown no interest in or concern with economic matters. He paid little attention even to the economy of his own household. Since becoming an assemblyman at the age of twenty-five, he had devoted his life to politics. His father, who was engaged in fisheries, financially supported his family.

---

[39] For details of the real-name financial system, see Soogil Young, "Korea's Financial Reform: Reshaping Society", *International Economic Insights*, V: 1 (Washington, D.C.: Institute for International Economics, January/February 1994); and Jongsoo Lee, "The Real Name Financial System and the Politics of Economic Reforms in the Republic of Korea", *Pacific Focus*, X:1 (spring 1995): 101-127.

[40] *Wolgan Chosun* (September 1993): 96-117.

[41] Diamond and Shin, *op. cit.*, 13-14.

[42] Chu Don-shik, *op. cit.*, 121-136; and Kim Young Sam, *Kim Young Sam daetongryong hoegorok* (Autobiography of Kim Young Sam) (Seoul: Chosun Ilbosa, 2001), 249-259.

Since his inauguration, Kim had displayed a remarkable lack of understanding of economic issues. In particular, he simply did not comprehend the sweeping changes engulfing South Korea brought on by globalization, and advisers and ministers were also not qualified to deal with these challenges. Many people were skeptical of Kim's capacity to manage economic policy; they believed he had few qualifications to make an accurate diagnosis of economic problems, or to offer solutions.[43]

At that time the Korean economy faced two contradictory challenges—globalization from without and democratization from within. With the end of the Cold War, the international economic environment was rapidly changing; the erosion of ideological barriers made international competition fiercer. Conclusion of the Uruguay Round negotiations in December 1993 resulted in the creation of the World Trade Organization and a set of rules that guaranteed freedom of investment and trade in all industrial sectors, including agriculture and services. That same year, the first summit meeting of the Asia Pacific Economic Conference (APEC) accelerated the process of economic globalization. The explosion of the Chinese economy provided an additional challenge to South Korea.

The acceleration and intensification of globalization posed serious challenges to a trading nation like South Korea. Korean products were already losing their competitiveness in the international market. With an extremely high trade/GDP ratio of 73 percent, Korea could not escape the payoffs and penalties of globalization. The South Korean economy needed to be fundamentally restructured in order to adapt to the emerging global economy. The danger associated with full exposure to foreign competition was serious. There was no quick fix for the challenges posed by globalization that would not entail economic disaster and serious political risks.

There was also a basic contradiction at work: while democratization pushed for reforms in favor of distribution, social welfare, and quality of life, globalization emphasized continuing growth and international competitiveness. How to balance two such conflicting imperatives provided a serious policy conundrum to the new Kim government.[44]

As part of his campaign strategy, and in an effort to maintain his popularity, Kim Young Sam had made it clear that he cared more about short-term economic growth than long-term economic stability and international competitiveness, abandoning Roh's stabilization program. Entering the Blue House, Kim pushed aside key long-term economic reforms and issued a number of expansionary economic policies meant to revive the economy, including a 100-day New Economy Plan. Highlights of the plan were cuts in bank interest rates and a proposal for a "more flexible" monetary policy in order to encourage business investment.

Earlier in January, then president-elect Kim had already forced the Roh administration to slash interest rates by three percentage points to fulfill his election campaign pledge to relieve a serious cash shortage among businesses. After its inauguration, the Kim government forced the governor of the Bank of Korea, Cho Soon, who had three more years left in his term, to resign. Cho, a renowned academic and former deputy prime

---

[43] Kirk, *Korean Crisis*, 43ff.
[44] Chung-in Moon, "Democratization and Globalization as Ideological and Political Foundations of Economic Policy", in Mo and Moon, eds. (1999), 1-13.

minister, had been at odds with president-elect Kim over the interest rate cuts. A senior researcher at the Bank of Korea expressed great concern over the inflationary pressures of the policy and warned that high inflation and a huge trade deficit could reappear as a result of the growth-oriented policy.[45]

In July 1993, the Kim government announced its Five-Year New Economy Plan (1993-97), which superseded the ongoing seventh Five-Year Economic and Social Development Plan (1992-96). The revised plan aimed at expanding the country's growth potential and solidifying the foundations of international trade. The nation's GNP was projected to grow at 7 percent annually, while the rise in consumer prices would be limited to 3.7 percent. The government also aimed to achieve a trade balance by 1995.[46] The spirit and scope of the plan were ambitious and encouraging, but details were lacking, and the implementation of key economic reforms, such as financial reform, corporate restructuring and labor reform, was not scheduled until 1996 and 1997. Thus, the policy invited the criticism that economic stability and fundamental restructuring were to be sacrificed for short-term growth. As one foreign diplomat commented, "there was no clear plan for the economy."[47]

Kim Young Sam was preoccupied with the anticorruption drive and had little time for economic troubles. He delegated most of the economic decision-making authority to his advisers and cabinet members. The economic team, neither particularly capable nor teamwork-oriented, was reshuffled ten months later.

Kim's slogan for the year 1994 was "strengthening international competitiveness."[48] Kim and his advisers seemed to believe that the business sector was more competitive than the government, and that the ropes of international competitiveness could be learned from the *chaebol*. The government asked some *chaebol* groups, such as Samsung, to set up special education programs for government officials. The idea was to show government what businesses do to strengthen international competitiveness. Some 1,500 high-ranking officials, including members of the Blue House staff, went to *chaebol* training institutes. As far as I remembers, the presentations were mostly business-related.[49] From the perspective of a government official, the education program was almost pointless since government and business have fundamental differences in goals and missions. Most of the participants were left disappointed or frustrated. Although reform was the "national goal," Kim and his advisers failed to provide a clear philosophy or guidelines for that goal.[50]

As part of its goal to enhance international competitiveness, the government promoted deregulation and liberalization. Although liberalization reduced governmental

---

[45] "Seeking to Regain Growth Potential", *Business Korea*, April 1993.
[46] Chong-Sik Lee and Hyuk-Sang Sohn, *op. cit.*, 5.
[47] Steve Glain, "South Korea's Corruption Crackdown Hinders Economy", *Wall Street Journal*, September 17, 1993.
[48] The presidential staff borrowed the concept from a report published in late 1993 by the Samsung Economic Research Institute.
[49] The author, with some fifty other officials of the Blue House, went to the training institute of Samsung Electronics in Suwon and spent a whole day. Many officials lacked any interest in listening to the speakers. Some of the officials were sleeping during the presentations.
[50] Yoo-Lim Lee, "Bureaucrats Learn from Local Business Leaders", *Business Korea* (March 1994).

intervention, it made it easier to "bend the rules" for political reasons. While bureaucratic intervention significantly weakened, political intervention dramatically increased. For example, the government allowed Samsung to enter the car-making business, thereby deepening over-investment in the South Korean auto industry. For economic reasons, Kim's chief economic adviser (Park Jae-yoon) and the minister of commerce and industry (Kim Chul-soo) at first opposed Samsung's entry into the automobile business. But they were under strong pressure from President Kim's close associates, many of whom came from Pusan, Kim's support base.[51] The Samsung Group submitted a shrewd plan to build a huge car-making plant near Pusan. At the time, the Pusan region was suffering a decline in its major industries, such as textiles and shoe manufacturing, owing to rising labor costs. As a result, political support for the Kim government in the region had dwindled. It was thus not surprising that the local constituency welcomed Samsung's proposal and pressured President Kim and his associates to support the plan. In order to ensure strong support in the coming elections, the government decided to offer a big gift to the region. In December 1994, the commerce and industry minister and the chief economic adviser were replaced, and within a few months Samsung was allowed to go into the auto-making business.

The rapidly emerging global economy required fundamental restructuring of the South Korean *chaebol*. But how could the *chaebol* downsize when they were the very entities with the capabilities needed for global investments for Kim's vision of enhancing international competitiveness? Apparently, Kim was unable to diagnose the real causes of the "Korean disease" (the *chaebol* problem). Owing to Kim's lack of understanding of economic issues and to aggressive lobbying by businesses, the economic policies of the Kim administration were overwhelmingly pro-*chaebol*. Measures to enhance global competitiveness allowed the big *chaebol* to expanded their businesses into often unrelated sectors and thus to overextend themselves. "Economies of scale" were emphasized for key sectors, which allowed some corporations to become multinational, acquiring government support and subsidies. Korea analyst Nicholas Eberstadt noted, "The Kim Young Sam government doesn't have a way to restructure the economy in any way that the *chaebol* don't have an enormous role."[52] The Kim administration, without enunciating a pro-*chaebol* policy, might actually have been more pro-*chaebol* than the preceding Chun and Roh governments.[53]

In an effort to adapt to the changing international economic order, on November 17, 1994, President Kim suddenly announced a globalization (*segyehwa*) policy. The announcement was made in Sydney, on the heels of his participation in the APEC meeting

---

[51] I attended many Blue House senior staff meetings. On several occasions debates between Park and other politically oriented staff members broke out. In response to President Kim's plunging popularity in the Pusan region, most senior members strongly supported providing Samsung with the necessary licenses to enter the auto business and pressured Park to give in. During a National Assembly hearing in January 1999, a lawmaker of the new ruling party (Millennium Democratic Party) accused the Kim Young Sam government of giving Samsung a license to obtain political gains ahead of the important elections. See "Lawmakers Say Former Government Favored Samsung for Auto Business", *Korea Herald*, January 23, 1999.
[52] Kirk, *Korean Crisis*, 74.
[53] Eun Mee Kim, "Reforming the *Chaebols*", in Diamond and Shin, eds. (2000), 171-183; Catherine Lee, "Unfinished Business", *Business Week*, September 9, 1996.

in Indonesia. His initial declaration stated that the globalization policy was meant "to brace the nation for cascading developments and sweeping changes in the world, to build the Republic into a first-rate nation in the coming century" by opening Korea to the world "in all fields including political, economic, and social activities," and by meeting "the global standards of excellence in all areas."[54] Kim made globalization the leading doctrine for national governance in the second half of his term. The Blue House spokesman said, "President Kim would like to be remembered for two things: his anticorruption drive and globalization."[55] Nevertheless, the task of globalization was proving difficult to define, and more so to accomplish.

Globalization means more uncertainty and an increasing complexity of decision making in the government. It also means intense international competition; globalization is thus seen as a threat by weak or capriciously governed states. Any mistake in policy is felt immediately. Therefore, effective government policy is essential for successful globalization. A state's ability to promote international competitiveness and to achieve economic growth may require particular conditions: a strong and effective government, autonomy from societal pressures, and high levels of political and bureaucratic unity. It was evident that the Korean government lacked most of these conditions. But the government was not seriously concerned about the immediate risks and dangers of globalization.[56]

On December 3, 1994, in an effort to support his globalization strategy, Kim Young Sam carried out a comprehensive government reorganization. The government eliminated two cabinet posts, three deputy ministerial positions, and twenty-three other high-ranking jobs. According to the Blue House spokesman, the aim of the reorganization was "a smaller but more efficient government in an age of global economy."[57] The office of senior secretary for policy planning was created at the Blue House to assist in the formulation of globalization policy. The highlight of the reorganization was the merger of the Finance Ministry with the Economic Planning Board (EPB) into the Ministry of Finance and Economy (MOFE), in charge of fiscal, budgetary, and other economic functions. This made economic planning and coordination more difficult. The powerful role of the EPB in national economic policymaking, which it had enjoyed for the past three decades, was significantly reduced. On December 21, 1994, only a year after the earlier cabinet reshuffle, Kim replaced the prime minister and seventeen other ministers in an attempt to make the government more "suited for the pursuit of globalization strategies."[58]

A Presidential *Segyehwa* Promotion Commission, chaired by prime minister Lee Hong-Koo, was established in January 1995 with a mandate to give shape and substance to globalization visions and goals that had been broadly delineated in the preceding weeks.[59]

---

[54] *Chosun Ilbo*, November 18, 1994.

[55] *Joongang Ilbo*, February 3, 1995.

[56] Yeon-ho Lee, "The Failure of the Weak State in Economic Liberalization: Liberalization, Democratization and the Financial Crisis in South Korea", *Pacific Review*, 13:1 (2000): 116-131.

[57] *Joongang Ilbo*, December 3, 1994.

[58] *Korea Times*, December 22, 1994.

[59] The Committee, headed by the prime minister, consisted of a set of committees on policy planning, administrative reform, educational reform, and science and technology. Its membership was composed of representatives from government ministries, research institutes, academia, and "socially eminent persons."

When the *segyehwa* commission met for the first time on January 25, President Kim identified a broad set of priority targets for globalization—"education, the legal and economic orders, politics and the news media, national and local administration, environment, culture and consciousness."[60] In August, after six months of study and debate, the *segyehwa* promotion committee prepared a plan. In the plan, the committee recommended economic, industrial relations, welfare, political, judiciary, environmental, and administrative reforms.[61] Accepting the recommendations, Kim ordered the establishment of presidential committees on economic, industrial relations, and judiciary reforms.

In August 1996, Kim again reshuffled his cabinet and Blue House staff and appointed conservatives to key positions, including the position of senior secretary for economic affairs. The new senior secretary for economic affairs, Lee Suk-chae, was a career technocrat from the Economic Planning Board, which had led the "growth first" policy for three decades. From the time of his appointment, there were serious disputes between Lee Suk-chae and the senior secretary for social development, Park Se-il, a former professor who emphasized redistribution and welfare.[62] But the president had no priorities in his globalization reform. The *segyehwa* reforms lost their momentum almost immediately. As a result, *segyehwa* was seen as nothing more than a political slogan. A globalization strategy requires "strategic choices."[63] Strategic choices involve not only prioritizing one set of policy goals over another, but also speed and logical sequence of prioritized reforms. The Kim government was pursuing two contradictory goals at the same time: quality-of-life reforms (educational, welfare, and labor reforms) and reforms for globalization (liberalization and economic competitiveness).

In an effort to make South Korea an advanced nation and to accelerate segyehwa reforms, in March 1995 Kim Young Sam decided his country should join the Organization for Economic Cooperation and Development (OECD), a Paris-based organization of industrialized states. Accession to the OECD was in fact motivated by Kim's political ambitions; although it was decorated with numerous economic reasons, the decision was not based on a purely economic rationale. The president thought it would be a significant political achievement of his term. In other words, South Korea would become a developed nation acknowledged by the international community via accession to the OECD. Kim also believed that OECD membership would contribute to the successful implementation of his globalization policy and to his party's platform as it went into the 1996 parliamentary and 1997 presidential elections.

However, an admission to the OECD club meant accelerating deregulation, a change that would bring greater competition with foreign firms, especially in the then-restricted financial markets. While some saw opening up as a solution to the country's economic problems, others believed the policy would worsen rather than cure the disease. Given the economic condition of South Korea, the risk of drastic internationalization was

---

[60] The Presidential Secretariat (1995), "The Blueprint for Globalization", 268-273.
[61] Presidential Segyehwa Promotion Committee, *Segyehwa ui bijeon kwa jeongchaek* (Globalization Vision and Strategy) (Seoul, August 1995).
[62] Se-Il Park, Reforming Labor Management Relations: Lessons from the Korean Experience (1996-97) (Seoul: KDI, 2000), 41-47; and Jeon Sung-Chul (2001), 124-169.
[63] Barry K. Gills and Dongsook S. Gills, "Globalization and Strategic Choice in South Korea: Economic Reform and Labor", in Samuel S. Kim, ed., *Korea's Globalization*, 29-53.

obvious. In fact, opening the national economy as fast as the OECD desired entailed major risks. Thus, economic bureaucrats, taking a more realistic view of the constraints that OECD membership imposed, were less enthusiastic about joining the organization than President Kim and his advisers. Those officials were concerned that too much "hot money," or speculative funds, sloshing in and out of the country could destabilize the economy. Mexico suffered a financial crisis several months after its entry into the OECD.[64] At the time, South Korea's conditions for globalization were deteriorating owing to: a growing trade deficit, dwindling foreign exchange reserves, and sharp increases in short-term foreign debts. Nonetheless, the government overemphasized the positive aspects of OECD membership.

As a condition of entry, the OECD demanded strict terms under which South Korea had to liberalize its economy and completely open its domestic markets, including the financial market, according to an agreed upon timetable. The United States announced that if South Korea agreed to financial liberalization, it would support its entry. But after having been so eager to join, the Kim government found itself being pressed to open up faster than it would have liked. As demanded by the OECD, in order to gain membership by December 1996, the South Korean government dramatically liberalized its foreign trade, banking and financial systems, and its foreign investment regimes. Especially in relation to foreign borrowing, an area that had traditionally been tightly controlled by the government, liberalization was considerable, and now there were virtually no restrictions. Many questioned whether Korean industries and banks could withstand open international competition, and whether Korean businesses had the discipline to attain a favorable trade balance when international trade restrictions were removed.[65]

Opening its financial market was challenging: South Korea was one of the most closed economies to foreign direct investment in Asia. Meanwhile, Korea's trade deficit increased dramatically and the current account deficit hit $24 billion in 1996, double that of 1995. Foreigners were eager to fund the deficit by investing in Korean stock and bond markets. The amount of South Korea's foreign loans doubled between 1994, when the country received its first signal to become an OECD member, and 1996, when its membership was officially granted.[66] Korea's OECD membership led the international financial community to assume that bank loans to the country carried no risk of default.[67]

The Kim government's choice of a capital liberalization process was a big mistake. The government found deregulation of long-term foreign direct investment too challenging, so it opened up short-term capital flows at a faster rate. The government paid no attention to the preconditions for financial liberalization, such as effective banking supervision and strong financial institutions. As part of financial liberalization, the government permitted the transformation of as many as twenty-four small investment and finance companies into merchant banks—nine of them in 1994 and

---

[64] David Pearson, "South Korea Faces Many Obstacles in Its Bid for OECD Membership", *Wall Street Journal*, March 30, 1995.
[65] Kim Joong-woong, "Korea's OECD Entry and the Road Ahead", *Korea Focus*, 4:5 (1996): 61-64. An editorial in a leading daily paper was concerned about the "challenges" of the "OECD era." See *Hankook Ilbo*, October 12, 1996, 3.
[66] *Joongang Ilbo*, April 11, 1998.
[67] *New York Times*, December 22, 1997.

fifteen of them in 1996, in contrast to the total of six that existed before 1994.[68] There was a controversy surrounding the granting of coveted licenses to operate merchant banks. It was later discovered that merchant bankers bribed those closely associated with President Kim to obtain licenses.[69] Moreover, the government allowed the inexperienced merchant banks to conduct international financial business, resulting in a rapid increase of short-term foreign loans.

In 1995, Korea's per-capita annual income was more than $10,000. A per capita income of $10,000 had symbolic importance for the government. This income was seen as the standard for an advanced country. The government could now brag that the country had achieved a per capita income of $10,000 during the Kim Young Sam administration. But in order to achieve a per capita income figure of $10,000, the government had artificially overvalued the South Korean *won*, triggering huge trade deficits. In October 1996 Korea achieved its long-held goal of membership in the OECD, the first East Asian country after Japan to join. The Kim government celebrated. Membership meant international recognition of South Korea's tremendous achievements since embarking on its First Five-Year Plan in 1962 with a per-capita income of only $87.

Bringing the country's political and economic institutions up to the level of those in advanced countries had now become an urgent task for South Korea. To open up its financial market—a condition of OECD entry—on January 10, 1997, President Kim announced the establishment of the Financial Reform Committee. The committee presented its final report to the president in early June, and the president approved most of the recommendations and instructed the Ministry of Finance and Economy to draw up legislation for the National Assembly. Some thirteen financial reform bills were submitted to the National Assembly during the summer, but without the president's strong commitment the assembly approved only four of the thirteen bills. The financial reform measures were not only too marginal but too late to deter the ongoing financial crisis.

Kim's globalization drive started with a bang but ended with a whimper. According to all economic indicators, during his five-year term in office South Korea's performance declined noticeably. The greatest irony of all was the fact that Korea's globalization ranking dropped from eleventh place among the fifteen emerging markets in 1993 to last place among the forty-six advanced and emerging market economies in the world in 1998. Its global competitiveness ranking also dropped from sixth place in 1993 to thirty-fifth place in 1998.[70]

THE NORTH KOREAN CRISIS

Kim Young Sam, an unskilled leader in national security and foreign policy, assumed office when relations with North Korea were at a low point. During his long political career as a dissident, his attention had always been focused on domestic politics; as a result he was considered somewhat naïve about external affairs.

The post-Cold War international environment was uncertain and challenging for South

---

[68] Five of the nine merchant banks were approved in the home region of President Kim Young Sam.
[69] Stephen Vines, "Financial Bribery Scandal Adds to Korea's Troubles", *The Independent*, April 16, 1998.
[70] International Institute for Management and Development, *World Competitiveness Yearbook 1998* (Lausanne, Switzerland).

Korea, because North Korea had become unstable and unpredictable. Following the demise of the Soviet Union and other socialist countries and West Germany's absorption of East Germany, many observers predicted that North Korea would face the same fate in the immediate future.[71] Members of the North Korean ruling circle had gone into shock and avoiding "absorption" had become their obsession. While South Koreans were distracted by the country's anti-corruption drive, a serious security crisis was brewing on the peninsula. Around the time of Kim's inauguration, the International Atomic Energy Agency (IAEA) found significant discrepancies between Pyongyang's initial report to the IAEA and the findings of six rounds of inspections. Increasing suspicion over the North's intentions drove the IAEA to ask for a special inspection of the North's two undeclared sites in Yongbyon, but North Korea resisted such an inspection.

Despite the growing menace of the North Korean nuclear issue, Kim Young Sam felt a compelling urge to make a breakthrough in inter-Korean relations during his term. In his inaugural address he surprised the nation and its allies by declaring, "No foreign ally can be equal in importance to our ethnic brethren in the North. No ideology can bring greater happiness than national kinship," and held out an olive branch to Kim Il Sung, proposing to meet him "at any time and in any place."[72] The remark, which implied a higher priority to South Korea's reconciliation with the North than with its alliance with the United States, created something of a sensation both at home and abroad. Kim Young Sam believed that a real breakthrough was only possible through a South-North summit. At his first Blue House meeting as president, Kim expressed his strong hope that a real breakthrough in the relations with the North would be accomplished during his term.[73]

With his lack of grounding in foreign and national security policies, President Kim was very dependent upon his foreign policy team. As described earlier, however, his initial foreign policy team was composed of former college professors who themselves had no experience in public service, but with different views ranging from radical to moderate. Considering the tremendous external challenges confronting the nation at the time, the appointment of the academics drew extraordinary concern. The deputy prime minister and concurrently unification minister, Han Wan-sang, a former campus radical and dissident accused of being a lackey for the regime in Pyongyang, was leader of the foreign policy team. During his first press conference as minister, he declared, "Cold War logic should be overcome by all means."[74] He had shown a sympathetic posture toward North Korea that was unprecedented for a senior official, and promoted a progressive policy in inter-Korean relations. Very soon, a private emissary from the

---

[71] Kyung-Won Kim, "No Way Out: North Korea's Impending Collapse", *Harvard International Review*, XVIII:2 (spring 1996); and Choong Nam Kim, "The Uncertain Future of North Korea: Soft Landing or Crash Landing", *Korea and World Affairs*, 21:4 (winter 1996): 623-636.

[72] The Presidential Secretariat (1995), "Inaugural Address", 9. The controversial sentence was originally suggested by Han Wan-sang and Kim Jung-nam, both of whom had been well-known dissidents, on the committee preparing President Kim's inaugural address. The author, who was a participant in the committee, pointed out the problems with the controversial sentence.

[73] Interview with Chung Chong-wook, on April 16, 2002.

[74] Steve Glain, "Maverick Minister", *Asian Wall Street Journal*, August 10, 1993.

North visited Han to tell him that Pyongyang had been favorably impressed.[75]

The Kim government, in an act initiated by the unification minister, tried to appease Pyongyang by repatriating Lee In-mo, a seventy-six-year-old North Korean prisoner of war. Lee was a North Korean reporter captured during the Korean War.[76] However, Kim Young Sam was betrayed by Pyongyang. On March 12, 1993, a day after Lee In-mo crossed the "bridge of no return" in Panmunjom, and fourteen days after Kim's inauguration, North Korea announced that it had "no choice but to withdraw from the Nuclear Nonproliferation Treaty (NPT)." The Kim government was deeply shocked and unprepared for such a foreign policy crisis. Kim's security adviser later recalled: "We had never imagined such a serious North Korean challenge as the withdrawal from the NPT."[77] The North Korean move raised new concerns about Pyongyang's suspected nuclear weapons program and heightened tension on the peninsula. Pyongyang's move exposed a weak link in Kim's three-week-old administration, something which deeply concerned the South Korean military and the general public.

Nevertheless, the pro-North Korean unification minister doggedly pursued direct talks with Pyongyang and advocated economic aid to defuse the crisis. He planned to send a delegation of business leaders to North Korea for economic cooperation. While the United States and its allies discussed sanctions against North Korea, the South Korean unification minister was talking about reconciliation and cooperation. The minister angered not only the conservatives but the general public as well. Kim's foreign policy team seemed conspicuously unseasoned.[78]

The Kim government had no well-planned policy toward North Korea; it tended to react to Washington's North Korea policy. It was also nervous about the possibility of direct negotiations between Washington and Pyongyang. The Clinton administration aimed to bring North Korea back into full compliance with its NPT obligations. In New York on June 2, 1993, the United States and North Korea initiated a series of meetings to resolve the crisis. Ten days later they issued a joint statement, which included a U.S. security guarantee to North Korea, a pledge of continued dialogue between the two countries, and suspension of Pyongyang's withdrawal from the NPT. The statement ignited a firestorm of debate and a sense of urgency in Seoul, which believed Washington had conceded too much to Pyongyang.[79] Very sensitive to his popularity at home, Kim criticized any U.S.-North Korea negotiations without South Korean participation. On July 1, during an interview with *The New York Times*, Kim criticized the expected U.S.-North Korea nuclear talks, charging that the North Koreans were manipulating the negotiations "to buy time to finish their projects."[80] The public denouncement by the

---

[75] Joel S. Wit, Daniel B. Poneman, and Robert L. Gallucci, *Going Critical: The First North Korean Nuclear Crisis* (Washington, D.C.: Brookings Institution Press, 2004), 23.

[76] During an interview, Chung Jong-wook said that other members of the foreign policy team had some reservations about the repatriation of Lee In-mo.

[77] Interview with Chung Jong-wook.

[78] Steve Glain, "Maverick Minister: One Lonely Voice in Seoul Calls for Helping the North", *Asian Wall Street Journal*, August 10, 1993.

[79] Donga Ilbosa (1999), vol. 2, 91.

[80] David E. Sanger, "Seoul's Leader Says North Is Manipulating U.S. on Nuclear Issue", *New York Times*, July 1, 1993.

South Korean president strained Seoul-Washington relations.

During the first Kim-Clinton summit at the White House on November 23, 1993, President Kim criticized the U.S.'s North Korea policy: "I believe the North Korean nuclear issue should be resolved by South-North dialogue. We may find out the details of the North Korean nuclear program only through simultaneous inspections by the IAEA and South Korea. The United States seems too naïve toward North Korea." Then he questioned the term, "comprehensive solution," which Seoul and Washington had agreed upon before the summit; he believed the term was similar to what North Koreans called the "package deal."[81] Owing to Kim's uncompromising stance, the two sides agreed to use a "thorough and broad approach." The Kim-Clinton meeting was originally scheduled for thirty minutes but the hot debate between the two leaders forced the meeting to continue for one and a half hours.[82]

Tensions on the peninsula were raised another notch when on March 19, 1994, Pyongyang's delegate to talks at the border village of Panmunjom blustered: "We are ready for a war. Seoul is not far from here. If a war breaks out, it [Seoul] will become a sea of fire."[83] Kim professed shock at the threat, which appeared to have been premeditated as the delegate had read from a prepared text. His immediate and angry reaction, which was broadcast, stunned his people because the president of the Republic of Korea was responding immediately to a statement by a mid-level North Korean official.

The shadow of war grew longer during the tense weeks of showdown between Washington and Pyongyang in May and June 1994. When North Korea removed the spent fuel rods from its Yongbyon reactor on May 8, it was widely believed that Pyongyang had crossed the Rubicon, signaling its determination to develop nuclear weapons. The United States was determined to stop North Korea's nuclear program. If its dialogue with Pyongyang failed, the United States was ready to shift to coercive diplomacy involving sanctions. Washington had already prepared a detailed contingency plan for bombing the nuclear facilities in Yongbyun, but such an air strike was highly likely to ignite general war. The South Koreans had the most to lose if North Korea lashed out, whether through an all-out assault or through random acts of terrorism.

The Pentagon requested that President Clinton authorize military reinforcements inside and outside South Korea for the preparation of a "surgical strike." Pyongyang might feel compelled to resort to a preemptive strike. On June 2, with tensions mounting, Clinton announced that he would seek UN Security Council sanctions against North Korea, provoking a response from the North Korean foreign ministry on June 5 that "sanctions means war, and there is no mercy in war."[84] At the time Kim Il Sung also said, "They decide to make war, we accept the war, the challenge we are prepared for."[85] The United States deployed an aircraft carrier off the Korean east coast at a distance proximate enough for its warplanes to strike the North's nuclear facilities at Yongbyon. U.S. warships were also ready for a naval bombardment of those facilities. The United

---

[81] Donga Ilbosa (1999), vol. 2, 88-89.
[82] Interview with Chung Chong-wook; and Donga Ilbosa (1999), vol. 2, 89.
[83] *Chosun Ilbo*, March 20, 1994.
[84] Quoted in Oberdorfer, *op. cit.*, 311.
[85] *Far Eastern Economic Review*, June 23, 1994.

States was within a day of applying major sanctions, undertaking new troop deployments and evacuating American citizens from South Korea.

According to Kim Young Sam, in June 1994, the United States was on the brink of renewed war on the Korean peninsula (in strict terms, the Korean War had never ended). Later, in a June 2000 interview with a Korean daily, Kim claimed he had stopped Clinton from launching an air strike against North Korea's nuclear facilities in June 1994. According to Kim, he had a thirty-two-minute telephone exchange with Clinton, during which he told the American president, "There will be no inter-Korean war while I am president. If a war broke out, so many soldiers and civilians would be killed, our economy would be devastated, and foreign capital would flow out of Korea. North Korean missiles and artillery would immediately bombard Seoul as soon as American bombers strike Yongbyon." Kim went on, "Clinton tried to persuade me to change my mind, but I criticized the United States for planning to stage a war with the North on our land." Kim stated that he had informed Clinton he would not commit any South Korean troops to such a conflict. Ultimately, Clinton backed off his plan, which had included naval and air bombardment. Kim continued, "One day, I heard [then U.S. Ambassador James] Laney was to hold a press conference the following day and announce the withdrawal of the families of U.S. embassy staff.... This is a step the United States usually takes on the eve of war." Kim called in Laney, warning the American ambassador that another war on the peninsula would turn Korea into a bloodbath, killing millions and destroying South Korea's prosperous economy.[86]

At the proverbial eleventh hour, former American president Jimmy Carter decided to visit Pyongyang to defuse the crisis. Carter's meeting with Kim Il Sung on June 17, 1994, succeeded in moving the situation from war's brink back to the negotiating table. Before Carter crossed the DMZ to visit Pyongyang, President Kim had requested he propose to Kim Il Sung a South-North summit. Upon returning to Seoul, Carter called on President Kim at the Blue House. Carter said he brought an important message from Kim Il Sung to President Kim. Taking out a small memo notebook, Carter read Kim Il Sung's message word-by-word: "I don't know why the top leaders of the North and South have never met. They should have met much earlier. If there had been summits, the situation on the peninsula would not come to such a critical state. I want to meet President Kim Young Sam anywhere, any time without conditions and at an early date."[87] When Carter conveyed Kim Il Sung's willingness to meet Kim Young Sam, Kim became visibly excited. As soon as Carter departed from the presidential mansion, the Blue House spokesman announced President Kim's acceptance of Kim Il Sung's summit proposal.

From that day on, President Kim's main preoccupation was preparing for the historic meeting with Kim Il Sung. The president spent days meeting with his ministers, staff, and experts on North Korea and reading materials on the meeting as well as on Kim Il Sung in preparation for the summit. To discuss the details of the summit, delegates of the South and the North negotiated at Panmunjom and agreed that the summit would be held in Pyongyang on July 25.

---

[86] Hankyoreh Shinmun, June 26, 2000.

[87] Chung Chong-wook, "If the 1994 South-North summit were realized", in Park Kwan Yong et al., *Gongjikenun machimpyoga upda* (There Is No End in the Career of an Official) (Seoul: Myungsol, 2001), 50.

Kim Young Sam

Unfortunately, at noon on July 9, North Korean media reported that Kim Il Sung was dead. President Kim and his advisers were shocked. Presiding over an emergency National Security Council meeting, Kim remarked that he was "sorry to hear the news because the leaders of the two Koreas were to meet in one place to frankly discuss peace on the Korean peninsula and the future of the nation."[88] Providence had stolen from Kim the opportunity of an historic summit with his North Korean counterpart.

Nevertheless, talks between the United States and North Korea resumed in August 1994. Finally, an Agreed Framework was signed between the United States and North Korea in Geneva on October 21, 1994, for the moment at least ending the North Korean nuclear crisis. In the brokered deal, the United States promised North Korea a light-water nuclear reactor in exchange for a promise to shut down its nuclear weapons program. But President Kim appeared to be frustrated with the deal because he believed he had been slighted during the Geneva negotiations, leading Seoul to oppose increased U.S.-North Korean engagement without some improvement in inter-Korean relations.

In December 1994, President Kim again replaced all members of his security and foreign policy team, this time with more capable personnel: the new unification minister, foreign minister, defense minister, director of the Agency for National Security Planning, and the senior secretary for diplomacy and security affairs were all people of expertise and experience. The outgoing diplomatic and security affairs team had come to perceive the huge gap that lay between their ideals and reality. During the critical period when the nation had to deal with both North Korean nuclear issues and Uruguay Round negotiations, squabbles and confusion reigned in decision-making and the implementation of external policies. As a result, it was not long before Kim's foreign policy lost the confidence of the people.

The most controversial issue in implementing the Agreed Framework was the source of the light-water reactors to be furnished. The United States called on South Korea to provide them and underwrite most of their $6 billion cost. The Kim Young Sam administration agreed on the condition that South Korean companies would play a major role in providing the reactors. President Kim saw the reactor project as the beginning of broader South-North economic cooperation. South Korea also demanded its role be openly acknowledged by reference to the "South Korean type" reactors to be furnished. Kim Young Sam was determined that Pyongyang accept the South Korean terms.

Pyongyang refused to accept South Korean-made reactors on security and technological grounds, and threatened to restart its idled nuclear reactors. Tensions rose again on and around the Korean peninsula. Kim Young Sam's plummeting popularity prompted him to take a hard-line stance toward North Korea to avoid any further loss of conservative support. The government intermittently threatened to withhold its funding for the North Korean deal. It said that South Korea would finance the reactor project only if it was allowed a primary role in constructing the reactors. Kim's unwillingness to compromise threatened to doom the Geneva agreement and aggravated tensions on the peninsula.[89] In June, after serious negotiations, the United States and North Korea

---

[88] *Korea Herald*, July 10, 1994.
[89] Steve Glain and Robert S. Greenberger, "South Korea's Kim Knows His Audience: Rigid Stance Threatens Pact with the North but Wins Votes", *Wall Street Journal*, April 17, 1995.

reached an agreement on the issue after Washington provided a face-saving solution to both North and South Korea.

While the regime in Pyongyang was playing a nuclear game, its people were starving. In January 1995, Pyongyang appealed to Japan and South Korea for food aid. Japan agreed to supply 500,000 tons of rice. Kim Young Sam was quick to seize the opportunity. Kim sent his close aide to Beijing to negotiate South Korea's food assistance to the North. On June 21, only four days before crucial local elections, the Kim government announced it would donate 150,000 tons of rice to the North. President Kim enthusiastically declared that the government would purchase the grain on the international market if domestic stocks were insufficient. The Blue House spokesman also announced, "The president hopes the rice will build trust with the North."[90] The president asked Prime Minister Lee Hong-Koo to go to the port to cerebrate the sending of the first rice shipments on June 25, the forty-fifth anniversary of the outbreak of the Korean War.

But Kim Young Sam's enthusiasm turned to anger when North Korean officials demanded the South Korean rice ship fly a North Korean flag as it entered the North Korean port. Two weeks later, another South Korea rice ship and its twenty-one-member crew were detained in North Korea for alleged "spying activities." These incidents infuriated South Koreans, and South-North relations again turned sour. President Kim was partly responsible for the incidents because he used his informal line for negotiations with North Koreans. The South Korean negotiator failed to discuss details of the shipment. Amid the controversy over the rice aid, the local elections resulted in a stunning defeat for Kim and his party. It was widely perceived that Kim had been manipulating the rice aid for his political gain.[91]

Meanwhile, the death of Kim Il Sung and two years of summer floods had sent North Korea even deeper into political and economic crises. Pyongyang's anti-South Korea rhetoric grew more hostile. For example, in early April 1996 the North Korean vice defense minister stated that the point was "not whether a war will break out but when it will be unleashed."[92] At the same time, the Kim Young Sam government was maintaining its hard-line policy toward the North until the parliamentary elections scheduled for April 11. In early September, North Korea staged a military adventure in which a submarine carrying twenty-six armed soldiers and agents ran aground off South Korea's east coast. All but one of the North Koreans were killed, captured, or committed suicide. The submarine fiasco led to the deaths of three South Korean civilians, shot by the fleeing North Koreans. As a result, Kim suspended South Korean support for the construction of nuclear reactors in the North and demanded an apology from Pyongyang.[93]

Kim had little command of foreign policy and is remembered as a leader ignorant of the "ins and outs" of diplomacy. Political considerations heavily influenced the government's actions as the mood of the public swung widely from event to event. The

---

[90] *Chosun Ilbo*, June 22, 1995.
[91] Donga Ilbosa (1999), vol. 2, 110-115.
[92] *Korea Herald*, April 4, 1996.
[93] "South Korea Demands Apology from North; Kim Suspends Nuclear Deal after Sub Incident", *Washington Post*, November 9, 1996.

media were merciless in their criticism of the government. The confrontation over the North Korea nuclear issue was fast pushing the Kim government into a corner. An editorial in one South Korean daily characterized the Kim administration's security policy and method of dealing with the North as "a total failure."[94] Much of this criticism was focused on the government's incompetence and lack of diplomatic capability. Thus, government policy bounced back and forth.[95] Kim's policy lines were also frequently influenced and disrupted by informal sources. For example, only a few days after receiving briefings on North Korea policy from his security adviser, Kim changed his position after talking with personal contacts—mostly followers from his days of opposition struggles or Christian ministers who had visited the Manchurian region across North Korea. An official explained, "President Kim's position changed whimsically since the beginning of U.S.-North Korea negotiation on the North Korean nuclear problem. When he received the progress of the talks from a hard-liner, he expressed strong discontent to the United States and North Korea. However, he soon changed his position when a soft-liner told him that tension on the peninsula would bring a war. There was a joke that whoever first contacts the president would influence his view."[96]

For Kim Young Sam, who was more concerned about his popularity at home, foreign policy was but an extension of domestic politics. His foreign policies shifted with the prevailing winds of public opinion. Kim was not afraid to say no to Bill Clinton, particularly when it suited his domestic political needs. In an attempt to mitigate the criticism that the Kim government was too dependent on the United States, the government tried to avoid sounding like an echo of Washington. Washington was frustrated with South Korea's failure to develop a coherent, comprehensive, long-range policy in dealing with North Korea. Thanks to Kim's markedly inconsistent policies and emotional approach toward North Korea, Seoul invited the criticism of the U.S. government, resulting in unnecessary conflict and a negative impact on U.S. confidence in the policy of the South Korean government.

Kim also played a perilous diplomatic game with Japan and in fits of temper sometimes made derogatory remarks about Korea's closest neighbor. At a joint news conference following a summit meeting with Chinese President Jiang Zemin at the Blue House in November 1995, Kim stated that he would "teach a lesson" to the Japanese. Kim's statement was in response to Japanese State Minister Takami Eto's praise of Japan's colonial past.[97] As the Korean term "teach a lesson" is normally used when a parent or teacher rebukes a trouble-making child, the statement did not sit well with the Japanese public. Kim's undiplomatic style would have serious implications for South Korea later on. For example, just before the outbreak of the 1997 financial crisis in Korea, the deputy prime minister for economic affairs flew to Tokyo in a hasty attempt to arrange a huge loan

---

[94] *Chosun Ilbo*, March 22, 1994.

[95] Yongho Kim, "Inconsistency or Flexibility? The Kim Young Sam Government's North Korea Policy and Its Domestic Variants", *International Journal of Korean Unification Studies*, 8 (1999).

[96] Donga Ilbosa (1999), vol. 2, 92.

[97] Regarding its colonial past, Takami had stated that Japan had done some "good things" during that time. See *Korea Herald*, November 7, 1995.

to avert the crisis. The Japanese refused.[98]

THE KOREAN FINANCIAL CRISIS

During the first year of his term, Kim Young Sam won kudos for his anticorruption drive and for implementation of the real-name financial transaction system. He also made progress in dismantling the legacies of past authoritarian governments and in keeping the military under firm civilian control. However, many of his reform announcements were merely slogans. What he described as reforms might be better described as purges and imprisonments, dismissals and reprimands.[99]

The problem was that the government essentially failed to tackle important national issues such as economic problems and market-opening pressures under the Uruguay Round negotiations. In addition, Kim promised to deliver a "new Korea" animated by a sense of justice. But he had become more self-asserting and arbitrary. Justice seemed to be determined by the president's whim, rather than objective standards and formal procedures. In April 1994, Kim abruptly fired Prime Minister Lee Hoi-chang, intensifying his image as a "civilian dictator." Before dismissal, the prime minister had asked the Ministerial Council on North Korea Policy to report its recommendations to him before sending them to the president. Lee, a former Supreme Court justice, in his interpretation of the constitution, felt he was fully within his rights and prerogatives. Kim, however, believed Lee was challenging his presidential authority. The peremptory removal of the prime minister after only four months in office underscored not only a personality clash at the top, but Kim's authoritarian perception of the presidency. By dismissing Lee, whose uncompromising stand against corruption had made him a popular hero, Kim earned plenty of criticism.[100]

The government was also blamed for scandals and man-made disasters. For example, in September through October 1994, a substantial number of tax officials in two western cities were found to have pocketed hundreds of thousands of dollars in what was becoming a nationwide tax scandal. [101] In October, a major bridge in Seoul collapsed, killing thirty-two people and triggering public anger over the government's failure to manage public facilities, especially when it came out that government inspectors had ignored repeated warnings of disaster. The president blamed his predecessors by saying, "The disasters are the results of the policy of rough-and-ready growth during the authoritarian regimes."[102] He did not seem to understand that the buck stopped at his desk. In order to defuse the evolving crisis, he again changed his prime minister seven months after his appointment and reshuffled his cabinet by replacing seventeen ministers. Critics argued that the action was partly aimed at bolstering his flagging popularity, which had dropped from 90 percent in mid-1993 to around 30 percent in late

---

[98] "Gong Ro-Myung Criticizes President Kim's Foreign Policy", *Wolgan Chosun* (June 2002).
[99] Kim's health and welfare minister, Sohn Hak-Kyu, made that point. See Hahm, ed. (2001), 273.
[100] "South Korea: Disposable Prime Ministers", *Economist*, April 30, 1994.
[101] "Cleansing the Government and Reform: Scornful 'Official Corruption'", *Donga Ilbo*, October 4, 1994.
[102] *Chosun Ilbo*, October 30, 1994.

1994, and diverting attention from a series of disasters and corruption scandals.[103]

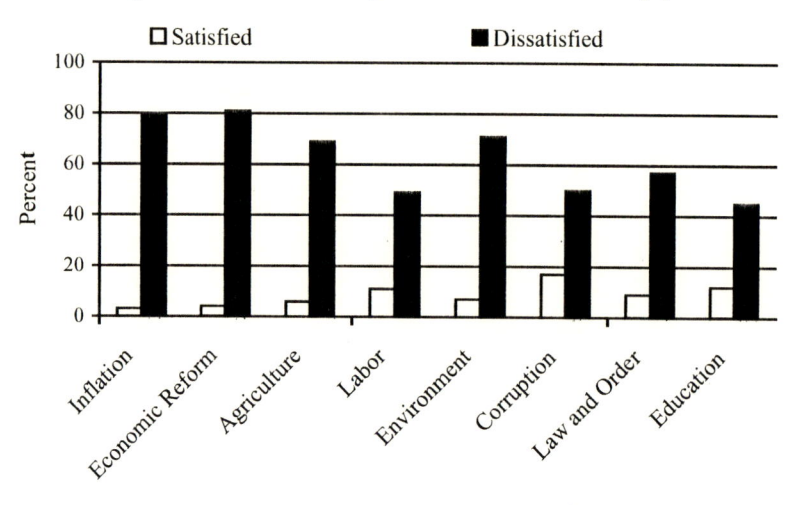

Figure 12. **Public Perception of Kim's Policies** (%)

□ Satisfied ■ Dissatisfied

Source: Joongang Ilbo, September 22, 1994.

However, 1995 proved another black year for the government. A series of man-made disasters dealt a serious blow to President Kim and his party as they prepared for crucial local elections. In April, two deadly gas explosions in Taegu and Seoul killed 113 people and injured 120 others. In June, the collapse of a five-story department store in Seoul killed 502 people and injured more than 900. These were the latest in a grim procession of incidents involving train, ferry, airliner and bridge that had claimed hundreds of lives since the beginning of his term. The disasters seriously undermined public confidence in the Kim government: the public believed that Kim paid too little attention to practical issues and that his government lacked the necessary capacity for effective national management. Public perception of the Kim administration's performance was extremely negative: according to an opinion survey the public was largely dissatisfied with major policies (see Figure 12).[104]

"Rectification Of History." The 1995 local election was a turning point in Korean democracy. Kim Young Sam needed a victory at the polls as the elections came at the midpoint of his term, and his approval rating had been plummeting. The public regarded the elections as a "midterm referendum" on the Kim government. The results of the elections would also influence the parliamentary elections in the following year and the presidential election the year after. Meanwhile, Kim Dae Jung had reemerged from his short and self-imposed political exile, eager to broaden the support base from which he might launch another presidential bid. Pressured by President Kim and his loyalists, Kim

---

[103] "Korean Leader Extends Change in Ministries", *Asian Wall Street Journal*, December 27, 1994.
[104] The figure is based on *Joongang Ilbo*, September 22, 1994.

Jong-pil resigned the chairmanship of the ruling party and established his own party, the United Liberal Democrats (ULD), in order to rebuild his own power base. The defection of Kim Jong-pil further dented President Kim's flagging popularity. Thus, local elections had once again become the field of a major showdown between the three Kims.[105]

In the local elections, Kim Young Sam and his party suffered a devastating defeat (see Table 11), creating a political crisis. The DLP lost ten of fifteen mayoralships and governorships, while the main opposition, the Democratic Party of Kim Dae Jung, won all the seats of the Cholla region and a landslide in Seoul. In the case of Seoul, the opposition mayoral candidate (Cho Soon) emerged as the decisive winner with some 42.3 percent of the vote; the ruling party's candidate suffered a humiliating defeat with 21 percent, far less than the support for the independent candidate. And in the Seoul ward chief elections, the opposition Democratic Party won twenty-three of twenty-five posts. Kim Jong-pil's ULD swept his native Chungchong region. The ruling DLP won a landslide only in Kim Young Sam's native Pusan-Kyongnam region.

Table 11. **Results of the 1995 Local Elections**

	DLP	DP	ULD	Independent	Total
Governors & Mayors	5	4	4	2	15
Heads of Counties & Small Cities	70	84	23	53	230
Members of Big Cities & Provincial Councils	286	355	83	151	875

Source: *Korea Annual 1995*, 58-59.

President Kim's anticorruption drive had affected many politicians in the Taegu-Kyongbuk region which had produced three presidents (Park Chung Hee, Chun Doo Hwan and Roh Tae Woo). As a result, voters in this region had become increasingly critical of Kim Young Sam and his party, and an independent won the mayoral post of Taegu. This disastrous defeat was a sobering manifestation of a rampant "anti-Kim Young Sam" sentiment.[106]

The ruling camp had been criticized for policy failures, corruption scandals, and a series of man-made disasters. It appeared that the ruling party would lose the upcoming parliamentary elections of 1996. Another electoral defeat might deal a fatal blow to Kim and to his party's chances in the 1997 presidential elections. Serious squabbles erupted within the ruling party. The DJP faction, mostly allies of Chun Doo Hwan and Roh Tae Woo, blamed President Kim for his massive purges and recklessness. However, Kim's followers demanded stronger reforms. Under the weight of overwhelming political and public pressure, it was imperative that Kim Young Sam, who was known for his ability to produce "surprise shows," divert the people's attention to another engrossing drama.

On October 19, 1995, an opposition lawmaker, Park Kye-dong, disclosed information on former president Roh Tae Woo's slush funds at a session of the National Assembly. Similar remarks had been made by a minister of government administration

---

[105] Oh, *Korean Politics*, 152-159.
[106] *Joonang Ilbo*, June 28, 1995.

(Suh Suk-jae) "off-the-record" during a meeting with reporters two months earlier. The minister had commented that a former president had 400 billion won in slush funds hidden at numerous banks and the president had fired him immediately. It was therefore widely believed that governmental authorities had provided the information to the opposition lawmaker.[107] Park's remarks gave the president, who was well known for his tendency to play hardball politics, the opportunity to "rectify the Korean history."

The disclosure had an immediate and dramatic effect on the national mood: students, labor and other activist groups waged street demonstrations demanding the imprisonment of Roh. At a press conference on October 27, Roh apologized to the nation for collecting some $650 million slush funds while in office. Roh's confessions triggered demonstrations around the country demanding punishment for Roh. Yielding to public pressure, on November 16, the government arrested Roh Tae Woo on bribery charges. A huge rally organized by opposition leader Kim Dae Jung demanded that President Kim Young Sam prove that he had not accepted money from Roh's slush fund. The contagion of anti-Roh protest immediately spread to another former president—Chun Doo Hwan. On December 3, Chun was also arrested on charges of corruption; the alleged crimes were in connection with the "December 12 incident" in 1979 and the Kwangju uprising in 1980.[108] These charges were far more serious, not only because they could lead to capital punishment, but also because they would deny legitimacy to Chun's administration and seriously hurt the legacy of his presidency.

However, there was a legal battle as to whether any crime committed in December 1979 and May 1980 by the two former leaders had already fallen under the statutes of limitations. The government concluded that additional legislation suspending the statutes of limitations was necessary. On November 24, President Kim ordered the ruling party to draft special legislation to punish the two former presidents who, he believed, were responsible for the military crackdown of the Kwangju uprising.[109] On December 19, a special law was passed in the National Assembly. Lawyers of the two former presidents argued that the special law was retroactive and that it was against the principle of prohibition for double jeopardy. They asked the Constitutional Court about the validity of the law. The court rejected the petition. Nevertheless, five of the nine judges considered the special law unconstitutional.[110]

In the name of "rectification of history" (*yoksa baro saeugi*), the government charged Chun Doo Hwan and Roh Tae Woo, along with sixteen other former generals, of corruption and insubordination. In connection with the charges against Chun and Roh, the head of nine big conglomerates were also convicted of bribing the former presidents. Throughout, the two former presidents remained defiant, alleging they were victims of a campaign that had nothing to do with history and everything to do with politics. The measures were very popular, but the charges against the two former presidents seriously shattered their images as well as the authority of Korean presidency itself. Thoughtful

---

[107] *Donga Ilbo* later reported that the prosecutor's office had secretly investigated Roh Tae Woo's "slush fund" during 1994 (see Donga Ilbosa (1999), vol. 1, 134-135).
[108] For "December 12 incident", refer to the first section, "A Turbulent Transition" of Chapter V.
[109] *Joongang Ilbo*, November 24, 1995.
[110] C Court.go.kr/English/case 44 (February 16, 1996).

observers wondered about the potentially fatal damage being done to the presidency. It was also a retroactive application of the law.

In December 1989, President Roh Tae Woo and leaders of the opposition parties (Kim Young Sam, Kim Dae Jung and Kim Jong-pil) had agreed to "settle the Fifth Republic's problems completely" in return for Chun's testimony at a National Assembly hearing, implicitly assuring that Chun's responsibility for wrongdoing during the Fifth Republic would no longer be a subject of inquiry. After inauguration, President Kim Young Sam announced that Chun and Roh had engineered a "coup-like" incident on December 12, 1979, but declared that the government would not prosecute them for the sake of national unity. He also urged the nation "to let history judge the December 12 incident."[111] Then in October 1994, after a yearlong investigation of the events after the death of Park Chung Hee (such as the "December 12 incident" and the Kwangju uprising), the Seoul District Prosecutor's Office had declared that it had decided not to indict the two former presidents because it was "feared to revive national divisiveness and confrontation in the course of legal disputes over the past, and what is taken into account is that they have already been judged by the people through parliamentary hearings on the Fifth Republic".[112] Finally, in July 1995, pointing to the statutes of limitations, the government announced its final decision not to pursue insurrection charges against Chun and Roh.[113] In January 1995, the Constitutional Court also found that the government had no jurisdiction to rule on the constitutionality of a "successful coup."[114] When President Kim decided to damage the heritage of the former presidents, however, the Constitutional Court reversed itself.[115]

The trials of the two former presidents and their co-defendant began on December 18, 1995. Chun and Roh were found guilty of the 1979 mutiny and of treason for the Kwangju tragedy. However, the trial found no one who actually ordered shooting in Kwangju. From a historical perspective, the trial could be seen as part of Korea's painful effort at establishing a rule of law under a democratic government. A leading Korean daily wrote that Korea "learned a lesson that even former presidents can be punished severely."[116] But "some have expressed concern that the trials were designed more to improve the political standing of the current president, Kim Young Sam, than to uncover the truth about past abuses."[117]

At the same time, Kim's move raised serious questions about his personal character. As a Machiavellian prince, Kim joined forces in 1990 with the heirs to authoritarian rule to forge a new winning electoral coalition, but then pressed charges of mutiny and corruption against the two former presidents only five years later in order to protect himself. Michael Breen, then a *Washington Times* correspondent in Seoul, wrote "[Public] cynicism reached its zenith at

---

[111] *Joongang Ilbo*, May 13, 1993.
[112] *Korea Times*, October 30, 1994.
[113] *Joongang Ilbo*, July 19, 1995.
[114] *Korea Herald*, January 20, 1995.
[115] Five of the nine judges considered the Special Law unconstitutional. At least six votes were necessary to declare the law unconstitutional.
[116] *Chosun Ilbo*, August 27, 1996, 3.
[117] *Washington Post*, August 27, 1996, A10.

the point at which the [anti-corruption] campaign seemed, to international society, to be most impressive—the arrests of the former presidents."[118] Opportunism had long been a hallmark of Kim's political career, and his latest actions seemed to be based more on desperation than on principle. By crushing the factions within the ruling party that remained loyal to the two former presidents, the trials paved the way for the disintegration of the ruling DLP and the creation of Kim Young Sam's party. Indeed, at the beginning of 1996 the ruling party changed its name to the New Korea Party (NKP).

The trials of former leaders were also perceived as acts of vengeance or acts of moral hypocrisy and betrayal: Kim Young Sam had reverted to the tradition of aggrandizing power by yielding the twin weapons of reform and anticorruption.[119] Korean history is replete with examples of political revenge and retribution. To the supporters of the former presidents, the trials appeared to be a disgraceful act of political patricide by a man who owed his presidency to the jailed leaders.[120]

A day after the arrest of Chun Doo Hwan, opposition leader Kim Dae Jung denounced Kim Young Sam's measures as nothing but "shock comedy." His party also charged that President Kim had taken political funds from former president Roh. President Kim declined to give a full account of his own dealings with Roh and the campaign funds he had spent in the 1992 presidential election.[121] Kim Dae Jung dropped a bombshell: he admitted he had received approximately $2.5 million from President Roh Tae Woo to help finance his 1992 presidential campaign.[122] If Roh gave money to the opposition leader, it seemed reasonable to assume that he had also funded his own party's candidate, Kim Young Sam. In one opinion survey, more than 70 percent of respondents believed this.[123] The results of the polls implied that many people wondered how Kim could indict former presidents for corruption when he himself had received huge campaign funds from Roh. From the beginning, Kim Young Sam did not have "moral legitimacy." In fact, he was elected by illegally spending huge amounts of money. Furthermore, since he had been active in politics for the last forty years, it is certain that he has to a great extent to share some responsibility for the misconduct of politics. Nevertheless, he behaved as if he had nothing to do with past wrong-doings.[124]

Kim looked like a hero in his crusade against corruption—until his own cabinet and his close associates were tried and jailed for bribery. In March 1996, a key aide to

---

[118] Breen, *Koreans*, 240-241.

[119] Byung-Kook Kim, "The Politics of Reform in Confucian Korea: Dilemma, Choice and Crisis", *Korean Journal of Area Studies*, 11 (1997): 112-113.

[120] Richard L. Parry, "Kim's 'Bloodless Coup' Shakes Korea to Core", *The Independent*, December 10, 1995.

[121] *Korea Herald*, October 27, 1995.

[122] Ahn Byung-ho, one of Roh Tae Woo's close aides, argued that the campaign funds delivered to Kim Young Sam from Roh during the presidential campaign reached as much as 146 billion *won* (about $200 million). See *Wolgan Chosun* (February 2002), 276-278.

[123] Gallup Korea survey of 1,000 adults conducted on October 27, 1995.

[124] Sung Deuk Hahm and Kwang Woong Kim, "Institutional Reforms and Democratization in Korea: The Case of the Kim Young Sam Administration, 1993-1998", *Governance*, 12:4 (October 1999), 485. Kim Hyun-chul, Kim Yong Sam's son, invested the remaining political funds, nearly $10 million from his father's 1992 presidential campaign, in the Hansol corporation.

the president (Chang Hak-ro), who had worked for him for nineteen years, was arrested for taking $900,000 in bribes in return for favors to businessmen. In June, the head of the Security Oversight Commission was arrested on charges of accepting bribes. In October, the defense minister was arrested for accepting money from a defense contractor, and in November the health and welfare minister resigned on suspicion of accepting a bribe. The series of corruption scandals seriously damaged the moral authority of the Kim administration.[125]

Facing crumbling popularity, Kim had become almost desperate and was determined to do well in the parliamentary elections scheduled for April 1996. The political warrior had to do whatever it took to win the elections, fair or foul. He recruited anyone electable as a candidate for his party, regardless of capacity and background. He believed that if his party failed to secure a comfortable majority in the coming elections, his government would become a lame duck and the prospects for victory in the 1997 presidential election would be bleak. Thus, the elections turned out to be less than clean—the candidates of the ruling party spent far more than the limit allowed by the new campaign finance law, which Kim had revised in 1994, and the government was even suspected of intervening in the elections.[126] The bold reforms, such as the Campaign Finance Law and real-name financial system, failed to change the corrupt practices of the elections. This meant that Kim chose an electoral victory by any means rather than by the "fair and clean" elections he advocated.[127] As a result, the ruling New Korea Party performed better than had been expected, winning 139 seats, eleven short of a majority. Kim created a majority by drawing in a handful of opposition members and independents.

In September 2003, Kang Sam-jae, then the ruling party's secretary general and a long-term loyalist of Kim Young Sam, was sentenced to four years in prison for illegal fundraising during the 1996 parliamentary elections. Kang had "embezzled" some 117 billion *won* (about $150 million) from the National Security Planning Agency (NSPA) to finance the election campaigns. The court also sentenced Kim Ki-seop, former deputy director of the spy agency, to five-years in prison on the same charge as that of Kang.[128] At the appeal court in February 2004, Kang surprised the nation by saying that he had received the money from President Kim at his office in the Blue House before the 1996 parliamentary elections. Kang was given a verdict of "not guilty," implying that the huge fund was Kim Young Sam's slush fund that had been hidden by the spy agency.[129] The point is that the illegal transaction was made while the government was trying two former presidents for corruption.

---

[125] "An Ex-aide to Kim Young Sam", *Wall Street Journal*, April 24, 1996; B. C. Koh, "South Korea in 1996", *Asian Survey*, 37:1 (January 1997): 1-9.

[126] Some argue that most politicians illegally spent 10 or 20 times more than the limits of political funding stated in the election law (Hahm and Kim, *op. cit.*, 487).

[127] Chu Don Shik (1997), 136-153.

[128] "Former NSPA Deputy Admits Money from Budget", *Chosun Ilbo*, February 22, 2001; and "GNP Lawmaker Sentenced to 4 Years", *Chosun Ilbo*, September 23, 2003.

[129] In January 2004, Kang's lawyer argued that the funds came from President Kim Young Sam, implying Kim had huge slush funds. See "Ex-President Diverted Funds", *Korea Herald*, January 13, 2004. The Supreme Court found them "not guilty" (*Donga Ilbo*, October 29, 2005).

The Financial Crisis. The year 1996 was a bad one for the South Korean economy. During Kim's term the rate of economic growth fell sharply and the current account deficit (balance on the trade of goods and services) became considerably larger, reaching $23.7 billion (the largest in Korean history), well over three times what was projected.[130] Nevertheless, the government did not want to devalue the Korean currency in order to reduce the trade deficit because that would set the country's per capita income back below the symbolic $10,000 benchmark achieved in 1995. Experts widely believed that the *won* was overvalued by 10 to 20 percent. As a result, foreign borrowing increased rapidly during the Kim administration; Korea's foreign debts rapidly increased from $44 billion in 1993 to $161 billion in 1996 and $153 billion in 1997.[131]

Political tensions arose in late 1996 when the government submitted its proposal for revision of the labor law. The opposition had been staging a sit-in at the National Assembly to block passage of the bill. But in order to meet the conditions of OECD membership, the ruling party had to pass the bill. On December 26, 1996, after gathering secretly at four hotels in the predawn hours, 155 members of the ruling party were bused to the National Assembly, where they passed eleven bills in six minutes without debate. The new labor law made it easier for companies to dismiss workers, hire replacements for striking workers, and adjust working hours.

The secret bill passages triggered several weeks of general strikes, the largest and costliest in the country's history. Labor was joined by tens of thousands of students and received support from other activist groups. South Korean and international press vociferously condemned the government's actions.[132] Many felt the government had returned to the undemocratic methods and spirit of its authoritarian past. Facing fierce resistance, the government feared it would be unable to implement the new labor law and sent it back to the National Assembly for revision.[133] In March 1997, a milder version, allowing companies to lay off workers only in certain circumstances, was passed. However, the new labor law was too weak, disappointing many investors.

While labor strikes continued, Hanbo Steel Co., the flagship company of the Hanbo Group, the fourteenth largest conglomerate, declared bankruptcy (with an enormous debt of $6.8 billion); later, the other companies in the Hanbo Group also went bankrupt. It was the largest corporate collapse in Korean history. There were fears that the collapse might trigger a chain reaction of bankruptcies among the conglomerates.[134]

The Hanbo bankruptcy was not merely a devastating financial blow, it also demonstrated serious weaknesses in financial supervision and in the banking sector as well as indicating endemic corruption. On February 13, 1997, the Hanbo chairman Chung Tai-soo) was arrested on charges of bribing bankers and politicians for loans.

---

[130] South Korea enjoyed a current account surplus of $380 million in 1993, but it deteriorated over time, with deficits mounting from $4.5 billion in 1994 to $8.9 billion in 1995 and a record of $23.7 billion in 1996. National Statistics Office, *Major Statistics of Social and Economic Indicators* (Seoul: National Statistics Office, 1996), 190.

[131] Samsung Economic Research Institute, *Principal Economic Indicators* (Seoul, November 1997).

[132] *Korea Herald*, December 28, 1996; January 7, 1997; January 14, 1997.

[133] "South Korea: Culture Clash", *Economist*, January 11, 1997, 35-36; and "Seoul Leader Fails to Halt Labor Strife", *New York Times*, January 23, 1997.

[134] "Meltdown in Korea", *Businessweek*, February 10, 1997.

Also arrested were the minister of home affairs, head of the ruling party's finance committee, one of Kim's senior aides in the Blue House, and three other lawmakers, all for accepting kickbacks to pressure banks into loaning Hanbo $6.2 billion—some 20 times its net worth. Prosecutors questioned and released President Kim's second son, Kim Hyun-chul. The Hanbo Group was accused of financing much of Kim Young Sam's 1992 presidential campaign in return for a license to manufacture steel and favors from government controlled banks.[135] On February 25, 1997, the fourth anniversary of his term, President Kim made a national apology: "I cannot even hold up my head because even those who used to work close to me were found to have been involved in the bribery scandal."

Opinion polls showed that the overwhelming majority of people believed the Kim administration was corrupt: nearly one-half (49 percent) of those polled in a May 1997 survey by Gallup Korea believed that the level of corruption in the Kim government was "high," while over a third (36 percent) of respondents described it as "very high."[136] The president's approval rating plunged to 14 percent in January 1997, and then to an unheard of 9 percent by March.[137] In March, only three months after his previous cabinet reshuffle, in a desperate attempt to defuse the grave political crisis stemming from the Hanbo scandals, Kim replaced his prime minister and eight ministers, including the economic ministers, and members of the Blue House staff.[138]

Persistent allegations that the president's son, Kim Hyun-chul, was a key player in the Hanbo scandal shredded Kim's remaining credibility. A month later prosecutors reopened an inquiry into charges that Kim Hyun-chul was on the receiving end of kickbacks from the Hanbo Group. In May, the junior Kim was arrested on charges of receiving illegal funds from businesses, of evading taxes, and illicitly influencing government policy through his private networks. On October 12, 1997, Kim Hyun-chul was sentenced to three years in prison and ordered to pay a fine of more than $1.5 million. The court also confiscated more than $500,000 in illegally amassed assets, which were hidden in over a hundred bank accounts.[139] The downfall of the son marked the downfall of the father as well. The president was accused of political hypocrisy, collecting political funds through his son and others while publicly portraying himself as a crusader for anticorruption. During the spring and summer of 1997, some questioned whether Kim would even be able to serve out his term. Some students and academics publicly called for the resignation of Kim Young Sam. Opinion polls showed that about 30

---

[135] During a National Assembly hearing on February 4, 1999, the former chairman of the Hanbo Group said he had secretly donated 15 billion won (about $20 million) for Kim Young Sam's presidential campaign. See "YS in Slush Fund Scandal", *Korea Times*, February 5, 1999.

[136] Doh C. Shin, *Mass politics*, 214. Only a small minority perceived it as either "not so much" (14 percent) or "very little" (1 percent).

[137] Jae Hoon Shim, "Hero to Zero", *Far Eastern Economic Review*, March 13, 1997.

[138] "Kim Terms Cabinet as an 'Emergency' Team", *Korea Herald*, March 25, 1997.

[139] *Chosun Ilbo*, October 14, 1999. In 1999 the Seoul Appeals Court granted Kim Hyun-chul a "partial" pardon, but confiscated $5.8 million remaining from his father's campaign fund for the 1992 presidential election that he had managed. Some reviewers raised questions whether I focus on corruption scandals of the Kim Young Sam and Kim Dae Jung administrations. I included those scandals because they occurred during the terms of the two presidencies.

percent of the respondents thought President Kim should step down to assume responsibility for the Hanbo scandal and his son's influence peddling.[140]

While Kim was struggling for the survival of his government, many South Koreans found themselves nostalgic for Park Chung Hee, the iron-fisted, charismatic leader, and Kim Young Sam's most loathsome political enemy. Nearly two decades after his death, Park's ghost was alive and overwhelming the current president. According to an April 1997 poll by *Donga Ilbo*, as many as 75.9 percent of those surveyed felt that Park Chung Hee was Korea's most effective president, ever. Kim Young Sam was selected by only 3.7 percent.[141]

The Hanbo bankruptcy accelerated the economic meltdown. Six medium-size conglomerates followed the Hanbo Group into bankruptcy; many others were experiencing severe financial difficulties. The economy seemed to have entered a freefall. The big blow came in July with the near-bankruptcy of Kia Motors, the second-largest carmaker and the main company of the Kia Group, the eighth largest conglomerate.[142] Like the Hanbo case, the Kia case damaged the government's credibility and foreign investors' confidence in Korea. But, in the Kia case, the hesitancy with which the government approached the problem aggravated the situation. The decision on the Kia case was long drawn out, from July 1997, when it filed for bankruptcy, until October, when the government finally decided to put it into court receivership. By this time, the financial crisis was in full swing. Kim Young Sam, who was struggling with the Hanbo bankruptcy and the arrest of his son, feared the fall of another *chaebol* and asked his advisers to save Kia from bankruptcy by any means. An IMF official said at the time, "The biggest reason for the worsening financial condition is mounting uncertainties derived from the Kia incident."[143] *The Financial Times* reported, "South Korea lacks leadership rather than dollars."[144]

Panicked by the Southeast Asian financial crisis, which began in Thailand in July and quickly spread to other countries in the region, frightened by the massive business failures within South Korea, and having lost confidence in the Korean government's capability to manage the economic crisis, foreign investors fled the South Korean stock market, initiating a sudden outflow of capital, and quickly leading to a currency tumble. From October 1997, the descent of the *won* was rapid: from about 900 *won* per dollar, it slumped to 1,650 *won* per dollar by December. The currency collapse was matched by a slump in the stock market, with stock prices dropping by 33 percent. Thousands of small firms went bankrupt.[145] In an attempt to shore up the *won*, South Korea's foreign exchange reserves were depleted from $22 billion to $4 billion between October and early December, an amount insufficient to carry the country through another day.

Despite the impending financial crisis, on November 18 the National Assembly

---

[140] Namju Cho and Michael Schuman, "Arrest of Son Deals New Blow to Kim's Regime", *Asian Wall Street Journal*, May 19, 1997.

[141] *Donga Ilbo*, April 10, 1997.

[142] In May 1997 the Kia Group owed the commercial banks 5.4 trillion *won* and the merchant banks 4.5 trillion *won*, a total of 11 billion dollars, about twice Hanbo's debt.

[143] "Overseas Borrowing Getting Tougher", *Business Korea* (Seoul), October 1997.

[144] Quoted in Donga Ilbosa (1999), vol. 2, 195.

[145] Finance and Economy Ministry, *Economic Trends and Statistical Data*, December 1997.

ended its regular session without passing a package of financial reform bills. Out of 13, only three relatively unimportant bills passed. Most of the bills foundered due to inter-party wrangling. The failure to pass urgently needed financial reform legislation added one more element of uncertainty to the deteriorating economic situation.

On November 19, the president fired the deputy premier for economy (Kang Kyung-shik) and his senior economic adviser (Kim In-ho), both of whom had inherited the failing economy only seven months previously, making them scapegoats for the crisis. Ignorant of the ongoing negotiations with the IMF, the new deputy premier for the economy (Lim Chang-ryol) attempted unsuccessfully to defuse the crisis by asking Washington and Tokyo for financial support. On November 28, President Clinton called President Kim to say, "We believe South Korea might be in default. It is better to settle the negotiations with the IMF."[146] On December 3, barely a year after joining the OECD, Seoul turned to the IMF for economic assistance. South Korea and the IMF agreed to a $57 billion rescue package. In return, Seoul agreed to tighten its fiscal and monetary policies and to engage in far-reaching, market-oriented reforms of its financial and corporate sectors and its labor market policies. It also agreed to open its economy further to foreign goods and investors.[147]

Most South Koreans viewed the acceptance of the IMF reform package as a humiliating infringement on national sovereignty; a devastating national tragedy surpassed only by the Korean War. Owing to their phenomenal success over the course of three decades, South Koreans had grown proud of themselves and their country. They found it difficult to swallow this newfound pride and yield to the IMF demands. The press called December 3 a "day of national humiliation"; a day when South Korea lost its economic sovereignty. An era of "IMF trusteeship" had come, lamented newspapers. On December 11, 1997, assuming full responsibility for the economic crises, President Kim told the nation he was "truly sorry" for the economic turmoil.[148]

The dawning of the "IMF era" coincided with the election of opposition leader Kim Dae Jung as president. The failure of the Kim Young Sam government and the consequent "IMF crisis" were the most important factors in Kim Dae Jung's victory. For his election, Kim Dae Jung was also indebted to former prominent leaders of the ruling party (such as Kim Jong-pil, Park Tae-joon, Lee Jong-chan and Park Joon-kyu) who had been purged by Kim Young Sam.

The 1997 Korean financial crisis reflected the economic mismanagement of the Kim government. First of all, the government accelerated opening of the financial market without adequate domestic preparations—that is, establishment of monitoring and supervision systems. The financial and capital liberalization without modern banking and legal systems in place proved to be a recipe for disaster, triggering a rush of short-term foreign loans.[149] The enormous sum of short-term capital inflow was the most significant

---

[146] Donga Ilbosa (1999), vol. 2, 232.

[147] Kang Bong-kyun, *Hankook kyongjae blajeon jeonryak* (Economic Development Strategy of Korea) (Seoul: Pakyoungsa, 2001), 28-29; "Program Emphasizes Restructuring Financial Sector, Corporations", *Economic Report* (Seoul: January 1998).

[148] *Joongang Ilbo*, December 11, 1997.

[149] Samuel Kim, "Korea's *Segyehwa* Drive: Promise versus Performance", Samuel S. Kim, ed. (2000), 255.

factor leading to the financial crisis. Foreign debt nearly trebled from $44 billion in 1993 to $150 billion in 1997, and the share of short-term debt (a debt with less than a year's maturity) in total debt rose from an already high 44 percent in 1993 to an astonishing 58.2 percent at the end of 1996, making South Korean short-term debt one of the highest among borrowers in Asia, Latin America and Eastern Europe.[150]

The entry of twenty-four new merchant banks was widely believed to be largely responsible for triggering the financial crisis by accumulating excessive short-term foreign debt and escalating reckless lending.[151] The new merchant banks were inexperienced in international banking and finance, yet they aggressively ventured into high-risk capital games: with borrowed short-term loans, they invested heavily in the high-risk "junk bonds" of Southeast Asia, Russia and Latin America. When these countries got into trouble, South Korean banks lost their money.[152]

The government also failed to monitor and supervise the business sector. Critics asserted that Korea ran into trouble because the government dismantled the very planning and coordination apparatus—the Economic Planning Board—that had successfully guided the economy for three decades. They argued that when the government merged the EPB with the Ministry of Finance, "it was the demise of industrial policy, driving the Korean economy into crisis."[153]

The 1997 Korean financial crisis is thus seen as "a product of government and policy failures."[154] The crisis resulted primarily from governmental mismanagement of the economy, not from flaws inherent in the state-led growth model. It is easy to dismantle an existing system but difficult to establish a new one. The Kim government weakened economic control mechanisms that were central to the efficiency of Korea's high growth model. There was neither an effective Economic Planning Board nor a capable and stable Blue House staff. As the Nobel Prize winning economist Joseph Stiglitz put it: "Many of the problems these countries face today arise not because government did too much, but because they did too little, and because they themselves had deviated from the policies that had proved so successful over preceding decades."[155]

---

[150] Ha-Joon Chang, "Korea: The Misunderstood Crisis", *World Development*, 28:8 (1998): 1556.

[151] As of March 1997, the financing pattern of nine merchant banks approved in 1994 was skewed toward short-term financing (63.4 percent of total financing). The pattern of the fifteen merchant banks established in 1996 was more severe; 92.9 percent was short-term. See Jin-Wook Choi, "Regulatory Forbearance and Financial Crisis in South Korea", *Asian Survey*, XLII:2 (March/April 2002): 261.

[152] Ha-Joon Chang, Hong-Jae Park, and Chul Gyue Yoo, "Interpreting the Korean Crisis: Financial Liberalization, Industrial Policy and Corporate Governance", *Cambridge Journal of Economics*, 22:6 (1999): 739. At a parliamentary panel probing the causes of the 1997 financial crisis, lawmakers of the new ruling party raised strong suspicions that "the government of Kim Young Sam might have allowed the small investment firms to become merchant banks in return for political donations." See "Former Government Accused of Raising Political Funds from Merchant Banks", *Korea Herald*, February 3, 1999.

[153] Ha-Joon Chang et al., *op. cit.*, 739.

[154] Chung-in Moon and Sang-young Rhyu, "The State, Structural Rigidity, and the End of Asian Capitalism", in Richard Robinson, Mark Beeson, Kanshka Jayasuriya, and Hyun-Rae Kim, eds., *Politics and Markets in the Wake of the Asian Crisis* (New York: Routledge, 2000), 78.

[155] *Wall Street Journal*, February 4, 1998.

Kim's frequent reshuffling of his economic team perhaps proved the most damaging to the economy. During his five-year term, he had seven different deputy prime ministers for economy—the average tenure was less than nine months! In addition, President Kim failed to establish an effective and stable Blue House staff: he had six different economic advisers with an average tenure of just ten months (see Table 12). It was virtually impossible for the government to formulate, implement, and coordinate consistent and effective policy with such short tenure.[156]

It is useful to compare South Korea's ministerial tenure with that of Taiwan and Singapore, South Korea's economic competitors in Asia. Unlike South Korea, these two nations avoided the devastation of the 1997 financial crisis. In Taiwan, the average tenure of economic ministers (finance minister and economy minister) was 44.5 months, four times longer than in South Korea.[157] These ministers also served as members on the Council for Economic Planning and Development before or after their ministerial posts. Thus, the Taiwanese economic team was kept stable and its economic policies consistent. The case of Singapore is astonishing. Richard Hu has served as finance minister since 1985, more than seventeen years. Other economy-related ministers were also experienced and had long tenures, averaging about ten years.[158]

Table 12. **Instability of Kim Young Sam's Economic Team**

EPB Minister	Months	Economic Adviser	Months
K. S. Lee (93.3-93.12)	10	J. Y. Park (93.3-94.10)	19
J. S. Chung (93.12-94.10)	9	Y. H. Han (94.10-95.12)	15
J. H. Hong (94.10-95.12)	15	B. Y. Koo (95.12-96.8)	7
W. B. Ra (95.12-96.8)	8	S. C. Lee (96.8-97.2)	7
S. S. Han (96.8-97.3)	7	I. H. Kim (97.2-97.11)	9
K. S. Kang (97.3-97.11)	8	Y. S. Kim (97.11-98.2)	3
C. R. Lim (97.11-98.2)	3		

Source: Civil Service Commission

Finally, Kim's lack of competence and knowledge was the most critical element in the precipitous escalation of the financial crisis.[159] Although Kim was decisive and courageous in politics, he proved a poor crisis manager. Kim was totally ignorant of economic policy and left its management to his economic policymakers. Answering questions by public prosecutors, the president's last chief economic adviser, Kim In-ho, revealed Kim Young Sam's lack of understanding and leadership in economic affairs. According to the unfortunate adviser, he always had to make oral reports to the president but the president never gave any instruction after his report: the only remark the president made was "do your best." He wondered whether the president had

---

[156] Jongryn Mo and Chung-in Moon, "Epilogue: Democracy and the Origin of the 1997 Korean Economic Crisis", in Mo and Moon, eds. (1999), 171-198.
[157] The data was provided by the Taipei Economic and Cultural Representative Office in Honolulu.
[158] See http://www.cabinet.gov.sg
[159] Chung-in Moon and Song-min Kim, "Democracy and Economic Performance in South Korea", in Diamond and Kim, eds., *Consolidating Democracy*, 154.

understood what he was reporting.[160] During the fall of 1997, in a last attempt to restore the confidence of the international financial community in the Korean economy, the deputy prime minister for economic affairs, Kang Kyung-shik, tried to persuade the ruling and opposition parties to pass the financial reform bills. Concerned over potential repercussions in the upcoming presidential election, the political parties were reluctant to pass the reform package. President Kim was the only person who might have been able to persuade the ruling and opposition parties; but despite Kang's repeated appeals, the president refused to take any initiative.[161]

Kim Young Sam entered office with a great blessing, but he stepped down from the presidency like a defeated warrior. His earlier pledge to elevate South Korea to a first-rate nation during his term proved but an empty slogan, and resulted only in the 1997 financial crisis and IMF trusteeship. Economic hardship, social trauma, and the loss of national pride implanted a deep sense of rage and betrayal in the minds of many South Koreans, fixing the image of Kim Young Sam as a "failed president."

LEADERSHIP FOR REFORM POLITICS

Context of the Presidency. During the early period of his term, Kim Young Sam enjoyed unprecedented legitimacy and public support, mainly because he was a life-long crusader for democracy and the first directly elected civilian president since 1961. After defeat in the presidential elections, Kim Dae Jung declared his political retirement and went to England, significantly weakening the opposition forces. Thus, Kim Young Sam faced no serious political challenges. He could also use broad reform rhetoric to appeal to progressives including students and labor.

However, the political foundation of the Kim presidency was not so solid. He garnered less than 42 percent of the presidential vote; of this, much support came from the loyal backers of Chun Doo Hwan and Roh Tae Woo, not exactly his natural power base. In addition, Kim inherited some serious problems: a flagging economy, the menace of the North Korean nuclear program, and the challenge of globalization.

Having suffered from the turbulent democratic transition, and having experienced a decline in economic growth under the previous administration, many Koreans now called for more law and order and efficiency. Moreover, Kim's capacity to lead was consistently questioned. He was known to have a poor understanding of major issues, in particular economic ones. Although he also lacked administrative experience, he surrounded himself with a hodgepodge of dissidents, who were loyal to their boss, but seriously unqualified to advise him.

At the time the world was undergoing sweeping changes that were beginning to have significant effects on South Korea. The country needed vision and a new paradigm in order to survive and prosper in a world that was becoming increasingly globalized and competitive. The window of opportunity was narrow: only a focused effort could significantly reduce the risk of being an administration in disarray. North Korea was also a serious concern for South Korea; it had become diplomatically isolated and

---

[160] *Oehwan wigi baeksu* (Korea's Financial Crisis Whitepaper), *Wolgan Chosun*, A Supplement (September 1999), 60-106.
[161] Ibid., 20-59; and "Korean Leadership", *Asian Wall Street Journal*, November 25, 1997.

economically weakened and was struggling for its very survival.

Agenda Setting. The relative success of a democratic transition under the Roh presidency gave Kim Young Sam a stable and predictable foundation for his presidency. A more sensible president would have maintained a great deal of continuity and stability. However, Kim declared his government would cure the "Korean disease" and build a "new Korea." His reform drive was usually geared towards getting quick results. He focused on weeding out the rotten apples rather than on reforming the system. The problem with the approach was his tendency to view corruption and other problems in the government and politics as an individual phenomenon, rather than as an institutional or systemic problem.[162]

Thus, his agenda was backward-looking rather than future-oriented: he intended to shake up or even dismantle the existing system. The government belittled the past and neglected the present. However, the purges and elimination of elements from the past were not enough to create a "new Korea." As one foreign observer noted, "It is one thing to push a couple of your enemies around and another thing to come up with a new system."[163] According to Gallup Korea surveys, most people were not concerned with Kim's agenda—anticorruption drive and democratic reform (see Figure 13).[164]

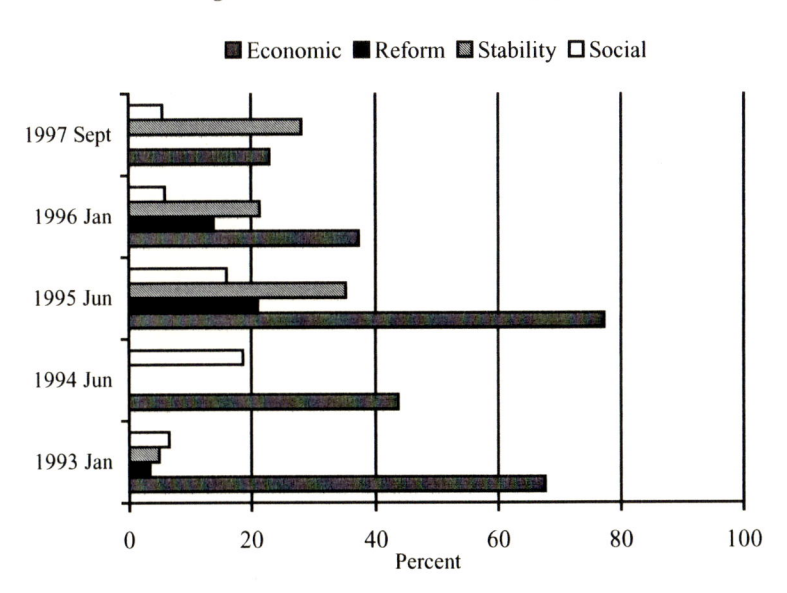

Figure 13. **Most Serious Issues** (%)

Source: Gallup Korea Surveys, 1993-97

---

[162] "Behind Stories of the Civilian Government (2)", *Donga Ilbo*, January 3, 1998, 3-4.

[163] Kirk, *Korean Crisis*, 74.

[164] Categories are: Economic Problems = inflation, economic growth, agricultural problems, and rich-poor gap; Reform Issues = corruption, and democratic reform; Stability = political and social stability; Social Problems= law and order, traffic jams, and pollution.

Their primary concern was economic. Two-thirds (68 percent) of the respondents in a survey taken before Kim's inauguration listed economic problems as the most serious problem the country faced. Although their concern over corruption increased after a series of corruption scandals, their concern over political stability also increased dramatically. In a different survey in November 1993, Koreans were asked to rate the priority of democratization as a national development goal in relation to economic development. While about one-half (49 percent) were in favor of economic development over democratic reform, about one-quarter (26 percent) chose democratization over economic development. In 1997, however, less than one-tenth (9 percent) replied that democratization was more important than economic development.[165]

Thus, Kim promoted what he thought important and neglected what was important to the people. Within a year after his inauguration, the public expressed discontent about the economic performance of the government. For example, according to a Gallup Korea survey conducted in early 1994, more than half of the respondents saw economic policy as the major failure of the government.[166] A leader should give priority to the nation's agenda rather than his own. Even in the late stages of economic development, economic performance appeared to be crucial for the success of a presidency. In short, Kim failed in the crucial task of agenda setting.

Another serious problem was Kim's relative neglect of external affairs. During his term, South Korea faced the formidable challenges of the post-Cold War era—a rapidly changing security environment, including North Korea's desperate attempt to develop nuclear weapons, and the emergence of a global economy. Kim focused his time and energy on domestic politics, in particular his anti-corruption drive.

Appointments and Leadership Style. Kim Young Sam had been a lifelong dissident but had no experience in government. Therefore, his appointments were crucial to the success of his government. From the beginning of his term, his appointments were one mistake after another.[167] He relied on recommendations of his informal aides rather than submitting them through official channels which were based on a screening system. The prime minister and presidential chief of staff played no role in appointment. Kim's appointments were heavily skewed toward his long-term followers, irrespective of their professional backgrounds. As a result, his appointments compromised the competence and efficiency of the government, undermined the expansion of his power base, and bred favoritism and corruption.

Without an effective presidential staff, it is impossible to assure appropriate decision-making and implementation of policies. The Blue House staff, which was composed of inexperienced outsiders, was incapable of preparing practical policies for Kim's major agendas and of monitoring and coordinating these policies. He did not realize that government experience and

---

[165] Shin, *Mass Politics*, 252-253.
[166] Gallup Korea survey, January 22-February 2, 1994.
[167] For an evaluations of Kim's appointment policy, see Kyung-hyo Park, "Minister- and Vice-Minister Level Staffing of the Kim Young-sam Administration", *Korea Journal* (summer 1999): 133-161; Chong-Bum Lee, "Traits of President Kim Young-sam's Leadership and National Management Style", *Proceedings of the Korean Public Administration Association* (spring 1994), 5-31; and Sok Hong Oh, "Is Appointment Everything or a Disaster?" *Shindonga* (October 1994): 218-223.

expertise were crucial qualifications for presidential staff. Presidential advice is too important to be limited to those the president has known intimately for many years.[168]

Kim had repeatedly pledged he would not make frequent changes in top administration posts. However, Kim appointed and replaced his prime minister and cabinet ministers any time he desired; government reshuffles became almost an annual ritual. During his five-year term, he reshuffled his cabinet six times. The average tenure of his ministers was less than twelve months (see Table 13). As a result, his cabinet never settled down to the work of devising long-term policies.[169] Before and after his inauguration, Kim had repeatedly said that he would borrow other people's brains. Thus, his frequent changes of senior officials led some South Koreans to joke that he "borrowed too many people's brains."

As one of Kim's advisers said, frequent and sudden changes of ministers and other high-ranking officials brought confusion, inconsistency, and unpredictability of policy.[170] His ministers and advisers never developed intimate working relationships with the president, and they were reluctant to tell the president something that was different from his position. Even within the Blue House, there were serious disputes among his senior advisers on the direction of policy.[171] In fact, while Kim appeared strong throughout his term, his staff and cabinet were weak.

Table 13. **Average Tenure of Kim Young Sam's Ministers**[172]

Ministers	Months	Ministries	Months
Prime Minister	10	Foreign Affairs	20
Finance & Economy	8.6	Defense	15
Trade & Industry	12	Justice	12
Agriculture	10	Education	12
Telecommunications	15	Home Affairs	8.6
Construction & Transportation	12	Culture & Sports	15
Science & Technology	12	Unification	10
Environment	10	Government Administration	8.6
Health & Welfare	7.5	Information	60
Labor	12	Political Affairs I	7.5
Presidential Economic Adviser	10	Political Affairs II	15
		Presidential Chief of Staff	15

Source: The Civil Service Commission

---

[168] Richard Neustadt argues that one critical component of the qualifications of White House staffers is governmental experience. See Neustadt, *op. cit.*, 54.

[169] According to comparative evaluations of Korean presidents, Kim Young Sam's personnel management ranks third with 49 points (maximum of 100%) after Park Chung Hee (69%) and Chun Doo Hwan (65%). In fact, Kim's score is similar to that of Syngman Rhee (48.6%) and Roh Tae Woo (47%). Hankuk daetongryong pyongga wiwonhoe (2002), 81.

[170] Choe Yang-bu, "*Nongrim haeyang soosuk sa yeon yigaewol yookil* (4 Years 2 Months and 6 Days as Senior Secretary for Agriculture)" in Sung Deuk Ham, ed. (2001), 242-246.

[171] Se-Il Park, *op. cit.*, 41-47; and Jeon Sung Chul, *op. cit.*, 121ff.

[172] It becomes 11.8 months if the exceptionally long term of the information minister is not included.

In South Korea, presidential power is perceived as unrestricted. As a result, the democratically elected president exercised his power without any constraints. He had a flair for daring political moves and a sensitivity to public opinion. He was thus often criticized as arrogant, capricious, and undemocratic. Even one of his top advisers, Chu Don-shik, later criticized Kim's leadership style:

> "President Kim decided by himself in secret most of the early reform measures and announced them by surprise. He rarely consulted about those "surprise" measures with his advisers…. Thus, even his close aides had no idea where the reform policies were going and what their contents were…. There was no unreserved discussion among the top leaders of the government on the philosophy and direction of the Kim Young Sam government; there was no consensus on major policies even inside the Blue House…. Such a leadership style resulted in virtual incapacitation of the staff system in the Blue House. The president neglected the most important element in the management of a modern government—organization."[173]

Kim Young Sam was well known for his loose organizational style. He had little respect for, or patience with, bureaucracy, hierarchy, or formal organizational structure. He conducted serious national business outside the formal governmental channels and thus made extensive use of personal networks such as his son and other young loyalists. His obsession with secrecy led him to exclude career bureaucrats from participating in policymaking. His management style carried a lack of system and structure too far. The Kim government operated as little more than "organized anarchy."[174] Kim Young Sam was accustomed to a "boss style" of leadership. Like Kim Dae Jung, Kim Young Sam was a long-term boss of his party. South Korean parties were far from democratic or policy-oriented; they were the political machines of their bosses. Considering his assertive personality and political success early on, it was not surprising that as president he would manage national affairs in his own style. Nobody could say "no" to him. He had no equal, only followers.

Before long, his leadership style began to trouble many observers. His anti-corruption measures were not based on laws and regulations but on personal enmities. Many of the targets of these measures were penalized retrospectively on moral charges, not on legal charges.[175] Although Kim had been a long-term pro-democracy activist, he had neither knowledge about nor belief in democracy. Just like his authoritarian predecessors, he was authoritarian in his mentality and psychology. The "democratic" government appeared overly centered on the person of Kim Young Sam: it was run more by persons than by institutions. The president was always at the top and at the forefront of all reform policies. As a result, not only was public participation hampered, but the bureaucracy and the ruling party were also relegated to the status of supporting

---

[173] Chu Don Shik (1997), 43ff and 99-100. Chu, who was a career journalist, served as senior secretary for political affairs, presidential spokesman, minister of culture and sports, and minister of political affairs under Kim Young Sam.

[174] Michael D. Cohen and James G. March, *Leadership and Ambiguity* (New York: McGraw-Hill, 1974), 3.

[175] Myoung-Soo Kim, "Government Reform in the Republic of Korea", in Christopher J. Sigur, ed., *Continuity and Change in Contemporary Korea* (New York: Carnegie Council, 1994), 44.

institutions, blindly carrying out the president's declarations and instructions.[176] Although he had served as a national assemblyman for more than thirty years, he belittled the role of the National Assembly. The personalization of the presidency and the role of patronage in politics reached new heights under Kim's leadership. His leadership style, often dubbed "rule of man," was denounced as "civilian dictatorship" by the press.[177]

Kim Young Sam was not satisfied to rule through 'legal legitimacy' but tried to base his legitimacy on 'morality.' He was criticized for being arrogant and self-assertive; by wielding the sword of morality against an establishment that he considered immoral and corrupt, he purged his enemies through presidential decrees and at his own discretion. Since his government was a legitimate one and was pursuing righteous missions, Kim believed the government and its policies should not be criticized. Anyone who pointed out problems in the reform policies was branded as part of the "anti-reform" forces. But the reformer could hardly claim moral superiority over the accused. As an American scholar pointed out, in a politics in which too much attention is given to moral standards, the capabilities of politicians and the government go unexamined.[178] The editor-in-chief of the *Chosun Ilbo* later described the dogmatism of President Kim Young Sam:

> "Once in charge he became too intoxicated with the legitimacy of his presidency and his self-invented correction of the history, and became convinced that everything he decided on was good and right, while anything opposing him was evil and anti-reform. He never escaped from this dogma throughout his term in office. As a result his authoritarianism was similar to or even worse than the previous governments', as there was no retreating or compromise."[179]

Through an aggressive anticorruption drive, Kim acquired a Mr. Clean image during the early period of his term. However, after a series of corruption scandals, particularly the scandals implicating his own son and close associates, his politics of morality crumbled.[180] Anti-government struggle is one thing and governing is another. His ambition overrode his talent. He was definitely reformist, even revolutionary, but lacked the necessary control capability and administrative skill to carry out reforms.

More than seven years after his retirement, an aspect of illegal spying operations was disclosed and has become an earth-shaking political issue. During the Kim administration the Agency for National Security Planning (KCIA) had conducted extensive eavesdropping on conversations of numerous influential figures at restaurants and other places of entertainment. The second son of President Kim had reportedly received regular reports from the spy agency along with a close aide of the president.

---

[176] Sunhyuk Kim, "The Political Origins of South Korea's Economic Crisis: Is Democratization to Blame?" *Democratization*, 7:4 (winter 2000), 92-93.

[177] Lim Seong-Ho, "A Paradox of Korean Democracy: 50 Years of Experience of the 'Imperial' Presidency and the 'Peripheral' Legislature", *Korea and World Affairs*, 22:4 (winter 1998): 533; and Hahm and Kim, *op. cit.*, 484.

[178] Barber, *Presidential Character*, viii.

[179] "Road for the Ruling Party", *Chosun Ilbo*, January 30, 1999.

[180] The ex-chairman of Kia Motors (Kim Sun Hong) handed over bribes of approximately $10 million to Kim Young Sam in three separate meetings, according to his parliamentary testimony on January 22, 1999. Kim had extended dinner invitations to businessmen in exchange for the equivalent in Korean *won* of more than $1 million, said one witness, while lesser donors were invited for tea. See *Yonhap News*, January 22, 1999.

Kim Young Sam, who repeatedly said he was a victim of the KCIA and promised to reform the agency, allowed such illegal operations.[181]

Achievements and Legacies. Kim Young Sam started with a grandiose plan to cure the deep-rooted "Korean disease" and build a new Korea. Reform was the central theme of the Kim presidency, and the scope of the reforms launched was broad. Starting with political and administrative spheres, the government launched a series of bold and comprehensive reforms. Certainly Kim made a significant contribution to the consolidation of Korean democracy.[182] He made progress in dismantling the power base of the authoritarian governments, de-politicizing and downsizing the security agencies, and establishing firm civilian control of the military. Despite the controversies surrounding the prosecution and imprisonment of two former presidents and the massive purges of military officers, political pacification of the military was perhaps the most important and long-lasting accomplishment of the Kim Young Sam years. The Kim government also revised laws to create greater local self-government, and in 1995 provincial governors and city mayors were elected for the first time since 1961.

Kim launched an aggressive anti-corruption drive. He was determined to terminate the collusive links between government and business. For this purpose, he introduced the real-name financial transaction system, which was hailed in both domestic and foreign media as a key to transparency in all economic transactions. The measures were also regarded as a significant step toward achieving a clean political system. To ensure freer, cleaner, and more frugal elections, the Kim administration enacted the Comprehensive Election Law, which increased government subsidies to campaigns and allowances for politicians with strict upper limits on what politicians could spend. Despite the short-term side effects, his globalization initiative, including Korea's entry into the OECD, also contributed to the country's adaptation to the age of borderless economy.

Although reform was Kim's top agenda, his reform efforts were not very effective. The magnitude of the reforms undertaken by the administration may have been unprecedented, but the reforms tended to be piecemeal and unsystematic: although some of the early reform measures were carried out resolutely, most other reforms were poorly planned, poorly implemented, or attempted and failed.[183] The public was tired of reform for reform's sake without tangible benefits.

The legacy of convicting two former presidents appears to be profound and serious; the convictions marred the authority and credibility of the presidency itself. The trials have made South Koreans believe that all political leaders are corrupt and frequently violate laws. At first, the people applauded the decisive act of convicting the most powerful of the previous governments. However, they soon questioned just how clean

---

[181] "Specter of Eavesdropping", *Korea Herald*, July 23, 2005; and "Eavesdropping: Dirty Games Should Face Full Probe", *Korea Times*, July 22, 2005.

[182] Bae-ho Hahn, "Assessing Kim Young-sam Administration's First Four Years", *Korea Focus*, 5:2 (1997), 1-17.

[183] Young-Jo Lee, "The Rise and Fall of Kim Young Sam's Embedded Reformism", in Diamond and Shin, eds.(2000), 97-125; and Stephan Haggard and David Kang, "The Kim Young Sam Presidency in Comparative Perspective", in Moon and Mo, eds., *op. cit.*, 118-129. For a self-evaluation by the architect of Kim's reform, see Se-Il Park, *op. cit.*, 63-93, and Jeon Sung-Chul (2001), 116-202.

and democratic President Kim Young Sam and his government were. If the top leaders were distrusted, how could they trust other leaders such as ministers and lawmakers? Before long, Kim himself was denounced by the public. As more and more scandals rocked the nation, distrust in leaders and government deepened.

Furthermore, Kim Young Sam interpreted Korea's history in his own way. He rejected the legitimacy of his predecessors, believing perhaps that this would strengthen the legitimacy of his own government. But if the people believed that leaders who had led South Korea through the Korean War and the country's astounding industrialization were illegitimate or worthy of distrust, how could they respect the authority of the Kim Young Sam presidency or any president that would follow? He overemphasized the legitimacy of his rule when he invoked heritage of the independence and democratic movements. History cannot be rectified by decisions of the head of state. Historical events and historical facts cannot be changed in retrospect.[184] We need to learn a lesson from Simone Weil, a French political philosopher, who wrote, "The destruction of the past is perhaps the greatest of all crime."[185]

The primary duty of a democratic leadership is to manage the nation and then pass the reigns to a successor. The rash and ambitious initiative "to rectify history" or "to build a new Korea" damaged rather than strengthened Korea's national institutions. Improving the image and legitimacy of the presidency will be an important task for Kim's successors. His successors will learn from Kim Young Sam that a "negative agenda" does not guarantee success.

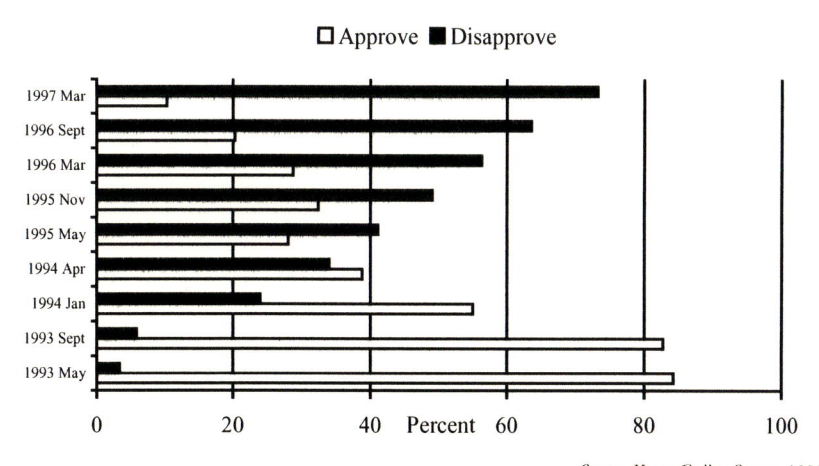

Figure 14. **Approval Rating of Kim Young Sam** (%)

Source: Korea Gallup Survey, 1993-97

Just after his inauguration, Kim's approval rating reached 90 percent. At the time of his departure from office it was at the single digit level (see Figure 14). His early popularity is

---

[184] Juergen Kleiner, *Korea: A Century of Change* (Singapore: World Scientific, 2001), 234-243.
[185] Lewis D. Eigen and Jonathan P. Sigel, *Dictionary of Political Quotations* (New York: Macmillan, 1993), 284.

a typical example of a "political bubble," created by the combination of his quixotic leadership style and the sensational media. Without tangible reforms and achievements, the presidency was destined to disaster. Kim was a successful fighter for democracy, but out of his element in the Blue House.

At the beginning, it seemed to be a perfect time for a new start. But it did not work out well. Economically, politically, and socially, Korea was in far worse shape in 1997 than it was in 1993—at home and abroad. Kim Young Sam misdiagnosed the "Korean disease" and brought his nation economic disaster, which seriously disrupted the momentum of Korea's nation building. The demise of the Cold War led to the dawning of a new era in which top priority is placed on the economy. Internally, democratization had made solving economic issues an even more critical task. Unfortunately, the economy was not on his agenda; from his inauguration to the final day of his term, he emphasized hollow slogans such as reform and anti-corruption. In the end, rampant political corruption, the 1997 financial crisis and consequent hardship, and unfinished reforms were lingering legacies of the Kim Young Sam presidency. Kim Young Sam has often been labeled South Korea's most ineffective leader.

His failure as president tarnished his lifelong contribution to Korean democratic development. It was a time to consolidate Korea's nation building rather than to start a "new nation building." Despite the retrogressions and failures of his reform efforts, Korean democracy made great strides under the leadership of Kim Young Sam. His lifelong struggle for Korean democracy as an opposition leader left a great mark on Korean history. If he had exhibited better management skills, he might have been a more successful president.

Kim Dae Jung

Chapter Eight
Kim Dae Jung
Groping for Reunification

> "The Government of the People will push democracy and economic development at the same time. Democracy and the market economy are two sides of a coin."
>
> "At last the sun is rising on national reunification, reconciliation and peace."
>
> – Kim Dae Jung

On February 25, 1998, Kim Dae Jung, the most renowned champion of Korean democracy, assumed the presidency of a nation in the maelstrom of financial crisis. His inauguration marked a major milestone in South Korea's quest for democracy. With his inauguration, South Korea became the first of East Asia's new democracies to peacefully transfer power to an opposition party. Kim Dae Jung's life as a freedom fighter had often been compared to that of South Africa's Nelson Mandela and Poland's Lech Walesa. The inauguration also represented the ultimate vindication of his turbulent political career. Before achieving victory in 1997, Kim had faced defeat in three presidential elections (1971, 1987 and 1992). At age seventy-three, the indefatigable Kim had finally achieved his life's ambition. He was the first South Korean president from outside the southeastern Kyongsang region in nearly forty years. As such, his presidency presented him with an opportunity to overcome the discrimination against the Cholla region from whence he hailed.

Kim Dae Jung was an unyielding leader: a lifelong dissident of international renown, a survivor of exile, imprisonment, a death sentence, and two alleged assassination attempts. Because of his longstanding commitment to democracy, he enjoyed a great deal of goodwill and support from abroad. Like the fall of the Berlin Wall and the election of Nelson Mandela as president of South Africa, the election of Kim Dae Jung was placed in the genre of those "impossible" political events that shake the world. An editorial in *The Washington Post* exulted:

> "You could write the latest South Korean election as a fairy tale: Once upon a time there was an evil ruler who oppressed his people, and a brave man who stood up to him. The ruler tried to kill the brave man, and threw him in prison; but the people rose up, put the ruler in jail, acclaimed the brave man as ruler—and lived happily ever after."[1]

Over the previous five years, Kim Dae Jung had watched the Kim Young Sam administration progressively flounder in a web of corruption and mismanagement. Many worried that Kim Dae Jung might repeat his predecessor's mistakes. Since Kim Young

---

[1] *Washington Post*, December 21, 1997.

Sam was regarded as a failed president, Kim Dae Jung immediately pledged not to repeat his predecessor's mistakes, promising a new style of leadership.

Kim Dae Jung inherited the nation at its worst possible moment. Also, he came to power with a number of handicaps. He had been accused for many years and by a succession of governments of being a leftist, and was mistrusted by conservatives and the military. He represented a minority government and therefore lacked a strong, broad power base from which to pursue national reform. Neither Kim nor his close associates had administrative experience. Finally, as he undertook the demanding position of president, a heavy burden for one at any age, Kim was seventy-three years old.

THE MAN AND HIS CHARACTER

Kim Dae Jung was born on January 6, 1924, the second of four sons in a poor family on a remote and underdeveloped island off Korea's southwestern tip.[2] The Kim family moved to the nearest port city of Mokpo, where Kim Dae Jung attended Mokpo Commercial High School and graduated in 1943. This was the end of his formal education. During 1943-45 he worked in a Japanese marine company. In 1945, at the age of twenty, he was married to Cha Yong-ae.

Just after the liberation, in October 1945, the already ambitious young Kim joined a leftist people's committee and a leftist political party (Sinmindang) which soon merged with the Korean Communist Party that was eventually renamed the South Korean Workers' Party. He was also actively involved in a leftist youth organization, the Democratic Youth Alliance (Minju chongyon dongmaeng), a front organization of the leftist party. In 1947 he established a small marine business. During the Korean War, when almost all young Korean youths were engaged in fighting, he did not fulfill the mandatory military service.[3] Instead, he reestablished the marine company and published a local newspaper. His business appears to have met with little success, leading him into a series of business ventures within a short period of time. In 1954 he ran unsuccessfully for a seat in the National Assembly. His second bid for an assembly seat in 1958 failed again. Her husband's electoral failures reportedly led his wife to suicide. The couple had two sons. Shortly thereafter he was elected as an assemblyman in the 1961 by-election, only to forfeit his seat within days when the military junta led by General Park Chung Hee dissolved the National Assembly.[4]

In 1962, an important turning point in Kim's life came with his marriage to thirty-nine-year-old Lee Hee-ho. At the time she was secretary general of the YMCA in Seoul. Two years older than Kim, Lee had graduated from the prestigious Seoul National University and gone on to study sociology at Lambuth College in Jackson, Tennessee, eventually receiving a master's degree from Scarritt College in Nashville.[5] Her American education

---

[2] For his autobiography, see Kim Dae Jung, *Yoksa wa hamkke sidae wa hamkke: Kim Dae Jung jaseojon* (With the History and the Time: Kim Dae Jung Autobiography), vol. 1 and 2 (Seoul: Indong, 1999).
[3] Cho Gapje, "*Jwaik jojikwon sijeolui sagondul* (Occurrences during the Time of a Leftist Activist)", *Wolgan Chosun* (April 2002).
[4] Kim Su-yong (1986), 14; Oh Kyung-hwan (1992), 194.
[5] Lee Hee Ho, trans. T.C. Rhee, *My Love, My Country* (Los Angeles, CA: Center for Multiethnic and Transnational Studies, University of Southern California, 1997).

and social activities in Korea became important elements in his political success.

Kim's political life became very active following his election to the National Assembly in 1963. From this time on, he became known as one of the most persistent and courageous democratic activists. He worked his way up through the ranks of the opposition party and, at the party's national convention in September 1970, the forty-six year-old Kim Dae Jung was nominated presidential candidate of the opposition New Democratic Party. His 1971 candidacy brought him international attention for the first time when he received 45 percent of the vote against the powerful Park Chung Hee, who won by nearly a million votes, a margin of 7.9 percent. Frustrated by the defeat, Kim went abroad. When Park Chung Hee managed a constitutional coup by adopting the *Yushin* system in 1972, Kim remained in the United States rather than joining the opposition's fight against the Park regime. While visiting Japan from the United States in August 1973, Kim was kidnapped from Tokyo by KCIA agents and brought back to his home in Seoul.

From then Kim was periodically put under house-arrest or jailed for his radical views and activities. He repeatedly asserted that the Park government had attempted several times to kill him (the first attempt, he believes, was in 1971, when a truck plowed into his car leaving him with a permanent limp).[6] Ironically, it was in great part due to his kidnapping that Kim earned international renown as a democratic crusader, as well as a victim of Park's iron-fisted rule. Ultimately this image contributed to Kim's success in winning the presidency. His strong anti-Park rhetoric attracted a large progressive and radical following. Thus, Kim acquired a reputation for being radical and even dangerous.[7]

After the assassination of Park Chung Hee, Kim was released from house arrest. After a brief period of political activity, in the spring of 1980 he was again arrested by the martial law command on charges of inciting riots in Kwangju. Sentenced to death by a military court, he saw the sentence later commuted to life imprisonment, and then to twenty years. In 1982, with the help of the Reagan administration, he was allowed to visit the United States for medical attention. As a condition of his release he pledged not to engage in politics. However, once in the United States he saw an opportunity to sell himself as a champion of Korean democracy and embarked on a campaign of speaking tours, galvanizing Korean-American support for his cause. On February 7, 1985, on the eve of crucial parliamentary elections, he returned to Seoul protected by a large group of American and Korean-American supporters and reporters.[8]

In the summer of 1987, Roh Tae Woo's declaration of democratic reforms provoked a rivalry between Kim Dae Jung and Kim Young Sam. Kim Dae Jung formed his own party and declared himself a presidential candidate, ultimately placing third with 27 percent of the popular vote. In 1992, Kim ran again for the presidency, and again met

---

[6] Kim Chung-yum, the chief of staff of President Park during the 1970s, said during an interview, "The accident occurred when Kim's car over-sped along a raining highway to catch a plane at Kwangju airport." Kim was behind schedule after he had a political meeting in a local city.

[7] Cotton, ed., *Politics and Policy*, 54.

[8] Cumings, *Korea's Place*, 381. Richard Walker, former U.S. ambassador to Seoul, at the time wrote: "Before and during Kim's return to Seoul, he (Walker) had witnessed Kim's numerous unkept pledges and statements not to enter politics again", leading him to believe that Kim Dae Jung was unpredictable. "Kim DJ Tried to Put Himself at Center of Media Attention", Ambassador Walker's Korean Remembrance (6), *Korea Times*, August 15, 1997.

defeat. But he never gave up. In September 1995, Kim formed a new party, the National Congress for New Politics (NCNP), to run again.

The Cholla region had a long anti-establishment tradition. Indeed, it had a distinctive history, going back at least thirteen hundred years to a time when it was the site of a separate Baekje dynasty. Eventually conquered by the more powerful Silla dynasty in the eastern part of the peninsula, the Cholla region had been disadvantaged and discriminated against ever since. Kim Dae Jung well understood the alienation the Cholla people felt, and used it to his own political ends. In a collection of essays he wrote: "I was born in Cholla province...that has maintained a long pangol [anti-establishment] tradition.... The tradition gave rise to the Donghak [Eastern Learning] uprising, which preached the egalitarian idea that 'all men are divine.' I believe this to be an astoundingly revolutionary idea." [9] He understood and used the grievances of the Cholla population. He became their advocate, their champion, and their unquestioned leader. Cholla was his long-time power base, but in the national context his regional background was largely perceived as a handicap.[10]

Kim Dae Jung is a man who generates both intense loyalty and intense antagonism. During his life-long struggle against the military-dominated governments, he acquired an image not only as a champion of democracy but also as a divisive leader with distinct "socialist" leanings. Most political observers agreed that Kim had outstanding political skill, a skill his detractors frequently labeled demagoguery. As a smart and accomplished survivor, he developed an ability to mobilize his supporters to pursue his goals without leaving traces of his own involvement. Many South Koreans distrusted him simply because they could not predict what he would do next. Thus, he was recognized as one of the most controversial political figures South Korea had ever produced.

POLITICS OF THE ECONOMIC CRISIS

Kim Dae Jung had been both a victim and a beneficiary of regionalism. Before his December 1997 victory, he had lost three presidential elections; the rise of regionalism, for which he had been partly responsible, had reduced his chances of victory. [11] The unswerving loyalty of the Cholla people automatically made Kim a major contender in Korea's presidential elections. However, as Kyongsang had double the population of Cholla, he was always at a disadvantage. Outside the Cholla region suspicion of Kim Dae Jung ran deep.

The political landscape for Kim Dae Jung was more favorable than ever during the 1997 presidential election. President Kim Young Sam's anti-corruption drive had virtually destroyed the ruling coalition that had propelled him into office in 1992. Kim Young Sam punished his two predecessors, Chun Doo Hwan and Roh Tae Woo, who

---

[9] Kim Dae Jung, *Hengdong hanun yangsim uro* (With a Conscience in Action) (Seoul: Kummundang, 1985), 39-42. The *Donghak* uprising originated in the Cholla region and swept the southwestern part of Korea during the first half of the 1860s, resurging in 1894 with strong anti-foreign (notably anti-Japanese) overtones.

[10] "Kim Dae Jung: A Political Profile", *BBC News*, February 24, 1998.

[11] For details of the 1997 presidential election, see David I. Steinberg, "Korea: Triumph Amid Turmoil", *Journal of Democracy* 9:2 (1998): 76-90; and Byung-Kook Kim, "Electoral Politics and Economic Crisis, 1997–1998", in Diamond and Kim, eds. (2000), 173-201.

both hailed from North Kyongsang Province. Kim Jong-pil and Park Tae-joon, co-chairmen of the ruling party with Kim Young Sam during the Roh administration, were forced out of the ruling party. In early 1995, Kim Jong-pil set up his own party, the United Liberal Democrats (ULD). Other leading figures purged from the ruling party joined the ULD.

Kim Dae Jung's primary rival in 1997 was Lee Hoi-chang, former prime minister in the Kim Young Sam government and the candidate of the ruling party. Lee's squeaky clean image was tarnished, however, when it was revealed that his two sons had been exempted from the military service ostensibly compulsory for all South Korean youths. Further, as the candidate and chairman of the ruling party, it was difficult for Lee Hoi-chang to distance himself from the ongoing economic crisis. Rhee In-je, after losing the ruling party's presidential nomination, launched his own party and declared his presidential candidacy, splitting the pro-government vote. The other leading opposition candidate was Kim Jong-pil, head of the ULD, who stressed a constitutional amendment to adopt a cabinet system.[12]

Now seventy-three, this was a last bid effort for Kim Dae Jung. To achieve his long-cherished goal, Kim Dae Jung had to forge an alliance with the conservative Kim Jong-pil, formerly a close associate of Park Chung Hee. Under the deal, Kim Jong-pil withdrew from the race and lent his support to Kim Dae Jung in return for the position of prime minister and an agreement that the coalition would revise the constitution by the end of 1999 to put Korea under a cabinet system. The alliance added the support of Kim Jong-pil's home provinces of Chungchong, and ensured that the conservative votes in other parts of the country would not necessarily all go to the candidate of the ruling party.

Kim Dae Jung and Lee Hoi-chang were running neck-and-neck until the campaign's final days. In the end, Kim achieved his lifelong ambition by the slimmest of margins—only 1.5 percent (390,000 votes out of 26 million votes cast)—the narrowest winning margin in any Korean presidential contest; Kim secured 40.3 percent of the vote, with Lee gaining 38.7 percent and Rhee placing a poor third with 19.2 percent. However, Kim's support was extremely uneven (see Figure 15).

Kim swept his power base of Kwangju City and the Cholla provinces with more than 93 percent of the vote, but received less than 15 percent of the vote in the more populated southeastern region of the country—the Kyongsang area, suggesting that antipathy against Kim Dae Jung was very strong there. Kim Dae Jung earned considerable support in the Chungchong region, the power base of Kim Jong-pil, which significantly contributed to his victory.[13] Moreover, if it had not been for Rhee In-je, Kim's victory would have been impossible. Thus, Kim's victory did not reflect his own strength as much as it did the many mistakes and weakness of the Kim Young Sam government and his party.

Kim Dae Jung, who had no time to celebrate his hard-fought victory, had cast

---

[12] *Chosun Ilbo*, June 25, 1997.

[13] The votes Kim Dae Jung received from Taejon and Chungchong provinces were some 11-20 percent higher than those he earned in the region in the previous presidential elections.

himself as a manager of economic crisis.[14] After being briefed by government officials, the president-elect "could hardly sleep," fearing the country might go bankrupt "tomorrow or the day after."[15] The deteriorating economic situation required urgent decisions, but the outgoing president had lost the authority to rule. Mainly because of the urgent need to address the worst economic crisis in decades, president-elect Kim virtually took full charge of the nation and its efforts to overcome the crisis during the two-month transition period.

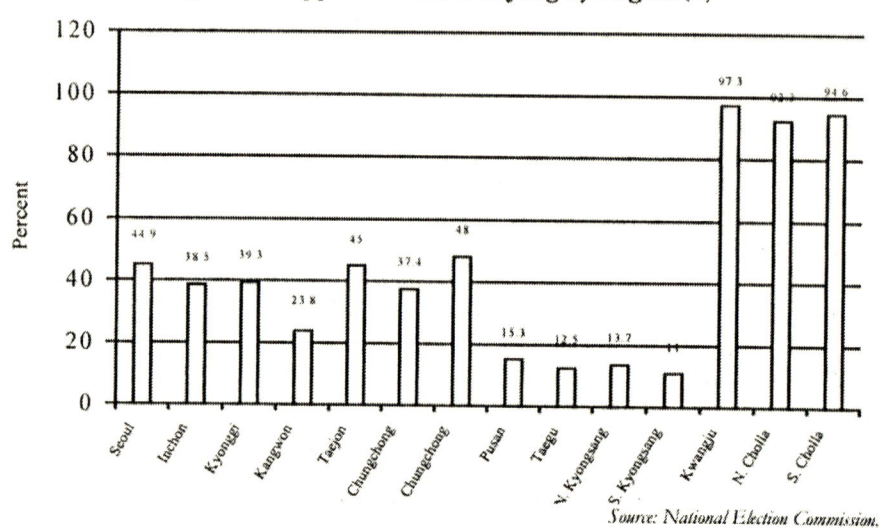

Figure 15. Support for Kim Dae Jung by Region (%)

Source: National Election Commission.

On December 20, only two days after the election, President Kim Young Sam and president-elect Kim Dae Jung met and formalized a six-point agreement, including the establishment of a joint economic crisis management committee consisting of Kim Dae Jung's aides and officials from the outgoing administration, to deal with the crisis and act as the nation's top economic policymaking body during the transition period.[16] The most pressing challenge the joint committee faced was the threat of national bankruptcy. On December 23, the won fell to a record low of 2,067 won to the dollar and rumors spread of an imminent national moratorium caused by a shortage of dollars. An immediate infusion of external funds to sustain the economy was the top priority. The country had foreign debts of $24.6 billion due by the end of December and a further $14.9 billion due to be repaid by the end of January 1998.

---

[14] "Korea: President-Elect Kim's Visions to Be Challenged under IMF Shadow", *Korea Economic Daily*, December 30, 1997.
[15] *Joongang Ilbo*, December 23, 1997.
[16] "Kim's De Facto Rule Focused on Crisis Management", *Korea Herald*, February 23, 1998.

What the Korean media was to dub "dollar diplomacy" became one of Kim Dae Jung's key activities during this period. He telephoned foreign leaders, such as American President Bill Clinton and Japanese Prime Minister Ryutaro Hashimoto, to assure them of his commitment to pull Korea out of its economic problems and to ask for their help. The U.S. undersecretary of the treasury, David Lipton, who visited Seoul only a few days after the Korean election to gauge Kim's support for the reform program, was particularly reassured by Kim's reform enthusiasm and helped encourage American banks to participate in negotiations to rollover short-term debt.[17] When international financier George Soros visited Seoul in early January 1998, he dined at the home of Kim Dae Jung, who encouraged him to invest in South Korea. This amicable meeting with Soros "worked wonders" in turning international perceptions of Kim Dae Jung in a favorable direction.[18] Unlike his predecessor, Kim Dae Jung was confident in dealing with Westerners, having lived three years in the United States during his self-imposed political exile.

A negotiating team was sent to the United States to discuss extensions for the short-term loans and, on January 28, 1998, it achieved a major breakthrough by concluding a formal rollover agreement with the major international creditor banks. Under the agreement, $24 billion in short-term loans was to be restructured into longer-term debt, ending the worst moments of the financial crisis.[19]

Kim Dae Jung and his advisers were quick to point out that the administrative failures of the outgoing government were a partial cause of the economic crisis, and to argue for the reform of government. On January 26, 1998, a month before his inauguration, Kim Dae Jung's Government Reform Committee submitted proposals calling for major reductions and changes in most ministries.[20] In February, the National Assembly passed a government reorganization bill. Under the new law, the vice-premier-level boards for economy and unification were downgraded to ministries, while the Ministry of Public Information and two state ministers for political affairs were abolished. The Planning and Budget Commission under direct supervision of the president was also established. Elimination of the vice-premier for economic affairs, who had been responsible for overseeing and coordinating economic policies since 1963, was the most significant change.

As part of his economic reform initiative, on January 13 the president-elect met the heads of the four largest *chaebol* and pressured them to drastically restructure their business groups.[21] They reached an agreement on principles of corporate restructuring. Big businesses bowed to political pressure and announced downsizing and restructuring programs. Soon afterward Kim met with another group of leaders representing thirty second-tier conglomerates, who also agreed to undertake restructuring efforts.

Using his influence with the labor unions, on January 15, 1998, Kim Dae Jung

---

[17] Scott Snyder, "Patterns of Negotiation in a South Korean Cultural Context", *Asian Survey*, 39:3 (May/June 1999): 414.

[18] Francois Godement, *The Downsizing of Asia* (London: Routledge, 1998), 81.

[19] Shalendra Sharma, "Asia's Economic Crisis and the IMF", *Survival* (summer 1998): 47.

[20] For details, see Kim Kwang-woong, "A Critical Reflection on the Reform of the Kim Dae-Jung Government", *Korea Journal* (summer 1999): 25-36.

[21] *Korea Herald*, January 14, 1998.

initiated a tripartite committee composed of labor, business and government representatives. On February 6, the committee announced an agreement reflecting a grand compromise between labor and business on issues of layoffs and restructuring. A week later the National Assembly passed a package of eighteen economic-related laws designed to implement these agreed measures.[22] The hard-won enactment helped bolster international confidence in the South Korean economy. Thus, even before his inauguration Kim Dae Jung had forged a basic institutional framework for economic reform by launching a triple program of debt rescheduling, government reorganization, and labor-management compromise.

In an effort to appeal to the people directly, Kim held a "conversation with the people" in January 1998. He answered questions from a live audience in the KBS television studio in Seoul and on the streets of South Korea. Asked by a businessman if Korea's economy might collapse, Kim responded, "Not in a year but in a few days the country can go bankrupt unless we cope with the situation." To the nation Kim projected confidence in the midst of crisis, reassuring his audience, "I have prepared for the presidency for many years. Just trust me, I know I can do it, just trust me."[23]

In order to overcome the main handicap of his new government, Kim repeatedly emphasized that he would cure one of Korea's long-standing social ills—regional antagonism. He publicly called on President Kim Young Sam to pardon two former presidents, Chun Doo Hwan and Roh Tae Woo. Kim Dae Jung's long-term cronies announced that they would not seek cabinet posts or other high-ranking government positions. Kim Dae Jung was widely seen as an outstanding president-elect. The international community recognized his pre-inauguration performance in adroitly rescuing the nation from the economic abyss.

The economic crisis was such a shock to the South Korean people that a broad national consensus emerged. Some even joked that Kim Dae Jung had "the mandate of heaven." Teetering on the brink of economic insolvency, Koreans pinned their hopes on the newly inaugurating president. Since the December election, the nation had quickly mobilized on a semi-war footing in response to patriotic appeals to overcome the economic crisis. More than $2 billion in gold had been collected from citizens to help pay the nation's foreign debt. A campaign had also been launched for blood donations to reduce imports of expensive plasma, while sales of foreign consumer goods dried up in an effort to cut the trade deficit. At the time of his inauguration more than twice as many South Koreans supported him as had voted for him only two months previously.[24]

On February 25, 1998, Kim Dae Jung was sworn in as president. In his inaugural address, the new president was frank about the "stupefying situation" facing the nation and the economic suffering that lay ahead. Sounding like Franklin D. Roosevelt in 1933, Kim asked the people to prepare themselves for difficulties and sacrifices: "All of us are being asked to shed sweat and tears."[25] He termed the current economic crisis "the most

---

[22] *Korea Newsreview*, February 21, 1998.
[23] Kim Dae Jung, "Conversation with Citizens", Korea Broadcasting System, January 19, 1998.
[24] "Kim stands tall before Korea", *Financial Times*, February 25, 1998; and *Overcoming A National Crisis: The Republic of Korea Rises Up Again*, the Blue House, February 25, 1998.
[25] "Inaugural Address", in the Presidential Secretariat (1999), vol. I, 5.

serious national crisis since the Korean War." Kim appealed to the public to support his efforts to overcome the economic crisis and pledged to achieve political and economic reforms. Rejecting the so-called "Asian values" that give priority to economic growth rather than democracy and human rights, the new president called for a new partnership between capitalism and democracy:

> "The Government of the People will push democracy and economic development at the same time. Democracy and the market economy are two sides of a coin or two wheels of a cart; if they were separated we could never succeed.... Nations...that have rejected democracy and accepted only a market economy have ended up suffering disastrous setbacks. When democracy and a market economy develop together in harmony, there cannot be collusion between politics and business, government-directed financing, irregularities and corruption."[26]

Tough tasks lay ahead: Kim was mandated to put a tattered economy back on track under the IMF framework.[27] However, his popular mandate was limited: his power rested on a weak coalition with the conservative ULD. Bipartisan efforts were necessary to get the nation through the economic difficulties and to fend off public concerns regarding massive layoffs and runaway inflation as a result of the bitter pill of IMF measures. Though confidence in his leadership was widespread, so were feelings of doubt and apprehension.

Figures released by the National Statistics Office put a numerical face on the economic crisis. More than 3,000 small and medium-sized companies went bankrupt in January 1998, and industries in general were operating at only 65 percent of total capacity.[28] Unemployment had nearly doubled within a few months and, by October 1998, almost a year into the crisis, unemployment had risen to 7 percent, the worst rate in more than a decade. In 1998 the country suffered the worst drop in annual growth since 1953, the last year of the Korean War, falling 6.7 percent in the first full year of the so-called "IMF era." Per capita income fell to $6,823 in 1998, two-thirds the 1997 figure of $10,379, effectively wiping out the gains of the past eight years.[29]

Entering the Blue House, the minority president felt the limits of his power. The opposition Grand National Party (GNP) held a majority (161) of the 299 seats in the National Assembly, while President Kim's National Congress for New Politics (NCNP) held seventy-eight seats and its coalition partner, the ULD, forty-three seats.[30] The day after the inauguration, the opposition party doused cold water on the new president's hoped-for honeymoon by refusing to confirm Kim Jong-pil, his coalition partner, as prime minister. President Kim appointed Kim Jong-pil as an acting prime minister and formed a new cabinet a day later. Pushing policy measures through a hostile National

---

[26] "Ibid., 7-8.
[27] For the first-year performance of the Kim Dae Jung administration, see Sunhyuk Kim, "The Politics of Reform in South Korea: The First Year of the Kim Dae Jung Government, 1998-1999", *Asian Perspective*, 24:1 (2000): 163-185.
[28] *Korea Economic Daily*, February 5, 1998.
[29] *Korea Economic Daily*, January 21, 1999.
[30] Byung-Kook Kim, "Electoral Politics and Economic Crisis, 1997–1998", in Diamond and Kim, eds. (2000), 192-194.

Assembly was clearly not going to be easy.

From the beginning, Kim Dae Jung was greatly frustrated and irritated by the opposition party's open and continued hostility toward the ruling bloc. His strategy was to neither negotiate nor compromise with the strong opposition. He pursued three interrelated political strategies.[31] The first was to manufacture a parliamentary majority in the National Assembly. The second was to mobilize civil society in support of his policies. The last was to fill the key positions in the government with his people. In an effort to create a parliamentary majority, he launched a campaign to lure opposition lawmakers to join the ruling coalition or to oust them from the National Assembly. The investigative powers of the Prosecutor's Office and the National Tax Administration were used against opposition lawmakers who were suspected of violating various laws. In order to control the opposition and critics, the National Intelligence Service (former KCIA) made use of the dubious practice of wiretapping on 3,580 occasions during the first six months of 1998, a considerable jump from the approximately 2,400 occasions in 1996 under Kim Young Sam.[32] Through such measures, hardly compatible with democratic principles, by September 1998 Kim Dae Jung was able to increase the strength of the governing coalition from 121 to 158.[33] The "manufactured majority" only made the opposition party even more recalcitrant, and they resorted to any means to block, delay, and subvert the government's legislative agenda.

Now controlling the National Assembly, the ruling coalition rammed through sixty-six bills in fifteen minutes amid opposition protest in January 1999, and then in May passed six bills in just eight minutes. The opposition reacted angrily. Branding the Kim government a dictatorial regime, opposition leader Lee Hoi-chang announced the start of what he called a war to restore democracy and prevent further administrative fiascos. The opposition then staged massive outdoor rallies in major cities.[34]

From this point onward, chaotic was the best way to characterize the South Korean political scene. Politics had been tainted by a series of political exposures by ruling and opposition camps looking to discredit one another. The front pages of newspapers were filled with accusations, counteraccusations, and scandals. The prolonged political wrangling overshadowed the debate on crucial pending issues, including the endemic economic crisis. Media coverage of the scandals and political squabbles reached such a point that the general public became weary of all political news.[35]

---

[31] Sunhyuk Kim and Doh Chull Shin, *Economic Crisis and Dual Transition in Korea*, 91.

[32] *Korea Herald*, October 19, 1998. In January 1999, the country was dismayed by the allegation that the National Intelligence Service was spying on the opposition party from a room inside the National Assembly building.

[33] *Korea Herald*, September 30, 1998.

[34] "Opposition Leader Declares War on 'Tyranny' to Restore Democracy", *Korea Herald*, May 7, 1999.

[35] "Chaos Has a Price", *Korea Herald*, November 26, 1999.

Economic Reform Drive

Kim Dae Jung had a mandate to tackle the urgent task of rescuing the nation from its economic crisis.[36] However, the crisis was really an opportunity for the new president; particularly with respect to economic reforms agreed upon with the IMF, it provided him with a once-in-a-generation opportunity to undertake fundamental economic reform. Several factors appeared to be favorable for his reform efforts.

The first was the gravity of the financial crisis itself. No one dared deny the urgent need for reform. The profound sense of national crisis forced South Korean society to rally behind the new president under the banner of economic recovery. The Korean people would have never accepted the radical economic restructuring in the absence of the economic, social, and political chaos created by the crisis.

The second factor was the intense international pressure for reform, especially from the IMF. The IMF demanded structural reforms from the ground up, with the potential consequence of *chaebol* breakup and the closing of many financial institutions. Without far-reaching economic restructuring, the IMF standby agreement and other foreign credits would have been placed in jeopardy. Thus, the government was able to use the IMF as a whipping post during the painful restructuring process.[37]

Finally, as a life-long dissident, Kim was an outsider to the networks of business-government relations that had been built up under his predecessors. He was therefore much less indebted to the business sector than his predecessors and free to break with Korea's prevailing model of economic growth.[38]

The Kim government and the IMF shared the view that over-expansion, mismanagement, and overall inefficiency of conglomerates was one of the most important causes of the 1997 Korean financial crisis. Such an anti-*chaebol* tone was unequivocally enunciated in his inaugural speech. His position on economic policy was also well reflected in his government's publication on "DJnomics."[39] However, broad corporate restructuring required massive layoffs. This was Kim's dilemma. Despite his political debts to labor, he had to restructure the economy as dictated by IMF conditionality. He struggled to juggle these two contradictory postures. "DJnomics" attempted to balance his populist ethos with the neo-conservative mandate for reform.

Since Kim Dae Jung lacked government experience, his selection of an economic team received great attention. As minister of finance and economy, he appointed Lee Kyu-sung who had served as finance minister under Roh Tae Woo. Kim also selected Lee Hun-jai, a former career bureaucrat of the finance ministry, as chairman of the Financial Supervisory Commission, and Jin Nyum, former labor minister during the

---

[36] This section is largely based on the author's interview with Kang Bong-kyun (Kim Dae Jung's economic adviser) on April 22, 2002. See also Kang Bong-kyun, *Hankukkyeongjae Baljeonjeonryak* (Development Strategy of Korean Economy).

[37] Seong-min Yoo, "Industrial Restructuring and Corporate Governance: Policy Issues before, during and after the Crisis", in Smith, ed., *Looking Forward*, 142-148.

[38] Eun Mee Kim. "Reforming the *Chaebols*", Diamond and Shin, eds. (2000), 193.

[39] DJ are the initials for Dae Jung, President Kim's first name. Ministry of Finance and Economy and Korea Development Institute, *DJnomics: Kukminkwa hamkk ae nailul yeonda* [Djnomics: Open Tomorrow with the People] (Seoul, 1998).

previous administration, as chairman of the Planning and Budget Commission. Surprisingly, the president's chief economic adviser was Kim Tae-dong, a liberal economics professor, who had no experience in government but was slated to manage the grave economic crisis nonetheless. Although most key members of the economic policymaking team were experienced, no one could play a leading role.[40] Thus, the government was not without differences in opinion over how to best deal with the economic crisis; in part this reflected the variant philosophies of the administration's economic advisers and ministers. Even President Kim was to later admit, "The economic team was a bit confused at the outset."[41]

Owing to Kim's governmental reorganization, the Ministry of Finance and Economy lost much of the traditional role it had played so successfully during the period of high growth. As a result, it was the president and his staff that tried to directly coordinate and control economic policies. Before long, Kim and his economic adviser, both of whom lacked field knowledge of the economy, encountered difficulties in managing the ongoing financial crisis and in controlling the economy-related ministries. The scholar-turned-economic-adviser was of no help to the president. Less than three months after his appointment, the president replaced his economic adviser with a career economic bureaucrat.

The first two months of the new administration were dominated by the need to focus on restoring financial stability; priority was placed on securing foreign currency liquidity in order to alleviate the immediate liquidity crisis. The government started on its economic reform plan, namely, giving priority to financial and corporate restructuring.[42]

Financial Reforms. It was providential that South Korea already had a plan in place to reform the financial sector during the last months of the Kim Young Sam government. On December 29, 1997, the National Assembly passed thirteen bills needed to carry out the IMF/government financial reform program. As a result, the fragmented financial regulatory bodies were consolidated into a new financial watchdog agency, the Financial Supervisory Commission (FSC), which covered the banking, securities, and insurance industries. In addition, the deposit-insurance system was reformed and a legal basis was established for reorganizing troubled financial firms. At the strong urging of the IMF, fourteen merchant banks were already suspended by December 1997.[43] On February 14, 1998, seventeen additional bills were enacted dealing with financial reform, corporate restructuring, and labor layoffs.

The key agency chosen for carrying out financial reform—and also more general

---

[40] Including Kim's senior secretary for policy planning (Kang Bong-kyun), Lee Kyu-sung, Lee Hun-jai, and Jin Nyum were career bureaucrats in the EPB or finance ministry.

[41] *Korea Herald*, September 29, 1998. See also "*Keongjaetim insaeui nanmaek*" (Confusion in the Appointments of the Economic Team), Series on *Bihwa: Kukmineui jeongbu* (Secret Stories of the Government of the People), *Donga Ilbo*, August 20, 2003.

[42] For details on South Korean economic reforms, see Chong Wa Dae [the Blue House], *The Road to Recovery in 1999*, and *Overcoming A National Crisis: The Republic of Korea Rises Up Again*, February 1999; and Ungsuh K. Park, "Economic Recovery and Future Challenges of Korea", *Korean and World Affairs*, XXV:1 (spring 2001): 65-66. For a critical evaluation of the economic reform, see James Crotty and Kang-Kook Lee, "Economic Performance in Post-crisis Korea: A Critical Perspective on Neo-liberal Restructuring", *Seoul Journal of Economics* (Seoul: summer 2001).

[43] Emery, *Korean Economic Reform*, 90-120.

corporate restructuring—was the FSC, which began work in April 1998. The FSC was designed to be independent of the Ministry of Finance and Economy, but not independent of the Blue House. The FSC was armed with wide-ranging powers to supervise the entire financial system. As a result, the first head of the commission, Lee Hun-jai, was named by Koreans in a poll as the country's most powerful economic manager after the president.[44]

Initiated by the FSC, the financial reforms were almost revolutionary. The restructuring objectives of the sector were to close weak banks and other financial firms, clean up the large volume of non-performing loans, recapitalize viable financial institutions, apply stronger regulation to force banks to avoid excessive risk, and induce foreign banks to take control of much of Korea's banking system in order to modernize its management techniques and raise its profitability.[45] Since the establishment of the Republic, few, if any, commercial banks had been closed. By tradition, banks did not fail and go out of business in Korea; so it was a wrenching experience for Koreans to realize that some banks would lose their identity and be taken over.

Despite the economic difficulties, the government established stricter prudential regulations immediately. Banks were required for the first time to meet the Bank for International Settlement standard (i.e., a bank's capital must be at least 8 percent of its total loans) by the end of 1999. The criteria for classifying non-performing loans were tightened significantly. Owing to the combination of massive bankruptcies and radical financial restructuring, banks were forced to sharply reduce loans to business in order to survive. In order to bail out some financial firms and recapitalize some viable ones, the government was thus required to inject huge public funds into the banking system. The government spent about $140 billion of public funds, an astonishing 29 percent of Korea's GDP in 2000, to bail out the ailing banking industry.[46] The government, which now owns about one third of the banking industry's assets, became the primary shareholder, and ultimate arbiter, of major banks as it injected tremendous public funds into banks whose capital bases were eroded. In effect, the old relationship between banks and government was resumed.[47]

Nevertheless, there was significant development in the reform and restructuring of the financial sector. The country strengthened and consolidated the banking system through the merger of five ailing banks with other stronger banks, reducing by about one third the number of employees, decreasing the number of bank branches, and finally liberalizing foreign investment in, and active ownership of, South Korean domestic banks.[48] Banks were then able to increase their capital and meet the mandated 8 percent minimum capital adequacy ratio. The number of merchant banks also declined from thirty prior to the crisis to nine. Out of fifty insurance firms, thirteen lost their licenses. Such a drastic reform was unprecedented in South Korean financial history. The reforms considerably strengthened the

---

[44] *Economist*, July 10, 1999.
[45] Korea Development Institute, *DJnomics*, 87-104.
[46] The amount is nearly twice the level required to save Mexico's financial system during its crisis in 1995.
[47] Kang Bong-kyun, *op. cit.*, 85-105.
[48] By the end of 1999, ten of twenty-seven commercial banks had been ordered to close, while sixteen of thirty merchant banks, six of thirty-four securities companies and four of fifty insurance companies had had their licenses either revoked or suspended. See Ministry of Finance and Economy, *The Year in Review: Korea's Reform Progress* (Seoul, November 1998), 28-29.

financial sector. However, two years after the reform efforts began some important problems remained. According to a February 2000 report, the country's financial restructuring was "only partially successful in making the banks clean and more efficient."[49]

Corporate Reforms. Next came the core of Kim's economic reform campaign—restructuring the *chaebol*. The *chaebol* had been the locomotive of the country's rapid economic growth over the past three decades, as well as the root cause of the 1997 financial crisis. Inevitably, the economic crisis led to finger-pointing. Just as the Ministry of Finance and Economy received much of the blame within the government, the conglomerates were the natural targets of public scorn.

Kim Dae Jung had made it clear that he strongly opposed "special favors for the *chaebol*."[50] Kim reinforced his position on the eve of his inauguration, when he stated bluntly: "The era of the *chaebol* is over." [51] Owing to the urgent imperative of the economic crisis and the IMF mandate, Kim was committed to restructuring the *chaebol*-dominated economy. As mentioned earlier, in January 1998, then president-elect Kim and the heads of the four top conglomerates reached a five-point accord regarding corporate restructuring.

As a result of the huge injection of public funds into the ailing financial system, major banks were nationalized and most other financial firms came under government dominance. Creditor banks maintained tight control over conglomerates throughout the restructuring process, while the government kept tight control over the major banks. Thus, the so-called bank-led restructuring was in fact government-led restructuring. The government directed the banks to negotiate financial restructuring agreements with conglomerates. The conglomerates now faced stark options: undertake drastic reform or perish. The FSC played a powerful role in deciding which ailing companies should be bankrupted through the denial of further credit. The FSC warned that banks would cut off new loans to, and even call back old loans from, the *chaebol* if they dragged their feet on restructuring.[52] These threats of bankruptcy were not hollow. In June 1998, banks forced fifty-five companies into bankruptcy, including twenty firms in the top five *chaebol*. After July 1998, twenty smaller *chaebol* went bankrupt.[53]

Not satisfied with the *chaebol's* restructuring progress, President Kim, at a breakfast meeting with the heads of the top five *chaebol* on December 7, 1998, called on them to come up with more detailed plans for comprehensive restructuring and the merger of various companies by December 15, 1998. On that date, each of the top five signed a Capital Structure Improvement Agreement with their creditor banks. The top five agreed: to cut in half the number of their subsidiaries, from 253 to 130 by the end of 1999, to clear cross-debt guarantees among affiliates by March 2000, to adopt combined financial statements from 1999 and to cut corporate debt-to-equity ratios to less than 200 percent by the end of 1999. To these ends, the conglomerates were required to submit blueprints of their restructuring

---

[49] "Remaining Challenges for Financial Restructuring in Korea", *Business Korea* (Seoul, February 2000).
[50] Kim Dae Jung, *Mass-Participatory Economy* (Lanham, Md.: University Press of America, 1996), 230.
[51] Su-hoon Kim, "Crisis in Korea and the IMF Control", in Eun Mee Kim, ed., *The Four Asian Tigers: Economic Development and the Global Political Economy* (San Diego: Academic Press, 1998), 215.
[52] *Wall Street Journal*, October 8, 1998.
[53] Crotty and Lee, *op. cit.*, note 18.

plans to the FSC.[54]

Yet by spring of 1999, some *chaebol* were still expanding their operations. Some critics charged that the *chaebol* were using the restructuring as a way to expand.[55] At a press conference on April 14, 1999, President Kim warned that the creditor banks would impose sanctions on the top five *chaebol* unless they abandoned their lukewarm approach to restructuring.[56] On April 27, 1999, Kim again called the chairmen of the top five *chaebol* to the presidential mansion and pressured them to accelerate their restructuring and pay off their debts. If they failed to do so, he warned, banks would start calling in their loans.[57] In a display of determination, in August, Kim approved decisive action to restructure the Daewoo Group, once the second largest conglomerate in the country and now on the verge of bankruptcy. The "too-big-to-fail" myth was discredited; even large conglomerates could collapse.

As a part of *chaebol* restructuring, the president pressured the heads of the top five to accelerate the so-called "Big Deal", wherein weak *chaebol* units merged with similar but stronger *chaebol* units. The concept of the Big Deal had its origin in the January 1998 agreements between Kim Dae Jung and heads of the top four *chaebol* to have the *chaebol* concentrate on only three to six core businesses. The government gave the Big Deals high priority, stating, "They are the key to the pace at which Korea regains global competitiveness."[58] The *chaebol* groups struggled to negotiate Big Deals but achieved very limited success. Although the government emphasized that the Big Deal plan was voluntary, government coercion was clearly behind the perceived willingness of the conglomerates to go through with it.

Corporate restructuring achieved some success. Some of the measures Kim employed would have been unthinkable only two years earlier. Some progress was made with medium-sized *chaebol* while the top *chaebol* also significantly reduced their average debt/equity ratio. But improvements came about not through serious restructuring but through new stock issues, asset sales, and asset revaluation. In the two years following the onset of the financial crisis, the debt of the top thirty *chaebol* fell only 26 percent while the value of their equity rose 125 percent.[59]

Although Korea's corporate reform was successful compared with other Asian economies that suffered under the same 1997 financial crisis, the process of reform was not based on any established rules or market principles, but on the discretion of a few top officials, including the president himself.[60] In other words, the government-led restructuring led to stronger governmental intervention in the economy. Despite Kim's avowed pledge to reduce government intervention in the economy, government control

---

[54] Kang Bong-kyun, *op. cit.*, 128-129.
[55] "*Chaebols* Move to Expand Empires", *Business Korea* (Seoul), April 1999, 43.
[56] "Kim Issues Ultimatum to Top *Chaebols*", *Economic Report* (Seoul), May 1999, 10.
[57] *The Economist*, May 1, 1999.
[58] "Establishing a Foundation for Recovery and Economic Integration", *Economic Bulletin* (Seoul: Ministry of Finance and Economy, February 1999): 33.
[59] Samsung Economic Research Institute, *Two Years after the IMF Bailout: A Review of the Korean Economy's Transformation* (Seoul, 2000), 66.
[60] Kim, Jong-han, "Reform: Process versus Outcome", *Korea Herald*, May 15, 1999; and Jongryn Mo and Chung-in Moon, "Korea after the Crash", *Journal of Democracy*, 10:3 (July 1999): 150-164.

over the economy became more pronounced than ever. Kim himself frequently made personal interventions, running the risk of drawing criticism that some of his methods were too authoritarian and arbitrary for an administration embracing democracy and a market economy.

Two policy directives were particularly criticized. The first involved the Big Deals, which were difficult to see as an economic success.[61] The Big Deals were not carried out according to the principles of a free market; they were government-designed programs in the name of private enterprise. To a large extent the Big Deals were an unfortunate revival of the industrial policies of Kim's predecessors, policies that Kim had criticized in the past. The Big Deals also did not address the main economic problems of the *chaebol*, such as excesses in capacity, debt, and workforce.[62] Another questionable directive was the setting of a debt/equity ratio target of 200 percent by the end of 1999. The *chaebol* had to sell assets to whoever would buy them, including foreigners, at a disadvantage, as everyone knew the *chaebol* were under pressure to sell by the end of 1999.

Foreign Direct Investment. Kim Dae Jung stressed the importance of attracting foreign direct investment as the primary means for alleviating the *chaebol*s' dire financial condition. In his inaugural address, he had declared, "Inducement of foreign capital is the most effective way to repay our foreign debts, strengthen the competitiveness of businesses and raise the transparency of the economy."[63]

In November 1998, the government revised the Foreign Investment Promotion Act. As a result, foreign investment restrictions were eased across a wide range of sectors. The law also provided ten-year tax exemptions for high tech and related industries, and for the investment projects in Foreign Investment Zones. The government also removed all remaining curbs on foreign participation in Korea's stock and bond markets.

The sharp decline of the value of the *won* made Korean assets extraordinarily cheap in U.S. dollars and other foreign currencies. As Korean economic conditions improved, foreign investors rushed in. Since many Korean companies were on the brink of bankruptcy, foreign firms and banks were the only possible large-scale buyers of ailing domestic companies. During 1999-2002 foreign direct investment totaled $60 billion— more than twice the total ($24.6 billion) invested from the early 1960s to December 1997 (see Figure 16).[64] The Kim government boasted that the tremendous inducement of foreign capital was one of its major achievements.

Foreign companies had finally gained the prize they had sought in vain for decades. One tragic aspect of this "fire sale" was that the overwhelming majority of inward foreign investment involved acquisitions of Korean firms, rather than new investment. Kim traded vast amounts of South Korea's hard-built and best manufacturing facilities for money. Foreign owner-ship of South Korean industry and finance increased dramatically. Foreign firms owned an estimated 40 percent of the value of the Korean

---

[61] Jae-Woo Lee, "Corporate Restructuring in Korea: Experience and Lessons", *Korea Journal* (autumn 1999): 253-255; and Lawrence B. Krause, "The Aftermath of the Asian Financial Crisis for South Korea", in Lee-Jay Cho et al., eds., *Korea and the Asia-Pacific Region*, 212.
[62] Emery, *Korean Economic Reform*, 147-148.
[63] Kim Dae Jung, "Inaugural Address", in the Presidential Secretariat (1999), vol. 1, 9.
[64] The figure is based on http://www.mocie.go.kr/index.jsp

stock market in 2004, and owned about one-third of the Korean banking industry. In early 2001, total foreign ownership exceeded that of domestic shareholders in twenty-nine of South Korea's major corporations. Foreigners also became major shareholders in more than half of the country's commercial banks.[65]

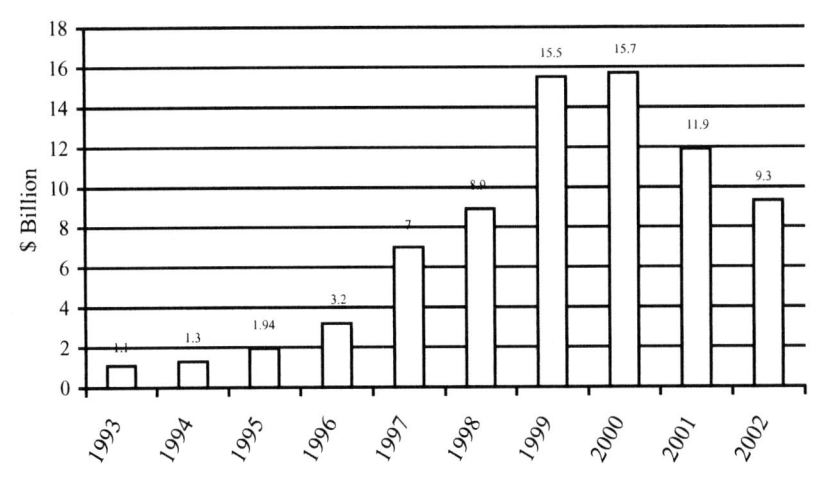

Figure 16. **Foreign Direct Investment** ($B)

Year	$ Billion
1993	1.1
1994	1.3
1995	1.94
1996	3.2
1997	7
1998	8.9
1999	15.5
2000	15.7
2001	11.9
2002	9.3

Labor Reforms and Social Safety Net. The main obstacle to economic reform was militant labor unions. In South Korea permanent full employment was taken for granted and, owing to rigid labor laws, firms could not fire workers even if necessary. Without massive layoffs, however, corporate restructuring was impossible. Kim took the public position that, since great sacrifice would be required of all Koreans in this time of economic crisis, tough decisions should be arrived at by consensus. Toward this end, in January 1998, then president-elect Kim initiated a tripartite committee composed of representatives of labor, business, and government.

On February 6, 1998, the committee reached an agreement and prepared a new law recognizing employer rights to lay off workers in times of economic duress. A week later the National Assembly passed a bill that legalized worker layoffs.[66] For the first time in modern Korean history, firms were allowed to fire workers in cases declared to be of "urgent managerial need," including mergers and acquisitions. The hard-won enactment contributed to accelerating corporate restructuring and improved international confidence in the South Korean economy. The radical financial and corporate restructuring and the dramatic increase of foreign investment in South Korea would have been impossible without the massive layoffs.

The bottom line of the economic crisis was that it hurt the average citizen, and most

---

[65] Foreigners owned 56 percent of the shares in Samsung Electronics, 63 percent of POSCO, and 57 percent of Hyundai Motors. Overall, they owned 42.2 percent of the listed shares of the top ten *chaebols*. (*Korea Herald*, May 25, 2001).

[66] *Joongang Ilbo*, February 15, 1998.

especially the laborer. As thousands of medium-sized firms went bankrupt and massive layoffs in the financial sector and among the mid-ranking *chaebol* ensued, the national unemployment rate rose sharply from 2.1 percent in October 1997 to 8.9 percent in February 1999, the highest level since 1966.[67] For Koreans, accustomed to a continually growing economy, to the practice of lifetime employment, and to unemployment rates of around 2 percent during most of the 1990s prior to the 1997 crisis, the sudden sharp rise of unemployment was both unfamiliar and terrifying.

To counter the anticipated sharp rise in the number of unemployed, and to secure the necessary support for implementing economic reforms, the government mounted a comprehensive set of social safety net programs.[68] The list of programs was impressive. It included: vocational training, job placement and information, job protection, social safety net efforts, and public works programs. During 1998, programs to assist displaced workers accounted for 2 percent of the GDP, a far higher share than had ever been allocated to such programs. In a move to broaden the safety net, the government's unemployment insurance program was expanded on October 1, 1998, to cover all displaced workers. During 1999 the government appropriated 16 trillion *won* ($12.6 billion) for unemployment measures.[69] It was estimated that some 1.3 million unemployed received some form of assistance out of approximately 1.5 million unemployed in 1999. As a result, total social welfare spending was increased threefold during the period 1997-1999.[70]

A Premature Toast. The first round of structural adjustment was painful but impressive, and the resulting economic rebound of 1999 was nothing if not remarkable. The Korean economy could boast a V-shaped recovery: during 1998, the economy had contracted 6.7 percent; but in 1999 and 2000 it made a dramatic turnaround, recording growth of 10.7 percent and 8.8 percent respectively. The trade balance improved from a deficit of $8.4 billion in 1997 to a surplus of $39 billion in 1998 and $24 billion in 1999, and inward foreign investment in 1999 grew to $15.4 billion, a record high and nearly double the amount in 1998. By 1999 the stock market had reached pre-crisis levels.[71] South Korea appeared to be the only country in Asia to successfully weather the financial crisis. International media and economists prematurely bestowed lavish praise on the Kim government for its rapid recovery, and the lion's share of credit was given to Kim Dae Jung. President Kim emerged as the East Asian leader most forthright in coming to grips with the economic crisis that had ravaged Asia.

In late 1999, as the second anniversary of the IMF agreement approached, the Kim government could boast that South Korea had overcome the economic crisis; Latin American nations would be unable to do so for over a decade. However, the government had uncorked the champagne prematurely. On December 12, 1999, Kim hosted a large IMF "graduation party" at the Blue House. Around 120 guests attended the celebration,

---

[67] National Statistical Office, *Monthly Statistics of Korea* (Seoul), March 2000.
[68] John P. Martin and Raymond Torres, *Korean Labor Market and Social Safety-Net Reforms: Challenges and Policy Requirements* (Paris: OECD), 2000.
[69] Emery, *op. cit.*, 86.
[70] Chris Manning, "The Korean Labor Market in Boom, Crisis and Recovery", in Smith, ed., *op. cit.*, 175-177.
[71] *Korea Herald*, December 17, 1999.

including leaders from business and financial sectors, all sporting bright and happy smiles. The president himself toasted the gathering: "We are completely out of crisis. I would like to congratulate and thank everyone for working through the excruciating structural reforms and allowing us to successfully graduate from the IMF program."[72] The rapid recovery had deluded not just Kim, but the average Korean as well; they were quick to shed the sense of urgency for a new economic paradigm and their commitment to economic reform.

It was as yet unclear whether the essential economic structure had undergone the kind of fundamental change required for sustainable growth and to safeguard against future crisis.[73] The unusually rapid recovery was rather the result of a technical rebound of the economy aided by a huge injection of public funds; the country had benefited as well from a general upswing in the global economy.[74] True to his populist credentials, Kim chose the easy path of an expansionary policy for a quick fix, rather than a sustained drive toward restructuring. The government was "creating bubbles in the economy by giving troubled firms access to public money through government bailout programs."[75] It also vigorously promoted venture capital industries, in part as an alternative to the *chaebol*-dominated economy. Spurred by the information technology (IT) boom in the United States in the later 1990s, South Korea's IT sector expanded rapidly. The number of startup ventures increased from 304 in May 1998 to more than 10,000 by April 2001, mainly supported by massive public funds. But the IT boom turned out to be a bubble.

The financial crisis had led to more than 100 percent depreciation in the official exchange rate—from 850 *won* to over 1,800 *won* per dollar, making Korean exports highly competitive. The operating ratio of Korean industry declined to nearly 60 percent, making real economic growth possible without spending a dime in industrial investment. These realities reduced South Korea's imports by one quarter of their pre-crisis total, and the trade account began to show $3 billion in surpluses every month for a year and a half. There was another contributing factor to this accelerated recovery. Among the various post-crisis liberalization measures, the Kim government promoted the stock market. By the end of 1999, total capitalization of the South Korean stock market reached a peak of nearly 100 percent of GDP, four times that of the pre-crisis market capitalization.

The announcement of the end of the crisis came just four months before the 2000 parliamentary elections. Kim was a "professional" politician and it was politics, rather than economics, driving his administration. Harsh proposals for economic restructuring were pushed into the background by political maneuvering. To ensure his ruling party won a majority, he found himself painting a rosier picture of the economy than was accurate. The government was more interested in showing off its economic achievements than in actually getting tough. Social anxieties quickly dissolved as banks and corporations, drunk on huge public funds, began enjoying the "moral hazard." Labor leaders declared, "Everybody is talking about the end of the economic crisis. Therefore, labor sacrifice is also over."[76]

---

[72] *Korea Herald*, December 13, 1999.
[73] Heather Smith and Sandra Eccles, "Lessons from Korea's Crisis", in Smith, *op. cit.*, 18-19.
[74] Ibid.
[75] *BusinessWeek*, May 8, 2000.
[76] Ibid.

Labor unions began to protest against economic restructuring, demanding higher pay and a shorter workweek.

Kim's ambivalent position of achieving two conflicting goals at the same time (promoting economic reform and winning labor support) led to indecisive and vacillating policies. In fear of possible electoral backlashes in the 2000 general elections, the government delayed important reforms in the public and financial sectors since the second half of 1999. The government frequently ended up modifying the restructuring packages in response to violent labor resistance. Such last-minute governmental retreat destroyed public confidence in the ability and willingness of the government to pursue the hard options.[77] Kim put off long-term reforms for short-term political expediency. He was no longer a great reformer but just another president with a half-finished agenda.

Changes that appeared sweeping turned out to have been perilously superficial. To a great extent the government was responsible for this loss of reform momentum by loudly proclaiming the end of the IMF crisis, and counting the proverbial eggs before they had hatched. In early 2001 a Korean economist wrote: "It is the commonly accepted view among the Korean public that roughly 80 percent of the restructuring in the private corporate sector is completed, whereas that in the public sector is near zero and that in the financial sector about 50 percent.... Labor sector reform is seen to have progressed almost not at all."[78] One foreign diplomat in Seoul remarked how he failed to see "any fundamental change in the structure of the economy" despite the government's policy of extreme intervention.[79] In fact, Kim's increasing attention to inter-Korean relations and domestic politics kept fundamental economic restructuring but a distant dream.

From 2000 on, the country began to suffer a recurrence of the problems that had dragged it down during 1997-98. In 2001, South Korea's economic growth was a poor 3.1 percent, a sharp decline from the 8.5 percent of 2000. Consumer spending was the easy, obvious answer to get the economy humming; but the government pursued shortsighted consumption policies by encouraging reckless allocation of credit cards with little regard to risk. Before 1998, it was virtually impossible to use a credit card outside international hotels in Korea, but by 2002 more than 100 million credit cards—more than double the national population—had been issued. Anyone, including the chronically unemployed, middle-school students, the incarcerated, and even the deceased could obtain a credit card. The Korean Board of Audit and Inspection reported that in 2002 more than 4 million cards were issued to 1.8 million customers who had no or negligible income.[80] In 2003 some 4 million people (one out of every five families) could not pay off their credit-card debts. The Korean consumer went from a net saver in 1997 to having an average family debt of about $27,000 in 2003. The result has been more than $375 billion in household debt (117 percent of household income and nearly 75 percent

---

[77] Ungsuh K. Park, "Economic Recovery", 69-70.
[78] Ibid., 71.
[79] "Despite All the Pain, Some Critics See No Real Changes in the Korean Economy", *Korea Herald*, September 8, 1999.
[80] "Finance Agencies Called Lax in Credit Card Crisis", *Joongang Ilbo*, July 16, 2004.

of the nation's gross domestic income), creating the risk of a second financial crisis.[81]

THE SUNSHINE POLICY

The Kim Dae Jung presidency marked an important turning point in inter-Korean relations. Kim's "sunshine policy," a policy of reconciliation with North Korea aimed at a unified Korea, was the main pillar of his foreign policy. His sunshine policy was a genuine departure from the policies of his predecessors. Where his predecessors had emphasized national security in inter-Korean relations, Kim Dae Jung adopted an approach that aimed at "genuine, long-term improvements in inter-Korean relations through peaceful coexistence and mutual cooperation and exchanges."[82] He had a forward-thinking and clear-headed vision for unification. He seemed to believe that inter-Korean reconciliation and reunification were the project of his calling. He had advocated a progressive unification policy since 1971 when he ran for president. He was an admirer of Willy Brandt and regarded his *Ostpolitik* as an inspiration for his own unification strategy.[83]

Kim Dae Jung appointed experienced and capable persons to the posts of foreign affairs. His diplomacy and security adviser, Lim Dong-won, a retired general and a diplomat, was an old hand in North Korea affairs: he had played an important role in inter-Korean relations during both the Roh Tae Woo and Kim Young Sam administrations. Lim, who later became director of the National Intelligence Service and then unification minister, was the main architect of the government's North Korea policy. Other key members of his foreign policy team were also considered qualified. He established the secretariat for the National Security Council and used the council as a consulting body for foreign policy in general, and North Korea policy in particular.

The term "sunshine policy" originated from the Aesop fable in which the sun competes with the north wind to see whether a traveler will take off his coat; the warming rays of the sun win out against the ferocious blasts of the north wind. Adapting this analogy to his policy toward North Korea, Kim argued that by providing economic and other benefits to North Korea, that state could be induced to change its anti-open door and anti-reform policies. When Pyongyang felt the warm sun of brotherly beneficence and cooperation, Kim believed, it would remove the straightjacket of a Stalinist system, reform its economy, open up to increased dialogue and contact with Seoul, and the result would be peaceful re-unification.

In his inaugural address, he emphasized that he would make the sunshine policy a top priority of his administration.[84] The policy was firmly based in an ideology of unconditional engagement with the North. In March 1998, the government announced the principle of separating economics from politics in order to create a more favorable environment for the improvement of South-North relations. In April, it simplified legal

---

[81] "Elements of 1997 Crisis Still Linger", *Korea Times*, July 29, 2004. Korea's household debt is almost double that of the United States, Japan, or the United Kingdom.
[82] Chung-in Moon, "Sunshine Policy Bearing Fruit", *Korea Times*, February 24, 2000.
[83] For a critical analysis of the sunshine policy, see Norman D. Levin and Yong-Sup Han, *Sunshine in Korea: the South Korean Debate over Policies toward North Korea* (Santa Monica, CA: RAND, 2002).
[84] The Presidential Secretariat (1999), vol. I, 12-13.

procedures for inter-Korean business interactions, ultimately lifting ceilings on South Korean investment in the North.[85] The policy allowed Chung Ju-yung, honorary chairman of the Hyundai Group, to negotiate a deal with on joint ventures, one of which was a cruise/tour of the Mt. Kumgang area, a premiere tourist site located on North Korea's east coast.[86] The tourism project involved a commitment by Hyundai to provide the North Korean government over $12 million a month—an amount totaling $1 billion over six years—in exchange for the rights to develop a tourist facility. In July Kim authorized the Hyundai group to proceed with the tourism project.

Earlier, both the Roh Tae Woo and Kim Young Sam governments had thrown cold water on Chung's resort project, blocking him from offering hard currency to Kim Jong Il. Kim Dae Jung, by contrast, encouraged Chung to offer terms attractive enough to open up Mt. Kumgang as soon as possible. Thus, the government and Hyundai Group became partners in the sunshine policy. The fact that Hyundai, one of the largest *chaebol*, became one of the key instruments of the sunshine policy was ironic given that the government was in the midst of *chaebol* restructuring. Hyundai's project in the North ensured financial support from the government for the nearly bankrupt conglomerate.[87]

But despite Seoul's conciliatory approach, Pyongyang was heading in the opposite direction. In September 1998, three years after the death of Kim Il Sung, the Kim Jong Il regime was officially inaugurated and a new socialist constitution was adopted. According to the constitution, the National Defense Committee (NDC) is "the highest ruling organ of state power." In fact, the chairman of the National Defense Commission is the top post in North Korea, in charge of all North Korea's political, military, and economic affairs. With the inauguration of Kim Jong Il as chairman of the NDC, the motto *Kangsong Taeguk*, a term meaning a "strong and prosperous great power," began to appear. In order to achieve such a goal, Kim Jong Il pursued a "military-first" policy.

Thus, Pyongyang did not trust Seoul's pledge to oppose the collapse-and-absorb formula for unification and strongly criticized the sunshine policy as a "sunburn policy."[88] Pyongyang responded to Seoul's positive measures with frequent military provocations. In June 1998, a North Korean spy submarine, packed with armed infiltrators on an unknown mission to the South, was found trapped in the net of a South Korean fishing boat along the east coast. All six crewmembers and three espionage agents found on board had committed suicide. Despite Seoul's stern admonition, three more infiltration attempts (July 1998, dead North Korean agent discovery; November 1998, submarine intrusion; December 1998, sinking of North

---

[85] *Korea Newsreview*, August 15, 1998.

[86] Other projects were a manufacturing plant, ship scrapping, oil exploration, and telecommunications (*Korea Herald*, November 4, 1998).

[87] While allowing the Daewoo Group to fail, the government provided special favors to the Hyundai Group. For example, a claim has been made that the government directed financial institutions to grant fresh loans to Hynix. Most analysts believe that these loans would not have been made in the absence of government direction. Likewise, there have been charges that Hyundai Heavy Industries was exempted from bailout after the company agreed to invest in North Korea. See Edward M. Graham, "Reform of the *Chaebol* in Korea", *Korea's Economy 2003* (Washington, DC: Korea Economic Institute, 2003), 24-25.

[88] Samuel S. Kim, "North Korea in 2000", *Asian Survey*, 41:1 (January 2001): 14.

Korean spy vessel) soon followed. Furthermore, on August 31, 1998, North Korea surprised the world by firing a multistage, long-range missile (*Taepodong* 1 missile) over northern Japan. In June 1999, two North Korean patrol boats sailed in and out of the Northern Limit Line of the Yellow Sea, a UN-declared border that both North and South had acknowledged since the end of the Korean War. In the next week both sides increased their naval presence in the region and military tensions heightened. Finally, a North Korean patrol boat opened fire and South Korean naval ships responded, sinking one North Korean boat and damaging five others. It was the worst inter-Korean naval conflict since the Korean War.[89]

Despite the strong negative public reaction to North Korean provocations, Kim Dae Jung remained firm in his resolution and doggedly pursued his sunshine policy. For instance, at the very moment of the naval skirmish, Hyundai's cruise ships were carrying South Korean tourists to Mt. Kumgang. The day after the naval shootout, South Korean government dispatched a shipload of fertilizer to the North.[90] The consistency and single-mindedness with which President Kim pursued engagement with the North sharply contrasted with the approach of most of his predecessors.

The year 2000, however, was to bring dramatic change to inter-Korean relations. Kim Dae Jung evidently decided to raise the tempo of his efforts for inter-Korean dialogue in the early months of the year. With the rapid recovery of the economy in 1999, he shifted his attention to his sunshine policy and the April 2000 parliamentary elections.

From the beginning of the year, Pyongyang showed signs of change as it launched a diplomatic offensive after years of isolation and suspicion of all contact with the outside world.[91] Stimulated by Pyongyang's seemingly positive move, Kim Dae Jung tried to create a favorable climate for an inter-Korean breakthrough by globalizing the sunshine policy and actively seeking international support. In an interview with Japanese television, the president described Kim Jong Il as a "pragmatist, a man of insight, a decisive leader with whom it is possible to negotiate."[92] In a major speech delivered at the Free University of Berlin on March 9, 2000, Kim Dae Jung reiterated his willingness to enter government-level dialogue and spoke in detail of his desire to assist North Korea's economic reconstruction through promoting large-scale economic collaboration in a broad range of industrial, infrastructure, and other areas.[93] After a ten-year contraction of its economy and a five-year famine, it had become increasingly untenable for Pyongyang to reject the olive branch being proffered by the South Korean government.

On April 10, 2000, a month after the Berlin speech, and just three days before parliamentary elections in the South, Seoul and Pyongyang surprised the world by announcing that an agreement had been reached on an historic North-South summit meeting to be held in Pyongyang on June 12-14, 2000. The announcement came as a shock to most Koreans.

---

[89] *Korea Times*, June 17, 1999.
[90] *Korea Herald*, June 15, 1999.
[91] Samuel S. Kim, "North Korea in 2000", 13.
[92] Kim Dae Jung, interview by Tetsuya Chikushi, Tokyo Broadcasting System Television Network, February 2, 2000. See also *Korea Herald*, February 3, 2000.
[93] "Lessons of German Reunification and the Korean Peninsula", in the Presidential Secretariat (2001), vol. III, 49-57.

The timing of the announcement provoked a political controversy. It infuriated the opposition parties, who saw it as an attempt to influence the outcome of the elections and manipulate the reunification issue for political purposes. It also ignited questions about the administration's trustworthiness and credibility as the government had been dealing with the North Koreans behind the scenes.

On June 13, the world's attention focused on Pyongyang. Kim Dae Jung flew on the first legal flight between the two capitals; he was the first South Korean president to step on northern land. History was made when the South Korean leader arrived at Sunan Airport in Pyongyang and declared, "We are one people." Kim Dae Jung was greeted on the tarmac by North Korean leader Kim Jong Il. They embraced each other like long-lost friends, and the two leaders inspected a military honor guard. Kim Jong Il said that President Kim had come a long way to Pyongyang, surmounting hardships, fear and danger. "June 13 will be recorded in history," the North Korean leader said. Kim Dae Jung replied, "Let's make history from now on."[94] The two leaders drove together in a Lincoln Continental limousine through the spacious boulevards of Pyongyang, as some 600,000 citizens lined the streets waving paper azaleas to the fervent chants of "Kim Jong Il!"

After an historic three-day summit, the two leaders signed a landmark agreement known as "the June 15 agreement," more of a general statement of common principles than a detailed roadmap for the future:

> 1. The South and the North have agreed to resolve the question of reunification independently and through the joint efforts of the Korean people.
>
> 2. For the achievement of reunification, we have agreed that there is a common element in the South's proposal for confederation and the North's proposal for a loose form of federation. The South and the North agree to promote reunification through these frameworks.
>
> 3. The South and the North have agreed to promptly resolve humanitarian issues such as exchange visits by separated family members and relatives...and the question of unswerving Communists serving prison sentences in the South.
>
> 4. The South and the North have agreed to consolidate mutual trust by promoting balanced development of the national economy through economic cooperation and stimulating cooperation and exchanges in all fields.
>
> 5. The South and the North have agreed to hold dialogues between relevant authorities in the near future and to implement the above agreements expeditiously.[95]

President Kim invited Kim Jong Il to visit Seoul, and Kim Jong Il agreed to do so at an appropriate time. It was a prosperous summit for Kim Dae Jung, who could now convincingly claim that his sunshine policy was making real progress. Immediate credit for the opening of a new chapter in inter-Korean relations went to President Kim, who for the two years since his inauguration had emphasized patience and openness over the traditional

---

[94] *Joongang Ilbo*, June 13, 2000.
[95] *Korea Herald*, June 16, 2000.

animosity that had characterized inter-Korean relations. One foreign observer extolled him as "the right man in the right place at the right time."[96]

Unfortunately, the June 15 agreement did not include provisions to reduce tensions caused by the massing of more than 1.7 million forces on both sides of the DMZ. Nor did it mention North Korea's controversial ballistic missile or nuclear weapons programs.[97] An unbalanced inter-Korean agenda that ignored potential sources of tension and instability was ultimately self-defeating. Many South Koreans wondered why Kim Dae Jung did not touch on security issues during the Pyongyang summit.[98]

After half a century of dangerous face-offs between the South and the North, the summit was unprecedented and raised hopes—at least in the South—for national reconciliation. The Pyongyang summit was greeted with euphoria in the South, and the disdain and distrust that had marred relations with the North showed signs of dissipating. For the moment, a "North Korea fever" swept the South. The trademark wide-framed sunglasses of Kim Jong Il even became a fashion craze. The summit made the impossible—peaceful reunification—suddenly seem possible. Public attitudes toward North Korea changed dramatically. According to a typical poll, only 4.6 percent of the general public said they viewed North Korea as an enemy. In contrast, nearly half (49.8 percent) saw North Korea as an equal cooperation partner to South Korea and another 44 percent said they considered the North a partner that South Koreans should help.[99] Greatly encouraged, Kim Dae Jung was determined while in office to banish the Cold War legacy from the peninsula "by all means," and to build a solid foundation of peaceful unification. During an interview with The New York Times, Kim was quoted as saying, "I hope that we can conclude a peace agreement with North Korea before I step down in 2003."[100] That is, he wanted to achieve the first stage of unification—confederation.

The summit propelled inter-Korean relations forward by leaps and bounds in the coming months. Seoul and Pyongyang negotiated agreements on the restoration of rail and road links across the DMZ, investment guarantees, and the provision of 600,000 tons of South Korean food aid to North Korea. A meeting of defense ministers also occurred, though with few tangible results. North and South Korean athletes marched hand-in-hand at the opening ceremonies of the 2000 Sydney Olympics. At September 18, 2000, groundbreaking ceremony for an inter-Korean railroad reconnection, Kim Dae Jung predicted a new era of an "Iron Silk Road" connecting the Korean peninsula with China, Russia, and Europe.

Kim's efforts to engage North Korea earned early international recognition. On October 13, 2000, the Nobel Peace Prize was awarded to Kim Dae Jung for his pursuit of democracy in South Korea and his efforts to promote peace and reconciliation with North Korea. The award elevated Kim Dae Jung into the pantheon of global peacemakers. At the award ceremony in Oslo on December 10, Norwegian Nobel Committee Chairman Gunnar Berge compared Kim Dae Jung to Nelson Mandela, Andrey Sakharov, and Mahatma Gandhi: "To

---

[96] Michael Breen, "Korean Summit: Avoiding Unification", *Asian Wall Street Journal*, April 18, 2000.
[97] For evaluation of the summit, see Jaeho Hwang, "North Korea's Arduous Trip: The North-South Summit Examined", *Security Dialogue*, 31: 4 (December 2000), 475-488.
[98] "Gong Ro-Myung Criticizes President Kim's Foreign Policy", *Wolgan Chosun* (June 2002), 100-118.
[99] *Joongang Ilbo*, August 3-6, 2000.
[100] *New York Times*, September 11, 2000.

outside observers, Kim's invincible spirit may appear almost superhuman."[101] In a speech before some 1,000 spectators in Oslo's City Hall, Kim pledged to dedicate the remainder of his life to "human rights and peace in my country and in the world, and to the reconciliation and cooperation of my people."[102] The Nobel Peace Prize, for which he had been nominated thirteen times over his life, was a personal honor that he had long dreamt of receiving. Kim Dae Jung was the first Korean to win a Nobel Prize, and its bestowment invoked a great outpouring of pride on the part of South Koreans.

Yet, returning home, Kim faced a grim national affairs picture, beset by a near-crisis situation in the economy and sustained political dissension. There was mounting criticism that the president kept himself more or less aloof from worsening domestic issues, while he was busily engaged in his sunshine policy. It was a great irony that the leader who had realized such an historic breakthrough in inter-Korean relations should face such mounting public discontent and criticism. Kim reportedly said that his two most ardent wishes were to achieve peace between the two Koreas and to win a Nobel Prize. One of his dreams had come true. But, many critics believed that Kim's unstated motivation for achieving détente with the North was an obsession with winning the Nobel Peace Prize.[103]

FROM ECONOMICS TO POLITICS

Unfortunately, the image of Kim Dae Jung as a reformer and peacemaker eroded quickly. With lingering economic problems, endless political bickering, failures in welfare reform and a slow response from Pyongyang, a series of scandals plagued the government and severely damaged its legitimacy. The scandals were especially embarrassing for Kim because he, as a former dissident, campaigned on a platform of stamping out corruption.

In the spring of 1999, the so-called "furgate" scandal, involving the wives of two ministers, occupied the front pages of major dailies. The scandal originated in the attempts of the wife of the jailed head of Korea Life Insurance to buy the influence of the prosecutor general (Kim Tae-jung) and other senior officials by offering expensive fur coats to their wives. Prosecutors cleared the prosecutor general's wife but arrested the wife of the unification minister. The government was widely criticized for mishandling the case. In one poll conducted by a Seoul daily, 74 percent responded that the probe was unfair and that the prosecutor general should resign.[104] Public opinion was also antagonized by the idea that ministerial wives could afford to frequent such expensive shops at a time when most people were suffering from the financial crisis.

In the midst of the graft scandals, on May 24, 1999, President Kim replaced eleven ministers, including major economy-related ministers. However, he faced public and opposition and criticism over the new appointments. The media described the new cabinet as "the same old face with a few doubtful names." Or in the words of one

---

[101] *Korea Herald*, December 11, 2000.

[102] The Presidential Secretariat (2001), vol. III, 280.

[103] Tim Larimer, "South Korea's Kim Can't Take His Eyes off the Prize", *Time*, October 16, 2000.

[104] B. J. Lee, "A Scandal Exposes Rich Wives' Spending Habits", *Newsweek*, June 14, 1999.

professor, the president appointed "all those guys who were close to him." [105] The opposition demanded that President Kim withdraw from what it said was the politically motivated appointment of Prosecutor General Kim Tae-jung, whose wife stood at the center of the "furgate" scandal, as justice minister.[106] In the face of such strong public pressure, the president retained the justice minister, angering the public and the media. The public was suspicious of the president's appointment not only as regional favoritism but also as an attempt to cover up the scandal. It was widely suspected that the new justice minister, who hailed from the Cholla region, would cover up the scandals related to the ruling circle. Two weeks after his appointment, however, President Kim was forced to dismiss the justice minister. The new environment minister, Sohn Sook, an actress, was also dismissed after a month in office because she accepted $20,000 from a representative of the Korean Federation of Industries. In July 1999, still reeling over the "furgate" scandal, prosecutors arrested the governor of Kyonggi Province (Lim Chang-ryol) and the mayor of Inchon City (Choi Ki-sun), both from the ruling coalition, with the charges of accepting bribes.[107]

In November 1999 an independent counsel's investigation into the "furgate" scandal disclosed that law-enforcement authorities, including the presidential secretary for legal affairs, had attempted to cover up the scandal to protect the wife of the former prosecutor general (Kim Tae-jung). The report disclosed a pattern of lies, cover-ups and false reports made to the president by his officials. President Kim proffered a formal apology to the nation over the government's mishandling of a series of scandals, and his legal aide subsequently resigned.[108]

An Eastward Policy. Suffering from minority status, Kim Dae Jung was determined to make his party a majority in the National Assembly in the April 2000 parliamentary elections. He was a "professional" politician; as the important elections approached, economic reform was replaced by a political agenda. The government did not want to take any actions unpopular with the public ahead of the elections.[109] Instead, with aggressive pursuit of the sunshine policy he now promoted three major programs—ambitious welfare policies, a reevaluation of Park Chung Hee, and the creation of a new party. The second and the third programs aimed to strengthen his support base in the southeastern region, a political strategy the media labeled an "eastward policy" (*dongjin jungchek*).

The support level of Kim and his party in the southeastern Kyongsang region was below 20 percent since his inauguration. In order to strengthen his power base, Kim had to broaden his support in southeastern Korea. In the midst of the economic difficulties, the late president Park Chung Hee was more popular than ever before. As a reconciliatory effort, Kim decided to reevaluate Park at the risk of political repercussion. Kim Dae Jung, the most prominent victim of the Park regime, publicly praised Park. Kim, while pledging government financial support for a memorial project for Park

---

[105] Donald Kirk, "Korean Crisis: Pride and Identity in the IMF Era", *Journal of East Asian Affairs*, XIII:2 (fall/winter 1999): 359.
[106] *Korea Herald*, May 26, 1999.
[107] Calvin Sims, "Graft Cases Remind South Koreans of Bad Old Days", *New York Times*, July 20, 1999.
[108] *Joongang Ilbo*, November 24, 1999.
[109] "Politics Jeopardizes Reform", *Chosun Ilbo*, November 7, 2000.

during his visit to Park's hometown, said that Koreans must recognize the former president's role in rebuilding Korea from the ruins of the Korean War and leading the nation toward modernization. After saying that past presidents had received negative historical evaluations, he remarked, "We should try to acknowledge them if they made some positive achievements."[110]

The president's remark, characterized by the media as an "historical reevaluation" of Park, was seen as a bold move, as a considerable number of people still held negative views of the late president. Many lauded Kim's decision to forgive and reconcile with his former oppressor, saying that it would contribute to promoting regional reconciliation between the country's southeastern region, Park's native area, and its southwestern region, where Kim originated.[111] Kim's move to endorse Park was also expected to boost the political position of President Kim and his ruling coalition in the southeastern region ahead of parliamentary elections.

On the eve of general elections, Koreans were all too accustomed to seeing parties broken apart, reassembled, and renamed solely for immediate electoral imperatives. Over its half century of constitutional democracy, South Korea had had more than 200 political parties. Kim Dae Jung was as responsible as anyone for the surfeit of parties; in his long political career he had inaugurated no less than four of them.[112] In an attempt to overcome the chronic maladies of regional antagonism, he established a new party, the Millennium Democratic Party (MDP) on January 19, 2000. In the past, a new party had always been the tailor made product of one man, and the creation of his new party appeared to fit the old pattern: artificial and orchestrated. A columnist described the "undemocratic" procedure of the party's creation—"the sudden declaration of creating a new party, a secret scouting of members, inviting popular figures to join, and the order to lawmakers of the government party that 50 percent of them will have to give up their seats."[113] Many wondered how a political party could be created in such a manner in the age of democracy and by a life-long democratic crusader.[114]

Two main domestic concerns dominated the parliamentary election campaigns: the economy and political corruption. The new government party, the MDP, clearly expected the first issue to work in its favor by capitalizing on the resurgence in the economy and the increasingly favorable figures on economic growth, foreign currency reserves, and trade balances. As for political corruption, the string of administrative scandals had apparently damaged the ruling coalition.

The results of the April elections were disappointing for the ruling coalition in every respect. It failed to secure a majority—the MDP winning 115 seats and its coalition partner (the ULD) only seventeen seats, a shocking loss of thirty-four seats for the ULD. The opposition won 133 seats, only four short of the 137 majority. The most striking

---

[110] *Korea Herald*, May 17, 1999. With only lukewarm government support, there was no progress in the construction of the memorial project of Park Chung Hee until the end of Kim's term.

[111] *Korea Herald*, May 18, 1999.

[112] A popular Korean saying goes something like this: if two Koreans lived in a desert they would create three parties: a ruling party, an opposition party, and a coalition party.

[113] Ryu Keun-il, "Tailor Made Party", *Chosun Ilbo*, September 18, 1999.

[114] Before the 2004 parliamentary elections, President Roh Moo Hyun and his loyalists deserted the MDP and created a new party.

phenomenon of the election was the aggravation of regionalism. The opposition GNP won sixty-four of sixty-five seats in the Kyongsang region, while the MDP won twenty-five of twenty-nine for the Cholla region. The four independents elected in Cholla supported President Kim during the campaign and joined the MDP immediately after the election.

Despite the president's commitment to dismantling regionalism, regional antagonism had apparently deepened. Although Kim Dae Jung's party had swept the seats for the southwestern region, never before had a party won such a decisive victory as the GNP had in the southeastern region. The MDP's desperate effort to secure a majority did not succeed and Kim Dae Jung had to maintain his cohabitation with the ULD. Kim's "eastward policy" had clearly failed.

Welfare Reform Blunders. Partly to boost support for the ruling coalition, the government embarked on pork-barreling welfare reforms to attract support from labor and low-income classes, Kim's traditional support base. Inspired by British Prime Minister Tony Blair's Third Way, which emphasized economic fairness rather than growth, Kim came up with the concept of "productive welfare" as an alternative to restoring the confidence of the working class.[115] In his Liberation Day speech on August 15, 1999, the president showered the nation with a series of new policy agendas such as national pensions, health care and unemployment support systems meant to drastically improve social welfare over the next several years.[116] But many wondered whether the government would be able to put into practice all the grand promises he was making. The government had no detailed programs and no plans on how to muster the enormous financial resources needed for the ambitious agenda.[117]

Kim's welfare reform initiatives were carried out in haste by rough-and-ready methods and resulted, not surprisingly, in mistakes and unexpected problems. As a result, the government suffered from a series of policy blunders—failures in the reform of education, medical insurance, and national pension systems.[118] Those failures were attributed not only to his "politics-first" approach, but also to poor policymaking and implementation. In a "politics-first" government, technocrats were not valued and amateurism prevailed.[119]

Medical insurance reform was one of the policy fiascos. President Kim took pains to introduce a new healthcare system that implemented the integrated medical insurance program and the system of differentiating between "over-the-counter" drugs and doctor-prescribed drugs. In an effort to oppose the reform, doctors went on an unprecedented

---

[115] "The Third Way, Korean Style", *Korea Herald*, May 10, 1999.

[116] For productive welfare policy, see the Presidential Secretariat, *DJ Welfarism* (Seoul: Samil Planning, 2003).

[117] The ratio of government debt to GDP increased from less than 10 percent in 1997 to 22.4 percent in 2001. When government debt-guarantees were included, the total public burden climbed to 40.4 percent of GDP. See Young-Sun Koh, "Fiscal Consolidation after the Crisis", a paper presented at the EWC/KDI conference on 'Macroeconomic Implications of Post-crisis Structural Changes', Honolulu, Hawaii, July 25-26, 2002.

[118] John Burton, "Series of Policy Blunders Hit South Korea", *Financial Times*, May 23, 2001.

[119] "Private Panel Points out Lack of Policy Coordination", *Korea Herald*, July 27, 2000.

general strike, bringing the medical system to a standstill for over six months. The solution to the strike was apparently cobbled together for a quick fix, a reckless move taken without careful preparation. The government twice allowed an increase in medical costs. The insured had to pay three to four times higher premiums with much reduced benefits. Nonetheless, the medical insurance plan led to near bankruptcy: it ate away $850 million in savings, and for the year 2000 alone suffered a deficit of $4 billion, a third of the plan's annual budget. The government was forced to subsidize national medical insurance, creating the danger of a black hole in national finance.[120]

National pension reform was another policy blunder. In early 1999 the government had put into force the state-run compulsory national pension plan. Then, in April it extended national pension coverage to include all South Koreans. The pension scheme attracted much criticism; wage earners and professionals complained they would pay a higher premium than the self-employed. But before long, an untenable combination of big pension benefits and small contributions put the nation's state-run pension system at risk of depleting reserves. According to an IMF report, in the near future the cash flow deficit of the national pension would amount to 5 to 8 percent of GDP.[121]

Education reform was the most controversial. At the beginning of its term, the Kim administration enforced education reform without carefully reviewing all of the consequences and developing action plans to redress them. The first education minister, Lee Hae-chan, one of Kim's confidants, had shaken the foundations of the education system by his radical and hasty reform programs. Presuming most teachers were corrupt, the minister adopted strict anti-corruption measures that humiliated teachers. He also lowered the retirement age of teachers from sixty-five to sixty. Within a year, schools throughout the nation were thrown into confusion: the outcome was a disaster; the quality of education dropped while schools suffered a teacher shortage. Lee was replaced after hundreds of thousand of teachers signed a petition for his resignation.[122]

Lee's successor tried to repair the damage but his term was very short. A quick series of four more education ministers within fifteen months ensured that education languished in a crisis of confused policies.[123] One national daily editorialized, "Every new education minister, whose average tenure has been less than a year, has introduced ambitious new policies. After so many reforms, the reality of Korean education is

---

[120] "South Korea: Health Insurance Needs Surgery", *Far Eastern Economic Review*, May 24, 2001. Kim Chong-dae, former assistant minister of health and welfare, estimated that the burden of the people had increased more than $15 billion during the Kim Dae Jung administration. See "Failed Medical Insurance Reform", *Wolgan Chosun* (March 2004).

[121] "State-run Pension Feared to Be Depleted", *Korea Herald*, September 6, 2001. Russell Dalton commented that, in old OECD nations, pension coverage took generations to get to full coverage.

[122] Kim had set a record when it came to education ministers, with as many as six in less than three years: Kim Duk-joong served for seven months, Moon Yong-lin for six months, Lee Don-hee for five months, and Song Ja for twenty-four days. In contrast, Richard W. Riley, Bill Clinton's secretary of education, served for eight years.

[123] In Kim's five-year term, he had seven different education ministers. During the Kim Young Sam administration, there had been five different education ministers. Thus, in ten years, Korea had twelve different education ministers.

wretched."[124] According to a public opinion survey conducted by the Korea Education Development Institute, a governmental think tank for education policy, an astonishing 93 percent of education experts and 88 percent of parents believed Korean education was in "serious crisis."[125]

The management of public funds was in dire straits.[126] The government had injected more than $128 billion in public funds into non-viable banks and other financial institutions to buy off non-performing loans and to help banks recapitalize. Nonviable businesses and banks, injected with public funds, found a haven under the corporate workout umbrella. Banks still suffered from an astronomical amount of non-performing loans. The government decided to delay the recovery of public funds for ten years. As a result, by 2003 the total government debt was estimated at $196 billion, 39.6 percent of South Korea's GDP.[127]

From a Hero to a Lame Duck

With reform efforts slackening, the economy slumping and unemployment still high, public discontent increased daily. Entering his fourth year in office (2001), Kim Dae Jung faced increasingly stronger challenges from within and without. The newly inaugurated George W. Bush administration adopted a hard-line North Korea policy, which in turn stiffened Pyongyang's posture toward Seoul, resulting in little progress in inter-Korean relations. Encouraged by the domestic and foreign troubles facing the Kim government, the opposition stepped up their political attacks. In order to revitalize his languishing government, Kim promoted two measures—government reorganization and media reform.

In late January 2001, three years after his initial reorganization, Kim initiated a second round of government reorganization. These reforms were in fact a reversal of those of 1998, recognition of the failure of the first reorganization which had lacked long-term vision and guiding principles.[128] Breaking his campaign promise of smaller government, the government under his leadership grew larger. The deputy prime minister for economic affairs was reinstated, the position of deputy prime minister for education and human resources development was created, and the Ministry of Women's Affairs was established. The Ministry of Public Information, which Kim had scrapped owing to concerns over government control of the media, was revived under a slightly different name—the Government Information Agency. The reinstatement of the deputy prime minister for economic affairs was primarily aimed at strengthening the efficiency of the economic team by giving the deputy prime minister authority to coordinate economic policy. With no deputy prime minister for economy during the three years of his term, the president and his economic advisers had to directly intervene to manage economic policies. Questions and criticisms were raised over how the government could inflate itself at a time when it was demanding that the private sector restructure itself and

---

[124] "Deserted Education", *Chosun Ilbo*, March 4, 2001.

[125] Ibid.

[126] "Financial Reform Seems like Money Pit", *Business Korea*, August 2000; "Editorial: Failed Public Funds", *Digital Chosun Ilbo*, September 20, 2001.

[127] *Joongang Ilbo*, September 8, 2003.

[128] Chung Jang-ryul, "Fading Promise of a Small Government", *Korea Focus* (January 2000): 30-36.

tighten its belt.[129]

Media Reform. Facing a decline in popularity, the Kim administration sought to divert the public's attention by waging an intensive war of attrition against the media under the guise of media reform. As major daily newspapers continued to criticize the government's policies, tensions between government and media rose. During his life-long struggle for democracy, the nation's major dailies—the Donga Ilbo and the Chosun Ilbo —were among Kim Dae Jung's closest allies and supporters. It was ironic that under the administration of this democratic crusader the government and press had become so confrontational.

As South Korea entered the year 2001, the government embarked on a campaign of so-called "media reform." On January 11, 2001, during his New Year press conference President Kim said, "There is a strong call for media reform among the people. We need to take reform measures to make the press transparent and fair."[130] Just a few weeks after his call for media reform, the government began to investigate tax evasion among twenty-three media companies. The government enlisted some trade unions and other civic groups to support his press reform.[131] These pro-government organizations accused major newspapers of being part of "the old establishment" and "anti-unification elements."

On August 24, three owners and executives of major newspapers were arrested on charges of embezzlement and tax evasion. The arrests were the harshest steps in a long campaign that the government had waged against the nation's press. The arrests finalized a four-and-half-month tax audit of media companies involving more than half of all available tax investigators in the National Tax Administration (NTA). The probe, the government claimed, was necessary to root out corruption in the press. Before the arrests, the NTA imposed unprecedented fines totaling $388 million against 23 media companies.[132] The Fair Trade Commission, in a separate investigation into monopolistic practices of leading newspapers, imposed fines of several million dollars each against the Chosun Ilbo and the Donga Ilbo. A foreign observer believed that the magnitude of the fines during the period of economic hardship was enough to force the closure of some newspapers.[133]

The tax probes damaged the reputation of Kim Dae Jung by exposing him to charges that he had reverted to the same dictatorial practices that he once opposed as a fighter for democracy. The Vienna-based International Press Institute said the investigation "was, in part, politically motivated" and was "instituted with the intention of intimidating the media" and included South Korea on its watch list.[134] Kim Dae Jung had made respect for

---

[129] "Why a Bigger Government?" *Donga Ilbo,* April 19, 2001.

[130] *Donga Ilbo,* January 11, 2001. In March 2002, investigators of the independent council found a document from the Kim Dae Jung Peace Foundation, which states, "It is urgent to overhaul Seoul-based newspapers in order to consummate President Kim's reform drive and bolster his power in running the administration." See "President's Confidant Suspected of Receiving Money", *Korea Herald,* March 11, 2002.

[131] According to Park Kwan-yong, chairman of the Press Freedom Committee of the opposition party, among the twenty-one civic groups which joined in calls for media reform, fourteen received 860 million *won* from the government (*Chosun Ilbo,* July 26, 2001).

[132] "A President Picks a Dangerous Fight with the Media", *Newsweek,* August 27, 2001.

[133] David I. Steinberg, "Kim Dae Jung vs. the Press Doesn't Make a Pretty Fight", *International Herald Tribune,* July 12, 2001.

[134] "South Korea papers face huge fines", *Financial Times,* July 3, 2001.

human rights and civil liberties the cornerstone of his political career. Kim's image as an autocrat contrasts sharply with his thirty-year history as a democratic fighter.[135]

Many worried that the "press reform" created more division in national opinion and that discord and the confrontational atmosphere in society would only get worse. Even at a Blue House meeting presided over by Kim Dae Jung, leading figures of the ruling party indirectly criticized his leadership: "The ruling party, which is preoccupied with the attack against the opposition and the media, does not do what it is supposed to do as a ruling party. There is no politics of dialogue and negotiation these days. There is only a dirty politics, politics of life-and-death confrontation."[136]

With half-finished reforms, numerous trials and errors in his policies, filling key positions in government with people from Cholla region or royal to him, and a series of bribery scandals complicated by his "hometown buddies," his moral legitimacy had quickly evaporated. Public opinion on the performance of the Kim administration was extremely negative. According to a poll, as much as 63.7 percent of the people were dissatisfied with the way Kim was running the country after three and a half years in office (see Table 14).[137]

Table 14. **Support for Kim's Major Policies** (%)

	Positive	Negative	Don't know / no answer
Parallel Promotion of Democracy & Market Economy	36.0	58.5	5.5
Resolution of Regionalism	35.6	63.4	1.0
Promotion of Parliamentary Democracy	30.8	66.5	2.7
Promotion of Market Economy	35.0	57.9	7.1
Social Welfare Policy	29.5	68.0	2.5
Media Reform	35.2	48.2	16.6
The Sunshine Policy	63.4	35.7	0.9

Source: *Donga Ilbo*, August 26, 2001.

According to the poll, the sunshine policy was the most successful policy of the administration: positive evaluation (63.4 percent) exceeded negative responses (35.7 percent). However, the public was generally dissatisfied with major domestic policies. Although Kim had emphasized regional reconciliation, parliamentary democracy and welfare policy, the majority of the people perceived these three policies negatively. President Kim's approval ratings plummeted from around 71 percent in June 15, 2000, the time of inter-Korean summit to just 19.7 percent in September 2001.[138]

---

[135] Jay Solomon, "Is Kim Dae Jung Trying to Muzzle the Press?" *Asian Wall Street Journal*, July 10, 2001.
[136] *Donga Ilbo*, August 9, 2001.
[137] *Donga Ilbo*, August 26, 2001.
[138] *JoongAng Ilbo*, September 21, 2001. If one excludes the devoted support of Cholla people who support regardless of his success or failure, his true popularity would be a single digit.

The "Sun" behind Dark Clouds. At the same time, Kim Dae Jung's top agenda, the sunshine policy, was experiencing increasing difficulties. The policy was based on the premise that North Korea would change very soon. Unless Kim Jong Il embarked on policies of economic reform and opening, the policy was likely to fail or to achieve little. In other words, the success of the policy hinged largely on Kim Jong Il's positive response.

Kim Dae Jung, who had staked his legacy on the success of the policy, had effectively made himself a hostage of Kim Jong Il. He could not afford to criticize Kim Jong Il for fear of antagonizing him. Once President Kim had mounted the tiger called inter-Korea reconciliation, he had to keep the tiger at a run, lest the tiger attack him. Since the inter-Korean summit, Kim had come under increased domestic pressure to deliver further and tangible progress. If Kim failed to show more results to the South Korean populace, it was quite feasible that all his investments in inter-Korean rapprochement might come to naught, and even work against him.[139] At the time, millions of unemployed demanded that money be spent at home rather than on propping up the North Korean regime with aid and investment. The deceleration of economic growth from 8.8 percent in 2000 to 3.8 percent in 2001 poured cold water on inter-Korean reconciliation. To most people, Kim Dae Jung's long-term vision of peaceful coexistence and unification was beginning to sound like pie-in-the-sky.

When South Koreans continued to see no clear indications of North Korean change, their distrust of the Kim government and its sunshine policy intensified. After a brief period of euphoria following the North-South summit, South Koreans grew increasingly frustrated with North Korean leader Kim Jong Il, who accepted economic assistance from the South only to cut off family reunion visits and ministerial talks; who demanded free electricity but refused to fulfill promises on opening North-South road and rail links. The promised reciprocal visit to Seoul by Kim Jong Il was delayed without explanation. Concerned with the possible political risks of reform and opening, the North had been reluctant to engage the South.[140]

The fundamental problem with the sunshine policy was that it failed to reduce the North Korean threat and to improve South Korean security. From the beginning, security issues had ranked far too low on the administration's negotiating agenda. The joint declaration issued after the South-North summit failed to even mention the word "security" and avoided addressing critical military issues. On the other hand, as it had given top priority to building a "militarily powerful" state, North Korea's military buildup continued. After the summit, North Korean procurement of arms actually increased and the percentage of its forward-deployed forces continued to grow. North Korea also followed up the summit by conducting its most extensive military exercises in a decade.[141] In his congressional testimony on March 27, 2001, General Thomas Schwartz, commander of U.S.-ROK combined forces in Korea, aid that North Korean forces over the past year

---

[139] "DJ on a tiger", *Chosun Ilbo* (English edition), July 1, 2000.
[140] Choong Nam Kim, "Pyongyang's Dilemma of Reform and Opening: How to Compromise Economic Benefits with Political Risks", *Korea and World Affairs*, 24: 2 (summer 2000): 247-276.
[141] Taewoo Kim, "Sunshine Policy and ROK-U.S. Alliance", *Korean Journal of International Studies*, XXVIII: 1(fall/winter 2001) 140.

had grown "bigger, better, closer, and deadlier."[142]

Naturally, public support for the sunshine policy evaporated quickly. It would be difficult for any government to pursue an effective engagement policy with the long-term enemy North Korea. The fundamental requirement for such a policy is a strong national consensus. But, Kim mistakenly used the policy to improve both his popularity and his minority party's electoral prospects. This approach angered his political opposition and politicized what had generally been considered a non-partisan issue—national reunification. Since the beginning, the policy had become a contentious core issue in a larger ideological and political conflict. Kim's confidence and conviction kept his policy focused and mobilized civil society in support of the policy, alienating general public and narrowing the potential base for political consensus. The government had been non-inclusive, intolerant of divergent views, and unresponsive to public opinion. It launched a major attack on the nation's leading newspapers which had been critical of the sunshine policy. The decision-making process of the policy was also closed and highly centralized; the government made unilateral decisions without required legislative approval or oversight.[143]

With his political clock ticking and his legacy at stake, seventy-six-year-old Kim seemed increasingly restless. The government tried to avoid anything that might offend Kim Jong Il, but in so doing it was angering South Koreans. Rather than trying to compromise with the opposition or to persuade a wary public, the government tried to suppress its critics. Those who expressed doubts or reservations about the policy were accused of being "anti-unification" and unpatriotic, further undermining the fragile base for national consensus. Some believed that the Kim government had better relations with North Korea than it did with the opposition.[144] The government was also putting all its efforts into making Kim Jong Il's return visit to Seoul a reality: for example, during the month of the first anniversary of the inter-Korean summit Kim Dae Jung urged Kim Jong Il to visit Seoul five times, and more than ten times by the end of 2001.[145] Critics argued that major policy decisions, such as those relating to subsidies for the failing Hyundai tourist business, media reforms, and other domestic political measures, were made in consideration of whether they would be conducive to the visit of Kim Jong Il. Kim Dae Jung's decision to depend on Kim Jong Il for his political success was a remarkable political risk, which could prove to be a failure if Pyongyang provided no concrete and positive response.

When George W. Bush was sworn in as president, a hostile attitude toward North Korea surfaced in the United States. Many of Bush's senior diplomatic and security advisers advocated policies toward North Korea that contrasted sharply with the strategy of the Clinton administration. Detente between North and South Korea lacked substance and could prove to be a mirage without Washington's involvement in reducing military tensions on the Korean peninsula. Washington's support for the sunshine policy was crucial. In early March 2001, President Kim rushed to Washington to meet with President Bush.

---

[142] Statement of General Thomas A. Schwartz Before the Senate Armed Services Committee, March 27, 2001.

[143] Levin and Han, *op. cit.*, 46.

[144] Manwoo Lee, "Sunset for Kim Dae-Jung's Sunshine Policy?" *Current History* (April 2002), 166-171.

[145] "Why Was Kim Dae Jung Preoccupied with Return Visit of Kim Jong Il", *Donga Ilbo*, November 23, 2005.

Unfortunately, the summit meeting was portrayed almost universally as a diplomatic disaster, dealing a fatal blow to Kim's sunshine policy.[146] In a joint press conference, Bush embarrassed Kim by saying, "I do have some skepticism about the leader of North Korea."[147] Assailing Bush's hard-line policy toward Pyongyang, North Korea broke off contacts with South Korea, plunging the sunshine policy into deep trouble.

Washington's North Korea policy stiffened after the September 11 terrorist attacks. The Bush administration expressed a fear that North Korea might sell nuclear, chemical, or biological weapons to a terrorist group like Al Qaeda. In his State of the Union address on January 29, 2002, Bush singled out North Korea, Iran, and Iraq as a members of an "axis of evil." Many Americans saw South Korean hopes for peaceful settlement with the North as hopelessly naïve. Karen Elliot House, The Wall Street Journal publisher, illustrated the extent of the U.S.-South Korea perception gap in a column. She wrote: "Remarkably, [South Korea] and its political leaders are more worried about George W. Bush than Kim Jong Il.... Regardless of how badly North Korea behaved, Kim [Dae Jung]'s response was more dialogue, more aid. It is this bankrupt policy that has brought South Korea to the current brink."[148]

Among South Koreans, the sunshine policy had created the illusion of a possible early unification. The naïve policy had the perverse effect of lulling many South Koreans into thinking war was now unthinkable. In a Gallup Korea survey conducted in February 2003, only 37 percent of respondents believed in the possibility of a North Korean invasion, down significantly from 69 percent in 1992.[149] When the North and South were truly reconciling, a considerable number of South Koreans wondered why the United States was considering North Korea a threat. As a result, Koreans' support for the alliance with the United States declined rapidly. According to the report of a Korean daily in May 2002, only 56 percent of the respondents wanted to maintain the alliance—a figure substantially down from 89 percent in 1999, a year before the inter-Korean summit.[150]

The sunshine policy proved to be less successful than initially believed in terms of eliciting North Korean reciprocity. The popular response was to look for scapegoats; the United States was used as a scapegoat for the failure.[151] Pro-sunshine elements believed that the United States was undermining inter-Korean reconciliation and unification. Some radicals declared: "There is no task more urgent than the reunification of the Korean nation.... The greatest obstacle to unification is the United States."[152] As former foreign minister Han Sung-joo concerned, anti-Americanism reached "a point where events could become uncontrollable."[153] Kim Dae Jung had overseen the sharpest decline in relations between South Korea and the United States since the Korean War.

---

[146] Levin and Han, *Sunshine in Korea*, 107-112.

[147] *Washington Post*, March 8, 2001.

[148] *Wall Street Journal*, November 13, 2002. For an analysis of the perception gap, see Choong Nam Kim, "Changing Korean Perceptions on the Post-Cold War Era and the U.S.-ROK Alliance", *Asia Pacific Issues* No. 67, East-West Center, April 2003.

[149] *Chosun Ilbo*, March 2, 2003.

[150] *Hankuk Ilbo*, May 28, 2002.

[151] Victor D. Cha, "The U.S. Role in Inter-Korean Relations", in Steinberg, ed., *Korean Attitudes*, 127.

[152] Kim Dae-joong, "A Leftist Hegemony", *Digital Chosun Ilbo*, July 28, 2001.

[153] *Far Eastern Economic Review*, September 28, 2001.

American columnist Robert Novak wrote that Kim Dae Jung was "the most anti-American president in Korean history."[154]

In August 2001, in the midst of a confrontation between pro- and anti-sunshine policy advocates, Unification Minister Lim Dong-won, with the consent of the president, approved a controversial visit to North Korea by 337 South Korean activists. Despite the South Korean government's order not to do so, more than 100 members of the delegation attended festivities at a site honoring Kim Il Sung's unification formula and engaged in other political activities praising Kim Jong Il; these actions were perceived as handing the North a valuable propaganda victory. The incident immediately turned into a political storm in South Korea. The opposition party drafted a no-confidence resolution against the unification minister in the National Assembly. Kim Jong-pil, leader of the junior coalition partner (the ULD), demanded the unification minister's resignation. Kim Dae Jung refused and the angered ULD joined the opposition party's motion. On September 3, 2001, the National Assembly approved a resolution of no confidence in Unification Minister Lim Dong-won, the primary architect of the sunshine policy, dealing a fatal blow to President Kim and his sunshine policy.[155] The vote resulted in the breakdown of the Kim Dae Jung–Kim Jong-pil coalition, effectively making Kim Dae Jung a lame duck. Lim was known to be one of the few South Korean leaders whom North Koreans trusted. Despite repeated warnings from the opposition, the unwavering president soon reappointed Lim as his special adviser for the sunshine policy.

Entering the last year of his term, Kim was determined to reactivate inter-Korean relations and in April 2002 he sent his special adviser Lim Dong-won to Pyongyang. After four days of talks, the two sides reached agreements on such issues as rail reconnections, development of an industrial complex in Kaesung (a city in North Korea), and South Korean food aid. Inter-Korean relations, which had been frozen for nearly a year, were back on track, at least for the time being.[156] However, the atmosphere of reconciliation was again shattered in June when North Korean patrol boats crossed the demarcation line in the Yellow Sea and fired on South Korean naval vessels, sinking one high-speed patrol boat, killing five sailors and injuring nineteen others. The military crisis was resolved when the North expressed regret over the incident. Thereafter, the two Koreas renewed their dialogue, resulting in a series of high-level meetings, reunions of separated families, groundbreaking ceremonies for the construction of railways and roads, and some social exchanges.

However, Pyongyang's decision in December 2002 to reactivate nuclear installations that had been shut down under the Agreed Framework of 1994, and its announced withdrawal from the NPT, again heightened tension on and around the Korean peninsula. North Korea's actions followed its disclosure in October 2002 that it was operating a secret nuclear program based on uranium enrichment. Tensions between the United States and North Korea became fearfully unpredictable. For Kim Dae Jung, this was a serious development; his legacy was dependent on the outcome of the sunshine policy. In January 2003, just one month before his retirement, President Kim again

---

[154] Robert Novak, "South Korea, A Time to Test Its Wings", *Washington Post*, January 6, 2003.
[155] *Joongang Ilbo*, September 4, 2001.
[156] *Joongang Ilbo*, April 18, 2002.

Kim Dae Jung

dispatched Lim Dong-won to Pyongyang to deliver a personal letter to Kim Jong Il. Lim waited three days to meet the North Korean leader only to be turned away.

During his last month in office, Kim was plagued by a 'cash-for-summit' meeting allegation.[157] In late January 2003, following a three-month investigation, the Board of Audit and Inspection announced that a secret transfer of at least $200 million to North Korea had occurred just prior to the inter-Korean summit of June 2000. Apparently, Park Jie-won, former culture and tourism minister and later Blue House chief of staff, had pressured then presidential economic adviser (Lee Ki-ho) and chairman of the Financial Supervisory Commission (Lee Keun-young) to get the state-run Korean Development Bank to advance the funds. The money transfer to the North was done in a cloak-and-dagger style, involving the National Intelligence Service (NIS, former KCIA), President Kim's aides, three Hyundai companies, at least three banks in three countries, and scores of laundered checks.[158] Under South Korean law, any secret financial transfer to North Korea is illegal. The Blue House and the NIS played a leading role in the illegal transfer. Most observers believed that the payments were a bribe to "buy the summit."[159] The scandal called into question both Kim Dae Jung's Nobel Prize and Kim Jong Il's sincerity about reconciliation.

On June 25, 2003, after a seventy-day investigation, an independent counsel concluded the Hyundai Group had sent $500 million to North Korea shortly before the June 2000 North-South summit, for which it was largely reimbursed by the South Korean government.[160] The counsel concluded, "it cannot be denied the money was linked to the summit given that all the cash was secretly remitted to the North shortly before the summit under the aggressive intervention of the government."[161] Park Jie-won, Lim Dong-won, and Lee Ki-ho, along with five others were indicted on charges of abuse of power and/or violation of laws on inter-Korean exchanges and cooperation. In September 2003 all were found guilty and convicted.[162]

In August 2003, yet another incident tarnished the reputation of the sunshine policy. Chung Mong-hun, fifth son of Hyundai founder Chung Ju-yung and chairman of the Hyundai group company that had developed the North Korean projects, leapt to his death from the 12th floor of the Hyundai Building in downtown Seoul. Apparently, death was the only escape from the burgeoning scandal and the financial drain of his company's North Korean venture. During their investigation, prosecutors found that just prior to the April 2000 parliamentary elections Chung had also paid political kickbacks to Park Jie-won ($13 million), then culture and tourism minister, and Kwon Ro-gab ($47 million), Kim Dae Jung's long-term right-hand man.[163] Chung's death shows how dangerously entangled the

---

[157] For details, see Cho Gab-je, *Daehanminkuki kimdaejung eul gobalhanda* (The Republic of Korea Charges Kim Dae Jung) (Seoul: Wolgan Chosunsa), 2003.

[158] Lee Dong-bok, "Sunset for Kim Dae Jung", *Asian Wall Street Journal*, February 13, 2003.

[159] "North Cash Called 'Payoff' by Counsel", *Joongang Ilbo*, June 26, 2003.

[160] Ibid.

[161] Ibid.

[162] Na Jeong-ju, "Six Key Figures in NK Payoff Scandal Convicted", *Korea Times*, September 26, 2003. Park Jie Won was sentenced to twelve years in prison in December 2003.

[163] James Brooke, "An Indicted Hyundai Heir Plunges to His Death", *New York Times*, August 5, 2003. Before his suicide, Chung reportedly told investigators that his company directly gave Kwon

chaebol remained in government affairs. During and after the North Korean summit, Kim Dae Jung's deft engineering of his meeting with Kim Jong Il had been lauded both at home and abroad as an act of rare courage and vision. Now the scandals involving money transfers to North Korea cast a shadow over Kim's North Korea policy.

Scandal upon Scandal. Since mid-2000, corruption scandals had also shaken the nation. The government had injected more than $128 billion in public funds into non-viable banks and other financial institutions to buy off non-performing loans. Corporations and venture firms were desperate to get the "easy money," resulting in a series of loan scandals. Since late 2000 three large-scale loan scandals, suffixed "gates," had plagued the Kim administration, casting a dark shadow over the legacy of the Kim presidency.[164] In the midst of scandals, the culture and tourism minister and one of the president's closest associates, Park Jie-won, resigned in September 2000 after being accused of using his position to help friends obtain huge bank loans.[165] A Blue House official was also arrested on charges of receiving $360,000. Even the Financial Supervisory Commission, a watchdog agency, was embroiled in bribery scandals. In November 2000, an assistant governor of the Financial Supervisory Commission was arrested on charges of accepting $300,000 in bribes for overlooking financial irregularities in companies under his jurisdiction. The watchdog agency was under fire after failing to avert a series of illegal loans, and the chairman of the commission apologized for the scandals.[166] President Kim's sons and relatives, close associates, lawmakers of the ruling party, and ministers were implicated in these or other high-profile graft and influence-peddling scandals. Coverage of corruption charges involving high officials appeared daily in the newspapers.

The string of corruption scandals fatally undermined the political neutrality of governmental agencies like the Public Prosecutor's Office. What infuriated the public most was that despite growing suspicions of a cozy link between business and politics, the Blue House and the Public Prosecutor's Office persistently failed to reveal the truth. Powerful insiders frequently influenced investigations of the scandals, damaging the integrity of the government. Some senior prosecutors and National Intelligence Service (NIS, former KCIA) officials resigned amid attempts to whitewash these scandals.[167] Public distrust in the NIS and the Public Prosecutor's Office deepened. According to a survey, 78 percent of respondents believed that the prosecution was not carrying out its

---

20 billion *won* ($16 million) and Hyundai subsidiary companies abroad deposited $30 million in Kwon's secret Swiss bank account (*Joongang Ilbo*, October 17, 2003). Kwon Ro-gab was sentenced to five years in prison with a fine of about $16 million in January 2004.

[164] Central figures of these scandals were the presidents of venture businesses—thirty-three-year-old Chung Hyun-joon of Korea Digital Line, twenty-eight-year-old Jin Seung-hyun of MCI Korea, and forty-three year old Lee Yong-ho of G & G. These scandals were called Chung-Hyun-joon-Gate, Jin-Seung-hyun-Gate, and Lee-Yong-ho-Gate. They managed to amass hundreds of million dollars in illegal loans by rigging stock prices, defrauding banks, or influence buying.

[165] Park was soon reappointed as Kim's special adviser and then chief of Blue House staff. He initially joined Kim's Blue House as Kim's spokesman. In the spring of 2000 Park secretly negotiated with the North Koreans for a South-North summit.

[166] "Korean Watchdog Apologizes for Scandals", *Asian Wall Street Journal*, November 30, 2000.

[167] *Business Korea*, October 2001.

duties properly.[168] The implicated businessmen and officials hailed largely from the Cholla region, and many had in fact attended the same schools in Kwangju, the capital of South Cholla Province. Regional and school ties made these government-business collusion scandals possible.

Giving in to opposition and public demands for a thorough investigation into the scandals, in late November 2001 President Kim was forced to appoint an independent counsel. After its 105-day probe into the nation-shaking graft scandals, the special counsel team reported that a large amount of money was confirmed to have flowed into six bank accounts of an assistant to President Kim's second son (Kim Hong-up), who was vice chairman of the Kim Dae Jung Peace Foundation. In March, the independent counsel arrested the director (Lee Soo-dong) of the foundation on charges of taking bribes. The director was believed to have received the money on behalf of the vice chairman.[169] In June Kim Hong-up was arrested on charges of taking bribes of some $2.2 million from businessmen in return for influence. He was also accused of managing some $23 million in secret funds. As a result, the foundation temporarily closed its operation, making it the epicenter of scandals. President Kim again offered an apology.[170]

It was reported that some of these financial scandals involving the heads of start-up companies were connected to the ruling camp's efforts to raise campaign funds for the 2002 presidential election. In December 2001, the deputy director of the NIS, Kim Eun-sung, was arrested and sentenced to two years in prison for accepting bribes to protect a jailed venture businessman (Jin Seung-hyun). The head of the economic information team of the NIS, Chung Sung-hong, was also arrested on bribery charges in connection with the financial and lobbying scandal. NIS officials had raised money through lobbyists and delivered it to deputy director Kim, who reportedly utilized the money for a "special project [probably the 2000 general elections]." It seemed that the spy agency was at or near the center of all of these scandals. In January 2002, the director of the NIS apologized for its role in the corruption scandals, after having purged fourteen senior officials.[171] The deputy prosecutor general (Shin Kwang-ok) and the former chief of the National Police Agency (Lee Moo-young) were also arrested in connection with the case.

On May 18, 2002, the prosecutor arrested the president's youngest son, Kim Hong-gul, on charges of receiving $3.1 million in bribes from a lobbyist (Choi Kyu-sun) who was under arrest on graft charges.[172] The arrest dealt a serious blow to President Kim, already reeling from a string of corruption scandals involving his family members, aides and high-ranking officials. Earlier in the month, Kim Dae Jung's once right-hand man

---

[168] Hong Yeong-lim, "People Lack Faith in Prosecution", *Digital Chosun Ilbo* (English), November 20, 2000.
[169] "President's Confidant Suspected of Receiving Money from Son's Close Associate", *Korea Herald*, March 11, 2002.
[170] Before his retirement, Kim Dae Jung was forced to donate the foundation to Yonsei University.
[171] John Larkin, "Spies out in the Cold", *Far Eastern Economic Review*, February 21, 2002.
[172] The forty-two-year-old jailed lobbyist Choi Kyu-sun was at the heart of the scandal. Choi was a close aide to President Kim during the early days of his term. Choi escorted hedge fund investor George Soros, Saudi investor Prince Al Wahid, and singer Michael Jackson to South Korea. See B. J. Lee, "Corruption: What Goes Around", *Newsweek*, May 27, 2002; and Kim Jung Min, "Rotten on Top", *Far Eastern Economic Review*, May 30, 2002.

and his most trusted fund-raiser (Kwon Roh-kap) was arrested on bribery charges.[173]

Just five years earlier, one of President Kim Young Sam's sons, Kim Hyun-chul, had been jailed on charges of bribery, influence peddling and tax evasion. At the time Kim Dae Jung blasted the first family for the scandal, and won the presidential race on a platform that vowed to erase corruption. But he trod the path of his predecessor. Throughout his lifelong democratic struggle, Kim Dae Jung had labeled corruption the ineluctable result of political dictatorship. Once democracy came to Korea, he asserted, corruption would cease to be a problem. However, during his administration corruption reached unprecedented levels.

Kim Dae Jung gave a sigh of great relief when Koreans elected the ruling party candidate Roh Moo Hyun his successor; Roh could protect Kim Dae Jung and his associates from investigation after his retirement. Widespread anti-American sentiment, especially among the younger generation who had not experienced the Korean War, contributed to the election of Roh Moo Hyun, whose campaign stressed criticism of the United States and its role in South Korea. During final months of his term, Kim Dae Jung was described as becoming "a lonely, almost tragic figure, deeply unpopular, politically spent and increasingly irrelevant."[174] He entered the Blue House as a hero but left office in disgrace and disappointment.

Corruption scandals lingered on even after Kim's retirement. In May 2003, Kim Hong-il, Kim Dae Jung's eldest son, was charged with receiving hundreds of million *won* from the president of a failed merchant bank, Nara Investment Banking Corporation, in return for exercising his influence to keep the troubled firm afloat. Among the arrested were Han Kwang-ok, Kim's former chief of staff in the Blue House and then former ruling party chairman, and Lee Yong-keun, former chairman of the Financial Supervisory Commission.[175] The Kim Dae Jung government has come to be seen as the most corrupt in Korean history.[176]

A belatedly disclosed wiretapping scandal dealt another serious blow to the image of Nobel Peace Prize winner, Kim Dae Jung, who was himself a victim of illegal wiretapping in the past and thus strongly opposed domestic intelligence operations and who, after his inauguration as president, declared such operations would come to an end. In July 2005, an investigation was touched off when a tape illegally recorded by the Korean spy agency under President Kim Young Sam became public. Hong Seok-hyun, then Korean ambassador to Washington and former chairman of the *Joongang Ilbo*, was one of the wiretapped and was forced to resign from the ambassadorship. The disclosure of Hong's conversation with the vice chairman of Samsung Group (Lee Hak-soo) about a plan to deliver money to Lee Hoi-chang, a presidential candidate in the 1997

---

[173] Hong Soon-il, "Seoul Perspective: Endgame Syndrome", *Korea Times*, April 24, 2002.
[174] Donald Macintyre, "For One Old Soldier, the Battle Is Over", *Time Asia*, 160:22 (December 9, 2002).
[175] *Korea Herald*, May 21, 2003.
[176] According to Transparency International Corruption Perception Index, South Korea's rank plummeted from 27th in 1996 to 50th in 1999, to 48th in 2002, and to 50th in 2003. See www.transparency.org/cpi.
Kim Hong-Il, was declared guilty of bribery by the Supreme Court and deprived of his position of national assemblyman. See "Kim Hong-Il Lost His Membership in the National Assembly", *Chosun Ilbo*, September 28, 2006.

presidential election, became a hot issue. The prosecutors who discovered the spy agency under Kim Dae Jung also conducted comprehensive bugging operations of at least some 1,800 important figures, such as politicians, including former president Kim Young Sam, business leaders, and high-ranking officials. Two former directors of the spy agency, Lim Dong-won and Shin Gunn, its former deputy director, Kim Eun-sung, were arrested on charges of ordering illegal eavesdropping.[177]

LEADERSHIP FOR FUNDAMENTAL CHANGE

Context of the Presidency. Short of war, Kim Dae Jung had inherited the nation at its worst possible moment.[178] The 1997-98 economic crisis was regarded as the most serious national crisis since the Korean War. To a good leader, crisis often means opportunity. The IMF mandate opened a golden opportunity for Kim to pursue difficult reforms. He came to power with the strongest chance of success. The crisis shocked South Koreans into abiding sacrifices and drastic reform. His record as a courageous dissident, and his consistent criticism of conglomerates, endowed him with the strong moral authority necessary to the pursuit of radical reform. Even a harsh reform program of economic downsizing and massive layoffs became a laudable act of great leadership.[179] There was a widely shared recognition that failure to reform would mean a collapse of the South Korean economy. South Koreans rallied behind the government to overcome the national crisis.[180]

However, doubts about his personality were planted deeply in the public mind; and he was also widely distrusted because of his alleged "leftist" leanings. His popularity was limited mostly to his home region. He also had a weak electoral mandate: Kim, who represented a minority government that held only 30 percent of the seats in the National Assembly, had won the presidential election by a narrow margin of 1.5 percent, and even then only with the cooperation of Kim Jong-pil's ULD, which sat at the most conservative end of the South Korean political spectrum. It was a coupling of two regionally and ideologically different political forces. The logic of the situation suggested the need for President Kim to broaden his base of support in order to build greater consensus behind his policies. Furthermore, bipartisan and popular support and cooperation were essential to implement the tough measures and sweeping reforms required to manage the financial crisis.

Agenda Setting. Entering office, Kim announced three major policy goals for his administration: economic recovery and renewal, improvement of relations with North

---

[177] "Wiretapping Probe Throws New Revelation", *Chosun Ilbo*, October 2, 2005; "Ex-Intelligence Chiefs Put to Jail", *Korea Times*, November 15, 2005; and "Ex-spy Chiefs Jailed in Wiretap Investigation", *JoongAng Daily*, November 16, 2005. Another deputy director (Lee Soo-il) of the agency committed suicide owing to the scandal. As opposition leaders, both Kim Young Sam and Kim Dae Jung had emphasized democracy and human rights. In power they also violated principles of democracy.

[178] For an evaluation of the Kim presidency, see Sung Deuk Hahm, "Presidential Politics in South Korea: An Interim Assessment for the Kim Dae Jung Presidency and Prospects for the Next Presidential Elections", *Korea Review of International Studies*, 4:1 (December 2001): 84.

[179] Byung-Kook Kim, "The Politics of Crisis and a Crisis of Politics: The Presidency of Kim Dae-Jung", in Kongdan Oh, ed., *Korea Briefing 1997–1999*, 35 74.

[180] Mo and Moon, "Korea after the Crash", *Journal of Democracy*, 10:3 (July 1999): 150-164.

Korea, and the fostering of democratic institutions. But among these, it was management of the economic crisis that constituted the public mandate given to him: his presidency would most likely be judged by its success or failure on the economic front. During the first year of his term, the economy appeared to be his top priority and he played a leading role in tackling the economic crisis.

After his hasty pronouncement of the end of the IMF crisis in late 1999, the sunshine policy became the primary policy on his agenda. Throughout his long political career, he had maintained a keen interest in unification. He believed that unification was the most important task in Korea's nation building. If he had succeeded in significantly improving relations with North Korea, he could have earned a place in history that would match (or even exceed) that of Park Chung Hee. Therefore, he rushed to gain as much momentum as possible in inter-Korean relations during his term.

Kim was obsessed with a breakthrough in inter-Korean relations and spent too much time and energy on his North Korea policy, neglecting domestic affairs. It is difficult, if not impossible, to have a successful foreign policy without strong public support, which in turn hinges on the success of domestic policies. This was particularly the case in his reconciliation initiative, considering the traditional anti-Communist sentiments in the country. With the South Korean economy in a lingering crisis and numerous unmet socio-economic needs, the massive flows of money and aid to the ungrateful North were seen as misplaced priorities. The sunshine policy might have been a good policy for the long term, but its timing was unfavorable given the economic and social crisis still rampant in the South. The policy was further dampened by an increasingly unfavorable international environment, such as the inauguration of the conservative Republican administration in the United States and the September 11, 2001, terrorist attacks.[181] Also, Pyongyang was not ready to engage itself with South Korea.

Kim's preoccupation with the success of the sunshine policy resulted in serious side effects—intensification of domestic cleavages and weakening of South Korean-American relations. The confusion reflected his problem in setting policy priorities. In inter-Korean relations, reconciliation cannot be separated from security, fundamentally the South Korea-U.S. alliance. In South Korea, which has faced immediate and continual threats from North Korea, the reality of security must precede the ideal of unification. Security is an immediate issue while unification remains a long-term and difficult process. Pyongyang's top priority continues to be the survival of the socialist regime, not unification. Kim Dae Jung skipped the intermediate process of peacemaking and agreed on principles of unification with Kim Jong Il during the June 2000 summit.

Kim Dae Jung repeatedly pledged he would promote democracy and a market economy in tandem. Considering the circumstances of an economic crisis, it was no easy task for him to harmonize the principles of democracy with a market economy. In fact, in attempting to do so, he frequently violated not only the principles of democracy but also those of a market economy. In other words, the parallel development of democracy and market economy was as difficult under the unstable and weak economic and social circumstances that prevailed under the Kim Dae Jung presidency, as it had been in earlier

---

[181] Choong Nam Kim, "The Sunshine Policy and Its Impact on South Korea's Relations with Major Powers", *Korea Observer*, 35:4 (winter 2004): 581-616.

decades. He gave priority to politics over economics. As major elections approached, he hesitated to push for painful reforms and slowed down economic restructuring. As a result, the economic reform was half-baked.

Appointments and Leadership Style. Considering the daunting tasks faced and his weak power base (concentrated mainly in the Cholla region), Kim Dae Jung's first priority was clear—expanding his support base. Considering the economic and social crisis the nation faced, it was expected that Kim's personnel administration would enlist qualified people from all levels of society and every part of the country—free from regional favoritism and prejudice. He might learn that appointments of inexperienced and incapable persons and frequent replacements were often regarded as the main reasons for the failure of the Kim Young Sam administration. Kim Dae Jung condemned the fierce regional loyalties that had long dominated Korean politics, and repeatedly pledged himself to eliminate regional favoritism in personnel management. From the beginning, many thought that if Kim Dae Jung showed overt favoritism to his home region, he would jeopardize the competence of his government and his goal of regional reconciliation.

It had become increasingly evident, however, that in running the country the president relied excessively on his long-time political vassals, who mostly hailed from Cholla and who lacked experience and expertise in government. It became evident that Kim used his own regional patronage network to strengthen his power base. This practice of rewarding loyal followers with government appointments alienated the public from the Kim administration.

The proportion of figures that hailed from Cholla in important government positions doubled during the Kim Dae Jung administration.[182] According to one survey of 100 important government posts in the Kim government, persons from Cholla occupied 37 percent, followed by those from Kyongsang at 25 percent.[183] According to a policy pamphlet issued by the opposition party, five out of nine presidential senior secretaries and four out of eight top officials at the National Intelligence Service hailed from the Cholla region. The same publication pointed out that five out of eleven important posts in the military, four out of seven at the Prosecutor's Office, five out of nine high-ranking police officers, and five out of seven top tax officials were from Cholla.[184]

Kwangju, a major city in the Cholla region, is relatively small compared with such southeastern urban centers as Pusan, Taegu, and Ulsan. Therefore, members of the ruling circle knew each other and many of them had intimate relations through school and regional ties. Informal networks of the president's associates and loyalists superseded official decision-making channels. The ostensible favoritism in personnel appointments undermined Kim's goal of regional reconciliation. "This upset the people and reinforced regional animosity," said Choi Jang-jip, former chairman of the Presidential Commission on Policy Planning in the Kim Dae Jung administration.[185] Because of regional and school ties, corruption and favoritism were widespread in the government. There was a long list of Kim's aides and cronies who had been implicated in a broad range of scandals. An

---

[182] *Joongang Ilbo*, March 17, 2001.
[183] *Wolgan Chosun* (April 2000).
[184] "Parachute Postings Attacked by Opposition", *Chosun Ilbo*, September 27, 2000.
[185] Quoted in *Far Eastern Economic Review*, May 24, 2001.

atmosphere of incest had enveloped the government. Power and spoils were shared by insiders, and this blocked rational relations between various government agencies.[186] The Kim Dae Jung government appeared to be one of the most corrupt since 1948.[187]

Table 15. **Major Reshuffles of the Kim Cabinet**

Period	Scope
February 1998	First Cabinet
May 1999	Replaced 11 Ministers
January 2000	Replaced 9 Ministers
August 2000	Replaced 11 Ministers
January 2001	Replaced 11 Ministers
September 2001	Replaced 6 Ministers
January 2002	Replaced 9 Ministers
July 2002	Replaced 7 Ministers

Another problem in Kim's personnel administration was frequent changes in cabinet ministers and advisers. Frequent cabinet reshuffles and resultant administrative instability were regarded as reasons for the failure of the Kim administration. Although he pledged not to repeat such mistakes, his record of cabinet reshuffles was worse than his predecessor's; during three years since January 2000, he reshuffled his cabinet six times at an average interval of once every six months (see Table 15).

Ministerial posts in the Kim government were like a revolving door: during his five-year term, Kim had seven different ministers for education as well as health and welfare, six ministers for unification as well as commerce and industry, and five ministers for finance and economy as well as foreign affairs. It would be difficult to find a similar case in any other modern government.[188] His frequent changes of ministers and Blue House staff seriously undermined the role of the cabinet and the whole administration. In addition to major reshuffles, there were numerous intermediate changes of ministers and other high-ranking officials. Cabinet instability and lack of teamwork fostered policy blunders. Ministers hurriedly came up with short-term measures, which fell short of dealing with the major national issues, leading to harsh criticism by the president. In an effort not to lose his or her position, a minister might opt to keep a low profile rather than take action.

Like Kim Young Sam, Kim Dae Jung was a powerful boss of his party and a

---

[186] Fukuyama argues that there is a greater propensity for political corruption in the government that is dominated by a group of the same regional background. Francis Fukuyama, "Asian Values and Democratic Consolidation", Diamond and Shin, eds. (2000), 328-329.

[187] According to an online survey of 12,824 persons by *Wolgan Chosun*, 64 percent believed the Kim Dae Jung government was the most corrupt, followed by the Syngman Rhee government (10 percent) and the Kim Young Sam government (8 percent) (http://monthly.chosun.com, October 4, 2001).

[188] Before German unification, West German foreign minister Hans Genscher served nineteen years. In France, which gives top priority to cultural policy, Andre Marlo served as minister of culture for eleven years. In Singapore, a top-tier nation in terms of economic competitiveness, the finance minister served for eighteen years.

charismatic leader to his followers. Kim Dae Jung had long been known as a democratic crusader, his followers called him, "*seonsaengnim* (teacher)". Many used to pledge their personal loyalty to him on their knees. After becoming president, his charisma was only augmented. He believed that he had strong credentials as an expert on economic and unification policies. He seemed to have a sense of superiority, believing that he knew best and most and, therefore, he selected ministers based on loyalty rather than expertise. In his mid-seventies, he was not likely to listen to good advice or constructive criticism. No one dared say "no" to the president at cabinet meetings or any other meetings; everyone present was there to carry out his orders. He rarely delegated authority and failed to handle state affairs in a systematic way. This left his cabinet and ruling party helpless and made them follow the president's intentions all the time. Being excessively self-confident and determined, he ruthlessly promoted major policies in a simple, slap-dash manner, without developing rational plans or public consensus. This resulted in unexpected side effects and errors, bringing one policy blunder after another. A Korean scholar says, "Kim has a knack for fighting. But fighting is different from leading."[189]

Kim Dae Jung spent much of his life struggling against authoritarian regimes. He, who had promised fundamental change in government and leadership style from those of his predecessors, was now accused of ruling in the same high-handed manner. As soon as he became president, he tried to simply bypass the National Assembly and the ruling party. He wielded presidential power with gusto. Politics under his rule was more a back-room exercise than an open debate with institutionalized checks and balances. Instead of using dialogue and compromise, he pressured and intimidated the opposition.[190] He was widely criticized for his abuse of government agencies—there were accusations of investigations and wiretaps of the opposition in order to "manufacture" a majority in the National Assembly, to suppress the critical press, and to break up labor strikes with police force. He was "becoming more like Khomeini and less like Mandela."[191] The all-powerful, "imperial" president often compromised the principles of democracy and market economy. As a result, his leadership failed to meet the expectations of the people. As public opinion polls showed, halfway through his term a majority of South Koreans evaluated his performance negatively, while less than a third viewed it positively (see Figure 17).[192]

Kim had some positive leadership characteristics but these qualities were not enough to surmount three inherent problems of the Kim Dae Jung leadership structure: an elderly president who micromanaged, a prevalence of "yes-men" as advisers and ministers, and a government that lacked checks and balances and sound teamwork.

Achievements and Legacies. The Kim Dae Jung presidency marked major turning points in political and economic development and in inter-Korean relations. Kim had been a lifelong democratic crusader and represented the unprivileged sector of society. He was

---

[189] Quoted in Donald MacIntyre, "Kim Dae Jung: The Halo Slips", *Time*, September 17, 2001.
[190] Sunhyuk Kim, *Politics of Democratization in Korea*, 173-179.
[191] Quoted in Howard W. French, "Korean Fights for Coalition and His Aims as a Reformer", *New York Times*, February 20, 2000.
[192] Kim's overall approval rate was higher as Cholla people overwhelmingly evaluated him positively (ranging from 73 percent to 95 percent).

also known as one of the few Korean politicians with special interests in, and visions for, the South Korean economy and national unification.

Kim was a master politician determined to leave his mark on history. He devoted his first year and a half in office to tackling the economic crisis and launched one of the most ambitious economic makeovers any country has ever attempted. Following the terms of the IMF bailout, he restructured the financial sector, pushed the big conglomerates to focus on core businesses, and passed laws encouraging transparency, competitiveness and foreign investment in the economy. The nation's foreign-exchange reserves reached more than $120 billion at the time of his retirement, which made Korea the fifth largest holder of foreign exchange holdings in the world. This testifies to South Korea's ability to withstand future external economic shocks.

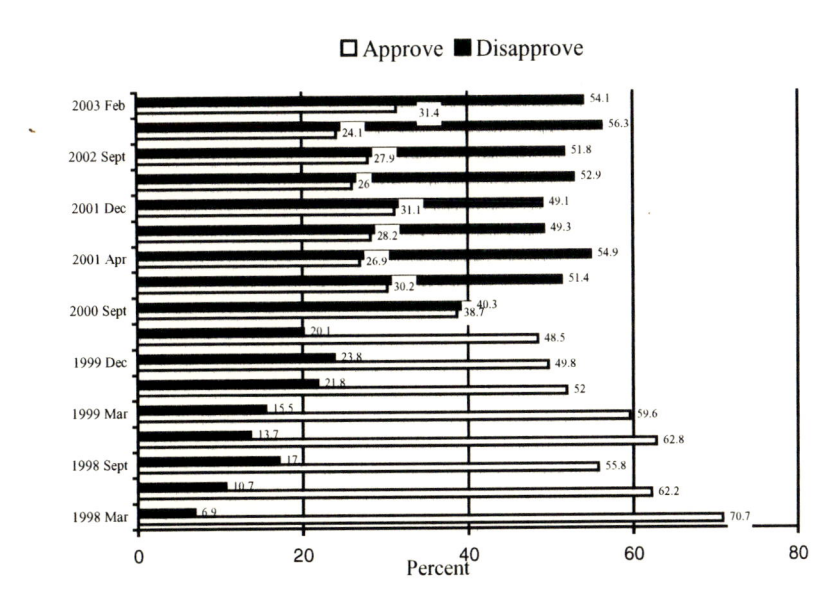

Figure 17. **Approval Ratings of Kim Dae Jung** (%)

□ Approve ■ Disapprove

Date	Approve	Disapprove
2003 Feb	31.4	54.1
	24.1	56.3
2002 Sept	27.9	51.8
	26	52.9
2001 Dec	31.1	49.1
	28.2	49.3
2001 Apr	26.9	54.9
	30.2	51.4
2000 Sept	38.7	40.3
	20.1	48.5
1999 Dec	23.8	49.8
	21.8	52
1999 Mar	15.5	59.6
	13.7	62.8
1998 Sept	17	55.8
	10.7	62.2
1998 Mar	6.9	70.7

Source: Gallup Korea Surveys, 1998-2003.

Among the crisis-stricken Asian economies, South Korea made far more progress in economic restructuring.[193] Kim was one of the few leaders in Asia to take an active and personal leadership role in restructuring the economy. A late 2002 IMF assessment of the South Korean recovery was very positive: "A key lesson from the recovery is the importance of political leadership. Kim Dae Jung was able to unify the country to overcome the crisis. Another lesson is that it is also very important to tackle structural issues, especially in the financial sector, early and with determination."[194] However, his

---

[193] Ministry of Finance and Economy, Republic of Korea, *Korea: A New Model Economy beyond the Crisis* (Seoul: December 2002).
[194] *IMF Survey*, November 4, 2002, 346.

economic reforms were left half-finished. Soon after he stepped down, the Korean economy experienced serious difficulties.

Kim Dae Jung also made a significant breakthrough in inter-Korean relations. His sunshine policy was a visionary, long-term policy for peace on the peninsula and ultimately unification. In order to preserve his legacy as the man who brought the two Koreas together, he initiated and sustained the difficult reconciliation process at considerable political risk at home with a great deal of wisdom and conviction, persistence and continuity.[195] Through the historic inter-Korean summit, he quickly succeeded in thawing the frozen wall between North and South Korea. He had every reason to bask in the success of the summit, and in the ensuing reunions of separated families, series of exchange and cooperation programs, and regular and high-level dialogue between the two Koreas. At least for a while he was one of Asia's most respected leaders, having staged an historic summit with the North Korean leader and having been recognized for his efforts by the Nobel Peace Prize. His North Korea policy looked as if it would be his greatest legacy.

Unfortunately, Pyongyang's "military-first" policy was ultimately incompatible with Seoul's engagement policy. North Korea still possesses one of the world's largest, most heavily fortified militaries and is suspected of possessing chemical, biological, and nuclear weapons. Nevertheless, in order to make the sunshine policy the legacy of his presidency, Kim Dae Jung attempted to achieve too much too quickly. His hasty and asymmetrical reconciliation policy brought about some damaging side effects—social and political cleavages, Washington-Seoul disputes over North Korea policy, and a concomitant rise in domestic anti-American sentiment.

Kim Dae Jung wanted to be an Asian leader for democracy. He had enjoyed a reputation as a lion-hearted defender of human rights and democracy in the international community. Ironically, after devoting his life and suffering much for the democratic cause, he failed to deliver a healthier democracy. He had repeatedly emphasized "the parallel development of democracy and a market economy" but his policies were far from consistent with these ideals. He weakened the opposition party by luring its lawmakers into the ruling coalition and prosecuting opposition members for violations of campaign-finance laws. As a result, Korean politics suffered from serious paralysis, primarily owing to the profound distrust and intense confrontation between the ruling coalition and the opposition GNP. The Kim administration was also accused of suppressing critical media. Although he promised to end the collusive link between business and politics, corruption scandals were more frequent than in previous administrations. A more troubling aspect of his leadership was his willingness to compromise the rule of law for the sake of consolidating power. After Kim's retirement, his administration was charged with conducting illegal wiretapping operations, and two chiefs and a deputy chief of the Korean spy agency were indicted.

When Kim left office in early 2003, South Korea was no more democratic than in 1998 when he had come in. Under his government, an all-powerful, "imperial presidency" continued to thrive with a "peripheral" legislature. As in the authoritarian past, it was the president who made most important decisions. Doh C. Shin, a long-term

---

[195] Petra Kolonko, "The Berlin Wall and the 38th parallel", *Asian Times Online*, June 30, 2001.

observer of Korean democratic evolution, concludes that under the Kim Dae Jung "imperial presidency," Korea regressed "from an influential consolidating democracy to a "broken-back democracy."[196] As the *Chosun Ilbo* daily noted in a editorial, what the country has today is "a government that listens to no one while ruling out of arrogance, self-righteousness, and an 'imperial mindset.'"[197] According to a 2001 survey, an absolute majority (82 percent) of the respondents believed that Korean democracy was in a state of crisis.[198]

Table 16. **Successful and Failed Policies of Kim Dae Jung**

Successful	%	Failed	%
The Sunshine Policy	30.6	Corruption	29.1
Management of the Economic Crisis	20.0	The Sunshine Policy	25.0
World Cup	3.4	Economic Instability	4.0
Welfare Policy	1.3	Health Reform	4.0
Political Stability	1.2	Political Reform	2.3

Source: Gallup Korea February 2003 Survey.

During his presidential campaign, Kim had repeatedly stressed that economic reform should conform to market principles. Once asked his view on the financial reform package of the Kim Young Sam government, Kim Dae Jung responded, "It can hardly succeed because it is led by the government. France also failed as it pursued financial reform by the government. The private sector initiated banking reform in Britain and it succeeded.... Financial reform led by the government is not a reform in real terms...the economy has to be operated under market mechanisms. The economy shouldn't be influenced by political logic."[199] Under Kim Dae Jung's administration, however, the reality was just the opposite. By trying to reform decades-old problems within a few years, the Kim government resorted to actions that came to be seen as illegal and arbitrary. Rationale for these actions was unclear and their processes were murky. The government dictated the terms of restructuring financial institutions, and some of the decisions, such as bank closings, were seen as politically motivated. Government control of the financial sector actually increased under the Kim Dae Jung government. The government also circumvented democratic procedures in carrying out corporate reform. Government interference in the economy rose to what many viewed as alarming levels.[200]

At the end of his term, the public evaluation of his presidency was mixed. According

---

[196] Doh C. Shin, "Mass Politics, Public Opinion, and Democracy", in Samuel S. Kim, ed., *Korea's Democratization*, 75. Four-fifths (80 percent) of respondents believed law enforcement in South Korea was unfair, and more than two-thirds (72 percent) of respondents believed that the Kim government was regionally biased.

[197] Quoted in Don Kirk, "South Korea's Conservative Press Takes Heat from the Liberals", *New York Times*, May 7, 2001, A7.

[198] Doh C. Shin, "Mass Politics, Public Opinion, and Democracy in Korea", in Samuel S. Kim, ed., *op. cit.*, 65.

[199] *Business Korea*, June 1997.

[200] Mo and Moon, "Korea after the Crash", 163-164.

to a Gallup Korea survey, 41 percent of the respondents evaluated his overall performance positively, while 47 percent evaluated it negatively. Since a large majority (65 percent) of the Cholla people viewed his presidency positively, the overall rating is relatively higher.[201] As successful policies, the sunshine policy (30.6 percent) and management of the economic crisis (20 percent) were listed most frequently and, as failed policies, corruption (29 percent) and the sunshine policy (25 percent) were suggested (see Table 16).

When Kim Dae Jung entered office, he was a towering moral figure—Asia's Nelson Mandela. For the South Korean nation, it was a soaring, hopeful moment, the first peaceful transfer of power to an opposition party in half a century. At the time many South Koreans placed great expectations on the new president. Before long, however, they recognized the gaping discrepancies between promises and performance, and this led to a loss of confidence in the government. Five years later, a deep sense of disappointment had supplanted earlier expectations. Kim left office a tragic figure—an unpopular, lonely, and alienated old man. The trajectory of his presidency was no different from that of his two democratically elected predecessors, Roh Tae Woo and Kim Young Sam. Both were popular at the beginning, but ended their respective presidencies with disappointment. Such repeated failures should provide sobering warnings to Kim Dae Jung's successors in the five-year, single-term presidency. Striking the balance, there is no doubt that Kim Dae Jung, who is a man of vision, courage and determination, had left long-lasting legacies such as inter-Korean reconciliation and economic reform.

---

[201] Doh C. Shin, "Mass Politics", 68.

Roh Moo Hyun

CHAPTER NINE
ROH MOO HYUN
A LEADER WHO ATTEMPTED
A SOCIAL REVOLUTION

BEGINNING OF A "NEW ERA"?

The election to the presidency of Roh Moo Hyun, a son of a poor farmer and a graduate of a vocational high school who became a self-taught labor and human rights lawyer, signaled a profound change in South Korea—its history, government, ruling elite, socio-economic structure, and foreign relations.[1] He narrowly won the 2002 presidential election on an ambitious reform agenda and with the support of a younger generation of Koreans, known as the "386 generation."[2] His humble background inspired hope among many young Koreans who have longed for an end to the old politics and the ushering in of an era of new, clean politics. They mobilized the power of the internet to encourage others to support Roh in the election. Two thirds of young voters supported him whereas he did not attract many older voters.[3] His victory represented a battle between the "old politics" and the "new politics" and was thus regarded as the beginning of a new era in South Korean political history.

During the presidential campaign, Roh and his 386 aides excelled in stirring up mass support by projecting his image as that of a principled underdog who challenged the powerful. In particular, they played to and took advantage of exploding anti-Americanism. When a U.S. military tribunal acquitted two U.S. soldiers whose armored vehicle accidentally killed two Korean schoolgirls, hundreds of thousands of people held anti-American demonstrations and candlelight vigils in Seoul and other major cities, demanding revisions to the Status of Forces Agreement. In his campaign, Roh vowed not to "kowtow" to the United States and even said that he might favor neutrality if a war ever broke out between North Korea and the United States, a country that saved South Korea in the Korean War and still deploys 32,000 soldiers to protect it from the

---

[1] For an overview of the 2002 presidential election and its implications, see Hun Jaung, "President Roh Moo-hyun and the New Politics of South Korea", *Asian Update*, February 2003, www.asiasociety.org/publications/update_korea.html; Kirk W. Larsen, "The End of the Beginning: Prospects and Problems for Political Reform in Roh Moo-Hyun's Republic of Korea", www.keia.org/2-publications/2-4-Adhoc/Adhoc2003/9larsen.pdf.
[2] "386 generation" refers to the activists of the democratic movement who are now in their thirties, were born in the 1960s and attended college in the 1980s.
[3] See Kang Won-Taek, "Generation and Electoral Politics in South Korea", *Dialogue + Cooperation* 1, 2005 (Singapore)

North.[4] Thus, massive anti-American demonstrations turned the presidential election into a referendum on Korea's relationship with the United States. Under the circumstances, the candidate perceived by the electorate as anti-American had an automatic advantage, and most Koreans clearly believed Roh Moo Hyun to be that man.

Roh, a left-wing and pro-unification reformer, took an unusually radical stance in the Korean political context. He is the first major candidate to publicly claim that his ideological stance is progressive.[5] In this respect, Roh and his 386 associates have much in common in terms of their experience in the anti-government movement and challenges to anticommunist ideology. They wanted to remove the negative legacies of the Cold War and the authoritarian past. Their progressive view supports the fundamental dissolution of the Cold War scheme, such as the repeal of the National Security Law, lifting all restrictions against North Korea, and moving away from an exclusive security dependence on the United States. The ideological pendulum suddenly shifted in a liberal, or leftist, direction.

Roh's political orientation was shaped largely by his personal experience as a lawyer who, in the 1980s, gained his legal reputation as an activist for the labor and democracy movement. He has shown personal sympathy for the socially disadvantaged and believes that participatory democracy can peacefully redress the unequal distribution of power and wealth. This view is typical of the progressive camp, which regards mainstream Korean society as conservative and the "privileged elite" with deeply vested interests in maintaining the status quo. Conservatives are also held responsible for all Korean problems. Thus, leftist ideology is strong in South Korea and has become an important element in the policies and public discourse of the Roh administration. The Roh administration was thus determined to pursue a radical reform in all aspects of South Korea, which is often dubbed a "social revolution."[6]

It soon turned out that managing national affairs was much more complicated than the anti-government struggle. The Transfer Team of president-elect Roh, responsible for preparing his policy agenda and counseling his choice of cabinet ministers, was composed of progressive intellectuals and former activists who are in general nationalistic, idealistic, ideologically oriented, and anti-establishment. It was unclear what the Roh administration was going to achieve; "one looks in vain for any overarching

---

[4] Tim Shorrock, "Roh's Election Victory and the Widening Gap between the U.S. and South Korea", *Foreign Policy in Focus,* January 7, 2003.

[5] According to an ideology survey by Sim Jiyeon in early 2002, Roh Moo Hyun was one of the most radical and isolated figures in Korean politics, far from not only the lawmakers of the MDP but also South Korean people. There were only four legislators who leaned more left than Roh. See Byung-kook Kim, "The Politics of National Identity: The Rebirth of Ideology and Drifting Foreign Policy in South Korea", in Jonathan D. Pollack, ed., *Korea: the East Asian Pivot* (Newport, R.I.: Naval War College, 2006), 102.

[6] David I. Steinberg, "The Roh Era: A Social Revolution Shakes South Korea", *International Herald Tribune,* November 10, 2004; David I. Steinberg, "The New Political Paradigm in South Korea: Social Change and the Elite Structure", *New Paradigms for Transpacific Collaboration* (Washington, D.C.: Korea Economic Institute, 2006).

vision or clear strategy."[7] Roh has very limited experience in government and lacks understanding of national issues. His only administrative credential is a seven-month stint as maritime minister. He speaks little English and has seldom traveled overseas. Therefore, appointments of capable and experienced persons would be crucial for his performance. However, the president intentionally appointed inexperienced 386 progressives to the key posts of the Blue House, presidential committees, and other governmental agencies, making former activists the core of the administration.[8] As he quickly learned, the pure principles and campaign pledges are tested, often severely, by the rough and tumble of actual governance.[9]

With crucial posts staffed with those from outside the mainstream, Roh's administration was self-defined as a "participatory government." This kind of a populist approach justifies the president's strategy of bypassing such institutionalized political organizations as the National Assembly and political parties to reach the people directly.[10]

EARLY TURBULENCE FOR THE PRESIDENCY

After taking office, Roh faced considerable obstacles and challenges.[11] He inherited, a minority government, a sluggish economy, the North Korean nuclear crisis, and strained relations with the United States, and was confronted by a hostile opposition. His Millennium Democratic Party (MDP) was a minority in the National Assembly, meaning he would face considerable difficulty in enacting any of his reform agenda. In addition, he had a weak power base; although he owed his electoral success to the support of his predecessor Kim Dae Jung, he nevertheless did not belong to Kim's inner circle. Questions were raised about whether he had the political skills and wisdom to manage the party and carry out his reforms, given his narrow base.

Second, the ever-present issue of dealing with North Korea would drown out other issues. The Sunshine Policy had itself been tarnished by the admission that the Kim Dae Jung government secretly paid $500 million to the regime in the North in order to secure an inter-Korean summit, attenuating the public ardor for continuing to provide significant amounts of aid in return for minimal concessions by Pyongyang, especially in light of continued threats over its nuclear program. Finally, the government inherited a sagging economy. Although Korea registered high growth in exports, the economy suffered from domestic problems such as high unemployment, low investment, and high household debt. In fact, the year 2003 also saw a low economic growth rate of 3 percent, the lowest except during the 1997-98 financial crisis.

With an outspoken leadership style, the president encountered numerous difficulties from the beginning. Most importantly, his presidency faced a difficult political landscape. The opposition Grand National Party (GNP) had the majority in the National Assembly,

---

[7] Aidan Foster-Carter, "Roh's Road: Is There a Map?" *Asia Times Online*, February 28, 2004; Steinberg, *op. cit.*, 90.
[8] Ihlwan Moon and Mark L. Clifford, "Korea's Young Lions", *Business Week*, February 24m 2003.
[9] Larsen, *op. cit.*, 117.
[10] Hong Yung Lee, "South Korea in 2003", *Asian Survey*, Vol. 44, No. 1, 130-138.
[11] See Ahn Byung-young, "*Kod jeongchi beorigo lideoship dasi sewoya*" (Drop 'Code Politics', Reestablish Leadership), *Sindonga*, November 2003.

and his own party, the governing MDP, was soon paralyzed by a factional rift between those who rose to power under the previous president and those who identified themselves with the new president.[12] When the pro-Roh faction left the MDP to form a new party (the Uri Party) in September 2003, Roh was not able to count on the MDP's support in the National Assembly, and his support base became even more fragile.[13] Meanwhile, the MDP, whose strength was halved as a result, turned squarely against Roh, forming an anti-Roh alliance with the GNP. The GNP (149 seats) and the MDP (63 seats) formed a supermajority of 272 members in the National Assembly.[14]

In addition, Roh's strength as a successful campaigner became a source of weakness as a president. He had to tackle the seemingly intractable tasks of governance in an ideologically polarized South Korea.[15] The campaign tactics of ambiguity and evasion no longer worked because he was the president responsible for making hard choices on urgent national issues. There was no way for him to meet the heterogeneous demands and interests of his supporters. When he completed 100 days in office, his approval rating was below 50 percent compared to his two immediate predecessors who recorded 60-80 percent support on their 100th day anniversary.

Roh held onto his rhetorically colorful but substantially shallow position on domestic and foreign policy. He was criticized for his reckless remarks and behavior, blunt and arbitrary leadership style, and policy inconsistency. In October 2003, his difficult job became even more difficult, as some of his closest aides were arrested for accepting illegal campaign contributions for his presidential campaign and taking one million dollars in bribes from a business group in exchange for favors.[16] Nevertheless, he was determined to win the upcoming parliamentary elections scheduled for April 2004. Finding himself in the middle of a political crisis with a small minority in the Assembly and plummeting job approval ratings, and anticipating the upcoming general elections, he made a series of moves to reassert his authority and lay the groundwork for a fresh mandate after the April general election.

First, on October 13, 2003, Roh suddenly declared: "I have no confidence in doing my job under the situation" and proposed a national referendum to ascertain the nation's confidence in his leadership, possibly a move at shoring up his crumbling support and vowed to resign if he lost the referendum.[17] He had no intention of holding a referendum or resigning from his office. Nevertheless, his announcement alarmed his

---

[12] Hwang Jang-jin, "Post-election Crisis Deepens in Ruling Party: Roh Supporters, Old Guards Off over Creation of New Party", *Korea Herald*, April 30, 2003.

[13] Lee Joo-hee, "Ruling Party Splits Today: About 40 Pro-Roh Lawmakers to Form New Party", *Korea Herald*, September 20, 2003.

[14] "GNP Flexes Muscle, MDP Reorganizes", *Korea Herald*, September 29, 2003.

[15] Byung-kook Kim, *op. cit.*

[16] Kim Kyung-ho, "Roh's Aide Faces Arrest on Bribery Charges", *Korea Herald*, October 16, 2003; and Anthony Faiola, "Crisis Widens for S. Korean Leader: Aides' Arrest in Bribery Scandal Is Latest in Roh's Brief Tenure", *Washington Post*, October 24, 2003; and Donald Macintyre, "Losing Face", *Time Asia*, December 1, 2003.

[17] "Roh: No Confidence in Doing My Job", *CNN*, October 12, 2003; Anthony Faiola, "S. Korean President Calls for Vote: Roh Offers to Quit If Referendum Goes Against Him", *Washington Post*, October 13, 2003, A16.

loyal supporters and unnerved the public. Second, in response to the campaign contribution scandal, he promised to resign if the amount of illegal contributions to his 2002 presidential campaign exceeded one-tenth the amount of illegal contributions the opposition GNP accepted for the same election.[18] At the same time, the Roh government focused on investigating the presidential campaign contributions to the GNP, making the opposition look very corrupt and his own problems minor. Third, although he had not formally joined the Uri Party, he made it clear that he might quit if the Uri Party did not make a strong showing at the upcoming general election. He again made clear his intention to tie the fate of his presidency to the election.[19]

The MDP, alleging that Roh's comments on the election amounted to a violation of the election law, filed a complaint with the National Election Commission which ruled that the president violated the law requiring neutrality of public officials in elections. The embittered MDP seized the opportunity to launch an aggressive impeachment campaign and gained the support of the GNP. The unusual coalition of old enemies passed a motion to impeach the president.[20] For the first time in Korean history, the National Assembly passed a motion to impeach a president, which led to an immediate suspension of Roh Moo Hyun's presidency. However, the impeachment was highly unpopular politically, with the polls indicating that seven out of ten Koreans were against it.[21]

The impeachment put Roh squarely back to where he is most comfortable, in the role of underdog, locked in battle with a more powerful foe.[22] He has been widely considered to be mediocre to ineffectual in his day-to-day governing of the nation, but the opposition handed him a redeeming crisis, a tool with which to rally the Korean people to the cause of the weak but "virtuous." The opposition once again ensured his position as the people's president, himself a victim of power and conspiracy. Roh and his followers stirred up and mobilized the young. As the Constitutional Court deliberated, the impeachment vote became a campaign issue in the general election. Influenced by the unpopularity of the impeachment, the Uri Party gained a majority in the general election. As in the 2002 presidential election, younger voters, in their late twenties and thirties, supported Uri Party candidates over GNP candidates by a 20-30 percent margin. After the election and presumably influenced by the election results, the Constitutional Court restored the status quo by dismissing the impeachment.[23]

---

[18] Sim Sung-tae, "Roh Takes Another Political Gamble: President May Resign If Campaign Spent Over 10% of GNP Funds", *Korea Herald*, December 15, 2003. Recently, a former prosecutor general, who was reportedly forced to resign by the government, said that prosecutors found that Roh's illegal campaign fund amounted to at least 20 to 30 percent of that of the GNP but they were pressured to scale down the investigation. See "*Daesunjageum susattae cheongwadae cheukguendul joosubu paeji apryok*" (Presidential Aides Pressured to Close the Central Investigation Office), *Hankook Ilbo*, April 20, 2007.
[19] "President's Gamble for Election Jackpot in April", *Korea Times*, January 9, 2004.
[20] Park Song-wu, "National Assembly Impeaches President Roh", *Korea Times*, March 12, 2004.
[21] Ryu Jin, "7 Out of 10 oppose Impeachment", *Korea Times*, March 13, 2004; Samuel Len, "President's Impeachment Stirs Angry Protests in South Korea", *New York Times*, March 13, 2004.
[22] David Scofield, "Drawbacks from South Korea's Impeachment", *Asian Times Online*, March 16, 2004.
[23] James Brooke, "Constitutional Court Reinstates South Korea's Impeached President", *New York Times*, May 14, 2004. The Court found that Roh was in violation of law in three instances. First,

Roh's first year in office yielded fewer positive results than many Koreans had expected. The realities of governing crisis-prone South Korea were daunting for him. Within six months after taking office, his support dropped from well over 70 percent to around 30 percent. Economic realities, high consumer debt, low consumer confidence, firmly entrenched regionalism, and myriad other problems dealt blow after blow to both the economy and the society. The president's casual, even reckless remarks on a wide range of issues helped to change the authoritarian political culture, but they also helped weaken legitimate state authority by generating unnecessary controversies and distracting from addressing the important issues facing the country. He also dismayed some of his ardent supporters with his changing positions on Korea-U.S. relations, labor unions, and the question of dispatching Korean troops to Iraq. He looked like a lame duck as he entered the second year of his term. According to a survey by EAI in February 2004, the perception of Roh's performance was very negative. When asked what Roh's best performance area is among the six areas of policy, 53 percent of the respondents and 55 percent of the government's advisors replied "none."[24]

THE POLITICS OF A NEW GENERATION

The attempted impeachment of President Roh and the consequent electoral victory of the governing party defined the dramatic political turnaround of 2004.[25] For the first time in South Korean history, both the president and the National Assembly were controlled by young progressives. The new political landscape gave Roh a free mandate to pursue his reform agenda. At a national press conference on May 15, 2004, a reinstated President Roh made it clear that he would vigorously pursue both political and economic reforms.[26]

Although the president and his associates excelled in criticizing, they were never clear about the system they wanted to build. Their reform agenda can be best summarized as building a participatory democracy based on social democratic ideas of protecting the weak in society (the poor, labor, farmers, and small business). Much of the next two years of his term saw him pursuing four controversial reform measures, namely, a failed bid to repeal the anticommunist National Security Law; reexamination of the periods of Japanese occupation and authoritarian governments (to delegitimize the opposition and conservatives); a law regulating private schools (to strengthen external control of private schools); and laws capping the market share of the major newspapers (to control critical newspapers).[27]

Roh violated the law mandating neutrality of public officials by openly advocating for the Uri Party. Second, he violated his duty to observe the constitution by challenging the validity of the election law that he was found to be in violation of the law. Third, he violated his duty to observe the constitution by proposing a national referendum without a constitutional basis. The Court then ruled that none of these violations were serous enough to justify removing him from office.

[24] The surveys were conducted by the East Asian Institute in late January and early February, 2004 in collaboration with *JoongAng Ilbo*. See Byung-kook Kim, *op. cit.*, 96.
[25] Eui Hang Shin, "Election Democracy, Populism, and Generational Politics: The Case of the April 15, 2004 General Election in South Korea", *East Asia*, Vol. 22, No. 1 (Spring 2005), 51-81.
[26] Blue House Briefings, "President Roh Moo-hyun's address to the nation on May 15", http://www.chongwade.go.kr.
[27] "Korea: Politics in Turmoil over Reform Bills", *Korea Herald*, October 19, 2004.

The president was a better fighter against his political enemies than a manager of a nation. He tried to strengthen the moral legitimacy of his administration by delegitimizing the opposition. Roh and his associates are leftists and historical revisionists. They argued that post-1945 Korean history was an era when injustice prevailed and pro-Japanese collaborators and opportunists dominated the country. Progovernment scholars rewrote South Korea's modern history from a revisionist perspective. Such moves delegitimize not only earlier governments but also the Republic of Korea itself.[28]

A "Special Law on Truths Concerning Anti-Korean Activities during the Japanese Occupation" and a "Basic Law on the Review of Past History for Truth and Reconciliation" were passed in July 2004 and March 2005, respectively. The former aims to investigate those who collaborated with the Japanese during the colonial era. It allegedly required an investigation of over a hundred thousand people. The latter seeks to investigate human rights violations and other wrongdoings of earlier governments during the Korean War and during the following decades.[29] The two bills were widely interpreted as attempts to damage the chairwoman of the GNP, Park Geun-hye, a daughter of Park Chung Hee.[30]

As part of its reform efforts, the administration enacted a law to ensure that *chaebols* (conglomerates) engaged in transparent management and refrained from old practices of accounting fraud and manipulation, as well as protecting minority shareholders from any unfair treatment. In March 2005, forty influential figures from the four sectors—public, political, private, and civil society—signed the Korea Pact on Anti-Corruption and Transparency that includes anticorruption agendas. Prosecutors have become more independent to pursue corruption cases involving business leaders and politicians. Investigations into political and business corruption have been conducted on a scale unprecedented in both size and scope. As a result, parliamentary and local elections have become more transparent.[31]

In December 2005 and the following months, the Presidential Truth and Reconciliation Commission and fifteen truth finding committees were established to probe into the wrongdoings of governmental ministries and agencies. These "truth-finding" organizations hired leftists with criminal records of espionage and other antigovernment activities.[32] The Truth Commission recognized one communist guerrilla and two North Korean spies as contributors to South Korea's democratization, inviting

---

[28] Norimitsu Onishi, "Korea's Tricky Task: Digging up Past Treachery", *New York Times*, January 5, 2005, 4.

[29] For most South Koreans, their leaders' violations of human rights were minor when compared with the atrocities of North Korean Communists during the Korean War. For some, even violations of human rights were justifiable in order to weed out Communists and their sympathizers and maintain order and stability.

[30] The initial law passed only called for a probe of those among the military collaborators who held the rank of lieutenant colonel in the Japanese military

[31] Victor Foo, "My Reflections on Roh Moo-hyun: His Achievements and Setbacks", *Ohmynews English*, November 26, 2006.

[32] Of the 178 members and 149 staffers in the 15 truth-finding committees, 49 percent and 55 percent are from leftist groups and conservative members and staff numbered less than ten ("Editorial: Reconciliation Indeed", *Donga Ilbo*, January 31, 2007).

strong condemnation from the opposition and conservatives.[33] The "truth-finding" committees investigated and revealed the wrongdoings of earlier governments, especially the Park Chung Hee government, one after another. The government also mobilized progovernment media and activist organizations to promote the campaign of historical rectification. For some time, the campaign of historical rectification benefited the Roh administration; it could arrest, if not reverse, Park Geun-hye's rising popularity by condemning her father as a traitor to the nation. Conservative newspapers and organizations strongly reacted and accused the Roh administration of making an infantile moralistic judgment on history without considering context. The government was blamed for "digging into the past rather than looking at the future." The euphoria of the ruling circle was brief. Less than half a year after his dramatic comeback, Roh's approval ratings dropped to just 26 percent in an October 2004 survey by Gallup Korea.[34]

The year 2005 began with a bombshell of a security crisis: Pyongyang announced on February 10 that it had developed nuclear weapons, dealing a severe blow to the government's reconciliatory North Korea policy. Rather than dealing with North Korea, President Roh began a "diplomatic war" against Japan, when that country claimed Dokdo (Takeshima) as a Japanese territory. Owing to territorial and historical disputes, the relations between the two neighbors soured. Thanks to his aggressive rhetoric against Japan, Roh's approval ratings improved to some extent. However, an absolute majority of the people were still dissatisfied with the government's national management including economic policy. Reflecting public discontent, all of the ruling party candidates were defeated by opposition GNP candidates in bi-elections in April and October, losing their majority status.

The public's disgust with the ruling camp was evidenced by the local elections held in May 2006 in which the Uri Party suffered humiliating defeats against the GNP. The ruling party won only on its home turf of North Cholla Province, the worst election performance by any governing party in South Korean history.[35] The main opposition (GNP) won 12 out of 16 large city and provincial contests. Political analysts described the election results as a vote of nonconfidence against the Roh administration, which was criticized for its amateurish and inconsistent management of state affairs and self-righteousness in managing the country.[36] According to a survey by *The Korea Times*, 44 percent of the respondents cited Roh's poor performance and policy failures as the main reason for the ruling party's electoral defeat, while 39 percent indicated the governing party was shunned by voters owing to its ceaseless factional discord and inability to carry out major policies.[37]

The electoral defeat rendered the Uri Party politically bankrupt; it lost its mandate and left Roh with little political capital. After the local elections, the approval ratings of President Roh and the ruling party plunged further. According to a survey, only 18 percent of respondents answered that Roh was doing well in the management of state

---

[33] In prison, they were tortured but they refused ideological conversion and died in prison.
[34] *Chosun Ilbo*, October 12, 2004.
[35] Choe Sang-Hun, "South Korean Election a Massive Defeat for Roh", *International Herald Tribune*, June 2, 2006.
[36] "Voters Turn Back on Governing Uri Party", *Korea Times*, June 5, 2006.
[37] Lee Jin-woo, "44% of People Say President Responsible for Election Defeat", *Korea Times*, June 6, 2006.

affairs, while 75 percent replied that his performance was poor. The survey showed some 61 percent of the respondents who supported the Uri Party in the 2004 parliamentary elections responded negatively to the Roh government. An expert on surveys said: "The simultaneous plummeting of public support for the president and the ruling party is the result of the people's discontent with the incompetent government and the insensitive ruling party that failed to deliver an economic turnaround among others."[38] After late 2004, Roh became increasingly unpopular, and came to be regarded as a political liability for the ruling party.

In late 2006 and early 2007, South Korea faced a leadership crisis as the popularity of Roh and his party plunged to record lows following a spate of scandals, policy failures, and political wrangling. His approval rating reached an all-time low of 11 percent in November 2006, and the ruling party's popularity plunged to under 10 percent.[39] In a move to prepare for the 2007 presidential election, key members of the ruling Uri Party appeared to have decided to divorce themselves from the maverick Roh and his loyalists and create a new political party. Roh's ups and downs mirror the alternating hope and disillusionment of the Korean people who elected an untested outsider in the expectation that he would revamp the staid and corruption-ridden political order. Roh's was the most unpopular administration in South Korean history.

ON THE BACK-BURNER: THE ECONOMY

Upon the Roh government's inauguration, South Koreans were very concerned over what economic policies it would enact. During his presidential campaign, Roh, a labor and human rights lawyer, talked about a wide-ranging progressive economic agenda.[40] Significant elements included economic reform aimed at reducing the power of the *chaebols* by limiting the level of corporate bank ownership and investment in subsidiaries and related enterprises and introducing class action lawsuits in cases of corporate malfeasance. He also advocated deregulation aimed at increasing competitiveness and growth. As the leader of progressives, he also supported labor rights, higher taxes for the rich, and a five-day workweek. Perhaps, most importantly, he wanted to distribute the national wealth more equally.

Nevertheless, Roh's economic policy during the election period was somewhat short on details.[41] His campaign pledge to "seek real economic growth of 7 percent annually over the next 10 years," was untenable, and his promise to relocate the capital to Chungchong area as part of balanced development plan was clearly seen as intended to attract the uncommitted votes in the region. His dearth of political and administrative experience also led to concerns that he lacked not only economic policy experience but

---

[38] Jung Sung-ki, "Uri Party's Approval Ratings Falls Again", *Korea Times*, June 15, 2006. The survey conducted by the Korea Society Opinion Institute on June 13.

[39] See "Editorial: Get Busy and Fix Things", *JoongAng Daily*, November 27, 2006; Norimitsu Onishi, "South Korea's President Sags in Opinion Polls", *New York Times*, November 27, 2006.

[40] Larsen, *op. cit.*

[41] For an evaluation of Roh's economic policy proposed in his inauguration address, see Yoshihisa Tsuruoka, "Inaugural Address by South Korean President Roh Moo-Hyun, Reconciliation Skills Will Be Needed to Execute Economic Policy", *R & I Asia Focus*, Rating and Investment Information, Inc., February 28, 2003.

the necessary support staff as well.

In his inaugural address, Roh did not mention his economic policy. Balanced development was one of three key goals of his administration. In this connection, Roh only emphasized decentralization and fairness. He also pledged that he would "make the country a favorable place to do business" and "promote uninterrupted innovation in science and technology."[42] However, he was elected president by winning the support of a younger generation that is unhappy over the uneven distribution of wealth. It was unclear how much priority would be given to the "even distribution of wealth" in his administration's economic policy as the severity of the economic environment worsened.

At that time, the overall state of the economy was less positive, for two reasons. First, although Korea registered high growth in exports, the economy suffered from domestic problems such as high unemployment, low investment, and high household debt. In fact, a credit-card bubble, the result of a "consumption boost" policy of the previous government, led to stagnation in private consumption. Second, the progressive nature of the Roh government was alien to the business community. The government's emphasis on labor relations and, in particular, its economic objectives of "income redistribution" and "balanced regional development" (as opposed to growth and profit) would scare off domestic investment.[43] Second, the geopolitical environment was unfavorable. Owing to a perceived rise in anti-Americanism and a rapidly escalating North Korean nuclear crisis, foreign investment in South Korea fell precipitously.[44]

Roh's inauguration undoubtedly raised the expectations of various social groups for their share of the pie, leading to an explosion of demands. Roh's first year witnessed intensified and spreading labor unrest, disputes, strikes, and social conflicts. Labor unions representing transportation, construction, the auto industry, farmers, and teachers have dominated the society. Foreign investors became reluctant to invest in Korea for fear of militant labor.[45] His supporters, mainly young, nationalists and militant labor unions demanded all that was promised during the election campaign. Where did he stand on two key issues of economic policy: corporate reform and union militancy? With Roh's populist past as a labor lawyer, he was expected to challenge the *chaebol* and favor the worker. However, as Roh faced conflicting demands and carried on without a clear policy priority, he vacillated on the two key issues of economic policy. Since he aimed to achieve economic growth and equitable distribution at the same time, he had to pursue inconsistent economic policies.

In order to reduce social and economic disparity, the Roh administration pursued the relocation of the capital, balanced regional development, and the rapid expansion of welfare benefits. The concentration of wealth and population in and around Seoul has long been a serious issue. Although the relocation plan was declared unconstitutional by the Constitutional Court, the government continues to build a new administrative city

---

[42] See "Inaugural Address", and "Address by President Roh Moo-hyun at an International Conference on the Economic Vision of the Roh Moo-hyun Administration", http://english.president.go.kr/cwd/en/archive.
[43] Victor D. Cha, "South Korea in 2004", *Asian Survey*, Vol. 45, No. 1 (January 2004), 34.
[44] Foreign investment in the first quarter of 2003 dropped to $1.2 billion from an average of about $2.5 billion in previous quarters (*Korea Insight*, Vol. 5, No. 7 [July 2003], 4).
[45] Hong Yung Lee, "South Korea in 2003", *Asian Survey*, 44:1, 133.

some sixty miles from Seoul. It also pushed various regional development programs and rapidly expanded welfare programs. Nevertheless, there was no visible improvement of decentralization under the Roh administration. Unexpectedly, owing to the astronomical amount in compensation to local people who sold their land for regional development, the money returned to the metropolitan area of Seoul, prompting a serious real estate bubble. As a result, the policy of closing the wealth gap has ironically widened it.

The economy has thus not performed well during the Roh administration. The main reason for public discontent was the perceived failure of government's economic policy. An absolute majority of the people believed that the nation's economy was in trouble during the Roh administration. In 2002 (the last year of the Kim Dae Jung administration), about 58 percent of the people believed the economy was undergoing hard times; that number grew to 87 percent in 2003 (the first year of the Roh administration). It remained steady in the 2004 survey, showing 86 percent, fell to 78 percent in 2005, and then rose to 81 percent in 2006.[46] Roh was elected on ideological issues and continued to dismiss a slumping economy as opposition chatter. But people tired of ideological issues and turned their attention to economic issues; they became increasingly frustrated with rising household debt, high education costs, and unaffordable real estate prices. According to a survey by *The Korea Times* in November 2006, more than eight in ten people (84 percent) wanted the president to focus on the economy instead of the political agenda.[47]

There are several reasons why the government was blamed for the poor performance of the economy.[48] First, the economy was never a primary agenda item for the Roh government. The Roh administration focused on political issues such as social and political reforms, the campaign for historical rectification, and an independent foreign policy. As a result, political and ideological confrontations dominated Korean political life. Polls consistently showed that more than 80 percent of respondents wanted the administration to focus on economic recovery rather than its dogged pursuit of political and social reforms. During the four years under the administration, an absolute majority of the people (from 72 percent to 80 percent) felt that the nation was unstable.[49] As a result, consumer confidence was shattered and businessmen refused to make investments, citing uncertainties.

Second, rather than managing the economy, the government has attempted to promote huge projects, such as a Northeast Asia economic hub and construction of a new administrative city and several "business" cities. It wasted resources and energy for these projects and made no serious effort to strengthen the economy. As a result, national debt has increased rapidly under the Roh administration; the sum of the national debt incurred during the four years of the administration—149 trillion won ($161 billion)—is larger than the debt amassed during all the years since the founding of the

---

[46] Shin Chang-un, "Koreans Sour Further on Administration's Record", *JoongAng Daily*, September 22, 2006.

[47] Ryu Jin, "84% of People Want Roh to Focus on Reviving Economy", *Korea Times*, October 31, 2005.

[48] "*Chongwadewa yeollinwooridangaks moleuneun 'nomuhyon kyongjewigi'*" (Only Chongwadae and Uri Party Do Not Know 'Roh's Economic Crisis) (Today's News), *Monthly Chosun*, August 23, 2004.

[49] "*Nodaetongryong jalhan il eopdd*" (Nothing Well Done by President Roh), *Joongang Ilbo*, September 22, 2006.

Republic.[50] Third, Roh and his 386 supporters, in general, are populist and antibusiness; they prefer a large role for government in the economy and are reluctant to reduce regulations. They have shown disdain for the rich and emphasize equitable distribution of wealth. Political considerations have frequently dominated economic considerations in economic policymaking. Under the circumstances, business has become reluctant to invest and has moved factories to countries more favorable for their investment.[51]

Finally, economic and labor policy has been inconsistent. Facing strong protests by labor unions and civil organizations, the government set back or delayed some reform measures and ongoing national projects. In the past, economic policies were in the hands of bureaucrats who had excessive control but at least were consistent. During the Roh administration, policy shifted according to political needs. Roh first talked about economic reforms, but several months later, his economic team said stability not radical changes was needed. He continuously emphasized fairer distribution of wealth but at a different time stressed growth. Confusion persisted on other issues such as labor relations as well. Such zigzagging increased uncertainties, worsening business confidence and delaying economic recovery.[52] As a result, the unemployment rate, particularly among the young, reached an all-time high as economic growth lagged.[53] Owing to the rapid rise in real estate prices, the perceived income gap between rich and poor widened.

From the first year of Roh's term, public discontent with the economy became a serious burden for his presidency. Public surveys singled out the sagging economy as the biggest policy failure under the administration. Although he pledged an average growth rate of 7 percent during his campaign, the economic performance under the administration was relatively poor.[54] During the period of 2003-2006, the average annual economic growth rate was 4.2 percent, lower than the 4.85 percent average economic growth rates of 181 countries evaluated by the International Monetary Fund.[55] Korea's rank was 106th, for a country whose rapid economic growth was once considered miraculous. Reflecting poor economic performance, household debt had doubled to 671 trillion won ($722 billion) in just five years, a dangerous level.[56] The overwhelming majority of the people believed Roh's economic policies had failed (See Table 17). Roh and his aides tried to pass the buck by arguing that the economic difficulties were triggered in part by the "false agenda" set by conservative media and scholars, who attributed the economic failure to the government's economic policy.

The government is largely to be blamed for the sagging economy because it hindered the recovery of domestic investment by obsessively emphasizing an artificially-balanced

---

[50] "Moo So-young, "National Debt Reaches New High", *JoongAng Daily*, April 19, 2007.

[51] Kim Byung-joo, "*Jeonmunga moosihan 'amatueo jeongchak' sinrae yireo*" (Amateurish Policies Lost Trust), *JoongAng Ilbo*, February 24, 2007.

[52] Ihlwan Moon, *op. cit.*

[53] During the Roh administration, the average unemployment rate among the young stood at 8 percent. ("Do Roh's Claims About the Economy Hold Up?" *Chosun Ilbo*, January 24, 2007.

[54] "Knowing What to Leave Undone", *Chosun Ilbo*, February 21, 2007.

[55] During the same period, China posted a 10.1 percent economic growth rate, India 8 percent, and Russia 6.9 percent. Asian countries of Hong Kong, Singapore, Indonesia and the Philippines saw their economies grow between 5.2 percent to 6.3 percent.

[56] "Our Debt Burden Is Growing", *JoongAng Daily*, April 20, 2007.

regional development.⁵⁷ Facility investments are very low; the top 600 companies in Korea decreased their investments over time. In 2006 Korea's facilities investments grew only 6.8 percent while Japan saw a 21.3 percent rise. During the last four years when the entire world pushed ahead with efforts to boost economic competitiveness, Korea regressed. The government focused only on redistribution policies by increasing taxes and expanding the public sector rather than trying to enlarge the pie. During 2003-2006 it increased the number of public officials by 50,000, and the number of regulations by 235, an increase of about 3 percent, in both cases.⁵⁸ The government failed not only to make the economy grow, but also to distribute wealth.⁵⁹

Table 17. **The Most Failed Policies of the Roh Administration**

	First	Second	Third
2003	Price stabilization	Job creation	Economic recovery
2004	Price stabilization	Economic recovery	Job creation
2005	Economic recovery	Job creation	Price stabilization
2006	Job creation	Real estate policy	Appointment policy

Although Roh has repeatedly emphasized competitiveness, South Korea's international competitiveness regressed. According to the Geneva-based World Economic Forum, the country's ranking fell five notches to 24th in 2006, slipping from the previous year's 19th.⁶⁰ A global competitiveness survey by the Swiss-based International Institute for Management Development (IMD) saw the country's ranking fall nine notches to 38th. The two institutes' assessment confirms that ineffective government, militant labor and uncompetitive education were dragging the country down. Since its inauguration, the government has repeatedly trumpeted government reform, labor reform, and education reform but its reforms failed.

Roh was also accused of failing to curb skyrocketing housing prices.⁶¹ Real estate speculation ran wild; the ordinary person's dream of owning one's own home was shattered. Roh repeatedly vowed stabilizing housing prices would be his top priority even

---

[57] "Editorial: Political Rhetoric", *Donga Ilbo*, February 14, 2007. During the four years of the Roh administration, the population of Seoul and its suburbs has only become more concentrated and the wealth disparity between Seoul and non-Seoul regions has grown. See "Balanced Development Policy is a Failure", *Chosun Ilbo*, January 25, 2007.

[58] "*Gongmuwon kyuje, gongseng aksoonhwan*" (A Vicious Circle of Officials and Regulations), *Joongang Ilbo*, April 25, 2007.

[59] "*Jeonmungadeul seongjang bunbae da notchin chot jeongbu*" (Experts: The First Government Which Failed in Both Growth and Distribution), *Chosun Ilbo*, January 25, 2007.

[60] "It Is Official: the Government's Reforms Have Failed", *Chosun Ilbo*, September 27, 2006. Korea's standing in labor relations slipped from 81st to 114th; government deregulation plummeted from 14th to 50th; and in quality of education, fell from 31st to 38th.

[61] "A Real Estate Policy in Ruins", *Chosun Ilbo*, November 11, 2006.

at the risk of sacrificing other policies, but his remarks to "do whatever he could" to calm the housing market have only triggered a buying spree, highlighting deep distrust of the public in government policies. During 2005-2006, the government adopted eight different measures to control the situation but failed. During the past few years, real estate prices doubled, or even tripled in some areas of Seoul and its suburbs. By pursuing massive local developmental policies such as balanced development, constructing an administrative city and numerous "business cities," the government also contributed to real estate speculation throughout the country.

On the other hand, Roh's determination and leadership played an important role in the Korea-U.S. Free Trade Agreement. Apparently, Roh made up his mind to pursue a free trade pact with the United States in the autumn of 2005, and in his New Year's address in 2006, he announced his intention to negotiate the FTA with Washington. Workers, farmers, and progressive movement activists who had backed him for president bitterly opposed it. However, he remained determined with the simple logic that if Korea opens its door it may succeed or it may fail, but if it does not open up, it will fail for sure. The agreed Korea-U.S. FTA will provide significant momentum for Korea to upgrade its overall economic system.[62] For politicians, betraying their support base is often political suicide.

PEACE AND PROSPERITY POLICY

Roh Moo Hyun was elected president in the midst of a two-pronged foreign policy crisis—the rapidly deteriorating North Korean nuclear crisis and shaky relations with the United States. Roh's victory significantly benefited from his unconventional pro-Pyongyang and anti-American positions because the Korea-U.S alliance and North Korea policy were the hottest campaign issues of the time. These two issues became Roh's major diplomatic challenges.[63]

During his televised talks in early 2003, president-elect Roh promised a sweeping change in Korea-U.S. security relations, including the Status of Forces Agreement, relocation of U.S. forces in Korea, and wartime operational control. Following up on his campaign pledge to stand between Washington and Pyongyang as a "neutral mediator," he openly criticized President Bush for a hawkish approach to North Korea and volunteered his "lead role" in peacefully resolving North Korean nuclear crisis.[64] However, massive anti-American demonstrations and Roh's critical remarks toward the United States brought immediate backfire. In early February 2003, U.S. Defense Secretary Rumsfeld called for relocating U.S. ground troops southward, bringing a shock wave to South Korea. The American move in the middle of the North Korean nuclear crisis was interpreted as a precipitous decline of American trust in South Korea, triggering foreign investors' concern over South Korea's security, downgrading Korea's

---

[62] "Korea-U.S. FTA: Il Sakong Interview", *East-West Wire*, April 11, 2007.
[63] See Chong Nam Kim, "The Roh Moo Hyun Government's Policy toward North Korea", *International Journal of Korean Studies*, Vol. IX, No. 2 (Fall/Winter 2005); and Choong Nam Kim, "Inter-Korean Relations and the Future of U.S.–ROK Alliance", *International Journal of Korean Studies*, Vol. X, No. 2 (Fall/Winter 2006).
[64] *Chosun Ilbo*, February 19 and February 20, 2003.

credit ratings, and leading to a nose-dive in the Korean stock market.[65] At the same time the second North Korean nuclear crisis was developing from October 2002. In early 2003 North Korea withdrew from the Nonproliferation Treaty (NPT), expelled International Atomic Energy Agency (IAEA) inspectors, and restarted the reactor. International tensions were also high surrounding the U.S. war against Iraq.

Notwithstanding, Roh made reconciliation with Pyongyang his top priority.[66] He labeled his North Korea policy a "Peace and Prosperity Policy," aiming to "reinforce peace on the Korean peninsula and seek the co-prosperity of both South and North Korea to build a foundation for a peaceful unification and a base for South Korea to become the economic hub of Northeast Asia."[67] The policy had a three-step strategy: it aimed to resolve the North Korean nuclear crisis in the short-term, bring lasting peace to the peninsula in the mid-term, and build a Northeast Asian economic hub in the long-term.[68] In regard to North Korea's nuclear program, Roh stressed that Pyongyang's acquisition of nuclear weapons was unacceptable, but that the problem must be resolved through peaceful dialogue.

Roh had a blank slate on foreign affairs and surrounded himself with inexperienced academics and politicians. Amateurism and idealism prevailed in foreign policymaking and implementation. He centralized policymaking power in the hands of the staff of the National Security Counsel, while foreign and defense ministers played second fiddle. His "386 generation" aides were less conversant with foreign affairs, more skeptical of U.S. motives and the American presence on the Korean Peninsula and elsewhere in the region, and had a strong desire to improve relations with the North Korean regime.[69] They saw the conspicuous U.S. military presence as a symbol of the past—a past when their country was poor, dependent, a pawn in great power politics—and they believed Korea should seek closer cooperation with neighboring China and loosen ties with the United States. They were unwilling to follow the dictates of the United States in their policies toward the North. As a result, the government experienced trials and errors in its foreign policies.

The Roh administration had a hard time reconciling his strategy for the North Korean nuclear crisis with Washington without damaging inter-Korean relations. It found itself in the delicate position of attempting a policy of "dual appeasement," simultaneously placating Washington and Pyongyang. The Roh administration provided Pyongyang with economic aid and continued inter-Korean economic projects, while minimizing policy differences with the United States. Roh also risked alienating many of his supporters by publicly supporting the U.S.-led war in Iraq and sending troops there.[70]

The Roh government looked for peace at all costs, it opposed any sanctions against

---

[65] *Chosun Ilbo*, February 11, 2003.
[66] During his presidential campaign, Roh said, that "he would not mind the failures of all other policies if only the North Korea policy were successful."
[67] "Inauguration Address of President Roh Moo-hyun", http://english.president.go.kr/cwd/en/archive.
[68] Ministry of Unification, *The Participatory Government's Policy of Peace and Prosperity* (in Korean) (Seoul, March 2003), 2.
[69] Ihlwan Moon and Mark L. Clifford, "Korea's Young Lions", *Business Week Online,* February 24, 2003.
[70] "Roh Trying to Mend Fences with US", *Korea Times,* March 13, 2003.

the North, and gave priority to a peaceful resolution while intentionally downplaying U.S.-South Korean relations and turning a blind eye to signs of North Korean nuclear development.[71] In the Six-Party Talks on North Korea's nuclear program, Seoul tended to share a similar position to China and to criticize the American hard-line position. At the same time, the Roh administration sped up three major economic cooperation projects: the construction of the Kaesong industrial park, the linking of railroads and roads, and the development of the Mt. Kumgang tourism project.[72]

Pyongyang's February 2005 announcement that it possessed nuclear weapons embarrassed the Roh government, which had advocated the North's cause even at the risk of sacrificing the 50-year-old alliance with the United States. It also made Roh's North Korea policy appear naïve, and it weakened Seoul's position vis-à-vis Washington. Nevertheless, Seoul repeatedly played down North Korean nuclear threats as a "bargaining chip."[73] Rather than focusing on the North Korean crisis, the Roh administration shifted its foreign policy focus to its traditional allies—the United States and Japan. Roh's foreign policy is partly an extension of his North Korea policy as well as domestic politics. Fixated on the improvement of inter-Korean relations, the Roh government often regarded growing South Korea-U.S. differences as an inevitable price for inter-Korean reconciliation.

The year 2005 saw rapidly deteriorating relations with Tokyo and Washington. In late February when the assembly of Shimane Prefecture in Japan declared a "Takeshima Day" and the Japanese Ambassador to Seoul reiterated Japan's claim of Dokdo (Takeshima) as its territory, the Roh administration reacted strongly. On March 1, Roh lambasted Japan for its handling of a wide range of revisionist history issues. At that time, as part of its "strategic flexibility," the United States also promoted the relocation of U.S. military bases in Asia-Pacific, transformation and reduction of U.S. troops in Korea, and strengthening U.S.-Japan security relations. Probably upset by the American and Japanese moves, in his speech on March 8, 2005, Roh stated that South Korea would begin to play a "balancing role" in Northeast Asia and that "the power equation in Northeast Asia will change depending on the choices we make," suggesting that support for its traditional allies, the United States and Japan, would not be automatic[74] He stated later that his country would maintain an equal distance between Tokyo and Beijing[75]

The declaration of Korea's role as a balancer was seen as a "revolutionary shift in Seoul's diplomacy."[76] The statement was interpreted as meaning that Seoul might advance its ties

---

[71] Doug Struck and Bradley Graham, "What Do U.S. and Allies Make of North Korea's Statement", *Washington Post*, April 25, 2003.

[72] In 2003, the total number of inter-Korean exchanges of people reached 16,000, and the total volume of inter-Korean trade stood at $720 million. See Se-Hyun Jeong, "Inter-Korean Relations under Policy for Peace and Prosperity", *Korea and World Affairs*, Vol. 28, No. 1 (Spring 2004), 7.

[73] Victor Cha, "Korea: A Peninsula in Crisis and Flux", in *Strategic Asia 2004-2005: Confronting Terrorism in the Pursuit of Power*, edited by Ashley J. Tellis and Michael Wills (Seattle, WA: The National Bureau of Asian Research, 2004), 152.

[74] "President Opposes Role for USFK in Regional Conflict", *Korea Times*, March 8, 2005.

[75] Reudiger Frank, "A New Foreign Policy Paradigm: Perspectives on the Role of South Korea as a Balancer", *Policy Forum Online* (Nautilus Institute), April 25, 2005.

[76] Ibid.

with Beijing at the expense of Tokyo and Washington. According to David Steinberg, the Pentagon seemed to wonder whether Seoul was willing to maintain its alliance with Washington.[77] Through a letter to the Korean people on March 23, Roh declared a virtual diplomatic war against Japan: "Now the South Korean government has no choice but to sternly deal with Japan's attempt to justify its history of aggression and colonialism and revive regional hegemony" and called into question the entire process of the 1965 normalization of relations with Japan, which was agreed on during the Park Chung Hee administration.[78] The Roh government's investigation of pro-Japanese collaborators also had a negative impact on bilateral relations. For its part, owing to strained relations with China and to the growing threat from North Korea, Japan became sensitive to Seoul's policies toward those two countries.[79] During the summit between President Roh and Japanese Prime Minister Koizumi in Seoul in June 2005, historical matters became the "hot topics," pushing aside all other issues of regional and global importance.[80]

North Korea's missile launches and the reported test of a nuclear weapon in July and October 2006, respectively, further strained U.S.–ROK relations. The United States and Japan spearheaded sanctions against the North, but Roh maintained its soft approach to Pyongyang. Amid mounting tensions on the peninsula, a transfer of wartime control of South Korean forces back to the Korean government became a hotly debated issue between Washington and Seoul. The Roh administration, which pursues an independent-oriented foreign policy, linked the issue of Korea's sole wartime operation control to national pride and sovereignty and demanded the transfer. Thus, the two countries agreed to transfer control by 2012 in October 2006, fundamentally changing the nature of their security relations.

Fortunately, Roh, perhaps the most anti-American president in South Korean history, showed good leadership during the negotiations for a Korea-U.S. free trade agreement (FTA), marking a turning point for the legacy of his presidency.[81] Not only did he bring to the FTA issue to the fore, but he also adhered to his belief that the Korea-U.S. FTA is a development strategy that will lead to a new leap for the Korean economy. Despite stubborn opposition from his own support base, he remained committed to the FTA. The FTA could also help consolidate the ROK-U.S. alliance, which is all the more important because the bilateral security relationship is undergoing a drastic transformation.[82] The FTA may be regarded as the most significant accomplishment of his presidency.[83]

---

[77] Steinberg's interview with a correspondent of *the Donga Ilbo*. See Seung-Ryun Kim, "U.S. Experts Assess Roh's Diplomacy", *Donga Ilbo*, November 15, 2005.
[78] *Korea Times*, March 24, 2005.
[79] "Seoul's 'Balancing' Role", *Asian Wall Street Journal*, May 31, 2005.
[80] Rozman and Lee, *op. cit.*, 763.
[81] Editorial: President Roh's FTA Leadership", *Donga Ilbo*, April 3, 2007: "A President Transformed", *JoongAng Daily*, April 5, 2007; Park Doo-sik, "More of This Roh, Less of the Other", *The Chosun Ilbo*, April 4, 2007.
[82] Lee Joo-hee, "Trade Deal to Bring Korea-U.S. Alliance to New Level", *Korea Herald*, April 3, 2007.
[83] Evan Ramstad, "U.S., South Korea Forge Major Free-Trade Alliance", *The Wall Street Journal Asia*, April 3, 2007; Park Young-chul, "The Korea-U.S. FTA Will Bring More Gain Than Pain", *Chosun Ilbo*, April 3, 2007.

The strain in U.S.-ROK relations concerned many in South Korea. According to a July 2005 survey by *Monthly JoongAng*, 57.4 percent of the respondents believe that current Korea-U.S. alliance relations are weak, while only 16.8 percent believe they are strong.[84] A large majority (72.3 percent) blames the Roh administration for the weakened alliance. An amateurish performance by its foreign policy team (46.6 percent) and its anti-American or "independent" policy (45.2 percent) are seen as responsible for the troubled relationship. An absolute majority of South Koreans (85.1 percent) believe that Korea-U.S. relations should be given priority.[85]

Although Seoul's post-Cold War readjustment of foreign relations may be necessary, it was not implemented through a well-prepared national strategy, planning, and careful deliberation. Lacking also was the sober policy appraisal needed to address the obvious limitations and risks involved in changing relations with former enemies and traditional allies. Diplomacy requires professional skills and thorough calculation of national interests, especially in South Korea which faces multiple geopolitical and economic challenges. But foreign policy in the Roh administration has been dominated by ideology, idealism, and amateurism. In addition, frequent undiplomatic remarks by the president himself resulted in unnecessary damage to Korea's foreign relations.

LEADERSHIP FOR A RADICAL REFORM

The strengths and weaknesses of President Roh's leadership are discussed here in terms of his vision, agenda setting, appointments and leadership style, managerial skills, and achievements.

Vision. The Roh administration set forth a broad policy agenda under the banner of participatory democracy. The web site of the Blue House presents a troika of its objectives: democracy for the people, a compassionate society through balanced development, and an era of peace and prosperity in Northeast Asia.[86] Within the troika are 12 policy goals that present a comprehensive attempt to reform and improve the nation. However, they appear to be a presentation of his hopes rather than achievable goals. The main themes of the administration's ideological orientation and policy directions were reiterated by Roh's address on the 60th anniversary of national liberation on August 15, 2005. He pledged to overcome three elements of division: the historical legacy (of pro- and anti-Japanese elements, leftists and rightists, and dictatorial and resistance elements); divisions in the political process (such as regionalism and partisan conflict); and divisions "caused by social and economic imbalance and disparity."[87]

His vision was ambitious but too idealistic. It might be impossible for him to dismantle the old structure and build a new one within a five-year single term. He has been brilliant in upsetting vested interests but weak in presenting achievable goals for the future.[88] South Korea has long defined itself as North Korea's polar opposite both

---

[84] According to an August 2006 survey of 395 opinion leaders in Korea, 74 percent believe that "the alliance has been deteriorated since the beginning of the Roh administration." See http://feature.media.daum.net/ politics/ article02417.shtm
[85] "Monthly JoonAng Survey Research on US-Korea Alliance", http://www.mansfieldfdn.org/polls/poll-05-5.htm
[86] See http://english.president.go.kr/warp/en/goals.php.
[87] "Address on the 60th Anniversary of National Liberation." See http://english.president.go.kr/cwd/en/archive.
[88] Ihlwan Moon, "Koreans to Roh: What's the Plan?", *Business Week Online*, August 31, 2004.

positively in terms of liberal democracy and market economy and negatively in terms of anticommunism. The Roh administration radically deviated from this historical trend. It defined South Korea's national identity in a very negative way. Rather than looking for a bright future, it looked backward to the dark side of South Korean history, seriously undermining the legitimacy and achievements of South Korea. He also failed to convince the public of his policy agenda; many Koreans did not have a clear understanding of what the Roh vision was.

Agenda Setting. Roh tried not only to achieve too many things but also to pursue conflicting policies at the same time. If a leader tries to solve all the problems, he could end up achieving nothing. The question is a matter of priority, which is one of the most important qualities of leadership. In terms of agenda setting, the Roh administration has shown some weaknesses.

First, he focused on ideologically and politically motivated policies. His campaign for historical rectification and a policy of "independent" diplomacy intensified social and political cleavages, pushing aside bread-and-butter issues, such as economic recovery, job creation, and stabilization of the housing market.[89] Although Korean people in general supported the campaign of historical rectification, they did not regard it as one of the most important items for the national agendas. In a survey of September 11, 2004, asking respondents to identify two out of nine contested issues deserving Roh's top priority, 88 percent of the respondents chose economic recovery and only 8 percent historical rectification.[90]

In fact, the public did not support Roh's major agendas. According to a November 2005 survey by Gallup Korea, the absolute majority of respondents (78 percent) saw social stability rather than a campaign for historical rectification as a much more important national goal. Answering which should receive greater emphasis, the majority (51 percent) answered that the economy should be followed by politics (29 percent), inter-Korean relations (7.3 percent), historical rectification (5.8 percent), and balanced regional development (3.5 percent).[91] They wanted a politics of compromise and dialogue rather than one of division and confrontation, a typical feature of politics during the Roh administration.

Second, an emphasis on negative issues not only created political enemies but also weakened Roh's power base. The conservatives reacted strongly when the ruling circle attacked the establishment. Under an unstable political and social environment, firms became reluctant to invest, and the public grew increasingly disappointed with the lack of tangible improvements in living conditions under the administration. Most importantly, the president's hostile attitude toward the establishment made it difficult to work with leading elements of society. Finally, Roh simultaneously pursued conflicting policies. For example, he promoted policies of high economic growth, expanding welfare, and balanced development. Without his own policy directions and facing conflicting

---

[89] The key members of the Uri Party confess their mistakes of emphasizing radial reforms and neglecting practical issues. See "*Yeolin wooridang jeongchi mooneungryokjadeuleui heowi gobaek* (Untruthful Confess of the Uri Party, a Group of Political Incompetence), November 10, 2006.
[90] *Donga Ilbo*, September 13, 2004.
[91] "*Kwageochoengsanboda sahoeanjeong joongyo*" (Social Stability Is More Important Than Historical Rectification), *DongA Ilbo*, November 30, 2005.

demands, he vacillated on major policies. He implemented a series of inconsistent policies that were often withdrawn when confronted by protest.

The Policy and Leadership Forum argues that the Roh government pursued anachronistic goals: Where people expected the government to consolidate security, stabilize politics, reinvigorate the economy, bring together society, and boost the nation's status on the world stage, Roh's administration instead gave top priority to overthrowing the old guard. In other words, it focused on correcting past wrongdoings, abolishing the decades-old security structure, revising private schools and media laws in order to regulate them, and taking over full operational control of Korean troops from the United States.[92]

Appointments and Leadership Style. Whether a political leader can achieve what he wants to do largely depends on what kind of people he works with. With limited experience in government and unproven managerial skills, Roh needed experienced and capable advisors. However, in his appointments, Roh gave a priority to ideology and personal connections rather than expertise. He appointed "386 generation" activists to important posts in government, especially the Blue House and presidential committees.[93]

Those former activists excelled in protest but were totally unprepared for governing. The Blue House staff seemed unable to provide objective information to the president in order for him to reach a balanced judgment, prepare and implement policies, coordinate ministries and other governmental institutions. Finding their performance unsatisfactory, Roh frequently changed his ministers and aides.[94] In fact, the average tenure of Blue House staffers was only about ten months.[95] As politically oriented inexperienced outsiders dominated the administration, capable technocrats became powerless, leading to inconsistent policies and creating frequent policy failures.[96] This shortcoming could be remedied by bringing in professional, experienced experts, but Roh consistently declined to do so. He obstinately rotated a handful of people for important government posts. By sticking to incompetent personnel, he perpetuated his failure.[97]

In order to understand his unusual leadership style, it is worthwhile to examine his personality. Roh lived the life of an underdog. He overcame his poor upbringing to

---

[92] "Academics Brand Roh Administration a Resounding Flop", *Chosun Ilbo*, February 21, 2007.

[93] According to a report of *Donga Ilbo*, there are around 100 former activists working in the Blue House and around 150 activists working in the ruling party and the National Assembly. Jeong Yong-kwan, "*Geudulmaneui hyokmyong... kwonryohaeksim jinyiphaettdeon 386 saede, jigeumeun*" (Their Revolution: 386 Generation Who Entered the Core of Power), *Donga Ilbo*, December 2, 2006.

[94] Within a year after their appointments, half of Roh's cabinet ministers were replaced.

[95] The number of the Blue House staff increased from 405 in the Kim Dae Jung administration to 531 in late 2006. See Jang Kyong-soo, "*Daetongryong biseosil jojik bidaehwa*" (Overexpansion of the Blue House Staff), *Chosun Ilbo*, November 15, 2006. According to a document reported to the National Assembly, the average work periods of 180 former middle and senior staffers are: less than 6 months (39); 7-12 months (32%); 1-2 years (24%); and more than 2 years (5%). See "*Daetongryong biseosil kukjanggeup yisang jaekikgigan 10gaewol*" (Average Work Period of Director-General and Above Is 10 Months), *Chosun Ilbo*, September 5, 2006.

[96] Kim Byung-joo, "*Jeonmunga moosihan 'amatueo jeongchak' sinrae yireo*" ('Amateurish Policies Lost Trust), *JoongAng Ilbo*, February 24, 2007; Kim Kwang-woong, "*Hyunjeongbu silpaenun jeonmunga bujok tat*" (Lack of Experts Brought Government Failure), *Donga Ilbo*, December 9, 2006.

[97] "Editorial: Shuffling the Same Deck", *Korea Herald*, May 8, 2006.

become a human rights lawyer and started his political career as an opposition lawmaker. He positioned himself to take advantage of a groundswell of righteous indignation—the plucky rebel, defender of the common man, standing up in defiance of larger, more powerful forces. His ascent to the presidency was full of fights against the odds. Even after he became president, his underdog mentality prevailed. He is also a populist: he inflamed and mobilized the young by employing rhetoric that was at once colorful but ambiguous, strong but elusive, and polarizing but shallow. Although he pledged to promote national integration, his favored tactic was division and confrontation between his allies and enemies. He polarized public opinion; he and his 386 aides deliberately magnified, inflamed, and organized it.

In addition, he is a moralist and emphasizes principles. Believing himself to be on a righteous mission, he prefers confrontation rather than compromise. He wielded the sword of morality against the establishment that he considered immoral and corrupt; he focused on the negative aspects of earlier governments and disregarded their strengths and achievements. Since his government was pursuing righteous missions, he believed the government and its policies should not be criticized. He was thus criticized for being arrogant and self-assertive. He is also a risk taker, "betting everything he had whenever challenged or given an opportunity," to quote his lecture before Yonsei students.[98] Faced with political crises and besieged by rock-bottom approval ratings, he frequently called for a national referendum for a vote of confidence and threatened to resign if he failed to win public confidence.[99] His frequent remarks on retirement deepened public distrust in him.

His undefined, even reckless remarks were regarded as one of the most frequently mentioned problems of his leadership. He not only says too much, but does so provocatively, recklessly, and with bluntness inappropriate for a president. He challenged some of the guiding precepts of the old political elite with provocative, even raw, statements. Although he emphasized compromise, dialogue and integration, he showed himself to be self-righteous, stubborn, and confrontational: he insisted on doing everything his own way. He blamed his political enemies for the failures of his government; and he promoted an aggressive public relations campaign that mobilized governmental institutions and a progovernment media for this purpose.

On the other hand, he showed courage and determination by adamantly pursuing a FTA with the United States. Despite strong opposition from his political allies and followers, Roh was determined to set a historical landmark in the course of his country's economic progress. During the negotiations on the FTA, he demonstrated leadership by taking a stand not for his political gain, but for the national interest.

Roh's leadership style could be better understood in terms of James Barber's active-negative character. Barber argues that "highly significant policy failures are rooted in a leader's character, which, expressing itself through and supported by his style and world view, pressed him to preserve rigidly in a disastrous policy."[100] Such a leader is concerned

---

[98] *Korea Herald*, May 27, 2004.
[99] At least fourteen times President Roh said he was considering quitting his post. See Kim Sungwook, *Roh Moohyunui nan* (The Rebellion of Roh Moo Hyun) (Seoul: Chogabje.com, 2007), 223-27. Juan Peron, a well-known Argentine populist, frequently used the same political tactics.
[100] James D. Barber, "*The Presidential Character*, Third Edition (Englewood Cliffs, NJ: Prentice-Hall, 1985), 81.

whether he is winning or losing, gaining or falling behind. He feels that the responsibility for success depends entirely on him. The policy becomes his policy; its defeat means his defeat. He has a perfectionist conscience which leads to an *all-or-nothing* mentality. He wavers between grandiosity and despair. This perfectionism imposes stringent guidelines for achievement—one is supposed to be good at everything all the time. For such a leader, an issue is highly moralized, a matter of principle, not prudence. To compromise is seen not only as mistaken but evil. "His stance toward the environment is aggressive, and he has a persistent problem in managing his aggressive feelings."[101] As such a leader, Roh helped arrange his own defeat, and left Korea worse off than it might have been.

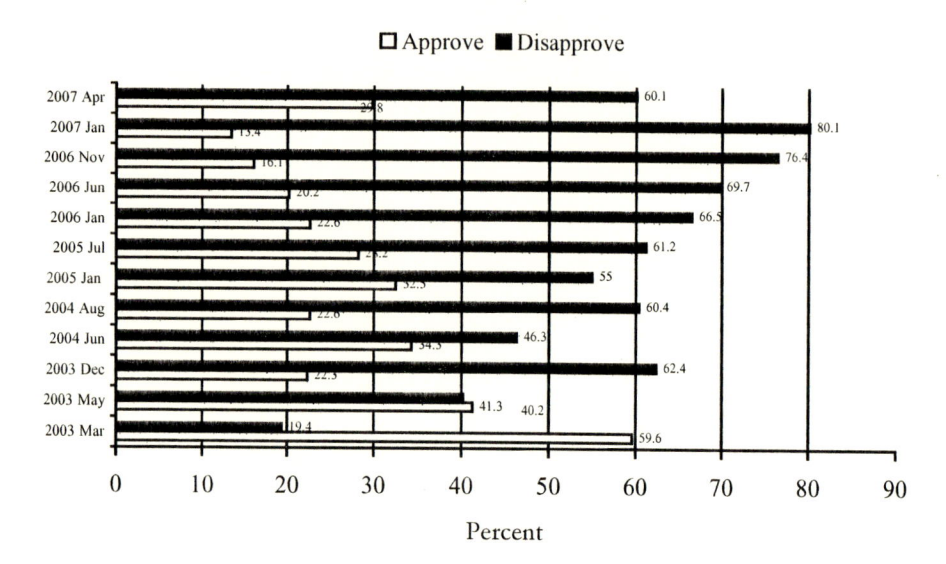

Figure 18. **Approval Rating of Roh Moo Hyun** (%)

☐ Approve ■ Disapprove

Date	Approve	Disapprove
2007 Apr	24.8	60.1
2007 Jan	13.4	80.1
2006 Nov	16.1	76.4
2006 Jun	20.2	69.7
2006 Jan	22.6	66.5
2005 Jul	24.2	61.2
2005 Jan	32.3	55
2004 Aug	22.8	60.4
2004 Jun	34.3	46.3
2003 Dec	22.3	62.4
2003 May	41.3	40.2
2003 Mar	19.4	59.6

Source: Gallup Korea Surveys, 2003-2007

Roh's was the most unpopular administration in South Korean history. According to Gallup Korea surveys (see Figure 18), the disapproval rating of Roh's performance as president surpassed the approval rating only two months after his inauguration. Since then, he has been very unpopular throughout his presidency. His popularity rebounded after Korea's agreement on an FTA with the U.S. in April 2007.

Managerial Skills. A leader's managerial capability matters. Unfortunately, Roh lacks such a quality. As discussed earlier, the Blue House was dominated by amateurs. The secretariat was the biggest among South Korean governments making it difficult for both the president and the chief of staff—who also lacked organizational skills—to manage it effectively. The secretariat was a very unstable organization: the president changed its

---

[101] Ibid., 9 and 13.

structure nine times during four years.[102] His management style made it worse; he frequently assigned missions in terms of a personal basis rather than official function.[103] Furthermore, the discipline of the Blue House staff was loose: sensitive secrets on national security were frequently leaked to political circles; some of them get involved in private business.[104]

The role of the presidential committees seemed to be counterproductive. There were 25 presidential advisory committees with more than 1,000 regular staff and with a strong influence in the government. A modern government is a complex organization. By establishing so many presidential committees Roh only added to the complexity, resulting in confusion and mismanagement. The mission of each committee sometimes overlapped with the missions or roles of ministries; they tended to propose new projects without consideration of administrative constraints. Some committees sent policy directions directly to the ministries.

His lack of leadership in managing the ruling party was also partly responsible for the poor performance of the administration. The lawmakers of the ruling party were so diverse in terms of political ideology and interests that the party was consumed by factional infighting for control over the direction of the party as well as policy directions of the government. Thus, the party continuously lacked discipline and consensual policies, became very unstable and mirred in confusion, and frequently changed its leadership.

The president also neglected coordination between the ruling party and the government and among the ministries and governmental agencies. The Blue House and the ruling party were in conflict on almost all major issues, resulting in frequent policy inconsistencies and failures. Under the circumstances, influential politicians also intervened in the decision making process of ministries. Thus, policymaking was hampered by amateurism, frequent changes in cabinet ministers, and government infighting. Surrounded by inexperienced idealists, President Roh continued to announce various road maps but failed to successfully implement them. The administration was labeled a "NATO" (No Action Talk Only) regime with more than 100 policy "road maps." According to a World Bank report, the ranking of Korean governance during the Roh administration fell measurably in several categories, including political stability, effectiveness of civil servants and administrative services, quality of regulation, and corruption control.[105]

Achievements. At this writing, the Roh government had one year left in its term. Therefore, the evaluation in this chapter may prove to be premature and unfair. Nevertheless, it is useful to provide general views of the Roh government performance. The way the Roh

---

[102] See "*Daetongryong biseosil kukjanggeup yisang jaekikgigan 10gaewol*" (Average Work Period of Director-General and Above Is 10 Months), *Chosun Ilbo*, September 5, 2006.

[103] For example, Roh asked his senior secretary for personnel management (Jeong Chan-yong) to lead a development project in southwestern Korea (so-called S Project) because the secretary comes from the region. Roh also asked his former aide (Ahn Hee-Jeong) to secretly contact North Korean officials to explore a second inter-Korean summit. Another influential aide (Lee Kwang-jae) was involved in a failed oil development project in Russia.

[104] "*Chongwadeeseo salinje naodani malideina?*" (A Killer at the Blue House?), *Yonhap News*, March 21, 2006.

[105] Bruce Klingner, *op. cit.*

government viewed itself was in contrast to the views of the public.[106] The government evaluated itself quite positively.[107] According to the chief of staff of the Blue House, the reduction in authoritarian political culture and balanced regional development represented successful policies. The chief of staff emphasized that the image of a Korean imperial presidency had disappeared completely; the economy was stabilized; the government succeeded in building a foundation for balanced regional development by decentralization of power and public finance and building an administrative city and a few "business" cities; and the welfare budget was doubled. In Korea's relations with the U.S., he argues, the two countries agreed on a free trade agreement, the relocation of American military bases in Korea, and the transfer of wartime operational control of Korean armed forces. The Korea-U.S. FTA will perhaps be remembered as President Roh's greatest achievement, along with breaking the corrupt bond between politicians and businessmen, making major government agencies independent, and discarding the remnants of authoritarianism.[108] However, the public perception of the Roh government's performance was very negative. Figure 19 shows the results of a survey by Gallup Korea on the four-year performance of the Roh administration.[109]

The Korean public perceived the Roh government's economic policy most negatively. But those who felt that corruption decreased compared with earlier governments outnumbered those who felt it had increased. Some 74 percent of respondents evaluated economic policy negatively, while only 11 percent rated it positively. On education policy, 63 percent evaluated it negatively, while only 13 percent saw it positively. Some 25 percent rated foreign policy positively, more than in other policies, but the negative assessment was still more than that at 48 percent. The next highest positive rating (23.8 percent) was given to his North Korea policy, still way below the negative assessment of 51.6 percent. On labor relations, only 14 percent perceived it positively, while 61.5 percent did negatively. Fortunately, more people (42 percent) felt corruption decreased, compared to 25.6 percent who felt it increased.

People seemed to be especially disappointed with his economic policy. Although equity and distribution were emphasized, about four out of five people (83.4 percent) felt the income gap had widened. In terms of living standard, 52.5 percent felt it worsened, while 36.6 percent felt it was similar and one out of ten people (9.6 percent) viewed it as improved. Even among the respondents who supported Roh and his party during

---

[106] The government's self-evaluation is 91.7% while the public satisfaction is 51.5%. See "*Jeongbuneun 92geom, kukmineun 52jeom jun jeongbu seongjeokpyo*" (On the Performance of the Government, the Government Gave 92 Points, the Public Did 52 Points), *Chosun Ilbo*, March 1, 2007.

[107] "President Roh Moo-hyun's New Year Address to the Nation: Review of Four Years of the Participatory Government and the National Development Strategies in the 21st Century", January 23, 2007. See http://english.president.go.kr/cwd/en/archive; "*21seki chotjeongbu jeongchijeok yubulli ddeona halileun haetta*" (The First Government of the 21st Century Has Done What Has to Be Done without considering Political Risks), Interview with Lee Byung-wan, former chief of staff of the Blue House, *Ohmynews*, January 14, 2007; and Victor Foo, "My Reflections on Roh Moo-hyun: His Achievements and Setbacks", *Ohmynews English*, November 26, 2006. .

[108] "Editorial: A Momentous Accord", *JoongAng Daily*, April 3, 2007.

[109] "Koreans Give Roh Government the Thumbs Down in Fresh Poll", *Chosun Ilbo*, February 21, 2007; "Roh Received Mixed Report Card", *Asia Times Online*, April 9, 2005.

previous elections, those who felt their economic circumstances worsened and the income gap had widened accounted for 69 percent and 74 percent respectively.

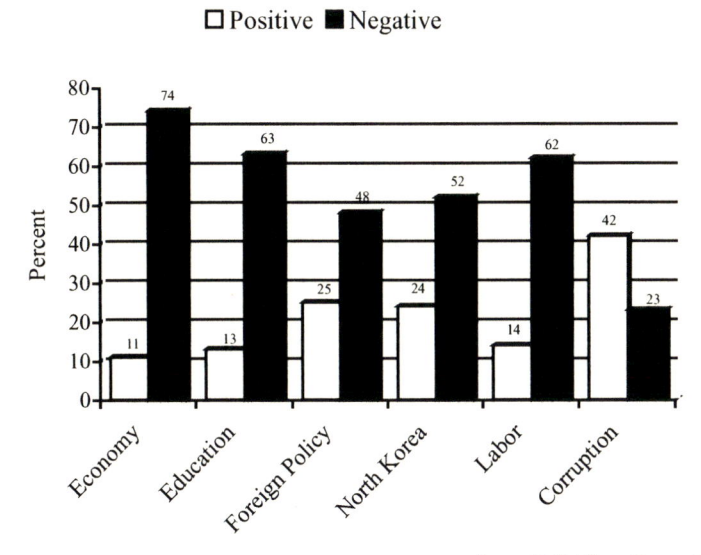

Figure 19. **Public Perception of Roh's Major Policies** (%)

☐ Positive ■ Negative

Policy	Positive	Negative
Economy	11	74
Education	13	63
Foreign Policy	25	48
North Korea	24	52
Labor	14	62
Corruption	42	23

Source: Gallup Korea Surveys, 2003-2007.

Asked about Roh's greatest achievement in office, 30.9 percent said nothing and 31 percent did not know. Of those who answered, anticorruption measures (7.2 percent), real estate policy (5.8 percent), welfare policy (3.8 percent), anti-authoritarianism measures (2.8 percent), shortening military service (2.4 percent), and balanced regional development (2.1 percent) were cited. Asked about his biggest failure, 26.9 percent cited real estate policy, followed by his inappropriate remarks and actions (15 percent), economic policy (4.7 percent), growing wealth gap (4.6 percent), divided public opinion and conflict (2 percent) and excessive tax (1.9 percent).[110]

Assessing the Roh government's policies, the Citizens' Coalition for Better Government gave poor marks to the government's management of national affairs during 2003-2005. It cited ideologically based personnel appointments, unilateral policy making and implementation, and exhaustive ideological conflicts as some of the reasons behind its failures. The Citizens United for a Better Society (CUBS) also criticized the overall failure of the national management of the administration, saying "The three years under the participatory government were days when they did not even know how to work." Some 400 experts—government officials, scientists, engineers, professors,

---

[110] Only 2.2 percent agreed with Roh's own assessment that he has done "nothing wrong". Asked about Roh's recent performance, 24 percent of the respondents rated it "good", 67.2 percent "poor" and 6.4 percent average. That was 10.5 percent rise in approval rating for him from the 13.4 percent he rated in a Gallup Korea poll on January 9, 2007.

teachers, businessmen and journalists—who replied to the CUBS survey gave the government a score of 2.43 points out of 5, or 48 out of 100, to the administration's management of state affairs during 2003-2005. Specifically, the administration failed in terms of appointments, efficiency, credibility, and democracy. All eight economic areas got very poor marks. The policy of making Korea an economic hub in Northeast Asia, the stabilization of housing prices, and the alleviation of the gap between the rich and the poor, items that the government had so far emphasized, got especially low marks of 2.12. The evaluation was the same for the government's attempts to create a business-friendly environment, reform education, and improve labor-management relations.[111]

Roh pursued lofty goals such as social justice and a participatory democracy. There was a big gap between what Roh wanted to do and what the people expected. Roh's ambition overrode his talent. He was a radical reformist, but lacked the leadership skills to carry out his agenda. It may be that it is impossible for a democratic government, which has a five-year single term, to achieve such grand tasks. From the Kim Young Sam administration to the Roh Moo Hyun administration, Korean governments failed not only in the campaign of historical rectification but also in the creation of a new order. Future leaders should learn the lesson that a single term presidency has no time for trial and error. In order to be successful, a president must be well prepared and effective: needed is a pragmatic agenda with clear policy priorities, an experienced and capable advisory group, systemic management of the government, and proactive role of the president. Nation building is a long-term difficult process. A president should work on the foundation built by predecessors and try to solve problems and improve conditions in a mature fashion.

---

[111] "Editorial: An 'F' for Roh", *Donga Ilbo*, February 17, 2006.

Chapter Ten
Lessons And Implications

"The difference between a statesman and a politician is that the former looks to the next generation and the latter to the next election."

—British proverb

"Progress, far from consisting in change, depends on retentiveness.... Those who cannot remember the past are condemned to repeat it."

—George Santayana

During periods of crisis and historical change, the quality of a nation's leaders can prove decisive. During the most difficult and challenging period in its history, South Korea produced some extraordinary leaders. Together, they preserved the nation from Communist rule, created "the miracle on Han," and built a dynamic democracy. Within a half-century, the country was transformed from a country of dire poverty to one of relative well being, from post-colonial chaos to dynamic democracy, from an underdeveloped society to a post-industrial one, and from a client state to a key economic and political powerhouse in East Asia. South Korea's spectacular success may be contrasted with the great failure of North Korea, which initially benefited from more favorable conditions, including more abundant natural resources and extensive industrial facilities that were built, then abandoned, by the Japanese.

In my introduction, I suggest criteria for evaluating political leadership for nation building—vision, agenda setting, appointments, managerial skill, crisis management, commitment, integrity, and achievement. Based on my analysis in the previous chapters, I have rated seven South Korean presidents according to these criteria (see Table 18).[1]

Agenda setting, managerial and organization skills, and appointments are emphasised as the most important qualities of leadership for nation building. It is no surprise that Park Chung Hee and Chun Doo Hwan made greater achievements than other presidents as they were superior in these qualities. Such leadership is vital in developing nations, where leaders attempt to promote short-cut modernization under difficult circumstances. To many foreign observers, Park Chung Hee and Chun Doo Hwan were brutal dictators, whereas Kim Young Sam and Kim Dae Jung were champions of democracy. Within South Korea, however, Park and Chun are not seen as unadulterated villains, nor are the two Kims considered saints of human rights and democracy. Other elements of leadership, such as commitment and integrity, are common qualities of good leaders.

---

[1] Table 18 was based on the results of an internet survey undertaken between May 2004 and December 2006. Sixty Korean scholars were asked to evaluate and thirty-seven responded in full. Based on American criteria, Sung Deuk Hahm evaluated five Korean presidents (Hahm, Sung-Deuk (1999), 291). His criteria were vision, appointments, morality, crisis management, leadership quality, and achievement. Hahm's findings were similar to those presented here.

and Implications

Table 18. **Overall Evaluation of South Korean Presidents**

	Rhee	Park	Chun	TW Roh	YS Kim	DJ Kim	MH Roh
Vision	3	3	1	1	2	2	1
Agenda Setting	2	3	2	1	2	2	1
Appointments	1	3	3	2	1	1	1
Managerial Skill	1	4	3	3	1	1	1
Crisis Management	1	3	3	1	1	2	1
Commitment	3	3	3	1	3	3	3
Integrity	3	2	1	1	2	1	2
Achievement	2	4	3	2	1	2	1

Notes:
excellent = 4
good = 3
average = 2
below average = 1

Vision, in its capacity to bind a people together for the sake of a common goal or ideal, plays a fundamentally important role in the early stage of nation building.[2] Considering the national division of post-colonial Korea, Syngman Rhee possessed a compelling vision of nationalism—an independent nation free from Communist and Japanese threats. His ideology of anti-Communism and anti-Japanism held his people together during the most difficult period of South Korean history. Park Chung Hee also had a great vision—the modernization of the fatherland. Kim Young Sam and Kim Dae Jung both made full use of democracy as a means of mobilizing support.

It must be emphasized that agenda setting, managerial and organizational skills, and talented appointments are important qualities for leadership for nation building. It comes as no surprise that Park Chung Hee and Chun Doo Hwan made greater achievements than other presidents since they were superior in these critical qualities. Such leadership is vital to success in developing nations, where leaders under difficult circumstances are frequently tempted by short-cut paths to modernization. To many foreign observers, Park Chung Hee and Chun Doo Hwan were brutal dictators whereas Kim Young Sam and Kim Dae Jung were champions of democracy. Within South Korea, however, Park and Chun are not seen as unadulterated villains nor are the two Kims considered saints of human rights and democracy.

No South Korean president measures up to Western standards of democracy, but South Korean presidents have been effective nation builders. Syngman Rhee, who inherited a South Korean state at its lowest point, promoted strong anti-Communist policies and helped preserve the country from Communist takeover. Park Chung Hee pushed aggressive economic development; he believed that economic growth was a basic precondition, not only for national survival and democracy but also for victory over North Korean Communists. Chun Doo Hwan inherited Park's unfinished program of modernization and led the nation to the doorstep of advanced nationhood. During the

---

[2] David E. Apter, ed., *Ideology and Discontent* (London, Free Press of Glencoe, 1964), 18ff.

late 1980s and the 1990s, building on economic and social foundations established by their predecessors, Roh Tae Woo and his successors succeeded in the transition to full democracy. Although the seven presidents pursued different goals and strategies, their presidencies appear to be complementary in terms of nation building.

In fact, each president made important contributions to nation building. If it weren't for Syngman Rhee, South Koreans might never have inhabited a free nation; without the efforts of Park Chung Hee, South Korea might have suffered from poverty, underdevelopment, and foreign dependency much longer than it did; if Kim Young Sam and Kim Dae Jung had not fought for democracy, the South Korean people might have continued to live under authoritarian rule. Of course, the Korean success is primarily a result of the enormous sacrifices and strenuous efforts of the South Korean people, often noted for their diligence, discipline, emphasis on education, drive for achievement, and strong sense of national identity. But without strong and effective leadership, the full potential of the people could not have been utilized.

In the introduction, I suggested four types of leadership—inactive, operational, frustrated, and effective (see Table 1 in chapter 1). Chang Myon (a short-term premier after the 1960 student uprising) and Choi Kyu-ha (an interim president after the death of Park Chung Hee) may be taken as examples of inactive leaders. Chang was passive and lacking in managerial capability, unable to control his divided administration. Choi was too passive and indecisive to manage the crisis after the death of Park Chung Hee. In contrast, general-turned-president Roh Tae Woo was an office holder or an operational leader. He had some administrative skills but he was passive. Rather than demonstrating true leadership, Roh allowed himself to be pushed and manipulated by his political enemies and activist groups. In contrast, Syngman Rhee, Kim Young Sam Kim Dae Jung, and Roh Moo Hyun were strong-willed fighters, but lacked organizational skills and failed to achieve their goals. Park Chung Hee demonstrated strong managerial skills and high levels of personal commitment which made him more effective than other presidents. To a lesser degree, Chun Doo Hwan demonstrated the same leadership strengths as Park.

Since the 1988 democratic transition, South Korea has experienced a lingering leadership crisis. What went wrong? Ineffective leadership is a large part of the answer. Recent democratically elected presidents delegitimized their predecessors, and failed to learn lessons from the past. Understanding the past is essential to mastering the future. Great leaders gain enormously by studying and drawing upon the experiences of others. Attention to history is indispensable to the preparation of most leaders. It is why we study the experiences of seven Korean presidents—to see what worked, what failed, and what can be learned by their successors. Eight such lessons for effective leadership for nation building have been drawn from this study.

LESSON ONE:
PRIORITY SETTING FOR NATIONAL GOALS IS MORE CRUCIAL IN DEVELOPING NATIONS.

Priority setting is important for leadership in general, but for leaders in developing societies in particular. Leaders of third world nations have to deal with a plethora of urgent and important tasks with limited governmental capabilities under unusual

Lessons and Implications

challenges and constraints. If a leader in such a country tries to solve all the problems, he could end up achieving nothing. To be effective and successful, the leader needs to choose a primary agenda and focus on achieving it.

In South Korea, as in most developing nations, the oft-extended process of modern nation building has been compressed into a period of a few decades. Relatively speaking, just about everything happened at once. In the beginning, the country lacked almost everything that counted in the West—workable institutions, basic infrastructure, natural and financial resources and trained manpower. Furthermore, Korean leaders have discovered that the tasks of nation building often conflict with one another, particularly when all must be accomplished hastily and almost simultaneously.

Like most developing nations, three major tasks of nation building—security, economic welfare, and democracy—have constituted the primary concerns of Korean presidents. Facing a North Korea determined to destroy the South, national security and social stability have always been requirements fundamental to South Korea's survival. In a poverty-stricken nation such as South Korea, economic growth has also been a critical issue. From its inception, South Korea adopted a Western democratic system, and democracy has continued to be a guiding national goal. In addition to the three main goals faced by developing countries, a fourth objective has faced South Korean leadership since liberation—the task of national unification. The priority given these four broad goals has differed under successive governments, according to the domestic and international circumstances predominant at the time of their leadership (see Table 19).

Table 19. **National Priorities of Korean Governments**

	Security	Economy	Democracy	Unification
Syngman Rhee	1	3	3	2
Chang Myon	3	2	1	n.a.
Park Chung Hee	1	1	3	n.a.
Chun Doo Hwan	1	1	3	n.a.
Roh Tae Woo	2	2	1	3
Kim Young Sam	3	2	1	n.a.
Kim Dae Jung	3	1	1	1
Roh Moo Hyun	n.a.	2	1	1

Notes:
primary goal = 1
secondary goal = 2
tertiary goal = 3

Syngman Rhee's anti-Communism and security-first policies were well founded, considering the daunting challenges to the very existence of the Republic that were prevalent during his presidency. His preoccupation with unification may be viewed as an extension of his security policy. Rhee's leadership was relatively successful as he was able to prevail over the most critical national threats—Communist insurgencies, civil and military uprisings, and the Korean War.

In contrast, the top priority of the Chang Myon administration was democracy. Prime Minister Chang sought to practice full democracy at the expense of security and stability. But security and economic conditions were not yet strong enough to sustain full democracy. As a result, economic and security situations were aggravated, providing justification for a military coup.

Park Chung Hee recognized the difficulty of attempting to achieve simultaneously national security, economic growth and democratic development. He was committed to what was possible (economic development) rather than what was desirable (democratic development). He believed that democracy could only be established on a healthy economic foundation. He also believed that establishing a sound economic base was the surest way of strengthening national security. Therefore, Park was ready, if necessary, to sacrifice democratic principles. Ultimately, Park succeeded in building a solid foundation of economic prosperity while strengthening the national defense. The Chun Doo Hwan administration maintained the same priorities.

By the late 1980s, South Korea had achieved a decisive victory in its competition with North Korea: it had succeeded in establishing the security, economic, and social foundations for democracy. Since that time, democracy has been the top national priority. In most historical cases, the establishment of a viable democracy has been a gradual, long-term process; an effective democracy is not easily achieved rapidly. More recently, South Korean leaders have not heeded this historical truth, putting too much emphasis on democratization and consequently weakening the economy and/or endangering security. In addition, Kim Dae Jung and Roh Moo Hyun placed too much emphasis on unification, compromising national security.

LESSON TWO:
MAINTENANCE OF NATIONAL SECURITY AND POLITICAL STABILITY
IS A PREREQUISITE FOR POLITICAL LEADERSHIP
IN NEWLY ESTABLISHED STATES.

Among all third world nations, South Korea, Taiwan, and Israel have been the most threatened in terms of national security. Exceptionally acute problems of insecurity in South Korea are due to the partition of the Korean peninsula. War, rebellion, and economic difficulties—"three types of crisis in the life of a democratic nation"[3]—have been largely attributable to continuing South-North confrontation. Yet despite its unique security condition, few Korean analysts have paid attention to security issues when examining South Korean leadership. South Korean presidents who have emphasized security have been denounced for justifying authoritarian rule. In particular, even though the Syngman Rhee administration spent most of its time and energy in fighting Communists, the vast majority of existing views on Rhee almost totally neglect his national security dilemma.

Syngman Rhee led a nation in a continual state of emergency. Without his staunch anti-Communism and security-first policies, South Korea might have disappeared even before the Korean War. During the Korean War, he maintained firm control of his government and military and mobilized human and other resources to fight the invaders. Without his firm resolve and dexterous diplomacy, the United States may not have

---

[3] Rossiter, *op. cit.*, 6-13.

agreed to sign a mutual defense treaty with South Korea, or agreed to the continued defense of South Korea after the war.

Most evaluations of former presidents Park Chung Hee and Chun Doo Hwan have paid limited attention to their legitimate security concerns. Many have blamed the two leaders for their anti-democratic measures. During the 1960s–1980s, North Korean threats became especially real and immediate, owing to the escalating war in Vietnam and concomitant weakening of American security commitments to South Korea. Both Park and Chun believed that national security would garantee social and political stability, which in turn enabled economic development. They realized that overseas investment in South Korea would be difficult to come by if the nation was perceived to be unstable in any respect. Finally, it was security and stability that enabled Korea to become an economic powerhouse and to develop a dynamic and viable democracy.

Newly independent states are insecure, unstable entities. Security is a necessary condition for state building. Without the assurance of national security, pursuit of other nation-building goals is difficult, if not impossible. Political leaders of newly independent states are preoccupied, even obsessed, by state and regime security, and security considerations commonly dominate their domestic and foreign policies. As a result, economic issues and democracy are often sacrificed, if necessary.[4]

Like their South Korean counterparts, Israeli leaders have been constrained by unique security problems. For instance, Ben Gurion and his successors have had to deal with the Arab-Israeli conflict and the dilemma of Palestinian statehood. In fact, the issue of national security has persistently been the top priority on the Israeli national agenda.[5] Ben Gurion invested most of his energy consolidating the military and enacting emergency regulations, rather than building up the democratic apparatus. His successors have maintained similar policies. Modern Taiwan, faced with an imminent military threat from Communist mainland China, has a history similar to South Korea's. In Taiwan a strong state emerged in response to military threat. The strong, militaristic state of Japan can also be attributed largely to foreign threat; after its forced opening following the Perry expedition of 1853, Japan set about modernization to protect the country against foreign invasion.[6]

The American Civil War of 1861-1865 was initiated to preserve the Union. To this end Abraham Lincoln did not shy away from breaking laws, violating the Constitution, usurping arbitrary power, and trampling on individual liberties. Woodrow Wilson during World War I and Franklin Roosevelt during World War II adopted similar measures. There is a tendency for the American people to rally around the president in times of security crisis, with little concern for the rightness or wrongness of the president's position, at least for a while.

---

[4] Job, *Insecurity Dilemma*, 28; Ayoob, *Third World Security Predicament*, 191.
[5] Jacob Abadi, *Israel's Leadership: from Utopia to Crisis* (Westport, CT: St John's University Press, 1981), 6ff.
[6] Joel S. Migdal, *Strong Societies and Weak States* (Princeton, NJ: Princeton University Press, 1988), 269-274.

LESSON THREE:
EFFECTIVENESS IS AS IMPORTANT AS LEGITIMACY FOR NATION BUILDING.

The political leader of a developing country is likely to be more successful and respected when he gives paramount importance to the enormous and pressing needs of the people. Park Chung Hee is a good example. Despite his authoritarian rule, more than two-thirds of respondents in many South Korean surveys believe Park to be one of the greatest leaders in their nation's history. It is also interesting to note that, according to surveys conducted by the daily *Donga Ilbo*, both the South Korean public and opinion leaders believe that Park made a greater contribution to their country's political development than any other president.[7]

For similar reasons, although Chun Doo Hwan was notoriously undemocratic, his achievements are evaluated to be second best by political scientists and the public.[8] Positive evaluations of Chun's performance have increased as democratically elected presidents have performed progressively more poorly.[9] Both Park and Chun were task-oriented and achievement-oriented leaders: they were very effective in ameliorating and solving economic and social problems.

Good management is essential to successful political leadership. Organizational and managerial skills are especially important for the leaders of developing nations because political institutions and policymaking processes are not well established. Both Park and Chun managed the government by institutions rather than personal whim. These two leaders learned organizational and managerial skills during military careers and established strong, effective national management teams by recruiting capable technocrats. The best presidents are ones who surround themselves with the best advisers. In his memoirs, Dwight Eisenhower emphasized the importance of organizational ability: "Organization cannot make a genius out of an incompetent, nor make the decisions that are necessary to trigger actions, disorganization can scarcely fail to result in inefficiency and can easily lead to disaster."[10]

Syngman Rhee, Kim Young Sam and Roh Moo Hyun pursued more ambitious but abstract goals and lacked managerial skills. They ultimately disappointed their people. Unification was the paramount goal of Rhee's government, but Rhee lacked realistic programs to achieve this goal. The South Korean people continued to languish under miserable living conditions and became increasingly disillusioned with his leadership. Kim Young Sam also pursued lofty ideals characterized by slogans such as the creation of a "new Korea," or globalization. But he had low organizational skills, an ineffective policymaking team, and no workable programs. This combination was echoed in the Roh Moo Hyun presidency which now seems to be even worse than that of Kim Young Sam.

---

[7] *Donga Ilbo*, August 14, 1998.

[8] Hahm (1999), 289-290.

[9] Supporters of the Chun Doo Hwan-style authoritarianism as the best method of tackling the country's serious problems increased steadily from 12 percent in 1996, to 24 percent in 1998, 31 percent in 1999, and 44 percent in 2001. See Doh C. Shin, "Mass Politics, Public Opinion, and Democracy in Korea", in Kim, ed., *Korea's Democratization*, 63.

[10] Dwight D. Eisenhower, *The White House Years: Mandate for Change, 1953-1956* (Garden City, NY: Doubleday, 1963), 114.

During the early stages of nation building, the people are preoccupied with basic needs of everyday life. Therefore, an effective leader must be successful in improving living conditions. A political leader who is out of touch with the pressing needs of his people can achieve minimal success. In addition, nation building among latecomers is typically short-cut modernization. Tasks which in the West were accomplished over centuries, now must be completed in a few decades, and under more challenging circumstances. Under such circumstances, a task-oriented and achievement-oriented leadership may prove more successful, as the primary concern is to get the job done in a quick yet effective manner. If people recognize some tangible progress in their lives, they will be much more willing to support and participate in the promotion of government policies.

In Korea, there is a tendency to give too much importance to legitimacy. For instance, Kim Young Sam, who was proud of his democratic legitimacy, exercised moralistic leadership. However, he became arrogant, neglected the real issues and disregarded the strengths and achievements of former governments. Again, Roh Moo Hyun seems to have exceeded the worse failings of Kim Young Sam. Democratic reform is by nature abstract, and ordinary people may not recognize any practical benefit from such reforms. Max Lerner, in an introduction to the works of Machiavelli, wrote: "Let us be clear on one thing: ideals and ethics are important in politics as norms, but they are scarcely effective as techniques."[11] As long as the economy and other such "mundane" issues are in trouble, the people will be dissatisfied with the government. For a five-year single term president, there is no room for trial and error; unless the president is well prepared and effective, his term is likely to be marred by mistakes and misjudgments he did not intend to commit.

Popular elections do not always guarantee the selection of competent leadership. Questions of legitimacy and effectiveness are interrelated: even a legitimate government may lose its legitimacy if the regime is incapable of functioning, just as an illegitimate regime may become acceptable if it proves to be effective, and may purchase legitimacy by such prolonged performance.[12] In fact, successful economic performance is the *sine qua non* for achieving stability and legitimacy in such a country as Korea. Using Korea Democracy Barometer surveys in 1993 and 2001, Doh C. Shin found that 68 percent of the general public defined economic prosperity, rather than political freedom (39 percent), as the most important element of democracy.[13] Furthermore, "supporters of authoritarianism, as the best method of tackling the country's serious problems, have increased steadily from 12 percent in 1996 to 24 percent in 1998, 31 percent in 1999, and 44 percent in 2001. Compared to the pre-[1997 financial]crisis period, nearly four times as many people expressed nostalgia for the way the Chun Doo Hwan government handled those problems."[14]

---

[11] Niccolò Machiavelli, *The Prince and The Discourses* (New York, NY : The Modern Library, 1950), iii.
[12] See Seymour M. Lipset, *Political Man* (Garden city, NY: Doubleday, 1981), 82-83; and Jorge I. Dominguez, "Political Change: Central America, South America, and the Caribbean", in Weiner and Huntington, eds., *Understanding Political Development*, 76-78.
[13] Doh C. Shin, "Mass Politics, Public Opinion, and Democracy in Korea", in Kim, ed., *Korea's Democratization*, 50.
[14] Ibid., 71.

Lesson Four:
A Strong and Determined Leader is More Likely to Succeed in the Initial Phase of Nation Building.

Strong presidents have dominated the Republic of Korea for fifty years. With the exception of Roh Tae Woo, all South Korean presidents were by and large strong-willed and authoritarian. To reach the top and survive in Korea during the most difficult period in its history, a leader needed to be tough and ruthless by nature. Post-1945 Korea was more receptive to a charismatic, authoritarian leader than a low-key one, regardless of his intention and ability. South Korean presidents governed according to one of the most realistic edicts of Winston Churchill, who once wrote, "People who are not prepared to do unpopular things and to defy clamor are not fit to be ministers in times of stress." In American history, great presidents were strong presidents.[15]

During the early phase of nation building, the main concern of leadership is likely to be the politics of personal and regime survival. The political capacities of leaders in developing nations are overloaded by the conjunction of many problems and challenges. The challenges include but are not limited to weak regime legitimacy, persistent domestic violence, explosive demands, and foreign military threat, including war. Moreover, the capabilities of the government are constrained by poor resources, incapable manpower and weak institutions. In order to survive and do his job, a leader should possess conviction, determination and courage. He must tell the country where he is heading so he can rally people behind him.

Syngman Rhee's leadership is a good example of the politics of survival.[16] Rhee fought the formidable challenges of a post-colonial and divided Korea with the same fierce intensity that he had employed against the Japanese. At times he was left with virtually nothing but his strong will. It is not too much to say that Rhee's charismatic leadership proved the most critical factor in holding the South Korean nation together and protecting what he saw as vital Korean interests during its most dangerous hours. Park Chung Hee was an iron-willed leader, determined to create a self-reliant industrial nation within a matter of decades. Despite strong protests and other obstacles, he pushed through with some historical decisions. Three other presidents—Chun Doo Hwan, Kim Young Sam, and Kim Dae Jung—also possessed strong convictions and determination. In contrast, a weak government under a passive leader like Roh Tae Woo failed to cope effectively with an outburst of economic and political demands. This man was simply catapulted into the leadership before he had a clear idea of what he wanted to do with it. More driven than driving, he succumbed to the pressures of party politics, military challenges and/or anti-government forces.

Economic hard times render an authoritarian leader far more probable. When the masses are abjectly impoverished or even economically insecure, they retreat to the shelter of strong leadership. Most successful leaders in nation building (such as Park Chung Hee, Chiang Kai-shek, Lee Kwan Yew, Mahathir Mohamad, and Augusto Pinochet) are authoritarian figures. Examples of successful democratic leaders during

---

[15] Burns, *Presidential Government*, 58 and 81.
[16] For politics of survival, see Migdal, *Strong Societies, Weak States*, chapter six.

nation building are rare and, in fact, I found none. The third world is full of failed leaders, and even today many such nations continue to experience a crisis in leadership. Although developing societies commonly express a preference for Western-style democratic leadership, it is uncertain whether such a leadership paradigm can meet the demands and expectations of these societies. It is meaningful to note that Lee Kwan Yew advised Philippine President Fidel Ramos: "Western-style democracy is simply not the best way for successful nation-building in Asia."[17]

There were times when Americans were more tolerant, even appreciative, of an authoritarian leadership style in their nation's highest office. During the Great Depression, Franklin Roosevelt was granted powers never before enjoyed by a president of the United States. The American public permitted some movement in the direction of more authoritarian rule.

LESSON FIVE:
LONG-TERM GOAL-SETTING IS REQUIRED FOR
SUCCESSFUL LEADERSHIP FOR NATION BUILDING.

Nation building requires transformational leaders. Park Chung Hee was a great leader, who transformed the Korean dream of a modern state into reality. Park, who ruled his country for eighteen years, had enough time and power to establish a strong and stable government. Owing to his prolonged presidency, he was able to promote the long-term goal of modernization with consistency and relative consensus. However, Park Chung Hee was no anomaly. Other long-term leaders in Asia—Chiang Kai-shek, Lee Kwan Yew, and Mahathir bin Mohamad—succeeded in building modern industrial states. Although Japan did not have a single dominant leader, its Liberal Democratic Party has run the country for most of the post-1945 period. Konrad Adenauer, who led post-war West Germany for fourteen years as chancellor, succeeded in reconstructing and revitalizing the nation's shattered economy.

Recent South Korean presidents wanted to go down in Korean history as greater leaders than Park Chung Hee and attempted to discredit his leadership while achieving credit for their own. For example, even though their rules were limited by a five-year single term, Kim Young Sam attempted unsuccessfully to forge a "new Korea," and Kim Dae Jung crusaded for a "second establishment of the Republic." The current president, Roh Moo Hyun, seems to tread in the steps of his immediate predecessors. Such unrealistic and unfocused approaches resulted in numerous trials, errors and policy blunders. Under a presidential system, any single administration is unlikely to make major contributions to the country's nation building.

In particular, South Korea's five-year single-term presidency is too short; it breaks the political process into discontinuous, rigidly demarcated periods, leaving no room for the continuous promotion of long-term policies. The limited time constrains the government's ability to make good on the promises it made in order to get elected. If these promises were far-reaching, including major programs of social change, the majority may feel cheated of their realization. A "sense of urgency on the part of the

---

[17] *Manila Chronicle*, November 19, 1992.

president may lead to ill-conceived policy initiatives, overly hasty attempts at implementation, unwarranted anger at the lawful opposition, and a host of other evils."[18] Since the democratic transition in 1988, four Korean presidents have suffered from this problem. Thus, an incumbent president respects his predecessors' legacies such as the direction of policy agenda so that thereby, later, his successor will respect his policy agenda too. This leads to policy consistency and stability.

In addition, frequent reshuffling of the policymaking team has become a distinctive feature of recent South Korean presidencies. The average tenure of South Korean presidential staff and cabinet ministers is about twelve months, possibly one of the shortest among nations in the world.[19] No one could stay in office long enough to be effective. Kim Young Sam, whose presidency ended with the humiliating 1997 financial crisis, had no less than six different ministers of finance and economy and six economic advisers over his five-year term. In contrast, the Singaporean finance minister served for seventeen years, from 1985 to 2002. Despite the fact that unification was Kim Dae Jung's top priority, he had six different unification ministers and five different foreign ministers during his term. In contrast, before German unification in 1990, Hans Genscher had worked for nineteen years as foreign minister of West Germany.

It is almost impossible for a single-term political leader to promote comprehensive and historical change, a reality current and future leaders of developing nations might take to heart. Even Park Chung Hee had to spend nearly five years before he could feel confident in his position. In order to promote viable reform and change, a leader needs to understand the past, be reconciled to it, and learn lessons from it. A leader should not be over-ambitious; he should recognize his own limited part in the division of labor for nation building. There are no thoroughly clean slates when it comes to nation building. A nation is not born anew as a new leader comes to office, and the past cannot be erased. There can be no meaningful progress without history and continuity. Before leaving the White House, Harry Truman said: "If a man is acquainted with what other people have experienced at this desk it will be easier for him to go through a similar experience. It is ignorance that causes most mistakes. The man who sits here ought to know his American history, at least."[20]

Nation building is a long-term phenomenon. Nation building in Europe required centuries. Also, there are dangers in democratic transition. Under a presidential system, in particular, as government changes, national goals and policies are more likely to change. Therefore, the maintenance of long-term developmental goals, strategies, and policies beyond one administration is critical to successful nation building.

---

[18] Juan J. Linz, "The Perils of Presidentialism", *Journal of Democracy* 1 (1990): 66.

[19] By comparison, the average tenure of ministers in Latin American countries over the period 1945-1981 was: 1.7 years in Chile, 2 years in Argentina, 2.2 years in Brazil, 2.5 years in Venezuela, and 4.4 years in Mexico. See Jean Blondel, *Government Ministers in the Contemporary World* (London: SAGE Publications, 1985).

[20] Quoted in Laurin L. Henry, *Presidential Transition* (Washington, DC: Brookings Institution, 1960).

LESSON SIX:
DOMESTIC POLICY SUCCESS OUTWEIGHS DIPLOMATIC PERFORMANCE.

Surrounded by powerful neighbors, facing constant North Korean threat, and with an economy heavily dependent on foreign markets, South Korea had to develop a strategic foreign policy. However, a president in South Korea is judged primarily for what he accomplishes in the economic sphere, and is not given as much credit for what he accomplishes in diplomacy.[21] Therefore, it is important to establish congruence between domestic and foreign policy.

Syngman Rhee put most of his time and energy into diplomacy. The survival of his nation was largely dependent upon foreign support. Rhee was successful in getting foreign assistance and forging and maintaining an alliance with the United States. Yet, despite his tremendous contribution to the survival of the nation, he is remembered as a president who failed to manage domestic affairs. Roh Tae Woo's "northern policy" was also very successful. His government opened formal relations with the Soviet Union, mainland China, and most other socialist countries. This policy improved South Korea's security conditions and expanded its exports market. Nevertheless, Roh is remembered as a leader who was unsuccessful in managing domestic affairs.

Kim Dae Jung demonstrated vision, determination, and consistency in his "sunshine policy" and he made a real breakthrough in inter-Korean relations. For foreign observers, Kim was seen as a great peacemaker. But preoccupied with the North Korea policy, he paid less attention to domestic issues, such as consensus building on the sunshine policy, continued economic reform, and maintenance of the U.S.-South Korea alliance. Now Pyongyang continues to develop nuclear weapons, and Kim's presidency is considered to have been a disaster.

In contrast, Park Chung Hee used foreign policy as a means of supporting his primary agenda—economic growth. His diplomatic initiatives induced Japanese loans and investments and he brought in millions of dollars in American aid through participation in the Vietnam War. These resources became fuel for the country's economic take-off. Chun Doo Hwan used Olympic diplomacy to accelerate economic growth and exports.

Successful nation builders such as Park Chung Hee, Lee Kuan Yew, and Mahathir Mohamad were not very popular abroad. In contrast, the progressive diplomacy of Mikhail Gorbachev (and perhaps Kim Dae Jung and Roh Tae Woo during their presidencies) was very popular internationally, but Gorbachev failed to manage domestic affairs effectively. In short, during the process of nation building, success in domestic issues is more important for the leaders of developing nations than for their Western counterparts.

LESSON SEVEN:
INTEGRITY IS AN IMPORTANT QUALITY FOR SUCCESSFUL LEADERSHIP.

To govern, a leader must have the trust of the people. It is vital that a leader be truthful and accountable and that his or her staff meet the same rigorous standards. However,

---

[21] Christopher J. Sigur, ed., *Continuity and Change in Contemporary Korea* (New York: Carnegie Council on Ethics and International Affairs, 1994), 12.

distrust in politics in general, and in the presidency in particular, is a serious problem in South Korea.[22] There are several sources of this distrust and discontent.

Political corruption appears to be the most lingering and damaging contributor. Recognizing the seriousness of the problem, successive presidents from Park Chung Hee on have embarked on anti-corruption campaigns. Yet, with the exception of Syngman Rhee and Park Chung Hee, all South Korean presidents or their close aides or relatives have been involved in corruption, virtually ruining the reputation of the presidency in question. From all of this, future leaders should learn a critical lesson: one who is found lacking in moral leadership earns the derision of history.

Another reason for the successive failures of anti-corruption drives is their highly moralistic nature. A high-minded approach to politics can have the contrary effect of prompting public distrust and alienation when the emphasis on public honesty is perceived as hollow and hypocritical, or when politicians are found to come up wanting when measured against very high ideals of public service and personal conduct. In Korean politics, it is more often the person rather than his or her policies, the behavioral mode rather than what is actually done, that attracts the interest of the public. As politics is generally judged by ethical standards, all behavior perceived as not absolutely right is perceived as being wrong.

Negative campaigning has been another source of public disillusionment with politics. In the politics of regionalism and personalities, political parties and politicians devote themselves to slandering and discrediting rivals, including outgoing presidents and previous national leaders. Politics has also been seriously tainted by a series of political exposures by ruling and opposition camps seeking to discredit one another. Indeed, media coverage of political infighting and scandal has reached critical levels, and the South Korean public has grown thoroughly weary of politics.

Perhaps the most important factor in public disillusionment has been the penchant for political revenge and scapegoating, which are often used to strengthen the legitimacy and consolidate the power of a new leader. Not only has this trend eroded public faith in government, it has seriously undermined the authority and legitimacy of the presidency itself. When a leader is in power, Koreans tend to fawn over him; once out of office, he becomes a scapegoat. The new leadership, joined by the media and populace, tends to dig out every possible incident of wrongdoing in the former leadership. Such "politics of the scapegoat" is self-defeating and counterproductive. If former leaders are routinely degraded, distrust in the government and in the chief executive threatens to become chronic. South Koreans can learn a lesson from former U.S. president Gerald Ford's courageous decision to grant a full and unconditional pardon to the disgraced Richard Nixon. His pardon of Nixon threatened to severely damage his prospects in the 1976 elections, yet he remained convinced that it was the right decision for the country. In 2001, Ford was awarded the John F. Kennedy Library Foundation's Profile in Courage

---

[22] According to a 1999 Gallup International Survey of ten Asian countries, nearly three quarters of South Koreans perceived their government as corrupt. A mere 8 percent of South Koreans felt their government was "efficient", while only 4 percent believed their government to be "just." See Chun-Si Ahn and Won-Taek Kang, "Trust and Confidence in Government in Transitional Democracies: South Korea in Comparative Perspective", *Journal of Korean Politics*, 11:1 (Seoul National University, 2002).

Award for his pardon of Nixon.[23]

In a presidential system, it is difficult to secure the stability and legitimacy of government. The system suffers from certain destabilizing and polarizing tendencies, and problems associated with presidentialism have led to breakdowns of democracy.[24] Monarchies have proved so useful as legitimizing devices that today "we have the absurd fact that ten out of twelve stable European and English-speaking democracies are monarchies."[25] In the case of Japan, monarchy has played a crucial role in legitimizing and stabilizing during the process of modernization. As an embodiment of Japan's sense of national identity, as the bridge linking traditional sources of legitimacy to the new state authority, as the father figure which justifies his subjects' self-discipline and sacrifice, the monarch is both a rallying point for his people and a means of concentrating authority behind the emerging national leadership.[26]

The president is the head of state and a national symbol. He must serve as a national unifier, much like a constitutional monarch. Koreans should learn from the Americans how to nurture the legitimacy of their presidency. In the United States, for the sake of preserving the authority and integrity of the office of president, an acting chief executive is reluctant to criticize his predecessors, just as his predecessors are careful of what they say about him. The United States boasts numerous monuments and memorials to its former leaders, and a score of presidential libraries. Airports, highways and roads, naval vessels, schools and other public buildings are often named after former presidents. In the United States, the president and the presidency occupy an important place in public education. South Korea may be unique in its lack of statues and memorials to its former presidents.

LESSON EIGHT:
INSTITUTIONALIZING THE ROLE OF CHIEF EXECUTIVE IS A KEY TO SUCCESSFUL PRESIDENTIAL GOVERNMENT.

Despite electoral democracy in South Korea, the nation suffers from under-institutionalization of democratic procedures. This is demonstrated by the extreme weakness of political parties and legislative institutions, a highly personalized and privatized nature of presidential power—based more on the "rule of man" than the rule of law—and a lack of tolerance, compromise, transparency and accountability in its leaders.[27] Presidential power has changed little since the 1988 democratic transition. Even life-long freedom fighters such as Kim Young Sam and Kim Dae Jung exercised highly personal leadership and were often criticized as "civilian dictators." As evidenced by a lingering, even growing, imbalance between the "imperial" presidency and the

---

[23] *USA Today*, May 1, 2001.
[24] See Linz and Valenzuela, eds., *Failure of Presidential Democracy*.
[25] Lipset, *Political Man*, 64-65.
[26] John W. Hall, "A Monarch for Modern Japan", in Robert E. Ward, ed., *Political Development in Modern Japan* (Princeton, NJ: Princeton University Press, 1968), 13-14.
[27] Samuel S. Kim, "Korea's Democratization in the Global-Local Nexus", in Kim, ed., *Korea's Democratization*, 39. For importance of institution building in developing countries, see Francis Fukuyama, *State-Building*.

"peripheral" National Assembly, under the leadership of the two Kims, personal presidency prevailed. Heavy reliance on the personal qualities of a political leader is a risky course, for one never knows if such a man can be found to fill the presidential office. Leadership must be balanced by institutions.

Good governance depends on the degree of institutionalization. As South Korea has succeeded in solving the most pressing problems of a developing nation, its politics now requires a higher level of institutionalization. The time has long since passed when one man could run an entire nation by himself. The process, rules, and mechanisms of policy making should be predictable, open and accountable. Korean political parties, which have been short-lived, should be stabilized and mobilized to play a leading role in politics.

There are institutional and cultural causes behind the under-institutionalization of the South Korean presidency. First of all, the one-term presidency is fundamentally flawed and has institutionalized political instability.[28] The term is characterized by a year or so of learning the ropes, a year of initiatives, and—should the government party lose the general elections occurring half way through the term—the remainder as a lame duck. Four Korean presidents since 1988 suffered setbacks and committed policy mistakes during the early phase of their terms and become early lame ducks. In order to meet challenges to his authority, a president naturally attempts to consolidate his power and becomes authoritarian.

The Korean political system also has the built-in defect of producing a divided government, engendering the problem of dual legitimacy. In most presidential systems, elections take place simultaneously. In South Korea the president's term is five years, but the term of all other elected politicians is four years. As a result, a new president is almost always elected to govern with his predecessor's National Assembly. Moreover, in all of the elections since 1988, no government party has succeeded in securing a majority in the National Assembly.

South Korean presidents with a divided government have to deal with a hostile and united opposition in the legislature. Owing to strong party discipline, individual lawmakers of opposition parties cannot freely cooperate with either the ruling party or the president. Problems arise when a government party fails to win a majority in the National Assembly. Disagreements between ruling and opposition parties often develop into serious showdowns between the president and the National Assembly. As a result, the president attempts to create a working majority, not through negotiation and compromise with the opposition, but by looking for leverage to coerce opposition members. On the other hand, if the government party comprises a majority in the National Assembly, the president controls the government in the absence of checks and balances.

Cultural factors also hinder the institutionalization of the South Korean presidency. The Confucian legacy has made Koreans idealize authority to such a degree that they fancy their rulers should be paragons—moralists rather than strategists.[29] This "Confucian"—and undemocratic—concept of the presidency is endemic to Korean society. The concept of "ultimate power" (*daekwon*) is frequently used in Korea to denote the power of the presidency; it assumes that political power is ultimately concentrated in

---

[28] R. J. Fouser, "Improving the Korean Political System", *Korea Herald*, August 22, 2001.
[29] Lucian W. Pye, *Asian Power and Politics* (Cambridge, MA: Belknap Press, 1985), 223-228.

a single individual—the president; hence, little room exists for ideas of checks and balances. Politicians and public alike tend to perceive presidential power as unlimited and unrestricted. The fact that the job of the president is extraordinarily ill defined and ambiguous contributes to this problem. The open-endedness of the president's responsibilities leaves him much latitude for initiative in national affairs. As a result, even democratically elected presidents frequently wield unconstrained and arbitrary power: the South Korean president may be more powerful than a king during the Yi dynasty.

Presidents can benefit from the lessons of those who have gone before. However, one of the problems in the Korean presidency is that it has no institutional memory. South Korea has no presidential library and studies of its presidencies are limited. In addition, each newly elected president has brought an enormous hubris to his office. Churchill was fond of citing the biblical quote that "pride goes before a fall." Each new president thinks that he is not going to stumble or fall and that his government should change everything the previous administration did. The concept of learning from the success and failures, the triumphs and tragedies of his predecessors is absent. This combination of ignorance and arrogance destroys the continuity of government and slows the progress of the nation.

An effective presidential staff is a necessary part of an institutionalized presidency. A South Korean president assumes office in an institutional vacuum. At his discretion, the structure of office and functions of presidential staff are changed. Inexperienced former activists have dominated the Blue House of recent presidents. Without an effective Blue House staff, a president is overly prone to personal leadership. One possible solution to the problem is to enact a law which stipulates the organization of the presidential agency and functions of presidential staff. Another solution would be to create an institutional presidential staff, composed primarily of civil servants whose main allegiance is to the office of the presidency, rather than to its current occupant, and whose tenure in office extends beyond that of any single presidential administration. Chief executives of some advanced nations can count on the advice of an extensive career civil service. The British prime minister's Private Office, for example, numbers about seventy officials of whom about 75 percent are civil servants with tenure preceding the current prime minister. The chief executives of Canada, Japan, and France have similar staff. [30]

More importantly, checks and balances on presidential power—as on other areas of government—must be provided for by a constitution. To this purpose, South Korea needs to consider a constitutional amendment which will provide for a four-year, two-term presidency and the synchronization of presidential and other national elections. Such a constitutional amendment also needs to provide for a legislative confirmation process of important political appointees and constrain presidential power in replacing ministers and other high-ranking officials on presidential whim. In return, the legislature's right to a no confidence vote of cabinet members should arguably be removed. In such a way, the cabinet might be stabilized and allowed to play its proper role in the executive.

There can be no meaningful progress without effective leadership. Nation building

---

[30] Matthew J. Dickinson, "No Place for Amateurs: Some Thoughts on the Clinton Administration and the Presidential Staff", *Presidential Studies Quarterly* 29:2 (fall 1998): 770.

demands effective political leadership, and the more rapid the process of nation building the more urgent that need. The world is witnessing a failure of nation building in many third world nations, and it is a serious global concern. In a developing state, good and effective leadership can make the difference between steady progress and early ruin. In a world undergoing revolutionary technological change, with an unprecedented degree of global interdependence, the call for creative leadership has been continual and ubiquitous. As Abraham Lincoln, who was also leading a developing country, communicated to the U.S. Congress: "The dogmas of the quiet past are inadequate to the stormy present. The occasion is piled high with difficulty, and we must rise — with the occasion. As our case is new, so we must think anew and act anew."[31]

The case of South Korea may provide valuable information for other developing nations, not only because the country has succeeded in the difficult task of nation building but also because we can learn lessons from the success and failure of the Korean presidency. These lessons may, I trust, prove beneficial for present and future leaders of Korea, and for students and leaders of other developing nations at a time when almost two-thirds of the earth's population continues to struggle for security, stability, prosperity, and democracy.

---

[31] Abraham Lincoln's Annual Message to Congress— Concluding Remarks, 1862.

ENGLISH BIBLIOGRAPHY

Abadi, Jacob. *Israel's Leadership: from Utopia to Crisis.* Westport, CT: Greenwood Press, 1993.

Acheson, Dean. *Present at the Creation: My Years in the State Department.* New York: Norton, 1969.

Allen, Richard C. *Korea's Syngman Rhee: An Unauthorized Portrait.* Rutland, VT: Tuttle, 1960.

Amsden, Alice H. *Asia's Next Giant: South Korea and Late Industrialization.* New York: Oxford University Press, 1989.

Armstrong, Charles K. *The North Korean Revolution, 1945-1950.* Ithaca: Cornell University Press, 2003.

Anderson, Charles W., Fred R. von der Mehden, and Crawford Young. *Issues of Political Development.* Englewood Cliffs, NJ, Prentice Hall, 1974.

Andrews, Henry L., Jr. et al., ed. *Security in Korea: War, Stalemate, and Negotiation.* Boulder: Westview Press, 1994.

Appleman, Roy E. *South to the Naktong, North to the Yalu.* Washington, D.C.: Office of the Chief of Military History, Department of the Army, 1960.

Ayoob, Mohammed. *The Third World Security Predicament: State Making, Regional Conflict, and the International System.* Boulder, CO: Lynne Rienner, 1995.

Azar, Edward E., and Chung-in Moon, eds. *National Security in the Third World: The Management of Internal and External Threats.* Aldershot: Edward Elgar, 1988.

Baldwin, Frank, ed. *Without Parallel: The American-Korean Relationship since 1945.* New York: Pantheon, 1974.

Bank of Korea. *The Banking System in Korea.* Seoul, 1969.

Barber, James D. *The Presidential Character.* Englewood Cliffs, NJ: Prentice Hall, 1992.

Bedeski, Robert E. *The Transformation of South Korea: Reform and Reconstitution in the Sixth Republic under Roh Tae Woo, 1987-1992.* New York: NY: Routledge, 1994.

_____. *State-Building in Modern China: The Kuomintang in the Prewar Period,* Berkeley: University of California, Berkeley, 1981.

Bell, Daniel A., David Brown, Kanishka Jayasuriya, and David M. Jones. *Toward Illiberal Democracy in Pacific Asia.* New York: St. Martin's Press, 1995.

Benjamin, Roger, and Stephen L. Elkin, eds. *The Democratic State.* Lawrence, KS: University Press of Kansas, 1985.

Bertsch, Leonard M. "Korean Partition Prevents Economic Recovery," *Foreign Policy Bulletin,* XXVIII, no.16 (January 1949).

Binder, Leonard, Lucian W. Pye, James S. Coleman, Sidney Verba, Joseph Lapalombara, and Myron Weiner. *Crises and Sequences in Political Development.* Princeton: Princeton University Press, 1971.

Boettcher, Robert, and Gordon L. Freeman. *Gifts of Deceit: Sun Myung Moon, Tongsun Park, and the Korea Scandal.* New York: Rinehart and Winston, 1980.

Bohlen, Charles E. *Witness to History, 1929-1969.* New York: W. W. Norton, 1973.

Breen Michael. *The Koreans.* New York: St. Martin's Press, 1999.

Breuer, William B. *Shadow Warriors: The Covert War in Korea.* New York: John Wiley, 1996.

Bridges, Brain. *Korea after the Crash: The Politics of Economic Recovery.* London: Routledge, 2001.

Bunge, Frederica M., ed. *South Korea: A Country Study.* Washington, D.C.: The American University, 1981.

English Bibliography

Burns, James M. *Presidential Government, the Crucible of Leadership.* Boston: Houghton Mifflin, 1965.

———. *Leadership.* New York: Harper & Row, 1978.

Cambell, Colin and John Halligan. *Political Leadership in an Age of Constraint: The Australian Experience.* Pittsburgh, University of Pittsburgh Press, 1993.

Campos, Jose Edgardo, and Hilton L. Root. *The Key to the Asian Miracle.* Washington, D.C., The Brookings Institution, 1996.

Cha, Dong-se, Kwang Suk Kim, and Dwight H. Perkins, eds. *The Korean Economy 1945-1995: Performance and Vision for the 21st Century.* Seoul: Korea Development Institute, 1997.

Chay, Jongsuk. *Unequal Partners in Peace and War: The Republic of Korea and the United States, 1948-1953.* Westport, CT: Praeger, 2002.

Cheon, Kum Sung, Trans. W. Y. Joh. *Chun Doo Hwan, Man of Destiny.* Los Angeles: North American Press, 1982.

Cheong, Sung-Hwa. *The Politics of Anti-Japanese Sentiment in Korea.* New York: Greenwood, 1991.

Cho, Lee-Jay and Yoon Hyung Kim (eds.). *Economic Development in the Republic of Korea: A Policy Perspective.* University of Hawaii Press, 1991.

——— and Yoon Hyung Kim, eds. *Korea's Political Economy.* Boulder: Westview, 1994.

———, Yoon Hyung Kim, and Chung H. Lee, eds. *Restructuring the National Economy.* Seoul: Korea Development Institute, 2001.

———, Myung-Kwang Park, and Choong Nam Kim, eds. *Korea and the Asia-Pacific Region.* Seoul: Kyunghee University Press, 2000.

———, Chung-si Ahn, and Choong Nam Kim, eds. *A Changing Korea in Regional and Global Contexts.* Seoul: Seoul National University Press, 2004.

Cho, Soon Sung. *Korea in World Politics 1940-1950: An Evaluation of American Responsibility.* Berkeley, University Of California Press, 1967.

Chu, Sok-Kyun. "Why American Aid Failed." *Koreanna Quarterly*, 4:1 (autumn 1962): 81-93.

Chung, Chung Kil. *Economic Leadership for Presidents: Economic Management of the Park Chung Hee, Chun Doo Hwan, and Roh Tae Woo Governments.* Seoul: Hankuk Kyungje Shinmunsa, 1994.

Chung, Henry, *The Russians Came to Korea,* Washington, D.C.: Korean Pacific Press, 1947.

———. *Korea and the United States through War and Peace,* Seoul: Yonsei University Press, 2000.

Chung, Kyung Cho. *Korea Tomorrow: Land of the Morning Calm.* New York: Macmillan, 1956.

———. *New Korea: New Land of the Morning Calm.* New York: Macmillan, 1962.

Clark, Mark W. *From the Danube to the Yalu.* New York: Harper & Brothers, 1954.

Clifford, Mark L. *Troubled Tiger: Businessmen, Bureaucrats, and Generals in South Korea.* Armonk, New York: M.E. Sharpe, 1994.

Cole, David C., and Princeton N. Lyman. *Korean Development: The Interplay of Politics and Economics.* Cambridge, MA: Harvard University Press, 1971.

Corbo, Vittorio, and Sang-Mok Suh, eds. *Structural Adjustment in a Newly Industrialized Country: The Korean Experience.* Baltimore: Johns Hopkins University Press, 1992.

Cotton, James, ed. *Korea under Roh Tae-Woo: Democratization, Northern Policy, and Inter-Korean Relations.* St Leonards, Australia: Allen & Unwin, 1993.

———, ed. *Politics and Policy in the new Korean State: From Roh Tae Woo to Kim Young Sam.* New York, NY: St. Martin's Press, 1995

——— and Ian Neary, eds. *The Korean War in History.* Atlantic Highlands, N.J.: Humanities Press International, 1989.

Courtois, Stephane. *The Black Book of Communism.* Cambridge, MA: Harvard University Press, 1999.

Crozier, Michel, Samuel Huntington, and Joji Watanuki. *The Crisis of Democracy*. New York: New York University Press, 1975.

Cumings, Bruce, ed. *Child of Conflict: The Korean-American Relationship, 1943-1953*. Seattle: University of Washington Press, 1983.

_____. *The Origins of the Korean War, Vol. II*. Princeton: Princeton University Press, 1990.

_____. *Korea's Place in the Sun*. New York: W. W. Norton, 1997.

Department of State, United States. *Foreign Relations of the United States*. Washington, D.C.: Government Printing Office, various years.

Diamond, Larry. *Developing Democracy: Toward Consolidation*. Baltimore: Johns Hopkins University Press, 1999.

_____ and Byung-Kook Kim, eds. *Consolidating Democracy in South Korea*, Boulder: Lynne Rienner, 2000.

_____, Linz, J. J., and Lipset, S. M., eds. *Democracy in Developing Countries: Volume Three, Asia*. London: Adamantine Press, 1989.

_____ and Doh C. Shin, eds. *Institutional Reform and Democratic Consolidation in Korea*. Stanford, Calif.: Hoover Institution Press, Stanford University, 2000.

Donovan, Robert J. *Tumultuous Years: The Presidency of Harry S. Truman, 1949-1953*. New York: W. W. Norton, 1982.

Douglas, William A., "South Korea's Search for Leadership," *Pacific Affairs*, 37:1 (Spring 1964).

Eckert, Carter J., Ki-baik Lee, Young Ick Lew, Michael Robinson, and Edward W. Wagner. *Korea: Old and New*. Seoul: Ilchokak, 1990.

Elcock, Howard. *Political Leadership*. Cheltenham, UK: Edward Elgar, 2001.

Emery, Robert F. *Korean Economic Reform*. Burlington, VT: Ashgate, 2001.

Elgie, Robert. *Political Leadership in Liberal Democracies*. New York: St. Martin, 1995.

Evans, M. Filmer. *The Land and People of Korea*. New York: Macmillan, 1963.

Fallows, James. *Looking at the Sun: the Rise of the New East Asian Economic and Political System*. New York: Pantheon Books, 1994

Farley, Miriam S. "Crisis in Korea". *Far Eastern Survey*, 19: 8 (August 1950), 149-156.

_____. "Crisis in Korea: Second Phase". *Far Eastern Survey*, 19: 11 (November 1950), 214-218.

Fordham, Benjamin O. *Building the Cold War Consensus*. Ann Arbor, Michigan: The University of Michigan Press, 1998.

Charles R. Frank, Jr., Kwang Suk Kim, and Larry E. Westphal. *South Korea*. New York: Columbia University Press, 1975.

Fukuyama, Francis. *State-Building: Governance and World Order in the 21st Century*. Ithaca: Cornell University Press, 2004.

Gergen, David. *Presidential Leadership: An Eyewitness Account—Nixon to Clinton*. New York: Simon & Schuster, 2000.

Gibney, Frank. *Korea's Quiet Revolution: From Garrison State to Democracy*. New York: Walker & Co., 1992.

_____. "Syngman Rhee: The Free Man's Burden". *Harper's Magazine* (February 1954).

Gills, B. K. *Korea versus Korea: A Case of Contested Legitimacy*. London: Routledge, 1996.

Gleysteen, William H., Jr. *Massive Entanglement, Marginal Influence*. Washington, D.C.: Brookings, 1999.

Greenstein, Fred I., ed. *Leadership in the Modern Presidency*. Cambridge, MA: Harvard University Press, 1988.

Haggard, Stephan, *Pathway from the Periphery: the Politics of Growth in the Newly Industrializing Countries*, Cornell University Press, 1990.

English Bibliography

_____ and Robert R. Kaufman. *The Political Economy of Democratic Transitions*. Princeton, New Jersey: Princeton University Press, 1995.

Hahm, Chaibong, Robert A. Scalapino and David I. Steinberg. *The 1997 Korean Presidential Elections*. New York: The Asia Society, 1997.

Hahm, Pyong-Choon. *The Korean Political Tradition and Law*. Seoul: Hollym, 1967.

Hahm, Sung Deuk and L. Christopher Plein. *After Development: The Transformation of the Korean Presidency and Bureaucracy*. Washington, D.C.: Georgetown University Press, 1997.

Han, Sung-Joo. *The Failure of Democracy in South Korea*. Berkeley: University of California Press, 1974.

Haptong News Agency, *Korea Annual*, various years.

Harrison, Selig S. *The South Korean Political Crisis and American Policy Options*. Washington, D.C.: The Washington Institute Press, 1987.

_____. *Korean Endgame: A Strategy for Reunification and U. S. Disengagement*. Princeton, N.J.: Princeton University Press, 2002.

Hart-Landsberg, Martin. *The Rush to Development: Economic Change and Political Struggle in South Korea*. New York: Monthly Review Press, 1993.

Henderson, Gregory. *Korea: The Politics of Vortex*. Cambridge, Mass.: Harvard University Press, 1968.

Helgesen, Geir. *Democracy and Authority in Korea: The Cultural Dimension in Korean Politics*. New York: St. Martin, 1998.

Henthorn, William E. *A History of Korea*. New York: Free Press, 1971.

Hermassi, Elbaki. *Leadership and National Development in North Africa*. Berkeley: University of California Press, 1972.

Hess, Stephen. *Organizing the Presidency*. Washington, DC: Brookings Institution, 1988.

Hill, Michael and Lian Kwen Fee. *The Politics of Nation-Building and Citizenship in Singapore*. New York: Routledge, 1995.

Hinton, H.C. *Korea under New Leadership: The Fifth Republic*. New York: Praeger, 1983.

Hollingsworth, J. Rogers. *Nation and State Building in America*. Boston: Little, Brown, 1971.

Hong, Sung-Chik. *The Intellectual and Modernization: A Study of Korean Attitudes*. Seoul: Korea University Press, 1967.

Hong, Yong-Pyo. *State Security and Regime Security: President Syngman Rhee and the Insecurity Dilemma in South Korea, 1953-60*. New York: St. Martin's Press, 1999.

Huer, Jon. *Marching Orders: The Role of the Military in South Korea's Economic Miracle, 1961-1971*. New York: Greenwood Press, 1989.

Huntington, Samuel P. *Political Order in Changing Societies*. New Haven: Yale University Press, 1968.

International Monetary Fund. *A Case of Successful Adjustment: Korea's Experience During 1980-84*. Washington, D.C., 1985.

Jayasuriya, J.E. *Education in Korea: A Third World Success Story*. Colombo: Associated Educational Publishers, 1980.

Job, Brian L., ed. *The Insecurity Dilemma: National Security of Third World States*. Boulder: Lynne Rienner, 1992.

Jones, Bryan D. ed. *Leadership and Politics*. Lawrence, Kansas: The University Press of Kansas, 1989.

_____. *Leadership and Politics*. Lawrence, Kan.: University Press of Kansas, 1989.

Jones, Leroy P., and Il Sakong. *Government, Business, and Entrepreneurship in Economic Development: The Korean Case*. Cambridge, MA: Harvard University Press, 1980.

Jung, Walter B. *Nation Building: The Geopolitical History of Korea*. New York: University Press of America, 1998.

Keon, Michael. *Korean Phoenix: A Nation from the Ashes*. Englewood Cliffs, NJ: Prentice Hall, 1977.

Kiewe, Amos, ed. *The Modern Presidency and Crisis Rhetoric.* Westport, CT: Praeger, 1994.

Kihl, Young Hwan. *Politics and Policies in Divided Korea.* Boulder: Westview, 1984.

_____. *Transforming Korean Politics: Democracy, Reform, and Culture.* Armonk, NY: M.E. Sharpe, 2005.

Kim, Bung Woong, David S. Bell, Jr., and Chong Bum Lee, ed. *Administrative Dynamics and Development: the Korean Experience.* Seoul: Kyobo, 1985.

Kim, C. I. Eugene, ed. *The Patterns of Korean Politics.* Kalamazoo, Mich.: Western Michigan University Press, 1964.

Kim, Chang Rok. "The Characteristics of the System of Japanese Imperialism in Korea from 1905 to 1945". *Korea Journal.* 36:1(Spring 1996).

Kim, Chum-Kon, ed. *The Korean War.* Seoul: Kwangmyong Publishing Co., 1973.

Kim, Chung-Yum. *Policymaking on the Front Lines: Memoirs of a Korean Practitioner, 1945-79.* Washington, D.C.: The World Bank, 1994.

Kim, Dae Jung. *Mass–Participatory Economy: Korea's Road to World Economic Power.* Lanham, MD: University Press of America, 1996.

_____. *Building Peace and Democracy: Kim Dae Jung's Philosophy and Dialogues.* New York: Korean Independent Monitor, 1987.

Kim, Hakjoon. "The American Military Government in South Korea, 1945-1948: Its Formation, Policies, and Legacies," *Asian Perspective,* 10:1 (Spring-Summer 1988).

Kim, Hyun-A. *Korea's Development under Park Chung Hee: Rapid Industrialization, 1961-1979.* New York: Rutledge Curzon, 2004.

Kim, Ilpyong J., and Young Whan Kihl, eds. *Political Change in South Korea.* New York: The Korean PWPA, Inc., 1988.

Kim, Kihwan. *The Korean Economy: Past Performance, Current Reforms, and Future Prospects.* Seoul: KDI, 1984.

Kim, Kwan Bong. *The Korea-Japan Treaty Crisis and the Instability of the Korean Political System.* New York: Praeger, 1971.

Kim, Kwang Suk, and Michael Roemer. *Growth and Structural Transformation.* Cambridge, MA: Council on East Asian Studies, Harvard University, 1979.

Kim, Jong-gie, Sang-woo Rhee, Jae-cheon Yu, Kwang-mo Koo and Jong-duck Hong. *Impact of the Seoul Olympic Games on National Development.* Seoul: Korea Development Institute, 1989.

Kim, Jong-Pil. "Modernization of Korea and a New Leading Force," *Koreana Quarterly.* 4:4 (Winter 1963).

Kim, Joungwon A. *Divided Korea: The Politics of Development 1945-1972.* Cambridge, MA: Harvard University Press, 1975.

Kim, Quee-Young. *The Fall of Syngman Rhee.* Berkeley, Calif.: Institute of East Asian Studies, University of California Berkeley, 1983.

Kim, Samuel S., ed. *Korea's Globalization.* Cambridge: Cambridge University Press, 2000.

_____, ed. *Korea's Democratization.* Cambridge: Cambridge University Press, 2003.

Kim Se-Jin. *The Politics of Military Revolution in Korea.* Chapel Hill: University of North Carolina Press, 1971.

_____ and Chang-hyun Cho, eds. *Government and Politics of Korea.* Silver Spring, Maryland: Research Institute on Korean Affairs, 1972

Kim, Sunhyuk, and Doh Chull Shin. *Economic Crisis and Dual Transition in Korea.* Seoul: Seoul National University Press, 2004.

Kim, Sunhyuk. *The Politics of Democratization in Korea.* Pittsburg, PA: Pittsburg University Press, 2000.

English Bibliography

Kim, Tscholsu, and Sang Don Lee. "Republic of Korea: The Influence of U.S.Constitutional Law Doctrines in Korea," in Lawrence W. Baer, ed. *Constitutional System in Late Twentieth Century Asia*. Seattle: University of Washington Press, 1992.

Kim, Young Sam, *Korea's Quest for Reform and Globalization: Selected Speeches of President Kim Young Sam*. Seoul: the Presidential Secretariat, the Republic of Korea, 1995.

_____. *Kim Young Sam and the New Korea*. Chicago: Bonus Books, 1992.

Kirk, Donald. *Korean Crisis: Unraveling of the Miracle in the IMF Era*. New York: St. Martin's Press, 2000.

Kleiner, Juergen. *Korea: A Century of Change*. Singapore: World Scientific, 2001.

Koh, Byung Chul. *Korea: Dynamics of Diplomacy and Unification*. Claremont, CA: Keck Center for International and Strategic Studies, 2001.

Kong, Tat Yan. *The Politics of Economic Reform in South Korea*. London: Routledge, 2000.

Koo, Hagen, ed. *State and Society in Contemporary Korea*. Ithaca: Cornell University Press, 1993.

Korean Pacific Press. *Korean Report*, Vol. I~VI (1948-1958). Washington, D.C.:

_____. *Korean Survey*, Vol. I~X (1952-1961). Washington, D.C.

_____. *Korea's Fight for Freedom: Selected Addresses by Korean Statesmen*, Vol. I~II. Washington, D.C., 1951 and 1952.

Krause, Lawrence B., and Kim Kihwan, eds. *Liberalization in the Process of Economic Development*. Berkeley: University of California Press, 1991.

Ku, Dae-yeol. *Korea under Colonialism*. Seoul: Seoul Computer Press, 1985.

Kwon, Ho-Youn, ed. *Contemporary Korea: Democracy, Economic Development, Social Change, Re-unification Process*. Chicago: Center for Korean Studies, North Park College, 1997.

Kruedener, Jurgen Baron von, ed. *Economic Crisis and Political Collapse: the Weimar Republic, 1924-1933*. New York: Berg, 1990.

Kwak, Tae-hwan, ed. *U.S.-Korean Relations, 1882-1982*. Seoul: Kyungnam University Press, 1982.

Kwon, Chan. "The Leadership of Syngman Rhee: The Charisma Factor as an Analytical Framework," *Koreana Quarterly*, 13:1-2 (spring-summer 1971): 31-48.

Larson, James F., and Heung-Soo Park. *Global Television and the Politics of the Seoul Olympics*. Boulder: Westview Press, 1993.

Lee, Chong-Sik. *The Politics of Korean Nationalism*. Berkeley: University of California Press, 1963.

_____. *Syngman Rhee: The Prison Years of a Young Radial*. Seoul: Yonsei University Press, 2001.

Lee, Hahn-Been. *Korea: Time, Change and Administration*. Honolulu: East-West Center Press, 1968.

_____. *Management of Change and Modernizing Leadership*. Seoul: Korean Council, ILCORK, 1970.

Lee, Kuan Yew. *From Third World to First, The Singapore Story: 1965-2000*. New York: Harper Collins, 2000.

Lee, Manwoo. *The Odyssey of Korean Democracy: Korean Politics 1987-1990*. New York: Praeger, 1990.

Levin, Norman D., and Yong-Sup Han. *Sunshine in Korea*. Santa Monica, Calif.: RAND, 2004.

Levi, Werner, "Fate of Democracy in South and Southeast Asia," *Far Eastern Quarterly*, 28 (February 1959).

Lewis, John P. *Reconstruction and Development in South Korea*. Washington, D.C.: National Planning Association, 1955.

Lie, John. *Han Unbound: The Political Economy of South Korea*. Stanford: Stanford University Press, 1998.

Liem, Channing. "United States Rule in Korea," *Far Eastern Survey*, XVIII (April 1949), 77-80.

Loewenstein, Karl. "The Presidency outside the United States: A Study in Comparative Political Institutions," *Journal of Politics*, 11:3 (1949): 448-496.

English Bibliography

Lijphart, Arend, and Carlos H. Waisman. *Institutional Design in New Democracies.* Boulder, Colo.: Westview Press, 1996.

Linz, Juan J. *The Breakdown of Democratic Regimes: Crisis, Breakdown, and Reequilibration.* Baltimore: Johns Hopkins University Press, 1978.

_____ and Alfred Stephan, eds. *The Breakdown of Democratic Regimes.* Baltimore: Johns Hopkins University Press, 1978.

_____ and Arturo Valenzuela, eds. *The Failure of Presidential Democracy.* Baltimore: Johns Hopkins University Press, 1994.

Lipset, Martin S. "George Washington and the Founding of Democracy," *Journal of Democracy,* 9:4 (October 1994).

Lyons, Gene M. *Military Policy and Economic Aid: The Korean Case, 1950-1953.* Columbus: Ohio State University Press, 1961.

MacArthur, Douglas. *Reminiscences,* London: Heinemann, 1964.

McCune, George M. *Korea's Postwar Political Problems.* New York: Institute of Pacific Relations, 1947.

_____. *Korea Today.* Cambridge, Mass.: Harvard University Press, 1950.

McCune, Shannon. *Korea: The Land of Broken Calm.* New York: Van Nostrand, 1966.

MacDonald, C. A. *Korea: The War before Vietnam.* New York: Free Press, 1986.

MacDonald, Donald. S. *The Koreans: Contemporary Politics and Society.* Boulder: Westview Press, 1988.

_____. *U.S.-Korea Relations from Liberation to Self-reliance.* Boulder: Westview Press, 1992.

_____. *Korea Today.* Cambridge, MA: Harvard University Press, 1950.

McGinn, Noel F., Donald R. Snodgras, Yung Bong Kim, Shin-Bok Kim, and Quee-Young Kim. *Education and Development in Korea.* Cambridge, MA: Harvard University Press, 1980.

Martin, Bradley K. *Under the Loving Care of the Fatherly Leader: North Korea and the Kim Dynasty.* New York: St. Martin's Press, 2004.

Mason, Edward S., Mahn Je Kim, Dwight H. Perkins, Kwang Suk Kim, David C. Cole.*The Economic and Social Modernization of the Republic of Korea.* Cambridge, MA: Harvard University Press, 1980.

Meade, E. Grant. *American Military Government in Korea.* New York: King's Crown Press, 1951.

Meltsner, Arnold J. *Rules for Rulers: The Politics of Advice.* Philadelphia: Temple University Press, 1990.

Merrill, John. *Korea: the Peninsula Origin of the War.* Newark: University of Delaware Press, 1989.

Migdal, Joel S. *Strong Societies, Weak States: State-Society Relations and State Capabilities in the Third World.* Princeton: Princeton University Press, 1988.

Mitchell, C. Clyde. *Korea: Second Failure in Asia.* Washington, D.C.: The Public Affairs Institute, 1951.

Mo, Jongryn, Chung-in Moon, eds. *Democracy and the Korean Economy.* Stanford: Hoover Institution Press, 1999.

Moon, Chung-in, and Jongryn Mo, eds. *Democratization and Globalization in Korea.* Seoul: Yonsei University Press, 1999.

Moon, Hyungpyo, Hyehoon Lee, and Gyeongjoon Yoo. *Economic Crisis and its Social Consequences.* Seoul: Korea Development Institute, 1999.

Murray, Robert K., and Tim H. Blessing. *Greatness in the White House. Rating the Presidents.* University Park, Pa.: Pennsylvania State University Press, 1994.

Nahm, Andrew C. ed. *Korea under Japanese Colonial Rule.* Kalamazoo, Mich.: Michigan State University, 1973.

_____. *Korea: Tradition and Transformation.* Elizabeth, N.J.: Hollym International,1988.

Nam, Hong-chin. *A Life Story of President Kim Young-sam.* Seoul: Bansuk, 1993.

English Bibliography

Robert Nathan Associates. *An Economic Program for Korean Reconstruction*. Washington D.C.: The U.S. Korean Reconstruction Agency, 1954.

Nazrul, Islam M. *Problems of Nation-Building in Developing Countries*. Dhaka, Bangladesh: University of Dhaka, 1988.

Neustadt, Richard E. *Presidential Power and Modern Presidents: The Politics of Leadership from Roosevelt to Reagan*. New York: Free Press, 1990.

Noble, Harold Joyce. *Embassy at War*. Seattle: University of Washington Press, 1975.

Oberdorfer, Don. *The Two Koreas*. Reading, MA: Addison-Wesley, 1997.

Office of Public Information, Republic of Korea. *Where Korea Stands*. Seoul, 1955.

_____. *Korea Flaming High*. vols. 1-2. Seoul, 1954-1955.

_____. *Handbook of Korea*. New York: Pageant Press, 1958.

Ogle, George E. *South Korea: Dissent with the Economic Miracle*. London: Zea Books, 1990.

Oh, John Kie-chiang. *Korea: Democracy on Trial*. Ithaca, NY: Cornell University Press, 1968.

_____. *The Dilemma of Democratic Politics with Economic Development in Korea*. Seoul: Korea Development Institute, 1990.

_____. *Korean Politics*. Ithaca, NY: Cornell University Press, 1999.

Oh, Kongdan. *Korea Briefing 1997-1999*. Armonk, New York: M. E. Sharpe, 2000.

Oliver, Robert T., ed., *Korea's Fight for Freedom*, Seoul: Korea Pacific Press, 1951.

_____. *A History of the Korean People in Modern Times: 1800 to the Present*. Newark: University of Delaware Press, 1993.

_____. *Syngman Rhee and American Involvement in Korea. 1942-1960*. Seoul: Panmun, 1978.

_____. *Syngman Rhee: The Man Behind the Myth*. New York: Dodd, Mead, 1954.

_____ *The Truth about Korea*. London: Unwin Brothers Limited, 1951.

_____. *Leadership in Asia*. Newark: University of Delaware Press, 1989.

Pae, S.M. *Testing Democratic Theories in Korea*. New York: University Press of America, 1986.

Paige, Glenn. *The Korean Decision June 24-30, 1950*. New York: The Free Press, 1968.

Paik, Sun Yup. *From Pusan to Panmunjom*. New York: Brassey's, 1992.

Pak, Chi-Young. *Political Opposition in Korea, 1945-1960*. Seoul: Seoul National University Press, 1980.

Park, Chang Jin. "The Influence of Small States Upon the Superpowers: United States-South Korean Relations as a Case Study, 1950-53," *World Politics*, 28:1 (October1975): 97-117.

Park, Chung-Hee, translated by Leon Sinder. *The Country, the Revolution and I*. Seoul: Hollym, 1970.

_____. *Our Nation's Path: Ideology of Social Reconstruction*. Seoul: Donga Publishing Co., 1962.

_____. "Korean Political Philosophy: Administrative Democracy," *Korean Affairs*, II (May-June, 1962)

_____. *To Build a Nation*. Washington, D.C.: Acropolis Books, 1971.

_____. *Korea Reborn: A Model for Development*. Englewood Cliffs, N.J.: Prentice Hall, 1979.

Paterson, Thomas G. *Meeting the Communist Threat: Truman to Reagan*. New York: Oxford University Press, 1988.

Pfiffner, James P. *The Strategic Presidency: Hitting the Ground Running*. Chicago: Dorsey Press, 1988.

_____. *The Modern Presidency*. New York: St. Martin's Press, 1994.

Pierpaoli, Paul G. *Truman and Korea: The Political Culture of the Early Cold War*.Columbia, MO.: University of Missouri Press, 1999.

Post, Jerrold M., and Robert S. Robins. *When Illness Strikes the Leader*. New Haven: Yale University Press, 1993.

The Presidential Secretariat, Republic of Korea. *The 1980s: Meeting a New Challenge: Selected Speeches of President Chun Doo Hwan.* Seoul: Korea Textbook Co., 1981.

_____. *Korea: A Nation Transformed: Selected Speeches of President Roh Tae Woo.* Oxford: Polity Press, 1990.

_____. *Korea's Quest for Reform & Globalization : Selected Speeches of President Kim Young Sam.* Seoul, 1995.

Pulparampil, John K. *Models of Nation-Building.* New Delhi: N. V. Publications, 1975.

Pye, Lucian W. *Asian Power and Politics: The Cultural Dimensions of Authority.* Cambridge, MA: Harvard University Press, 1985.

Pyun, Yung Tai. *Korea, My Country.* Seoul: International Cultural Association of Korea, 1953.

Rees, David. *Crisis and Continuity in South Korea.* London: Institute for the Study of Conflict, 1981.

Reeves, W. D. *The Republic of Korea.* London: Oxford University Press, 1963.

Rhee, Seungkeun. "Evolution of Korean Nationalism I: The Political Views of Syngman Rhee," *Korea Observer,* 6: 4 (autumn 1975), 395-404.

Rhee, Syngman, trans. Han-Kyo Kim. *The Sprit of Independence.* Honolulu: University of Hawaii Press, 2001.

Ridgway, Matthew B. *The Korean War.* Garden City, N.Y.: Doubleday, 1967.

Roh, Tae Woo. *Blueprint for a Bright Future: Roh Tae Woo's Promises.* Seoul, Democratic Justice Party, 1988.

_____. *Korea, A Nation Transformed: Selected Speeches of Roh Tae Woo.* New York, Pergamon, 1990.

_____. *Korea in the Pacific Century: Selected Speeches, 1990-1992.* Lanham, MD: University Press of America, 1992.

Root, Hilton L. *Small Countries, Big Lessons: Governance and the Rise of Asia.* New York: Oxford University Press, 1996.

Rossiter, Clinton L. *Constitutional Dictatorship: Crisis Government in Modern Democracies.* Princeton: Princeton University press, 1948.

Rotberg, Robert I. ed. *State Failure and State Weakness in a Time of Terror.* Washington, D.C.: Brookings Institution Press, 2003.

Rustow, Dankwart A. *A World of Nations.* Washington, D.C.: Brookings Institution, 1967.

Sakong, Il. *Korea in the World Economy.* Washington, D.C.: Institute for International Economics, 1993.

Sawyer, Robert K. *Military Advisors in Korea: KMAG in War and Peace.* Washington, D.C., 1962.

Scalapino, Robert A. and Chong-sik Lee. *Communism in Korea.* Berkeley: University of California Press, 1972.

Selochan, Viberto, ed. *The Military, the State and Development in Asia and the Pacific.* Boulder: Westview Press, 1991.

Seoul Sinmunsa. *Hankuk oekyo birok* (Secret Stories of Korean Diplomacy). Seoul: Seoul Sinmunsa, 1984.

Shin, Bum Shik. *Major Speeches by Korea's Park Chung Hee.* Seoul: Hollym, 1970.

Shin, Doh C. *Mass Politics and Culture in Democratizing Korea.* Cambridge: Cambridge University Press, 1999.

_____, Myeong Han Zoh, and Myung Chey, eds. *Korea in the Global Wave of Democratization.* Seoul: Seoul National University Press, 1994.

Shin, Inseok. *The Korean Crisis: Before and After.* Seoul: Korea Development Institute, 2000.

Shin, Gi-wook. *Peasant Protest and Social Change in Colonial Korea.* Seattle: University of Washington Press, 1996.

Shin, Jae-hong, et al., eds. *Collections of Historical Materials of the Republic of Korea.*

English Bibliography

Kwa Cheon City, 1996.

Shinn, Bill. *The Forgotten War Remembered, Korea: 1950-1953.* Elizabeth, NJ: Hollym International, 1996.

Simonton, Dean Keith. *Why Presidents Succeed.* New Heaven: Yale University Press, 1987.

Skowronek, Stephen. *The Politics Presidents Make: Leadership from John Adams to George Bush.* Cambridge, MA: Belknap Press, 1993.

_____. *Building a New American State: the Expansion of National Administrative Capacities, 1877-1920.* New York: Cambridge University Press, 1982.

Smith, Heather, ed. *Looking Forward: Korea after the Economic Crisis.* Canberra: Asia Pacific Press, 2000.

Sohn, Hak-Kyu. *Authoritarianism and Opposition in South Korea.* London: Loutledge, 1989.

Song, Byung-Nak. *The Rise of the Korean Economy.* Hong Kong: Oxford University Press, 1990.

Song, Kwang Sung. "The Impact of U.S. Military Occupation on Korean Liberation, Democratization, and Unification." Ph. D. Thesis, University of California, Los Angeles, 1989.

Stamps, Norman L. *Why Democracies Fail: A Critical Evaluation of the Causes for Modern Dictatorship.* Notre Dame, Indiana: University of Notre Dame Press, 1957.

Steinberg, David I. *Korea: Nexus of East Asia.* New York: American-Asian Educational Exchange, 1968.

_____. *The Republic of Korea: Economic Transformation and Social Change.* Boulder: Westview Press, 1989.

_____, ed. *Korean Attitudes toward the United States.* Armonk, NY: M.E. Sharpe, 2005.

Strauss, Julia C. *Strong Institutions in Weak Polities: State Building in Republican China, 1927-1940.* New York: Oxford University Press, 1998.

Stueck, William W. Jr. *The Road to Confrontation: American Policy toward China and Korea, 1947-1950.* Chapel Hill: University of North Carolina Press, 1981.

Sunwoo, Harold H. *20th Century Korea.* Seoul: Nanam, 1994.

Taranto, James and Leonard Leo, eds. *Presidential Leadership: Rating the Best and Worst in the White House.* New York: Wall Street Journal Books, 2004.

Taylor, John M. *General Maxwell Taylor: The Sword and the Pen.* New York: Doubleday, 1989.

Tewksbury, Donald G., ed. *Source Materials on Korean Politics and Ideologies.* New York: Institute of Pacific Relations, 1950.

Trimberger, Ellen K. *Revolution from Above: Military Bureaucrats and Development in Japan, turkey, Egypt, and Peru.* New Brunswick, N.J.: Transaction Books, 1978.

Truman, Harry S. *Memoirs: Years of Trial and Hope.* New York: Doubleday, 1956.

Tsurutani, Taketsugu. *The Politics of National Development: Political Leadership in Transitional Societies.* New York: Chandler, 1973.

Tucker, Robert C. *Politics as Leadership.* Columbia: University of Missouri Press, 1981.

UNESCO. *Rebuilding Education in the Republic of Korea: Report of the UNESCO- UNKRA Educational Planning Mission to Korea.* Paris, 1954.

U.N. Korean Reconstruction Agency. *An Economic Program for Korean Reconstruction.* New York: United Nations, 1954.

United States Armed Forces in Korea, *Official Gazette,* April 15, 1948.

U.S. Department of State. *Korea: 1945-1948.* Washington, DC, Government Printing Office, 1948

U.S. Department of State, Historical Office. *American Foreign Policy: Current Documents 1960.* Washington, DC: Government Printing Office, 1964.

U.S. Senate. *Background Information on Korea.* Washington, D.C., Government Printing Office, 1950.

English Bibliography

Vinocour, Seymour M. "Syngman Rhee: Spokesman for Korea (June 23, 1951-October 8, 1952): A Case Study in International Speaking," Ph. D. dissertation. Pennsylvania State College, 1953.

Wade, James. *One Man's Korea*. Seoul: Hollym, 1967.

Wagner, Edward W. "Failure in Korea," *Foreign Affairs*, 40:1 (October, 1961).

Ward, Robert E., and Dankwart A. Rostow, eds. *Political Modernization in Japan and Turkey*. Princeton: Princeton University Press, 1964.

Watanuki, Joji. *Some Reflections on the Typology of Nation-Building in Asia*. Tokyo: Sophia University Press, 1973.

_____. *Formation and Survival of Japanese Democracy after the Second World War*. Tokyo: Sophia University Press, 1975.

Whicker, Marcia Lynn, and Raymond R. Moore. *Why Presidents Are Great*. Englewood Cliffs: Prentice Hall, 1988.

Whitfield, Stephen J. *The Culture of the Cold War*. Baltimore: Johns Hopkins University Press, 1991.

Wickham, John A. *Korea on the Brink: From the 12/12 Incident to the Kwangju Uprising*. Washington, D.C.: Brassey's, 2000.

Williams, Phil, Donald M. Goldstein, and Henry L. Andrews, Jr. *Security in Korea*. Boulder: Westview Press, 1994.

Woronoff, Jon. *Korea's Economy: Man-made Miracle*. Arch Cape, OR: Pace International, 1983.

Wright, Edward. R., ed. *Korean Politics in Transition*. Seattle: University of Washington Press, 1975.

Yang, Sung Chul. *The North and South Korean Political Systems*. Boulder, CO: Westview Press, 1994.

_____. *Korea and Two Regimes: Kim Il Sung and Park Chung Hee*. Cambridge, MA.: Schenkman, 1981.

Yaniv, Avner, ed. *National Security and Democracy in Israel*. Boulder: Lynne Rienner, 1993.

Yim, Louise. *My Forty Year Fight for Korea*. Seoul: Chungang University, 1951.

Korean Central Yearbook, 1949 edition. *Seoul*.

Korean Unification Yearbook 1956-1966. Seoul.

KOREAN BIBLIOGRAPHY

Ahn, Chung-si, and Duck-kyu Chin, ed. *Jeonhwanki ui hankuk mijujuui* (Korean Democracy in Transition). Seoul: Bupmunsa, 1994.

Ahn, Young Sup, Kim Ik Hee, and Park Kyong Suh. *Yokdae daetongryong ui peosnality wa jeongchijok lideusip bikyo yongu* (Comparative Study of Presidential Personality and Political Leadership). Seoul: Hyundai Sahoe Yonkuso, 1986.

Cho, Gab-je. *Park Chung Hee 1: Bulman kwa bulun ui saewol, 1917-1960* (Park Chung Hee, vol. 1: the Era of Frustration and Bad Luck, 1917-1960). Seoul: Kkachi, 1992.

———. *Nae mudomae chimul battura* (Spit on My Grave). Seoul: Chosun Ilbosa, 1998.

Cho, Lee-Jay and Carter J. Eckert, eds. *Hankuk Geundaehwa, gijeokui kwajeong* (Modernization of the Republic of Korea: A Miraculous Achievement). Seoul: Wolgan Chosunsa, 2004.

Cho, Pyong-Ok, *Naui Hoegorok* (My Recollections), Seoul: Omungak, 1952.

Choe, Po-sik. "Che-o konghwakuk chonya: 12.12 pyon" (The Eve of the Fifth Republic: The 12.12 Phase), *Wolgan Choson* (May 1996): 497-631.

Choi, Dong-Kyu. *Sungjang sidaeui jeongbu: kwanryo jojikui yokhwal* (Government in the Age of Growth: The Role of Bureaucratic Organization in Leading Korean Miracle). Seoul: Hankuk Kyongjae Sinmunsa, 1991.

Choi, Pyong-gil. *Daetongryonghak* (The Study of Presidency). Seoul: Pakyoungsa, 1998.

Chosun Ilbosa. *Pirok: Hanguk ui taetongryong* (Hidden Record: the Korean Presidents). Seoul: 1993.

Chough, Pyong-ok. *Naui hoekorok* (My Memoir). Seoul: Minkyosa, 1959.

Chu, Don Shik. *Moonmin jeongbu chunyibaekil* (1200 Days of the Civilian Government). Seoul: Saram Gwa Chaek, 1997.

Chun, Mok Ku. *Chungi Park Chung Hee* (Biography Park Chung Hee). Seoul: Kyoyuk Pyongron-sa, 1966.

Chung, Chae-Kyong. *Park Chung Hee sasang seosul* (An Introduction to Park Chung Hee's Philosophy). Seoul: Chimundang, 1983.

———. Chung Chae-kyung, *Park Chung Hee silgi* (Real Records of Park Chung Hee). Seoul: Jimundang, 1994.

Chung, Il-Kwon. *Conjaeng-Gwa Hyujon* (War and Truce). Seoul: Dong-A Ilbo, 1986.

Chung, Jung-kil. *Daetongryong ui kyungje lideoship* (Economic Leadership of Presidents: Economic Management of the Park Chung Hee, Chun Doo Hwan, and Roh Tae Woo Governments). Seoul: Hankuk Kyungje Shinmunsa, 1994.

Donga Ilbosa. *Iruburin oyon* (The Lost Five Years). Seoul: Donga Ilbosa, 1999.

———. *Bihwa: Kukmineui jeongbu* (Secret Stories of the Government of the People). Seoul, 2003.

Hahm, Sung-Deuk. *Daetongryonghak* (The Korean Presidency). Seoul: Nanam, 1999.

———, ed. *Kim Young Sam jeongbuui sunggonggwa silpae* (The Kim Young Sam Presidency: Success and Failure). Seoul: Nanam, 2001.

———. *Daetongryong biseosiljang ron* (A Study of the Chief of Staff in the Blue House). Seoul: Nanam, 2002.

Han, Pyo-uk. *Yi Sung-man kwa han-mi oegyo* (Syngman Rhee and Korea-US Relations). Seoul: Joongang Ilbo-sa, 1996.

———. *Han-mi oekyo yoramki* (The early year of the Korean-American diplomatic relationship). Seoul: Choongang Ilbosa, 1984.

Hanguk daetongryong pyongga wiwonhoe, ed. *Hankukui yokdae daetongryong pyongga* (Evaluation of Korean Presidents). Seoul: Chosun Ilbosa, 2002.

Hanguk Ilbo. *Silrok: Chongwadae* (Veritable Records: The Blue House). Seoul, 1994.

Ho, Chong. *Unam Yi Sung-man* (Syngman Rhee). Seoul: Taekuk Chulpansa, 1970.

Im, Pyong-jik. *Im Pyong-jik hoegorok* (Im Pyong Jik Memoior). Seoul: Yowon-sa, 1964.

_____. *Kundae oekyo ui imynsa* (The inside history of modern diplomacy). Seoul: Yowonsa, 1956.

_____. "Rhee Paksawa topulo Pusan kaaji" (To Pusan with Dr. Rhee), *Shindonga*, June 1970, 174-178.

Jeon, Sung-Chul. *Chongwadae ga boinda daetongryongi boinda* (Looking into the Blue House, Looking into the President). Seoul: Chosun Ilbos, 2001.

Kang, Bong-kyun. *Hankukkyeongjae baljeon jeonryak* (Development Strategy of Korean Economy). Seoul, Pakyoungsa, 2001.

Kim, Chin-Hak and Chol-Yong Han. *Chaehon kukhoe sa* (A History of the Constitutional Assembly). Seoul: Shinjo Publishing Co., 1954.

Kim, Chong-bom and Kim Tong-un. *Haebang Chonhu ui Choson Chinsang (The Actual Situation of Korea Before and After Liberation)*. Seoul: Chosun Chongkyong Yongusa, 1945.

Kim, Choong Nam. *Sunggonghan daetoryong silpaehan daetongryong* (Successful Presidents, Unsuccessful Presidents). Seoul: Doongji, 1998.

Kim, Do-Yon, *Naui insaeng paekso* (A White Paper of My Life), Seoul, 1967.

Kim, Hak-Joon and Yeom Hong-Chul, ed. *Sunjin Hankukui mosek* (The Politics of the Sixth Republic). Seoul: Donghwa, 1993.

Kim, Ho-chin. *Hankuk jeongchi chaejeron* (A Study of Korean Political System). Seoul: Pakyoungsa, 1994.

Kim, Sung-ik, *Chon Tu-hwan yuksong chungon* (The Spoken Testimonies of Chun Doo Hwan), Seoul, Choson Ilbo-sa, 1992.

Kim, Su-yong, *Kim Dae Jung: Ku ui sengae wa chungchi* (Kim Dae Jung: His Life and Politics) (Seoul: Tongbang Chulpansa, 1986.

Kim, Woon-tae. *Hankook jungchiron* (On Korean Politics). Seoul: Pakyoungsa, 1994.

Kim, Young Sam. *Kim Young Sam daetongryong hoegorok* (Kim Young Sam Memoir) Vols. 1-2. Chosun Ilbo-sa, 2001.

_____. *Sin Han'guk 2000: Sin Han'guk changjo rul wihan kaehyok chonsajin* (New Korea 2000: the Blueprint of Reforms for the Creation of a New Korea). Seoul: Tonggwang Chulpan-sa, 1993.

_____. *Na wa choguk ui chinsil* (The Truth of Fatherland and I). Seoul: Irwol Sogak, 1984.

_____. *Kim Yong-sam hoegorok : minjujuui rul wihan na ui t`ujaeng* (Memoirs: My Struggle for Democracy). Seoul: Paeksan Sodang, 2000.

Korean Political Science Association, ed. *Nambukhanui choegojidoja* (Top Leaders of South and North Korea). Seoul: Baeksan Sudang, 2001.

Koo, Kwangmo. *Daetongryongron* (A Study of Presidents). (Seoul: Koreawon, 1984.

Lee Byong Joo. *Daetongryongdeuleui chosang* (Portraits of Presidents). Seoul: Seodang, 1991.

Lee, Chae-Jin and Young Ick Lew, eds. *Hankuk kwa 6.25 Jeonjaeng* (Korea and the Korean War). Seoul: Yonsei University Press, 2003.

Lee, Dong Won. *Daetongryongeul geuriwo hamyo* (Longing after President Park Chung Hee). Seoul: Koreawon, 1992.

Lee, Jang-kyu, *Kyongjaenun dangshini daetongryongiya* (You Are the Economic President). Seoul: Joongang Ilbo Sa, 1992.

Lee, Kyung-Nam. *Yonggiitnun botongsaram Roh Tae Woo* (A Courageous Common Man, Roh Tae Woo). Seoul: Elyoo Publishing Co., 1987.

Korean Bibliography

Lee, Sangu. *Pak Jeongkwon 18 Yeon* (The Eighteen Years of the Park Regime). Seoul: Donga Ilbo-sa, 1986.

Lee, Suk Jae. *Gakha, uri hyokmyong hapsida* (General! Let's Take Over the Government). Seoul: Seujukpo, 1995.

Lew, Young-Ick. *Yi Sung-man yon'gu: tongnip undong kwa Taehan Min'guk kon'guk* (Studies on Syngman Rhee: His Independence Activities and Establishment of the Republic of Korea). Seoul: Yonsei University Press, 2000.

_____. *Yi Sung-man ui sam kwa ggum* (Life and Dreams of Syngman Rhee). Seoul: Choongang Ilbo Sa, 1996.

Lho, Shin Yong, *Lho Shin Yong hoegorok* (Shin Yong Lho Memoirs). Seoul: Koryo Publishing Co., 2000.

Moon, Chae Chol, *Chongwadae bimil memo* (Secret Notes in the Blue House). Seoul: Gapin chulpan, 1993.

Office of Public Information, Republic of Korea. *Taet'ongnyong Yi Sung-man Paksa tamhwajip* (A Collection of Statements by President Syngman Rhee). Seoul, 1953.

Oh, Kyong Hwan, *Daetongnyung kaui saramdul* (People on the Presidential Street). Seoul: Myungjisa, 1992.

Paik, Nam-ju. *Hyongmyong chidoja Pak Chong-hi non* (On Park Chung Hee, the Revolutionary Leader). Seoul: Inmulkaesa, 1961.

Paik, Sun Yup. *Kunkwa na: 6.25 Hankuk Chunchang hoekorok* (The Army and I: The Korean War Memoirs). Seoul: Daeryuk Yonkuso, 1989.

Paik, Tu-jin. *Paek Tujin hoegorok* (Reminiscences of Tu-jin Paik). Seoul: Daehan Gongron Sa, 1976.

Park, Bo-kyun. *Chongwadae Bisushil 3* (The Blue House Secretariat 3). Seoul: Joongang Ilbo Sa, 1994.

Park, Sung-ha. *Unam nosun* (Political Philosophy of Syngman Rhee). Seoul: Donga, 1958.

Rhee, Francesca. "6.25 wa Rhee Syngman Taetongryong" (The Korean War and President Syngman Rhee). Choongang Ilbo, June 24, 1983.

Rhee, In Soo. *Daehan minkukui geonguk* (Establishment of the Republic of Korea). Seoul: Chotbool, 1988.

Son, Se-il, ed. *Kim Dae Jung kwa Kim Young Sam* (Kim Dae Jung and Kim Young Sam). Seoul: Ilwol Sogak, 1985.

So, Chong-ju. *Unam Yi Sung-man chon* (A Biography of Syngman Rhee). Seoul: Hwasan Munhaw Kihoek, 1995.

Song, In-sang, *Songinsang Hoegork: Buheung kwa sungjang* (Song In-sang Memoir: Reconstruction and Growth) (Seoul: 21 Saeki books, 1993.

The Presidential Secretariat, Republic of Korea. *Park Chong-hui Taetongnyon yonsolmun chip* (Speeches of President Park Chung Hee), vols. 1~8, Seoul, 1965-1979.

Unam Chongi Pyonchan Wiwonhoe, *Unam noson* (Selected Speeches of President Syngman Rhee), Donga Chulpan Sa, 1958.

Yi, Han-u, *Yi Sung-man 90-yon: Kodaehan saengae* (90 Years of Syngman Rhee: A Great Life), Seoul: Chosun Ilbo Sa, 1995.

Yi, Won-sun. *In'gan Yi Sung-man* (Biography: Syngman Rhee). Seoul: Sintaeyangsa, 1965.

Yu, Chin-o, *Honpop kicho hwoegorok* (Recollection of Constitution Drafting), Seoul: Ilchogak, 1980.

Persons Cited

A
Abe, Nobuyuki
Acheson, Dean
Agnew, Spiro
Aquino, Benigno
Aquino, Corazon
Atatürk, Kemal

B
Barber, James David
Ben-Gurion, David
Benjamin, Roger W.
Berge, Gunnar
Berger, Samuel
Blair, Tony
Bonifas, Arthur
Brandt, Willy
Breen, Michael
Brown, Harold
Bundy, McGeorge
Burns, James McGregor
Bush, George

C
Carter, Jimmy
Cha Chi-chol
Chang Ki-young
Chang Myon (John M. Chang)
Chang Se-dong
Chang Taek-sang
Chiang Kai-shek
Cho Bong-am
Cho Pyong-ok (Pyong-ok Chough)
Cho Soon
Choi Byung-ryol
Choi Jang-jip
Choi Kyu-ha
Chun Doo Hwan
Chun Kyung-hwan
Chung Chong-Wook
Chung Il-kwon, General
Chung Ju-yung
Chung Mong-hun
Chung Seung-hwa
Churchill, Winston S.

Clark, Mark W., General
Clinton, Bill
Conally, Tom
Cumings, Bruce

D
Dean, William F.
de Gaulle, Charles
Deng Xiaoping
Diem, Ngo Dinh
Dobrynin, Anatoly
Donner, Francesca (see also Francesca Rhee)
Dulles, John Foster
Duvall, Raymond

E
Eberstadt, Nicholas
Eisenhower, Dwight D.
Erhard, Ludwig

F
Fiedler, Fred E.
Ford, Gerald R.
Fukuyama, Francis

G
Gallucci, Robert L.
Gandhi, Mohandas
Genscher, Hans
Gleysteen, William J.
Gorbachev, Mikhail
Gong Ro-myung
Gregg, Donald

H
Hahm Pyong-choon
Han Kwang-ok
Han, Sung-joo
Han Wan-sang
Harriman, Averell
Hashimoto, Ryutaro
Hay, John
Hideyosh Toyotomi
Hirohitho, Emperor
Huh Shin-haeng
Ho Dam
Hodge, John R., Lieutenant General
House, Karen E.

Persons Cited

Hu, Richard
Humphrey, Hubert H.
Huntington, Samuel P.
Hwang Jang-yop
I
Ignatenko, Vitaly
Ikeda, Hayato
J
Jessup, Philip
Jiang Zemin
Jin Nyum
Johnson, Lyndon B.
K
Kang Bong-kyun
Kang Min-chul
Kang Myung-do
Kang Kyong-shik
Kang Sam-je
Kapitsa, Mikhail
Kennedy, John F.
Kim Chong-in
Kim Chong-whi
Kim Chul-soo
Kim Chung-yum
Kim Dae Jung
Kim Deok
Kim Dong-jo
Kim Eun-sung
Kim Hakjoon
Kim Hong-gul
Kim Hong-il
Kim Hong-up
Kim Hyun-chul
Kim Hyun-hee
Kim Il Sung
Kim In-ho
Kim Jae-ik
Kim Jae-kyu
Kim Jai-soon
Kim Jong Il
Kim Jong-Pil
Kim Ku
Kim Kye-won
Kim Kyu-Shik (Kimm Kiusic)
Kim Kyung-won
Kim Man-jae
Kim Sung-su

Kim Tae-dong
Kim Tae-jung
Kim Young Sam
Kirkpatrick, Jeanne J.
Kishi Nobusuke
Kissinger, Henry
Kohl, Helmut
Kojong, Emperor
Kwon Roh-kap
Kubota Kanichiro
L
Laney, James
Lee Bum-suk
Lee Byung-chull
Lee Dong-won
Lee Hee-ho (Mrs. Kim Dae Jung)
Lee Hoi-chang
Lee Hong-koo
Lee Hu-rak
Lee Hun-jai
Lee Hyon-jae
Lee Jong-chan
Lee Kwan Yew
Lee Ki-poong (Yi Ki-bung)
Lee Kon-hui
Lee Kyu-sung
Lee Sang-ok
Lee Seung-yoon
Lee Soon-ja (Mrs. Chun Doo Hwan)
Lee Suk-chae
Lee Suk-jae
Lee Won-kyong
Lee, Yoon-yungs
Lho Shin-yong
Lim Chang-ryol
Lim Dong-won
Lim Pyong-jik
Lincoln, Abraham
Lipton, David
Lyuh Un-hyung
M
MacArthur, Douglas A., General of the Army
Machiavelli, Noccolò
McCune, Evelyn
McCune, George
McNamara, Robert
Magruder, Carter

Persons Cited

Mahathir, Mohamed
Mandela, Nelson
Mao Tse-tung
Marcos, Ferdinand
Maslyukov, Yuri
Min, Queen
Montesquieu, Charles-Louis de
Muccio, John
N
Nakasone, Yasuhiro
Nasser, Gamal Abdel
Napoleon
Nam Duck-woo
Nixon, Richard M.
Novak, Robert,
O
Oberdorfer, Don
Oh Myung
Ohira, Masayoshi
Oliver, Robert T.
P
Paik Sun-yup, General
Paik Tu-jin
Park Choong-hoon
Park Chul-un,
Park Chung Hee
Park Hon-yong
Park Jae-yoon
Park Jie-won
Park Joon-kyu
Park Kwan-yong
Park Kye-dong
Park Se-il
Park Seh-jik
Park Seung
Park Sung-chul
Park Tae-joon
Park Tong-sun
Przeworski, Adam
Pyun Yung-tai
Q
Qian Qichen
R
Rabin, Yitzhak
Ramos, Fidel
Rankov, Andrei
Reagan, Ronald

Reston, James
Rhee, Francesca (Mrs. Syngman Rhee)
Rhee In-je
Rhee, Syngman
Ridgway, Matthew B., General
Robertson, Walter S.
Roh Jae-bong
Roh Moo Hyun
Roh Tae Woo
Roosevelt, Franklin D.
Roosevelt, Theodore
Rossiter, Clinton L.
Rostow, Dankwart A.
Rostow, Walter W.
Rusk, Dean
S
Sakong Il
Schwartz, Thomas, General
Shah Pahlavi
Shin Byung-Hyun
Shin, Doh C.
Shin Hyun-hwack
Shin Ik-Hui (P. H. Shinicky)
Shin Kwang-ok
Shin Sung-mo
Shtykov, Terenti, Colonel General
Shultz, George
Soros, George
Stalin, Joseph
Steinberg, David I.
Stiglitz, Joseph
Suh Chae-Pil (Philip Jaisohn)
Sukarno
T
Taylor, Maxwell
Thatcher, Margaret
Tokukawa Iyeyasu
Truman, Harry S.
V
Van Fleet, James A., General
Vance, Cyrus R.
W
Walesa, Lech
Walker, Richard
Walker, Walton, Lieutenant General
Ward, Robert E.
Washington, George

Persons Cited

Weinberger, Casper
Weizman, Ezer
Wickham, John A., Jr., General
Wilson, Harold
Wilson, Woodrow
Y
Yeltsin, Boris
Yim, Louise

Yon Hyong-muk
Yook Young-Soo (Mrs. Park Chung Hee)
Yoon Po-sun
Yoon Song-min
Yoshida, Shigeru
Z
Zenko, Suzuki
Zin Mo

THE KOREAN PRESIDENTS
Leadership for Nation Building

Choong Nam Kim earned the Ph. D. from the University of Minnesota and has been a researcher at the East-West Center in Honolulu since 1997. He served three Presidents of the Republic of Korea as an assistant and earlier was professor of political science at the Korea Military Academy.

EastBridge
SIGNATURE BOOKS

The *Signature Books* imprint of EastBridge is dedicated to presenting a wide range of exceptional books in the field of Asian and related studies. The principal concentrations are texts and supplementary materials for academic courses, literature-in-translation, and the writings of Westerners who experienced Asia as journalists, scholars, diplomats, and travelers. Doug Merwin, a founding director and publisher emeritus of EastBridge, has more than thirty years' experience as an editor of books and journals on Asia and was the founding editor of East Gate Books.